THE COMPLETE
JAMES BOND
MOVIE ENCYCLOPEDIA

THE COMPLETE
JAMES BOND
MOVIE ENCYCLOPEDIA

STEVEN JAY RUBIN

CONTEMPORARY
BOOKS
A TRIBUNE NEW MEDIA COMPANY

Library of Congress Cataloging-in-Publication Data

Rubin, Steven Jay, 1951–
    The complete James Bond movie encyclopedia / Steven Jay Rubin.
       p.   cm.
    ISBN 0-8092-4161-7 (cloth)
        0-8092-3268-5 (paper)
    1. James Bond films—Encyclopedias.   I. Title.
PN1995.9.J3R78   1990
791.43'651—dc20   90-41735
                                                              CIP

Published by Contemporary Books, Inc.
Two Prudential Plaza, Chicago, Illinois 60601-6790
Manufactured in the United States of America
International Standard Book Number: 0-8092-4161-7 (cloth)
                                          0-8092-3268-5 (paper)

For my wife, Elisa, who brings me joy every day

ACKNOWLEDGMENTS

Writing an encyclopedia is an enormous challenge and a never-ending task. There's always one more fact to check, one more biography to write, one more rare photograph to identify. Just as you're finalizing one entry, you discover two more that need more cross-checking. New information is continuously available, especially on an ongoing film series such as the James Bond films.

This book could never have been assembled without the cooperation of the film community. Many artists came forward with enthusiasm to lend a hand. In London, New York, Los Angeles, Miami, and many other cities, they consented to interviews, consulted their own references for facts that escaped them, and found rare photographic materials, most of which have never been published. Many are old friends who helped me assemble my first book on 007, *The James Bond Films* back in 1977.

I would like to especially thank Terence Young, Jack Schwartzman, Richard Maibaum, Maurice Binder, Ronnie Udell, John Stears, Burt Kwouk, Andy Bradford, Willy Bogner, Cec Linder, Syd Cain, Claire Russhon, Jordan Klein, Bruce Glover, Manning Redwood, Ricou Browning, Mrs. Johnny Jordan, the late Mignon (Mrs. Ted) Moore, Ken Adam, Roald Dahl, Max Youngstein, Donna Garratt, Peter Bayliss, Rose Alba, Corkey Fornof, Barry Champagne, Tom Sanders, Wally Potts, Tetsuro Tamba, Mie Hama, Richard Schenkman and the James Bond 007 Fan Club in New York, and Graham Rye and the James Bond British Fan Club in London.

For putting me in touch with several key 007 people, I also thank Mr. Eddie Jaffe of New York City. And for suggestions, criticisms, and notes, special nods to Jeff Kalmick, Steve Mitchell, and Kent Shocknek.

For photographs and additional editorial information, I owe a debt of gratitude to the following individuals, publications, corporations, photo agencies, production companies, and artists' representatives: Robert Short, Fred Clark and *Cinefantastique* magazine, Frank Herbert, Paul Deeson, John Brosnan, Marit Bern-hardt of Willy Bogner Public Relations, Pippa White at British Actor's Equity, Rex Features Limited of London, Globe Photos, People in Pictures Ltd., Terry Norman of *Express Newspapers* of London, the *Los Angeles Times*, Stephen Allen of the Las Vegas News Bureau, Carole E. Stewart of the Las Vegas Hilton, United Press International, *San Francisco Chronicle*, Associated Press/Wide World, *Life* magazine, Marshak-Wyckoff & Associates, NASA, Donna Woodward of Tom Jones Enterprises, A&M Records, Kai Rosenthal of Moet & Chandon, Malcolm Forbes Collection, ICM London, ICM Los Angeles, Hugh Sidey, Mark Hollingsworth of the Royal Air Force, Northolt, The Amberley Chalk Pits Museum, Clifford Elson Publicity Ltd., San Diego Museum of Art, Capitol Records, Arista Records, MCA Records, Warner Brothers Records, William Morris Agency of London, Miller Agency, Triad Artists, Inc., Ford Motor Company, Jeremy Conway Ltd, Vernon Conway Ltd, John Redway and Associates, L'Epine Smith, Marmont Management Ltd, London Management, Lou Coulson, CCA Personal Management Ltd., Peter Charlesworth Limited, Associated International Management Ltd., Michael Whitehall Limited, Michelle Braidman Associates, MacNaughton Lowe Representation Ltd., Patrick Freeman Management, David White Associates, Caroline Dawson, Patrick Freeman, Stephen P. Oxenrider.

I also thank the research staffs of the British Film Institute in London and the Academy of Motion Picture Arts and Sciences in Los Angeles for their generous support.

I owe a special debt of gratitude to a true artist and friend, Erik Hollander of Jacksonville, Florida, who was my graphics department on this book. His drawings and logo depictions were an important contribution.

At Contemporary Books of Chicago, I would like to thank Nancy Crossman for believing strongly in the project and Kathy Willhoite for helping to shape the final product.

I would also like to thank my agent, Sherry Robb of Sherry Robb Literary Properties, for her continuing support. Her enthusiasm is contagious.

Most importantly, I would like to thank my own research team, who helped me create this book. In Los Angeles, Barbara Petty, a published author in her own right, was my library detective and computer genius who stayed glued to the screen even when her eyes were turning into chewing gum. Ben Harper also combed the libraries, battled the books, and found the facts. He deserves a toast for his skill. In London, Terry Baxter played detective, tracking down invaluable information on even the most elusive artists. His enthusiasm for the James Bond films never quit. A special thanks to Terry's family for putting up with the long-distance communication and strange requests.

Finally, a special note of gratitude to my mother, Eve Rubin, who is always in my corner and who still makes the best Sunday-night dinners (now vegetarian) in America.

Thanks, everybody—we made it!

INTRODUCTION

Who is a Bond fan? Is it someone who stands patiently in the rain for three hours outside New York City's Winter Garden theater to catch a glimpse of actress Jane Seymour? Is it someone who is delighted to possess the complete collection of 007 films on videotape? Is it someone who trades Bond dialogue lines with friends, or is it someone who owns every poster, every publicity still, and every Bond toy ever manufactured?

Of course the answer is all of the above. I can predict that when any fan hears the famous staccato beat of the James Bond theme, his or her pulse will begin to quicken in expectation. For Bond fans, it's the call of the wild.

As we enter the 1990s, it's hard to believe that Bond fans have been around since the 1950s when the first Ian Fleming books were published. I was one of them. If you had wandered into my seventh-grade classroom in 1963, you would have seen many Signet paperbacks. Remember the colorful covers and the tiny artwork?

I can still see Gala Brand pointing the automatic at me from the cover of *Moonraker*, the fat ugly face of Mr. Big staring back at me from *Live and Let Die*, and those Aston Martin headlights from *Goldfinger*. I can still smell the pages of those paperbacks—my "E" tickets to adventure.

Simultaneously, the films began to appear. *Goldfinger* came on like gangbusters over Christmas 1964. Then *Dr. No* and *From Russia with Love* were re-released as the biggest double feature of all time. *Thunderball* fever captured the covers of *Life* and *Look* magazines. Next came the first Bond toys.

The Complete James Bond Movie Encyclopedia is a memory trigger. It's a literal encyclopedia—007 from A to Z—a compendium of thousands of facts, character biographies, definitions, behind-the-scenes information, and bloopers. It's a computer-age information blitz on our favorite subject—the Bond movies.

Why, after writing *The James Bond Films: A Behind the Scenes History* in 1981, did I return to the same topic? That book did not delve into the mythology of the character, the backgrounds of the villains and women, the identities of the principal filmmakers, or the bits of trivia I have discovered over the years. Also, the idea of putting all of this material together in a new form appealed to me. Here was the opportunity to actually define the specifics of the series. It would also give me the opportunity for a return visit with some of my favorite actors and filmmakers. A film historian doesn't need much more incentive than that.

I'm also a film archaeologist—someone who's always digging for new information. I've learned that if you go to the trouble to find a fresh story, a huge audience is waiting to hear it. As a staff writer for *Cinefantastique* (CFQ) in the 1970s, I specialized in the science-fiction films of the 1950s. I was particularly fascinated by the writer's story. How were the characters created? What inspired the story? How was it sold to the studio? I also collected a number of rare behind-the-scenes photographic stills, and I was stunned by the fans' reaction to them.

When I researched *Them* in 1974, I went to Warner Brothers and found the original still book for that 1954 science-fiction film classic. I purchased three shots and sent them to Fred Clark, CFQ's editor in chief in Chicago. The photos were extremely interesting. One showed director Gordon Douglas standing in knee-deep water in the L.A. storm drains speaking to actress Joan Weldon. Another showed Douglas shouting at Weldon in the middle of the Mojave Desert while a wind machine roared. It was the first time, to anyone's recollection, that a behind-the-scenes shot from *Them* had been published.

What I had uncovered was more than just a story about the making of a popular film. I had opened a movie door that had remained locked prior to my story. For the fans of *Them*, I had provided an opportunity to approach their favorite subject from an entirely new perspective. It was thrilling. I received fan mail and offers to write additional stories. It was an inspirational moment that has led to works such as *The Complete James Bond Movie Encyclopedia*.

If you love a particular subject, you simply

want to learn as much as you can about it. This applies to everything in life, from relationships to cooking, from automobile technology to comic-book characters. *The Complete James Bond Movie Encyclopedia* is a bible for Bond lovers everywhere.

It's for the many different kinds of Bond fans. Some speak their own 007 language. They know their favorite scenes, including the dialogue, by heart. Other fans simply enjoy seeing the films over and over again; thanks to unedited videotapes, they have that opportunity. Since the series has lasted so many years, Bond films also appeal to a wide audience. I would be surprised if there were a single person on the North American continent, let alone in Europe and in parts of Asia, who did not recognize the name James Bond, his code name, 007, and the Bond musical theme. Grandfathers who remember their first 007 film are now sharing that experience with their grandsons and granddaughters.

Why is Bond still with us? There are two reasons. First, the filmmakers have maintained an extremely high level of quality that is unprecedented in the history of movies. The public expects an epic show with an incredible gallery of beautiful women, nasty villains, exotic locations, breathtaking stunts, and catchy music combined with the world's most famous secret agent, played by actors who have carried on the tradition established by Sean Connery in 1962. Whether they feature Sean Connery, George Lazenby, Roger Moore, or Timothy Dalton, the Bond films have never let the fans down. Some have been less than memorable, but as a series, no others come close.

The second reason that Bond has survived is the character's durability. James Bond is the most famous motion-picture hero of the 20th century. He hasn't been alone in the spotlight. From time to time, his throne has been usurped by Batman, Superman, Indiana Jones, Conan, the *Star Wars* gang, and E.T., but Bond has surpassed all of them.

But, unlike the comic-book and serial heroes, Bond is a flesh-and-blood human being who deals with realistic situations. Although *Moonraker* bordered on pure science fiction, most of the films have featured outrageous villains with very believable schemes.

Bond is also flexible. He's grown with the times. He's a modern hero who is capable of understanding and using everything supplied to him by Q Branch. If the job calls for him to pilot a space shuttle, he'll figure it out. He doesn't have any super powers, he's not impervious to pain, and he has an appetite for healthy, voluptuous women. He's not a comic-book character. His life story is also not a headline in the *National Enquirer*.

Sex has played a part in the success of the series, but the filmmakers wisely kept their stories from turning away the family audience. James Bond movies are the ultimate family entertainment. You won't see nude women running around in a Bond movie. Nor will you see gratuitous violence. Although they're tougher films today, reflecting the violent world in which we live, they have never crossed the line into exploitation. Once that happens, the series will be finished.

Movies are our literature. Whereas our ancestors quoted Shakespeare, we trade movie dialogue. There are those who might look down their nose at such trivia, but we have nothing to be ashamed of. Shakespearean scholars are nothing more than fans. They love Shakespeare, they love his writing, and they can't get enough of it. Fans of the James Bond movies are just as dedicated.

A couple of questions plagued me as I was writing *The Complete James Bond Movie Encyclopedia*. First of all, I wondered if the fans would appreciate a detailed breakdown of the series. I decided to use myself as the weather vane. I'm a fan. I love the films. I quote the dialogue. I know that Disco Volante means "flying saucer" in Italian.

I also knew that I could bring a great deal of new information to the book, culled from new interviews, new research trips, and a great deal of digging.

Another question I had to answer was whether to add *Casino Royale* (both the 1954 TV version and the 1967 feature version) to the book. I decided that both films belonged in the encyclopedia. This is *The Complete James Bond Movie Encyclopedia*, and both are James Bond films.

For the record, my favorite James Bond is Sean Connery; my favorite Bond film is *Goldfin-*

ger, although *From Russia with Love* had the best story; my favorite Bond villain is Goldfinger; my favorite Bond girl is *Thunderball's* Claudine Auger, although *Licence to Kill's* Carey Lowell is a close second; and my favorite stunt sequence is the ski jump in *The Spy Who Loved Me*. I think the worst Bond movie ever made was the *Casino Royale* spoof and that the worst United Artists Bond was *The Man with the Golden Gun* (although *Moonraker* and *A View to a Kill* are competitive in that category). John Barry's best score was the one for *On Her Majesty's Secret Service*, but all of his 007 work has been outstanding. The worst score was a "non-score"—Michel Legrand's for *Never Say Never Again*. The best Bond song is Shirley Bassey's "Goldfinger," with honorable mentions going to Duran Duran's "A View to a Kill" and Carly Simon's "The Spy Who Loved Me." I also think Rik Van Nutter was the best Felix Leiter.

I hope you enjoy the book.

INTRODUCTION TO THE UPDATED EDITION

Welcome to the updated edition of *The Complete James Bond Movie Encyclopedia*. I'm thrilled to present this revised volume on the eve of an epic new James Bond movie and the dawn of the Pierce Brosnan 007 era. *Goldeneye* is the name of the 17th film in the fabulously successful series of United Artists James Bond movies that span 33 years of film history. In honor of *Goldeneye*, I've carefully assembled a dossier of inside information on the new 007 adventure, which you will find at the back of this book. You'll find all the new characters, from luscious and lethal Xenia Onatopp to the mysterious double-0 operative Alec Trevelyan. There's new director Martin Campbell, a new team of writers, and other faces new to the Bond scene. The cold war may be over, but James Bond is still the free world's most potent weapon.

The new *Goldeneye* information isn't the only reason to crack open these pages. Throughout this volume and in an Addendum are adjustments to the 1990 text: key changes and fine-tuning based on six years' worth of letters, telephone calls, criticisms, comments, and new research information.

The history of the James Bond movies is a living history. Every day new pages are being written in the never-ending story of the movie 007. Even as Pierce Brosnan carries the 007 banner to new heights (we hope!), exciting events are rekindling the spark of Bond fever for fans around the world, including conventions, new organizations, and plans for additional films in the series.

The new Ian Fleming Foundation is charting a course with its wonderful magazine *Goldeneye* and its preservation efforts. Steadfast Graham Rye continues to turn the James Bond Fan Club into an international organization of significance and respect, and producers Barbara Broccoli and Michael G. Wilson and MGM/UA are charting the course of James Bond movies into the 21st century. The James Bond movies were conceived as an ongoing franchise and, despite years of legal problems, it looks like they still are.

The computer revolution even allows me to present this material in CD-ROM format, so look for *The Complete James Bond Movie Encyclopedia* on CD-ROM (with video and audio interviews with many Bond veterans) this fall from Villa Crespo Software of Highland Park, Illinois.

We've all come a long way from John Strangways, Crab Key, and Dr. No. But there is evidence that Bond is forever. I don't know about you, but I personally look forward to watching new James Bond movies into the 2050s—any further than that and I'm going to have to brush up on my reincarnation skills. Then again, with Q Branch, is anything really impossible?

See you at the movies . . . James Bond movies!

Steve Rubin
Summer 1995

A

ACADEMY AWARDS The Bond series has scored rarely in the annual awards derby of the Academy of Motion Picture Arts and Sciences. In the entire history of the series, up to 1989, Bond films have been awarded ten nominations and only two wins:

Wins
1964 *Goldfinger*, Best Sound Effects—Norman Wanstall
1965 *Thunderball*, Best Visual Effects—John Stears

Nominations Only
1967 "The Look of Love" (from *Casino Royale*), Best Song—Burt Bacharach and Hal David (It lost to "Talk to the Animals" from *Doctor Dolittle*.)
1971 *Diamonds Are Forever*, Best Sound—Gordon McCallum, John Mitchell, and Alfred E. Overton (It lost to *Fiddler on the Roof*.)
1973 "Live and Let Die," Best Song—Paul and Linda McCartney (It lost to "The Way We Were.")
1977 Best Art Direction *The Spy Who Loved Me*, "The Spy Who Loved Me" Best Art Direction: Ken Adam, Peter Lamont, Set Decoration: Hugh Scaife (It lost to *Star Wars*.)
1977 "Nobody Does It Better" (from *The Spy Who Loved Me*) Best Song—Marvin Hamlisch and Carole Bayer Sager (It lost to "You Light Up My Life.")
1977 *The Spy Who Loved Me*, Best Original Score—Marvin Hamlisch (It lost to *Star Wars*.)
1979 *Moonraker*, Best Visual Effects—Derek Meddings, Paul Wilson, and John Evans (It lost to *Alien*.)
1981 "For Your Eyes Only," Best Song—Bill Conti and Mick Leeson (It lost to "Arthur's Theme: The Best That You Can Do" from *Arthur*.)

ACHMED'S TEA PARTY British Secret Service operation in Cairo mentioned by Q (DESMOND LLEWELYN) in *The Spy Who Loved Me*, during which a newly designed razor-sharp food tray/weapon is supposed to be deployed.

ACKRIDGE, BILL American actor who portrayed O'Rourke, an irritable San Francisco Bay crab fisherman who objects to Zorin's (CHRISTOPHER WALKEN) oil pumping activities in *A View to a Kill*. *See* O'ROURKE, MR.

ACME POLLUTION INSPECTOR Bond's (SEAN CONNERY) cover when he arrives on Blofeld's (CHARLES GRAY) oil rig in *Diamonds Are Forever*. His comment to the head of S.P.E.C.T.R.E. when he arrives is "We're cleaning up the world and we thought this was a suitable starting point."

ACROSTAR MINI-JET (aka Bede jet) Miniature jet aircraft flown by James Bond (ROGER MOORE) in the *Octopussy* teaser. After his plan to destroy a top secret South American radar system goes awry, Bond escapes in his plane, hotly pursued by a heat-seeking anti-aircraft missile. Diving into the radar system's hangar, he's able to maneuver his acrobatic plane through to the other side, just as enemy soldiers are closing the hangar doors. As the doors close, the missile, enters the hangar and explodes against them—obliterating the hangar, the radar system, and everything else.

The Acrostar/Bede jet, designed, manufactured, and flown by veteran stunt pilot Corkey Fornof, is slightly more than three meters in length and boasts a top speed of 310 mph. It's powered by a Micro-turbo TRS 18 engine.

The jet was originally scheduled to make its screen debut in *Moonraker*. In that film's original script, Bond and CIA agent Holly Goodhead (LOIS CHILES) arrive in Brazil and discover that a fleet of cargo planes owned by Hugo Drax (MICHEL LONSDALE) are disappearing into the hinterlands. Determined to find them, Bond and Holly climb into their own mini-jets and take off for a run across the jungle surrounding Angel Falls.

During one planned action-sequence, the two friendly agents engage in a bit of acrobatics that takes them through tight crevices and, at one point, behind Angel Falls itself. Then, just as they're about to find Drax's hidden base, they're jumped by a flight of black twin-boom Vampyre jets that try to shoot them down.

However, the viability of the sequence depended on the water level in and around Angel Falls. Unfortunately, when it came time to shoot the scene, the riverbed was completely dry. So the Acrostar jet sequence was eliminated from the script, only to be resurrected for the *Octopussy* teaser, where only one jet was used. *See* FORNOF, J. W. "CORKEY."

ADAM One of Kananga's (YAPHET KOTTO) motorboat drivers in *Live and Let Die*, portrayed by Tommy Lane. Adam steals the swift motorboat from Sheriff J. W. Pepper's (CLIFTON JAMES) brother-in-law, Billy Bob. Trapped in an old navy shipyard, 007 (ROGER MOORE) manages to sneak up to Adam and fling gasoline in his face. Bond then flips the accelerator on the boat and Adam goes hurtling out of control toward a head-on collision with an old navy landing ship.

ADAM, KEN (Berlin, Germany, 1921–) (real name, Klaus Adam) Colorful, innovative British production designer and 007 veteran who, starting with *Dr. No* in 1962, gave the interior sequences he designed a vibrant, exciting style and look that would become the hallmark of the James Bond series for nearly three decades. Adam came to the series on the recommendation of producer Cubby Broccoli, who had worked with him on *The Trials of Oscar*

Production designer Ken Adam. (Charles Sherman)

Wilde in 1960. Broccoli knew that Adam was innovative and could work within the minuscule production-design budget available on *Dr. No*. Given that budget, Adam's design output was nothing short of extraordinary. Dr. No's (JOSEPH WISEMAN) marvelous "reactor room," his eerie Crab Key waiting area, and the undersea observation living room were design gems. His more realistic full-size settings—M's office, the Secret Service communications room, Bond's apartment, the casino, and Miss Taro's bedroom—also belied their actual cost. Adam's designs, along with Terence Young's understated direction, Peter Hunt's slam-bang editing, and John Barry's throbbing score, contributed heavily to the success of *Dr. No* and the emergence of the James Bond films as a pop cultural triumph of the 1960s.

Adam's location art director on *Dr. No*, Syd Cain, took over production-design chores on the next Bond film, *From Russia with Love*, while Adam toiled for Stanley Kubrick on *Dr. Strangelove*. Adam returned to the Bond fold on *Goldfinger*, once again stretching the limits of contemporary production design with his glittering Fort Knox interior (*see* FORT KNOX, KENTUCKY), the enormous exterior of the repository built on the Pinewood Studios lot, and the sprawling Auric Stud ranch with its intricate and electronically enhanced planning room interior, manipulated by Goldfinger (GERT FROBE) himself. Working with special effects supervisor John Stears, Adam also contributed heavily to the design of the customized Aston Martin sports car. Weapon and gadget design, always a vital part of the Bond movie experience, was part of Adam's responsibility, especially on the next film, *Thunderball*, which featured huge working elements such as the *Disco Volante* hydrofoil and a number of underwater devices employed by the villain, Largo (ADOLFO CELI). Adam's S.P.E.C.T.R.E. briefing room, with its modern stainless-steel look, was another design triumph of the period, along with his immense Secret Service conference room, complete with animated wall charts and a drawing-room feel.

The continuing international box-office success of the Bond movies in the early 1960s meant that the films' budgets also began to increase dramatically. With extra money in the bank, Adam began to take on tasks that only the ancient pharoahs would have understood. On *You Only Live Twice* he created the famous volcano set, an enormous, fully operational S.P.E.C.T.R.E. rocket base, hidden inside an extinct Japanese volcano and built full size on the Pinewood Studios lot in 1966 (*see* VOLCANO ROCKET BASE).

Syd Cain took over production-designer chores on the next film, *On Her Majesty's Secret Service*, but Adam returned on *Diamonds Are Forever*. He designed Blofeld's (CHARLES GRAY) garish penthouse suite at the Whyte House in Las Vegas, the interior of the moon-buggy testing facility, and the oil-rig advance base in the Gulf of Baja, which was actually a portable rig placed off the southern California coast near Oceanside (*see* OIL-RIG BATTLE).

With Syd Cain handling production-design chores on *Live and Let Die* and Peter Murton (another former associate of Adam) taking on *The Man with the Golden Gun*, Adam took a five-year 007 hiatus, returning on the mammoth *The Spy Who Loved Me* in 1976. This time, working with a design concept built around the circular and ellipse patterns he discovered on a location trip to Sardinia's Costa Smeralda resort, Adam created the marvelous Stromberg (CURT JURGENS) marine laboratory sets built inside the amphibian Atlantis structure.

But his blockbuster on *Spy* was the *Jonah* set—the incredible interior of the *Liparus* super-tanker that was built inside its own specially constructed soundstage—the 007 stage, which became the largest soundstage and tank in the world. The glimmering, shimmering interior, with five-eighths scale nuclear submarines, an armored control room, catwalks, a monorail, and assembly and weapons rooms, became one of the most celebrated motion-picture interiors of all time, rivaling Adam's own volcano creation for *You Only Live Twice* (*see* JONAH SET, THE).

Following *The Spy Who Loved Me*, Adam came aboard for one more 007 adventure (to date)—the first film with a strong space angle—*Moonraker*. This time, his designs were strongly influenced by three elements: the triangular architecture of the ancient Mayan civilization, the unusual design of a Nemar cathedral that Adam discovered during a location "recce" to Brasilia in 1978, and the work of the painter Mondrian.

All of these elements would come together inside Hugo Drax's (MICHEL LONSDALE) fascinating rocket base, that included the "Great Chamber," an enormous junglelike atrium constructed under a Mayan pyramid; the triangular control room with its perspex floor and colorful viewing panels; and the boxlike space shuttle launching pad. Adam also designed the tubelike structure of Drax's radar-proof satellite, a multilevel maze of engineering and scientific bric-a-brac that becomes a battleground in the finished film.

ADAMS, MAUD (Lulea, Sweden, February 12, 1945–   ) (real name, Maud Wikstrom) A former ex-model-turned-actress who is the only woman in the Bond series to play two different leading characters—Andrea Anders in *The Man with the Golden Gun* and the title character in *Octopussy*—Adams is also seen briefly in the background of the Fisherman's Wharf sequence in *A View to a Kill*. On *Octopussy*, she was originally called to do a screen test with actor James Brolin, who was being considered for the role of Bond.

In August 1982, prior to the start of principal photography, she told *Los Angeles Times* columnist Roderick Mann, "The test went well but I was confused—I knew it was policy never to use an actress twice and I'd already been in *The Man with the Golden Gun*. So what was I

Actress Maud Adams.

doing there? Then they called me in for a makeup test and darkened my hair and eyebrows.

"That was when I realized they had me in mind for *Octopussy*, the villainess of the picture. She's half Indian. I was very excited. After all, a woman has never before played the title role in a Bond film, or been in two films.

"I came home and waited and then I got the telephone call saying I had the part. And it's a marvelous one. Everyone says it's the best role ever written for a woman in a Bond film.

"Remember, when I did *Golden Gun* all those years ago, I had no acting experience at all. I've done a lot since then so I feel I'm ready to tackle a much more challenging role." *See* ANDERS, ANDREA; OCTOPUSSY.

ADEN A country on the Arabian Peninsula between Yemen and Oman that is the refueling stop for a NATO aircraft delivering the diamond ransom in *Thunderball*. During World War II, title designer Maurice Binder helped build a military airfield here.

A-5 Bond's (ROGER MOORE) and Anya's (BARBARA BACH) suite number at Sardinia's Cala di Volpe Hotel in *The Spy Who Loved Me*. It has a single sitting room and two bedrooms.

AFRICAN JOB, THE Where 007 (ROGER MOORE) is coming from when he's on his "last leg" to London in the *Moonraker* teaser.

A.F.S.D. Acronym for Anti-Female Spy Device, Sir James Bond's (DAVID NIVEN) secret weapon in *Casino Royale*. Faced with a rash of assassinations attributable to a group of female agents, Bond determines that the British Secret Service needs an agent who is immune to a woman's charms.

Miss Moneypenny's daughter (BARBARA BOUCHET) is recruited to test the candidates by kissing each one and determining their attractiveness to the opposite sex. Agent Cooper (TERENCE COOPER) appears to have the edge, and they withdraw to Moneypenny's bedroom to resume the testing.

While Cooper passes the test and is given the name James Bond, simultaneously a second man—mild-mannered card expert Evelyn Tremble (PETER SELLERS)—also becomes an A.F.S.D. after he's seduced by Vesper Lynd (URSULA ANDRESS). Tremble is sent to Monte Carlo to play baccarat against Soviet spymaster Le Chiffre (ORSON WELLES). *See* TREMBLE, EVELYN.

AGENT 326 Code name of Nicole (SASKIA COHEN TANUGI), James Bond's (SEAN CONNERY) Secret Service contact in the South of France in *Never Say Never Again*. She's murdered by S.P.E.C.T.R.E. assassin Fatima Blush (BARBARA CARRERA).

A-HA Norwegian rock & roll trio who performed the title tune to *The Living Daylights* in 1987. The trio previously scored with the international number-one smash "Take on Me,"

a-ha, the Norwegian rock & roll band that performed the title song in *The Living Daylights*. (a-ha, John Paul)

which featured a most extraordinary video that combined live action with animation. The group consists of three natives of Oslo, Norway: Pal (pronounced "Paul") Waaktaar, Morten Harket, and Mags.

AIR FRANCE CONCORDE The famous supersonic aircraft that transports James Bond (ROGER MOORE) to Rio de Janeiro in *Moonraker*.

AIR VICE MARSHAL The Royal Air Force officer, portrayed by Edward Underdown, who receives the news about the missing NATO bomber in *Thunderball*. Addressed as "Sir John" at the MI-7 briefing, he later informs all double-0 agents that a thorough search has turned up nothing.

AKBAR SHAH One of the famous diamonds viewed by James Bond (SEAN CONNERY) and M (BERNARD LEE) at the showroom of a London diamond syndicate in *Diamonds Are Forever*. It's 116 carats, rough.

AKI Beautiful and resourceful Japanese Secret Service agent, portrayed by Akiko Wakabayashi in *You Only Live Twice*. Agent 007's (SEAN CONNERY) guardian angel in Tokyo, she drives an exotic Toyota 2000 sports car, wears fancy Western outfits, and works for Tiger Tanaka (TETSURO TAMBA), head of S.I.S.—the Japanese Secret Service. In many ways, she was screenwriter Roald Dahl's tribute to the Japanese woman of the 1960s who was gradually breaking away from traditional restraints. Unfortunately, while sleeping with Bond, she's killed when a S.P.E.C.T.R.E. assassin, in a botched attempt on 007's life, dribbles liquid poison into her mouth from a string suspended from a skylight above their bed.

ALBA, ROSE British actress who portrayed the shapely Madame Boitier, who is seen entering a Lincoln Continental limousine in the *Thunderball* teaser. It's all a sham. In actuality, she's S.P.E.C.T.R.E. agent Jacques Boitier, who is masquerading at his own funeral in order to escape British intelligence. In the Chateau D'Arnet, his true identity is revealed during a vicious fight with James Bond (SEAN CONNERY). Stuntman Bob Simmons portrayed the real Boitier.

ALBANIAN COAST Location of Aris Kristatos's (JULIAN GLOVER) heroin-smuggling operation in *For Your Eyes Only*. In order to convince Bond (ROGER MOORE) that Kristatos is his enemy and the employer of Locque (MICHAEL GOTHARD), assassin Milos Columbo (TOPOL) launches a night raid on Kristatos's warehouse. The mission is successful and Bond eventually corners Locque on a mountain roadway and kills him. The wreck of the *St. Georges* surveillance ship is located near the Albanian coast.

A.L.C.M. Abbreviated designation of the cruise missiles carried by a U.S. Air Force B-1 bomber in *Never Say Never Again*. For a test designed to "assess distance and accuracy of cruise missile release from the support country," two missiles are loaded into the bomb bay of the B-1, based at Swadley Air Force Base in Britain. Officers on the base assume that the missiles are dummies, but thanks to traitorous Captain Jack Petachi (GAVAN O'HERLIHY), they're actually armed with W-80 thermonuclear warheads. *See* PETACHI, CAPTAIN JACK.

ALGERNON (aka Algy) James Bond's (SEAN CONNERY) dry-witted equipment officer in *Never Say Never Again* and writer Lorenzo Semple, Jr.'s, version of Q, portrayed by Alec McCowen. A victim of the British Secret Service's new budget constraints, poor Algy works in a cluttered, air-conditioned workshop that plays havoc with his sinuses, let alone his department's capabilities. Still, he's able to provide 007 with some formidable items, such as a rocket-propelled motorcycle, a laser-equipped watch, and a very lethal fountain pen that comes in extremely handy during Bond's climactic confrontation with Fatima Blush (BARBARA CARRERA). Now that Bond's back on the job,

British actress Rose Alba portrayed Madame Boitier in *Thunderball*. (Rose Alba Collection)

Algy also hopes that "some gratuitous sex and violence" will also return to the ranks of the Secret Service.

"ALIMENTARY, DR. LEITER" Bond's (SEAN CONNERY) comical medical response in *Diamonds Are Forever* when Felix Leiter (NORMAN BURTON) asks him where the diamonds are hidden on Peter Franks's (JOE ROBINSON) body. According to screenwriter Tom Mankiewicz, when he first read the script, Cubby Broccoli felt that no one would get the line. However, Mankiewicz forced him to keep it in. On opening night when Bond said the line, a man in the fourth row laughed out loud. According to Mankiewicz, Broccoli turned to him and whispered, "It's probably a doctor."

ALLEN, IRVIN Actor who portrayed Che Che, one of Draco's (GABRIELE FERZETTI) henchmen, who fights Bond (GEORGE LAZENBY) in a Portuguese hotel room in *On Her Majesty's Secret Service.*

ALLEN, WOODY (Brooklyn, New York, December 1, 1935–   ) (real name, Allen Stewart Konigsberg) Superstar American comedian and film director who portrayed the villainous Dr. Noah in *Casino Royale*, as well as his alter ego, bumbling Jimmy Bond, the nephew of Sir James Bond (DAVID NIVEN). *See* NOAH, DR.; BOND, JIMMY.

Woody Allen.

ALPERT, LORD The British Foreign Secretary in *Never Say Never Again*, portrayed by Anthony Sharp. *Note:* In the credits, this character is mistakenly referred to as "Lord Ambrose."

ALPINE ROOM The name given to the huge dining room at Piz Gloria, Ernst Stavro Blofeld's (TELLY SAVALAS) Swiss mountain hideaway in *On Her Majesty's Secret Service.*

ALVAREZ Latin lothario, portrayed by stunt supervisor Gerardo Moreno, who, while in bed with Lupe Lamora (TALISA SOTO), is surprised and captured by drug runner Franz Sanchez (ROBERT DAVI) in the *Licence to Kill* teaser. Convinced that Alvarez promised Lupe his heart, Sanchez orders his killer, Dario (BENICIO DEL TORO), to literally cut it out, which is, thankfully, completed offscreen.

AMA ISLAND A secluded Japanese island that is home to a community of beautiful pearl divers and fishermen in *You Only Live Twice.* Disguised as a Japanese, and determined to find the secret S.P.E.C.T.R.E. rocket base, Bond (SEAN CONNERY) travels to Ama where he "marries" Kissy (MIE HAMA), a stunningly beautiful Ama pearl diver who is one of Tiger Tanaka's (TETSURO TAMBA) top agents. Undercover as fisherman and pearl diver, they eventually find their way through the Rosaki Cave and onto the extinct volcano that is the cover for Blofeld's rocket installation.

AMASOVA, MAJOR ANYA A beautiful but deadly Russian KGB agent portrayed by Barbara Bach in *The Spy Who Loved Me.* Codenamed Triple X, she's partnered with James Bond (ROGER MOORE) on a hunt for freelance madman Karl Stromberg (CURT JURGENS), whose supertanker, the *Liparus*, has been swallowing British and Russian nuclear submarines. Both agents are also looking for a British submarine tracking system that has been developed by Stromberg.

Major Amasova is, in effect, the first liberated woman in the James Bond series, reflecting well the mid-1970s movement for more believable and realistic female characters in all films. Having been introduced in the 1960s, when 007's chauvinism was given a free rein, the

James Bond films, as they entered their second decade, were given a considerably more contemporary outlook. Although there would continue to be playmates for Bond in every film, the main female characters began to be drawn with elements of intelligence, independence, and strength.

Major Amasova certainly reflected this trend, as demonstrated in the ruined-temple sequence in *The Spy Who Loved Me* where Bond and Anya are trailing Jaws (RICHARD KIEL). Moving stealthfully among the pillars, Anya (accompanied by Marvin Hamlisch's moody score) shows off a few extremely impressive martial arts stances while dressed in a clinging evening gown. This is no breathless female waiting to be rescued. Later, aboard a train bound for Sardinia, she's no match against Jaws, but she still fights back.

Later, she even threatens to kill Bond in return for murdering her lover (MICHAEL BILLINGTON) in Berngarten, Austria. The strength and determination in her threat was unprecedented in the series. Bond women were beginning to hold their own at 007's side, and Amasova was the first.

Recalled director Lewis Gilbert, "Anya is a very independent woman; she's a major in the KGB and Russia's top agent. She's capable of scoring off Bond, and she does. In *The Spy Who Loved Me*, 007 doesn't always win. Sometimes she's smarter than he. This type of interplay makes Bond more human, more like one of us. Being vulnerable with the girl allows Bond's other accomplishments in the film to appear that much more impressive." *See* BACH, BARBARA.

AMC HORNET The American car that Bond (ROGER MOORE) steals from a Bangkok showroom in *The Man with the Golden Gun*. Chasing Scaramanga (CHRISTOPHER LEE), with J. W. Pepper (CLIFTON JAMES) in the passenger seat, 007 races through town with half the Bangkok police on his tail. Outdistancing the local authorities, Bond finds himself on one side of a Thai river while Scaramanga and Nick Nack (HERVE VILLECHAIZE) are inexplicably on the other. Spying a ruined bridge, Bond does the unthinkable by using the bridge's superstructure for a 360-degree spiral jump

across the river, landing on all four tires and continuing the chase.

Unfortunately, in my opinion, this incredible stunt, performed by British stuntman Bumps Willard, was ruined when in post-production a kazoo sound effect was added over the jump. It served to cheapen what was actually one of the most incredible stunts ever performed on any film.

AMC MATADOR The basis for Francisco Scaramanga's (CHRISTOPHER LEE) flying car in *The Man with the Golden Gun*. It transports Scaramanga, Nick Nack (HERVE VILLECHAIZE), and Mary Goodnight (BRITT EKLAND) in the trunk to a strange, prehistoric island off the Chinese mainland which is actually Khow-Ping-Kan Island, off the coast of Thailand. Bronze-colored with a black landau top, its license plate number is 7543.

AMRITRAJ, VIJAY World-class professional tennis player who portrayed Vijay, James Bond's (ROGER MOORE) Secret Service associate in *Octopussy*.

ANDERMATT A small village in Switzerland, about 50 miles due south of Zurich, that served as a key exterior location in *Goldfinger*. In the shelter of the Leopontine Alps and not far from the Simplon Tunnel, Bond (SEAN CONNERY) tails Goldfinger's (GERT FROBE) Rolls-Royce and later encounters the Mustang convertible of fast-driving Tilly Masterson (TANIA MALLET). The warmly romantic instrumental strains of John Barry's score in this sequence are a definite highlight.

ANDERS, ANDREA Super-assassin Francisco Scaramanga's (CHRISTOPHER LEE) girlfriend in *The Man with the Golden Gun*, portrayed by Maud Adams, who would go on to play the title character in *Octopussy* in 1983. Involved in a loveless relationship, Anders sleeps with Scaramanga prior to every kill—a ritual that is also popular among bullfighters. It's supposed to improve their eye.

A virtual slave to Scaramanga's will, Anders's only hope is to find the one man—James Bond (ROGER MOORE)—capable of defeating Scaramanga at his own game. So Anders sends an inscribed golden bullet to the British Secret Service. In return, she also receives a golden bullet, but at a much higher muzzle velocity. *See* ADAMS, MAUD.

ANDERSON-GIMBEL, ELGA (1939–1994) German actress who was director Terence Young's first choice for the Tatiana Romanova part in *From Russia with Love.*

Many actresses were tested for the part, but, Young said, "a German actress, Elga Anderson, was our first choice. She was in a film called *Bird of Paradise*, and she got the part on those merits. She was going to be announced the next day, but there was a disastrous screening of a new Judy Garland film, *I Could Go on Singing*, and no one was in the mood for announcing anything.

"Then a top United Artists (UA) executive who had been trying to climb in the sack with her told us plainly that we couldn't use her because of her reputation. It was completely untrue.

"I found out later that she was a woman of impeccable character. But between the bad taste in everyone's mouth at UA about the Judy Garland film, and this character's unfounded accusations, I couldn't get anyone to approve her casting.

"Our second choice was an Italian girl who had been the runner-up in the 1960 Miss Universe pageant. This was Daniela Bianchi, whom I liked very much, but at the time I thought she was a very limited actress. The role, of course, didn't call for much, but Elga would have been better."

ANDRESS, URSULA (Berne, Switzerland, March 19, 1936–   ) Swiss actress who portrayed Honey Ryder in *Dr. No.* (Her name was Honeychile Ryder in the book.) A stunning presence in the first Bond film and the fantasy figure for many male college students of the 1960s, her entrance on the beach—coming out of the water in a white bikini that she designed herself—is considered one of the great screen introductions.

Unfortunately, thanks to screen morals of

Ursula Andress poses for husband John Derek in the Falmouth Swamp of Jamaica during the filming of *Dr. No* in 1962. (UPI)

the period, the producers could not recreate the scene as Fleming wrote it. In the book Honey wears only a belt that contains a knife around her waist. When she sees 007 for the first time, she covers her crotch and her broken nose, allowing her magnificent breasts to jut out at Bond, certainly one of Fleming's most erotic sequences.

The author originally described her as the incarnation of Botticelli's Venus, quite a chore for the casting director. A photograph of Andress in a wet T-shirt eventually won her an audition, although her then-husband, John Derek, had to persuade her to take the part. Andress was entirely re-voiced in post-production.

The same woman who did her voice in *Dr. No* can be heard as the desk clerk in James Bond's Istanbul hotel in *From Russia with Love*. Andress also portrayed seductress and double agent Vesper Lynd in *Casino Royale*. See RYDER, HONEY; LYND, VESPER.

ANGEL CAKE What Moneypenny (LOIS MAXWELL) offers 007 (SEAN CONNERY) in *Goldfinger* if he'll come home to her place for dinner. As always, Bond passes on the date.

ANGELIS, PAUL Actor who portrayed Karageorge, one of Milos Columbo's (TOPOL) nimble Greek fighters in *For Your Eyes Only*. He takes part in the assault on the monastery.

ANGELS OF DEATH The nickname that Ernst Stavro Blofeld (TELLY SAVALAS) gives to the beautiful allergy patients from his Bleuchamp Institute who are brainwashed and given orders to disperse the deadly Virus Omega germ-warfare strain worldwide in *On Her Majesty's Secret Service*. Each girl is given an atomizer filled with the virus and a radio transmitter through which Blofeld can signal her to destroy the agricultural and animal husbandry productivity of an entire country. The targeted countries include England, Germany, the United States, Scandinavia, China, Australia, Italy, India, Jamaica, and Israel.

APOLLO AIRWAYS Airline flown by James Bond (ROGER MOORE) in the *Moonraker* teaser. Returning from his African job, and on his "last leg" to London, 007 finds himself the victim of another assassination attempt perpetrated by three characters aboard his turboprop airliner: the stewardess, who holds a gun on him; the pilot, who shoots out the controls, disabling the plane; and Jaws (RICHARD KIEL), who tosses Bond out of the plane without a parachute, precipitating the wildest teaser in the series.

APOSTIS Henchman of Aris Kristatos (JULIAN GLOVER), portrayed by Jack Klaff, who is killed by Bond (ROGER MOORE) during a fight atop the rock cliff of St. Cyril's monastery in *For Your Eyes Only*.

AREA FINANCIAL REPORTS International business briefing conducted by Ernst Stavro Blofeld at S.P.E.C.T.R.E.'s Paris headquarters in *Thunderball*. When called upon by Blofeld, the participating agents tally their recent receipts from various S.P.E.C.T.R.E. operations.

At this meeting we hear from Agent No. 5 (250,000 pounds sterling as a consultation fee for the British train robbery), No. 7 (40 million yen for the blackmail of double agent Matsu Fugiwa), No. 10 (3 million francs for the assassination of Peringe, the French anti-matter specialist who defected to the Russians), and No. 11 ($2.3 million for the distribution of Red Chinese narcotics in the United States collected by No. 9 and No. 11). The latter transaction is considered suspect by Blofeld, who fingers No. 9 as an embezzler. Calmly sitting at his desk while his partner, No. 11, sweats it out, the agent is then electrocuted by Blofeld. In S.P.E.C.T.R.E., justice is swift.

ARK ROYAL British aircraft carrier where James Bond (ROGER MOORE) once saw active service, according to Admiral Hargreaves (ROBERT BROWN), Flag Officer Submarines in *The Spy Who Loved Me*. It's the first time in the series that mention is made of Bond's previous naval service.

ARMENDARIZ, PEDRO (Churubusco, Mexico, May 9, 1912–1963) Mexican leading man who, despite a terminal illness, portrayed the exuberant British spymaster Ali Kerim Bey in *From Russia with Love*.

If I picked my favorite character actor in

Actor Pedro Armendariz portrayed Bond's friend, Ali Kerim Bey, in *From Russia with Love.*

the series, it would be Armendariz, who was perfectly cast. Kerim Bey was properly charming, his line delivery was crisp as a sword point, and he gave the film a marvelously exotic flavor in the manner of the great character actors—Peter Lorre, Sydney Greenstreet, and Orson Welles.

You believe that he is a Turk working for the British Secret Service in Istanbul who was recruited out of the circus where he was a strongman who broke chains for a living. You're sure that he knows every inch of the city, including all his enemies and their daily habits, that all of his sons are on the company payroll, and that he doesn't hesitate to invite his lady friends for trysts in the office.

Armendariz had just finished playing the evil caliph in the King Brothers' production of *Captain Sinbad* when Director Terence Young signed him to play Kerim Bey. Because he wanted to improve his family's financial condition, Armendariz told no one that he had cancer when he came aboard on the Bond picture.

During the final weeks of location shooting in Istanbul, however, Armendariz began to develop a bad limp, and Young finally discovered

the truth. His imminent incapacity forced the producers to make some hasty decisions. Could they finish the film with Armendariz or would they have to find a new actor to portray Kerim Bey?

Young visited Armendariz at his London hotel and asked him about his own plans. The stricken actor mentioned his poor wife and her need for financial security. "Help me," he asked. "I think I can give you two more weeks. Can you finish with me in that time? I would like to get the money and finish the picture."

Young, who felt he couldn't do the film without Armendariz, convinced the producers that he could shoot all the Pinewood Studio sequences with Armendariz in the remaining time. A meeting was called, and art director Syd Cain and his assistant, Michael White, were told to begin construction immediately on everything that would require Armendariz, including the sprawling gypsy camp.

Young and cinematographer Ted Moore planned to film all of the Armendariz close-ups by shooting onto the actor over a stand-in's shoulder. Weeks later, Connery would finish his scenes with Terence Young playing Ali Kerim Bey.

The atmosphere was heavy at Pinewood Studios during those last weeks of May 1963. For everyone concerned with the production, it was as if *From Russia with Love* had taken on a new seriousness. On Sunday, June 9, 1963, Terence Young held a going-away party for Armendariz at his mid-London townhouse.

Most of the production crew was there, and Ian Fleming, himself dying of heart disease, arrived in the late afternoon. The two stricken men had met for the first time in Istanbul and had taken a considerable liking to one another. They spent much of the afternoon on a couch in Young's living room, discussing Armendariz's good friend, the late Ernest Hemingway. Armendariz mentioned that he had gone to Cuba to visit Hemingway in 1961 before coming to Europe for a part in *Francis of Assisi*, for Michael Curtiz. He remembered that final meeting well. He told Fleming, "On the morning that my boat left for Europe, Ernest came down to my little launch to see me off. We embraced and said farewell. It was sad because I knew he was dying. As the boat started off, Ernest ran back, jumped into the boat, almost fell in the sea, and put his arms around me, yelling 'Don't leave! Don't leave me!' He told me that he wouldn't suffer through a long illness. He didn't want to be a vegetable for the rest of his life. He could hardly control himself. But eventually, with a number of people trying to help him, Ernest left the boat and returned to shore. That was the last time I saw him. Two weeks later he went to Idaho and shot himself.''

After Armendariz had finished his story, Fleming, who was terribly impressed, turned to him and said, "You know, [Hemingway's] right; you can never be a vegetable in this life. You've got to go at the right moment.'' Armendariz nodded, tapped an ash from his long cigar, and said, "You're right, Ian.''

On June 18, nine days later, Pedro Armendariz, lying deathly ill with cancer of the lymph glands in a hospital bed in UCLA Medical Center, sent his wife out to have lunch, then took a .357 Colt Magnum that he had smuggled in his luggage and shot himself through the heart with an armor-piercing bullet.

In a strange mixture of fate, Ian Fleming would not last much longer himself. He too would choose the right moment to go.

ARMENDARIZ, JR., PEDRO Son of the late actor Pedro Armendariz, who portrayed Ali Kerim Bey in *From Russia with Love*. Pedro Armendariz, Jr., portrayed Hector Lopez, the puppet president of the fictional Isthmus City in *Licence to Kill*. *See* LOPEZ, PRESIDENT HECTOR.

ARMORED MOTORBOAT James Bond's (ROGER MOORE) transportation up Brazil's Tipperapi River in *Moonraker*. Built by Glastron, the company that had previously manufactured all of the motorboats in *Live and Let Die*, the armored motorboat had a futuristic design and such defense mechanisms as torpedoes and mines. The weapons come in handy when 007 is attacked by a small flotilla of enemy villains led by the intrepid Jaws (RICHARD KIEL).

Like many of James Bond's gadgets, the armored motorboat was also convertible. Just as he's about to go over the falls, Bond pushes a button and triggers a hang glider that propels him within striking distance of Hugo Drax's (MICHEL LONSDALE) jungle space-installation.

ARMORLITE III Brand of bulletproof glass, two inches thick, that coats the outer windows of drug runner Franz Sanchez's (ROBERT DAVI) upper-story office in *Licence to Kill*. In order to assassinate Sanchez with his signature sniper's rifle, Bond (TIMOTHY DALTON) first has to blow out the windows with plastic explosive. That works, but before he can pull the trigger, he's jumped by a pair of Ninja-dressed Hong Kong narcotics officers who are outraged at Bond's rogue actions, which will jeopardize their own operation.

ARMSTRONG, LOUIS (New Orleans, Louisiana, July 4, 1900–1971) Legendary trumpet player who sang "We Have All the Time in the World" in *On Her Majesty's Secret Service*. Armstrong had been in a New York hospital for nearly a year when composer John Barry and lyricist Hal David decided, in 1969, that he was the best person to sing the main song in the film. They needed a man in the autumn of his years who could, with true emotion, sing the line, "We've got all the time in the world," which was taken from the last scene in Ian Fleming's novel.

"Louis Armstrong was the sweetest man alive," recalled Barry solemnly, "but having been laid up for over a year, he had no energy left. He couldn't even play his trumpet. And still he summoned the energy to do our song. At the end of the recording session in New York City, he came up to me and said, 'Thank you for this job.' He was such a marvelous man. He died soon after that.

"The song didn't do a thing when the film came out. It was a very heavy song, so we couldn't use it as the title track. It was buried inside the film and that probably hurt its chances for success. Interestingly, two years later, it suddenly became number one in Italy."

AR-7 FOLDING SNIPER'S RIFLE A .25 caliber rifle carried in James Bond's trick briefcase in *From Russia with Love*. Q Branch has also equipped it with an infrared telescopic sight. With this rifle, Ali Kerim Bey (PEDRO ARMENDARIZ) kills Krilencu, the Bulgarian agent (FRED HAGGERTY) who was sneaking out of his apartment's emergency exit, which is located in the billboard featuring Anita Ekberg in *Call Me Bwana*. Bond also makes use of the gun. He uses it to wound a hand grenade-wielding, helicopter-borne S.P.E.C.T.R.E. assassin who drops the grenade—obliterating the chopper.

ARTIFICIAL HEART Animal rather than human, it's sitting in a Red Cross ice chest in *The Living Daylights* atop $50 million in diamonds disguised in the ice crystals that General Koskov (JEROEN KRABBE) is about to give to the Snow Leopard Brotherhood in exchange for a huge cache of raw opium. *See* $50 MILLION.

ASCOT RACECOURSE Famous British racetrack featured in *A View to a Kill*. It's where Bond (ROGER MOORE), M (ROBERT BROWN), and Sir Godfrey Tibbett (PATRICK MACNEE), dressed formally in top hat and tails, first lay eyes on billionaire industrialist Max Zorin (CHRISTOPHER WALKEN) and his bodyguard, May Day (GRACE JONES). Zorin is there to watch his prize thoroughbred, Pegasus, win another race. *See* PEGASUS.

ASGARD JUMP, THE The celebrated July 1976 ski/parachute jump accomplished by stuntman Rick Sylvester for $30,000 off Baffin Island's Asgard Peak in *The Spy Who Loved Me*.

The idea for this stunt, the most daring of the James Bond series, came to producer Albert R. Broccoli via a Canadian Club Whiskey advertisement in which ace ski-jumper Sylvester was pictured flying off the Asgard. Sylvester later admitted that the Asgard jump had been faked for the advertisement and that he had really jumped off El Capitan in Yosemite Valley, California.

For *The Spy Who Loved Me*, Sylvester accepted the $30,000 fee to jump the Asgard. He would be doubling Bond (ROGER MOORE). While on a mission in Berngarten, Austria, Bond is attacked on the ski slopes by four Russian agents carrying machine guns. After killing their leader (MICHAEL BILLINGTON) and performing some amazing stunt maneuvers himself, Bond reaches the edge of an enormous cliff that he jumps without hesitation, eventually losing his poles and skis.

Will he plunge to his death? Of course not. At the perfect moment, a parachute billows forth with the Union Jack insignia of his country fluttering in the wind. For the James Bond fan, it is one of the most incredible moments in the entire series.

Rick Sylvester explained why Baffin Island's Asgard Peak was chosen in the first place: "The first requirement is a vertical cliff. Not vertical in the layman's sense, but in the climber's denotative, meaning a true 90 degrees. Overhanging would be even nicer. Once I sail over the edge with the skis and a closed parachute, I achieve very little horizontal distance.

"Second, there has to be skiable terrain—snow—leading to the edge.

"Third, the cliff should be high, the higher the better. In fact, the higher, the more spectacular—but actually safer too. More vertical means more time to get rid of the skis and deploy the chute, not to mention more time to react if something goes wrong, like bindings not releasing, chute malfunctioning—the usual unthinkables.

"Fourth, I need a suitable landing area, and fifth, suitable wind conditions."

For Sylvester, the Asgard proved ideal. It was a 3,000-foot narrow-ledged peak in the Auquittuq National Park, an arctic wonderland on Canada's Baffin Island, 1,500 miles north of Montreal in Eskimo country. The Asgard's summit was a football field's length, covered with a carpet of snow and accessible only by helicopter.

While the world girded for the 1976 Summer Olympics in Montreal to the south, second-unit director John Glen assembled his crew of 14. In addition to Sylvester, there were his friend Bob Richardson, an expert climber who would handle safety on the Asgard, working with the camera rigs and keeping a watchful eye on those less experienced in mountain work; Jim Buckley, a parachute expert, who would be in charge of repacking Sylvester's chute, if need be, and keeping track of wind conditions; Monsieur Claude, the proprietor of a Montreal film production company, who would serve as local liaison; a doctor; Rene Dupont, the film's production coordinator in Canada; Alan Hume, the principal cameraman; two other cameramen and one assistant cameraman; two helicopter pilots; one helicopter mechanic; and director, Glen.

Glen's crew was airlifted out of Montreal in early July 1976, and headed north across Greenland to Frobisher Bay—Baffin Island's largest settlement. From Frobisher Bay, they boarded a DC-3 for a two-hour ride over Cumberland Sound to the little village of Pangnirtung, which in the local vernacular means "place where the Bull Caribou meet." Here in Pang, ensconced in a comfortable ex-Hudson Bay hunting lodge, the advance guard of *The Spy Who Loved Me* waited for the appropriate weather conditions.

The Asgard was 50 miles away or a quick hop in the unit's $400-a-day rent-a-copter. For 10 days, they waited for the perfect conditions that would allow Sylvester to make the jump. During the interim, Glen shot some test footage, as well as the approach shot showing Sylvester skiing to the takeoff point.

Long hours were spent in determining responsibilities and camera positions. Glen had to make sure the stunt was captured on film. After 10 days of waiting, the calls began to come in from London: "Has he done it yet?" Back came the negative replies and the grumbling. But there was no other choice. Sylvester wasn't going to risk his life unless the conditions were perfect, and Glen wasn't going to be able to shoot the stunt unless the clouds cleared away from their perch above the Asgard.

The crew remained in Pang, playing cards, watching the Olympics with a decidedly Canadian slant on the cable television, exercising, and making the twice-daily reconnaissance to the Asgard. Sylvester had to continually refurbish the prepared run with ice rakes to assure a smooth takeoff.

On a crisp Monday morning, after a night of late television and beer, a tired, grumpy Sylvester took the morning patrol up to the Asgard. After 5:00 A.M., the helicopter entered the valley. But the clouds were still there, and a heavy rain had set in. Sylvester yawned. Glen frowned and the crew returned to base. Sylvester went back to sleep.

Six hours later, the noon reconnaissance returned to the peak and found the Asgard spotlighted in sunshine and the clouds backing off. Glen phoned the base camp and ordered the crew to scramble. It was time. "What?" mumbled Sylvester into the shortwave. "It's okay," replied Glen. "The wind's died down and the clouds are staying away."

The wind was Sylvester's biggest fear. A harsh breeze could push him against the cliff face, making his parachute useless. He recalled those moments of preparation: "The operation suddenly geared up. I was on the first shuttle.

We flew in and found the Asgard surrounded by clouds, but standing out. And somehow hardly any wind stirred. We had to hurry, though; the clouds looked like they were regrouping for another move."

At midafternoon, the cameramen were in position. The Jet Ranger helicopter hovered nearby, out of range of the cliff face so that the propeller draft wouldn't interfere with Sylvester's parachute. Alan Hume manned the helicopter camera, which was to take the master shot of the sequence. The other two cameras were of secondary importance.

Exactly three minutes before a huge cloud blotted out the sun and enshrouded the Asgard in shade, Sylvester received his confirmation from Glen, drew in a sharp breath, dropped down into the egg position, and started his ski run. He bumped across a mini-ice bulge, remained steady, and then shot over the cliff, virtually inches above the head of one of the cliff-positioned cameramen.

"Down, drop poles," his mind cried mechanically, and the ski poles went shooting off into space.

"Pull off the skis," and the skis fell.

"Pop open the chute," and it opened.

"I see the skis rush by. Hmmm, seemed to take a long time for them to catch up with me. How am I doing? Not bad. Heading out from the wall beautifully, toward the broad silky glacier below.

"I see one ski hit at the wall's base, roll down, then get stuck somewhere on a series of ledges.

"The other one schusses down the steep snow-slope leading from the base of the wall. A strange spectacle. Now gently gliding to a stop. And down I come, under the nylon. Lower, lower, lower, touchdown! Up to my knees in snow. It's over. Again?"

On top of Asgard Peak, Glen was too busy cueing his cameramen to actually see Sylvester's stunt. He was already learning that despite the tests and the painstaking precautions, Hume, in the helicopter, had lost Sylvester soon after he dropped over the cliff wall. It was up to the ledge cameramen to save the day.

After the doctor confirmed that Sylvester was okay, the film was rushed by helicopter back to Pang, where Rene Dupont personally transported it to Montreal and to a Canadian processing facility. All hands waited for the news. Sylvester anxiously wondered whether the stunt would have to be performed again.

In a very emotional moment, the telephone rang in the crew's converted hunting lodge, and everyone crowded around Glen. "Really!" Glen smiled as Dupont described the film as adequate. The helicopter had lost Sylvester, but one of the ledge cameramen had found him and had caught the entire stunt intact. The parachute had opened, if not perfectly, to reveal the Union Jack—and it looked beautiful.

Glen hung up and smiled at everyone. A cheer went up and Sylvester bought a round of drinks. It was time to pack up and go home.

ASTON MARTIN DB-5 WITH MODIFICATIONS James Bond's (SEAN CONNERY) fabulous sports car in *Goldfinger* and *Thunderball*. Although, in his 1960 novel, Ian Fleming had introduced an Aston Martin DB-3 that had a few secret compartments and a homing device, 007 producers Albert R. Broccoli and Harry Saltzman, fresh from their success with the rigged briefcase in *From Russia with Love*, were ready to introduce a vehicle with more elaborate defense mechanisms.

Buying three silver cars from the Aston

Martin plant in England, production designer Ken Adam and special effects supervisor John Stears went to work. As Q (DESMOND LLEWELYN) instructs, the car has the following features:

(1) revolving license plates, valid in all countries; (2) bulletproof front-and-rear wind screen, which Goldfinger's elderly lady gatekeeper (VARLEY THOMAS) later invalidates by peppering Bond's windshield with a blast from her machine gun; (3) audiovisual reception on the dashboard, tied to a magnetic homing

One of the Aston Martin cars makes its debut at the New York World's Fair in 1965. (Frank Herbert)

Two of *Thunderball*'s key props—the Aston Martin DB-5 and the BSA rocket-firing motorcycle. (John Stears Collection)

Side view of the Aston Martin DB–5. (Aston Martin Lagonda)

Front view of the Aston Martin DB–5. (John Stears Collection)

device—with a range of 150 miles—placed in the car 007 is tailing; (4) defense mechanism controls built into the armrest, including left and right front-wing machine guns, smoke screen, oil slick, and a switch to raise the rear bulletproof screen; (5) electrically operated and retractable tire shredders, built into the wheel hubs; and (6) a passenger ejector seat activated by a red button hidden atop the gear shift.

In reality, the special effects department gave these modifications an assist. The machine guns were actually thin metal tubes activated by an electric motor connected to the automobile distributor. Acetylene gas (the kind used in a blow torch) was discharged into the tubing to give the impression of the guns firing. Insert shots of actual machine guns were also used.

The tire shredder, or "chariot scythe" (named for the same device on Messala's chariot in *Ben Hur*), was really an enormous screw knife welded to a spare knock-on wheel nut. The car had to be stopped to exchange the nut, but cinematographer Ted Moore's photography and Peter Hunt's editing show it emerging automatically from the hub center.

Bond's radarscope, which allows him to track Goldfinger, was another nonworking feature that appears in the film as an insert shot, showing the lighted map, its dialing feature and the moving blip that indicates the position of Goldfinger's Rolls.

The ejector seat worked, but it was more a prop than part of the real Aston Martin. The actual ejector seat came from a fighter plane. The seat was spacious and could be mounted only immediately before the actual shot, where a Chinese guard is thrown through the roof. As in a plane, the ejector seat in the Aston Martin was triggered by compressed air cylinders.

For close shots of the car's interior, the air force seat was replaced by a nonejecting passenger seat. The working features included the electrically operated rotating license plate, which gave Bond three alternative numbers for his car.

Bond's smoke screen also worked and was operated by army-type smoke canisters that were discharged into the exhaust tailpipe. The bulletproof screen, which wasn't really bulletproof, was built into the car's trunk and could be raised or lowered electrically.

The special effects department attached electronic squibs to the car's metal to simulate ricocheting bullet hits. Into the car's rear light cluster, the special effects department built two chambers that could be opened to reveal an oil-slick sprayer that contained 15 gallons of colored water and a supply of three-point nails that were blown out onto the highway by compressed air. The car was completed on schedule in the spring of 1964.

According to Aston Martin, the nail ejector was never used in the film, because it might have given children the wrong kind of inspiration. Only one car contained all of the special modifications, and it was sold to Eon Productions, rather than given away free as was originally believed. However, all the subsequent interest in the car, once *Goldfinger* was released, forced Aston Martin to build two more replicas. These were sent to events, shows, carnivals, and festivals until the early 1970s when they were sold to collectors. If you look into the replicas' interiors, you can see features that weren't showcased in the film, including a telephone built right into the driver's door, a five-speed manual transmission, a reserve gas tank, a speedometer toplined at 150 mph, a hand-crafted body, and a very luxurious antelope-hide interior.

The modified Aston Martin DB-5 replaced Bond's Bentley, which is seen briefly in *From Russia with Love*.

In *Goldfinger*, after winning the golf match and planting the homing device in his adversary's Rolls, Bond has the Aston Martin transported to the European mainland via the British United Air Ferry. He then follows Goldfinger's Rolls-Royce Phantom 337 to Switzerland, where he meets and shreds the tires of the very attractive Tilly Masterson (TANIA MALLET), the revenge-seeking, poor-shooting sister of the late Jill Masterson (SHIRLEY EATON).

Having accidentally heard Goldfinger utter "Operation Grand Slam" to the Red Chinese agent Mr. Ling (BURT KWOUK), Bond (with Tilly in tow), hops in his DB-5 and attempts to escape from the Swiss factory complex, with three Mercedes Benz on his tail. His defense-mechanism controls are immediately put to work.

The smoke screen eliminates one Mercedes, which smashes blindly into a tree; a second Mercedes runs into Bond's manufactured oil slick, skids off the road, and explodes into the side of Goldfinger's factory; but the third corners Bond at a dead end.

After Tilly is decapitated by Oddjob (HAROLD SAKATA), Bond surrenders to his Chinese and Korean captors. In one of the great blunders, they allow him to drive his own car back to the factory, guarded by one gun-toting Asian in the passenger seat. Make that one ex-gun-toting Asian, since Bond immediately triggers the ejection seat.

Back in business, he nonetheless is stymied by the gun-toting lady gatekeeper and forced back into the factory compound, where he leads two enemy Mercedeses on a high-speed chase punched up in editing by Peter Hunt.

Finally, blinded by what he thinks are automobile headlights headed straight for him, 007 crashes his Aston Martin into a brick wall. Oddjob has rigged a mirror that reflects Bond's own headlights back at him; 007 is captured again.

The Aston Martin DB-5 is also featured briefly in the *Thunderball* teaser when 007 activates his rear bulletproof screen and then unleashes a powerful jet of water at a group of S.P.E.C.T.R.E. bodyguards.

A 1968 Aston Martin is featured during the Portuguese sequences of *On Her Majesty's Secret Service*. It's the car Bond (GEORGE LAZENBY) is driving in director Peter Hunt's striking opening sequence when he first sees Tracy (DIANA RIGG) passing him in her Cougar.

Driving the Aston Martin onto the actual beach, 007 rescues Tracy before she can drown herself. At the end of the film, the Aston Martin becomes the honeymoon car for newlyweds Bond and Tracy. Because friends have attached a conspicuous *Just Married* sign to the car's rear, Bond stops on the highway to remove it. At that very moment, Blofeld (TELLY SAVALAS) and Irma Bunt (ILSE STEPPAT) race by, spraying the car with machine gun fire that kills Tracy.

In *The Living Daylights*, the new James Bond (TIMOTHY DALTON) is assigned a brand-new 1986 Aston Martin, which is equipped with a parcel of customized defense mechanisms designed for snow warfare, including retractable skids that can maneuver the vehicle on ice. A laser mounted in the wheel hubs

performs practically the same maneuver, albeit more cleanly, as the spinning chariot-scythe knives in *Goldfinger*; a rocket launcher has a visible target display in the windshield; and a rocket-boosted engine allows the car to virtually fly over a towering roadblock. Like the later-model Lotus Esprit, this Aston Martin is also equipped with a self-destruct mechanism so that the gadgety vehicle doesn't fall into the wrong hands.

A.T.A.C. The acronym for Automatic Targeting Attack Communicator, a device employed by the *St. Georges*, a British surveillance and communications ship in *For Your Eyes Only*. The top secret device uses an ultra-low-frequency coded transmission to order nuclear submarines to launch ballistic missiles. When the *St. Georges* is sunk off the coast of Albania, the A.T.A.C. becomes a salvageable prize for the British and the Russians. Deploying Timothy Havelock's (JACK HEDLEY) two-man submarine, the *Neptune*, Bond (ROGER MOORE) with Melina's (CAROLE BOUQUET) help enters the sunken *St. Georges* and retrieves the A.T.A.C.

Unfortunately, it is soon recovered by Russian agent Kristatos (JULIAN GLOVER), who plans to turn it over to General Gogol (WALTER GOTELL). When Bond triumphs, in the film's conclusion, atop the Meteora in Greece, he tosses the A.T.A.C computer over the cliff, where it smashes into a million pieces.

ATKINSON, ROWAN British actor and television personality who portrayed bumbling

British comedian Rowan Atkinson portrayed fumbling Nigel Small-Fawcett in *Never Say Never Again.* (Taliafilm)

foreign officer Nigel Small-Fawcett in *Never Say Never Again*.

ATLANTIC IRON AND METAL COMPANY Miami auto-wrecking yard featured in *Goldfinger*. The firm's crane and electromagnet lifts the body of Oddjob's (HAROLD SAKATA) Lincoln Continental and places it into the metal compactor, crushing it into a small metal lump that fits nicely into the bed of Oddjob's Ford Ranchero. As the Lincoln is being lifted, you can see through the front hood that this car has no engine; only a body shell was crushed.

ATLANTIS (aka Stromberg Marine Research Laboratory) Huge spiderlike amphibian structure located off the coast of Sardinia in *The Spy Who Loved Me*. It's the centerpiece of billionaire shipping magnate Karl Stromberg's (CURT JURGENS) undersea city of the future. Explained production designer Ken Adam, "The idea for Atlantis was not in the original script for *The Spy Who Loved Me*. Cubby (Broccoli), Lewis Gilbert, and I went out to Okinawa because we had heard about a Japanese structure that could rise out of the water.

"When we got there, it turned out to be a white elephant. It was something the Japanese government had spent $77 million on for Expo

'75, a huge floating exhibition hall called the *Aquapolis*.

"It looked like a big floating oil platform, and since it looked so much like an oil rig, I didn't like it. It was gigantic, though, and at first I tried to make it work for us by designing it in a way to make use of models and matte paintings. But I never could get anywhere on that. It had an immense heliport on the top of the structure, which wasn't necessary. You didn't need a heliport that big.

"When we were in Okinawa, the *Aquapolis* wasn't quite completed. They were still planning to give it huge solar panels. Since the *Aquapolis* was a big disappointment, I decided to design something entirely new.

"And for the interiors, I wanted to get away from my old straight-line concepts. This time I was going to use circles and ellipses, a concept partly influenced by our location scouting in Sardinia, where much of the architecture along the Costa Smeralda utilizes that style.

"As it turned out, this concept was in line with the future of design in which we see a lot of plastic furniture and prefabricated housing in those shapes. All of the fish tanks in Atlantis were elliptical, the escape corridors featured elliptical exit ways, and Stromberg's big shark pond was circular in shape."

Derek Meddings's Atlantis model for *The Spy Who Loved Me*. To gauge its actual size, look at the camera lens placed in the bottom left hand corner. (Don Griffin, Perry Oceanographics)

AUBERGINE, ACHILLE Detective hired by the French Jockey Club to look into the possibility that Max Zorin (CHRISTOPHER WALKEN) may be involved in a horse-fixing scheme in *A View to a Kill*. Meeting James Bond (ROGER MOORE) for lunch in the Eiffel Tower Restaurant, Aubergine (JEAN ROUGERIE) tells Bond that drug tests on Zorin's horses have come up negative. He plans to continue his investigation at Zorin's annual horse sale at his stud farm near Paris. Before Aubergine can continue, however, he's struck in the side of the face by a poisonous-barb-carrying butterfly dangled on a puppeteer's line by the murderous May Day (GRACE JONES), who escapes James Bond's clutches by diving off the Eiffel Tower and parachuting to safety.

AUGER, CLAUDINE (Paris, April 26, 1942-   ) French actress and former Miss France (1958) who perfectly portrayed Dominique "Domino" Derval in *Thunderball*. Her measurements in 1965 were 36–23–37.

AUGSBURG According to the London College of Arms, it's the ancestral home of the de Bleuchamp, a royal family that may or may not be related to Ernst Stavro Blofeld (TELLY SAVALAS) in *On Her Majesty's Secret Service*. Blofeld is trying to lay official claim to the title: Count Balthazar de Bleuchamp.

Bond (GEORGE LAZENBY), posing as Sir Hilary Bray of the London College of Arms, insists that Blofeld journey to Augsburg, where the final research can be done. Bond knows that if he can entice Blofeld out of Switzerland, the British Secret Service can arrest him.

Unfortunately, even the best information from the London College of Arms can be incorrect. Blofeld later trips up Bond when he explains that the de Bleuchamp tombs are not located at Augsburg at all, but at the St. Anna Cathedral at Kirsche.

French actress Claudine Auger played sultry playgirl Domino in *Thunderball*.
(Loomis Dean/Camera Press, Globe Photo)

AUGUST 10, 1982 The first day of filming on *Octopussy*. The sequence is James Bond's (ROGER MOORE) arrival at Checkpoint Charlie in West Berlin.

AU-1 The license plate of Goldfinger's (GERT FROBE) Rolls-Royce Phantom 337.

AURIC ENTERPRISES A.C. Sign on the roof of Goldfinger's (GERT FROBE) factory in Switzerland.

AURIC SPECTROMETER A device in *Goldfinger* that detects the presence of Delta Nine nerve gas in the atmosphere. When the reading comes up negative, Kisch (MICHAEL MELLINGER) knows it's okay for his unit to remove their gas masks. What he doesn't know is that, thanks to Pussy Galore (HONOR BLACKMAN), no gas was sprayed in the first place, and all the supposedly dead soldiers that are lying around are faking it.

AURIC STUD Goldfinger's (GERT FROBE) estate in Kentucky, built full scale in England at the Pinewood Studios paddock, where he raises racehorses and plans Operation Grand Slam. His huge ranch house is equipped with a game room where a "hoods convention" assembles to hear the plan.

Designed by Ken Adam, the room is rigged

The Auric Stud "rumpus room," a game room where the "hood's convention" takes place in *Goldfinger*. (Ronnie Udell Collection)

Auric Stud, Goldfinger's Kentucky ranch, built on the Pinewood Studios lot in England. (Ronnie Udell Collection)

with a number of electronic controls that can transform it into a high-tech war room, replete with huge maps and photographs, and a model of Fort Knox that rises majestically from the floor. Escaping from his holding cell, James Bond (SEAN CONNERY) eavesdrops on Goldfinger's briefing and learns enough to send a message to the CIA.

After the briefing, while the hoods are digesting the complex plan that could net each of them $10 million, Goldfinger orders his lieutenant, Kisch (MICHAEL MELLINGER), to spray Delta Nine nerve gas into the room, which has been sealed tight. He does and the convention adjourns—forever.

AU 603 License plate of the green Rolls Royce in Hong Kong that transports Scaramanga (CHRISTOPHER LEE) and Andrea (MAUD ADAMS) in *The Man with the Golden Gun*. The automobile actually belongs to the Peninsula Hotel, which operates a fleet of Rolls-Royces.

AUSTRIAN BORDER Where Q (DESMOND LLEWELYN) plucks defecting Russian General Georgi Koskov (JEROEN KRABBE) out of the Trans Siberian Pipeline pipe after his escape from Bratislava in *The Living Daylights*. He's then shoved into a British Harrier jump-jet and flown to England. It's also where Bond (TIMOTHY DALTON) and Kara (MARYAM D'ABO) escape to after their hair-raising battle with Czechoslovakian snow troops.

AUTHORITY Name given to the female agents in *Casino Royale* who supervise the espionage activities of Dr. Noah (WOODY ALLEN).

AVA CIA agent, portrayed by Dulice Liecier, who is working in Tangier for Felix Leiter (JOHN TERRY) in *The Living Daylights*. Along with her colleague, Liz, she helps James Bond (TIMOTHY DALTON) escape from local police after he "assassinates" Russian General Pushkin (JOHN RHYS-DAVIES).

AWACS U.S. Air Force surveillance aircraft that helps shadow Maximillian Largo's (KLAUS MARIA BRANDAUER) *Flying Saucer* yacht in *Never Say Never Again*.

B

BACARDI ON THE ROCKS KGB Major Anya Amasova's (BARBARA BACH) favorite drink, as ordered by James Bond (ROGER MOORE) at Cairo's Mojaba Club in *The Spy Who Loved Me.*

BACCARAT Blackjack-like card game, popular in European casinos, that is the focal point of the TV film "Casino Royale." Soviet masterspy Le Chiffre (PETER LORRE) has been losing heavily at the game. Unless he comes up with the 80 million francs he's illegally borrowed from Soviet coffers, the KGB will target him for assassination. With 26 million francs left, Le Chiffre plans to assume the bank and win back his fortune. James Bond (BARRY NELSON) is assigned the task of bankrupting Le Chiffre at the tables.

As in blackjack, the object of baccarat is to get two cards closest to a specific number—in this case, the number nine, as compared with blackjack's 21. Picture cards are worth nothing. Players are allowed to draw one card. If a player draws two picture cards, he has zero, which is called "baccarat." If a player draws one card and acquires a total higher than nine, he is busted, which is also called "baccarat."

Unlike blackjack, there is no house dealer. A player can assume the deal by becoming the "bank" and offering a specific amount of money that becomes the total in that bank. A player is the bank until he or she is busted or decides to quit by passing the shoe. Any player who arrives at the table starts his or her play by saying, "Banco," meaning he or she challenges the bank to a game. The player may cover all or part of the bank's total.

In the TV film "Casino Royale," the bets are for the total amount of the bank. (No chintzing on Bond's part—he's playing for keeps.) Here's the baccarat game on the night Le Chiffre must win back his money. Both Bond's and Le Chiffre's hands are featured, plus the individual stake, or pot, of each game and the rise and fall of Le Chiffre's winnings. Having won two preliminary hands against another opponent, Le Chiffre's stake is up to 29 million francs when Bond enters the game.

BACCARAT HANDS IN "CASINO ROYALE"

LE CHIFFRE	BOND	STAKE (in francs)	LE CHIFFRE'S WINNINGS (in francs)
baccarat	9	4 million	25 million
7	5	2 million	27 million
9	7	4 million	31 million
6	3	8 million	39 million
9	7	16 million	55 million

(At this point, Bond is broke—but he suddenly receives a mysterious envelope filled with 35 million francs that replenishes his own coffer.)

LE CHIFFRE	BOND	STAKE (in francs)	LE CHIFFRE'S WINNINGS (in francs)
3	4	32 million	23 million
baccarat	9	23 million	busted

In the 1967 feature version of *Casino Royale*, Le Chiffre (ORSON WELLES) was matched against baccarat expert Evelyn Tremble (PETER SELLERS), who was impersonating James Bond. Their match lasted only three hands. In the first, Le Chiffre beats "Bond" 9–6; in the second, Le Chiffre wins 7–5. However, in the third match, worth 50 million francs, "Bond" and Le Chiffre both draw fives. While Bond chooses to stand, Le Chiffre takes a card and draws another five giving him a total of ten or zero ("baccarat"). "Bond" wins the 50 million francs.

BACH, BARBARA (New York City, August 27, 1947–   ) American actress, and wife of former Beatle Ringo Starr, who portrayed resourceful KGB agent Major Anya Amasova in *The Spy Who Loved Me.*

Said director Lewis Gilbert, "Barbara was a very serene kind of girl, very quiet, and thus very effective as the Russian agent. We didn't want anyone flashy or loud. And we couldn't have someone too young either—a girl in her early twenties—because she wouldn't match up with Roger. She had to be a mature woman, especially since she was playing a top KGB assassin."

Beginning with Major Amasova in *The Spy Who Loved Me*, the Bond filmmakers began to give the women in 007's life a stronger dose of reality. The chauvinistic approach to the breathless, bosomy female of the 1960s was replaced with a more believable female protagonist who could defend herself and show 007 a thing or two. Major Amasova, as she demonstrates throughout *Spy*, had these qualities. *See* AMASOVA, MAJOR ANYA.

BACKGAMMON GAME A spirited contest between Kamal Khan (LOUIS JOURDAN) and James Bond (ROGER MOORE) in *Octopussy*. Structured like the golf match in *Goldfinger*, it's the first real face-to-face encounter between the two enemies in the film. Bond has actually been observing Kamal's game with the losing Major Clive (STUART SAUNDERS), who announces that he cannot accept the challenge when Kamal raises the stakes to 100,000 rupees. 007 also notices that Kamal is using loaded dice.

Bond takes over the game, only to lose the full amount when Kamal rolls double sixes. This time, 007 doubles the bet to 200,000 rupees. Asked for collateral, he produces the genuine Fabergé egg he stole from Sotheby's. A smug Kamal agrees to the bet and explains that Bond can win only with double sixes.

As a large crowd observes the encounter, Bond remarks that he needs some of Kamal's luck, so he takes his opponent's dice. After shaking the dice in their container, he rolls them out on the table, producing winning double sixes. Asked to pay Bond in cash, Kamal Khan stares daggers across the table and says with a Bond movie villain's typical malice, "Spend the money quickly, Mr. Bond."

BAINES The British agent killed by a snake bite on San Monique island in *Live and Let Die*. He shared the same bootmaker as 007.

BAJA The site off the Mexican coast of Ernst Stavro Blofeld's (CHARLES GRAY) oil-rig headquarters in *Diamonds Are Forever*. Bond (SEAN CONNERY) and billionaire Willard Whyte (JIMMY DEAN) discover the base when they notice that Blofeld has made an oil-well addition to the floor-size map in Whyte's Las Vegas penthouse. "Baja!" says Whyte. "I haven't got anything in Baja."

BAKER, GEORGE (1929–   ) British leading man who portrayed heraldry expert Sir Hilary Bray in *On Her Majesty's Secret Service*. Baker also dubbed George Lazenby's voice for the sequences in which Bond impersonates Bray at Blofeld's (TELLY SAVALAS) mountain hide-

Actor George Baker was Sir Hilary Bray in *On Her Majesty's Secret Service*. (Dennis Selinger)

away. He returned briefly as Captain Benson in *The Spy Who Loved Me*. According to director Terence Young, Baker was one of the actors considered for the part of James Bond prior to *Dr. No*. *See* BRAY, SIR HILARY.

BAKER, GLYN British actor who portrayed 002 in *The Living Daylights* teaser. *See* 002.

British actor Glyn Baker portrayed 002 in *The Living Daylights*. (ICM)

BAKER, JOE DON (Groesbeck, Texas, February 12, 1936–   ) American tough-guy actor who portrayed shady arms dealer Brad Whitaker in *The Living Daylights*. Fascinated by arms and armies, Whitaker has turned his home into a museum of wax dummies, military miniature dioramas, and historical arms. In reality, he's a pathetic little weasel who was thrown out of West Point. Baker, one of Hollywood's most physical actors—he shined in the first *Walking Tall* (1973)—has very little to do in *The Living Daylights* except strut around his house in a thoroughly starched uniform and mouth historical platitudes. *See* WHITAKER, BRAD.

BAMBI One of the acrobatic ladies assigned the task of guarding Willard Whyte (JIMMY DEAN) in *Diamonds Are Forever*. Bambi (DONNA GARRAT) and her partner Thumper (TRINA PARKS) give James Bond a handful of trouble when he arrives to rescue Whyte. Agent 007 finally gets the better of them in the swimming pool. *See* GARRAT, DONNA

BANCO DE ISTHMUS The largest bank in fictional Isthmus City, where South American drug runner Franz Sanchez (ROBERT DAVI) launders his money in *Licence to Kill*. Arriving in town with $4.9 million in stolen drug loot, James Bond (TIMOTHY DALTON) becomes an instant high roller when he deposits the sum in the bank that's owned by Sanchez. The money helps legitimize Bond's cover as an ex-British agent and a gun for hire.

BARDOT, BRIGITTE (Paris, September 28, 1934–   ) Sexy French actress who was director Peter Hunt's first choice for the part of Tracy Vicenzo in *On Her Majesty's Secret Service*.

Said Hunt, "She would have looked a lot like the Tracy in the book. So Harry Saltzman and I went down to the south of France to see her. We had dinner, twice actually, and she was delightful. But on the second night she informed us that she had just signed a deal to do *Shalako* with Sean Connery."

Diana Rigg was eventually signed to play the woman who marries James Bond at the film's conclusion.

BARNES, PRISCILLA (Fort Dix, New Jersey) American actress and light comedienne who portrayed Della Churchill, CIA agent Felix Leiter's (DAVID HEDISON) doomed bride, who's murdered by drug lord Franz Sanchez's (ROBERT DAVI) henchmen in *Licence to Kill*. Barnes is best known for her running part on the "Three's Company" television series. *See* CHURCHILL, DELLA.

BARR, LEONARD (1903–1980) Wisecracking comedian who portrayed nightclub entertainer and diamond smuggler Shady Tree in *Diamonds Are Forever*.

BARR, PATRICK (1908–1985) British character actor who portrayed the British ambassador to East Germany in *Octopussy*. He receives the Fabergé-egg forgery from mortally wounded 009 (ANDY BRADFORD).

Actor Patrick Barr played the British Ambassador to East Germany in *Octopussy*.
(National Film Archive, London)

BARRELHEAD BAR Seedy watering hole in Bimini where Bond (TIMOTHY DALTON) meets CIA undercover agent Pam Bouvier (CAREY LOWELL) in *Licence to Kill*.

Equipped with a formidable Mossberg Rogue shotgun, Pam is observing the activities of some of Franz Sanchez's (ROBERT DAVI) drug runners when she's joined by Bond. When villainous Dario (BENICIO DEL TORO) joins the party, a brawl breaks out, with Bouvier and

Bond putting on a good show until Pam blasts a hole in the barroom wall so they can make good their escape. Dario eventually shoots Pam in the back, but she survives, thanks to some body armor.

The Barrelhead Bar was actually an interior designed by Peter Lamont and filmed at the Churubusco Studios in Mexico City. The exterior where Bond's motorboat arrives at the dock was filmed at the Harbor Lights Bar in Key West, Florida.

BARRY, JOHN (York, England, 1933-) (real name, John Barry Prendergast) Four-time Oscar-winning British film composer best known for his work on the James Bond films. Barry's contribution to the series has been enormous, especially in the early days when the tenor of the films was more serious.

His Bond theme, credited to Monty Norman, is arguably the most famous signature theme in film history and a trademark of the Albert R. Broccoli–produced Bonds. When the Jack Schwartzman–produced *Never Say Never Again* film opened in 1983 without the signature theme, one of the common complaints was the lack of "real James Bond music."

Barry's show-business influence probably dates back to his maternal grandfather, a sea captain who used his pension to purchase the Repertory Theater in Lancaster, England, which he owned and operated until his death. Barry's mother was an accomplished piano player, and his father, John Xavier Prendergast, took over his father's theatrical operation, later expanding it into a chain of theaters and cinemas.

Young Barry attended convent school until the age of nine when he left for a public school education in London. He followed his mother's tutelage at first and practiced piano, but by the time he was 16 he had taken a liking to the trumpet. He was also studying harmony and orchestration with Dr. Francis Jackson, the master of music at Yorkminster Cathedral, while also playing trumpet in a local dance band. In 1952 Barry was drafted and spent three years in the Green Howard Regiment of the First Infantry Division, which was sent to Egypt and Cyprus. Draftees were required to spend only two years in the service, but Barry wanted to continue to study music in the regimental band, so he agreed to sign on for the extra year in order to get his assignment.

On Cyprus, he started a practical correspondence course with Bill Russo, Stan Kenton's orchestra arranger in the United States. He began to arrange the music for his regiment, and when he left the Army in 1955, he was practically guaranteed a good orchestral job in London.

It was at this point, in 1955, that Bill Haley and Elvis Presley appeared on the music scene, affecting the futures of all young musicians everywhere, especially Barry, who spent every spare moment listening to the new sound and preparing his own first rock and jazz rendition.

In 1956 Barry formed the John Barry Seven in London with three army buddies and their friends. He was the first bandleader in England to employ an electric bass guitar player. Barry and his jazz-oriented group dived headfirst into the rock & roll revolution, and within two years they were the leading group in England.

Their success led directly to movie offers, the first of which was a little film titled *Beat Girl*, which was released by Renown Films in 1960. Between 1960 and 1963, Barry and his group toured England and worked on the scores of three more films: *The Amorous Mr. Prawn* (1962), *The L-Shaped Room* (1963), and *Never Let Go* (1963).

Barry's involvement with the Bond movies began in late 1962 when he received a call from Noel Rogers of United Artists Records. Barry had recorded two hit records for United Artists. One called "Hit and Miss" was a signature tune for a BBC program called "Juke Box Jury," and the other was an English version of the American hit "Walk Don't Run."

With two important instrumentals on the charts, UA was interested in Barry for the first Bond film, *Dr. No*. Barry learned from Rogers that 007 producers Broccoli and Saltzman were disenchanted with a Bond theme created by composer Monty Norman and that *Dr. No* needed a vibrant theme as soon as possible.

Considering the impact his theme would have on the future of the series, it is ironic that Barry completed his job without ever having seen *Dr. No*. He simply was handed a timing sheet and told to come up with a two-and-a-half-minute theme that could fit conveniently into the film's title track. Although he composed the piece from scratch, it was not entirely original. He borrowed from his own instrumental repertoire, especially a little tune titled "Bea's Knees," which featured that same distinctly plucked guitar.

Little did Broccoli and Saltzman know when they first heard the Bond theme how popular it would become. Barry's fee for the James Bond theme was 200 pounds, less than $1,000. Contractually, because of Monty Norman, Barry would never receive credit for creating the most famous theme in movie history. In fact, it is Norman's name—not Barry's—that always appears on the credits if the Bond theme is used.

Still, the success of the first film encouraged a creative relationship to develop between Barry and the Bond films that continues to this day.

Barry's 007 scores: *Dr. No* (theme only), *From Russia with Love, Goldfinger, Thunderball, You Only Live Twice, On Her Majesty's Secret Service, Diamonds Are Forever, The Man with the Golden Gun, Moonraker, Octopussy, A View to a Kill,* and *The Living Daylights.*

BARRY MANILOW RECORDS The music with which the new Miss Moneypenny (CAROLINE BLISS) attempts to lure the new James Bond (TIMOTHY DALTON) to her apartment in *The Living Daylights.*

BARSOV, SERGEI Handsome Russian KGB agent, portrayed by Michael Billington, who dies during an abortive assassination attempt on Bond (ROGER MOORE) in Berngarten, Austria, in *The Spy Who Loved Me* teaser. Later 007 learns that Barsov was Major Anya Amasova's (BARBARA BACH) lover.

BARTLETT, RUBY A British allergy patient, portrayed by actress Angela Scoular, at Piz Gloria in *On Her Majesty's Secret Service.* Ruby's from Morecamb Bay, Lancashire, and she's terribly allergic to chicken. She also develops a passionate interest in Bond's cover as heraldry expert Sir Hilary Bray, Baronet. She astutely refers to his title as "inferior baron," but Hilary doesn't take it as an insult. According to Irma Bunt (ILSE STEPPAT), patients are not allowed to give their room assignments to strangers. Unable to verbally pass her room number to Bond (GEORGE LAZENBY) at dinner, Ruby writes her room number in lipstick on his inner thigh.

Later, Bond manages to sneak into her room. They're about to make love when Blofeld's (TELLY SAVALAS) brainwashing begins.

BASE COMMANDER Steadfast U.S. Air Force general, portrayed by Bruce Boa in *Octopussy,* who commands the U.S. Air Force base at Feldstadt, West Germany, where a Russian atomic bomb has been placed for detonation. At first treating James Bond's (ROGER MOORE) warning as a joke, the commander becomes an instant believer when Octopussy (MAUD ADAMS) shoots the lock off the base of the circus cannon, revealing the ticking atomic device. Ordering his MPs to let Bond go, he quiets the crowd and watches as 007 carefully removes the detonator with nary a second to spare.

BASIL Tall blond henchman of Russian masterspy Le Chiffre (PETER LORRE) in the TV film "Casino Royale." He's later killed by James Bond (BARRY NELSON).

BASINGER, KIM (Athens, Georgia, December 8, 1953–   ) American actress and former model who portrayed Maximillian Lar-

On the beach with Sean Connery and Kim Basinger in *Never Say Never Again.* (Taliafilm)

Bond (SEAN CONNERY) confronts Domino (KIM BASINGER) in *Never Say Never Again.* (Taliafilm)

go's (KLAUS MARIA BRANDAUER) mistress, Domino Petachi, in *Never Say Never Again.* The spectacularly proportioned Basinger, who would go on to play Vicki Vale in *Batman,* was the perfect love interest for returning 007 (SEAN CONNERY).

Unlike Roger Moore, who spent a limited amount of lovemaking time with his leading ladies, Connery in *Never Say Never Again* is very much attached to Basinger in the film's second half. The steamy highlights include their massage rendezvous in the south of France, their shower in the American nuclear sub, and their hot tub scene at the film's conclusion. *See* PETACHI, DOMINO.

BASSEY, SHIRLEY (Tiger Bay, Cardiff, England, January 8, 1937–   ) International recording artist and a diva of rhythm and blues who recorded the title songs for three James Bond films: *Goldfinger* (1964), *Diamonds Are Forever* (1971), and *Moonraker* (1979). Bassey was discovered in 1955 at the Aston Club by music impresario Jack Hilton, who signed her to

appear in "Such Is Life," a show built around the comedian Al Read. Bassey was making records by 1956 and had a run of respectable hits by the time she was 23.

Diva Shirley Bassey, who warbled the title tracks to *Goldfinger, Diamonds Are Forever,* and *Moonraker.* (Shirley Bassey)

BATHOSUB Ernst Stavro Blofeld's (CHARLES GRAY) one-man submarine in *Diamonds Are Forever*. Terming his situation aboard the oil rig "hopeless," Blofeld enters the sub and orders his crane driver to lower him into the ocean. Bond (SEAN CONNERY), however, knocks out the driver and gains control of the sub himself. Literally in the driver's seat, he begins to play with his longtime nemesis, eventually smashing the sub into the wall of a building, where it explodes.

"Originally," recalled screenwriter Tom Mankiewicz, "in my first version of the ending, Blofeld was escaping underwater in his bathosub when Bond sees the submarine idling in 12 feet of water. Bond dives off the oil rig, holding the long string of a huge weather balloon, which he ties to the sub's conning tower. . . . And they were going to wind up in a giant salt mine. But this was all very long and involved . . .

"First of all, Blofeld was going to die in the salt mine . . . . At that particular point, nobody knew what was going to happen in the next film. . . . Blofeld might have been in the next film, especially if somebody had a good idea.

"The picture was quite long at the time and . . . something had to go. So we said, 'Let's deal with Blofeld on the rig.' Because, as you remember, we still had to get to our tag with Mr. Wint and Mr. Kidd on the ocean liner."

BAUCHAU, PATRICK French actor who portrayed Scarpine, Max Zorin's (CHRISTOPHER WALKEN) head of security, in *A View to a Kill*. *See* SCARPINE.

BAUER, DAVID (1918–1973) British actor who portrayed soft-spoken mortuary owner/ diamond smuggler Morton Slumber in *Diamonds Are Forever*.

Actor David Bauer portrayed mortician Morton Slumber in *Diamonds Are Forever*. (National Film Archive, London)

BAUXITE MINE The perfect cover for Dr. No's (JOSEPH WISEMAN) operations on Crab Key. The scenes were filmed at an actual bauxite mine located on the Jamaican coast near Ocho Rios. In Fleming's original *Dr. No* novel, the operations were disguised within a guano, or "bird dung," factory.

BAYLDON, GEOFFREY (1924–   ) British character actor who portrayed Q as a foppish bureaucrat in the *Casino Royale* spoof. *See* Q.

BAYLISS, PETER (Kingston-upon-Thames, England, June 27, 1927–   ) British character actor who portrayed Commissar Benz, the Rus-

Actor Peter Bayliss portrayed Benz, the mustachioed Russian security man, in *From Russia With Love*. (Peter Bayliss Collection)

sian security man in Istanbul, in *From Russia with Love*. Bayliss had worked with Sean Connery the previous year in a stage production of *Judith*, performed at Her Majesty's Theater. *See* BENZ.

BECHMANN, DR. Doomed nuclear physicist, portrayed by Cyril Shaps, who, with his partner Professor Markovitz (MILO SPERBER), is responsible for the design of a nuclear-submarine tracking system in *The Spy Who Loved Me*. Working for fanatical billionaire shipping magnate Karl Stromberg (CURT JURGENS), Bechmann and Markovitz will each receive $10 million for their work. However, once they leave Atlantis, their helicopter is blown out of the sky by Stromberg, who cancels the transfer of the $20 million. Among the James

Bond villains, scientific help usually has one reward—death.

BECKWITH, REGINALD (1908–1965) Chubby British character actor who portrayed Kenniston, the Home Secretary's assistant in *Thunderball*.

BEDI, KABIR (India, 1946–   ) Half-English, half–East Indian actor who portrayed Gobinda, Kamal Khan's (LOUIS JOURDAN) bodyguard, in *Octopussy*. See GOBINDA.

"BEFORE SETTING OUT ON REVENGE, YOU FIRST DIG TWO GRAVES" Chinese proverb related to Melina Havelock (CAROLE BOUQUET) by James Bond (ROGER MOORE) in *For Your Eyes Only*. It doesn't have much effect on Melina, who has just witnessed the brutal machine-gunning of her parents.

BELGRADE, YUGOSLAVIA The Orient Express's first stop after it leaves Istanbul, Turkey, in *From Russia with Love*. Arriving in the train station at precisely 6:32 P.M., James Bond (SEAN CONNERY) leaves the train and meets with one of Ali Kerim Bey's (PEDRO ARMENDARIZ) sons, who learns that his father's been killed.

Bond thinks that Kerim Bey was killed by the Russian agent Benz (PETER BAYLISS). He doesn't realize Red Grant (ROBERT SHAW) killed both operatives. Bond hands over Kerim Bey's effects to his son, including his wallet and cigar holder. He then asks that a message be sent immediately to M in London, requesting reinforcements at the next stop: Zagreb.

BELL JET PACK A one-man, jet-propelled flying apparatus worn by James Bond (SEAN CONNERY) during his escape from Jacques Boitier's (BOB SIMMONS) French chateau in the *Thunderball* teaser. As 007 remarks to his French contact (MITSOUKO), "No well-dressed man should be without one." In reality, the suit was worn by a U.S. Army jet-pack specialist assigned to the film crew. The stunt was performed on the afternoon of February 19, 1965. Bond's escapade with the jet pack became

a prominent element of the film's poster, along with his underwater antics.

BELL, MRS. Terrified elderly Louisiana flying student, portrayed by Ruth Kempf, whose training plane is commandeered by James Bond (ROGER MOORE) in *Live and Let Die*. Without uttering a word, Bell is subjected to Bond's intervention (she had been expecting her normal trainer, Mr. Bleeker), a chase through a crowded airport, gunfire from the henchmen of Mr. Big (YAPHET KOTTO), and finally a crash that severs both of the plane's wings.

BELLY DANCER Given its exotic locations and beautiful women, it's not surprising to find belly dancers in the James Bond series. With their jingling costumes, voluptuous figures, and alluring artistry, they keep the Bond movies within their PG ratings, too.

Belly dancers figure prominently in *From Russia with Love*. Not only does Leila dance for Bond (SEAN CONNERY) at the gypsy camp, but she is featured in the title credits designed by Robert Brownjohn and Trevor Bond.

According to cinematographer Frank Tidy (*Dracula, Spacehunter: Adventures in the Forbidden Zone*), who broke into the film business as an assistant to Brownjohn and Bond, the idea for the *From Russia with Love* titles came when Brownjohn's wife walked in front of a slide show he was projecting. From that idea came the concept of projecting the titles on the undulating, highly erotic form of a belly dancer. Among cinematographers, the in-joke on the *From Russia with Love* credits was projecting cinematographer Ted Moore's credit on the girl's posterior.

In *The Man with the Golden Gun*, on the trail of Francisco Scaramanga (CHRISTOPHER LEE), Bond (ROGER MOORE) tracks to Beirut a golden bullet that killed British agent Bill Fairbanks. The bullet belongs to a beautiful belly dancer named Saida (CARMEN SAUTOY). The dumdum bullet that flattens on impact for maximum wounding effect is her lucky charm, and she will not dance without it. Bond swallows the bullet during a fight with enemy agents.

Belly dancers also appear as ornaments in the tent of Sheik Hosein (EDWARD DE

SOUZA), Bond's British agent contact in Egypt in *The Spy Who Loved Me.*

BELMONDO, JEAN-PAUL (Paris, April 9, 1933–) French superstar actor who had a cameo role in *Casino Royale.* Belmondo is the brawling French foreign legionnaire who joins forces with Sir James Bond (DAVID NIVEN) in the climactic fight in the Monte Carlo casino. Belmondo was also the star of the great 007 spoof *That Man from Rio,* which was directed by Philippe De Broca in 1964. Filmed on location in Brazil at a breakneck pace, the film was one of the few imitators to develop a cult following of its own, along with Daniel Mann's *Our Man Flint* in 1966.

BELUGA CAVIAR Exotic appetizer ordered by Bond (SEAN CONNERY) but never served, during a romantic evening encounter with Domino (CLAUDINE AUGER) in *Thunderball.* It's also a prominent item in 007's gourmet suitcase at Shrublands in *Never Say Never Again.* Rather than commit himself entirely to a healthy vegetarian diet, Bond's emergency rations include the Beluga, quail's eggs, foie gras from Strasbourg, and vodka.

BENNETT, CHARLES (Shoreham, England 1899–) British screenwriter and playwright who cowrote the 1954 live-TV adaptation of "Casino Royale" with Antony Ellis. It's not known whether it was the writer's decision or that of producer Bretaigne Windust, but for American television James Bond became an American agent, with the ridiculous nickname "Card Sense Jimmy Bond." Interestingly, American CIA agent Felix Leiter became British Secret Service agent Clarence Leiter, and French agent of the Deuxieme Bureau Rene Mathis became Valerie Mathis, a beautiful double agent. When "Casino Royale" was broadcast live on the night of October 21, 1954, the adventures of James Bond were still unknown in the United States, thus no one paid much attention to the changes in the story.

Casino Royale is still the only Ian Fleming novel that has never been properly adapted to the big screen. The 1967 feature from producer Charles K. Feldman doesn't qualify because it was a spoof.

BENNETT, JILL (Penang, Malay, December 24, 1931–1990) British character actress who portrayed Jacoba Brink, an ice skater coach who is preparing Bibi Dahl (LYNN-HOLLY JOHNSON) for the Olympics, in *For Your Eyes Only.* See BRINK, JACOBA.

BENSON, CAPTAIN British nuclear-submarine staff officer who is the first to learn about the mysterious disappearance of the HMS *Ranger* in *The Spy Who Loved Me.* After informing the First Sea Lord (GEORGE BAKER), Benson later briefs Bond (ROGER MOORE) on the disappearance.

BENSON, MARTIN (1918–) Sinister-looking British character actor who portrayed doomed Mafia kingpin Mr. Solo in *Goldfinger.* See SOLO, MR.

BENZ Mustachioed Russian agent based in Istanbul, portrayed by actor Peter Bayliss, in *From Russia with Love.* As the agent in charge of surveillance at the local railroad station, Benz spots Bond (SEAN CONNERY) and Tanya (DANIELA BIANCHI) as they board the Orient Express with Ali Kerim Bey (PEDRO ARMENDARIZ).

To ensure a safe journey for his friends, Kerim Bey later tricks Benz into opening his door for the ticket agent, only to brandish a loaded pistol in the Russian's face. Trussed-up like a turkey, Benz is left alone with Kerim Bey, who will keep the Russian company until Bond escapes across the Turkish/Bulgarian border.

Unfortunately, these events are observed by S.P.E.C.T.R.E. assassin Red Grant (ROBERT SHAW), who eventually murders both Kerim Bey and Benz, making it appear as if they killed each other.

BENZALI, DANIEL Actor who portrayed W. G. Howe, a corrupt California official with the Division of Oil and Mines, who is on the payroll of Max Zorin (CHRISTOPHER WALKEN) in *A View to a Kill.* See HOWE, W. G.

BERETTA Agent 007's (SEAN CONNERY) handgun prior to *Dr. No.* He's used it for 10 years, since 1952. Major Boothroyd (PETER

BURTON), the armorer, doesn't like the Beretta because he thinks the gun's too light and has no stopping power. He terms it more of a "lady's gun." Agent 007 disagrees, but M (BERNARD LEE) overrules him and issues him the Walther PPK instead.

BERETTA 950 CIA undercover operative Pam Bouvier's (CAREY LOWELL) handgun in *Licence to Kill.* A .25-caliber automatic known as the Jetfire, it's carried in a special lace garter leg holster designed by Jodie Tillen.

BERKOFF, STEVEN Prolific theatrical director, playwright, and character actor who portrayed fanatical Russian Army General Orlov in *Octopussy.* Berkoff's unusual look, plus his wild mannerisms and gestures, contributed to a bravura performance in a film laced with interesting characters and mysterious events. Even his dialogue, delivered in a measured tone from an obnoxious strutting carriage, is given additional impact, especially during his lecture to the Soviet leadership on the possibility of a military breakthrough in the West.

Berkoff's impact as a textured villain has been employed in other films, especially in the miniseries "War and Remembrance," in which he portrayed Adolf Hitler.

BERNE, SWITZERLAND Location of the legal offices of Gebruder Gumbold (JAMES BREE), a Swiss attorney who represents the interests of Ernst Stavro Blofeld (TELLY SAVALAS) in *On Her Majesty's Secret Service.* Tipped off by Union Corse Chief Marc Ange Draco (GABRIELE FERZETTI), Bond (GEORGE LAZENBY) breaks into Gumbold's safe and removes documents that he duplicates on a safe-cracking photocopier supplied to him by Campbell, a local British operative (BERNARD HORSFALL).

BERNGARTEN, AUSTRIA Alpine setting in *The Spy Who Loved Me* teaser where James Bond (ROGER MOORE) escapes from a KGB assassination plot; kills the leader, Sergei Barsov (MICHAEL BILLINGTON); and ski jumps off a mountaintop, parachuting to safety. Later in the story we learn that Barsov is Major Anya Amasova's (BARBARA BACH) lover. The famous mountaintop ski jump was actually filmed atop the Asgard Peak on Baffin Island in Canada. Stuntman Rick Sylvester doubled 007.

BESWICK, MARTINE (1941–   ) Lovely Jamaican actress who portrayed Zora, one of the gypsy girls who is matched against Vida (ALIZA GUR) in the celebrated girl fight in *From Russia with Love.* A favorite of director

Actress Martine Beswicke veteran of *From Russia with Love* and *Thunderball.* (Century Artists)

Terence Young, Beswick returned to the James Bond film series in *Thunderball,* portraying Paula Caplan, Bond's (SEAN CONNERY) doomed assistant in Nassau. In *Thunderball* she is captured in her hotel room by Fiona Volpe (LUCIANA PALUZZI) and her S.P.E.C.T.R.E. thugs, drugged, and brought to Largo's (ADOLFO CELI) Palmyra estate. Tortured by Vargas (PHILIP LOCKE), she takes a cyanide pill and kills herself to avoid revealing any information. *Note:* In the *From Russia with Love* opening credits, her name is misspelled as Martin Beswick.

BEZANTS Ornamental gold balls featured on various medieval coats of arms, including James

Bond's. Bond has three bezants on his, according to the research done by Sir Hilary Bray (GEORGE BAKER), in *On Her Majesty's Secret Service*. During his conversation with Ruby Bartlett (ANGELA SCOULAR) at Piz Gloria, 007 (GEORGE LAZENBY) incorrectly tells her that his coat of arms has four bezants, instead of three. Whether this was an unintentional blooper or Bond is simply inflating his ball count is not clear. *Note:* The 007 coat of arms was created by production designer Syd Cain.

BIANCA Bond's (ROGER MOORE) sultry assistant, portrayed by statuesque Tina Hudson, in the *Octopussy* teaser. After Bond is captured and thrown into an army truck, Bianca drives by in a convertible attached to the phony horse trailer. Opening her dress enough to reveal her naked thighs, she's able to distract two South American paratroopers long enough for Bond to make his escape by pulling their rip cords. As she drives off, he climbs into the Acrostar mini-jet hidden in the phony horse trailer.

BIANCHI, DANIELA (1942 -   ) Voluptuous Italian leading lady, a former Miss Rome (1960), who won the part of defecting Russian cipher clerk Tatiana Romanova in *From Russia With Love*, a character described by Fleming as a "young Greta Garbo." Definitely one of the most beautiful and sexy women in the series, Bianchi was entirely re-voiced for the part.

Her seduction scene in the bridal suite of the Istanbul hotel was pretty steamy for 1963, especially with S.P.E.C.T.R.E. movie cameras recording it from inside the *cabinet de voyeur*. Sean Connery worked extremely well with her. Their scenes have a polish and a realism that is uncommon in the series, probably because this is the best Bond script.

BIATHLON A sporting event held in Cortina D'Ampezzo, Italy, in *For Your Eyes Only* that combines cross-country skiing with rifle shooting. One of the competitors is East German champion Eric Kriegler (JOHN WYMAN), an enemy agent working for heroin smuggler Aris Kristatos (JULIAN GLOVER), who later tries to kill James Bond (ROGER MOORE).

BIDDING PROCEDURES Wacky auction rules related by the individual country representatives that attend a sale of compromising military photos at the Mata Hari School of Dancing and Spying in *Casino Royale*.

According to the Russian representative, when the Russians are sitting, they're bidding. When they're standing, they're not bidding.

The American officer says, "We'll do our bidding sitting down; when we're standing, we're not bidding"—exactly what the Russian said.

The Chinese representative (BURT KWOUK, of *Goldfinger* and *You Only Live Twice*) says, "We stand, we bid. We no stand, we no bid."

As for the British procedures, their representative (RICHARD WATTIS) says, "We'll do a little bit of both." The auction is actually one of the comic high points of the film.

BIG, MR. Tough Harlem drug kingpin portrayed by actor Yaphet Kotto in *Live and Let Die*. Mr. Big is actually Dr. Kananga, the sinister island diplomat and drug smuggler from mythical San Monique. The Mr. Big camouflage allows him to maintain a disciplined crime syndicate in the States while performing the sensitive duties of a diplomat in New York City.

Moving between the two identities can be difficult, so Kananga keeps a number of hideouts, secret passageways, and electronic ruses that are used to confuse the CIA surveillance teams. Kananga/Big is eventually killed on San Monique when, in an underwater scuffle with Bond (ROGER MOORE), he is forced to swallow a "bitter pill"—a compressed air bullet that literally blows him to smithereens.

BILLINGTON, MICHAEL Handsome British leading man who portrayed KGB assassin Sergei Barsov in *The Spy Who Loved Me*. Because of his Bondian good looks, Billington had been considered for the part of 007 in the past.

BILLY BOB Sheriff J. W. Pepper's (CLIFTON JAMES) brother-in-law who owns the fastest boat on the bayou and who works for the State Wildlife Department at Ranger Station Number One in *Live and Let Die*. Adam

(TOMMY LANE), one of Kananga's (YAPHET KOTTO) henchmen, goes there, clubs Billy Bob, and steals the boat.

BINDER, MAURICE (New York City, December 4, 1925–1991) Famous American title designer, trailer maker, marketing specialist, and artist, long residing in England, whose stylishly photographed nude models and world-famous title sequences have perfectly symbolized the unique world of James Bond since 1962.

The pattern was established practically from the beginning. Composer John Barry's staccato 007 theme rings out as Binder's twin white dots roll across the screen, gradually turning into the through-the-gun-barrel portrait of James Bond. Agent 007 walks across the screen, turns, and fires his Walther PPK. The barrel wavers and a red shroud washes across it. Is there a more recognizable animated logo in the world? Following such a send-off, an incredible pre-title sequence—a true teaser—sends the audience to the edge of their seats. Then as they recover, Binder's titles strike, perfectly matched to the title songs performed by a who's who of popular recording artists.

Like a circus ringmaster's oratory, Binder's titles prepare the audience for the adventures to come. They've become as much an accepted part of the United Artists series as the phrase "Bond. James Bond."

What would the films be like without them? Just look at the opening sequence of *Never Say Never Again*, the rival Bond from 1983. Lani Hall's title song isn't the most vibrant piece of music ever recorded, but it's catchy. However, it plays over a bland helicopter shot of the Bahamas that's underwhelming.

Bond movies should always open with a tremendous send-off—akin to medieval trumpets blowing or a cannonade—because they're such a phenomenon. No other series in the history of movies has been so durable.

The son of a New York City manufacturer, Maurice Binder grew up studying ship and architectural design.

Attending Stuyvesant High School, his ambition was to become a naval architect. He was a precocious, energetic youngster, and his mother shipped him off to the Art Students' League and sketching classes to quiet him down.

In 1939, at the age of 14, Binder began to edit a company newspaper produced by the advertising department of Macy's department store. He also produced a radio program on WOR in Newark called the "Macy-Bamburger Boys' Club." As a teenager working on the show, Binder received an education in radio production, sound effects, and special effects.

Graduating from high school at the age of 15, Binder attended City College of New York and night school at St. John's University. At 17 he became the assistant art director at Macy's, in charge of catalog and mail order.

"In those days," he remembered, "we had dozens of publications. There were piles of advertising layouts to do and it took someone who could work quickly."

His burgeoning art career, however, was put on hold as the war in Europe began. In 1941, as a civilian administrative assistant attached to the War Department on a diplomatic passport, he embarked on a two-and-a-half-year building program throughout the Middle East and North Africa. Binder helped build airports, hospitals, roads, and military bases in Aden, Oman, Masirah Island, Syria, Lebanon, Palestine, Cairo, and Dakar. From the Allied air bases he helped construct, military aircraft were shuttled into the China/Burma/India theater.

In 1943, as Rommel's German forces were being forced out of North Africa, Binder returned to the United States and enrolled in sea navigation school. When the war ended in Europe in May 1945, Binder was a lieutenant (J.G.) on the LT-60, a salvage tug. He served on the tug until VJ Day, then navigated from what he refers to as "the Panama Canal to Universal Pictures' back lot."

Still in the navy, Binder began to do freelance advertising work for Mischa Kallis at Universal, the only studio that created its own advertising on the West Coast. (Everyone else did it in New York.) Kallis was dubious about Binder's qualifications, but he gave him a test on a cheap little western called *The Daltons Ride Again*. Binder returned to his ship with pad and pencils and put together 35 designs in one night.

He remembered, "My job at Macy's had primed me for pressure. We were doing 35 pages of advertising a day at one time, so Kallis's assignment wasn't extreme."

Binder was given $125 for his sketches and another assignment, on an Yvonne DeCarlo western, *Frontier Gal* (1945). Discharged from the navy, Binder worked for Arthur A. Schmidt, who was the assistant to Harry Cohn at Columbia Pictures. Schmidt needed a sketch artist to help him visualize ad campaigns. Binder posed the stars for photo layouts and sketched ads. His first full campaign was for the classic *Gilda* (1946). He eventually became West Coast art director for Columbia, working on films such as *The Jolson Story* (1946), *Down to Earth* (1947), *Dead Reckoning* (1947), and *The Lady From Shanghai* (1948). As a freelance consultant, Binder worked for various production companies.

Although Binder had been introduced to Albert R. Broccoli when the latter was an agent with Charles Feldman, their creative relationship didn't begin until 1961, when Broccoli and his partner, Harry Saltzman, attended the premiere of a Stanley Donen film titled *The Grass Is Greener*. Binder's title sequence, which featured a group of infants, was considered so charming by the audience that Broccoli and Saltzman immediately thought of him for their new James Bond series.

Binder's storyboard for the James Bond logo—designed in 10 minutes—consisted of a series of white sticky-backed price tabs placed to simulate the bullet holes of gunshots going off across the screen. One of the bullet holes would appear as if you were looking through a gun barrel—the barrel, not the gunsight. At a miniatures studio, Binder filmed his through-the-gun-barrel spiral logo shot.

The shot of 007 walking and firing was a separate piece of film shot later. For that sequence, stuntman Bob Simmons doubled Sean Connery. The portrait of Simmons was used in the first three films: *Dr. No*, *From Russia with Love*, and *Goldfinger*, which were shot in 1:85 ratio (flat). When *Thunderball* was lensed in Cinemascope, or "scope," Binder was forced to reshoot his logo. This time, he used Sean Connery. In the Bob Simmons/Sean Connery, and later George Lazenby, walks, Bond always wore a fedora. When Roger Moore entered the series in 1973, the hat was discarded.

Binder's work was exemplary for *Dr. No* but he did not work on the next two films in the series, *From Russia with Love* and *Goldfinger*. He came back in *Thunderball* with an idea he had seen in Raymond's Review Bar in Soho, where a woman swam in a tank above the bar. From that springboard, Binder designed his first live-action title sequence using carefully photographed nudes. Binder's use of slow-motion, colorful lighting, rippling bubbles, and the silhouettes of shapely female bodies—a pattern that has remained virtually unchanged throughout the entire series—were all elements that worked perfectly against Tom Jones's rousing theme song.

One of the most interesting stories associated with the title sequence shoots occurred at Pinewood on *The Man with the Golden Gun*. Binder was shooting a nude woman's silhouette. Conscious of rating codes and censors, he noted that from a certain angle the woman's privates were a little too noticeable on camera. When the model refused to shave, Binder realized that the only way to make the shot work was to brush her pubic hair into place and use Vaseline to hold it there. "You do it," she said, and Binder dutifully got down on his knees and put things right. At that exact moment, Roger Moore and Cubby Broccoli walked onto the stage. Roger turned to Cubby and said, "I thought you were the producer on this picture." And Cubby replied, "It doesn't seem right, does it?"

As he attempted to avoid a repetitive approach to the title sequences his creativity has been tested throughout the years. For the Roger Moore films, he enlisted the actor's cooperation for the title sequences, and Moore became a prime character in them. In *For Your Eyes Only* he was impressed with singer Sheena Easton's beauty and wanted to use her on-screen, which he did.

He worked with composer Bill Conti so that the title song meshed with the titles. "I've always wanted the song synchronized so that when I show the title of the film, the singer sings it," Binder said. "Unfortunately, on *For Your Eyes Only*, the song title came in 90 seconds after the song began. I asked Bill Conti to help, and we rewrote the song in two days."

In addition to the title sequences, Binder has also been heavily involved in designing the trailers, or previews, for most of the Bond movies. Binder created the sequence in which the Dobermans track down and kill Corinne Dufour (CORINNE CLERY) for the *Moonraker* teaser trailer, which was narrated by actress Lise Hilboldt.

BIRDS OF THE WEST INDIES A book that became one of author Ian Fleming's prime reference sources during his vacations in Jamaica. In 1952, searching for a name to christen his hero, Fleming noticed the simple name of the author of *Birds of the West Indies*, ornithologist James Bond. The name struck a chord and the world's greatest secret agent was born. *See* BOND, JAMES.

BISERA, OLGA Middle Eastern actress who portrayed Felicca, Aziz Fekkesh's (NADIM SAWALHA) secretary, in *The Spy Who Loved Me*.

BISHOP, ED Comical character actor who first appeared as an American space-tracking technician in *You Only Live Twice*. Later he returned in *Diamonds Are Forever*, as radiation-shield inspector Klaus Hergesheimer, who's impersonated by James Bond (SEAN CONNERY).

BISSET, JACQUELINE (Waybridge, England, September 13, 1944–   ) British actress who portrayed seductive Miss Goodthighs in *Casino Royale*—one of her first films. She's the one who slips Evelyn Tremble/James Bond (PETER SELLERS) a Mickey Finn in his Monte Carlo hotel room. *See* GOODTHIGHS, MISS.

BLAAZER, LOUIS British actor who portrayed Principal Secretary Playdell-Smith, the diplomat stationed at Government House in Jamaica in *Dr. No*. He was also a member of the regular bridge foursome that included murdered British Secret Service agent John Strangways (TIM MOXON), Professor R. J. Dent (ANTHONY DAWSON), and Colonel Potter.

BLACK, INGRID Actress who portrayed the German allergy victim in *On Her Majesty's Secret Service*.

BLACK PARK An area of rural England, not far from Pinewood Studios, where the *Goldfinger* Aston Martin chase was filmed. The factory element of that chase was filmed on the Pinewood grounds. *See* PILATUS AIRCRAFT FACTORY.

BLACK ROSE Unusual flower growing in Sir James Bond's (DAVID NIVEN) garden in *Casino Royale*. It's destroyed, along with Bond's manor house by M (JOHN HUSTON), who feels that it's the only way to motivate 007 to accept one final dangerous assignment.

BLACKING The golf club "starter," portrayed by Victor Brooks, in *Goldfinger*, who introduces Bond (SEAN CONNERY) to Goldfinger (GERT FROBE).

BLACKMAN, HONOR (1927–   ) British actress who starred in *Goldfinger* as Pussy

Pussy gets her kicks. Honor Blackman prepares for judo activity in *Goldfinger*. (Loomis Dean/ Camera Press, Globe Photos)

Galore, the title character's resourceful pilot and confederate in Operation Grand Slam. Blackman won the part after impressing producers Albert R. Broccoli and Harry Saltzman with her continuing role as the leather-clad, judo-proficient Cathy Gale in the first three seasons of "The Avengers" television series in Britain. Leaving the series, she was replaced by Diana Rigg, who would later star in *On Her Majesty's Secret Service* (1969). The male half of "The Avengers," Patrick Macnee, would join the 007 series in *A View to a Kill* (1985). *See* GALORE, PUSSY.

BLANC DE BLANC The French champagne ordered by James Bond (SEAN CONNERY) for himself and Tatiana Romanova (DANIELA BIANCHI) on the Orient Express in *From Russia with Love*. In Tanya's glass, Red Grant (ROBERT SHAW) places a chloral hydrate sleeping potion (the proverbial Mickey Finn).

BLAYDEN SAFE HOUSE Heavily guarded British Secret Service property in rural England that hosts defecting Russian General Georgi Koskov (JEROEN KRABBE) in *The Living Daylights*. Protected by dozens of agents and electronic surveillance equipment, the house is still penetrated by Koskov's associate Necros (ANDREAS WISNIEWSKI). While impersonating the milkman, Necros kills two British agents and wounds two more before he and Koskov are plucked to safety by their own men—disguised in a Red Cross helicopter.

BLEEKER, MR. New Orleans airport flight instructor in *Live and Let Die* whose appointment with student Mrs. Bell (RUTH KEMPF) is interrupted when James Bond (ROGER MOORE) commandeers the training plane.

BLEUCHAMP INSTITUTE OF ALLERGY RESEARCH S.P.E.C.T.R.E. Chief Ernst Stavro Blofeld's (TELLY SAVALAS) cover organization in *On Her Majesty's Secret Service*. Located at Piz Gloria, an Alpine peak accessible only by funicular, the privately run institute treats allergy victims—in this case, a group of beautiful women. As part of Blofeld's scheme to blackmail the free world, the girls are systematically brainwashed so that they will distribute a terrifying germ warfare toxin that can completely destroy the agricultural and livestock capabilities of selected nations. Blofeld is masquerading as Count Balthazar de Bleuchamp, a royal moniker that he claims. This association allows James Bond (GEORGE LAZENBY), posing as London College of Arms heraldry expert Sir Hilary Bray, to infiltrate the institute. The institute is eventually obliterated in a dawn helicopter assault by Union Corse gunmen led by Bond and Marc Ange Draco (GABRIELE FERZETTI).

BLISS, CAROLINE Statuesque blond actress, and the granddaughter of composer Sir

Bond (Timothy Dalton) meets his new Moneypenny, portrayed by actress Caroline Bliss. Beware of her Barry Manilow collection!
(Express Newspapers, London)

Arthur Bliss, who made her debut as the new Miss Moneypenny—M's proud but love-starved secretary—in *The Living Daylights*. She returned to that role in *Licence to Kill* (1989). Bliss made her film debut on ABC Television in 1982 as Princess Diana in "Charles and Diana, a Royal Love Story."

BLOFELD, ERNST STAVRO Bond's longtime nemesis and the head of the Special Executor for Counter-Intelligence, Terrorism, Revenge, and Extortion (S.P.E.C.T.R.E.)—an enormous criminal organization introduced in Ian Fleming's *Thunderball* novel and based on a film story created by Jack Whittingham, Kevin McClory, and Fleming. S.P.E.C.T.R.E. and Blofeld are also featured in the novels *On Her Majesty's Secret Service* and *You Only Live Twice*.

In the movies, Blofeld is first featured with his back to the camera in *From Russia with Love* (portrayed by *Dr. No* veteran ANTHONY DAWSON). Eric Pohlmann is Blofeld's voice in both *From Russia with Love* and *Thunderball*.

He makes his on-camera debut in *You Only Live Twice*, with Donald Pleasence in the role, complete with an incredible scar supplied by the makeup department. Quoting film critic Alexander Walker, *James Bond in the Cinema* author John Brosnan wrote, "Pleasence resembles 'an egg that had cracked on the boil.'"

Hatching a scheme to start World War III on behalf of the Red Chinese, Blofeld in *You Only Live Twice* builds a secret rocket base inside a dormant Japanese volcano. From this enormous conclave, he launches his *Intruder* rocket—a jaw-opening spaceship that captures Soviet and American capsules. When Bond (SEAN CONNERY) invades the base with the help of an army of Ninja warriors, Blofeld escapes to appear in the next film, *On Her Majesty's Secret Service*, in the guise of Telly Savalas.

This time Blofeld is sequestered in the Swiss Alps, posing as a world-famous allergist. In reality, he is developing a terrifying germ warfare strain that will destroy the agriculture and livestock of the world's leading nations. His agents are young female allergy victims who have been brainwashed to perform their deadly deed. Once again, Bond (GEORGE LAZENBY) comes in to mess up the works. During a climactic chase in the bobsled run, Blofeld appears to

Max von Sydow portrayed Blofeld in *Never Say Never Again*. (Taliafilm)

have been killed when his skull is cracked by an overhanging branch, but he returns in the climax with Frau Irma Bunt (ILSE STEPPAT) to murder Bond's bride, Tracy (DIANA RIGG).

In *Diamonds Are Forever*, Blofeld is portrayed in a very sophisticated manner by Charles Gray. With his smart uniforms, cigarette holder, and sparkling quotations, this Blofeld is the most fantastical of them all. His plot is nothing less than nuclear blackmail from outer space, thanks to his diamond-powered laser satellite. Blofeld gets trapped in his own bathosub, with Bond (SEAN CONNERY) controlling the crane that lowers it into the water. The sub later explodes, but Blofeld's body is never found or seen.

Although he was never identified by name in the credits, a bald-headed, wheelchair-bound, beige-uniformed Blofeld appears in the *For Your Eyes Only* teaser with his trademark white cat. Snared by Bond's (ROGER MOORE) helicopter skid, he's deposited in the nearest industrial smokestack, which would appear to be his final and utter demise.

In fact, it would take the rival Bond group

in *Never Say Never Again* to resurrect the S.P.E.C.T.R.E. chieftain in the guise of actor Max Von Sydow. Like the never-fully-seen Blofeld in the early 007 films, this one simply announces the latest extortion plan and keeps in touch with his field commander, Largo (KLAUS MARIA BRANDAUER).

Blofeld was supposed to have been featured as the key villain in *The Spy Who Loved Me*, but because of threats from *Thunderball* producer Kevin McClory, who claims all rights to Blofeld and the S.P.E.C.T.R.E. organization, producer Albert R. Broccoli had screenwriter Richard Maibaum change the character to the purely independent villain Karl Stromberg (CURT JURGENS).

BLOMBERG, DELLA An Argentine industrialist's daughter who was kidnapped by S.P.E.C.T.R.E., which received 1 million pesos in ransom. This incident, mentioned by S.P.E.C.T.R.E. No. 12 during Blofeld's area financial briefing in *Thunderball*, was featured in an early draft of the film but was later cut from the final shooting script.

BLUE Maximillian Largo's (KLAUS MARIA BRANDAUER) color in the Domination video game featured in *Never Say Never Again*. Bond (SEAN CONNERY) played red. *See* DOMINATION.

BLUE GRASS FIELD, KENTUCKY The final destination of Goldfinger's (GERT FROBE) private Lockheed Jetstar that carries the recently captured and tranquilized 007 (SEAN CONNERY). From the airport, Bond is driven to Auric Stud, the Kentucky home of Goldfinger.

BLUE MASK/BLACK MASK A continuity error in *Thunderball*. During the furious battle with S.P.E.C.T.R.E. frogmen, Bond (SEAN CONNERY) loses his blue diving mask. Diving to the ocean floor, he rips the black mask from a dead enemy and puts it on. However, in the next close-up he is again wearing his blue mask.

BLUE MOUNTAIN GRILL Bond's restaurant choice in *Dr. No* after making love to Miss Taro (ZENA MARSHALL) in her cottage. It's the type of place that makes him feel "Italian and musical."

BLUE-RINGED OCTOPUS TATTOO The sign of the Octopus Cult, an old secret order of female bandits and smugglers that is revived by the title character in *Octopussy*. Magda (KRISTINA WAYBORN) has one of these tattoos on her buttocks. Octopussy's (MAUD ADAMS) barge flies the symbol on its pennant. The blue-ringed octopus, of the genus *hapolochaena*, produces a venom that is usually fatal in seconds.

BLUEBEARD REEF, BAHAMAS According to the British embassy, this is the reported location of Maximillian Largo's (KLAUS MARIA BRANDAUER) marine archaeology activities in *Never Say Never Again*. In actuality, it's where his yacht, the *Flying Saucer*, recovers the hijacked cruise missiles.

BLUSH, FATIMA Truly wicked S.P.E.C.T.R.E. executioner, portrayed by Barbara Carrera in *Never Say Never Again*. No. 12 in the S.P.E.C.T.R.E. chain of command, Fatima is introduced as a private-duty nurse assigned to Captain Jack Petachi (GAVAN O'HERLIHY), a U.S. Air Force communications officer who has been turned by S.P.E.C.T.R.E.

Bribed, seduced, drugged, and beaten into submission by Fatima, Petachi has undergone an eye operation (a corneal implant) so that he now possesses the same eye print as the president of the United States. With that startling characteristic, he can bypass a top-level security check and arm two cruise missiles with nuclear warheads. Petachi succeeds in his mission and is promptly eliminated by Fatima who tosses a snake into his car—distracting Petachi into a head-on collision with a stone wall.

Turning her attentions to James Bond (SEAN CONNERY), Fatima meets him at a "wet" bar in Nassau and takes him for a diving excursion off Bluebeard's Reef. After they make torrid love, she attaches a homing device to Bond's diving gear that summons a group of radio-controlled sharks, ready for the kill. Bond eludes them, hooks up with a sexy deep-sea diver (VALERIE LEON), and evades another attempt on his life when Fatima detonates a

Wicked Fatima Blush, a S.P.E.C.T.R.E. assassin in *Never Say Never Again*. (Taliafilm)

bomb in his hotel suite.

In Nice, she leads a motorcycle-riding 007 on a merry chase that ends up in a tunnel, where Bond is surrounded by her henchmen. Employing the rocket-motor capability of the bike, Bond escapes from the nest of enemies, only to be cornered by Fatima in a warehouse. Forced to his knees, Bond is about to have his genitals blown off, when Blush orders him to confess in writing that their sex was the best he ever had.

Stalling for time, Bond deploys and fires his rocket-loaded fountain pen, plunging an explosive dart into Fatima's chest. For an agonizing moment, nothing happens, but then she's blown to kingdom come. Like a latter-day wicked witch, only her high heels remain. *See* CARRERA, BARBARA.

BOA, BRUCE British character actor who portrayed the commanding general at the U.S. Air Force base at Feldstadt, West Germany, in *Octopussy*. *See* BASE COMMANDER.

BOGNER, JR., WILLY (Munich, January 23, 1942–) Famous German filmmaker and ex-Olympic skier whose uncanny ability to capture skiers in action has provided the James Bond series with some of its most breathtaking action sequences. Bogner gained prominence during *On Her Majesty's Secret Service*, most of which takes place in the snows of Switzerland.

Equipped with a modified Arriflex and an adapted Hasselblad viewfinder, Bogner held his camera while skiing backward to catch the swiftly moving Olympic skiers as they flew down the slopes above Murren. Sometimes he shot backward looking through his legs. His skis were modified with curved tips at both ends to allow him the proper mobility. *OHMSS* director Peter Hunt said, "I've never seen anyone manipulate skis and a camera like Willy. Of course, in the rushes, we got lumps of sky, bits of his bottom, and somebody's shoe—things like that—but when you took all of the best pieces, you had some exciting material."

Producer Albert R. Broccoli saw one of Bogner's early films, *Fascination with Skiing* (1965), a 47-minute 35mm documentary that won first prize at sports festivals in Cortina D'Ampezzo and Grenoble. After the success of his work in *On Her Majesty's Secret Service*, Bogner was hired to handle the acrobatic ski sequences on *The Spy Who Loved Me*, once again photographing his stunt performers while skiing himself.

He explained his unusual technique: "I hold the camera between my legs, absorbing the shocks with my knees. We use a wide-angle lens to give you the impact of speed. There's no illusion, because the guys actually do the stunts. The only illusion is that it's not James Bond himself, but a stunt skier."

For the close-ups of Bond (GEORGE LAZENBY or ROGER MOORE), Bogner placed his actors on a sled that was pulled forward at 40–50 mph while the cameras rolled. Bogner returned to handle ski stunts on *For Your Eyes Only* in 1981. Four years later, he journeyed to Iceland to shoot the teaser sequence for *A View to a Kill*, which not only involved ski scenes but also "snow surfing" to the Beach Boys' tune, "California Girls."

When he's not skiing, Bogner runs one of the most successful activewear companies in the world.

BOITIER, COLONEL JACQUES S.P.E.C.T.R.E. agent (aka No. 6) portrayed by stuntman Bob Simmons and assassinated by Bond (SEAN CONNERY) in the *Thunderball* teaser. Attending the Colonel's supposed funeral at a cathedral outside Paris, Bond and his French contact (MITSOUKO) notice that upon leaving, Boitier's widow (ROSE ALBA) suspiciously opens a car door by herself—something French widows are obviously not supposed to do. Bond follows her back to a French chateau and promptly offers his personal condolences with a solid punch to the face. The widow is none other than Boitier in drag.

A particularly vicious fight ensues, especially for Bond, who knows that Boitier has already murdered two double-0 agents. Whacked by a fireplace poker, Bond finally gets the best of Boitier and breaks the enemy agent's neck. He then escapes from the chateau in a Bell jet pack.

There is a certain mystery about the pronunciation of Colonel Boitier's name. As spoken, it sounds like "Bow-vard," while the spelling suggests "Bwah-tee-ay."

BOLLINGER 1969 Astrophysicist Dr. Holly Goodhead's (LOIS CHILES) champagne at Venice's Hotel Danieli in *Moonraker*. James Bond (ROGER MOORE) shares a glass as he unveils her true cover as a CIA agent on Drax's (MICHEL LONSDALE) trail.

BOLLINGER 1975 Champagne identified by Bond (ROGER MOORE) in the Eiffel Tower Restaurant in *A View to a Kill*. Agent 007's luncheon guest, French detective Achille Aubergine (JEAN ROUGERIE), then orders a bottle of Lafitte Rothschild 1959.

BOLTON, EMILY Beautiful, exotic actress who portrayed Manuela, Bond's (ROGER MOORE) Rio de Janeiro–based secret service assistant, in *Moonraker*.

BOMBE SURPRISE The dessert delivered to James Bond (SEAN CONNERY) and Tiffany Case (JILL ST. JOHN) by phony ocean liner waiters Mr. Wint (BRUCE GLOVER) and Mr. Kidd (PUTTER SMITH) in *Diamonds Are Forever*. It's actually a time bomb. During a fight with the two S.P.E.C.T.R.E. assassins, Bond attaches the bomb to Wint and kicks him overboard, where he is blown to bits.

BOND, JAMES (Philadelphia, 1899–1989) American ornithologist and author of the famous book *Birds of the West Indies*. His name was chosen in 1952 by author Ian Fleming for the fictional British Agent 007.

Fleming wrote years later to Mr. Bond's wife, Mary Fanning Wickham Bond, "It struck me that this brief, unromantic, Anglo-Saxon, and yet very masculine name was just what I needed, and so a second James Bond was born. In return, I can only offer you or James Bond unlimited use of the name Ian Fleming for any purposes you may think fit. Perhaps one day your husband will discover a particularly horrible species of bird which he would like to christen in an insulting fashion by calling it Ian Fleming."

James Bond the ornithologist, a native of Philadelphia and a graduate of Cambridge University, was a former curator of ornithology at the Academy of Natural Sciences in Philadelphia. He was the leading authority on birds of the West Indies for more than half a century, and he is best known among scientists for proving that birds of the Caribbean originated in North America, not South America.

Actress Emily Bolton portrayed Bond's Rio contact, Manuela in *Moonraker*. (ICM)

BOND, MRS. JAMES Short-lived identity of the Countess Teresa (Tracy) de Vicenzo (DIANA RIGG) in *On Her Majesty's Secret Service*. She's murdered by Ernst Stavro Blofeld (TELLY SAVALAS) only a few minutes after her wedding to Bond (GEORGE LAZENBY). It's also CIA agent Rosie Carver's (GLORIA HENDRY) cover in *Live and Let Die*. She uses it to register in James Bond's (ROGER MOORE) San Monique hotel room. In actuality, she's an agent of Kananga (YAPHET KOTTO).

BOND, SIR JAMES Retired British Secret Service agent portrayed by David Niven in *Casino Royale*. In this undisguised parody, which has nothing to do with any of Ian Fleming's original books, Sir James's heyday was during World War I when spying was an art form. Stealthy secretive agents were forced to use their wits and courage rather than the supersonic gadgets of the modern world that Sir James disdains.

In his prime, Bond was the top agent in the world. What caused his downfall? The woman he loved dearly—Mata Hari, the famous World War I spy who was working for the Germans. When duty called, Bond lured her across the Spanish frontier into France, where she was arrested and later put before a firing squad.

Before she died, Mata Hari gave birth to their child, Mata Bond (JOANNA PETTET).

Now retired to private life in rural England, a stuttering and melancholy Sir James spends most of his time playing Debussy on the piano; watering his rose garden, which includes a rare black rose; standing on his head; and cleansing his intestines with royal jelly.

When he refuses to help M (JOHN HUSTON) stop a mysterious plot that is killing dozens of Allied agents throughout the world, the head of the British Secret Service orders his home destroyed. Bond's beautiful rural mansion is then obliterated by mortar bombs—a barrage that also kills M.

Forced to accept the assignment, Sir James also assumes M's job as the head of the British Secret Service. He eventually discovers twin evils—the nefarious activities of Soviet masterspy and super gambler Le Chiffre (ORSON WELLES) and the more deadly international scheme of Bond's own nephew, Jimmy Bond (WOODY ALLEN). In reality, the latter is Dr. Noah, a fiend who plans to rule the world with an army of robots who are exact duplicates of every world leader.

Sir James Bond's plan involves confusing his enemies by giving his name to dozens of agents. There are male Bonds and female Bonds. All roads eventually lead to the baccarat table in Monte Carlo, where agent James Bond/Evelyn Tremble (PETER SELLERS) beats Le Chiffre in a high-stakes card game.

When Mata Bond is kidnapped by Dr. Noah, Sir James arrives on the scene with the French foreign legion, American cowboys, American Indian paratroopers, and every British agent that can stand. The entire casino, however, is blown to pieces by Dr. Noah, who inadvertently self-destructs when the last tiny time pill explodes in the tablet-form nuclear bomb he swallowed. *See* NIVEN, DAVID.

BOND, JIMMY Sir James Bond's (DAVID NIVEN) bumbling nephew, portrayed by Woody Allen in *Casino Royale*. The son of Sir James's sister Nelly, Jimmy is sent to the Caribbean as an agent with the British Secret Service, where he's captured and nearly executed by a firing squad. Escaping, he turns to a life of crime, transforming himself into Dr. Noah, a fiendish villain who sets out to conquer the world with an army of beautiful female agents. Jimmy cannot speak in his uncle's presence, however. According to Sir James, it's a psychological block based on hero worship. *See* NOAH, DR.

BOND, MATA Sir James Bond's (DAVID NIVEN) illegitimate daughter, portrayed by sexy Joanna Pettet in *Casino Royale*. The product of 007's World War I love affair with German spy Mata Hari, Mata Bond was born shortly before her mother's execution. Deposited in an orphanage at the age of three, she's been living in India where her title is Celestial Virgin of the Sacred Altar.

She's recruited by Sir James to infiltrate the Mata Hari Dance and Spy School in West Berlin and learn all she can about a Soviet spymaster named Le Chiffre (ORSON WELLES) and his organization. Mata arrives by cab from London and greets two old friends of her mother—Frau

Hoffner (ANNA QUAYLE), who was Mata Hari's dance teacher and who now runs the spy school, and Polo (RONNIE CORBETT), Hoffner's diminutive assistant whose faulty pacemaker keeps him perpetually nervous.

Using her considerable feminine charm, Mata worms her way into Polo's confidence and learns that Le Chiffre is preparing to raise currency by selling off his unusual collection of compromising photographs. The auction will be conducted at the spy school that very evening by one of Le Chiffre's associates (VLADEK SHEYBAL).

During the frenetic auction for American, British, Russian, and Chinese military men, Mata sneaks into the projection booth and steals the box of slides, dumping them in a toilet. She then escapes from the school with the help of her cabdriver, Carlton Towers (BERNARD CRIBBINS) of the Foreign Office. Back in London, she's kidnapped by a spaceship and taken to the Monte Carlo hideaway of Dr. Noah (WOODY ALLEN), who is planning world conquest with a thousand robot duplicates—some of whom will take over the duties of the world's political leaders.

Sir James and Agent Cooper (TERENCE COOPER) eventually rescue her. However, like everyone else, she's blown to bits when Dr. Noah's tablet-sized atomic bomb explodes. *See* PETTET, JOANNA.

BONDON, JERZY Captured 007's (TIMOTHY DALTON) identity on forged documents that will allow him to leave Tangier for Afghanistan in *The Living Daylights*. Drugged by Kara Milovy (MARYAM D'ABO), who mistakenly believes him to be a KGB agent, Bond—disguised as a critically ill heart transplant patient—is taken aboard a Russian transport plane by Koskov (JEROEN KRABBE).

In Afghanistan, he's incarcerated in the jailhouse of a Soviet air force base, where he's charged with the assassination of General Pushkin (JOHN RHYS-DAVIES), whose death was actually faked by Bond and Pushkin to expose Koskov's plot. Bond and Kara escape from the base, join up with Mujahedeen rebels, and discover that the renegade Russian general is planning a huge diamonds-for-opium swap with the Snow Leopard Brotherhood.

BOND'S OFFICE Featured only once—in the sixth James Bond film, *On Her Majesty's Secret Service*. Resigning from the British Secret Service when M (BERNARD LEE) fails to permit him to continue his search for the missing Blofeld (TELLY SAVALAS), Bond (GEORGE LAZENBY) retreats to his own office to clean out his desk.

In screenwriter Richard Maibaum's homage to the series's rich history, 007 pulls out three souvenirs from previous adventures—Honey's (URSULA ANDRESS) knife from *Dr. No*, Red Grant's (ROBERT SHAW) strangler's watch from *From Russia with Love*, and the miniature rebreather from *Thunderball*. He then takes out a flask and toasts a portrait of the Queen.

When Moneypenny (LOIS MAXWELL) summons him back to M's office, Bond learns that his resignation has turned into a much-needed vacation.

B-1 BOMBER Supersonic U.S. Air Force plane that carries the cruise missiles that are hijacked in *Never Say Never Again*. In actuality, the B-1 was a three-foot model designed and animated by effects supervisor David Dryer and his Apogee effects team. A larger six-foot model, incorporating the plane's bomb bay, was used for the sequence in which the missiles are launched.

BONITA The fiery flamenco dancer portrayed by actress Nadja Regin in the *Goldfinger* teaser. A double agent, she lures Bond (SEAN CONNERY) to her dressing room after he blows up Mr. Ramirez's heroin operation. There he picks her up out of the bathtub, kisses her, and then sees assasin Capungo (ALF JOINT) reflected in her pupils. Whirling around, Bond shoves Bonita in front of Capungo's billy club, and she gets a good thwacking.

BOOTHROYD, MAJOR (aka Q) Bond's equipment officer. Peter Burton portrayed him in *Dr. No* in no-nonsense fashion, supplying 007 with his new firearm—the Walther PPK. Tall, aristocratic Desmond Llewelyn portrayed him as the long-suffering technician in every other 007 adventure except *Live and Let Die*, where no Q was featured; *Never Say Never Again*, where Alec McCowen portrayed him as witty Alger-

Choreographer Selina Wylie takes a moment to give Nadja Regin flamenco dancing lessons for her part in the *Goldfinger* teaser. (National Film Archive, London)

non; and *Casino Royale*, where he was portrayed as a fop by Geoffrey Bayldon. Llewelyn's stiff no-nonsense bearing was often a humorous contrast to 007's playfulness. But it went a little overboard in *The Man with the Golden Gun* when he was reduced to buffoon status.

Q has always been and will always be a staple of the series—in essence, the voice of Ian Fleming, whose original novels were filled with the type of technical references that became the gist of the Q equipment briefings. His introduction in *From Russia with Love* when he demonstrates the trick briefcase, and his appearance in *Goldfinger* when he reveals the modifications to the Aston Martin are high points of the series.

Q's appearance in *Licence to Kill* was his most lengthy as he joins rogue agent James Bond (TIMOTHY DALTON) on location in fictional Isthmus City. His bag of tricks proves to be the difference for outnumbered and outgunned 007. *See* LLEWELYN, DESMOND.

BORCHOI The curator of Leningrad's Hermitage Museum, portrayed by Gabor Vernon, who exposes the jewel forgeries of Lenkin (PETER PORTEOUS) in *Octopussy*. Brought as a consultant to the Kremlin Art Repository by a suspicious General Gogol (WALTER GOTELL), Borchoi scrutinizes what is supposed to be a genuine Romanoff Star. Without hesitation, he then drops it onto the floor, smashing its phony glass texture to bits with his boot.

BOREN, LAMAR (1918–1986) Veteran cinematographer and underwater specialist who was responsible for the large-scale battle sequences in *Thunderball*, the opening underwater sequences in *You Only Live Twice* (in Hong Kong Harbor), and the adventures of Little Nellie, the Lotus submarine car in *The Spy Who Loved Me*. He also filmed James Bond's (ROGER MOORE) duel with a giant snake in *Moonraker*.

Unlike dozens of "diving for sunken treasure" and "monsters from the deep" exploitation films, *Thunderball* was a wide-screen underwater epic.

United Artists, balancing on a tidal wave of 007 interest in early 1965, was ready to pour nearly $6 million into the next Bond adventure. It was going to be the biggest Bond film yet, and Lamar Boren was given the task of photographing its trademark underwater sequences. There were underwater battles with dozens of CO_2 spear gun–carrying frogmen, a trip to an underwater garage where the stolen atomic bombs were hidden, a romantic swim with Bond (SEAN CONNERY) and the sensuous Domino (CLAUDINE AUGER), and a tense encounter between Bond and an underwater sentry guarding the *Disco Volante* yacht.

Boren, who claimed his first dive at 11 years old, had been photographing underwater films since the late 1940s. He knew of *Thunderball* because Broccoli contacted him in the summer of 1961 when *Thunderball* was scheduled as the first Bond film. When *Thunderball* was shelved because of Kevin McClory's lawsuit, Boren returned to the Bahamas to wind up his fourth season on the popular "Sea Hunt" television series. As the Bond films grew in size and importance, he remained in the Caribbean working for the Ivan Tors Studios, a Miami-based production team that specialized in underwater adventure shows and films, including "Sea Hunt" and *Flipper*.

Underwater photography had come a long way since 1914 when a photographer named Ernie Williamson hand-cranked the original version of Jules Verne's *20,000 Leagues under the Sea* off Nassau. In those days, Williamson worked on a specially built catamaran on which a photosphere was balanced between two pontoons. The photosphere—a glass canopy in which Williamson placed himself and his camera—was then lowered into the water to photograph the various divers and props that had

Underwater photography master Lamar Boren. (Miller Agency)

been assembled for the film. Boren knew Williamson and he admired his techniques, but his own dream was to physically follow the underwater action with an airtight camera that could operate under its own power.

In his early days at RKO (around 1950), Boren designed an airtight stainless steel camera case for an old Eymo camera, and he was followed around the studio tank by a stagehand carting a car battery for the power supply. This worked well enough in the studio tank, but when Boren began filming "Sea Hunt" in the Caribbean, something more practical was needed. The key to his problem was an independent power source. He didn't want generator cords or battery cables to inhibit his progress underwater.

The solution came in 1957 when he acquired some miniature silver cells from a friend. The tiny batteries were part of the guidance system to an air-to-air missile and were being manufactured in limited quantities by the Yardney Company of New York. Boren incorporated the little batteries into his Eymo and created one of the first independent underwater camera units. He was now free to explore the ocean on his own. The quality of his work and the variety of his subject matter improved considerably, and it was not long before a number of producers were hiring him to do underwater work.

By the early 1960s, he had replaced his

The self-contained Panavision underwater camera that Lamar Boren used to film *The Spy Who Loved Me* and *Thunderball*. (Don Griffin, Perry Oceanographics)

Eymo with a watertight Panavision camera, two of which would film all the underwater action in *Thunderball*. "*Thunderball* was the most ambitious underwater film in history," Boren recalled. "Cubby and Harry were so pleased with our footage that they kept increasing its importance in the film. One thing that made the whole project even more interesting was the creation of so many functional underwater props and gadgets."

The Ivan Tors unit, working closely with Boren, would eventually number more than 60 professional divers and $85,000 worth of Voit diving equipment. Production designer Ken Adam and art director Peter Lamont also designed several futuristic underwater vehicles, including several one-man, electric-powered CO_2 spear gun–equipped scooters and the two-man sled designed to carry the hijacked A-bombs that were built by Miami underwater engineer and cameraman Jordan Klein. (*See* KLEIN, JORDAN).

In *Thunderball*, Boren put to good use the filming techniques he had perfected earlier on "Sea Hunt." To adjust the level of his camera, he used his lungs like an elevator. To rise up, he took a deep breath of oxygen. And to drop down, he exhaled. By controlling his breathing in such a fashion, he achieved a perfect balance—a factor that contributed to the steadiness

of his camera and the clarity and effectiveness of his underwater sequences.

Thunderball, thanks to Boren, played to the sea. The ocean itself became a character in the story, just as exotic Jamaica had enlivened the first Bond entry, *Dr. No*. With the beauty of Boren's crystal-clear underwater photography married to composer John Barry's beautifully mellow musical score, the underwater sequences took on an enchanting quality that gave the film a huge dose of needed atmosphere.

This freshness and otherworldliness is evident from the start, in the early sequence where James Bond (SEAN CONNERY) meets Domino (CLAUDINE AUGER) in the sea off Nassau. Agent 007 sees her swimming underwater among the exotic tropical fish that inhabit the Caribbean coral. As she glides through the underwater tapestry, Bond is entranced by her wonderful form. When her foot gets caught in an outcropping of coral, Bond comes to her rescue. He helps her to the surface, where he introduces himself. It's a short sequence, but it perfectly captures the magic of the tropics and the romance that is such an important part of *Thunderball*.

BORIENKO, YURI Actor/stuntman who portrayed Grunther, Irma Bunt's tall, silent assistant in *On Her Majesty's Secret Service*. He's the opponent that Tracy (DIANA RIGG) defeats in the climactic battle inside Piz Gloria.

"BORN FREE" Appropriate theme played when M's (JOHN HUSTON) party, surrounded by roving lions, arrives at Sir James Bond's (DAVID NIVEN) country home in *Casino Royale*. This type of musical motif would later become a comic trademark of some of the Bond films starring Roger Moore.

BORODIN'S STRING QUARTET No. 2 IN D What scholarship cellist Kara Milovy (MARYAM D'ABO) plays at the Academy in Bratislava when 007 (TIMOTHY DALTON) attends her daytime concert in *The Living Daylights*.

BOTTOM BUTTON Located on the back of British agent Mary Goodnight's (BRITT EK-

LAND) dress in *The Man with the Golden Gun*, it contains a homing device that allows Bond (ROGER MOORE) to track her when she's captured and thrown into Scaramanga's (CHRISTOPHER LEE) trunk in Bangkok.

BOTTOMS UP CLUB Hong Kong strip joint in front of which Francisco Scaramanga (CHRISTOPHER LEE) assassinates British solar energy expert Gibson in *The Man with the Golden Gun*. Bond (ROGER MOORE) learns of the site from Miss Anders (MAUD ADAMS) but is unable to prevent the killing.

BOUCHET, BARBARA (Reichenberg, Germany, August 15, 1945–   ) German-born American actress who portrayed the beautiful daughter of Miss Moneypenny in *Casino Royale*. See MONEYPENNY'S DAUGHTER.

Actress Barbara Bouchet portrayed Moneypenny's daughter in *Casino Royale*.

BOUQUET, CAROLE (1957–   ) Hauntingly beautiful French actress who portrayed the revengeful Melina Havelock in *For Your Eyes Only*. Bouquet was a definite casting coup for the Bond producers—perfectly suited to play a young Greek archaeologist's daughter whose parents are brutally murdered early in the film.

When Havelock's beautiful eyes were featured in close-up after her parents' deaths, one could easily sense the seething Greek blood, thirsting to avenge her family. Armed with a crossbow, she's an impressive sight skulking in the woods of Spain in pursuit of Cuban hit man Hector Gonzales (STEFAN KALIPHA). *See* HAVELOCK, MELINA.

"BOURBON AND WATER, NO ICE" James Bond's (ROGER MOORE) drink order in Harlem's Fillet of Soul nightclub in *Live and Let Die*. In this joint, "no ice is extra, man."

BOUVIER, PAM American CIA undercover operative and ex-U.S. Army pilot portrayed fabulously by Carey Lowell in *Licence to Kill*. In the Michael G. Wilson–Richard Maibaum screenplay, Bouvier is an ode to the woman of the 1980s—a tough, no-nonsense player who doesn't like warming her behind on the sidelines. Glimpsed briefly in Felix Leiter's (DAVID HEDISON) office in Key West, her true introduction occurs in Bimini's seedy Barrelhead Bar—and quite an introduction it is. Tipped off by Leiter's computer that Bouvier is shadowing Sanchez's (ROBERT DAVI) drug operatives in Bimini, Bond (TIMOTHY DALTON) joins her at the Barrelhead.

Surrounded by the slime of the Caribbean, Pam is seated at a table, sporting a hidden double-barreled shotgun. She's very unimpressed with Bond's own firepower—his trusty Walther. But there's no time for reinforcements, as the two are quickly joined by Sanchez's henchman Dario (BENICIO DEL TORO), who is very suspicious of Pam and her English friend.

After Pam shoves her shotgun up against Dario's crotch, a brawl breaks out. Outgunned and outnumbered, 007 holds back the tide until Pam creates her own escape route by blasting a hole in the barroom's wall.

CIA pilot Pam Bouvier (CAREY LOWELL) keeps watch on the highway in *Licence to Kill*. (Barry Champagne)

They escape in Bond's motorboat. Pam is shot by Dario, but fortunately she's wearing body armor. After a rather abrupt moonlight tryst in the boat, Pam agrees to fly 007 into the dragon's den—Isthmus City, Sanchez's stronghold.

Posing as 007's secretary, with a new hairdo and wardrobe to match, Pam becomes a passive observer, as Bond gradually infiltrates the drug empire. Her skills come in handy, though, when she impersonates the Isthmus harbor pilot and rams the *Wavekrest* vessel into the dock—a diversion that helps Bond plant the drug loot in the decompression chamber.

She's also very handy at Joe Butcher's (WAYNE NEWTON) Olimpatec Meditation Institute, where she seduces the hapless televangelist, locks him in his bedroom, and goes off to help Bond escape from the drug laboratory. Later, while piloting the crop-dusting plane, Pam drops 007 on top of one of the liquid cocaine–carrying tanker trucks.

As Bond systematically obliterates Sanchez's cocaine convoy, Pam keeps watch from above—a sort of friendly guardian angel version of Naomi (CAROLINE MUNRO) from *The Spy Who Loved Me*. With Sanchez dead and his empire ruined, there's a major celebration at the drug lord's home, where Pam sees Bond kissing Lupe Lamora (TALISA SOTO).

Unaware it's a good-bye kiss—(Lupe is now a fixture on President Lopez's (PEDRO ARMENDARIZ, JR.) arm—a teary-eyed Pam stalks off. Bond sees her and jumps into Sanchez's pool where they enjoy a climactic embrace in the water, where most Bond movies seem to end.

BOWE, JOHN British actor who portrayed Colonel Feyador, the Soviet Air Force base commander whose Afghanistan installation is overrun by Mujahedeen rebels in *The Living Daylights*.

BOX 274 Parisian bank safe-deposit box that allows Fatima Blush (BARBARA CARRERA) access to S.P.E.C.T.R.E. headquarters in *Never Say Never Again*. Her key, plus the key of a bank employee, triggers an electronic switch, which opens a secret passageway to S.P.E.C.T.R.E.'s inner sanctum. A further security check—an electronic eye that scans her entire body—prevents unauthorized personnel from entering at this point.

BOYER, CHARLES (Figeac, France, August 28, 1899–August 26, 1978) French romantic leading man who appears briefly in *Casino Royale* as Deuxieme Bureau Chief Le Grand. *See* LE GRAND.

BRACHO, ALEJANDRO Mexican actor who portrayed Perez, one of drug runner Franz Sanchez's (ROBERT DAVI) henchmen in *Licence to Kill*.

BRADFORD, ANDY (Cambridge, England, September 7, 1944–   ) Top British stuntman who portrayed one of Kristatos's (JULIAN GLOVER) guards atop the Meteora in *For Your Eyes Only* and clown-suited Agent 009 in *Octopussy*. In the former film, Bradford was the guard who was shot by one of Melina Havelock's (CAROLE BOUQUET) crossbow arrows during the assault on St. Cyril's. He spent four weeks in Greece, also participating in the fight in Kristatos's warehouse and in the car stunts involving Melina's Citroen Deux Cheveux.

On *Octopussy*, Bradford spent two weeks near Checkpoint Charlie in West Berlin, where 009 attempted to steal a Fabergé egg from the Octopussy Circus. Chased through the woods near the circus, 009 fought with the twin assassins Mischa and Grischka (TONY AND DAVID MEYER), took a knife in the back, and fell into the flood-control channel.

Interestingly, because he was attached to Alf Joint's stunt team, then shooting on *The Keep* (1983), Bradford was unable to return to the production to re-create 009's fall through the British ambassador's East German office window. It was completed by another stuntman.

BRANDAUER, KLAUS MARIA Marvelous Austrian character actor who made his English-speaking screen debut as Maximillian Largo in *Never Say Never Again*. The previous year, Brandauer had attracted worldwide attention with his starring role in Istvan Szabo's *Mephisto*, which won the 1982 Academy Award for Best Foreign Film and the notice of producer Jack Schwartzman. Brandauer's Largo was the most interesting 007 villain since Auric Goldfinger. Youthful, handsome, and urbane, he also had a touch of the psychotic that made his on-screen appearances fascinating to watch, particularly his moments with Domino (KIM BASINGER). *See* LARGO, MAXIMILLIAN.

Stuntman Andy Bradford played clown-suited 009 in *Octopussy*. (Andy Bradford)

Actor Klaus Maria Brandauer played a slick but psychotic Largo in *Never Say Never Again*. (Taliafilm)

BRANDT, HELGA Agent 007's (SEAN CONNERY) female nemesis in *You Only Live Twice*, portrayed by German beauty Karin Dor. Posing as Osato's (TERU SHIMATA) confiden-

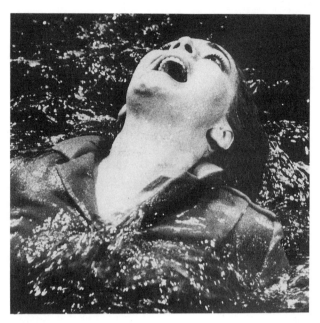

Helga Brandt (KARIN DOR) becomes fish food in *You Only Live Twice*. (UPI)

tial secretary, the spectacularly built Brandt is in reality S.P.E.C.T.R.E. agent No. 11.

Schooled in the Fiona Volpe–style of assassination, she unsuccessfully tries to kill Bond by leaving him trapped in a disabled private plane. Her failure spells her own doom when a dissatisfied Ernst Stavro Blofeld (DONALD PLEASENCE) opens a mechanical footbridge, causing her to fall into his private piranha pool. When it comes to their agents' failed assassination attempts against 007, the Bond villains seldom have a kind word or a forgiving heart.

BRATISLAVA, CZECHOSLOVAKIA City, originally behind the Iron Curtain, where Bond (TIMOTHY DALTON) first meets defecting Soviet General Georgi Koskov (JEROEN KRABBE) in *The Living Daylights*. In helping Koskov across the border, Bond disrupts the assassination attempt by cellist Kara Milovy (MARYAM D'ABO).

In actuality, Kara is not a KGB sniper—she's been duped by her patron/lover Koskov to help him convince British intelligence that his defection is genuine. Rather than kill the beau-

tiful woman, Bond merely shoots the rifle out of her hand.

After Koskov is whisked out of Czechoslovakia via the Trans Siberian oil pipeline, Bond returns to Bratislava to question Kara, who is being shadowed by the KGB. When Kara is arrested on a tram, Bond retrieves her cello case, throws her sniper's rifle into the river, and returns the case to her apartment.

Now aware that Koskov has been spirited out of England by unknown parties, Bond poses as Koskov's friend to determine if Kara knows his whereabouts. She gives him one clue: her cello is called "The Lady Rose."

Thanks to Austrian Section Chief Saunders (THOMAS WHEATLEY), Bond later learns that Kara's cello is an expensive Stradivarius, purchased at auction in New York by Brad Whitaker (JOE DON BAKER), a notorious arms dealer based in Tangier. Bond eventually breaks through several KGB roadblocks and spirits Kara out of Bratislava and into Vienna.

BRAUN One of South American drug runner Franz Sanchez's (ROBERT DAVI) henchmen in *Licence to Kill*, portrayed by Cuban actor Guy de Saint Cyr. Braun is present on Cray Cay when Dario (BENICIO DEL TORO) cuts out the heart of Lupe Lamora's (TALISA SOTO) unfortunate lover, Alvarez (GERARDO MORENO).

He's also in the Wavekrest warehouse when Felix Leiter (DAVID HEDISON) is thrown to the sharks. Braun is killed during the tanker-truck chase when Bond (TIMOTHY DALTON) single-handedly obliterates Sanchez's cocaine convoy.

BRAUSCH The brand of silencer attached to Bond's (SEAN CONNERY) Walther PPK in *Dr. No.*

BRAY, SIR HILARY (aka Sir Hilary Bray, Baronet) Heraldry specialist, portrayed by actor George Baker, at the London College of Arms, whose identity Bond (GEORGE LAZENBY) assumes in *On Her Majesty's Secret Service*. Bray is busy determining whether fugitive criminal Ernst Stavro Blofeld (TELLY SAVALAS) has a claim to the royal bloodline of the de Bleuchamp family.

Sensing an opportunity to apprehend Blofeld, Bond learns all he can from Bray about heraldry and the London College of Arms and takes on Bray's identity for a trip to Blofeld's Swiss hideaway—Piz Gloria. His mission: for research purposes, get Blofeld to the de Bleuchamp ancestral home in Augsburg. There the British Secret Service can arrest him. Unfortunately, Bond's cover is blown during his stay in the Alps, especially when he begins bed-hopping among the luscious allergy victims that Blofeld is brainwashing.

BRAYHAM, PETER   Actor who portrayed Rhoda, the S.P.E.C.T.R.E. agent driving the Chevrolet stake truck that is intentionally stalled on the railroad tracks to stop the Orient Express and establish Red Grant's (ROBERT SHAW) escape route in *From Russia with Love*. Having killed Grant in a vicious fight on the train, Bond (SEAN CONNERY) surprises Rhoda, knocks him out, ties him up, and captures the truck.

Later, after he's destroyed a S.P.E.C.T.R.E. helicopter, Bond arrives at the dock where Rhoda has tethered a motorboat. When Bond and Tanya (DANIELA BIANCHI) head for Venice, Rhoda is untied and tossed into the water off Illystria, where he cusses unintelligibly. It just wasn't his day.

BREE, JAMES   British actor who portrayed Swiss lawyer Gebruder Gumbold, who helps Blofeld (TELLY SAVALAS) establish a blood connection to the royal de Bleuchamp line in *On Her Majesty's Secret Service*.

BRENNAN, MICHAEL (1912–   )   Tough British supporting actor who portrayed Janni, a S.P.E.C.T.R.E. henchman in *Thunderball*.

BRIDAL SUITE   Bond's choice for a new room in *From Russia with Love* when he discovers that his reserved hotel room is filled with listening devices. In actuality, the hotel desk clerk who recommends the new room is working for S.P.E.C.T.R.E. The bridal suite has been chosen as the site for Tatiana Romanova's (DANIELA BIANCHI) night of seduction, which will be filmed from a *cabinet de voyeur* situated behind the bed.

BRIEFCASE (aka trick briefcase)   A smart piece of luggage supplied to Bond by Q Branch in *From Russia with Love*. The briefcase saves his life in the final duel with Red Grant (ROBERT SHAW) on the Orient Express. Equipped with a number of lethal weapons, the briefcase was such an important element of the story that it influenced all future Bond films. From this point on, every film contained a Q Branch sequence in which Bond is outfitted with various gadgets. Even the Aston Martin car that became a sensation in the next film, *Goldfinger*, was

Years before he played Janni in *Thunderball*, actor Michael Brennan, *second from right*, appeared with Desmond Llewelyn in Terence Young's rousing war film, *They Were Not Divided*. (National Film Archive, London)

simply an "automotive briefcase."

As science gained a strong impetus during the space-race era, it is not surprising that Bond's gadgets were so important to the films. This was 1963, and mankind was already preparing to land a man on the moon by the end of the decade. Technology was on the march, and in every facet of human life, machines were beginning to do jobs previously accomplished by man. Thanks to producers Harry Saltzman and Albert R. Broccoli, the Bond movies were always looking for the latest items that might be developed in the Q Branch arsenal. Having once searched for vaudeville acts in New York City in the 1930s, Saltzman was especially adept at finding new toys that would work wonders in the latest Bond movie. The briefcase was the first.

Bond's briefcase figured in the first day of shooting on *From Russia with Love* (April 1, 1963), during a scene in which Q comes to M's office to explain the case's various elements and trick compartments: .25-caliber AR-7 folding sniper's rifle, 20 rounds of ammunition hidden in two metal rods, 50 gold sovereigns hidden in the back, a flat-bladed throwing knife hidden in the front, and a metal tin of talcum powder that was actually a tear-gas cartridge that magnetically rested against an inside wall of the case.

As Q (DESMOND LLEWELYN) explains, when you ordinarily open a briefcase like this one, you move the catches to the side and open. If you do this, the tear-gas cartridge will explode in your face. Bond is advised to first turn the catches horizontally and then move them to the side. The case can then be opened without triggering the gas.

Whimsical editor Peter Hunt actually played a trick on director Terence Young during one of the screening sessions where this footage was shown. During the screening, when Bond attempts to properly open the briefcase using Q's instructions, Hunt cut in a sequence where there is an actual explosion obliterating Bond, M, and Q, all in one blast. According to Hunt, it gave Young quite a start and, of course, kept everyone in stitches for days.

In the movie, the briefcase is identified as standard field issue. In addition to Bond, it is carried by Captain Nash (BILL HILL), Bond's doomed Yugoslavian contact who is murdered by Red Grant. The briefcase is then involved in one of the most thrilling sequences in the entire series—inside the train compartment on the Orient Express when 007 is about to be murdered by Grant.

On his knees, staring into Grant's silenced automatic, Bond plays his final card. He asks for a cigarette, but Grant refuses. Bond then offers to pay for it. Considering that Grant has already taken Bond's bankroll, the question is intriguing to the S.P.E.C.T.R.E. assassin. Grant asks him how he's going to pay for the cigarette, and Bond replies that there are 50 gold sovereigns in his briefcase. Grant then makes his worst mistake by letting Bond retrieve them.

Knowing how the trick case works, Bond opens it correctly and retrieves the sovereigns, which he throws on the floor for Grant. The ever-greedy Grant then asks if there are any more in the other case, to which Bond adroitly replies in the affirmative, even taking the step of offering to open the other case himself. Grant falls right into the trap, thinking that Bond has a weapon hidden in the other case. When Grant decides to open the case himself, he gets tear gas sprayed in his face. The most exciting fight in the series—one that is always cut on network television—then begins.

Despite his prowess in fisticuffs, 007 is about to be strangled with Grant's watch when he trips a catch on the briefcase, revealing the hidden knife. Bond stabs a surprised Grant in the arm and strangles him with his own watch.

The briefcase is mentioned one other time in the series, on the *Goldfinger* private jet, when Mei Ling informs Bond that his briefcase was damaged upon examination. "So sorry," she says. Not surprisingly, the briefcase became a popular toy when it was later commercially introduced in a plastic version.

BRIGADIER The American officer, portrayed by John McLaren, who leads the U.S. Infantry assault against Goldfinger (GERT FROBE) at Fort Knox. Another Brigadier, portrayed by Paul Carpenter, bids farewell to Bond (SEAN CONNERY) at the airport after the battle.

BRINK, JACOBA Tough but not entirely unlikable ice-skating coach employed by ruthless heroin smuggler and Soviet agent Aris Kristatos (JULIAN GLOVER) in *For Your Eyes*

Only. Assigned the task of preparing Bibi Dahl (LYNN-HOLLY JOHNSON) for the Olympics, Brink is a taskmaster. But unlike other Teutonic ladies in the Bond series, such as Rosa Klebb (LOTTE LENYA) and Irma Bunt (ILSE STEPPAT), she's not involved in the villain's nefarious activities.

BRITISH AMBASSADOR TO EAST GERMANY Diplomat, portrayed by Patrick Barr in *Octopussy,* who receives the phony Fabergé Easter egg from mortally wounded Agent 009 (ANDY BRADFORD).

BRITISH EMBASSY, EAST BERLIN Where mortally wounded 009 (ANDY BRADFORD) takes the phony Fabergé egg he stole from the circus in *Octopussy.*

"BRITISH NAVAL COMMANDER MURDERED" *Evening Standard* newspaper headline featured with a photograph of James Bond (SEAN CONNERY) in *You Only Live Twice.* It's all part of an elaborate ruse to convince 007's enemies that he's dead and out of the way. The fake murder in a seedy Hong Kong hotel room, the phony burial at sea, and the manufactured obituary give Bond a head start on his investigation into the disappearance of a U.S. spacecraft.

BRITISH TRAIN ROBBERY A crime mentioned at a S.P.E.C.T.R.E. briefing in *Thunderball.* According to S.P.E.C.T.R.E. agent No. 5, the organization received a consultation fee of 250,000 pounds for its services in the robbery.

BRITISH UNITED AIR FERRY/FLIGHT VS-400 The airline flight that transports Goldfinger (GERT FROBE), Oddjob (HAROLD SAKATA), and the Rolls-Royce Phantom 337 to Geneva, Switzerland. Tracking his adversaries' progress, thanks to a homing device that has been placed in the Rolls, 007 (SEAN CONNERY) and his Aston Martin sports car follow them a half hour later on the next Air Ferry to Geneva.

BRITTANY Where Sir Hilary Bray (GEORGE BAKER) is headed when Bond (GEORGE LAZENBY) assumes his identity in *On Her Majesty's Secret Service.* A specialist in heraldry, Bray plans to lose himself among the ancient churches of Brittany, where he hopes to do some brass rubbings. With Bray conveniently gone, it will be easier for Bond to proceed with his plan to infiltrate Blofeld's (TELLY SAVALAS) Swiss allergy clinic.

BROCCOLI, ALBERT ROMOLO "CUBBY" (New York City, April 5, 1909–) American film producer who has been exclusively devoted to the production of the James Bond films since 1962. Originally partnered with Harry Saltzman in the first nine films in the series, Broccoli now shares producing chores with his stepson, Michael G. Wilson. Other family members—including his daughters, Barbara and Tina, and son, Tony—are closely involved in the productions, making the adventures of 007 a true family affair.

Broccoli is the son of Giovanni Broccoli, who, along with his brother, emigrated to Long Island from Calabria, Italy, at the turn of the century. According to research done in Florence by Broccoli's wife, Dana, the brothers are descended from the Broccolis of Carrera who first crossed two Italian vegetables—cauliflower and rabe—to produce the vegetable that took their name and eventually supported them in the United States.

Although Giovanni made a comfortable living as a civil engineer, his plan to retire to truck farming in the early 1900s did not prove successful. The Broccoli children thus were forced to toil in the family garden and sell their vegetables in the Harlem produce market. It was not an easy life. Expenses mounted, and when the market was flooded with too many vegetables, prices plummeted. Many times, Albert and his brother had to dump their vegetables in the sewers rather than truck them sixty miles back to the family farm in Astoria.

For a time, Albert's father operated a successful citrus farm in Florida, but the venture proved disastrous in the late twenties when the farm was bombarded by hurricanes. Albert Broccoli soon realized that he could not survive in America by following in the footsteps of his ancestors. He would have to seek another calling.

After his father died, he went to live with his grandmother in downtown Astoria and began working as an assistant pharmacist. After a

Producer Cubby Broccoli, *facing camera*, chairs film discussions with Japanese officials during the shooting of *You Only Live Twice* in 1966. Joining him on the dais, *left to right*, are Ken Adam, Roald Dahl, and military liaison Charles Russhon. (Claire Russhon Collection)

few months, he quit to work for a cousin named DiOrta who ran a casket company. DiOrta needed an office manager, so 18-year-old Broccoli began a successful new career as a casket salesman and accountant.

Although young Cubby made a great deal of money working for his cousin, he was not happy. In 1934 his wealthy cousin Pat DeCicca invited him out to California. DeCicca, then married to actress Thelma Todd, introduced Broccoli to the movie industry, and it wasn't long before the casket salesman from Astoria was hobnobbing with such Hollywood notables as Howard Hughes, Howard Hawks, and Joe Schenck.

When his vacation time ended, Broccoli decided to uproot himself from the coffin business and move west. It was not easy to make a living in Hollywood unless you were in the entertainment business. And Broccoli was not in the business. He was, however, a very good salesman, and he soon amassed a bankroll selling beauty supplies in the Los Angeles area. His movie contacts paid off when Howard Hawks

offered him a "gofer" job on Howard Hughes's new film, *The Outlaw*.

As Hawks's able assistant, Broccoli plunged into the film business, learning the business end of the creative medium, meeting new people, getting married, and continuing to socialize with the upper strata of Hollywood. When Howard Hawks was fired from *The Outlaw* project in 1941, Broccoli stayed on the film. He worked closely with Howard Hughes, who took over personal control of the film, which starred his buxom girlfriend Jane Russell.

Upon the recommendation of Joe Schenck, Broccoli later transferred over to 20th Century Fox to become Henry King's production assistant on such classics as *A Yank in the RAF* (1941), *The Black Swan* (1942), and *The Song of Bernadette* (1943). In 1942 Broccoli left Fox to join the navy.

After VJ Day in September 1945, Broccoli returned to Hollywood to become a successful agent. His boss was Charles K. Feldman, who would later produce the 1967 Bond spoof *Casino Royale*. As a member of Feldman's extremely successful Famous Artists Agency, Broccoli resumed his film education. He learned about casting, bargaining, contract negotiations, and percentages—in short, a lawyer's course in how to make movies and turn a profit.

Broccoli and his wife mingled freely with the Hollywood community, giving sumptuous parties and acquiring an impeccable social standing. Broccoli still couldn't hide a desire to try something else. He wanted to enter the creative side of show business. Feldman had already started to produce on the side as early as 1942, and Broccoli began considering a career as a producer. Friends encouraged him, but it wasn't easy to begin a producing career in Hollywood after the war. Money was extremely tight, and the studios were relying on their own proven talent. The time of the independent producer was still a good decade away, so Broccoli bided his time at Famous Artists. In 1951 he resumed a high school friendship with Irving Allen, a Polish-born director who was then between jobs. With slim prospects of landing a film project on their own, the disgruntled pair decided to pool their talents and resources, form their own company, and move to London. Their company was called Warwick Pictures, named after the New York hotel where they made the deal. With the backing of the British government—which, through its Eady subsidy plan, traded financial backing for the employment of British artists—and a hard-won distribution deal with Columbia Pictures, Broccoli and Allen hired Alan Ladd to a three-picture contract.

After establishing himself in a town house in London's Portland Place, Broccoli began acquiring British talent so that Warwick could benefit from the Eady plan. Broccoli told the *Los Angeles Times* in 1989, "If you went over to England to make a picture and you hired 80 percent British technicians, you got a slice of what they called Eady money. In other words, you got a British subsidy and it could amount to two or three million pounds."

Warwick's first project was a little war drama titled, *The Red Beret.* Budgeted at $1.1 million, written by Richard Maibaum, and directed by Terence Young, it told the story of a young paratrooper (Alan Ladd) who fights to clear his cowardly reputation. Retitled *Para-*

trooper for its American debut, this first Warwick entry became an overnight sensation for Columbia Pictures at a time when the production company desperately needed revenue to counter the postwar slump at the box office.

The surprising success of the film was encouraging to Broccoli and Allen, who were still relative newcomers to the producing business. For their second Alan Ladd feature, they returned to the action element by purchasing American director Mark Robson's novel *Hell Below Zero,* which was about a two-fisted sailor who helps a young lady search for her father's killer in Antarctica. With Ladd in the lead and the veteran Robson directing, Warwick scored again. It was the second in a string of successes that would last for seven years, making the transplanted Americans the kings of the independent film business in England.

The features were all strong on American actors, British supporting players, colorful location backgrounds, and action-packed plots. And during those successful years, Broccoli established lasting relationships with many artists who would later contribute heavily to the success of the Bond pictures. Warwick's personnel included cinematographer Ted Moore, who started as a camera operator on *The Red Beret;* screenwriter Maibaum, who wrote *The Red Beret* and the very successful *Cockleshell Heroes;* and art director Ken Adam, who designed the last Warwick feature, *The Trials of Oscar Wilde.*

Two years before future partner Harry Saltzman acquired an option from Ian Fleming for his Bond novels, Broccoli was given the opportunity to start a 007 project. In the summer of 1958, while he was still partnered with Allen, he received a call from Ned McLaine, a wealthy London businessman who was a good friend of Ian Fleming. Broccoli was in New York taking care of his two children while his first wife fought a losing battle with cancer. It was a trying time for the production executive, and had the project been anything else, Broccoli would probably have said no. But the Bonds were a different story.

Ever since reading *Dr. No,* Broccoli had become fascinated by Fleming's writing style and the exciting life of Britain's most famous Secret Service agent. Thus, not surprisingly, the chance of doing an action-packed James Bond film appealed to him. McLaine advised Broccoli to contact his partner, Irving Allen, as soon as possible. Fleming, he was told, was anxious to make a deal.

Two weeks later, a luncheon was arranged at Les Ambassadeurs, which would later host the Harry Saltzman/Ian Fleming tête à tête. Accompanying Fleming were the McLaine brothers—Ned and Jacque—and Fleming's MCA agent, Bob Fenn, who prefaced the meeting by discussing the recent CBS Television deal for 32 half-hour episodes (a deal that would promptly collapse), the latest publishing figures on *Dr. No*, and Mr. Fleming's eagerness to make a lucrative film deal.

Fifty-three-year-old Irving Allen seemed content to let Broccoli do all of the talking. He listened to Fenn, nodding occasionally to Fleming, who seemed to have a voracious appetite for scrambled eggs, but the whole proceeding seemed to bore him. After Fenn declared that the rights to all of the Bond books could be optioned for $50,000, Allen couldn't stand it anymore.

"Come on," he said, "how can you talk figures like that?" Fenn replied, "Excuse me?" Allen then declared, "I'm sorry, gentlemen, but these books aren't even television material." Broccoli tried to argue the point, but it was hopeless.

Having said his piece, Allen grabbed his hat and left the luncheon. Broccoli mumbled an apology and also left. For a few seconds, the remaining gentlemen sat in stunned silence, wondering why they had journeyed to London to hear such claptrap. Even more exasperating to Ned McLaine was the fact that Allen had left him with the luncheon check. Allen's failure to support a project that was deep in Broccoli's heart contributed to the gradual disintegration of their partnership and the final collapse of Warwick Films in 1960. Alone, but extremely wealthy and resourceful, Broccoli began to search for a new project. For two years he thought about how the Bonds had slipped from his hands, his memory rekindled each time Fleming wrote a new novel.

Then, in the summer of 1961, Broccoli was approached by screenwriter Wolf Mankowitz, whose friend, producer Harry Saltzman, held an option on the Bond novels. With only 28 days left on the option, Saltzman needed a production deal fast. Extremely dubious about making any deals with Fleming after the fiasco at Les Ambassadeurs, Broccoli reluctantly agreed to meet Saltzman in Audley Square in June 1961. A deal was struck, creating a partnership on the project, and Eon Productions was born (E.O.N. stands for "Everything or Nothing").

Soon after the meeting at Audley Square, Broccoli took the Fleming option to his old cohorts at Columbia Pictures. He left copies of the Bond novels with Mike Frankovich, then the production chief. Frankovich gave the novels to a story editor for an opinion, who quickly advised him that James Bond was a poorly conceived British version of Mike Hammer and that the character would never work in the United States. Frankovich, though, had a great deal of respect for Cubby Broccoli and his track record. He decided to call a board meeting and briefly postpone making a final decision.

Meanwhile, there were rumors going around that the story editor had never even read the Bond books and that someone had even mistakenly given him copies of Peter Fleming's travel novels instead. Broccoli waited in London for an answer, and when the phone failed to ring, he decided to take the project to his friend Arthur Krim at United Artists.

On June 20, 1961, Broccoli and Saltzman, accompanied by their wives, Dana and Jacqueline, and Broccoli's one-year-old daughter, Barbara, flew into New York City for a meeting with Krim. Frankovich had called the previous week, stating that Columbia could not pick up the Bond option, so it was either UA or back to square one. Fortunately for the future of James Bond, United Artists was ready to deal.

Broccoli told the *Los Angeles Times* in 1989, "Twenty-eight years ago, Harry Saltzman and I walked into 729 Seventh Avenue, in New York, to United Artists for a meeting with Arthur. I found 10 people at the meeting, including young David Picker, who had just been given the job of head of production. Arthur said, 'Now, Cubby, tell me about James Bond,' and I did. I was the salesman. But Picker said, 'I'm very familiar with James Bond.' He wanted to know how I planned to make the pictures. I had budgeted the first one at $1.1 million. They agreed to $1 million. In 45 minutes we put together a deal for six pictures.

"When Arthur and I shook hands, I suddenly remembered that it was my second wedding anniversary. I thought, I'm here in New York with my wife Dana and our baby daughter Barbara—and I've got a deal to make James Bond pictures. I'm flying high.''

Since 1975, when Harry Saltzman sold his share of Eon to United Artists, Broccoli has been the sole film conduit for James Bond's adventures—except for the 1983 film *Never Say Never Again*, which is a remake of the *Thunderball* novel, the rights to which he does not own. Even when the Fleming titles ran out, Broccoli had permission from Fleming's estate to create new Bond stories. *Licence to Kill*, Broccoli's 16th 007 film, released in 1989, was the first that was not based on a Fleming title. *Goldeneye*, released in 1995, was the second.

In 1981 the Academy of Motion Picture Arts and Sciences awarded Broccoli its prestigious Irving G. Thalberg Award for his illustrious producing career. Broccoli has also received the Order of the British Empire from the Queen of England, as well as the French Commandeur des Arts et des Lettres.

Since 1962 it is estimated that more than two billion tickets—about one for every two people on earth—have been sold to Broccoli's Bond movies. And there appears to be no end in sight. The catchphrase that appeared after his first film, *Dr. No*, still rings true: "James Bond Will Return."

BROOKE, PAUL British actor who portrayed Contessa Lisl Von Schlam's (CASSANDRA HARRIS) card-playing friend Bunky, in *For Your Eyes Only*.

BROOKS, VICTOR British character actor who portrayed Blacking, the golf club "starter" in *Goldfinger*.

BROSNAN, PIERCE (Ireland, May 16, 1952-) Handsome Irish actor who, in *Goldeneye*, became the fifth man to portray James Bond in the United Artists series of 007 adventures. Brosnan was originally signed to play James Bond in *The Living Daylights*, but in a well-publicized decision, NBC Television executives refused to let the actor out of his contract for the "Remington Steele" television series. *Note:* Brosnan was married to the late Cassandra

Harris, who appeared in *For Your Eyes Only*. See ADDENDUM.

BROWN, EARL JOLLY Portly actor who portrayed the extremely soft-spoken Whisper in *Live and Let Die*.

BROWN, JANET Actress and Margaret Thatcher look-alike who portrayed the British prime minister in a humorous sequence at the end of *For Your Eyes Only*.

BROWN, ROBERT (1918-) British character actor who became the second actor to portray M in the James Bond series. Brown was actually introduced as Admiral Hargreaves, flag officer, Submarines, in *The Spy Who Loved Me*. When Bernard Lee, the first M, died prior to the making of *For Your Eyes Only*, his part was temporarily replaced by Chief of Staff Tanner (JAMES VILLIERS). Brown became M in *Octopussy* and played that part in every film since until he was replaced by Dame Judi Dench in *Goldeneye*.

BROWN, WILLIAM H. Director who helmed the 1954 one-hour CBS live television adaptation of Ian Fleming's *Casino Royale*.

BROWNING, RICOU (Fort Pierce, Florida, February 16, 1930-) Underwater director, cameraman, actor, and stuntman who worked on both *Thunderball* and *Never Say Never Again*. Although he achieved international popularity as the gruesome Gill Man in *The Creature from the Black Lagoon* (1954), Browning has spent most of his professional life behind the underwater cameras.

While directing *Thunderball* Browning began a typical shooting day at 9:00 A.M. "We needed sunlight," he explained. "Then we would rehearse the sequence before we went into the water. Everything on *Thunderball* was orchestrated underwater with hand signals—no radio communicating like we can do today. If we had a problem, we would never correct it underwater. We'd surface, discuss it, and go back down to complete the sequence."

Most of the time, the underwater team filmed in shallow water—between 15 and 20 feet. The deepest they went on *Thunderball* was 50 feet when they worked around the ditched NATO bomber. The final battle sequence was conducted off Clifton Pier in Nassau in 15 to 20 feet of water around an old wrecked U.S. Navy landing craft.

Eighteen years later, Browning began work on *Never Say Never Again*—a shoot that was bedeviled by bad weather. For the sequence in which Bond is chased by sensor-equipped sharks, the crew shot around a wrecked fishing boat that was located only 200 feet from the carcass of the *Thunderball* NATO bomber, only the framework of which remains. The crew also shot off Silver Springs, Florida, where Jordan Klein had constructed the exterior superstructure of the *Flying Saucer* yacht, through which a new generation of underwater scooters travels. *See* KLEIN, JORDAN; UNDERWATER BATTLE.

BRUNSKILL Colonel Smithers's (RICHARD VERNON) servant, portrayed by Denis Cowles, at the Bank of England dinner attended by Bond (SEAN CONNERY) and M (BERNARD LEE) in *Goldfinger*. He's the one who serves the "rather disappointing brandy."

BT F 608 License plate of the West German Audi that James Bond (ROGER MOORE) steals in *Octopussy* from a woman who stops to make a phone call. Agent 007 is on his way to Feldstadt to deactivate an A-bomb set to explode at 3:45 P.M. Arriving at a U.S. Air Force base with a convoy of German police on his tail, Bond crashes through the main gate, eludes his pursuers for a brief moment, sneaks into a clown's dressing room, dons a complete disguise in record time, and makes a mad dash for the tent where Octopussy's (MAUD ADAMS) troupe is performing.

BT RS 1730 License plate of the teenager-filled, red West German Kharmann Ghia that fails to stop for James Bond (ROGER MOORE) during his desperate trek to Feldstadt to deactivate an A-bomb in *Octopussy*.

BT-36-72 License plate of General Orlov's (STEVEN BERKOFF) Mercedes in *Octopussy*. After Soviet troops load a cache of stolen Kremlin jewels into the trunk, the car is stolen by Bond (ROGER MOORE), who attempts to follow the Octopussy Circus train.

When his tires are shot to shreds by enemy machine-gunners, Bond amazingly maneuvers the car's steel wheels onto a railroad track, and continues the chase. Climbing onto the train, Bond leaves the car just seconds before an oncoming train strikes it head-on, catapulting the Mercedes into a nearby lake.

Raised quickly by Russian salvagers, the Mercedes is plucked out of the water and placed on land, where General Gogol (WALTER GOTELL) finds the stolen cache of Kremlin jewels. He then orders Orlov's arrest.

BUCCELLA, MARIA A former Miss Italy and Miss Europe who was one of the finalists for the part of Domino in *Thunderball*.

BULGARIAN FRONTIER James Bond's (SEAN CONNERY) planned destination when he escapes from the Orient Express with his captured Lektor decoder and defecting Soviet cipher clerk Tatiana Romanova (DANIELA BIANCHI) in *From Russia with Love*. According to this plan formulated by Kerim Bey (PEDRO ARMENDARIZ), the head of the British Secret Service in Turkey, the Express will make an unscheduled stop near the Bulgarian frontier at 6:00 P.M. A car will then take Bond to the airstrip 20 miles away, where he will catch a plane that is chartered to Athens. A jet will then take him directly to London with his prizes.

Unfortunately, when Red Grant (ROBERT SHAW) murders Kerim Bey on the train, the plan is abandoned. The train does not stop and Kerim Bey's sons—who were waiting for Bond—must scurry back to a phone to find out what the hell happened.

BULLION BOULEVARD TO GOLD VAULT ROAD The motor route taken by Goldfinger (GERT FROBE) and his Grand Slam Task Force during their assault on Fort Knox.

BULLION KILL Code name for a British Secret Service operation conducted in November 1964 in which three of the Union Corse's top operatives were liquidated, as related by M (BERNARD LEE) to Marc Ange Draco (GABRIELE FERZETTI) at James Bond's (GEORGE LAZENBY) wedding to Tracy Vicenzo (DIANA RIGG) in *On Her Majesty's Secret Service*.

BULLOCK, JEREMY British actor who portrayed Smithers, Q's (DESMOND LLEW-ELYN) assistant in New Delhi in *Octopussy*. He had previously portrayed one of the British submarine crew members in *The Spy Who Loved Me*.

BUNGALOW 12 James Bond's (ROGER MOORE) San Monique hotel room number in *Live and Let Die*. Rosie Carver (GLORIA HENDRY) has already registered as Mrs. James Bond.

BUNKY Card-playing friend, portrayed by Paul Brooke, of Contessa Lisl Von Schlam (CASSANDRA HARRIS) in *For Your Eyes Only*. They're introduced at a chemin de fer table at Milos Columbo's (TOPOL) club in Corfu.

BUNT, FRAU IRMA Ernst Stavro Blofeld's (TELLY SAVALAS) ruthlessly efficient personal secretary in *On Her Majesty's Secret Service*. Bunt was perfectly portrayed by German actress Ilse Steppat, who, unfortunately, died soon after the film's release. Showing off some of his knowledge of family trees and heraldry, Bond (GEORGE LAZENBY), masquerading as Sir Hilary Bray of the London College of Arms, informs Irma that *bunt* is a nautical term referring to the "baggy, swollen parts of a sail." However, it is Bunt who pierces Bond's cover when she discovers him sneaking into luscious allergy patient Ruby Bartlett's (ANGELA SCOULAR) bedroom.

Surviving the Union Corse helicopter assault on the Piz Gloria fortress, Bunt is the one who machine-guns Tracy (DIANA RIGG) to death in the film's tragic conclusion. *See* STEPPAT, ILSE.

BUOY POINT, FLORIDA Fictional location off the coast of Miami of a wrecked ship where S.P.E.C.T.R.E. intends to place one of the two hijacked A-bombs in *Thunderball*. It is also the site of an underwater battle between Emilio Largo's (ADOLFO CELI) black-suited frogmen and a platoon of orange-suited U.S. Navy Aquaparas led by James Bond (SEAN CONNERY). Thanks to 007, who performs the same chores he did at the gypsy camp in *From Russia with Love*—in other words, he's everywhere—the Americans win and the bomb is captured.

BURTON, NORMAN American character actor who portrayed Felix Leiter in *Diamonds Are Forever*. Burton's Leiter was a throwback to the jacket-and-tie CIA bureaucrat introduced by Cec Linder in *Goldfinger*. In *Diamonds Are Forever*, however, Leiter is a little funnier and a bit more exasperated than usual with his buddy 007 (SEAN CONNERY). The fact that Bond has broken every law in the Las Vegas vehicle code has something to do with Leiter's annoy-

Author Steve Rubin hosts a *Diamonds Are Forever* reunion at The James Bond Weekend luncheon in July 1981. (right to left: Lana Wood, Rubin, Norman Burton, and Bruce Glover)

ance. Leiter, himself, is the one who, after deploying an army of agents at Circus Circus to keep an eye on Tiffany Case (JILL ST. JOHN), still manages to lose her.

BURTON, PETER British actor, and a member of director Terence Young's stock company, who portrayed Major Boothroyd, the armorer from Q Branch in the first James Bond film, *Dr. No.* When Burton proved unavailable, actor Desmond Llewelyn took over the role in *From Russia with Love* and has portrayed Boothroyd ever since.

BUSH, GRAND L. Actor who portrayed Hawkins, a DEA agent who attempts to halt the unauthorized investigation of James Bond (TIMOTHY DALTON) into the mutilation of his friend Felix Leiter (DAVID HEDISON) in *Licence to Kill. See* HAWKINS.

BUTCHER, JOE Soft-spoken, gentle international televangelist, portrayed by Wayne Newton, who is actually a sleazy, lecherous member of Franz Sanchez's (ROBERT DAVI) South American cocaine empire in *Licence to Kill.* In the tradition of Jim and Tammy Bakker, Butcher is a high-rolling charlatan who lives in a pleasure palace called the Olimpatec Meditation Institute, which houses the laboratories that dilute Sanchez's cocaine into gasoline.

Through a code developed by Sanchez's financial expert, William Truman-Lodge (ANTHONY STARKE), Butcher's television show actually broadcasts the current price of cocaine to an international clientele. Thus, in addition to receiving donations from devoted viewers, Butcher's telephone operators also take major drug orders.

The cushy lifestyle is disrupted when Bond (TIMOTHY DALTON) and Pam Bouvier (CAREY LOWELL) destroy the Institute and its cocaine cargo. Pam enters the well-guarded grounds by posing as an innocent devotee of Butcher. Invited to his bedroom, she turns the tables on the sleazoid, holds him up at gunpoint, and locks him in his room.

BUTLER, DICK American stuntman who doubled Sean Connery in sections of the fight between Bond and Bambi (DONNA GARRATT) and Thumper (TRINA PARKS) in *Diamonds Are Forever.* In one sequence, Butler is kicked into the metal tubes (actually cardboard) in Willard Whyte's living room, and in another he's thrown into the swimming pool. According to writer/director and special effects expert Robert Short, who in 1971 visited the Axelrod residence in Palm Springs where this sequence was filmed, Sean Connery did most of his own stunts and enjoyed every minute of it.

BUTTERCUP Enticing enemy agent, portrayed by Angela Scoular, who attempts to seduce the celibate Sir James Bond (DAVID NIVEN) in a Scottish bathtub in the 1967 *Casino Royale* spoof. She's posing as one of M's (JOHN HUSTON) twelve daughters. Scoular would join the cast of *On Her Majesty's Secret Service* two years later as Ruby Bartlett. *See* SCOULAR, ANGELA.

BUZZ-SAW YO-YO Terrifying razor-sharp, retractable weapon deployed by a Udaipur mugger, portrayed by William Derrick in *Octopussy.* Normally, the bandits from Udaipur prefer not to bother the women on Octopussy's (MAUD ADAMS) island. However, evil Prince Kamal Khan (LOUIS JOURDAN), determined to destroy Bond (ROGER MOORE), has enough gold to make it worth their while.

First they deal with poor Vijay (VIJAY AMRITRAJ), who is brutally murdered while on guard. Stealthfully making their way into the "floating palace," three muggers approach Octopussy's bedroom, where Bond is asleep. The yo-yo–yielding man hovers above the bed. Fortunately, a drop of water from the tip of the buzz saw alerts Bond and Octopussy, and they dive out of the way of its destructive path. When his weapon is caught in a piece of furniture, Bond pulls the yo-yo man's wire, and he comes crashing down from the balcony and is throttled.

BYRON LEE BAND An all-Chinese band from Jamaica that performed the Jamaican songs featured in *Dr. No,* including "Underneath the Mango Tree," "Jump Up," and the calypso version of "Three Blind Mice."

C

CABINET DE VOYEUR The French term for a secret anteroom or chamber connected to the bedroom of a hotel suite, in which sexually frustrated men and women can watch the love-making of various guests.

In *From Russia with Love*, S.P.E.C.T.R.E. uses such a room connected to an Istanbul hotel bridal suite in order to catch the lovemaking of James Bond (SEAN CONNERY) and Tatiana Romanova (DANIELA BIANCHI) on film. The footage is part of an intricate blackmail scheme perpetrated by S.P.E.C.T.R.E. in order to humiliate and murder 007 after the death of S.P.E.C.T.R.E. agent Dr. No.

CABLE CAR Cable cars play dramatic roles in both *On Her Majesty's Secret Service* (1969) and *Moonraker* (1979). In OHMSS, a cable car connects the tiny Swiss village of Murren with the Bleuchamps Institute of Allergy Research (aka Piz Gloria), the cover for Ernst Stavro Blofeld's (TELLY SAVALAS) latest plot to blackmail the free world.

His cover as a British heraldry expert blown, James Bond (GEORGE LAZENBY) is imprisoned by Blofeld in the cable car's wheelhouse—a complicated mass of cables and gears that resembles the mechanism of a watch. Bond realizes that if he can make it through a window to the outside, he can escape.

Tearing out the pockets of his pants to create a pair of ersatz gloves, Bond carefully winds his way through the gear system, catches hold of the departing cable, and is whisked out of the mechanical prison. Once he's in the open air, 007 holds onto the cables and then jumps aboard an arriving cable car that takes him back into the Piz Gloria reception area, where he steals a pair of skis and heads for Murren.

The interior of the wheelhouse was filmed at Pinewood Studios on a set designed by Syd Cain. Stuntmen Chris Webb and Richard "Dicky" Graydon did the dangerous location work in which Bond clings to the icy cables. Said stunt coordinator George Leech, "I was supposed to be George Lazenby's double in that

sequence, but when I started doing the cable climb, I fell off and twisted my arm. It was a dangerous stunt to do in freezing cold weather, 10,000 feet up. We were working on the last station of the Schilthorn cable run. Below was at least a 100-foot drop, and the cables were extremely greasy and caked with ice."

Since Leech was injured, he employed Chris Webb and Dicky Graydon to double for Lazenby. To protect them, Leech fastened a metallic rigging device inside their sleeves. In case they lost their grip, the metal hook would prevent them from falling. As a second safety precaution, a drop bed was placed below the cable to catch the stuntmen if their primary device failed them. Director Peter Hunt asked Leech if the stunt was possible without the metallic aid, but as the day wore on and it became colder, Leech felt it was impossible to do the stunt without some metallic safeguard. The use of the safety device almost killed Graydon.

"It was so cold," said Leech, "that Dicky couldn't get a grip on the moving wire. He began to slide down the mountain on the cable. Luckily, I had stationed somebody at the first piling who stuck his foot out in time and prevented Dicky from sliding any farther. He could have eventually slid all the way to Murren down that rope."

A much larger cable car is featured in *Moonraker*, during a hair-raising sequence filmed partially on stage and partially in Rio de Janeiro. Bond (ROGER MOORE) and Holly Goodhead (LOIS CHILES) are making their way from Sugarloaf Mountain to the Brazilian mainland, when a crony of Jaws (RICHARD KIEL) halts their cable car midway on its run. Jaws then climbs aboard a second car, which is carefully maneuvered alongside a trapped Bond and Holly.

A fight ensues between 007 and his steel-toothed nemesis, with each jumping in, around, and between the two stalled cars. Eventually 007 grabs hold of one of the cables, and using a chain, he slides downhill with Holly in tow. Jaws follows in a cable car controlled by his wheelhouse assistant and nearly runs Bond down. At the last possible moment, Bond and Holly jump to safety, while Jaws, the controls on his cable car shot, crashes spectacularly into the wheelhouse—later emerging unscathed.

The fight between Bond and Jaws was performed on a stage at Pinewood, with the actors trading blows in front of a blue screen where the Brazilian skyline was matted in. Master shots of the stalled cable cars and the wheel house were shot on location in Brazil.

CABOT, BRUCE (Carlsbad, New Mexico, April 20, 1904–May 3, 1972) (real name, Jacques Etienne Pellissier de Bujac) American character actor and former 1930s adventure hero who portrayed casino boss Burt Saxby in *Diamonds Are Forever*. Cabot's rugged features were perfectly suited to the Las Vegas atmosphere, crowded with underworld diamond smugglers, tough-talking women, and mysterious assassins. Cabot made 15 films with his friend John Wayne. *See* SAXBY, BURT.

"CAFE COMPLAIT FOR TWO WITH FRESH ORANGE JUICE" Bond's (GEORGE LAZENBY) breakfast order at the Portuguese hotel/casino where he meets and beds Tracy (DIANA RIGG) in *On Her Majesty's Secret Service*. Unfortunately for Bond, the following morning Tracy is gone, and he must eat alone.

CAFE MARTINIQUE Romantic outdoor Nassau nightclub, featured in *Thunderball*, where Bond (SEAN CONNERY) dances with Domino (CLAUDINE AUGER) and discovers that she is leaving Nassau in two days' time. The Cafe Martinique lies on Paradise Island, a two-mile strip of sand and rock that forms the outer edge of Nassau Harbor. Here, every evening, Nassau's elite arrive in their motor launches to eat, drink, and dance to the wonderful melodies of the tropics. In this lush atmosphere, Domino begins to fall in love with James Bond.

How do you get 150 extras to resemble a group of rich socialites and tourists? If you're Cubby Broccoli and Harry Saltzman, you don't use extras at all. With the help of Patty Turtle of the Nassau Tourist Board, and an offer to donate a sum of money to the local Red Cross, a group of Nassau's social elite agreed to portray themselves for the two all-night parties, during which Terence Young shot his key sequences. Eon Productions threw in a bucket of the finest caviar, as well as several cases of Dom Perignon champagne. The same group was later hired to attend the special Junkanoo Parade which was organized especially for *Thunderball*.

CA52H6 The California license plate of the red 1971 Mustang driven by James Bond (SEAN CONNERY) and Tiffany Case (JILL ST. JOHN) in *Diamonds Are Forever*. Technically speaking, this license plate is a blooper. A Mustang rented in Nevada should have Nevada plates.

CAIN, SYD Top British production designer who joined the James Bond series (as location art director) on *Dr. No* and later worked as production designer on *From Russia with Love*, *On Her Majesty's Secret Service*, and *Live and Let Die*.

Returning to the scene of the crime. Production designer Syd Cain, *right*, joins director Terence Young in September 1989 for a visit to the lawn behind the Pinewood Studios administration building, which was used as S.P.E.C.T.R.E. Island headquarters in *From Russia with Love*.

CAIRO Egyptian capital featured in *Diamonds Are Forever* and *The Spy Who Loved Me*. In *Diamonds*, the city is the second stop on James Bond's (SEAN CONNERY) ruthless search for Ernst Stavro Blofeld (CHARLES GRAY), the man who murdered Bond's wife in the previous film.

Tipped off in Tokyo, Bond goes to a Cairo casino and meets a fez-wearing blackjack player whose card request, "Hit me," is followed by a 007-size punch instead. To avoid a beating, he in turn directs Bond to Marie (DENISE PERRIER), a bikini-clad jet-setter who tells Bond everything when he rips her top off and nearly strangles her with it. The information eventually leads him to the jungles of South America and to Blofeld's cloning experiments.

In *The Spy Who Loved Me*, Cairo becomes the scene of a number of strange encounters between Bond (ROGER MOORE) and KGB Major Anya Amasova (BARBARA BACH), who are both competing for a nuclear-submarine tracking system that is being offered on the open market by mysterious sources. Following a briefing in the desert with Sheik Hosein (EDWARD DE SOUZA), an old college friend and fellow Secret Service agent, Bond learns that his contact is a man named Aziz Fekkesh (NADIM SAWALHA). At Fekkesh's Cairo apartment, Bond finds only the seductive Felicca (OLGA BISERA) and Sandor (MILTON REID), one of billionaire shipping magnate Karl Stromberg's (CURT JURGENS) assassins.

Disposing of Sandor, but not before the bald bodybuilder tells him that Fekkesh can be found at the pyramids, Bond, that night, attends a magnificent outdoor show at the pyramids where he sees Fekkesh. Unfortunately, the Egyptian is murdered by Jaws (RICHARD KIEL), another one of Stromberg's assassins. On the body, Bond finds an appointment book that shows Fekkesh's planned meeting that same night with a certain Max Kalba (VERNON DOBTCHEFF) at the latter's Cairo nightclub.

Outside the pyramids, Bond has his first encounter with KGB Major Anya Amasova, whose two male assistants are unable to subdue 007. At Kalba's club, Bond and Anya formally introduce themselves and then vie for the tracking system in Kalba's possession. However, Kalba is soon called to the phone, where he's killed by Jaws, who takes the microfilm containing the plans. Bond and Anya then chase Jaws into the desert.

Recovering the microfilm from the steel-toothed assassin during a moody encounter in an old ruin, and surviving his physical assault on their pathetically brittle stolen utility truck, Bond and Anya cross the desert—to the appropriate theme from *Lawrence of Arabia*—and

board a sailing vessel to Cairo. After a romantic moment, Anya blows knockout smoke in Bond's eyes, which puts him to sleep for several hours. When he awakens, Anya and the microfilm are gone. Fortunately, as 007 discovers when he enters the Egyptian tomb-turned-headquarters of the British Secret Service in Cairo, Anya is now on his side, as Russia and Britain are cooperating in the search for the tracking system.

"CALIFORNIA GIRLS" This classic song by the Beach Boys is performed by Gideon Park in the teaser for *A View to a Kill*. It accompanies the sequence in which Bond (ROGER MOORE) takes the runner from a disabled snowmobile and surfs down a glacier.

Continuing a trend toward including memorable musical bits as comic relief in the James Bond movies starring Roger Moore, the use of "California Girls" was, nonetheless, a low point in this arena. In the old days, the filmmakers created incredible stunt sequences that were almost too believable. Afterward, a little throwaway humor was tossed in to bring the audience back into their seats. Musical bits like a Beach Boys song tended to undercut the audience's belief in a very well-directed action sequence—just as the humorous musical bit destroyed the believability of the 360-degree car jump in *The Man with the Golden Gun*.

CALL, ED American actor who portrayed Maxie, Plenty O'Toole's (LANA WOOD) Las Vegas cowboy boyfriend who loses her affection to high-rolling James Bond (SEAN CONNERY) in *Diamonds Are Forever*.

CALL ME BWANA A 1963 Bob Hope/Anita Ekberg comedy-in-the-jungle produced by Albert R. Broccoli and Harry Saltzman. To publicize the movie, Broccoli and Saltzman featured the film on the billboard containing the trapdoor to Krilencu's (FRED HAGGERTY) apartment in *From Russia with Love*. In the film, Krilencu crawls through Anita Ekberg's mouth and is promptly shot by his longtime nemesis, Kerim Bey (PEDRO ARMENDARIZ).

In the original novel, the billboard was from the 1953 Twentieth Century Fox film *Niagara*, starring Marilyn Monroe, whose billboard mouth was used as the trapdoor getaway. Monroe died from an overdose of sleeping pills shortly before *From Russia with Love* went into production. It is doubtful that *Niagara* would have been used anyway, since the billboard sequence provided an excellent promotional opportunity for *Call Me Bwana* and Anita Ekberg.

CAMBRIDGE James Bond's (ROGER MOORE) college alma mater, according to the recollection of Sheik Hosein (EDWARD DE SOUZA), in *The Spy Who Loved Me.*

CAMERON, EARL (1925–) Jamaican actor who portrayed Pinder, Bond's (SEAN CONNERY) able Nassau contact in *Thunderball. See* PINDER.

British actor Earl Cameron portrayed Pinder in *Thunderball.* (National Film Archive, London)

CAMPARI An Italian aperitif offered to Bond (GEORGE LAZENBY) by Draco (GABRIELE FERZETTI) in the latter's office in *On Her Majesty's Secret Service.* Draco's usual drink is Corsican Brandy.

CAMPBELL Switzerland-based British agent, portrayed by Bernard Horsfall, who comes to Bond's (GEORGE LAZENBY) assistance in *On Her Majesty's Secret Service.* It is Campbell, working a construction crane, who delivers the safe-cracking computer/photocopier to Bond in Gumbold's (JAMES BREE) office in Berne.

Later, while attempting to follow Bond to Blofeld's (TELLY SAVALAS) Piz Gloria fortress, Campbell is killed by S.P.E.C.T.R.E. guards.

"CAN I BORROW A MATCH?" The opening phrase in the British Secret Service recognition code used in *From Russia with Love.* The proper sequence is (a)"Can I borrow a match?," (b)"I use a lighter," (c)"Better still," and (d)"Until they go wrong." Bond first hears the opening phrase from one of Kerim Bey's sons in the Istanbul airport. He hears it again in the Belgrade, Yugoslavia, train station when he informs another one of Kerim Bey's sons that his father has been murdered. Grant uses it to trick and murder British agent Captain Nash (BILL HILL) in Zagreb, Yugoslavia, and Bond and Grant use the recognition code one last time in the same station. Grant knows the code because S.P.E.C.T.R.E. "sweated" it out of a British agent in Tokyo before he died.

CANADIAN CLUB WHISKEY ADVERTISEMENT Where producer Albert R. Broccoli first heard about ski-jumper/parachutist Rick Sylvester and his death-defying jump off Canada's Asgard Peak—a stunt he would recreate for *The Spy Who Loved Me* teaser. To Broccoli, though, Sylvester admitted that the Asgard jump had been faked for the advertisement. Sylvester said he had instead jumped off the much smaller El Capitan Peak in Yosemite Valley, California. He had attempted to jump the Asgard, but weather conditions had made it impossible. For $30,000, Sylvester returned to the Asgard in July 1976 and achieved the impossible for the 007 cameras.

CAPE COM Coded reference in *You Only Live Twice* to Cape Canaveral, where scientists are tracking *Jupiter 16* as it heads for its fourth orbit.

CAPLAN, PAULA Bond's (SEAN CONNERY) Nassau assistant in *Thunderball,* portrayed by Martine Beswick, who had earlier appeared as one of the gypsy girls in *From Russia with Love.* Introduced on 007's motorboat during Bond's first encounter with Domino

Sean Connery and actress Martine Beswicke, who portrayed Paula Caplan in *Thunderball*. (Rex Features, Ltd./RDR Productions)

(CLAUDINE AUGER), Paula is later kidnapped by S.P.E.C.T.R.E. and taken to Largo's (ADOLFO CELI) Palmyra estate, but she takes poison before divulging any information. She is referred to as Paula Roberts in the original script.

CAPONE, AL Chicago gangster of the 1920s whose pop-up wooden likeness is featured in Francisco Scaramanga's (CHRISTOPHER LEE) private fun house maze in *The Man with the Golden Gun*. The figure looks amazingly like character actor Bruce Gordon, who portrayed Frank Nitti in "The Untouchables" television series.

CAPRI An island off the coast of Italy, mentioned in *Thunderball*, where Domino (CLAUDINE AUGER) says she first met Emilio Largo (ADOLFO CELI).

CAPUNGO Spanish word for "thug," also the Latino assassin portrayed by stuntman Alf Joint in the *Goldfinger* teaser. Capungo sneaks up behind Bond (SEAN CONNERY) while he is embracing Bonita (NADJA REGIN), the flamenco dancer, but 007 sees Capungo's approach reflected in Bonita's pupils. As they struggle, Capungo gets thrown into the bathtub and reaches for Bond's gun, which is hanging on a peg. Bond then tosses an electric heater into the tub, electrocuting the assassin.

CARD SENSE JIMMY BOND James Bond's (BARRY NELSON) nickname in TV's "Casino Royale." It's mentioned by British agent Clarence Leiter (MICHAEL PATE), who knows Bond's reputation as an expert baccarat player. Bond's card-playing ability is actually a cover for his secret agent work with America's Combined Intelligence. *See* NELSON, BARRY.

CARLIEZ, CLAUDE Stunt coordinator who portrayed the man in the coffin, one of Drax's (MICHEL LONSDALE) Venice assassins in *Moonraker*. Carliez was also a stunt coordinator on *A View to a Kill*. *See* MAN IN THE COFFIN, THE.

CARLOS & WILMSBERG, INC. Huge import/export company, based in Rio de Janeiro, that's another subsidiary of Drax Enterprises Corporation in *Moonraker*. On the trail of Hugo Drax (MICHEL LONSDALE) and a plot that could destroy human life on earth, Bond goes to the C & W warehouse on Carioca Avenue in Rio, where he finds some Drax air freight labels and the lurking presence of Jaws (RICHARD KIEL).

CARRERA, BARBARA Nicaraguan actress and former model who shined in *Never Say Never Again* as S.P.E.C.T.R.E. executioner Fatima Blush. A latter-day Wicked Witch of the West, Carrera exuberantly approached the part of the S.P.E.C.T.R.E. assassin. In her delightfully animated hands, Fatima is a colorful psychotic who revels in her killing—a pure comic-book villainess.

Cackling like a witch, dancing down stairways and across hotel lobbies, employing every possible approach to assassinate Bond (all unsuccessful, of course), Carrera is such a lively element in *Never Say Never Again* that the film's pacing never recovers from her character's death. Deprived of her presence in the film's final third segment, the movie stumbles along with very little drama. Like *Thunderball*, the movie's remaining villian Largo (KLAUS MARIA BRANDAUER) does not make a very formidable opponent for Bond—nothing approaching the hysterically fiendish zeal in killing that is the essence of Fatima Blush. *See* BLUSH, FATIMA.

CARTER, COMMANDER Efficient U.S. Navy nuclear submarine skipper, portrayed by Bond veteran Shane Rimmer, who commands the USS *Wayne* in *The Spy Who Loved Me*. With Bond (ROGER MOORE) and Anya (BARBARA BACH) on board as observers, Carter is ordered to trail the suspicious *Liparus* supertanker—the pawn in billionaire shipping magnate Karl Stromberg's (CURT JURGENS) plan to destroy the world. Unfortunately, the cat soon becomes the mouse as the *Wayne* is disabled and captured by the *Liparus*, ending up in the belly of the tanker along with two other missing subs and crews.

With Bond's help, Carter and his men later escape in the *Wayne*, which sails directly to Stromberg's amphibian Atlantis home. When 007 fails to return from his mission to kill Stromberg and rescue Anya, Carter fires two torpedoes at Atlantis, which destroy the facility—but not before Bond and Anya get away in a cocktail-glass–shaped escape pod.

CARTER, REGGIE Actor who portrayed Mr. Jones, the mysterious chauffeur in *Dr. No*, who poisons himself with cyanide rather than submit to 007's line of questions.

CARTLIDGE, WILLIAM P. (1945-   ) Longtime associate of director Lewis Gilbert and an associate producer on *The Spy Who Loved Me*, Cartlidge began his career as an assistant director on *Born Free* in 1966, the same year he went to work for Gilbert on *Alfie*. Prior to *The Spy Who Loved Me*, he was an assistant director on two other Lewis Gilbert films, *The Adventurers* (1970) and *Friends* (1971), and an associate producer on *Paul and Michelle* (1974).

On *Spy*, he was the associate producer, working closely with Albert R. Broccoli and Michael Wilson on that film's complicated international shooting schedule. Said Cartlidge, "We had found that we couldn't get access to Sardinia until the tourist season ended in September (1976). And we couldn't shoot in Egypt in the summer because of the incredible heat. So we ended up starting in the studio, on the smaller sets.

"The big 007 stage was still under construction and wasn't going to be ready until Christmas. What we decided to do was build all the smallish sets, the ones that would require only a day's shooting or less; and when they were finished, we could strike them down and go off to locations. This procedure gave the studio back its valuable space for other productions, and it allowed us to get rid of a lot of actors who were only scheduled for a short period.

"You can't book supporting players for a shot in August and another shot in November. You have to take them when they're available. So we got rid of the little scenes that take place in, say, Gogol's (WALTER GOTELL) office in Moscow, in the pyramid complex when M (BERNARD LEE) and Gogol supervise the search operations, the Q (DESMOND LLEW-ELYN) laboratories, and the ski chalet where you first see Bond (ROGER MOORE). When we came back from Egypt and Sardinia, the only things we had left to do were the Atlantis and supertanker sets, which were just about finished."

CARVER, ROSIE Inept CIA liaison of Bond's (ROGER MOORE) in *Live and Let Die*, portrayed by former Playboy bunny Gloria Hendry. In actuality, Carver's CIA cover is a sham; she's really working for Kananga (YAPHET KOTTO). Solitaire's (JANE SEY-MOUR) tarot-card clue—the Queen of Cups in the upside-down position—warns Bond that Carver is not what she says. Rosie is eventually killed when she blunders into one of Kananga's jungle booby traps.

CARUSO, MISS Lovely Italian Secret Service agent portrayed by Madeline Smith in *Live and Let Die*. She's the buxom brunette who is hiding in James Bond's (ROGER MOORE) closet when M (BERNARD LEE) pays an early morning visit. When M leaves, Bond opens the closet door and unzips Miss Caruso with the help of his hypersensitive magnetic watch.

CASE, TIFFANY Cocky redheaded diamond smuggler portrayed by Jill St. John in *Diamonds Are Forever*. When Bond (SEAN CONNERY) questions the derivation of her name, she explains that she was born on the first floor of Tiffany's in New York while her mother was looking for a wedding ring.

Based in a third-floor apartment in Amsterdam, Case is a crafty courier for an international diamond-smuggling syndicate that is being decimated by Ernst Stavro Blofeld (CHARLES GRAY). Tiffany's mission is to supervise the smuggling of a huge diamond cache into the United States through Los Angeles. British smuggler Peter Franks (JOE ROBINSON) will

be the courier, but 007 kills Franks and assumes his identity.

When Bond hides the real diamonds and substitutes fake ones, Case joins her smuggling cohorts in Las Vegas to track down the real stuff. Later she reluctantly joins forces with Bond against Blofeld, who kidnaps her. She winds up on Blofeld's oil rig in the Gulf of Baja, where Bond and the CIA disrupt S.P.E.C.T.R.E.'s latest caper to blackmail the planet with a laser satellite—powered by diamonds.

In the film's conclusion, Case joins Bond on a romantic cruise to England that is disturbed by the arrival of the homosexual assassins Mr. Wint (BRUCE GLOVER) and Mr. Kidd (PUTTER SMITH). Bond disposes of the assassins and joins Case, who, ever the opportunist, wonders how they can retrieve the diamond satellite from outer space.

Voluptuous Madeline Smith portrayed Miss Caruso, an Italian agent who is Roger Moore's first bedmate in the Bond series. (George Whitier/Camera Press, Globe Photos)

Actor and former professional football player Bernie Casey portrayed Felix Leiter in *Never Say Never Again*. (Bernie Casey)

CASEY, BERNIE Actor and former professional football player who portrayed CIA agent Felix Leiter in *Never Say Never Again*. Casey was the first black to play James Bond's opposite number in the Central Intelligence Agency. His part was small and underwritten by writer Lorenzo Semple, Jr.

Joining Bond (SEAN CONNERY) in the South of France, where Largo's *Flying Saucer* yacht is under surveillance, Leiter helps Bond escape from local authorities after 007 eliminates Fatima Blush (BARBARA CARRERA) with his rocket pen. He later joins Bond in the climactic assault on Largo's (KLAUS MARIA BRANDAUER) archaeological dig in the Tears of Allah, where he keeps some S.P.E.C.T.R.E. operatives pinned down with machine-gun fire.

CASINO DE MACAO Crowded Portuguese-island gambling house featured in *The Man with the Golden Gun*. It's where Bond (ROGER MOORE) first sees Andrea Anders (MAUD ADAMS), who's on a munitions pickup for her live-in lover, Francisco Scaramanga (CHRISTOPHER LEE). After Andrea receives a supply of golden bullets, 007 follows her to the waterfront where she boards Scaramanga's junk.

"CASINO ROYALE" (The Live Television Version) ★ ★ TV adaptation of Ian Fleming's first James Bond novel, which aired at 8:30 P.M., EST on Thursday, October 21, 1954, as the third live one-hour episode of the CBS Climax Mystery Theater. Technically the first Bond movie, "Casino Royale" is a small-scale, studio-bound thriller that introduces James Bond (BARRY NELSON) as an American agent up against a Russian masterspy named Le Chiffre (PETER LORRE). The battlefield: a Monte Carlo baccarat table.

Terribly dated and low-key, the story nonetheless conveys a sense of Fleming's style and that of the Bond films to come—the larger-than-life villain, the high-stakes gambling, the beautiful woman (double agent Valerie Mathis, portrayed by Linda Christian), and the loyal friend—in this case, British agent Clarence Leiter, portrayed by Michael Pate. The film is also introduced in an unusual fashion by series host William Lundigan, who brings out a baccarat "shoe" at the beginning of the show and explains its significance to the story.

Directed by William H. Brown from a script by Antony Ellis and Charles Bennet, "Casino Royale" was produced by director Bretaigne Windust. CBS had purchased the rights to Fleming's novel for $1,000.

Lost for nearly thirty years, "Casino Royale" surfaced in 1981 when a Chicago airline executive named Jim Shoenberger unearthed an original 16mm kinescope copy of the 1954 show. Shoenberger, a film collector and a member of the Cliffhangers of America society, was rummaging through some old film canisters that were marked "Casino Royale." Thinking that the print was a battered 16mm copy of the 1967 Columbia Pictures feature-length comedy *Casino Royale*, he was about to cut up the film for leader when he noticed that it was in black and white. Remembering that the David Niven/Woody Allen spoof was a color film, he was curious enough to run the film, and discovered that it was a perfectly preserved copy of the 1954 show.

The film was first shown publicly in July 1981 at the James Bond Weekend in Los Angeles—a 007 luncheon and trivia marathon. Barry Nelson was a featured guest.

CASINO ROYALE (Columbia Pictures, 1967) ★ James Bond spoof produced by Charles K. Feldman and Jerry Bresler. U.S. release date: April 19, 1967. Budget: $9 million. U.S. film rental: $10.2 million.

With five directors, eight writers (only three credited), two second-unit directors, and a galaxy of name talent, *Casino Royale* is still one of the worst film spoofs ever made. When Charlie Feldman was unable to make a deal with Albert R. Broccoli and Harry Saltzman to produce Ian Fleming's first novel as a serious James Bond entry (Feldman turned down half a million dollars for the rights), he decided to produce a spoof instead—a big lumbering satire on the world of Bond that comes across like a misfired television variety special.

Filled with plot holes you could drive Aston Martins through, and long set pieces that are not the least bit funny, *Casino Royale* is the ultimate stepchild of the 007 series. By 1967 Bond spoofs were a dime a dozen. There was the *Our Man Flint* series, the *Matt Helm* series, the Belmondo *That Man* series. Television was producing "The Man From U.N.C.L.E.," "I Spy," "Get Smart," and dozens more.

When questioned about the viability of using different directors, Feldman replied, "We're trying to stress a different quality in each sequence." What emerges instead is an approach that stumbles and gasps its way through much of the film. John Huston's "Deborah Kerr in Scotland" sequence is a total misfire that serves only to showcase David Niven as a bumbling boob. Joe McGrath's "Peter Sellers/Ursula Andress Seduction" sequence just barely works, thanks to the always inventive Sellers. Ken Hughes's "Mata Bond in Berlin" sequence is appropriately surreal, but ends up like a Mack Sennett Keystone Cops sketch, suffering the same fate as Richard Talmidge's "Casino Brawl" sequence.

High points: a few. The Herb Alpert score. The Dusty Springfield song "The Look of Love." Barbara Bouchet as Moneypenny's luscious daughter. Peter Sellers and Woody Allen. Otherwise a thoroughly forgettable film.

CASINO ROYALE CAST

Evelyn Tremble/James Bond	Peter Sellers
Vesper Lynd	Ursula Andress
Sir James Bond	David Niven
Le Chiffre	Orson Welles
Mata Bond	Joanna Pettet
The Detainer/Lady James Bond	Daliah Lavi
Jimmy Bond/Dr. Noah	Woody Allen
Agent Mimi/Lady Fiona	Deborah Kerr
Ransome	William Holden
Le Grande	Charles Boyer
McTarry/M	John Huston
Smirnov	Kurt Kasznar
Himself	George Raft
French Legionnaire	Jean-Paul Belmondo
Cooper/James Bond	Terence Cooper
Miss Moneypenny	Barbara Bouchet
Buttercup	Angela Scoular
Eliza	Gabriella Licudi
Heather	Tracey Crisp
Peg	Elaine Taylor
Miss Goodthighs	Jacqueline Bisset
Meg	Alexandra Bastedo
Frau Hoffner	Anna Quayle
Hadley	Derek Nimmo
Polo	Ronnie Corbett
Casino Director	Colin Gordon
Taxi Driver	Bernard Cribbins
Fang Leader	Tracey Reed
Casino Doorman and M.I.5	John Bluthal
Q	Geoffrey Bayldon
Q's Assistant	John Wells
Inspector Mathis	Duncan MacRae
Casino Cashier	Graham Stark
Chic	Chic Murray
John	Johnathan Routh
British Army Officer	Richard Wattis
Chinese Army Officer	Burt Kwouk
Le Chiffre's Representative	Vladek Sheybal
1st Piper	Percy Herbert
Recognizable Piper	Peter O'Toole
Control Girl	Penny Riley
Captain of the Guards	Jeanne Roland

72

CASINO ROYALE CREW

Presented by ....Charles K. Feldman
Producer ....Charles K. Feldman
Producer ....Jerry Bresler
Director ....John Huston
Director ....Ken Hughes
Director ....Val Guest
Director ....Robert Parrish
Director ....Joseph McGrath
Additional Sequences ....Val Guest
Screenplay by ....Wolf Mankowitz,
       John Law, Michael Sayers
Suggested by the novel *Casino Royale* by Ian Fleming
Director of Photography .....Jack Hildyard, B.S.C.
Additional Photography......John Wilcox, B.S.C.,
       Nicholas Roeg, B.S.C.
Music Composed and Conducted by ....
       Burt Bacharach
Main Title Theme Played by ....Herb Alpert
       and the Tijuana Brass
"The Look of Love" Sung by ...Dusty Springfield
Music by ....Burt Bacharach
Lyrics by ....Hal David
Production Designer ....Michael Stringer
Costume Designer ....Julie Harris
Film Editor ....Bill Lenny
Titles and Montage Effects ......Richard Williams
Associate Producer ....John Dark
Production Managers ....Douglas Peirce,
       John Merriman, Barrie Melrose
Art Directors....................John Howell,
       Ivor Beddoes, Lionel Couch
Assistant Directors ....Roy Baird,
       John Stoneman, Carl Mannin
Second Unit Directors ....Richard Talmadge,
       Anthony Squire
Choreographer ....Tutte Lemkow
Set Dresser ....Terence Morgan
Casting ....Maude Spector
Costumes for Ursula Andress and Joanna Pettet by
       Bermans of London
Chief Makeup Artist ....Neville Smallwood
Makeup for Ursula Andress ......John O'Gorman
Chief Hairdresser ....Joan Smallwood
Wardrobe Supervisor............Betty Adamson
Special Effects ....Cliff Richardson,
       Roy Whybrow
Special Matte Work..................Les Bowie
Technical Adviser ....David Berglas
Sound Editor ....Chris Greenham
Dialogue Editor ....James Shields
Assistant Film Editor ....Alan Strachan
Sound ....John W. Mitchell, Sash Fisher,
       Bob Jones, Dick Langford, Chris Greenham
Assistant Art Directors ....Norman Dorme,
       Tony Rimmington

Construction Manager ....Bill MacLaren
Production Company ....Famous Artists
       Productions Ltd.
Distribution Company ....Columbia Pictures

CASINO ROYALE COMPETITION

Competitive films in release when *Casino Royale* opened in Los Angeles on April 28, 1967:
The Busy Body
Hombre
Alfie
The Endless Summer
Horrors of Spider Island/The Fiendish Ghouls
Hurry Sundown
Night Games
Grand Prix

"CASINO ROYALE IS TOO MUCH . . . FOR ONE JAMES BOND" Advertising catchphrase used to sell the 1967 *Casino Royale* spoof. It was accompanied by the film's logo—a colorfully tatooed nude woman—designed by Joseph Mack.

CASTALDI, JEAN PIERRE Actor who portrayed the private-jet pilot, in the *Moonraker* teaser, who attempts to assassinate Bond (ROGER MOORE) by disabling his own plane. Leaving Bond behind while he parachutes to safety, the pilot is later jumped by 007—who has been pushed out of the plane by Jaws (RICHARD KIEL). In an amazing midair fight sequence, Bond steals the parachute of the unfortunate pilot, who then falls to his doom.

CAVENDISH Hugo Drax's butler in *Moonraker*, portrayed by Arthur Howard (the brother of *Gone with the Wind*'s Leslie Howard). *See* HOWARD, ARTHUR.

CELESTIAL VIRGIN OF THE SACRED ALTAR Mata Bond's (JOANNA PETTET) Indian title in *Casino Royale*. *See* BOND, MATA.

CELI, ADOLFO (Messina, Sicily, July 27, 1922–February 19, 1986) Heavyset Italian character actor who played the ruthless one-eyed S.P.E.C.T.R.E. agent Emilio Largo in *Thunderball*. Celi was well cast as Largo, a big operator who can easily turn from charmer to killer when S.P.E.C.T.R.E. business is at stake.

Realistic in bearing and mannerisms, Celi's

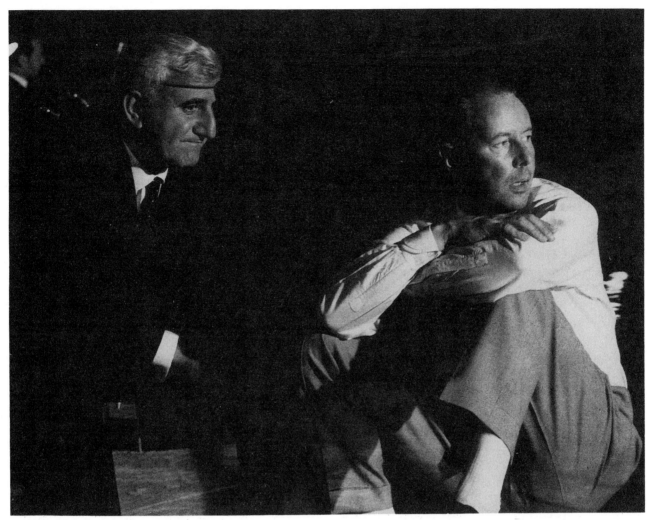

Director Terence Young takes a breather with Adolfo Celi during filming inside the S.P.E.C.T.R.E. conference room in *Thunderball*. (Terence Young Collection/The Swarbricks of London)

nonetheless villainous character has varied turf extending from the regal card rooms of the Nassau casino to the crystal-blue waters of the Caribbean, where his underwater army maneuvers the hijacked A-bombs. Unlike many Bond villains, who sit around and delegate authority, Celi's Largo is a true field commander, donning wet suit and personally leading his men in their underwater schemes.

CENTRIFUGE TRAINER A gravitational-force simulator, sabotaged in *Moonraker*, found at Hugo Drax's (MICHEL LONSDALE) industrial space complex outside Los Angeles. Touring the facilities with Dr. Holly Goodhead (LOIS CHILES), Bond (ROGER MOORE) takes her offer to test his skills on the simulator. According to Goodhead, the maximum speed of

the trainer is 20g, a fatal force. 3g is equivalent to takeoff pressure, and 7g is the point at which most people pass out.

Unbeknownst to Holly, who is called away from the training area to receive a bogus phone call, Chang (TOSHIRO SUGA) plans to sabotage the trainer and kill Bond with a lethal force. As the trainer builds speed like an amusement-park attraction to a 7g force, Bond begins to push a "chicken switch," which is supposed to automatically shut down the system. It doesn't work.

As the force begins to build, rippling the skin on 007's traumatized face, Bond tries to use his wrist-activated dart gun. He finally shoots out the controls of the trainer after living through a 13g pressure. A returning Holly rushes to his side, but Bond wants none of her comforting. He staggers away—totally disoriented, but alive.

It's one of the few times in the film (along with Corinne Dufour's death in the forest) that the film takes on a chilling realism. Otherwise, most of the action sequences in *Moonraker* are either unbelievable (the gondola chase, the space-station assault), overstaged (the glass museum fight with Chang), or just plain dull (the motorboat chase in South America). *Note:* The centrifuge trainer sequence owes a great deal to the motorized traction table incident in *Thunderball.*

CEYLAN, HASAN Turkish actor who portrayed the persistent, mustachioed Bulgar agent with the beret in *From Russia with Love.* It is Ceylan who tails 007 (SEAN CONNERY) from the Istanbul airport to Kerim Bey's (PEDRO ARMENDARIZ) office. And it is Ceylan who tails defecting cipher clerk Tatiana Romanova (DANIELA BIANCHI) to the St. Sophia Mosque, where he is killed by Grant (ROBERT SHAW) before he can intercept the map of the Russian consulate that Tanya is leaving for Bond. One sequence, in which Ceylan tails Bond to the Bosphorus ferryboat but gets into an automobile accident planned by Bond and Kerim Bey, was cut from the film when the son of director Terence Young pointed out that Ceylan had already been killed in the Mosque.

CHAIN SAW What the Drug Enforcement Administration says mutilated CIA agent Felix Leiter (DAVID HEDISON) in *Licence to Kill.* Bond (TIMOTHY DALTON) and Leiter's friend Sharkey (FRANK MCRAE) know that a shark attack was responsible, but no one in Key West will believe them.

CHAMPAGNE, BARRY (Houma, Louisiana, June 18, 1952–   ) An assistant aerial stunt coordinator and an engineer on *Licence to Kill* who worked closely with Corkey Fornof. One of Champagne's key sequences was the stunt where CIA pilot Pam Bouvier (CAREY LOWELL) maneuvers her Piper Cub crop-dusting plane so that James Bond (TIMOTHY DALTON) can jump onto a moving tanker trailer-truck.

For that sequence, shot in the mountains outside Mexicali, Mexico, English stuntman Simon Crane doubled Dalton, and aerial stunt coordinator Corkey Fornof flew the Piper. A padded ''bed'' was placed atop the tanker, and Fornof slowed the aircraft down to about 70 mph so that Crane could jump onto the truck.

For the teaser sequence, where Bond captures Sanchez's Cessna 172 private plane, Champagne explained that three aircraft were actually used. Fornof flew the in-flight Cessna, a second plane was hung upside-down in the Coast Guard helicopter snare, and a third was mounted on the ground rig (where close-ups of Dalton were shot). All three aircraft were purchased from a Florida aircraft junkyard. The plane that the Coast Guard helicopter snares was equipped with an engine built by John Richardson's special effects department. Its tail section was also reinforced to accommodate the helicopter's winch cable.

CHAMPAGNE SECTION Flight ID for the five Piper Cherokee monoplanes that participate in Operation Rockabye Baby in *Goldfinger.* Trained in stunt flying by Pussy Galore (HONOR BLACKMAN), the five voluptuous women flyers, dressed in black jumpsuits, are led by Sydney, the Champagne leader.

CHAN YIU LAM Actor who portrayed tough, muscle-bound Chula, Bond's (ROGER MOORE) second and more formidable opponent in the kick-boxing segment of *The Man with the Golden Gun.*

CHANG One of Dr. No's (JOSEPH WISEMAN) rocket technicians, in charge of controlling the fuel elements of the nuclear reactor. Bond (SEAN CONNERY) knocks him out, dons his radiation suit, gains entry to Dr. No's reactor room, and destroys the reactor by raising the temperature of the atomic pile beyond the danger level.

Chang is also the name of Hugo Drax's (MICHEL LONSDALE) bodyguard in *Moonraker,* portrayed by Toshiro Suga. Chang's first job, on Drax's orders, is to ''see that some harm'' comes to James Bond (ROGER MOORE). Following these orders, Chang sabotages the centrifuge trainer that is taking 007 on what is supposedly a sample journey. Thanks to his wristwatch dart gun, however, the controls are shot away before 007 loses consciousness and his life.

Later in Venice, Chang, equipped with a mighty samurai sword, battles Bond in the Venice Glass Museum, a sequence that was originally written as a Cairo Museum of Antiquities "mummy room" fight in *The Spy Who Loved Me*. Bond wins that fight, tossing Chang through an upper-story window and onto the piano of an outdoor evening concert.

CHARLES Maximillian Largo's (KLAUS MARIA BRANDAUER) financial expert aboard the *Flying Saucer* yacht in *Never Say Never Again*.

CHARLIE Bond's doomed CIA chauffeur in *Live and Let Die*, portrayed by stunt driver Joie Chitwood. Charlie is bumped off by a deadly dart fired from the side-view mirror of Whisper's (EARL JOLLY BROWN) pimpmobile.

CHARLIE ONE Code name for Felix Leiter's (NORMAN BURTON) command helicopter during the raid on Blofeld's oil rig in *Diamonds Are Forever*.

"CHARTS, PEESTOL, SOME FLARES" The contents of the motorboat supply locker, as described to Bond (SEAN CONNERY) by defecting Russian cipher clerk Tatiana Romanova (DANIELA BIANCHI), during their escape from Illystria to Venice in *From Russia with Love*.

CHATEAU CHANTILLY, FRANCE Ornate French estate that doubled as Max Zorin's (CHRISTOPHER WALKEN) home and stables in *A View to a Kill*. The buildings were completed in the 18th century by an aristocrat who was convinced he would be reincarnated as a horse. Zorin relates that story in the film to Bond (ROGER MOORE), but he incorrectly dates his home as being from the 16th century.

CHATEAU D'ANET, FRANCE Glitzy location used in the *Thunderball* teaser to portray S.P.E.C.T.R.E. agent Jacques Boitier's (BOB SIMMONS) estate. Located near Paris, the elegant surroundings were the jump-off point for James Bond's (SEAN CONNERY) flight in the Bell jet pack. The chateau is also the historic residence of Diane de Poitiers. Principal photography on *Thunderball* began here on February 16, 1965.

CHE CHE One of Marc Ange Draco's (GABRIELE FERZETTI) Union Corse henchmen in *On Her Majesty's Secret Service*, portrayed by actor Irvin Allen. Che Che surprises 007 (GEORGE LAZENBY) in Tracy's hotel room in Portugal and starts a brawl that he eventually loses. Shaken but not stirred, Bond then goes to find Tracy (DIANA RIGG) for a night of intimate lovemaking. Joining Bond in the Rolls-Royce for a drive to Draco's headquarters, Che Che becomes a comrade of Bond during the Union Corse helicopter assault on Blofeld's (TELLY SAVALAS) Piz Gloria fortress.

CHECKPOINT CHARLIE Famous German border crossing-point, featured in *Octopussy*, where James Bond (ROGER MOORE) takes his leave of M (ROBERT BROWN) and enters East Germany. Posing as Charles Morton, a furniture manufacturer's representative from Leeds, 007's on the trail of Kamal Khan (LOUIS JOURDAN) and the Octopussy Circus, which is still behind the Iron Curtain and headed for a performance on a U.S. Air Force base in Feldstadt, West Germany.

CHEOPS Ancient Egyptian pharaoh whose pyramid tomb provides the backdrop for a spectacular nightly show at Giza, outside Cairo, in *The Spy Who Loved Me*. Searching the grounds for black-market trader Aziz Fekkesh (NADIM SAWALHA), Bond (ROGER MOORE) finds his corpse instead and a notebook that leads 007 to his next stop—the Mojaba Club. *See* FEKKESH, AZIZ.

CHEVRON OIL SIGN One of the casualties of James Bond's (ROGER MOORE) madcap hook-and-ladder fire truck chase through San Francisco in *A View to a Kill*.

"CHICKEN SWITCH" The button you push in Hugo Drax's centrifuge trainer in *Moonraker* when you reach your maximum pressure threshold. It's supposed to automatically shut down the system. Unfortunately in Bond's (ROGER MOORE) case, the button doesn't work because Chang (TOSHIRO SUGA) has sabotaged the machine. See CENTRIFUGE TRAINER.

CHIEF OF THE SNOW LEOPARD BROTHERHOOD Afghan drug wholesaler, portrayed by Tony Cyrus in *The Living Daylights*, who makes a huge opium-for-diamonds deal with arms dealer Brad Whitaker (JOE DON BAKER) and renegade Russian General Georgi Koskov (JEROEN KRABBE). Only the Afghans make anything on the deal.

The drugs themselves are destroyed when Bond (TIMOTHY DALTON) and Kara (MARYAM D'ABO) hijack a Soviet transport plane and dump the opium bundles out of the cargo hatch. The Soviets also lose the $50 million advance they gave Whitaker for an arms shipment that was turned into diamonds for the freelance opium deal. Koskov is captured and sent to Siberia.

CHIFFRE, LE (aka Herr Ziffer) Soviet masterspy and obsessed gambler, portrayed by Peter Lorre in the 1954 TV film "Casino Royale." Le Chiffre's name comes from the French word, meaning "cipher" or "number." According to British Secret Service records and author Ian Fleming's own text, Le Chiffre was a displaced concentration camp survivor after World War II who could not remember his name. Since he became a simple number on a displaced person's list, he took the name Le Chiffre as an appropriate moniker.

He eventually becomes a top agent for the Soviet Union working in the area of southern France and Monte Carlo. His penchant for high-stakes gambling and high-stakes losing (using Soviet funds) comes to the attention of both the Soviets and Allied Intelligence. Bond (BARRY NELSON) is sent to Monte Carlo to bankrupt Le Chiffre in one last grand game of baccarat.

Having lost 80 million francs, Le Chiffre is down to a sum of 26 million, which he plans to use to make back the money he stole from the Soviets. If Bond can bankrupt Le Chiffre, British intelligence is convinced that the Soviets will take matters into their own hands and liquidate Le Chiffre before he becomes a source of international embarrassment to his country.

In the TV film "Casino Royale," Bond beats Le Chiffre at cards with the help of the Deuxième Bureau's double agent, Valerie Mathis (LINDA CHRISTIAN). However, while searching for Mathis, Bond is captured and tortured by the Russian masterspy, who is determined to take back a check worth 87 million francs that Bond won at the tables. When Le Chiffre briefly leaves Bond alone while he goes off to search for the missing check, 007 manages to free himself, and he eventually shoots and kills Le Chiffre and one of his thugs (see LORRE, PETER).

The same character, in a comic vein, was portrayed by actor Orson Welles in the *Casino Royale* spoof. In that film, the Soviet masterspy still plays baccarat in Monte Carlo with stolen Soviet funds, but he's also a magician who practices his tricks right at the table. To raise currency for his gambling habit, he sends his agent/auctioneer (VLADEK SHEYBAL of *From Russia with Love*) to West Berlin with a cache of compromising photographs that will be auctioned off to Soviet, American, British, and Chinese military men. The auctioneer loses the photos to Mata Bond (JOANNA PETTET), and he's blown up when Le Chiffre detonates his phone booth. Le Chiffre is defeated at the baccarat table by Evelyn Tremble/James Bond (PETER SELLERS) and later killed by the KGB. See WELLES, ORSON.

CHILES, LOIS American leading lady who portrayed brainy and slinky CIA agent Holly Goodhead in *Moonraker*. See GOODHEAD, DR. HOLLY.

CHIN, ANTHONY Chinese actor who portrayed the Taiwanese tycoon in *A View to a Kill*. Like Mr. Solo (MARTIN BENSON) in *Goldfinger*, his desire to *not* participate in Max Zorin's (CHRISTOPHER WALKEN) microchip scheme guarantees him one thing: death—in this case, a quick unscheduled exit from Zorin's blimp. Chin also appeared in *You Only Live Twice* as the guard who Bond (SEAN CONNERY) shoots with his cigarette rocket gun.

CHIN, TSAI Chinese actress who portrayed Ling, Bond's (SEAN CONNERY) Hong Kong girlfriend in *You Only Live Twice*.

CHINESE JUNK Scaramanga's (CHRISTOPHER LEE) vessel in *The Man with the Golden Gun*. It transports him to and from his island home off the coast of mainland China. Bond (ROGER MOORE) and Mary Goodnight (BRITT EKLAND) use it to escape from the island when Scaramanga's solar energy station is obliterated. After his attempt to kill Bond is foiled, Nick Nack (HERVE VILLECHAIZE) is netted and hoisted into the rigging of the junk for safekeeping.

Speaking of junks, one is reminded of a line of dialogue from the 1953 Richard Widmark World War II adventure film *Destination Gobi*. When one of the enlisted men asks, "Why is it called a junk?," a friend replies, "What else would you call it?"

CHITWOOD, JOIE Stunt daredevil whose Greatest Show on Wheels troupe was featured prominently in *Live and Let Die*. Chitwood, among other things, portrayed Charlie, the doomed CIA chauffeur who is killed by Whisper (EARL JOLLY BROWN) while driving Bond (ROGER MOORE) into New York City.

CHLORAL HYDRATE A sleeping powder that Red Grant (ROBERT SHAW) places in Tatiana Romanova's (DANIELA BIANCHI) champagne glass on the Orient Express in *From Russia with Love*. According to Grant, posing as British agent Captain Nash, the drug is "quick, but mild." As to why he drugged the defecting Russian cipher clerk, Grant explains to Bond (SEAN CONNERY) that his escape route is only for one. This tidy bit of information delivered by Grant appears to satisfy Bond, who then lowers his gun—one of 007's biggest mistakes in the series.

Chloral hydrate is also used by Kara Milovy (MARYAM D'ABO) to drug James Bond (TIMOTHY DALTON) in *The Living Daylights*. She's been told, mistakenly, by renegade Russian General Georgi Koskov (JEROEN KRABBE) that Bond is a KGB agent.

CHONG, MONA Actress who portrayed the Chinese allergy victim in *On Her Majesty's Secret Service*.

CHOPIN Composer of classical piano music playing loudly on the radio in James Bond's (BARRY NELSON) Monte Carlo hotel room in the TV film "Casino Royale." It prevents Russian masterspy Le Chiffre (PETER LORRE) from using a bug planted in Bond's room to listen in to his conversation with Valerie Mathis (LINDA CHRISTIAN).

CHRIS American astronaut who is on an EVA (Extra Vehicular Activity) maneuver during the teaser for *You Only Live Twice*. When the S.P.E.C.T.R.E. intruder craft envelops the *Jupiter 16* spacecraft, Chris's lifeline is snapped, catapulting him to his doom.

CHRISTIAN, LINDA (Tampico, Mexico, November 13, 1924–   ) (real name, Blanca Rosa Welter) Mexican-born leading lady who portrayed Valerie Mathis, a French double agent who became the first James Bond girl, opposite Barry Nelson's 007 in the live television version of "Casino Royale" in 1954. Although she appears to be working for Soviet masterspy Le Chiffre (PETER LORRE), Mathis is actually an agent with the French Deuxième Bureau who supplies Bond with 35 million crucial francs during the climactic baccarat game with Le Chiffre. *See* MATHIS, VALERIE.

Actress Linda Christian portrayed French secret agent Valerie Mathis in the TV "Casino Royale." (Columbia Pictures Corp.)

British actress Julie Christie, age twenty-one. In 1965 she was considered for the role of Domino in *Thunderball*, but she lost the part to Claudine Auger. (Philip Pearman)

CHRISTIE, JULIE (Chukua, Assam, India, April 14, 1941–   ) Charismatic English leading lady who was one of the early choices for the role of Domino in *Thunderball*. Cubby and Dana Broccoli first spotted her on British television in the fall of 1964. Recalled Broccoli, "I marked her name down because she was beautiful, and both Dana and I were raving about her acting. So I brought her into the office a few days later to see Terence and Harry.

"She was very nervous. She came in wearing a pair of jeans and she was terribly disheveled and didn't look at all like she did on television. I was disappointed in seeing her this way. In fact, I couldn't believe it was the same girl."

Said director Terence Young, "It wasn't the ideal place for a shy young actress to meet the powers that be. There were a lot of people hanging around Audley Square in those days, mentally undressing every girl who walked in, and I immediately thought this chick wasn't destined for such an atmosphere. She had class and was more than a pretty face."

Whether she had class or a pretty face was not the question, apparently. It was the size of her breasts that was of more consequence, and according to Broccoli and Saltzman, that is where the extremely talented Christie fell a bit short. She eventually lost out to the quite voluptuous Claudine Auger.

CHUCK, OSWALD Actor who portrayed the Korean guard on the U.S. presidential jet that is commandeered by Auric Goldfinger (GERT FROBE).

CHULA Tough, muscle-bound kick-boxer portrayed by Chan Yiu Lam in *The Man with the Golden Gun*. After 007 (ROGER MOORE) takes care of his first opponent by kicking him in the face during a ceremonial bow (a little touch of the old ruthless Bond), he faces Chula, who is a more formidable opponent. The fight seesaws until Bond sees an opportunity for escape and takes it, crashing through a wall in the process.

CHU MI Poolside bathing beauty who is one of Hai Fat's (RICHARD LOO) harem in *The Man with the Golden Gun*. Bond (ROGER MOORE) meets her on the grounds of Hai Fat's estate in Bangkok when he impersonates Scaramanga (CHRISTOPHER LEE). Some sources spell her name Chew Mee.

CHURCHILL, DELLA The doomed bride of Bond's (TIMOTHY DALTON) long-time friend and compatriot Felix Leiter (DAVID HEDISON), portrayed by "Three's Company" veteran Priscilla Barnes, in *Licence to Kill*. Married to Leiter in Key West, Della is later murdered when the henchmen of escaped drug lord Franz Sanchez (ROBERT DAVI) break into her house. Leiter himself is thrown to the sharks in Milton Krest's (ANTHONY ZERBE) marine warehouse, where he loses his left leg. Della's murder and Felix's mutilation send a revenge-crazed Bond after Sanchez.

CHURUBUSCO STUDIOS Studio complex in Mexico City that was the base of operations for *Licence to Kill*. Financial considerations forced Cubby Broccoli's team to investigate alternatives to their usual base—England's Pinewood Studios.

CIAO Italian word for "good-bye" and a favorite of doomed NATO aerial observer Major Francois Derval (PAUL STASSINO) in *Thunderball*.

CINCINNATI MOOSE LODGE Sign draped over a New Delhi sightseeing boat that Bond (ROGER MOORE) swims to during his escape from Kamal Khan's (LOUIS JOURDAN) tiger trackers in *Octopussy*. When the tourists ask him how he got into such a fix, Bond explains that he's on the "economy tour."

CIRCUS CIRCUS CASINO Colorful, raucous Las Vegas hotel and casino chosen by Bond (SEAN CONNERY) for his rendezvous with Tiffany Case (JILL ST. JOHN) in *Diamonds Are Forever*. Tipped off by Bond, Felix Leiter (NORMAN BURTON) fills the place with radio-equipped CIA agents who monitor Tiffany's every move.

Circus Circus is known for the high-wire show that goes on above the casino and its many sideshow games designed for younger tourists left to wait while their parents gamble. The film features a virtual guided tour of the casino, including stops at the blackjack table, where Tiffany receives a card saying, "Why don't you play the water balloons?"; the water balloon game, where she wins a stuffed animal filled with diamonds; and the Zambora transformation show, a carny attraction featuring a female changeling who becomes a huge rampaging gorilla—after which Tiffany escapes from Bond and his CIA associates.

CITROEN H31854 Make and license number of the car driven by Bulgar agents in Istanbul that tails Bond (SEAN CONNERY) from the airport to Kerim Bey's (PEDRO ARMENDARIZ) office in *From Russia with Love*.

CITROEN 2CV aka Deux Cheveaux Melina Havelock's (CAROLE BOUQUET) compact getaway car in *For Your Eyes Only*. When Bond's (ROGER MOORE) deluxe Lotus Esprit self-destructs, he's forced to drive Melina's vehicle in a wild chase through the backcountry outside Madrid. Pursued by heavily armed enemy agents of hit man Hector Gonzales (STEFAN KALIPHA), Bond and Melina somehow survive, putting the frail little vehicle through some very unlikely maneuvers—including a calculated roll.

CLAUS One of Kristatos's (JULIAN GLOVER) Greek henchmen in *For Your Eyes Only*, portrayed by Charles Dance. Involved with Locque (MICHAEL GOTHARD) in the dune-buggy attack on Bond (ROGER MOORE) and Lisl (CASSANDRA HARRIS) on the beach in Corfu, Claus is about to shoot Bond, when he's in turn killed by Columbo's (TOPOL) men. *See* DANCE, CHARLES.

CLAVELL, MICHAELA British actress who was introduced as Penelope Smallbone, Miss Moneypenny's (LOIS MAXWELL) new assistant in *Octopussy*. Initially, it was thought that Clavell would replace Maxwell as M's (ROBERT BROWN) secretary; however she did not return in *A View to a Kill*. When Timothy Dalton took over the role of Bond in *The Living Daylights*, he was greeted by an entirely new Moneypenny, portrayed by actress Caroline Bliss.

CLEMENT, DICK Screenwriter who, along with Ian Le Frenais, was called in to do some uncredited "bridging" work on Lorenzo Semple, Jr.'s script for *Never Say Never Again*.

CLERY, CORINNE (1950–   ) Beautiful French actress who portrayed Corinne Dufour, Hugo Drax's (MICHEL LONSDALE) doomed helicopter pilot and executive assistant in *Moonraker*. Clery is actually one of the highlights of the film. Cool and resourceful, she has all the classic attributes of a Bond girl. Unfortunately, in Christopher Wood's screenplay, she also has an extremely short life span.

Her death scene in the forest where she's attacked and killed by Drax's trained Dobermans became the basis for *Moonraker's* unusual teaser trailer. It's one of the best-directed scenes in the film and totally out of sync with the rest of the movie's numbing mindlessness.

CLEVELAND, MURRAY American stuntman who worked on the Louisiana motorboat chase sequences in *Live and Let Die*.

CLIFTON PIER Nassau Harbor installation off of which the final underwater battle takes place in *Thunderball*. This sequence, the most ambitious of all the film's underwater sequences, was handled by the full Ivan Tors crew—60 divers strong. It was filmed by Lamar Boren, who single-handedly paddled through the underwater war zone.

CLIVE, MAJOR Retired British army officer, portrayed by Stuart Saunders in *Octopussy*, who has been losing steadily to Kamal Khan (LOUIS JOURDAN) in a series of high-stakes backgammon games. Down 200,000 rupees, Clive is unable to continue the game when Kamal raises the stakes. James Bond (ROGER MOORE) then offers to take over the major's position, and he finally beats Kamal at his own game by using his "loaded" dice to score winning double sixes. The backgammon game, which was originally considered for *The Spy Who Loved Me* for a sequence in Max Kalba's Mojaba Club, was brought back to *Octopussy* and plays like the golf match from *Goldfinger*. *See* BACKGAMMON GAME.

CLOSE ENCOUNTERS OF THE THIRD KIND Classic 1977 Steven Spielberg-directed science-fiction film featuring a five-note alien musical tone that surfaces as a Venice laboratory entry code in *Moonraker*.

COBALT AND IODINE The principal ingredients in the "atomic device" given to Goldfinger (GERT FROBE) by the Red Chinese government. Enabled by Ling (BURT KWOUK), the specialist in nuclear fission, the bomb is set to detonate inside the American gold repository at Fort Knox, Kentucky, with the goal of irradiating America's entire gold supply for 58 years.

COCOON The stern section of the *Disco Volante* yacht in *Thunderball* that becomes a heavily armed decoy when its aft section is transformed into a swift-moving hydrofoil craft. Dead in the water with a U.S. Coast Guard flotilla closing in, the doomed cocoon fights a delaying action with machines guns and a naval artillery piece until one well-placed shell from an American warship obliterates the decoy and its crew.

COFFEY, AL World-class springboard diver whose ability is on brief display at the Fontainebleau pool in *Goldfinger*.

COLTHORPE Ballistics expert, portrayed by actor James Cossins, who works for the British Secret Service in *The Man with the Golden Gun*. Colthorpe identifies Francisco Scaramanga

(CHRISTOPHER LEE) as the man who sent James Bond (ROGER MOORE) an engraved golden bullet—a sign that 007 is the million-dollar-a-shot hit man's next victim. *See* COSSINS, JAMES.

COLUMBO, MILOS Pistachio-chewing Greek smuggler, ex–resistance fighter, and casino owner on Corfu, expertly portrayed by Topol in *For Your Eyes Only*. James Bond's (ROGER MOORE) first impression of Columbo is based on the lies of Soviet agent Aris Kristatos (JULIAN GLOVER), who claims Columbo is a drug smuggler, white slaver, and contract murderer. In reality, Columbo is a smuggler, known as The Dove, but his activities are limited to gold, diamonds, cigarettes, and pistachio nuts—not heroin, which is Kristatos's domain. He runs a fleet of intercoastal freighters in the Aegean.

There is a blood feud between Columbo and Kristatos, dating back to World War II, when both fought the Nazis as resistance fighters on Crete. Unfortunately, Kristatos was a double agent who betrayed his countrymen to the Germans—an act that Columbo will never forget.

Columbo eventually captures Bond on a beach in Corfu—after Kristatos's henchman, Locque (MICHAEL GOTHARD), runs down Columbo's mistress, Lisl (CASSANDRA HARRIS), and sets the record straight about Kristatos. Joining forces with 007, Columbo and his men help Bond track Kristatos to St. Cyril's in Greece, where a wounded Columbo fatally puts a knife in Kristatos's back.

COMBINED INTELLIGENCE A CIA-type organization that's James Bond's (BARRY NELSON) American employer in the TV film "Casino Royale." Bond's card-playing skills, which have won him the sobriquet Card Sense Jimmy Bond, are a front for his intelligence activities.

COMEAUX, JERRY American stuntman whose skill with a motorboat is displayed in *Live and Let Die*. Comeaux jumped his jet-pump powerboat across the Crawdad Bridge, outside Phenix, Louisiana, on October 16, 1972.

COMMANDANT The term used by Domino (CLAUDINE AUGER) in *Thunderball* to describe the rank of her brother, NATO aerial observer François Derval (PAUL STASSINO). In actuality, he is a major.

"COMMANDER JAMAICA" Title proposed by producer and multimillionaire Henry Morganthau III for a 1956 NBC-Television series. Morganthau collaborated on the story with Ian Fleming.

Set aboard a 30-foot yacht moored at Morgan's Harbor, Jamaica, the story pitted an agent named James Gunn against a gang threatening to deflect the course of American missiles from nearby Cape Canaveral. If the plot sounds familiar, it should. When NBC failed to pick up Morganthau's proposed series, Fleming took the plot outline back and wrote his sixth James Bond novel, *Dr. No*.

"COMMANDO TACTICS, MINIMUM OFFENSIVE FIRE" Attack orders for U.S. Army infantry elements assigned the task of stopping Goldfinger's (GERT FROBE) assault on Fort Knox. Until the A-bomb is neutralized by the bomb disposal unit, the army cannot afford a more violent attack.

CONCH CHOWDER Seafood entree served to Bond (SEAN CONNERY) and Domino (CLAUDINE AUGER) at the hotel pool in *Thunderball*. Domino thinks that Bond thinks that conch chowder is an aphrodisiac.

CONLEY, BOB Irresponsible oil executive, portrayed by Manning Redwood, employed by Max Zorin (CHRISTOPHER WALKEN) in *A View to a Kill*. In charge of Zorin's oil reclamation project in the East San Francisco Bay, Conley is actually pumping seawater into the Hayward Fault, an activity that can lead to a major earthquake in the region. He's also making final preparations for a huge explosion under the Main Strike Mine near San Francisco, which will also cause major seismic activity. The twin quakes are designed to carry out Zorin's ambitious Project Main Strike, which will utterly destroy Silicon Valley.

Conley's last job was as chief engineer on a South African gold mine. He left in a hurry after a cave-in killed 20 miners. Unfortunately, Conley runs afoul of another mine disaster when Zorin orders the Main Strike Mine flooded before his men have been evacuated. Protesting the senseless massacre, Conley becomes the first victim—killed by Zorin's security chief, Scarpine (PATRICK BAUCHAU).

CONNERY, MICHELINE French wife of Sean Connery, who not only encouraged her husband to return to the role of James Bond in *Never Say Never Again*, but also coined the film's title.

CONNERY, SEAN (Edinburgh, Scotland, August 25, 1930-   ) (real name, Thomas Sean Connery) For many, Connery is the best of all possible Bonds. He was the first actor to portray 007 in the Broccoli-Saltzman–produced series, and one of the screen's true natural resources.

A great actor who has recently come into his prime in character parts, Connery also developed early in his career a unique screen presence and a dashing romantic manner à la Cary Grant and Errol Flynn that became overwhelmingly appealing to both men and women. It was this quality that led to the success of the early James Bond series, both commercially and critically.

Today Connery is finally getting some of the credit he has always richly deserved, including the recent Oscar for his critically acclaimed role as Chicago cop Jimmy Malone in *The Untouchables*. What he brought to the character of Bond was a sense of danger combined with a sexual magnetism that few actors possess.

As screenwriter Tom Mankiewicz once said, "When Connery walks into a bar, you know he could probably kill somebody if he had to. When Roger Moore walked into a bar, you knew he would probably say something glib to get out of a situation." Both actors were successful 007s, but Connery was the tougher, more serious agent and a tremendous success with audiences of the 1960s.

Although a London newspaper's popularity poll picked Connery as the perfect actor to play the first Bond in a feature film, it was his appearance in two separate films that brought him to the attention of the producers. Albert R. Broccoli spotted him in the Walt Disney fantasy *Darby O'Gill and the Little People*, while Harry Saltzman saw him in *On the Fiddle*, playing an English comic opposite British comedian Alfie

One of actor Sean Connery's first publicity photos. (Express Newspapers, London)

Sean Connery escorts his first wife, actress Diane Cilento, to a premiere in London. (Express Newspapers, London)

Sean Connery returns to his most famous role in the 1983 film *Never Say Never Again*. (Taliafilm)

In 1959, a youthful Sean Connery takes actress Janet Munro for her ride in California during shooting on *Darby O'Gill and the Little People*—the film that brought Connery to the attention of Bond producer Cubby Broccoli.

A pre-Bond caper in which Sean Connery hits the trenches with British comedian Alfie Lynch in *Operation Snafu* (aka *On the Fiddle*)—the film that brought Connery to the attention of Bond producer Harry Saltzman. (American International)

In between 007 assignments, Sean Connery chose serious roles in extremely offbeat films like Sidney Lumet's acclaimed 1965 military drama, *The Hill*.

Lynch. Saltzman had screened the latter film upon the suggestion of editor Peter Hunt, who was friendly with *On the Fiddle* producer Ben Ficz.

The odds were against Connery, who was referred to at that time by American film executives as "the truck driver" (he had driven a truck at one time in his native Edinburgh). But Broccoli was especially impressed by Connery's stature and the fact that for a big man, he moved like a cat. For Broccoli, Bond had to be an Englishman who was good with his fists—a combination he could sell to U.S. film audiences who were used to the two-fisted handiwork of American detectives such as Mike Hammer and Sam Spade.

When Connery was eventually signed to a seven-year contract, he underwent a transformation, thanks to director Terence Young. Having grown up in the slums of Edinburgh, the very rugged and wild Connery was hardly Fleming's dashing upper-class hero. Young brought him to his own tailor and carefully outfitted him for the role of Bond.

Connery may not have been Fleming's prototypical Bond, but from the fans' point of view—and there would soon be millions—he was the best possible choice for the film series. Serious, sexy, deadly, and unbeatable, he was also extremely glib with writer Richard Maibaum's throwaway humor, a factor that contributed to the series' long-standing success.

From 1962 to 1967, Connery appeared in five films in the series: *Dr. No* (1962), *From Russia with Love* (1963), *Goldfinger* (1964), *Thunderball* (1965), and *You Only Live Twice* (1967). Tired of the extremely long shooting schedules that prohibited him from doing more than a handful of non-Bond films, plus the grueling pressures of being an international media star, Connery departed the series after *You Only Live Twice*.

Following George Lazenby's solo performance as 007 in *On Her Majesty's Secret Service* (1969), Connery returned to the series in *Diamonds Are Forever* (1971) when United Artists film executive David Picker offered to back two of Connery's personal film projects, in addition to giving him a salary of $1.4 million plus profits on *Diamonds*. (Connery donated $1 million of his fee to the Scottish Education Trust, a

The key to Sean Connery's success hinged on his ability to balance humor, sexuality, and menace. In this scene from Miss Taro's cottage in *Dr. No*, the menace is on good display. (Rex Features, Ltd./RDR Productions)

charity he founded to aid deprived Scottish children.)

Connery left the series after *Diamonds Are Forever*, ushering in the Roger Moore era. However, thanks to producer Jack Schwartzman and the *Never Say Never Again* project, Connery returned to play 007 one more time in 1983. Connery's long-standing passion for the game of golf dates from the early days prior to *Goldfinger* when he was first learning the sport for a key sequence in that film.

CONNERY VERSUS JAPAN One of the major reasons why actor Sean Connery decided to leave the James Bond series after *You Only Live Twice* was his experience and treatment in Japan in July and August 1966 during that movie's location filming. For an actor who was rapidly tiring of the James Bond films' long and difficult shooting schedules, the Japanese location was the proverbial last straw.

His frustration began on July 27, 1966, when Connery and his first wife, Diane Cilento, arrived in Tokyo and were soon mobbed by 007 fans. Already hugely popular in Japan, James

Bond enthusiasm tripled when it was announced that the latest film would be shot practically in Japanese fans' own backyard.

Hundreds of journalists and photographers—virtually anyone who could handle a camera—were sent to record the six-week-long Bond invasion. The torrent of coverage began at 5:00 P.M. on July 27, 1966, at the Hilton Hotel, where a hasty press conference was arranged to greet the exhausted Connery. Agent 007 appeared rumpled and bleary-eyed, minus his toupee, and dressed in baggy, knockabout trousers, shower sandals and a blue shirt open at the neck to reveal his hairy chest.

"Is this the way James Bond dresses?" asked one arrogant reporter who had waited in the hotel lobby for six hours. "I'm not James Bond," Connery replied politely. "I'm Sean Connery and I like to dress comfortably, except for formal occasions."

Sensing that an international incident was brewing unless he appeared more cordial, Connery summoned his patented Bond charm and even managed a few weak jokes about his fondness for Scotch cooking and whiskey. He let the

Crowds disrupted the filming of *You Only Live Twice* in Japan. Here photographers and onlookers are barely restrained as Sean Connery and Akiko Wakabayashi prepare for action on the Kobe docks. (Rex Features Ltd./RDR Productions)

reporters inspect the tatoos on his arms—one reading "Scotland Forever," and the other, "Mother and Father"—and offered some words of praise for Japanese cooking.

Connery particularly liked the O-Furo, the Japanese bath. "It's wonderful," he beamed, "all that splashing around after you've washed yourself clean, and then getting back into a deep tub of hot water. The soaking is marvelous."

After about 20 minutes of good-natured discussion, everyone was smiling, even publicity chief Tom Carlisle, who was nervous about the awesome crowd of camera-clicking reporters.

And then the bombshell was dropped.

A reporter asked, "What do you think of Japanese women?" Connery thought for a second, according to a reporter from *Asian Adventure* who attended the press conference, and then smiled, answering the question honestly, if not too diplomatically. "Japanese women are just not sexy," he said. "This is even more so when they hide their figures by wearing those roomy kimonos."

After Connery's comment, the reporter related, "There was a rather strained silence in the room. The Japanese often display something of

Sean Connery celebrates his 36th birthday on the set of *You Only Live Twice* on August 25, 1966. Director Lewis Gilbert has his plate ready. (Rex Features Ltd./RDR Productions)

an inferiority complex toward the West in many matters. But they generally consider their women beautiful and amply sexy. This time national pride was aroused.''

To avoid a confrontation, Carlisle stepped in quickly, asking the crowd's indulgence so that Connery could get some rest after the long jet flight from London. Connery offered to pose once more for the cameras, and retired to his room. The press conference was a bad omen, and it was only the beginning of a series of press assaults on *You Only Live Twice* that could rival the ''banzai'' charges of World War II.

During the six weeks of filming in Japan, reporters were everywhere—hiding behind fences, hanging from trees, lurking in rest rooms—all armed with cameras, ready to capture their own private scoop. Such coverage made the film front-page news for weeks, and at times put the Eon Productions crew under a microscope.

Every move was scanned by hundreds of reporters. When a stuntman mistimed his throw and catapulted a steel dart into the wall of historic Himeji Castle, it seemed that every paper in Japan had wind of it. Official protests were lodged, the Eon crew was banned from the castle grounds—where the Ninja training was being shot—and it was only after a judicious amount of apologizing and repeated offers to pay for any damages that the crew was once more permitted inside the grounds of the historic fortress.

Filming on the streets of Tokyo was at times impossible. No sooner would director Lewis Gilbert's hidden camera begin recording Connery's progress than the actor would be mobbed by his fans. After location filming was completed in Japan, Connery returned to London to finish the picture. However, the seeds of revolt were already sown. After 1967, producers Albert R. Broccoli and Harry Saltzman would be looking for a new actor to play Bond.

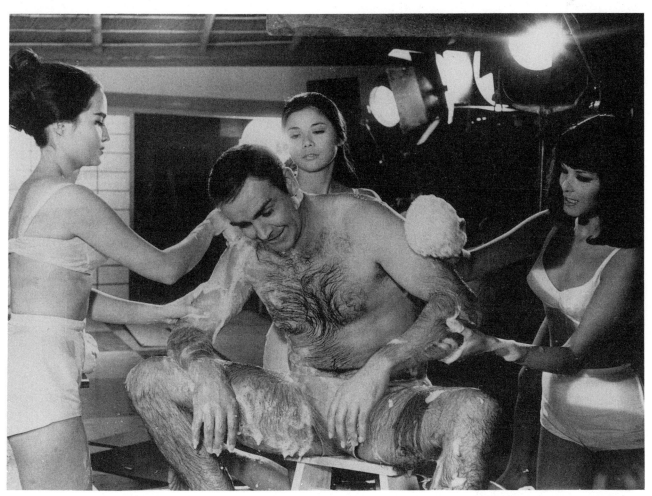

Sean Connery is in hot water again, during another grueling session before the cameras in *You Only Live Twice*. (Rex Features Ltd./RDR Productions)

CONTI, BILL (Providence, Rhode Island, April 13, 1942–   ) American composer, well known for his *Rocky* music, who contributed the sound-track score to *For Your Eyes Only* in 1981. Considering the ominous mood of the film, his music was at times too lighthearted, especially during the ski chase between Bond and Kriegler.

COOLIDGE, RITA (Nashville, Tennessee, May 1, 1944–   ) Soulful American pop singer with country music roots who sang "All Time High," the title tune in *Octopussy*. Before

Singer Rita Coolidge who sang "All Time High" in *Octopussy*. (A&M Records)

embarking on a solo career, Coolidge sang with Delaney and Bonnie and Friends, Joe Cocker, Leon Russell, and Kris Kristofferson. When it was released overseas in 1983, "All Time High" became a Top 10 hit in nine countries.

COOPER British agent, portrayed by Terence Cooper, who, thanks to Miss Moneypenny's daughter (BARBARA BOUCHET), becomes a

British Secret Service Anti-Female Spy Device (A.F.S.D.) in *Casino Royale*. A judo/karate expert, Cooper wins the assignment when he kisses Moneypenny with such vigor that she immediately summons him to her bedroom for additional testing. The A.F.S.D. is a ploy of Sir James Bond (DAVID NIVEN) to neutralize the effectiveness of enemy female agents employed by Dr. Noah (WOODY ALLEN). Cooper is also given the name James Bond—another trick to confuse the enemy.

COOPER, TERENCE (Cairmoney, County Antrim, Northern Ireland, July 5, 1933–   ) Rugged, handsome Irish actor who portrayed Cooper, the A.F.S.D. who became James Bond in *Casino Royale*. *See* A.F.S.D.; COOPER.

Rugged British actor Terence Cooper played Cooper, one of the many James Bonds in *Casino Royale*.

COPPOLA, FRANCIS FORD (Detroit, Michigan, April 7, 1939–   ) American film director who contributed script ideas to *Never Say Never Again*, a film produced by his brother-in-law, Jack Schwartzman. *See* SCHWARTZMAN, JACK.

CORBETT, RONNIE (Edinburgh, Scotland, 1930–   ) Diminutive British television comic who portrayed Polo, the spy school assistant with the faulty pacemaker in *Casino Royale*. *See* POLO.

CORFU Greek island in the Aegean Sea that is a principal location in *For Your Eyes Only*. Corfu's sandy beach proved to be difficult terrain for assassin Emile Locque's (MICHAEL

GOTHARD) dune buggies, which are supposed to run down and kill Bond (ROGER MOORE) and his lady friend, Lisl (CASSANDRA HARRIS). It was a particularly difficult location for fledgling director John Glen, who quickly fell three days behind schedule. Despite the delay, producer Cubby Broccoli stood by Glen, and somehow the crew managed to unstick themselves and finish the frenetic dune-buggy chase.

CORNEAL IMPLANT Surgical operation that gives *Never Say Never Again*'s Captain Jack Petachi (GAVAN O'HERLIHY) an exact duplicate of the cornea from the President of the United States' right eye. Petachi's "new" extremely blue eye allows him to breach a top-level security check and arm two U.S. Air Force cruise missiles with nuclear warheads.

CORNELL, PHYLLIS Actress Tania Mallet's stand-in during the Aston Martin car chase in *Goldfinger*. She worked in the Black Park area of rural England.

CORSICAN BRANDY Marc Ange Draco's (GABRIELE FERZETTI) usual drink in *On Her Majesty's Secret Service*. During his meeting with Bond (GEORGE LAZENBY) at his Draco Construction offices, he forgoes the brandy for a glass of Campari, an Italian aperitif.

CORTINA D'AMPEZZO Winter resort city in the Italian Alps that is a key location in *For Your Eyes Only*. Tipped off by the Italian Secret Service that Emile Locque (MICHAEL GOTHARD) is in Cortina, Bond (ROGER MOORE) goes there and meets Aris Kristatos (JULIAN GLOVER), who claims to be an ex–World War II resistance fighter and Anglophile. He's actually a Russian agent preparing to retrieve the A.T.A.C. device from the sunken hulk of the *St. Georges* surveillance ship.

Kristatos lies and tells Bond that Locque is working for Columbo (TOPOL), a man he also claims is involved in drug smuggling, white slavery, and contract murder. Bond also meets Kristatos's protege, ice skater Bibi Dahl (LYNN-HOLLY JOHNSON); her teacher, Jacoba Brink (JILL BENNETT); and another enemy agent, East German biathlon champion Eric Kriegler (JOHN WYMAN), who is working for Kristatos.

Bond's local Secret Service contact, Luigi Ferrara (JOHN MORENO), is later murdered by Locque, who leaves Columbo's symbol—the white dove—on the body. Bond, meanwhile, has been chased on skis by Kriegler, assaulted by ski-borne motorcycles, and, later, at a hockey rink, attacked by three hapless hockey players who end up sprawled in their own net.

COSSINS, JAMES (1932–   ) British character actor who portrayed Colthorpe, the Secret Service ballistics expert in *The Man with the Golden Gun*.

COURTLEIGH MANOR HOTEL The base of operations in Kingston, Jamaica, for the crew of *Dr. No* in January 1962.

COUSIN PAM How James Bond (TIMOTHY DALTON) introduces CIA agent Pam Bouvier (CAREY LOWELL) to Q (DESMOND LLEWELYN) in *Licence to Kill*. For purposes of security, Q is then referred to as "Uncle."

COVENTRY An English city whose name is painted on the side of the Auric Stud forklift that loads gold bars into the Lincoln Continental that will take Mr. Solo (MARTIN BENSON) to the airport in *Goldfinger*. Although this scene takes place in Kentucky, it was actually shot on the Pinewood Studios backlot in England. Purists will note that the Coventry sign on the forklift is a clue to the scene's true location.

COWARD, SIR NOEL (Teddington, England, December 16, 1899–March 26, 1973) British actor-writer-composer-director who was author Ian Fleming's first choice to play Dr. No. However, after receiving Fleming's cable, the actor replied, "Dear Ian, the answer to Dr. No is No! No! No! No!"

COWLES, DENIS British actor who portrayed Brunskill, Colonel Smithers's (RICHARD VERNON) servant at the Bank of England dinner in *Goldfinger*.

CP3-2008 Identification number on the S.P.E.C.T.R.E. fishing boat that helps hijack two U.S. Air Force cruise missiles in *Never Say Never Again*. On board the vessel is Dr. Kovacs (MILOW KIREK), a nuclear physicist in

S.P.E.C.T.R.E.'s employ, who helps jam and adjust the guidance system that controls the missiles' trajectories. With Kovacs in control, the cruise missiles are thrown off course and land gently in the Bahamas, where they're recovered by Largo (KLAUS MARIA BRANDAUER).

CPW 654W The license plate of James Bond's (ROGER MOORE) Lotus Esprit in *For Your Eyes Only*. When the henchmen of Cuban hit man Hector Gonzales (STEFAN KALIPHA) tamper with the car outside a villa in Madrid, it self-destructs, forcing Bond to escape in Melina Havelock's (CAROLE BOUQUET) clunky Deux Cheveux.

CPW 678W The license plate of James Bond's (ROGER MOORE) red turbo Lotus Esprit in *For Your Eyes Only*. It's assigned to him for use in Cortina D'Ampezzo, Italy.

CRAB KEY A fictional island off the coast of Jamaica that was turned into a fortress by S.P.E.C.T.R.E. operative Dr. No (JOSEPH WISEMAN). Disguised inside a bauxite mine, the operation centers on a nuclear-powered radio beam that is tampering with the guidance systems on U.S. rockets fired from nearby Cape Canaveral, Florida.

Protecting the operation are a diesel-powered amphibious flame-thrower vehicle disguised as a dragon in order to frighten off the locals, and Dr. No's private army, which is equipped with machine guns, guard dogs, and high-powered boats. The entire operation is obliterated by 007 (SEAN CONNERY) when he sabotages Dr. No's nuclear reactor, causing a meltdown.

CRAY CAY Island in the Bahamas where drug runner Franz Sanchez (ROBERT DAVI) lands his private plane in the *Licence to Kill* teaser. With two of his thugs—Dario (BENICIO DEL TORO) and Braun (GUY DE SAINT CYR)—in tow, Sanchez takes the chance of slipping back onto American soil to interrupt a tryst between his girlfriend, Lupe Lamora (TALISA SOTO), and local lothario Alvarez (GERARDO MORENO), whose own heart becomes Sanchez's "little valentine."

While Sanchez is engaging in this dastardly business, the Drug Enforcement Administration (DEA) tracks his private plane to the key. DEA agents attempt to catch the wanted drug lord, aided by James Bond (TIMOTHY DALTON) and Felix Leiter (DAVID HEDISON), both of whom are on their way to Felix's wedding. Sanchez escapes in his plane, but thanks to a Coast Guard jet helicopter, Bond is able to give chase and disables the aircraft by fastening a winch hook to its tail section.

CRETE Island in the Aegean Sea that was a World War II battleground for resistance fighters Milos Columbo (TOPOL) and Aris Kristatos (JULIAN GLOVER), as revealed in *For Your Eyes Only*. Columbo later tells James Bond (ROGER MOORE) that Kristatos became a traitor by working as a double agent for the Nazis.

CREWDSON, CAPTAIN JOHN Royal Air Force officer who flew the S.P.E.C.T.R.E. helicopter that chases Bond (SEAN CONNERY) across the foothills of Illyria in *From Russia with Love*. The sequence was actually filmed in Lochgilphead, Scotland. He also flew Draco's helicopter in *On Her Majesty's Secret Service*.

CRIBBINS, BERNARD (1928–) British comedy actor who portrayed Carlton Towers, the Foreign Service officer who masquerades as Mata Bond's (JOANNA PETTET) cab driver in *Casino Royale*. See TOWERS, CARLTON.

CRINAN A coastal town in Scotland that was the site of the motorboat chase finale in *From Russia with Love*. The scene was originally to be shot in Turkey's Bay of Pendik, but bad weather, malfunctioning motorboats, and inexperienced support crews shifted the location to Scotland.

CROCODILE FARM A principal location in *Live and Let Die*, where James Bond (ROGER MOORE) is left to die by Tee Hee (JULIUS

HARRIS). Captured in New Orleans, Bond is brought out to the farm, where he is stranded on an island in the middle of a small stream infested with hundreds of crocodiles and alligators. Convinced that his enemy is doomed, Tee Hee chuckles and returns to the drug lab where Kananga's (YAPHET KOTTO) heroin is being refined. As the crocodiles prepare for their human lunch, 007 sees his chance by jumping to safety over their aligned backs.

This sequence was shot at an actual Jamaican crocodile farm owned by part-Seminole Ross Kananga. To determine how Bond could escape from a stream full of crocs, screenwriter Tom Mankiewicz went to the real Kananga and asked him what he would do if he found himself in a similar predicament. Kananga told him that he would try to jump over their backs, a stunt that could be done only if the crocodiles were immobilized. Kananga succeeded in tying the feet of half a dozen reptiles to weights on the bottom of the pond so they couldn't move, while their jaws and tails remained free. When the crocodiles were finally tethered in place, creating a reptilian bridge of snapping teeth and swishing tails, Kananga prepared to jump their backs—a stunt he had never before attempted.

The entire pond was later cleared of excess crocodiles so that director Guy Hamilton could bring in his small team of filmmakers, including a contingent of London construction workers who fashioned the little retractable bridge that strands Bond on the island. For the stunt, Kananga had to wear a pair of pants and shoes resembling the outfit worn by Moore, who would be watching his own escape from a safe distance.

The first four times Kananga tried the stunt, he slipped and fell into the pond. On the third time, one of the crocs actually nipped at his foot. He soon discovered that the street shoes were preventing him from getting across the strange, slippery surfaces. Even with specially prepared soles, which were designed to give him traction, he continued to slip and land in the water. Each time, he had to return to the wardrobe shack, change into a fresh pair of dry trousers, and row out to the little concrete island.

Kananga also told Hamilton that each time he failed, it made the stunt more difficult, because the crocodiles knew he was coming the next time. The element of surprise was especially important with those huge jaws only inches away. On the fifth try, Kananga finally managed to keep his footing and raced to the shore across the crocs' backs.

CT5-828 License plate of Professor-Dr. Metz's (JOSEPH FURST) Ford Van in *Diamonds Are Forever*. When Tiffany Case (JILL ST. JOHN) distracts Metz at a Shell gas station in Las Vegas, Bond (SEAN CONNERY) climbs into the van and is transported to Willard Whyte's (JIMMY DEAN) Techtronics installation.

CUBA Goldfinger's (GERT FROBE) destination when he commandeers the special plane provided for James Bond's (SEAN CONNERY) trip to the White House. According to his flight plan, Cuba is two hours from Kentucky. Unfortunately, during the vicious fight with Bond, Goldfinger shatters a window with his golden gun and is sucked into the stratosphere when the cabin undergoes violent decompression.

CUBBY BROCCOLI'S DREAM The inspiration for the main plot of *Diamonds Are Forever*. Producer Albert "Cubby" Broccoli had always maintained a friendship with his first boss in the film business, billionaire industrialist Howard Hughes, whom he referred to as Sam. In the dream, he visited the aging Hughes at his luxurious suite in Las Vegas. It was midafternoon, and Broccoli found himself peeking through a window in Hughes's suite, where he saw a familiar figure sitting behind a huge oak desk. The man turned around, and Broccoli started. It wasn't Hughes at all, but an imposter.

Broccoli described the dream and its eerie details at his next script conference with writer Richard Maibaum. Said Broccoli on that day, "What would happen, Dick, if someone kidnapped Howard Hughes and substituted an imposter for him? Since no one has seen the real Howard Hughes for years, no one would even know that he was gone." "Sounds like just the right caper for Blofeld," agreed Maibaum, and *Diamonds Are Forever* was born.

Venerable Roland Culver brought dignity to *Thunderball* as the harried Home Secretary. (National Film Archive, London)

CULVER, ROLAND (London, England, August 31, 1900–February 29, 1984) British character actor who portrayed the stalwart home secretary in *Thunderball*.

CUMMINGS, BILL British character actor who portrayed Quist, one of Emilio Largo's (ADOLFO CELI) henchmen in *Thunderball*. *See* QUIST.

CUNEO, ERNEST (1906–1988) American friend of Ian Fleming and a partner in Ivar Bryce's Xanadu Productions, who contributed early story elements to the *Thunderball* project in 1959. A former legal adviser to Franklin D. Roosevelt, Cuneo wrote a memorandum to Bryce, dated May 28, 1959, that was, in effect, the film's first story outline.

In it, a Russian agent poses as a U.S. Army sergeant working on board a celebrity-filled USO airliner that is constantly flying to top secret U.S. bases. James Bond discovers that the Russians plan to detonate atomic bombs on these same bases.

When the sergeant transfers to the Caribbean USO, Bond follows, disguised as a British entertainer. In Nassau, he discovers that a mysterious power is commanding a fleet of Bahamian fishing boats, all of which are equipped with watertight underwater hatches just like those used by the Italian navy during World War II. Atomic bombs are to be delivered by Russian submarines to these fishing boats and hoisted through their watertight trapdoors by frogmen.

Cuneo finished the outline by detailing an underwater battle between the enemy frogmen and Bond's unit that takes place during an outdoor USO concert in Nassau. Cuneo had based his outline on the heavy use of both American and British celebrities, an idea given to him by Kevin McClory, who had used a number of names for cameo roles in casting *Around the World in 80 Days*. Cuneo also felt that the American government would be willing to cooperate by allowing a British camera crew to film at certain U.S. installations, perhaps even aboard their new aircraft carrier, the *Independence*.

Bryce showed Cuneo's outline to Fleming, who scribbled his own pointed comments. His two biggest criticisms concerned the lack of a Bond heroine and the use of the Russians as the principal villains. "It might be very unwise," wrote Fleming, "to point directly at Russia as the enemy. Since the film will take about two years to produce, and peace might conceivably break out in the meantime, this should be avoided."

Following Cuneo's initial story, Fleming created a film treatment in which the Russians are replaced by the Mafia in the A-bomb conspiracy. The latter are headed by a capo mafioso named Cuneo, whose principal lieutenant is a huge bear of a man named Largo. Largo would be played by American actor Burl Ives, who was already very interested in the project.

Largo and his handpicked team break into an American atomic base in Britain and steal an A-bomb. They transfer the bomb to a helicopter, which transports it to a tramp steamer anchored in the English Channel. The steamer passes the bomb on to a Sunderland flying boat, which then speeds across the Atlantic and deposits its cargo in the water near Largo's huge yacht, the *Virginia*, where a complement of divers transfer it through the yacht's watertight underwater hatch.

Much of the early action in Fleming's treatment takes place at a public house in the British countryside, where Bond tracks Largo and meets a British agent named Domino Smith, who has infiltrated the Mafia gang. Screenwriter Jack Whittingham would later alter many of these story elements, and the Mafia villains would be replaced by Fleming's own S.P.E.C.T.R.E. organization. *See* WHITTINGHAM, JACK.

CURLING A shuffleboard-like ice game played at Piz Gloria by the girls of *On Her Majesty's Secret Service*. Bond (GEORGE LAZENBY), posing as brainy and not brawny heraldry expert Sir Hilary Bray, tries his hand at the game and lands flat on his face.

CURLY Nickname of the Shell gasoline station attendant who attempts to help Tiffany Case (JILL ST. JOHN) in *Diamonds Are Forever*. Ordered by Bond (SEAN CONNERY) to block the exit of Dr. Metz's (JOSEPH FURST) van, Tiffany drives into the station and parks her car sideways. She then gets out and walks off, distracting everyone long enough for Bond to sneak into Metz's van. When Bond succeeds, the very cocky Tiffany walks back and says, "Sorry, Curly, you had your chance and you blew it." She then drives off.

CUSTOM .38 Rosie Carver's (GLORIA HENDRY) handgun in *Live and Let Die*. Bond (ROGER MOORE) notes that it's standard CIA issue—a Smith and Wesson, with a corrugated three-inch stock and no serial number. It identifies Carver as an ally, even though she's really an agent of Kananga (YAPHET KOTTO).

CYRUS, TONY Middle Eastern actor who portrayed the Chief of the Snow Leopard Brotherhood—the biggest opium dealer in the Golden Crescent in *The Living Daylights*. *See* CHIEF OF THE SNOW LEOPARD BROTHERHOOD.

D

D'ABO, MARYAM English actress of Dutch and Russian heritage who portrayed Kara Milovy, the Czechoslovakian cellist who falls in love with James Bond (TIMOTHY DALTON) in *The Living Daylights*. Playing opposite Dalton, who was making his auspicious debut as

Actress Maryam d'Abo who portrayed cellist Kara Milovy in *The Living Daylights*. (Georges Beaume/Jeremy Conway)

007, d'Abo was the perfect mate—an elegant, well-mannered, soulful woman dedicated to her musical craft and dreams of a solo career who is tossed headlong into the adventure of a lifetime.

Romance, a key element missing from many of the Roger Moore James Bond movies, is present in *The Living Daylights* in large doses as a definite on-screen chemistry develops between Bond and Milovy. It's helped, of course, by the fact that both characters spend a great deal of time together on-screen. Not since *Thunderball*, *On Her Majesty's Secret Service*, and *The Spy Who Loved Me* has Bond been given the special time

to develop a believable relationship with a woman. *See* MILOVY, KARA.

DACCA STREET New Orleans address of the Fillet of Soul nightclub, a front for Dr. Kananga's (YAPHET KOTTO) illegal drug-smuggling operation in *Live and Let Die*. It's along this street that the solemn funeral procession passes each time it kills an Allied agent.

DAHL, BIBI Randy Olympic ice-skating hopeful portrayed by blond Lynn-Holly Johnson in *For Your Eyes Only*. The teenage protege of sinister millionaire Aris Kristatos (JULIAN GLOVER), Bibi meets James Bond (ROGER MOORE) in Cortina D'Ampezzo, where she is training under the tutelage of Jacoba Brink (JILL BENNETT). 007 returns to his hotel at one point and finds Bibi waiting invitingly in his bed. Ever the wit, Bond offers her an ice-cream cone instead.

Bibi eventually discovers that her patron is a ruthless Soviet agent who virtually imprisons her in his fortress at St. Cyril's in Greece. When Kristatos is killed, Bibi discovers a new and more suitable patron, amiable Milos Columbo (TOPOL).

DAHL, ROALD (1916–1990) British short-story writer who was enlisted to write *You Only Live Twice* in 1966. Recalled Dahl, "I remember the phone ringing and this man saying his name was Broccoli. I thought he was joking. After all, a man with the last name of a vegetable? It was funny. I really hadn't heard of him.

"He told me about the Bond films and about *You Only Live Twice*, the latest in the series. And then he asked me if I would like to write a script. Now that was an exciting proposition because I had admired the films. I had seen one or two and I had known Ian Fleming well. My wife (actress Patricia Neal) and I had often stayed at his home in Oracabessa.

"So I went up to London right away, to Audley Square, where I met Cubby and Harry Saltzman. And they asked me right off whether I could deliver a first draft in eight weeks, a second in four more, and a complete script in 20 weeks. I said I could, and that was that.

"*You Only Live Twice* was the only Fleming book that had virtually no semblance of a plot

You Only Live Twice screenwriter Roald Dahl. (Mark Gerson)

that could be made into a movie. The concept of Blofeld patrolling his garden of poisonous plants in a medieval suit of armor and lopping off the heads of half-blinded Japanese was ridiculous.

"When I began the script, I could retain only four or five of the original novel's story ideas. Obviously, the movie had to take place in Japan. We kept Blofeld and Tiger Tanaka and Bond's pearl-diving girlfriend, Kissy Suzuki. And we retained the Ninjas—those masters of oriental martial arts who use their talents to raid Blofeld's hideout. But aside from those bits, I had nothing except a wonderful Ian Fleming title."

DAILY GLEANER A newspaper in Kingston, Jamaica, that is the supposed employer of Little Miss Freelance, the photographer (MARGARET LeWARS) in *Dr. No.*

DALTON, TIMOTHY (Colwyn Bay, North Wales, England, March 21, 1946–) Classically trained British actor, known for his costume films and stage work, who became the fourth actor to portray James Bond in the United Artists 007 series. Having replaced Roger Moore, Dalton's appearance on the scene, starting with *The Living Daylights* in 1987, prompted a major about-face in the approach to the films. Moore's comfort with witty lines, light comedic situations, and fantasy plots was replaced by a hard-edged reality and some unflinching violent episodes that were better suited to Dalton's more realistic approach to the character of 007.

Dalton told film journalist Craig Modderno in 1989: "I think Roger was fine as Bond, but the movies had become too much techno-pop and had lost track of their sense of story. I mean, every movie seemed to have a villain who had to rule or destroy the world. If you want to believe in the fantasy on screen, then you have to believe in the characters and use them as a stepping stone to lead you into this fantasy world. That's a demand I made, and Albert Broccoli agreed with me."

Although humor hasn't completely disappeared from the stories, it has taken a backseat. Whether it comes back will depend on how closely Eon Productions listens to fans' reactions to the recent Bond films.

One thing is certain, and it's based on more than a decade of Roger Moore Bond films: people like to laugh in a James Bond movie. It's not that they're looking for comedy but instead it is a defensive reaction to how Bond survives the most deadly encounters. In the Connery Bonds, such comedic moments were called throwaway humor. Connery played the character seriously, and he took the audience on a roller coaster ride during the action sequences, but he also had the uncanny ability to let them off the hook at the end—giving the audience time to catch its breath, feel the seat cushions, and wait for the next bit of nonsense to begin. Humor helped the pacing of the film, just as it does in any tense dramatic situation.

In the Moore films, the writers played to Moore's comfort with light comedic situations. It wasn't so much that Bond was funny, but the people who surrounded him took on a fantastic, larger-than-life quality. Action sequences lost their deadly flavor and took on a madcap flavor. In battles with characters such as J. W. Pepper, Nick Nack, Jaws, and May Day, it was hard to keep too straight a face—and Bond didn't.

There were exceptions with the Moore

Actor Timothy Dalton brought a serious side to James Bond that had been missing during the Roger Moore years. (Erik Hollander)

films, especially in *For Your Eyes Only* and *Octopussy*. But the sense of humor was always there, tied to an incredible plot played out against a spectacular globe-trotting canvas—an unbeatable combination for worldwide audiences.

Timothy Dalton has the perfect Bond qualities. He's handsome, athletic, commanding. He's believable as a British secret agent with a license to kill, who can bed any lady he wants. His fisticuffs appear genuine—Roger had a tendency to use too much kick-boxing—and he can underplay situations. Most of all, he's an excellent actor who brings a wealth of experience to the set.

Dalton's debut in *The Living Daylights* is extraordinary. His first close-up on the Rock of Gibraltar is riveting as he spies the death of a fellow agent. His arrival via parachute onto the yacht of a playgirl is equally perfect. There is no hesitation in his performance.

He doesn't play humor well, but the humor was not written well—especially in the virtually humorless *Licence to Kill*. In *The Living Day-*

lights, Dalton can be forgiven his punning remarks because they were probably written for Pierce Brosnan to deliver instead. In *Licence to Kill*, he was saddled with a dead-serious story with very little room for humor. It was a James Bond circus without the clowns. Everyone was much too serious, especially the villains. Dalton did the best he could, but the film's problem was its approach. That will change.

Interestingly, the producers' interest in Timothy Dalton as a potential Bond dates back to 1971, following the release of *Diamonds Are Forever*, Sean Connery's final film for Cubby Broccoli. But Dalton was too young then—only 25—and he wasn't interested in sidetracking his emerging career.

For *The Living Daylights*, he was the second choice. Pierce Brosnan had already been signed, sealed, and delivered, when NBC stormed into the picture and demanded he fulfull his "Remington Steele" contract and remain in that role. Dalton won the role by default, but the Bond producers won a major victory.

In interview after interview, the new Bond

told reporters that he was rereading the Fleming novels, especially his favorite, *Casino Royale*, in order to research his new role. This James Bond was not going to play second fiddle to gadgets and breathless females.

Unlike Moore, who always seems to be in command, Dalton's Bond sometimes looks like a candidate for the psychiatrist's couch—a burned-out killer who may have just enough energy left for one final mission. That was Fleming's Bond—a man who drank to diminish the poison in his system, the poison of a violent world with impossible demands. In fact, Timothy Dalton's 007 may be responsible for eventually resurrecting Fleming's Secret Service psychiatrist, Dr. James Maloney. His is the suffering Bond.

A youthful Timothy Dalton escorts actress Imogen Haddell to a London premiere. (Express Newspapers, London)

A jubilant Timothy Dalton celebrates his new role in *The Living Daylights* with costars Maryam D'Abo, *left*, and Caroline Bliss, *right*. (Express Newspapers, London)

Top character actor Charles Dance appeared briefly as one of Kristatos's henchmen in *For Your Eyes Only*. (Caroline Dawson)

DANCE, CHARLES (Plymouth, England, 1946–) Top British actor who had a bit part in *For Your Eyes Only* as Claus, one of Kristatos's (JULIAN GLOVER) henchmen, who is killed on the beach in Corfu by Columbo's (TOPOL) men. *Note:* Dance recently played 007 author Ian Fleming in a British telefilm based on John Pearson's biography.

DANIELI Dr. Holly Goodhead's (LOIS CHILES) Venice hotel in *Moonraker*. It's where she introduces herself to Bond (ROGER MOORE) as an undercover CIA agent who is following Hugo Drax (MICHEL LONSDALE).

DARIO Cold-blooded killer and ex-Contra rebel, portrayed by Benicio del Toro, employed by drug lord Franz Sanchez (ROBERT DAVI) in *Licence to Kill*. Knife-carrying Dario is introduced almost immediately as the man who cuts out the heart of Alvarez (GERARDO MORENO), Lupe's unfortunate lover. He later confronts Bond (TIMOTHY DALTON) and Pam Bouvier (CAREY LOWELL) in the Barrelhead Bar and takes a major punch from 007.

As Pam escapes to 007's waiting motor boat, Dario shoots her in the back. She survives, thanks to her body armor. During a laboratory demonstration at the Olimpatec Meditation Institute, Dario recognizes Bond, who, up until this point, has been trusted in Sanchez's company. 007 is quickly disarmed and nearly thrown into a cocaine-bundle shredder, when Pam arrives to save him. As the laboratory explodes in flames, Bond and Dario engage in a desperate fight above the shredder, which 007 eventually wins. Dario, the cowardly killer, is given his just desserts in the shredder.

DART-FIRING WRISTWATCH A weapon supplied to James Bond (ROGER MOORE) by Q (DESMOND LLEWELYN) in *Moonraker*. The watch is equipped with ten darts. Five are blue-tipped and have armor-piercing heads. Five are red-tipped and coated with cyanide, which causes death in 30 seconds. Later trapped in the out-of-control centrifuge trainer, Bond uses one of the armor-piercing darts to disable the machine.

DAUNTLESS Name of a U.S. Coast Guard vessel docked near the DEA interrogation block where captured drug lord Franz Sanchez (ROBERT DAVI) is being held in *Licence to Kill*. This sequence was filmed on the Coast Guard Pier in Key West.

DAVI, ROBERT (Astoria, New York, 1951–) Charismatic leading man who portrayed ruthless South American drug lord Franz Sanchez in *Licence to Kill*. Davi was a breath of fresh air after the comic-book Bond villains of the Roger Moore films and the buffoons in *The Living Daylights*. In effect, he's the best Bond villain since Gert Frobe's Goldfinger.

Like Dalton's portrait of Bond, Davi's Sanchez is a darker, more realistic character who is totally immersed in his corrupt world. Such a portrait of Sanchez was necessary in order to give Bond's revenge mission credibility. The relationship between Bond and the villains in the James Bond series was established in Ian Fleming's first novel, *Casino Royale*.

Said Davi, "There's a chapter in that book on the nature of good and evil, where Fleming talks about how Bond and the villain at a certain

Actor Robert Davi, *right*, drops his sinister side as Franz Sanchez to pose with Erik Hollander during shooting in Key West on *Licence to Kill*. (Erik Hollander)

point become mirror images of each other. I like that. I saw both of these characters as existential nihilists, improvisers of a moral code. Bond is much more on the right side of the truth. What we discussed during filming with John Glen was to capture this crossover and to bring in underlying subtleties." *See* SANCHEZ, FRANZ.

DA VINHO ESTATE The actual location in Zambuljal, Portugal, of Marc Ange Draco's (GABRIELE FERZETTI) home in *On Her Majesty's Secret Service*. Used for Draco's birthday celebration in the film, the estate sported a private bullring and sumptuous gardens. Said screenwriter Richard Maibaum, who departed somewhat from Fleming's description of the head of the Union Corse crime syndicate, "What I thought we should do to Draco, our sympathetic mafioso, was to give him some in-

terest in livestock. In this case, we made him a cattleman, someone who raised bulls as a pastime. Such a background gave some weight to Draco's decision at the end of the film to support Bond's (GEORGE LAZENBY) attack on Blofeld. The birthday sequence was also helped when we discovered the Da Vinho estate in Portugal, which I thought was absolutely right for this man's background."

DAWES The British agent who is assassinated at the United Nations in *Live and Let Die*. He receives a lethal dose of sound through his translation earphones.

DAWSON Royal Air Force officer who informs Sir John (EDWARD UNDERDOWN), the air vice-marshal, about the missing NATO bomber in *Thunderball*.

Before he joined the *Dr. No* cast, actor Anthony Dawson (with map) appeared in *They Were Not Divided*, the first of many films he's done for director Terence Young. (National Film Archive, London)

DAWSON, ANTHONY (1916–   )
Lean-faced Scottish character actor who portrayed Professor R. J. Dent in *Dr. No*. He also portrayed Ernst Stavro Blofeld (back to camera) in *From Russia with Love* (his voice was dubbed by Eric Pohlmann). Prior to his Bond experience, Dawson had the memorable role of Grace Kelly's attempted murderer in Hitchcock's 1954 thriller *Dial M for Murder*.

DEA Acronym for the U.S. Drug Enforcement Administration, which attempts to nab South American drug lord Franz Sanchez (ROBERT DAVI) in the *Licence to Kill* teaser. After James Bond (TIMOTHY DALTON) helps disable his private plane, Sanchez is put into protective custody, only to be freed by Killifer (EVERETT MCGILL), a DEA agent who succumbs to a $2 million bribe.

DEAN, JIMMY American actor who portrayed kidnapped billionaire Willard Whyte in *Diamonds Are Forever*.

DEATH, HIGH PRIESTESS, MOON The three tarot-card clues that Solitaire (JANE SEYMOUR) leaves for Bond (ROGER MOORE) when Felix Leiter's (DAVID HEDISON) CIA agents raid Kananga's (YAPHET KOTTO) Fillet of Soul nightclub in New Orleans in *Live and Let Die*. The cards lead 007 on a dangerous night mission to rescue Solitaire and to blow up Kananga's San Monique poppy fields.

DEAUVILLE CASINO Where Clarence Leiter (MICHAEL PATE) claims he first saw the card-playing skills of James Bond (BARRY NELSON), in the TV film "Casino Royale." Reminiscing at the baccarat table in Monte

Carlo, Leiter mentions the card-playing skills Bond had used against a maharaja of India and that earned 007 the sobriquet Card Sense Jimmy Bond.

DEBEERS Famous European diamond broker that, should it become necessary, will supply NATO with the $280 million ransom in *Thunderball*.

DE BLEUCHAMP, COUNT BALTHAZAR Title to which Ernst Stavro Blofeld (TELLY SAVALAS) aspires in *On Her Majesty's Secret Service*. Masquerading as a world-famous allergist who runs an exclusive clinic high in the Swiss Alps, Blofeld has also been tracing his ancestral line and now wishes to claim the de Bleauchamp title. He hopes that the London College of Arms will validate such a claim—dealings that lead James Bond (GEORGE LAZENBY) to impersonate Sir Hilary Bray (GEORGE BAKER) of the College of Arms.

It is 007's hope that he can lure Blofeld to Augsburg, the ancestral home of the de Bleuchamp, where he can be arrested by the British Secret Service. Unfortunately, Blofeld is too busy to travel—he's about to unleash a deadly

Actor Jimmy Dean portrayed kidnapped billionaire Willard Whyte in *Diamonds Are Forever*. (National Film Archive, London)

germ strain onto the world's livestock and agricultural industries—and Bond/Sir Hilary is ordered by Blofeld to finish his research within the walls of Piz Gloria.

DEBUSSY French composer whose work is a favorite of Sir James Bond (DAVID NIVEN) in *Casino Royale*. Retired and living in rural England, Bond spends each afternoon at his own piano playing his favorite Debussy selections.

DECOMPRESSION CHAMBER The final resting place of boozy drug runner Milton Krest (ANTHONY ZERBE) in *Licence to Kill*. Located aboard his marine research vessel, the *Wavekrest*, the chamber becomes the repository of $4.9 million in drug loot that is stolen by James Bond (TIMOTHY DALTON).

As part of his plan to infiltrate Franz Sanchez's (ROBERT DAVI) cocaine empire and destroy the drug runner's relationship with his key associates, 007 plants the money in the chamber as the *Wavekrest* is entering the port of Isthmus City. Tipped off by 007 that Krest may be a traitor, Sanchez searches the vessel and—to Krest's astonishment—finds the money. Krest is then tossed into the decompression chamber, where he super-inflates and explodes. When asked what they should do with the bloody loot, Sanchez deadpans, "Launder it."

DEHN, PAUL (Manchester, Lancashire, England, November 5, 1912-1976) Academy Award–winning British screenwriter and lyricist who received cowriting credit with Richard Maibaum on *Goldfinger*. When the script won an Edgar Award from the Mystery Writers of America in 1964, the witty Dehn sent a telegram to Rex Stout, president of the Mystery Writers, expressing his thanks, but claiming that his contribution was only .007 percent of the finished script. Dehn went on to write four sequels for the *Planet of the Apes* series.

DEIGHTON, LEN British mystery writer who, according to director Terence Young, wrote the first draft of *From Russia with Love* in 1962 and accompanied Young on the first location trip to Istanbul. Richard Maibaum wrote the final script on the picture and receives sole screenplay credit. Deighton also collaborated with Sean Connery and Kevin McClory on an early draft of *James Bond of the Secret Service* (aka *Warhead*), the proposed remake of *Thunderball* that was never to be shot (*See JAMES BOND OF THE SECRET SERVICE*). Deighton is also the author of the popular Harry Palmer series of spy novels, three of which were made into films by producer Harry Saltzman: *The Ipcress File*, *Funeral in Berlin*, and *Billion Dollar Brain*.

DE KEYSER, DAVID Actor who portrayed Dr. Tynan, the plastic surgeon who was in charge of creating Blofeld clones in *Diamonds Are Forever*. De Keyser also dubbed the voice of Auric Goldfinger (GERT FROBE) in *Goldfinger*. And in 1969, he dubbed the voice of Marc Ange Draco (GABRIELE FERZETTI) in *On Her Majesty's Secret Service*.

"DELICATESSEN IN STAINLESS STEEL, A" Wheelchair-bound Ernst Stavro Blofeld's desperate and basically ludicrous bribe to prevent Bond (ROGER MOORE) from dumping him into the industrial chimney in the *For Your Eyes Only* teaser. It is certainly one of the most ridiculous lines of dialogue ever uttered by a Bond villain. Interestingly, it is a line that screenwriter Richard Maibaum denies ever writing. Whoever was responsible for it deserves a good thrashing, because it put a rude cap on what was, at best, a mediocre teaser sequence. *Note:* Although he was dressed like Blofeld, the wheelchair-bound villain was uncredited in the film.

DEL MATEO, SIGNORINA One of Drax's (MICHEL LONSDALE) ladies of the hunt in *Moonraker*, portrayed by actress Chichinou Kaeppler. Introduced, along with Mademoiselle Deradier, during a pheasant shoot on the grounds of Drax's estate in California, del Mateo and her friend are later revealed to be two of Drax's master-race astronauts.

DELTA NINE A nerve gas that Goldfinger (GERT FROBE) intends to spray into the atmosphere above Fort Knox, Kentucky, in order to immobilize the garrison of 41,000 U.S. soldiers. Although he informs Pussy Galore (HONOR BLACKMAN), as well as his gangster associates, that the gas is a mere sleep-inducer, in actuality it is a deadly poison gas that is effectively tested on the "hoods convention." Fortunately, thanks to her interest in James Bond (SEAN CONNERY), Pussy switches the canisters at the last minute.

DEL TORO, BENICIO (Puerto Rico, February 19, 1967–   ) Puerto Rican/American actor who portrayed Dario, one of Franz Sanchez's (ROBERT DAVI) killers in *Licence to Kill*. Prior to the Bond movie, del Toro played a character in *Big Top Pee-wee* (1988). *See* DARIO.

Actor Benicio del Toro portrayed Dario, a cool assassin who's shredded in *Licence to Kill*. (Benicio del Toro)

"DEMOLITION DEAL" James Bond's (GEORGE LAZENBY) code phrase for the early-morning helicopter assault on Piz Gloria and Ernst Stavro Blofeld (TELLY SAVALAS) in *On Her Majesty's Secret Service*. The phrase is spoken to his future father-in-law, Marc Ange Draco (GABRIELE FERZETTI).

DENEUVE, CATHERINE (Paris, October 22, 1943–   ) French actress who was director Peter Hunt's second choice for the part of Tracy Vicenzo in *On Her Majesty's Secret Service*. After Brigitte Bardot turned down the role in favor of a part with Sean Connery in *Shalako*, the director offered it to Deneuve, who unfortunately didn't see herself as a Bond girl. Sexy Diana Rigg, star of TV's "The Avengers," later won the role.

DENT, PROFESSOR R. J. Dr. No's (JOSEPH WISEMAN) spymaster, portrayed by Anthony Dawson, in Kingston, Jamaica. An oily-haired, suspicious-looking local geologist who runs Dent Laboratories in Kingston, Dent leads a team of assassins that kills John Strangways (TIM MOXON) and his secretary, but bungles all attempts on 007's (SEAN CONNERY) life.

After Bond disposes of the famous tarantula in the bed, Dent tries again to kill Bond at Miss Taro's cottage in the Blue Mountains. But 007 is sitting behind Dent in the darkened bedroom when Dent pumps six shots from his Smith and Wesson automatic into a bundle of sheets and pillows designed to look like Bond and Taro. Ordered to drop his gun, Dent confesses that Strangways was killed, and starts to explain other details in the hopes of distracting Bond long enough so that he can retrieve his pistol.

Finally diving for the gun, Dent comes up empty, prompting 007's classic remark, "That's a Smith and Wesson, and you've had your six!" Dent is then promptly blown away by Bond in a manner that pretty much defines his 00 prefix—licensed to kill—although it would be the last time that 007 would shoot down an unarmed assailant. Regarding such confrontations, the series was headed in a much lighter direction. See DAWSON, ANTHONY.

DENTONITE TOOTHPASTE Plastic explosive disguised in a toothpaste tube—another one of the useful little gadgets that Q (DESMOND LLEWELYN) brings to Isthmus City in *Licence to Kill*. Bond (TIMOTHY DALTON) uses it to blow out the windows in Sanchez's (ROBERT DAVI) office so that he can shoot the drug lord with his signature gun.

DERADIER, MADEMOISELLE One of Drax's (MICHEL LONSDALE) ladies of the hunt in *Moonraker*, portrayed by actress Beatrice Libert. Together with Signorina del Mateo, they observe the industrialist's pheasant-shooting on the sumptuous grounds of his California estate. Later in the story, Deradier and del Mateo are revealed as two of the master-race astronauts headed for Drax's radar-proof space station.

DERMATONE A plastic surgeon's tool that Helga Brandt (KARIN DOR) wields as a torture device in *You Only Live Twice*. However, thanks to 007's (SEAN CONNERY) significant charm and sex appeal, she puts the tool aside and kisses him instead. If only all torture scenes could be handled in such a manner!

DERVAL, DOMINIQUE Largo's (ADOLFO CELI) French mistress in *Thunderball* and the sister of murdered NATO aerial observer François Derval (PAUL STASSINO). Portrayed by actress and former Miss France Claudine Auger, her nickname is Domino, which appears on her ankle bracelet.

Bond (SEAN CONNERY) first sees Dominique's photograph in his official dossier. Their first meeting is a very romantic one, occurring underwater, in the Caribbean when Bond gallantly removes her trapped foot from the coral. He gradually learns that she's Largo's unhappy mistress and that she has no idea that he's S.P.E.C.T.R.E.'s No. 2.

Later, when Bond tells Domino that Largo had her brother murdered, she becomes revengeful. In the film's dramatic conclusion, she kills Largo with a spear gun.

Domino is my favorite Bond girl and probably the most beautiful woman in the series (in my opinion, of course). She also appears in one of the most romantic films in the series. Her encounters with Bond on Love Beach, in the casino, underwater, and at the Palmyra pool are all wonderfully romantic sequences that work particularly well with John Barry's intimate musical score.

Helping her along are a series of breathtaking bikinis and bathing suits. It's no wonder that Broccoli and Saltzman turned down consummate English actress Julie Christie as their choice for Domino. Claudine Auger definitely filled the requirements for the part.

DERVAL, FRANCOIS A NATO aerial observer, portrayed by actor Paul Stassino, who is murdered by S.P.E.C.T.R.E. in *Thunderball*. Assigned to a nuclear bomber squadron based in rural England, Derval is seduced by S.P.E.C.T.R.E. assassin Fiona Volpe (LUCIANA PALUZZI) and murdered by Angelo Palazzi (also STASSINO), a mercenary who, thanks to plastic surgery, is now an exact duplicate of Derval.

James Bond (SEAN CONNERY) discovers Derval's body at the Shrublands health clinic. This clue leads him to Nassau and to Derval's sister Domino (CLAUDINE AUGER), who happens to be the mistress of the mysterious Emilio Largo (ADOLFO CELI), a Nassau multimillionaire and S.P.E.C.T.R.E. spymaster.

Swimming to a downed NATO bomber that had been hijacked to the Bahamas by Palazzi, Bond finds the former's body in the plane's cockpit, where he drowned when Largo cut his air hose. Among his effects, Bond finds Derval's identification disk and watch—clues that finally convince Domino that Largo is her enemy. See PALAZZI, ANGELO.

DE SAINT CYR, GUY Cuban-born actor who portrayed Braun, one of South American drug runner Franz Sanchez's (ROBERT DAVI) henchmen in *Licence to Kill*. See BRAUN.

DESK CLERK She works in the Istanbul hotel that is under S.P.E.C.T.R.E.'s control in *From Russia with Love*. If you listen carefully, you'll notice that her voice is exactly the same as Honey's voice in *Dr. No*. In actuality, the actress who dubbed the desk clerk's voice is the same one who dubbed Ursula Andress's voice in the latter film.

DE SOUZA, EDWARD (1933–) British actor who portrayed Sheik Hosein, a Secret

Actor Edward de Souza was suave Sheik Hosein in *The Spy Who Loved Me*. (ICM)

Service agent masquerading as a desert chieftain in *The Spy Who Loved Me*. See HOSEIN, SHEIK.

DEVON, LADY VICTORIA One of Hugo Drax's (MICHEL LONSDALE) drawing room ladies in *Moonraker*, portrayed by actress Francoise Gayat. Together with Countess Labinsky, they're the women who are listening to piano music when Bond (ROGER MOORE) arrives from London. Later in the story, we discover that Devon and Labinsky are two of Drax's master-race astronauts.

DE WOLFF, FRANCIS (South Minister, England, January 7, 1913–) British character actor who portrayed Vavra, the fiery Gypsy leader in *From Russia with Love*. See VAVRA.

DIALOGUE, FIRST The first-ever line of dialogue in a James Bond movie was heard on the night of October 21, 1954, when "Casino Royale" made its debut as a one-hour, live drama on CBS Television's Climax Mystery Theater. Following host William Lundigan's introduction (See LUNDIGAN, WILLIAM), James Bond (BARRY NELSON) appears onscreen, walking into the casino in Monte Carlo. Bullets are fired, missing Bond and prompting the doorman to rush to 007's side. "Are you hurt?" he asks. "No," Bond replies. "Still in one piece, but I wouldn't know how."

DIAMONDS ARE FOREVER (United Artists, 1971) ★ ★ ★ The seventh James Bond film produced by Albert R. Broccoli and Harry Saltzman. U.S. release date: December 17, 1971. U.S. film rentals: $19.7 million. Running time: 119 minutes.

Having lost their box-office momentum with *On Her Majesty's Secret Service*, producers Broccoli and Saltzman offered Sean Connery a sizable incentive to return to his 007 role. Connery returned in another epic Bond film that was a huge success at the box office.

After the relative box-office failure of *On*

Sean Connery takes a break during location shooting in Las Vegas on *Diamonds Are Forever*. (Stephen Allen, Las Vegas News Bureau)

Her Majesty's Secret Service ($25 million gross was considered a major disappointment), the producers knew that a return to the seriousness of *From Russia with Love* was not a wise move. They were more intent on taking the *Goldfinger* approach to Bond filmmaking, which meant an outrageous caper, plenty of gorgeous women to dally with Bond, and action sequences that bordered on the unbelievable.

Diamonds Are Forever has these elements in good quantity. Blofeld returns in a plot to place a laser-equipped satellite—a laser powered by a refracting solar shield made entirely of diamonds—into outer space. Much of the story takes place in the perfect 007 playground—Las Vegas, Nevada.

Bond has liaisons with Tiffany Case and Plenty O'Toole, and battles bodyguards Bambi and Thumper. He performs unbelievable stunts with a stolen moon buggy and a swift Mustang fastback. And he faces some of his most unusual enemies, including the gay assassins, Mr. Wint and Mr. Kidd; the burly diamond smuggler, Peter Franks; and, of all things, a foppish Blofeld, played in ham fashion by Charles Gray, who was deadpan in *You Only Live Twice*. This *Goldfinger* approach to Bond would continue uninterrupted for a decade until the tenor changed in *For Your Eyes Only*.

DIAMONDS ARE FOREVER CAST

James Bond	Sean Connery
Tiffany Case	Jill St. John
Ernst Stavro Blofeld	Charles Gray
Plenty O'Toole	Lana Wood
Willard Whyte	Jimmy Dean
Burt Saxby	Bruce Cabot
Mr. Wint	Bruce Glover
Mr. Kidd	Putter Smith
Felix Leiter	Norman Burton
Professor-Dr. Metz	Joseph Furst
M	Bernard Lee
Q	Desmond Llewelyn
Sir Donald Munger	Laurence Naismith
Maxwell	Burt Metcalf
Slumber	David Bauer
Shady Tree	Leonard Barr
Mrs. Whistler	Margaret Lacey
Miss Moneypenny	Lois Maxwell
Peter Franks	Joe Robinson
Bambi	Donna Garratt
Thumper	Trina Parks
Klaus Hergersheimer	Edward Bishop
Barker	Larry Blake
Dentist	Henry Rowland
Dr. Tynan	David de Keyser
Doorman (Tropicana)	Nicky Blair
Aide to Professor-Dr. Metz	Constantin de Goguel
Aide to Professor-Dr. Metz	Janos Kurucz
Tom	Shane Rimmer
Immigration Officer	Clifford Earl
Agent	Karl Held
Airline Representative	John Abineri
Blofeld's Double	Max Latimer
Controller (Moon Crater)	Bill Hutchinson
Guard (Moon Crater)	Frank Mann
Sir Donald's Male Secretary	Mark Elwes
Man in Fez	Frank Olegario
Marie	Denise Perrier
Vandenburg Launch Director	David Healy
Vandenburg Aide	Gordon Ruttan
Houseboy	Brinsley Forde
Gangster #1	Marc Lawrence
Gangster #2	Sid Haig
Gangster #3	Michael Valente
Maxie	Ed Call
Helicopter Pilot	Raymond Baker
Boy	Gary Dubin
Welfare Worker	Catherine Deeney

DIAMONDS ARE FOREVER CREW

Producers	Harry Saltzman and Albert R. Broccoli
Director	Guy Hamilton
Screenplay by	Richard Maibaum, Tom Mankiewicz
Associate Producer	Stanley Sopel
Music Composed by	John Barry
Title Song Sung by	Shirley Bassey
Lyrics by	Don Black
Director of Photography	Ted Moore, B.S.C.
Production Designer	Ken Adam
Editors	Bert Bates, John W. Holmes
Production Managers	Claude Hudson, Milton Feldman
Main Titles Designed by	Maurice Binder
Wardrobe Supervisors	Elsa Fennell, Ted Tetrick
Sound Recordists	John Mitchell, Al Overton
Dubbing Editors	Teddy Mason, Jimmy Shields, Gordon McCallum
Location Managers	Bernard Hanson, Eddie Saeta
Second Unit Cameraman	Harold Wellman
Miss St. John's Costumes	Donfeld
Special Effects	Leslie Hillman, Whitney McMahon
Visual Effects	Albert Whitlock, Wally Veevers
Stunt Arrangers	Bob Simmons, Paul Baxley
Set Decorators	Peter Lamont, John Austin
Art Decorators	Jack Maxsted, Bill Kenney

Camera Operators . . . . . .Bob Kindred, Bill Johnson
Continuity . . . . .Elaine Schreyeck, Del Ross
Assistant Directors . . . . .Derek Cracknell,
Jerome M. Siegel
Production Company . . . . .Eon Productions
Distribution Company . . . . .United Artists

DIAMONDS ARE FOREVER COMPETITION

Competitive films in release when *Diamonds Are Forever* opened in Los Angeles on December 17, 1971:

Sometimes a Great Notion

The Boy Friend

Straw Dogs

Play Misty for Me

Bedknobs and Broomsticks

Fiddler on the Roof

Made for Each Other

The Last Picture Show

A Clockwork Orange

The French Connection

The Hospital

Lady and the Tramp (reissue)

Chandler

DINK Blond masseuse, portrayed by Margaret Nolan, seen briefly in *Goldfinger* administering to Bond (SEAN CONNERY) at the Fontainebleau Hotel pool in Miami.

DI PORTANOVA, SANDRA AND RICKY American owners of the fabulous Acapulco house that became Franz Sanchez's (ROBERT DAVI) Isthmus City home in *Licence to Kill*. With its Moorish arcades, wide decks, and terraces, the house became the perfect Bond location.

"DISCIPLINE, 007, DISCIPLINE" What Bond (SEAN CONNERY) whispers to himself on a Swiss mountain highway in *Goldfinger* after he realizes that chasing a beautiful brunette (TANIA MALLET) in a Mustang convertible is not his proper mission.

DISCLAIMER Legal phrasing featured at the beginning of *A View to a Kill*. It read: "Neither the name Zorin nor any other name or character in this film is meant to portray a real company or actual person." The phrase was employed because of possible legal complications with a real company called Zoran Ladicorbic Ltd.—a fashion design company. Although Max Zorin's microchip entity was conceptually a million miles away from such a company, the legal departments at Eon Productions and United Artists asked for and received permission to feature the unusual disclaimer that appears before the teaser. Another disclaimer concerning the use of the Red Cross insignia was featured at the beginning of *The Living Daylights*.

DISCO VOLANTE Italian name for Emilio Largo's (ADOLFO CELI) fabulous yacht in *Thunderball*. In English, the name means "flying saucer." Equipped with a false bottom through which S.P.E.C.T.R.E. frogmen can deposit the hijacked A-bombs, the yacht's normal speed is 20 knots. However, at the drop of a switch, the *Volante* can jettison its rear superstructure—the cocoon—and become a swift hydrofoil craft. To fight a delaying action, the cocoon is equipped with machine guns and an artillery piece.

In *Thunderball*, the *Disco Volante*'s false bottom is discovered by 007 (SEAN CONNERY), who photographs it with an infrared underwater camera. The pictures convince him that the yacht could have picked up the stolen A-bombs without generating surface activity. When 007 later disrupts Largo's NATO Project, Largo orders the cocoon jettisoned and makes his escape in the hydrofoil, which later grounds on a coral reef and disintegrates. The cocoon is eventually obliterated by U.S. Coast Guard warships.

To build such a vessel, production designer Ken Adam was sent to Puerto Rico in December 1964 to purchase *The Flying Fish*, an old Rodriguez hydrofoil that had once carried passengers between Venezuela and Mexico. Rodriguez was the manufacturing firm in Messina, Sicily, that had originally built the swift hydrofoils for use in the Adriatic.

The rusty craft was driven under its own power to a Miami shipyard for a complete overhaul. Its 1,320 HP Mercedes Benz diesel was put into top condition to propel the extra 50-foot cocoon that Adam was constructing nearby.

"We had two slip bolts holding the cocoon," said Adam, who used a real pleasure yacht as the prototype for his own creation.

The Old Flying Fish hydrofoil, soon to be the dazzling *Disco Volante*, is refitted in Miami. (Ronnie Udell Collection)

"Some of our naval experts thought it wouldn't work, but we had less trouble with the *Disco* than with any other gadget.

"The cocoon itself was about 50 feet long. We fitted it out with a yellow smokestack, two lifeboats, and a functional sun deck. Once the hydrofoil drove off, we were able to turn the cocoon into a floating arsenal. I installed the type of armament you would find on a destroyer, including an anti-aircraft cannon, heavy machine guns, and armor plating."

Special effects expert John Stears later constructed a model of both the hydrofoil and the cocoon. Both were blown apart in the Pinewood tank.

The completed *Disco Volante* with its "cocoon." (Ronnie Udell Collection)

DOBTCHEFF, VERNON French character actor who portrayed black market trader and Cairo nightclub owner Max Kalba in *The Spy Who Loved Me. See* KALBA, MAX.

DR. NO (United Artists, 1962) ★ ★ ★ ½ The first James Bond movie produced by Albert R. Broccoli and Harry Saltzman. U.S. release date: May 8, 1963, in 450 theaters in the Midwest and Southwest. Los Angeles opening: May 29, 1963. Budget: $1.1 million. U.S. film rentals: $6.4 million. Running time: 111 minutes.

In the beginning, there was *Dr. No.* Long before *Batman, Ghostbusters, The Road Warrior, Superman,* and Indiana Jones, James Bond, Secret Agent 007, appeared on the scene and ushered in a new genre of high-tech thrillers, loaded with sex and violence. But to intimate that James Bond introduced sex to the cinema would not be fair or accurate.

Moral codes had begun to relax toward the end of the 1950s, especially when Elvis Presley, Marilyn Monroe, James Dean, "Peyton Place," and *Playboy* magazine entered the scene. However, no film series initiated sex on the big screen quite like the Bond movies. And it started with *Dr. No.*

Sylvia Trench, Miss Taro, Honey Ryder—they were extremely desirable women, filmed in various states of dress and undress—all in big-screen color. Ursula Andress coming out of the water on Crab Key, dressed in a skimpy bikini, is the most famous introduction for a performer

James Bond's (SEAN CONNERY) night visitor arrives at Miss Taro's cottage in *Dr. No.* (Rex Features Ltd./RDR Productions)

in screen history—paralleling Omar Sharif's arrival on camel in *Lawrence of Arabia*, the same year.

However, producers Broccoli and Saltzman were shrewd enough to maintain a suggestive rather than an explicit approach to sex, which guaranteed that their film series would not turn off the family audience. Like P. T. Barnum, the producers were selling a circus to everyone in town.

But it wasn't just the hint of sex that guaranteed the success of the first Bond movie. *Dr. No* (and *From Russia with Love*, which followed) tells a very realistic story—a story that begins innocently enough with a bridge game in Jamaica. What remains fascinating about the first 007 movie is its almost documentary-like flavor and, at times, dead seriousness.

A British agent is murdered in Jamaica. London is calling on all radio frequencies, to no avail. The head of MI7 is alerted. His top agent arrives for a meeting in the early morning hours, where there's some serious brainstorming about the agent's unknown fate; an assignment; and a predawn tryst in his apartment with a comely playgirl. You also see the last trappings of the 1950s reflected in the conservative clothing of the Secret Service communications personnel (sweaters and bow ties), the elegantly dressed women (evening gowns in major motion pictures were on their way out, too), and the businesslike approach to investigating a crime in the tropics.

Helping maintain the film's credibility are a group of colorful, extremely interesting background characters: Strangways, Professor Dent, Quarrel, M, Boothroyd, Leiter, even Sylvia Trench. And Joseph Wiseman brought to life Dr. No—the first megalomaniac supervillain of the atomic age.

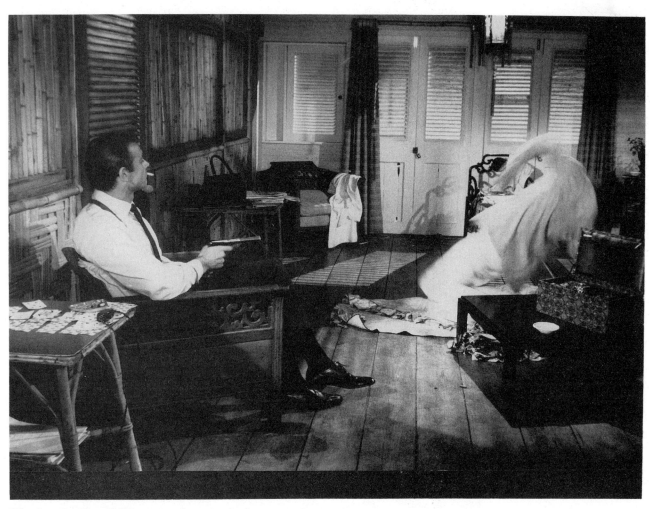

"That's a Smith and Wesson, and you've had your six." (Rex Features Ltd./RDR Productions)

The prop department outfits Sean Connery with the proper holster during interior shooting in Miss Taro's cottage in *Dr. No.* (Rex Features Ltd./RDR Productions)

No's modus operandi was pure Fu Manchu, Professor Moriarty, and Ming the Merciless. But his high-tech island fortress, along with its ruthlessly efficient garrison, were trappings of the machine age. America had invented the bomb and other superweapons, and Dr. No was the first in a gallery of supercrooks who were prepared to abuse them.

Dr. No introduced Sean Connery to international audiences—the perfect actor to bring Bond to life. He was handsome, enormously charismatic, a big-screen hero-type, and when he punched someone, they stayed down. For the American audience, such a two-fisted approach to the character was a key ingredient in the film's success. Producers Albert R. Broccoli and Harry Saltzman had been pushing all along for a tough, Mickey Spillane/Raymond Chandler-esque style to the Bond series—with Connery in the role, they got it.

Credit Broccoli and Saltzman for also assembling a fine creative team to put the first adventure together. Director Terence Young was mostly a B-film director until the Bond series. With 007, he found a character with whom he had plenty in common. Young himself was a dashing tank commander with the Irish Guards during World War II. A contemporary of Ian Fleming, Young had his own stylish savoir faire that blended perfectly with the author's creation.

Working with Young was screenwriter Richard Maibaum, a talented, extremely witty ex-playwright who could perfectly capture the essence of Bond on the printed page, but with a touch of humor that wasn't present in any of the books. That Maibaum wrote with a light touch guaranteed that the Bond films would never be spoofed into oblivion (the fate of many adventure series).

Also on the Bond team was editor Peter Hunt, whose urge to bring commercial cutting styles to the feature-film business would be a tremendous boon to the production. Ted Moore's camera work, Bob Simmons's stunt arranging, John Barry's theme music, Maurice Binder's titles, John Stears's special effects—everything added up to a powerful sendoff.

Still, due to the reluctance of United Artists to give the film a big splash in the United States, the film opened in America with no premiere and little fanfare. If you'd have called a San Fernando Valley theater in Los Angeles that spring of 1963, you would have been told that the picture was *Doctor Number* and the star was *Seen* Connery.

Despite its lackluster release, *Dr. No* made a tidy profit and guaranteed the production of a second Bond film, *From Russia with Love*. After the success of *Goldfinger* in 1964-65, *Dr. No* and *From Russia with Love* were re-released and became the most successful double feature in film history.

DR. NO CAST

James Bond	Sean Connery
Honey	Ursula Andress
Dr. No	Joseph Wiseman
Felix Leiter	Jack Lord
M	Bernard Lee
Professor Dent	Anthony Dawson
Quarrel	John Kitzmiller
Miss Taro	Zena Marshall
Sylvia Trench	Eunice Gayson
Miss Moneypenny	Lois Maxwell
Puss-Feller	Lester Prendergast
John Strangways	Tim Moxon
Girl Photographer	Margaret LeWars

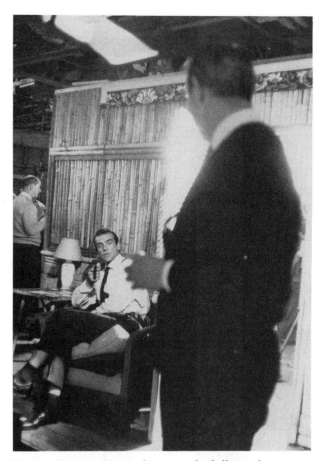

Director Terence Young discusses the killing of Professor Dent with Sean Connery. (Rex Features Ltd./RDR Productions)

Sean Connery and Zena Marshall, who played Miss Taro, attend the premiere of *Dr. No* in London in 1962. (Express Newspapers, London)

Mr. Jones	Reggie Carter
Major Boothroyd	Peter Burton
Duff	William Foster-Davis
Playdell-Smith	Louis Blaazer
Sister Rose	Michele Mok
Sister Lily	Yvonne Shima
Mary	Dolores Keator

DR. NO CREW

Producers	Harry Saltzman, Albert R. Broccoli
Director	Terence Young
Screenplay by	Richard Maibaum, Johanna Harwood, Berkely Mather
From the Novel by	Ian Fleming
Music Composed by	Monty Norman
Orchestrated by	Burt Rhodes
James Bond Theme played by the John Barry Orchestra	
Conducted by	Eric Rodgers
Director of Photography	Ted Moore, B.S.C.
Production Designer	Ken Adam
Art Director	Syd Cain
Production Manager	L. C. Rudkin
Editor	Peter Hunt
Main Titles Designed by	Maurice Binder
Animation	Trevor Bond, Robert Ellis
Makeup	John O'Gorman
Special Effects	Frank George
Continuity	Helen Whitson
Assistant Director	Clive Reed
Camera Operator	Johnny Winbolt
Hairstylist	Eileen Warwick
Sound Recordists	Wally Milner, John Dennis
Production Company	Eon Productions
Distribution Company	United Artists
"Three Blind Mice," "Jump Up, Jamaica," "Underneath the Mango Tree" performed by	Byron Lee Band

DR. NO COMPETITION

Competitive films in release when *Dr. No* opened in Los Angeles on May 29, 1963 (*Note*: in L.A., *Dr. No* opened on a double feature with *The Young and the Brave*, costarring Rory Calhoun and William Bendix):

The List of Adrian Messenger
Lawrence of Arabia
To Kill a Mockingbird
55 Days at Peking
Battle of the Worlds
Bye Bye Birdie
My Six Loves

DR. SHATTERHAND'S CASTLE A feudal stronghold introduced by author Ian Fleming in his original novel *You Only Live Twice*. Honeycombed with deadly volcanic fumaroles, poisonous plants, and terrifying insects, the castle becomes a magnet for suicide-crazy Japanese citizens. Its owner is none other than S.P.E.C.T.R.E. chieftain Ernst Stavro Blofeld, now retired to private life and masquerading as the very neutral Swiss Dr. Shatterhand. Producer Cubby Broccoli tried to replicate this medieval bastion on a location scout to Japan in March 1966. Crisscrossing the island of Kyushu in a French-built Alouette helicopter that spring were Broccoli, director Lewis Gilbert, cinematographer Freddie Young, production manager Ken Adam, and military liaison Charlie Russhon. Nowhere could they find the location described in Fleming's book.

Remembered Gilbert, "We didn't see one castle on the Japanese coastline, for the very simple reason that the Japanese don't build castles on the coast. Because of the typhoons, it's too dangerous. Any castles were built inland to defend strategic mountain passes and valleys. It was frustrating for us because we couldn't find the most important setting in Fleming's book. We searched every inch of the Japanese coastline and drew an entire blank. Not one battlement . . ."

The recce was not entirely without results. During one of the helicopter scouts, the crew came across a Japanese national park filled with dormant volcanos, one of which was a crater lake. The scenery inspired Ken Adam to build Blofeld's base inside the cone of one of the volcanos. Its roof would be made out of solid metal, camouflaged to appear as the surface of a crater lake. *See* VOLCANO ROCKET BASE.

DOG COMPANY A unit of the U.S. Army infantry assigned the task of escorting a bomb disposal unit inside Fort Knox in *Goldfinger*. *See* FORT KNOX, KENTUCKY.

DOLEMAN, GUY (1923–) Australian character actor who portrayed S.P.E.C.T.R.E. agent Count Lippe in *Thunderball*. After bungling his mission at Shrublands, Lippe is assassinated on the highway by motorcycle-riding Fiona Volpe (LUCIANA PALUZZI). *See* LIPPE, COUNT.

DOLLY The buxom blond who falls for Jaws (RICHARD KIEL) in *Moonraker*. She is portrayed, without any dialogue, by Blanche Ravalec.

DOMINATION A fascinating 3-D video game featured in *Never Say Never Again* and played by Maximillian Largo (KLAUS MARIA BRANDAUER) and James Bond (SEAN CONNERY). A mid-1980s equivalent of the obligatory game of chance between 007 and his nemesis, Domination is a high-tech battle for power as opponents fight for countries chosen at random by the machine.

Seated at opposite ends of a long table, both players face a 3-D map of the world that adjusts to a specific country as the game proceeds. Target areas light up on the map. Whoever hits them first with the hand-controlled laser beam scores points.

Another way to win is to employ missiles. The left hand controls two nuclear missiles, and the right hand controls a shield to block the missiles. Fail to block the incoming missile, and you lose the game. Score totals are calculated in dollar amounts.

Largo chooses blue and 007, red. When Bond begins a game against Largo, who's fighting for France, he loses quickly and gets an electric shock. Largo apologizes and informs 007 that, like a real battlefield general, the player gets an electric shock if he loses. As the stakes increase, so does the level of pain.

In the first game, fighting for Spain and a value of $9,000, Largo wins. In the second game, fighting for Japan and a value of $16,000, Largo wins again. In the third game, fighting for the United States and a value of $42,000, Bond begins to get used to the apparatus but loses anyway, getting a powerful shock this time that throws him to the floor.

Getting to his feet, Bond is informed by Largo that he owes $67,000. Bond then says he'll play one more game, fighting for the rest of the world, with a value of $325,000. This time Bond masters the machine and beats Largo at his own game, giving his nemesis an incredibly

powerful electrical shock. He then tells Largo that he'll forgo his winnings in return for one dance with Domino (KIM BASINGER).

The live-action element of the Domination game sequence was filmed in a huge French rococo room inside Waddesdon Manor, the Rothschild home in England. David Dryer's effects team then spent months creating the game effects with elaborate laser effects matted into the live-action photography.

DOMINIQUE AND THE ENCHANTED PAPILLON Eiffel Tower Restaurant cabaret act featured in *A View to a Kill*. While Bond (ROGER MOORE) and French detective Achille Aubergine (JEAN ROUGERIE) discuss Max Zorin's (CHRISTOPHER WALKEN) possible horse-fixing activities, Dominique (DOMINIQUE RISBOURG) performs onstage with dozens of butterflies—some of which are animated like puppets by her dark-suited puppeteers on the balcony. Unbeknownst to Bond and Aubergine, May Day (GRACE JONES), Zorin's murderous bodyguard, has knocked out one of the puppeteers and assumed her identity. Only, her butterfly is equipped with a poisonous barb that strikes Aubergine in the face and kills him. Bond chases after May Day, but she escapes by jumping off the Eiffel Tower and parachuting to safety—an incredible stunt performed by stuntman B. J. Worth.

DOMINO The nickname of Dominique Derval (CLAUDINE AUGER) in *Thunderball*. The name, given to her by her friends, appears on

Claudine Auger enjoys the publicity on *Thunderball*. Her Domino is the author's favorite Bond girl. (Rex Features/Ltd./RDR Productions)

Kim Basinger brought Domino back to the screen in *Never Say Never Again*. (Taliafilm)

her ankle bracelet. (*See* DERVAL, DOMINIQUE; AUGER, CLAUDINE.) It's also the name of Maximillian Largo's (KLAUS MARIA BRANDAUER) mistress, portrayed by Kim Basinger in *Never Say Never Again*. *See* PETACHI, DOMINO; BASINGER, KIM.

DOM PERIGNON '52 The champagne found by Bond (ROGER MOORE) and Anya (BARBARA BACH) in Stromberg's escape pod in *The Spy Who Loved Me*.

DOM PERIGNON '53 The champagne served by James Bond (SEAN CONNERY) to

Jill Masterson (SHIRLEY EATON) in his Miami Beach hotel suite in *Goldfinger*. Agent 007 refers to it as "passion juice" and says that it should never be consumed above the temperature of 38 degrees Fahrenheit. However, before he can retrieve a chilly second bottle from the refrigerator, he is knocked out by Oddjob (HAROLD SAKATA).

DOM PERIGNON '55 The champagne served by Dr. No (JOSEPH WISEMAN) at his dinner with Bond (SEAN CONNERY). Agent 007 says he prefers the '53 vintage, although this preference doesn't deter him from ordering the '55 champagne by the pool in *Thunderball*.

DOM PERIGNON '57 The champagne ordered by Bond (GEORGE LAZENBY) for Tracy (DIANA RIGG) and himself after he rescues her from heavy gambling losses in *On Her Majesty's Secret Service*.

DOM PERIGNON '59 The champagne offered to James Bond (SEAN CONNERY) by S.P.E.C.T.R.E. agent Helga Brandt (KARIN DOR) in *You Only Live Twice*.

DOM PERIGNON '64 The champagne offered to James Bond (ROGER MOORE) by Nick Nack (HERVE VILLECHAIZE) on Scaramanga's island in *The Man with the Golden Gun*. Agent 007 indicates that he prefers the '62 vintage.

DOODY, ALISON Blond actress who portrayed Max Zorin's (CHRISTOPHER WALKEN) assistant, Jenny Flex, in *A View to a Kill*. See FLEX, JENNY.

DOR, KARIN German actress who portrayed S.P.E.C.T.R.E. agent Helga Brandt in *You Only Live Twice*. Masquerading as Osato's (TERU SHIMADA) confidential secretary, she fails in her attempt to assassinate Bond and ends up as fish food in Blofeld's (DONALD PLEASENCE) private piranha pool.

DOUBLE BLOODY MARY WITH PLENTY OF WORCESTERSHIRE SAUCE The hefty drink that Domino (KIM BASINGER) orders when she meets Bond (SEAN CONNERY) at Largo's (KLAUS MARIA BRANDAUER) charity benefit in Nice in *Never Say Never Again*. Having deceived her at the massage parlor—where 007 impersonates a masseuse and gives Domino a very erotic "hard" massage—Bond apologizes and offers to buy her a drink. "Shall it be hard or soft?" he asks. Domino says "soft" and proceeds to order the double Bloody Mary.

DOUBLE SIX A reference to a specific dice combination featured in the rigged backgammon game in *Octopussy*. In order to cheat Major Clive

(STUART SAUNDERS) out of 200,000 rupees, Kamal Khan (LOUIS JOURDAN) has been using loaded dice that can produce a double six at will. When challenged on his uncanny ability to throw that number, Kamal shrugs and says, "It's all in the wrist."

When Bond (ROGER MOORE) takes over the Major's position, Kamal throws another double six and 007 loses a quick 100,000 ru-

German actress Karin Dor brought Helga Brandt to life in *You Only Live Twice*. (UPI)

pees. However, when the bet is doubled, Bond calls "player's privilege" and uses Kamal's loaded dice to score a double six and win the game. Such trickery recalls the golf course shenanigans in *Goldfinger*.

DOVE, THE   The nickname of Greek smuggler Milos Columbo (TOPOL) in *For Your Eyes Only*. The moniker dates back to his days with the resistance during World War II. A white dove symbol adorns the wetsuits of his divers.

In an attempt to confuse James Bond (ROGER MOORE), Emile Locque (MICHAEL GOTHARD)—a ruthless assassin working for Aris Kristatos (JULIAN GLOVER)—leaves a white dove symbol on the body of murdered Secret Service agent Luigi Ferrara (JOHN MORENO) in Cortina. After Locque kills Columbo's mistress, Lisl Von Schlam (CASSANDRA HARRIS), on the beach in Corfu, 007 is captured by Columbo's divers and brought to Columbo, who tells him the truth about the allegiances of Kristatos and Locque.

Agent 007 wounds Locque during the raid on Kristatos's heroin-smuggling operation in Albania. He then approaches the assassin's disabled car, which is sitting on the edge of an ocean cliff, tosses him the white dove symbol that had been left with Ferrara's corpse, and kicks the car over the edge. *See* COLUMBO, MILOS.

"DO YOU EXPECT ME TO TALK?"   The question James Bond (SEAN CONNERY) asks Auric Goldfinger (GERT FROBE) after a laser beam begins to approach a particularly vulnerable part of 007's anatomy. Goldfinger's memorable reply: "No, Mr. Bond, I expect you to die!"

"DO YOU HAVE A MATCH?"   A variation of the initial phrase of the British Secret Service recognition code in *From Russia with Love*. *See* "CAN I BORROW A MATCH?"

"DO YOU KNOW HOW CHRISTMAS TREES ARE GROWN?"   Cheery Christmas tune sung by songstress Nina during the ice-skating sequence in *On Her Majesty's Secret Ser-*vice when Bond (GEORGE LAZENBY) escapes from Piz Gloria.

DRACO, MARC ANGE   Head of the notorious Union Corse—one of the biggest crime syndicates in Europe—and the father of Contessa Teresa "Tracy" de Vicenzo (DIANA RIGG) in *On Her Majesty's Secret Service*. He is portrayed by Italian actor Gabriele Ferzetti. One of the most sympathetic Mafia dons ever to grace the screen, Draco runs several legitimate business fronts, including construction, electronics, and agricultural concerns. Bond (GEORGE LAZENBY) meets Draco at his offices at Draco Construction in Portugal. A native of Corsica, Draco met Tracy's mother, an English girl, when he was on the run from the authorities. She died when Tracy was 12.

Draco likes the fact that Bond is interested in his daughter, and he's determined to help her find the right husband (her first killed himself in a Maserati with one of his mistresses). He thus offers Bond a dowry of a million pounds sterling if 007 will wed his daughter. Bond declines the generous offer but does mention an interest in Draco's intelligence sources, particularly in regard to the whereabouts of the mysterious S.P.E.C.T.R.E. chief, Ernst Stavro Blofeld (TELLY SAVALAS). Draco will only admit that some of his men have defected to S.P.E.C.T.R.E.

However, when Tracy threatens to run away unless he tells Bond what he needs to know, Draco admits that there may be a lead through a lawyer named Gumpold (JAMES BREE), who has offices in Berne, Switzerland. Later when Tracy is captured by Blofeld, Draco joins Bond in a full-scale assault on S.P.E.C.T.R.E.'s Piz Gloria mountain fortress. And true to his promise, he gives Bond a check for a million pounds when 007 weds his daughter at the film's conclusion. Bond, of course, returns the money.

DRAGON   Dr. No's primary antipersonnel, diesel-powered, all-terrain vehicle on Crab Key. Equipped with a flamethrower, headlights, and armor plate, and painted with dragon markings to frighten superstitious locals, the vehicle doesn't deter Bond and Quarrel, who launch an ill-fated, all-out assault. The vehicle was based on a swamp vehicle first seen by Ian Fleming on the island of Inagua in 1956.

DRAGON GARDEN, CASTLE PEAK

Bangkok, Thailand, location of Hai Fat's (RICHARD LOO) estate in *The Man with the Golden Gun.*

DRAX, HUGO

Fanatical billionaire industrialist, portrayed by Michel Lonsdale in *Moonraker*, who plans to destroy the human population of Planet Earth with a strain of toxic nerve gas dispersed from outer space. His plan for mass murder completed, Drax will then repopulate the planet with his own master race.

Drax is the head of Drax Enterprises, a multinational corporation that, among other things, manufactures the space shuttle in California, using components from countries around the world. His fleet of shuttles—the Moonrakers—which are based in South America, will transport his master race into space. There they will live on a radar-invisible space station until Earth's depopulation has been completed. When his orbiting installation is overrun by U.S. astro forces, Drax is cornered by James Bond (ROGER MOORE) and tossed out of the station's air lock into outer-space oblivion.

DRAX INDUSTRIES

The California-based division of Drax Enterprises. It is responsible for the manufacture of the Moonraker space shuttle fleet.

DRESDEN

East German city that is the birthplace of Max Zorin (CHRISTOPHER WALKEN) in *A View to a Kill*. Trained and financed by the KGB as a top agent, Zorin left East Germany in the 1960s and was set up in France, where Zorin Industries was founded. *See* ZORIN, MAX.

DRINKA PINTA MILKA DAY

Sign atop the remote-control explosive-laden Wright's Dairies milk truck that chases Sir James Bond (DAVID NIVEN) in *Casino Royale*. It eventually slams into a female agent of Dr. Noah's (WOODY ALLEN) and explodes.

"DROP IN THE OCEAN"

The fate of a carload of S.P.E.C.T.R.E. operatives who make the mistake of tailing Bond (SEAN CONNERY) and Aki (AKIKO WAKABAYASHI) in *You Only Live Twice*. To reinforce "Zero Zero," Tanaka (TETSURO TAMBA) sends over a twin-rotor Japanese Secret Service helicopter equipped with an electromagnet. Maneuvering over the speeding S.P.E.C.T.R.E. vehicle, the helicopter attaches the magnet to its roof and lifts the car into the air. The car and passengers are then neatly dumped into Tokyo Bay.

DUFF

British police officer, portrayed by William Foster-Davis, who was assigned to help 007's investigation in Jamaica in *Dr. No.*

DUFOUR, CORINNE

Hugo Drax's (MICHEL LONSDALE) beautiful helicopter pilot and executive assistant, portrayed by Corinne Clery, in *Moonraker*. Based at the enormous Drax French estate, which has been rebuilt brick by brick near Drax's Los Angeles space-shuttle manufacturing plant, Dufour becomes one of Bond's (ROGER MOORE) early bedmates. Unfortunately, in Drax's eyes, her dalliance with Bond also marks her for early assassination.

After being unceremoniously dismissed, she is chased through a nearby forest and devoured by Drax's vicious Dobermans. This latter sequence was used effectively in the film's unusual teaser trailer/preview campaign, which contrasted the tranquility of a picturesque forest scene with the deadly hounds killing their human prey.

DUGGAN, GERRY

British actor who portrayed Bond's (SEAN CONNERY) caddy, Hawker, in *Goldfinger.*

DUKE OF WELLINGTON PORTRAIT

A painting by Goya found in the living room of Dr. No's underground fortress on Crab Key in the Caribbean Sea. The Duke of Wellington portrait was actually stolen prior to the start of principal photography on *Dr. No* in February 1962. Hence, Bond's double take upon seeing the portrait in Dr. No's lair is appropriate.

The choice of the Wellington was suggested

by director Terence Young's script girl, Johanna Harwood, who received co-credit on the script with Richard Maibaum and Berkely Mather. Harwood's idea came after the production was about to use a stolen Picasso, which had also been recently heisted from the Aix-en-Provence Museum in France.

DUNAWAY, FAYE (Bascom, Florida, January 14, 1941–   ) (real name, Dorothy Faye Dunaway) American leading lady who was one of the early choices for the part of Domino in *Thunderball* but who chose to make her film debut in the low-budget clunker *The Happening* (1967) instead.

DURAN DURAN British pop supergroup who recorded the rousing title track to *A View to a Kill* in 1985. Duran Duran (Simon Le Bon, Nick Rhodes, and John Taylor) take their name from the wacky character with the "orgasmatron" in the science-fiction film, *Barbarella*. The band first surfaced in 1978 in a club called Barbarella's.

The rock group Duran Duran—*left to right*, John Taylor, Nick Rhodes, and Simon Le Bon—sang the title song in *A View to a Kill*. (Capitol Records)

E

EAST BERLIN Performing site of the Octopussy Circus when 009 (ANDY BRAD-FORD) successfully steals a phony Fabergé egg at the beginning of *Octopussy*.

EASTON, SHEENA (April 27, 1959–) Scottish pop singer who sang the title track to *For Your Eyes Only* (1981). Thanks to title producer Maurice Binder, Easton is the only musical performer ever to sing on camera in the series.

The type of look that won British comedy actress Shirley Eaton the part of golden girl Jill Masterson in *Goldfinger*. (National Film Archive, London)

Pop singer Sheena Easton, who sang "For Your Eyes Only," was the first musical artist to appear on camera in a Bond title sequence. (Aaron Rapoport)

EATON, SHIRLEY (1936–) The famous "golden girl" of *Goldfinger* who portrayed the villain's seductive Girl Friday, Jill Masterson, who dies of skin suffocation when her entire body is painted gold. Who could ever forget Eaton's introduction in the film? She's lying on a chaise longue on the balcony of Goldfinger's Miami Beach hotel suite, attired in black bra and panties, while she observes Mr. Simmons's (AUSTIN WILLIS) gin hand through binoculars.

When 007 (SEAN CONNERY) sneaks into the suite and turns off the radio transmitter to Goldfinger's hearing aid, she whirls around, showing plenty of cleavage, and utters, "Who are you?" Bond gives his standard retort, "Bond. James Bond" while, thanks to John Barry, the moody James Bond Theme rises in the background. Definitely one of the great moments in the series. *See* MASTERSON, JILL.

EGE, JULIE Actress who portrayed the Scandinavian allergy victim in *On Her Majesty's Secret Service*.

EGG SPINES Poisonous thorns, imbedded in a coral reef, that spear Domino's (CLAUDINE AUGER) foot in *Thunderball*. Ever the gentleman, Bond (SEAN CONNERY) pulls the spines out of her foot with his teeth.

8 English allergy patient Ruby Bartlett's (ANGELA SCOULAR) room number at Piz Gloria in *On Her Majesty's Secret Service*. In order to get Bond (George Lazenby, posing as Sir Hilary Bray) to come to her room, she writes the number in lipstick on his inner thigh at dinner. While sneaking into her room for a second night of passion, Bond blows his cover when he finds Irma Bunt (ILSE STEPPAT) there instead.

EIGHT AGENTS CIA casualties inflicted in *Casino Royale* by female agents of Dr. Noah (WOODY ALLEN). Two died right in the Pentagon, according to CIA Chief Ransome (WILLIAM HOLDEN).

18 Identification number on the opium-loaded Soviet transport plane that Bond (TIMOTHY DALTON) hijacks in *The Living Daylights*.

18TH CENTURY The real era of France's beautiful Chateau Chantilly, which serves as Max Zorin's (CHRISTOPHER WALKEN) estate and stables in *A View to a Kill*. While speaking to Bond (ROGER MOORE), Zorin incorrectly refers to the chateau as coming from the 16th century.

EIGHT MINUTES The amount of breathing time at a depth of 584 feet, using a mixture of oxygen and helium, that James Bond (ROGER MOORE) and Melina Havelock (CAROLE BOUQUET) have while diving on the *St. Georges* wreck in *For Your Eyes Only*.

89632 The first five numbers of Swiss lawyer Gepruder Gumpold's (JAMES BREE) safe combination in *On Her Majesty's Secret Service*. Bond (GEORGE LAZENBY) cracks the safe with the help of a computerized safecracking photocop-

ier supplied to him by Campbell (BERNARD HORSFALL). While the computer figures out the combination. Bond sits back and reads the latest issue of *Playboy*.

8:00 P.M. Dinnertime at Kamal Khan's (LOUIS JOURDAN) Monsoon Palace in *Octopussy*. For 007 (ROGER MOORE) the entree is the delectable stuffed sheep's head. Beware, Mr. Bond, Kamal likes the eyeballs!

879-432 The telephone number for Felix Leiter's (CEC LINDER) Miami Beach hotel in *Goldfinger*. He's staying in Room 119. Bond (SEAN CONNERY) calls him there when he discovers the body of Jill Masterson (SHIRLEY EATON), covered in gold paint.

8:30 A.M. Agent 007's departure time for Istanbul in *From Russia with Love*.

EIGHT WEEKS The amount of time that the kidnapped millionairess (WENDY LEECH) has supposedly been held captive by the fanatical revolutionaries during the opening war-game sequence in *Never Say Never Again*. During that period, she's also been brainwashed à la Patty Hearst—a fact that leads her to stab Bond (SEAN CONNERY) in the arm even though he's rescued her.

80 DEGREES The temperature of the mud bath, in the *Diamonds Are Forever* teaser, where an Ernst Stavro Blofeld (CHARLES GRAY) double is recovering.

88 Honey Ryder's (URSULA ANDRESS) geiger reading when she enters Dr. No's radiation decontamination center on Crab Key.

87 MILLION FRANCS The total sum won by James Bond (BARRY NELSON) in the Monte Carlo baccarat game with Soviet masterspy Le Chiffre (PETER LORRE) in the TV film "Casino Royale." That amount is given to Bond in the form of a check, which he hides behind the brass number-plate on his hotel suite door.

Desperate to get back his money, Le Chiffre captures Bond and tortures him to find out where he's hidden the check. Also captured is

Valerie Mathis (LINDA CHRISTIAN), Bond's ex-lover and an agent with the French Deuxième Bureau who can't bear seeing 007 tortured. She eventually admits that she saw Bond with a screwdriver in his hand, information that leads Le Chiffre to recover the check.

Incarcerated in his hotel suite bathroom and left alone for a key moment, Bond uses the razor blade hidden in Le Chiffre's cigarette case—which the Russian leaves on the edge of the bathtub—and unties himself. In a desperate fight, he manages to shoot and kill Le Chiffre and one of his thugs.

EKBERG, ANITA (Malmo, Sweden, September 29, 1931–   ) Statuesque, blond Swedish actress whose mouth became a key plot point in *From Russia with Love*. Alerted to an unannounced police search, Bulgar assassin Krilencu (FRED HAGGERTY) attempts to sneak out of his Istanbul apartment by using a trapdoor built inside a billboard featuring an advertisement for the 1963 film *Call Me Bwana*. The door actually opens right into the mouth of Ekberg, who is prominently displayed on the billboard. Krilencu never makes it to safety, as he is gunned down by Kerim Bey (PEDRO AR-MENDARIZ).

EKLAND, BRITT (Stockholm, Sweden, October 6, 1942–   ) (real name, Britt Eklund) Swedish actress—ex-wife of Peter Sellers, ex-lover of rocker Rod Stewart, and current wife of Jim McDonnell of the rock group the Stray Cats—who portrayed daffy Mary Goodnight in *The Man with the Golden Gun*. Ekland impressed producers Albert R. Broccoli and Harry Saltzman with her vital statistics, although the producers were later surprised to discover that she was pregnant at the time.

Ekland's problem in the ninth Bond film was the pure silliness of her part. She spends most of the film either locked in the trunk of Scaramanga's flying car or stuck in the closet of Bond's (ROGER MOORE) hotel room while 007 makes love to Andrea (MAUD ADAMS). Still, those full sensuous lips, gorgeous eyes, and enticing accent were strong assets to the film. And if her part was mostly that of a buffoon, it couldn't distract viewers from the fact that she was still one of the most beautiful women in the world. In the Bond books, by contrast, Goodnight was nothing more than Bond's secretary, the successor to Miss Moneypenny. *See* GOODNIGHT, MARY.

ELECTRA The avenging daughter from Greek mythology who is the inspiration for orphaned Melina Havelock (CAROLE BOUQUET) in *For Your Eyes Only*.

ELECTROMAGNETIC RPM CONTROLLER A comical gadget that Q (DESMOND LLEWELYN) uses to beat Las Vegas slot machines in *Diamonds Are Forever*. I wonder what the Nevada Gaming Commission thought of this device.

11 AGENTS British Secret Service casualties inflicted by female agents of Dr. Noah (WOODY ALLEN) in *Casino Royale*. They include seven dead, four missing.

11 DAUGHTERS M's (JOHN HUSTON) progeny in *Casino Royale*, all of whom are impersonated by the agents of Dr. Noah (WOODY ALLEN). Their mission: destroy the celibate image of Sir James Bond (DAVID NIVEN). Their ages: 16–19.

11:00 A.M. AND 3:00 P.M. The appointed hours for Ali Kerim Bey's (PEDRO ARMENDARIZ) daily boat trips across a fourth-century underground, rat-infested Byzantine reservoir in *From Russia with Love*. The atmospheric journey leads him under the Russian embassy in Istanbul, where a British naval periscope allows him to spy into a KGB conference room.

11:25 A.M., March 14 The exact time and date that Evelyn Tremble (PETER SELLERS) visits Q's (GEOFFREY BAYLDON) workshop in *Casino Royale*. The time appears on Tremble's new wristwatch communicator, which contains a miniature television.

11:30 A.M. The time of James Bond's (ROGER MOORE) arrival from London at John F. Kennedy International Airport in New York in *Live and Let Die*. He arrives on a Pan American flight.

11:45 A.M. The time at which Kamal Khan (LOUIS JOURDAN) prepares the A-bomb for detonation in *Octopussy*. Given a four-hour delay, the bomb is set to go off at 3:45 P.M.

11½–11½ The posted score in the Venice chess match between MacAdams (PETER MADDEN), representing Canada and playing black, and Kronsteen (VLADEK SHEYBAL), representing Czechoslovakia and playing white, in *From Russia with Love*. Kronsteen eventually wins.

ELLERY, MARGARET A pretty BOAC stewardess—playing herself on the morning of Tuesday, January 16, 1962—who competes with 007 for a taxi at Kingston, Jamaica's Palisadoes Airport. It was the first day of shooting on *Dr. No.*

ELLIS, ANTONY Screenwriter who co-wrote the script for the TV film "Casino Royale" in 1954 with Charles Bennett. *See* BENNETT, CHARLES.

EL SCORPIO NIGHTCLUB The tough South American bar, featured in the *Goldfinger* teaser, where Bond (SEAN CONNERY) arrives in a completely dry white dinner jacket after setting demolition charges that will destroy Mr. Ramirez's illegal drug operation. In that sequence, shot on Pinewood Studios' Stage D, Jack Dawkes, Sid Abrams, and Harry Thorne portrayed the dummy musicians—who played John Barry's incidental flamenco music. Selina Wylie choreographed Bonita's (NADJA REGIN) dance. The extra crowd consisted of 35 men and 15 women.

EMI STUDIOS, ELSTREE British studio where the interior sequences for *Never Say Never Again* were shot in 1982 and 1983.

EMPEROR CONSTANTINE The fourth-century Byzantine monarch who commissioned an underground reservoir in Istanbul that is Ali Kerim Bey's (PEDRO ARMENDARIZ) clandestine route to the Russian embassy in *From Russia with Love*.

EMPIRE CHEMICALS Bond's (SEAN CONNERY) employer, according to the cover story he gives Mr. Osato (TERU SHIMADA) during a visit to the latter's Tokyo headquarters in *You Only Live Twice*. He identifies himself as a managing director interested in the bulk purchase of fermentation chemicals.

ENCO Brand of South American gasoline being sold at the tiny Mom and Pop roadside station visited by James Bond (ROGER MOORE) in his Acrostar mini-jet in the *Octopussy* teaser.

EON PRODUCTIONS, LTD. Producer Albert R. Broccoli's film production company. It's actually an acronym that stands for "Everything or Nothing." Producer Harry Saltzman sold off his interest in the company in 1975. Eon is a subsidiary of Danjaq S.A., a European company named after the wives of Broccoli and Saltzman—Dana and Jacqueline, respectively.

E-667 License plate of Aris Kristatos's (JULIAN GLOVER) white Rolls-Royce, with the black top, seen on the island of Corfu in *For Your Eyes Only*.

ESTHER WILLIAMS Code name for the Lotus Esprit submarine car in *The Spy Who Loved Me*. The sobriquet was featured in an early draft of the screenplay but was dropped from the final film. The car was also called Wet Nellie—a reference to Little Nellie, the autogyro from *You Only Live Twice*. *See* LOTUS ESPRIT SUBMARINE CAR.

EXPLODING ALARM CLOCK One of the ingenious little gadgets that Q (DESMOND LLEWELYN) brings to Isthmus City in *Licence to Kill*. The sleeping subject is guaranteed *never* to wake up.

EXPLOSIVE GROUSE Bomb-laden mechanical birds used by female agents of Dr. Noah (WOODY ALLEN) to assassinate Sir James Bond (DAVID NIVEN) in *Casino Royale*. They're attracted to a magnetic homing device in one of Bond's buttons.

F

FABERGE EGGS The extremely rare jeweled eggs originally designed by Carl Fabergé as Easter gifts for the Russian royal family. One of the eggs becomes a key plot element in *Octopussy*.

The story begins when 009 (ANDY BRADFORD) steals a phony Coronation egg from the Octopussy Circus in East Berlin. Agent 009 dies with a knife in his back, and the jeweled egg falls into the hands of the British ambassador. It is eventually sent to Secret Service headquarters, where it is branded a fake.

The real egg, which contains a tiny model of the Russian imperial state coach, is up for auction at Sotheby's. Suspiciously, it is the fourth egg to be auctioned in a single year. Secret Service experts have determined that the seller is anonymous and has a numbered Swiss bank account—possibly a Soviet front.

Meeting with James Bond (ROGER MOORE), M (ROBERT BROWN) and Defense Minister Freddie Gray (GEOFFREY KEEN) reason that the egg could be part of a Soviet plot to raise currency for covert operations abroad or payoffs. What they don't know is that renegade Soviet General Orlov (STEVEN BERKOFF) is trading a huge cache of Kremlin jewelry for the services of ruthless Afghan Prince Kamal Khan (LOUIS JOURDAN) and his associate Octopussy (MAUD ADAMS) and her circus performers.

This huge "fifth column" cover force is going to help engineer Orlov's terrifying plan to detonate a nuclear device on a U.S. Air Force base in Feldstadt, West Germany. With unilateral disarmament a foregone conclusion after such a calamity, Orlov can then complete his plan to invade the West with Soviet armies.

The phony Fabergé egg stolen by 009 is part of a fake trove that Orlov's jewel forgery expert, Lenkin (PETER PORTEOUS), is substituting for the real jewels in the Kremlin Art Repository. Curious about the identity of the high bidder at the Sotheby auction, M orders Bond to accompany Secret Service art expert Jim Fanning (DOUGLAS WILMER) on a trip to the auction gallery, where they will scrutinize the fate of the egg, which is identified in the program as "The Property of a Lady." The mission: Operation Trove.

At Sotheby's the auction begins, and Kamal Khan is quickly identified as a principal bidder. Fanning doesn't like what Kamal Khan usually sells at auctions—what he refers to as "marginal quality from dubious sources." But, as a buyer, it looks this time as if Kamal Khan will win the egg—that is, until Bond, to Fanning's astonishment, starts to bid against him.

At one point, Bond asks the auction assistant if he can see the egg up close. Unbeknownst to anyone in the gallery, 007 then substitutes the phony egg stolen by 009 for the real gem.

The bidding continues, reaching an unimaginable 500,000-pound figure, until Bond lets Kamal Khan win. Fanning, about to suffer a heart attack, can't believe what he's seen. "He had to buy," says Bond. Determined to find out why, Bond follows Kamal Khan to Udaipur, India, later using the real Fabergé egg he switched at the gallery as collateral in a high-stakes backgammon game with Kamal Khan, which he wins.

Like the golf match in *Goldfinger*, the Sotheby egg auction in *Octopussy* is one of those perfectly dramatized sequences that matches

The actual Coronation Egg and its jeweled carriage surprise, now in the *Forbes* Magazine Collection, which were copied for use in *Octopussy*. (The *Forbes* Magazine Collection, New York)

007 against a villain without the typical gunplay and mayhem associated with secret agent derring-do. Sumptuously re-created by producer Cubby Broccoli's top production designer, Peter Lamont, the auction house sequence stands out in the Bond series as another breath of fresh air.

FAIRBANKS, BILL (aka 002) British Secret Service agent, mentioned in *The Man with the Golden Gun*, who was supposedly assassinated by Francisco Scaramanga (CHRISTOPHER LEE) in a Beirut cabaret in 1969. The bullet was never recovered. His girlfriend, Saida, the belly dancer (CARMEN SAUTOY), now wears the bullet as a lucky charm in her belly button.

FAIRY MARINE A boat rental service in Glasgow, Scotland, that supplied the swift motorboats to the *From Russia with Love* crew in 1963. The boats, which were driven by Bond (SEAN CONNERY) and a group of S.P.E.C.T.R.E. agents in the film's finale, were loaded onto trucks and taken to the coastal village of Crinan, Scotland, where they were deposited on an estuary and then motored out into the Atlantic. Fairy Marine's Peter Twiss, a former air force pilot who is credited as the first Englishman to break the sound barrier, was in charge of the flotilla.

FAKE RUBBER SEAGULL Perched on 007's head, the seagull was Bond's (SEAN CONNERY) camouflage while he was swimming up to an enemy dock in the *Goldfinger* teaser. From this point on, the tone of the series changes.

Up until *Goldfinger*, the James Bond series had followed author Ian Fleming's lead by presenting serious spy stories with a touch of screenwriter Richard Maibaum's self-mocking humor. Humor was an important element in American suspense films at that time, and Maibaum reasoned, correctly, that to make the American audience accept the completely preposterous 007 plots, there had to be moments in which the story took a "we know this is completely ridiculous, but isn't it also extremely fun?" approach—an approach similar to the one employed by Alfred Hitchcock in most of his films, including the very Bondlike *North by Northwest*.

In the early films, Sean Connery mastered the deadpan "throwaway" line that presented Maibaum's humor to the masses. Unfortunately, with the "fake rubber seagull" bit in *Goldfinger*, the series began to take a less subtle approach. Putting a rubber seagull on 007's head was like popping a giant red ball on his nose—something they would do, in fact, years later in *Octopussy*.

In *From Russia with Love*, 007 was a British Secret Service agent. But in *Goldfinger*, he began to take on the trappings of a clown. It was an unfortunate change in the character, which even the technicians on the set during the seagull scene realized (there was considerable grumbling when the prop department brought out the phony seagull rig).

FALLON British agent, portrayed by Christopher Neame, who is allied with Hong Kong narcotics operative Kwang (CARY-HIROYUKI TAGAWA) in *Licence to Kill*. When Kwang and his associate, Loti (DIANA LEE-HSU), disrupt James Bond's (TIMOTHY DALTON) attempt on Sanchez's (ROBERT DAVI) life, Fallon identifies 007 as a rogue agent.

FALMOUTH A tropical quagmire on Jamaica's north shore—about 20 miles east of Montego Bay—that served as the location for the swamp country where Bond (SEAN CONNERY), Quarrel (JOHN KITZMILLER), and Honey (URSULA ANDRESS) run into Dr. No's "dragon" tank.

FANNING, JIM Fussy British Secret Service art expert portrayed by Douglas Wilmer in *Octopussy*. Determined to scrutinize the high bid on a rare jeweled Fabergé Easter egg, the price of which could be supplying currency for covert Soviet intelligence operations abroad or payoffs, Fanning and Bond (ROGER MOORE) attend a Sotheby's auction in London.

In the gallery, 007 spots exiled Afghan Prince Kamal Khan (LOUIS JOURDAN) and his gorgeous assistant, Magda (KRISTINA WAYBORN). Fanning, meanwhile, predicts that the egg—identified in the catalogue as "The Property of a Lady"—will probably fetch between 250,000 and 300,000 pounds. Any more would be crazy, he claims.

Kamal Khan turns out to be the most interested bidder for the egg. It looks like he has it, when, to Fanning's astonishment, 007 suddenly joins in the bidding. As the art expert sweats next to him, Bond asks to see the egg up close. Unbeknownst to anyone in the hall, Bond switches a phony egg—one stolen by the late 009—for the real article.

Bond enthusiastically continues his bidding war against Kamal Khan until bidding on the egg has reached an astronomical 500,000 pounds. He then relents, and the Afghan wins the egg. At the conclusion of the bidding, Fanning looks like he's going to have a heart attack. *See* WILMER, DOUGLAS.

FAN-TAN PARLOR SEQUENCE The original teaser, written by Richard Maibaum, for *Thunderball*. It takes place in a Hong Kong fan-tan parlor (aka strip joint), where a beautiful girl dressed from head to toe like a peacock sits in a golden cage above the main ballroom.

Bond gives her the eye and later follows her into a dressing room, where he enters into polite conversation with her and then slugs her in the mouth. Her peacock head comes off, revealing a male—the very enemy agent Bond is searching for. This teaser was abandoned in favor of a similarly themed sequence that takes place at the Chateau d'Arnet in France. *See* BOITIER, JACQUES.

FASLANE SUBMARINE BASE An actual British Royal Navy Polaris submarine base located on the Clyde River near Glasgow, on the southwest coast of Scotland. It served as a background for an exterior sequence in *The Spy Who Loved Me*, where Bond (ROGER MOORE) is briefed about a missing nuclear submarine while an actual British nuclear submarine navigates the channel behind him.

FEARING, PATRICIA Bond's (SEAN CONNERY) randy physical therapist, portrayed by blond British actress Molly Peters, in *Thunderball*. At the Shrublands health clinic in rural England, Patricia not only helps Bond recover from the nasty poker scars wielded by Jacques Boitier (BOB SIMMONS) in the teaser, but

she's involved with S.P.E.C.T.R.E. agent Count Lippe (GUY DOLEMAN), who's enrolled at the clinic while a plastic-surgery-aided duplicate is substituted for NATO aerial observer François Derval (PAUL STASSINO).

When Lippe nearly kills Bond by increasing to killer force the tension on 007's motorized traction table, Patricia pleads with 007 not to tell her boss about the "accident." It could mean her job. The price of Bond's silence is a tryst that occurs in the steam room and later in 007's suite, where he works a mink glove over Patricia's nude back.

The Patricia Fearing character resurfaces in *Never Say Never Again*, with actress Prunella Gee in the role. This time, Bond (SEAN CONNERY) seduces her with a suitcase full of gourmet foods, including Beluga caviar, quail eggs, foie gras from Strasbourg, and vodka. While sleeping with Patricia, Bond hears a scuffle in another room, where S.P.E.C.T.R.E. agent Fatima Blush (BARBARA CARRERA) is beating up nervous airman-turned-drug-addict-and-sex-slave Jack Petachi (GAVAN O'HERLIHY).

FEKKESH, AZIZ Egyptian black-market trader, portrayed by Nadim Sawalha in *The Spy Who Loved Me*, who is one of the mysterious characters involved in the peddling of a nuclear-submarine tracking system. James Bond (ROGER MOORE) learns of Fekkesh's identity from Sheik Hosein (EDWARD DE SOUZA), a British agent masquerading as a desert chieftain outside Cairo.

Unfortunately, Fekkesh is murdered by Jaws (RICHARD KIEL) during a huge outdoor show at the pyramids. Inside the dead man's coat, Bond finds a datebook that indicates a meeting with Max Kalba (VERNON DOBTCHEFF), a Cairo nightclub owner who may or may not have the missing microfilm copy of the tracking system.

In an early draft screenplay of *The Spy Who Loved Me*, Fekkesh was first identified as a curator for the Cairo Museum of Antiquities, and Bond goes to the museum instead of to the pyramids for his first rendezvous. In the museum, he encounters the two Russian agents, and a big fight occurs in the mummy room. Glass cases are smashed, mummies disintegrate, and inane one-liners prevail. (In one sequence, after one of the Russians hurls a bust of King Tutankhamen at Bond and misses, Bond replies, "Tut Tut.")

Bond is eventually overpowered by the Russian and knocked out. The idea of fighting in such a delicate atmosphere was later used in *Moonraker*, where Bond fights Chang (TOSHIRO SUGA) in the Venice Glass Museum.

FELDKIRSCH Swiss village featured in *On Her Majesty's Secret Service*. After escaping from Ernst Stavro Blofeld's (TELLY SAVALAS) Piz Gloria mountain hideaway, Bond (GEORGE LAZENBY) discovers that the nearest pay telephone is located at the post office in Feldkirsch. Unfortunately, before he can make a desperate international call to M (BERNARD LEE), Blofeld's thugs arrive.

FELDMAN, CHARLES K. (New York City, April 26, 1905–May 25, 1968) (real name, Charles K. Gould) American film producer and former movie agent who purchased the feature-film rights to *Casino Royale* from Gregory Ratoff for $75,000 and brought it to the big screen in 1967 as a $9 million spoof for Columbia Pictures. His coproducer on the project was Jerry Bresler.

FELDMANSTRASSE Fictitious West German street that is the location of the Mata Hari Dance and Spy School in *Casino Royale*. Also an inside reference to producer Charles K. Feldman.

FELDSTADT, WEST GERMANY Site of a U.S. Air Force base targeted for nuclear destruction in *Octopussy*. In order to force Western Europe to disarm unilaterally, renegade Russian General Orlov (STEVEN BERKOFF) is determined to detonate an A-bomb at Feldstadt and make it look like an accident. With the borders free of American atomic weapons, he reasons that a massive invasion of the West can succeed.

Unbeknownst to Octopussy (MAUD ADAMS), who thinks she's involved in a typical jewel-smuggling operation with her partner Kamal Khan (LOUIS JOURDAN), her own circus is being used as a cover for the bomb, which has been planted in the base of a circus cannon. Despite being thrown off the circus train and left far behind, James Bond (ROGER MOORE)

manages to steal a car and head for Feldstadt to prevent the "accident." Pursued by angry West German police and a platoon of MPs, 007 disguises himself as a clown and quickly enters the circus tent. There he fights his way to the cannon's base and, with Octopussy's help (she shoots the lock off), deactivates the bomb.

FELICCA Egyptian secretary, portrayed by beauty Olga Bisera, who works for Aziz Fekkesh (NADIM SAWALHA) in *The Spy Who Loved Me*. She's kissing Bond (ROGER MOORE) in the living room of Fekkesh's Cairo house when the assassin Sandor (MILTON REID) opens fire.

FELTON, NORMAN (London, England, April 29–) American television producer who, in New York during the spring of 1962, began a short-lived collaboration with author Ian Fleming on what would eventually become "The Man from U.N.C.L.E." television series. The sum of Fleming's involvement in the series consisted of notes written hurriedly to Felton on a pad of Western Union telegram blanks. Much of it was useless, but Felton did make note of the names Fleming gave to his two principal agents: Napoleon Solo and April Dancer.

Returning to Hollywood and working with his associate, Sam Rolfe, Felton created a pilot script, titled "Solo," about an international crime-fighting organization named U.N.C.L.E. (United Network Command for Law and Enforcement) and its various operatives, one of which, Napoleon Solo, was a secret agent like James Bond.

One year later, Felton tried to interest Fleming in the venture, but this time the author was advised to stay away from any television projects that involved secret agents. Already embroiled in one lawsuit over *Thunderball*, Fleming was not about to get involved in another, especially since producers Albert R. Broccoli and Harry Saltzman were already aware of the Felton series and were dead set against it.

In January 1964, Eon Productions brought a suit against Felton's production company, claiming that by using the title "Solo" for their proposed series, they were in effect stealing an actual character name from *Goldfinger*, then in production at Pinewood. Felton pointed out that Mr. Solo in *Goldfinger*, a Mafia chieftain, was certainly not the same man as Napoleon Solo in their series. After he brought MGM's best lawyer into the case, Eon Productions backed down, demanding only that Felton change the name of the series. Felton's Arena Productions agreed, and "Solo" was changed to "The Man from U.N.C.L.E.," which made its debut on American television in the fall of 1964.

FERMENTATION CHEMICALS What Bond (SEAN CONNERY) claims to be interested in purchasing when he poses as Mr. Fisher of Empire Chemicals in Osato's (TERU SHIMADA) office in *You Only Live Twice*. His exact need is a bulk shipment of monosodium glutamate and ascorbic acid.

FERRARA, LUIGI British Secret Service agent, portrayed by John Moreno, based in Milan in *For Your Eyes Only*. Ferrara meets Bond (ROGER MOORE) in Cortina D'Ampezzo, a resort city in the Italian Alps where Bond hopes to find Emile Locque (MICHAEL GOTHARD), the man he spied paying off Cuban hit man Hector Gonzales (STEFAN KALIPHA) for the murder of the Havelocks. Ferrara is later killed by Locque, who, to confuse Bond, leaves the white dove symbol of Milos Columbo (TOPOL) on the body.

FERZETTI, GABRIELE (1925–) (real name, Pasquale Ferzetti) Italian leading man who portrayed Marc Ange Draco, the head of the Union Corse crime syndicate, in *On Her Majesty's Secret Service*. He's also the father of Bond's (GEORGE LAZENBY) wife-to-be, Contessa Teresa "Tracy" de Vicenzo (DIANA RIGG). Well groomed and impeccably mannered, Ferzetti's Draco is probably one of the most sympathetic Mafia dons ever presented on-screen. His voice, however, was dubbed by actor David de Keyser. *See* DRACO, MARC ANGE.

FEYADOR, COLONEL Soviet Air Force base commander, portrayed by John Bowe, whose Afghanistan installation is overrun by Mujahedeen rebels in *The Living Daylights*.

FH-3 Identification number on the helicopter that guards Kananga's (YAPHET KOTTO) camouflaged poppy fields in *Live and Let Die*. It

eventually takes some potshots at Bond (ROGER MOORE) and Solitaire (JANE SEYMOUR).

$15 BILLION The amount of gold deposited in the Fort Knox gold repository (circa 1964), which becomes the target of Auric Goldfinger's (GERT FROBE) Operation Grand Slam.

15 MINUTES The amount of time that physical therapist Patricia Fearing (MOLLY PETERS) tells Bond (SEAN CONNERY) she will spend away from the motorized traction table he is strapped to in *Thunderball*. She leaves at 12:45 P.M., and the machine is immediately sabotaged by S.P.E.C.T.R.E. agent Count Lippe (GUY DOLEMAN). Fortunately, she returns in time to save Bond from the machine.

$15,000 The amount of money that Goldfinger (GERT FROBE) must lose to Mr. Simmons (AUSTIN WILLIS) in the rigged Miami Beach gin game in order for James Bond (SEAN CONNERY) *not* to call the Miami Beach police and turn him in for cheating.

15 YEARS The amount of time that Auric Goldfinger (GERT FROBE) has devoted to his planned assault—code named Operation Grand Slam—on Fort Knox.

50 The number of glass globes, containing a deadly nerve gas, that will be dropped into Earth's atmosphere from Drax's (MICHEL LONSDALE) space station, in *Moonraker*. Each globe is capable of killing 100 million people, but animal life will be spared. With the Earth's population eliminated, Drax plans to repopulate the planet with his own "master race."

50 CONTAINERS OF LOX Appearing on a naval-store order that Bond (SEAN CONNERY) steals from Mr. Osato's (TERU SHIMADA) Tokyo safe, this shipment refers to liquid oxygen—a rocket propellant—not to smoked salmon. The shipment is headed by freighter to Blofeld's (DONALD PLEASENCE) secret rocket base in *You Only Live Twice*.

$50.00 The dollar value in Miami of one of the seashells Honey Ryder (URSULA ANDRESS) finds on Crab Key in *Dr. No*. Also, the winning answer in the first James Bond Trivia Marathon in Los Angeles (1981).

$50 MILLION The advance given to arms dealer Brad Whitaker (JOE DON BAKER) by the KGB for a huge shipment of high-tech weapons in *The Living Daylights*. Instead of fulfilling, Whitaker and his partner, renegade Russian General Georgi Koskov (JEROEN KRABBE), convert the money into diamonds and plan a huge freelance drug deal with the Snow Leopard Brotherhood of Afghanistan.

Once they get their hands on the drugs, Koskov and Whitaker can make a huge profit and still have enough money to provide the Soviets with their arms. The diamonds-for-opium deal will take place as soon as the British Secret Service assassinates Russian General Leonid Pushkin (JOHN RHYS-DAVIES), who has canceled his country's high-tech arms order and demands an immediate refund of the money. *See* PUSHKIN, GENERAL LEONID.

58 DAYS The number of days it took to shoot *Dr. No* in 1962. It is also the exact number of days, owing to bad weather in Switzerland and a complicated script, that *On Her Majesty's Secret Service* went over schedule in 1969.

58 YEARS The amount of time the entire American gold reserve will stay radioactive if Goldfinger (GERT FROBE) successfully explodes an atomic device inside Fort Knox, Kentucky.

55 MINUTES The amount of time James Bond (ROGER MOORE) has to catch his plane flight from London to New Delhi in *Octopussy*.

53 The number of James Bond's (BARRY NELSON) Monte Carlo hotel suite in the TV film "Casino Royale." He hides a check for 87 million francs behind the brass number-plate on the door.

50,000 CARATS The weight of the huge diamond cache that James Bond (SEAN CONNERY) will smuggle from Amsterdam to Los Angeles in *Diamonds Are Forever*. Surprised when Tiffany Case (JILL ST. JOHN) mentions the size of the cache, Bond, posing as diamond smuggler Peter Franks, calculates that there are 142 carats to the ounce—what he terms "a lot of ice." That "ice" eventually falls into the hands of Ernst Stavro Blofeld (CHARLES GRAY), who will use it to power his laser satellite.

$50,000 Bond's (SEAN CONNERY) fee for smuggling 50,000 carats of diamonds from Amsterdam to Los Angeles in *Diamonds Are Forever*. Posing as diamond smuggler Peter Franks (JOE ROBINSON), he kills the real Franks, convinces fellow smuggler Tiffany Case (JILL ST. JOHN) that Franks is really James Bond, and then plants the diamonds on the body—actually, in the body along the alimentary canal.

Arriving in Los Angeles, he's whisked through customs, thanks to his friend Felix Leiter (NORMAN BURTON), and escorted to Las Vegas by henchmen from the diamond syndicate. There he begins a cat-and-mouse game with the smugglers, which eventually leads him to a rival ringleader—Ernst Stavro Blofeld of S.P.E.C.T.R.E. (CHARLES GRAY).

Also, $50,000 was actress Deborah Kerr's salary for one week's work on the *Casino Royale* spoof in 1967.

FILLET OF SOUL A chain of fictional U.S. restaurants that are used as distribution points for illegal narcotics in *Live and Let Die*. The Harlem and New Orleans franchises are featured in the film.

FINLAND Where a British agent is stabbed to death in a ladies' sauna in *Casino Royale*. It's one of many agent assassinations reported to Sir James Bond (DAVID NIVEN) by Hadley (DEREK NIMMO).

FINMERE, SCOTLAND Location in *You Only Live Twice* where Bond (SEAN CONNERY) manages to crash-land Helga Brandt's (KARIN DOR) Aero Commander private plane.

FIRST IN ORIENTAL LANGUAGES The reason why James Bond (SEAN CONNERY) doesn't need a Japanese phrase book in *You Only Live Twice*. His first-class honors degree came during studies at Cambridge, according to his brief conversation with Moneypenny (LOIS MAXWELL) aboard the British submarine.

FISHER, MR. James Bond's (SEAN CONNERY) alias when he visits Mr. Osato's (TERU SHIMADA) Tokyo headquarters in *You Only Live Twice*. Agent 007 is posing as the managing director of Empire Chemicals. According to Bond, Williamson, the previous manager, was killed when he fell into a pulverizer.

$5.00 A POINT The stakes for the rigged gin game between Mr. Simmons (AUSTIN WILLIS) and Goldfinger (GERT FROBE) that is being observed by James Bond (SEAN CONNERY). In an effort to recover the $10,000 he has already lost, Simmons has just doubled the bet from $2.50 a point to $5.00.

555-LOVE The call-in number for Reverend Joe Butcher's (WAYNE NEWTON) phony religious show in *Licence to Kill*. It's actually a front for a major international cocaine empire run by Franz Sanchez (ROBERT DAVI). Drug distributors in the United States call in their price guarantees on that line.

5:40 P.M. Quitting time on *Dr. No's* first day of shooting—January 16, 1962—at Kingston, Jamaica's Palisadoes Airport.

5:48 A.M. The time that M (BERNARD LEE) comes to visit James Bond (ROGER MOORE) at his London apartment in *Live and Let Die*.

545 BBB The New York license plate of the car CIA agent Charlie (JOLIE CHITWOOD) uses to collect James Bond (ROGER MOORE) at Kennedy International Airport in *Live and Let Die*. How does Bond know that it's the right car? It matches the claim tags on 007's luggage.

When Whisper (EARL JOLLY BROWN) murders Charlie with a dart from his side-view-mirror gun, Bond is left practically helpless in the backseat as the car goes out of control. Steering to save his life, 007 eventually drives the car over a curb and to a stop in midtown Manhattan.

500 FEET The British nuclear submarine *Ranger's* depth when it's swallowed by the *Lipa-*

rus supertanker in the teaser for *The Spy Who Loved Me*.

584 FEET Depth in the Ionian Sea, off the coast of Albania, at which James Bond (ROGER MOORE) and Melina Havelock (CAROLE BOUQUET)—traveling inside the two-man *Neptune* submarine—find the wreck of the British surveillance ship the *St. Georges* in *For Your Eyes Only*.

$500,000 What United Artists offered American producer Charles K. Feldman for the screen rights to *Casino Royale* in 1965. He refused and produced his spoof two years later.

500,000 FRANCS The bank when James Bond (BARRY NELSON) first approaches the baccarat table in the TV film "Casino Royale." Bond explains to interested onlooker and British agent Clarence Leiter (MICHAEL PATE) that 500,000 francs equals about $1,500, or 500 pounds (in 1954 equivalents). Bond waits until the bank reaches one million francs before he says "Banco" and matches the bank. He wins with a nine, versus the bank's "baccarat," or zero.

500,000 POUNDS The purchase price of the jeweled Fabergé egg in the Sotheby auction in *Octopussy*. The high bidder is sinister exiled Afghan Prince Kamal Khan (LOUIS JOURDAN), who expected to pay only 250,000 pounds. But thanks to 007 (ROGER MOORE), who raised the ante by entering the bidding himself, the price has been inflated beyond all reason. As Bond says to Secret Service art expert Jim Fanning (DOUGLAS WILMER), "He had to buy." *See* FABERGE EGGS.

$5 MILLION What Max Zorin (CHRISTOPHER WALKEN) is offering Stacey Sutton (TANYA ROBERTS) for her shares of Sutton Oil in *A View to a Kill*. Zorin stole the company from Stacey's father in a rigged proxy fight. Now he's offering the money to her on the condition that Stacey drops her lawsuit against him and keeps her mouth shut.

While a guest of Zorin at his horse sale in France, Bond (ROGER MOORE) peers into his office with trick sunglasses and observes Zorin writing out the $5 million check to Stacey. He later slips unseen into the room, finds Zorin's checkbook in the desk, and makes a copy of the check—#000131, dated May 3, 1985, and drawn on the Zorin International Bank. The transaction encourages Bond to go to San Francisco to investigate Stacey's association with Zorin. Stacey takes the check but eventually tears it up. She will not give in to Zorin's pressure tactics.

5 MINUTES, 10 SECONDS The amount of time set on Union Corse high explosives before Ernst Stavro Blofeld's (TELLY SAVALAS) Alpine hideaway is obliterated in *On Her Majesty's Secret Service.*

593 The numercial designation of the nuclear submarine U.S.S. *Wayne* in *The Spy Who Loved Me.*

5:00 P.M. According to what James Bond (SEAN CONNERY) tells Domino (KIM BASINGER) in the Jacuzzi at the conclusion of *Never Say Never Again,* it's 007's daily appointed hour for a martini.

$5.6 MILLION The production budget for *Thunderball* (1965).

5,000 POUNDS The value of the gold bar loaned to 007 (SEAN CONNERY) by the Bank of England, which becomes the prize in his high-stakes golf challenge match with Goldfinger (GERT FROBE).

5,000 YEARS The age of the underwater ruins being researched by Timothy Havelock (JACK HEDLEY) off the coast of Albania prior to his murder in *For Your Eyes Only.*

FLAME-THROWING FOUNTAIN PEN Gadget in the possession of M (JOHN HUSTON) when he comes to visit Sir James Bond (DAVID NIVEN) in *Casino Royale.*

FLEMING, IAN LANCASTER (London, May 28, 1908–August 12, 1964) Clever British author, newspaper columnist, travel writer, and ex-intelligence officer who invented the character of James Bond, Secret Agent 007.

Fleming's novels and short stories were fairy tales for adults—fantastic globe-trotting adventures about a British Secret Service agent with a license to kill. Loaded with sexual innuendo, sadomasochistic violence, and edge-of-your-seat suspense, they captured the imagination of thrill-seeking readers around the world.

President John F. Kennedy was a big Fleming fan, as was author Raymond Chandler, who encouraged Fleming to continue his writing career even though his first books were not big sellers. Fleming based many of his novels on his experiences as a naval intelligence officer during World War II. It wasn't until 1975, though, that Fleming was identified as a close associate of British spymaster Sir William Stevenson, whose Ultra Network had broken the German diplomatic code in 1939. With Ultra, Fleming was involved in some of the greatest espionage capers in military history.

In 1944, during a wartime trip to Jamaica, Fleming decided that he would make the island his postwar retreat. Before returning to London, he asked his good friend American millionaire Ivar Bryce to purchase some Jamaican beach property for him. Goldeneye was born that year when Bryce purchased a beachfront parcel near the deserted donkey track at Oracabessa, a fruit-trading center on Jamaica's beautiful north shore.

Two years later, Fleming was hired by newspaper magnate Lord Kemsley to manage the foreign news section of a large group of English papers. He took the job on the condition that his contract include a two-month vacation each year. With his little beach house completed, Fleming began a routine that was to continue for the rest of his life and that produced all of the James Bond thrillers.

For nearly six years, he toyed with the idea of writing. He even completed a few local color articles for *Horizon* magazine, but it was not until a few weeks before his 1952 marriage to Lady Anne Rothermere that Ian Fleming decided to write a novel in the tropics. He took the name of his main character from the author of a book that graced his coffee table—*Birds of the West Indies* by American ornithologist James Bond. Within six weeks, *Casino Royale* was completed, and Fleming was off to find a suitable publisher.

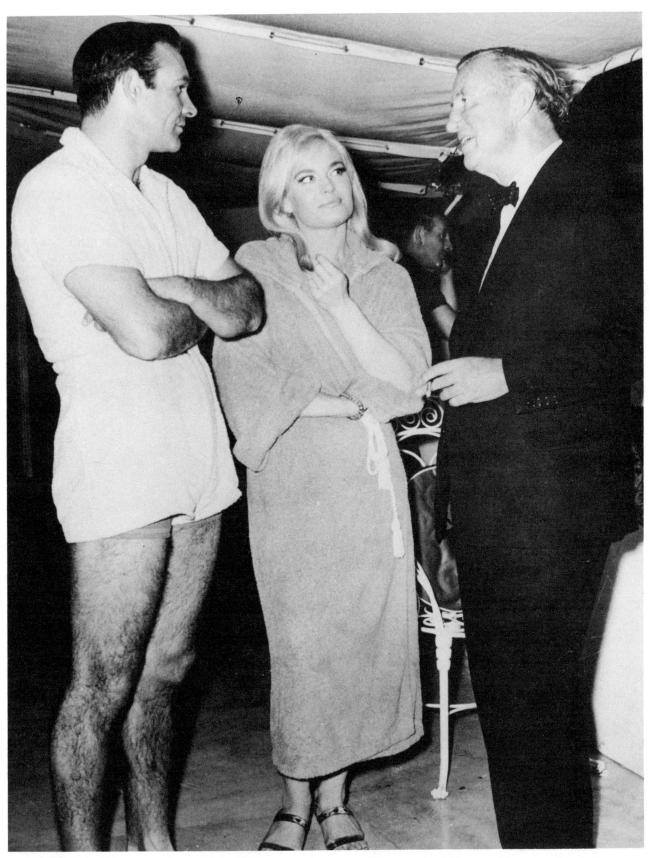

Shortly before his death in August 1964, author Ian Fleming visited the set of *Goldfinger* and conversed with Sean Connery and Shirley Eaton. (Rex Features Ltd./RDR Productions)

Ian Fleming visits the Istanbul location of *From Russia with Love.* (Wide World Photos)

The exterior of *Goldeneye*, Ian Fleming's Jamaican retreat. (Richard Schenkman)

Inside Goldeneye today. Note the addition of appropriate poster art. (Richard Schenkman)

The desk in Ian Fleming's bedroom at Goldeneye where he wrote many of his James Bond novels. (Richard Schenkman)

He approached venerable old Jonathan Cape, who had published several of his brother Peter's travel books. Cape accepted the manuscript on the recommendation of several people, including Fleming's good friend William Plomer, and scheduled the book for publication in England in the spring of 1953.

Between 1952 and his death in 1964, Fleming wrote twelve 007 novels and two collections of short stories. In order of their publication dates, they are: *Casino Royale* (1953), *Live and Let Die* (1954), *Moonraker* (1955), *Diamonds Are Forever* (1956), *From Russia with Love* (1957), *Dr. No* (1958), *Goldfinger* (1959), *For Your Eyes Only* (1960, short stories), *Thunderball* (1961, based on a screen treatment by Fleming, Kevin McClory, and Jack Whittingham), *The Spy Who Loved Me* (1962), *On*

Her Majesty's Secret Service (1963), *You Only Live Twice* (1964), *The Man with the Golden Gun* (1965) and *Octopussy/The Living Daylights* (1966, short stories).

In 1961 producers Albert R. Broccoli and Harry Saltzman acquired film rights to all of Fleming's novels, except for *Casino Royale*, which had been sold to Gregory Ratoff in 1956 (Ratoff later sold the rights to Charles K. Feldman, who produced a 007 spoof in 1967), and *Thunderball*, whose film rights were won by producer Kevin McClory in a copyright infringement suit (McClory joined forces with Broccoli and Saltzman to produce *Thunderball* in 1965). Fleming's James Bond character continued in literature after his death, first in *Colonel Sun* by Kingsley Amis (1968) and then in a series of books authorized by the Fleming estate and written by John Gardner, beginning with *License Renewed* (1981).

FLEX, JENNY One of Max Zorin's (CHRISTOPHER WALKEN) beautiful but dangerous assistants in *A View to a Kill*, portrayed by Alison Doody (*Indiana Jones and the Last Crusade*). Bond (ROGER MOORE) meets her when she escorts him to his suite at Zorin's sumptuous French chateau. She's later double-crossed and left to die, along with May Day (GRACE JONES) and her fellow assistant Pan Ho (PAPILLON SOO SOO), when Zorin floods the Main Strike silver mine.

FLIGHT 759 Flight number of the NATO bomber hijacked by S.P.E.C.T.R.E. in *Thunderball*.

FLOATING PALACE, THE Nickname for Octopussy's (MAUD ADAMS) lavish island home. Surrounded by watery gardens, streams, bathing ponds, and pools, it appears to be floating on the lake. In actuality, the floating palace is an island in the middle of Udaipur's Lake Pichola. Unfortunately, Octopussy's defenses are bereft of serious walls or barricades. Thus, a group of tough muggers from downtown Udaipur can gain entrance with little trouble.

FLOOD, JOE American actor who portrayed the unfortunate San Francisco Police Department captain who has to chase James Bond's (ROGER MOORE) hook-and-ladder truck in *A*

View to a Kill. Like his cousins in Las Vegas who had a similiar chore in *Diamonds Are Forever*, all he ends up with is a squadron of wrecked police cruisers.

FLOWER GIRL IN CORTINA Beautiful northern Italian shopkeeper portrayed by American actress and *Playboy* magazine playmate Robyn Young, in *For Your Eyes Only*. Her brief scene occurs when James Bond (ROGER MOORE) defeats a team of enemy motorcyclists, one of whom goes flying through the window of the flower shop.

FLYING PLACIOS, THE The high-wire act that is performing above the Circus Circus Casino when Tiffany Case (JILL ST. JOHN) arrives for her rendezvous with 007 (SEAN CONNERY) in *Diamonds Are Forever*.

FLYING ROULETTE WHEEL Monte Carlo casino game that becomes airborne in *Casino Royale*, expelling laughing gas as it goes.

FLYING SAUCER The name of Maximillian Largo's (KLAUS MARIA BRANDAUER) fabulous yacht in *Never Say Never Again*. In Italian, flying saucer translates to *disco volante*—the name Ian Fleming, Kevin McClory, and Jack Whittingham gave to the yacht in the original novel, *Thunderball*. For *Never*, producer Jack Schwartzman received permission to film aboard Arabian billionaire Adnan Khashoggi's yacht, the *Nabila*. Nearly 300 feet long, the *Nabila* had a helicopter pad and 11 guest suites, many of which had gold bathroom fittings. *See* NABILA.

FONTAINEBLEAU The famous Miami Beach hotel that served as a key location at the beginning of *Goldfinger*. It is first seen from an aerial view as a plane tows a promotional banner proclaiming "Welcome to Miami Beach."

James Bond (SEAN CONNERY) thinks he's been booked into "the finest hotel in Miami Beach" as a holiday gift from M (BERNARD LEE). In actuality, he's been ordered to observe the suspicious activities of Auric Goldfinger (GERT FROBE). Bond's orders are delivered via CIA agent Felix Leiter (CEC LINDER), who makes his film introduction while walking through the hotel's famous ice rink and pool area. There he finds 007 getting a massage from Dink (MARGARET NOLAN), a fabulously proportioned blond.

Leiter briefs Bond on his mission and then points to a spot near the Fontainebleau pool where Goldfinger is cheating a Mr. Simmons (AUSTIN WILLIS) at gin. Equipped with a radio transmitter disguised as a hearing aid, Goldfinger is being aided by his Girl Friday, Jill Masterson (SHIRLEY EATON), who, while looking out a window of Goldfinger's hotel suite, spies on Simmons's hand with a pair of binoculars. Masterson is discovered by Bond, who orders Goldfinger to start losing or else he'll be turned over to the Miami Beach police. Helpless to defend himself, lest he give himself away, Goldfinger then proceeds to lose back $15,000 to Mr. Simmons.

Cec Linder told a funny story about filming at the Fontainebleau Hotel pool in 1964. Said Linder, the scene in which Felix Leiter strolls past the pool in search of Bond called for a background of voluptuous bathing beauties in bikinis. However, this is not the usual clientele at the Fontainebleau pool. On an average day, the pool instead is populated by a huge crowd of older, silver-haired ladies and their card-playing husbands. Because of hotel restrictions, the film crew could not prevent the vacationers from relaxing by the pool, so the production company had to do some quick thinking to get their second-unit shots. What they decided to do was pure subterfuge.

At the pool that morning, it was an-nounced that at five o'clock in the afternoon, the crew would be shooting the pool area and that since the vacationers were going to be on camera, it would be a good idea for the women to go out and have their hair done. No sooner did all the older ladies leave the area than the crew brought in their voluptuous extras and shot Linder's walk-by. When the older ladies returned at 4:30 P.M., the crew shot the pool area a second time—but there wasn't any film in the camera. M couldn't have planned a more successful mission. See LINDER, CEC; MASTERSON, JILL.

FOOL, THE A tarot card selected by James Bond (ROGER MOORE) from Solitaire's (JANE SEYMOUR) deck in *Live and Let Die*. After the selection, she replies, "You've found yourself."

FORD II, HENRY Grandson of the world-famous auto manufacturer and a friend of director Terence Young. He played an extra during the Nassau casino sequence in *Thunderball*. His fee: $35.00 for the day.

FORD RANCHERO A light blue 1964 model was driven by Oddjob (HAROLD SAKATA) in *Goldfinger*. In the truck's bed, he transports the remains of a 1964 Lincoln Continental that has been crushed into a neat pile of metal by a compactor in a Kentucky auto wrecking yard.

Oddjob (HAROLD SAKATA) drove a 1964 Ranchero in *Goldfinger*. It carried the crushed remains of a Continental and Mr. Solo (MARTIN BENSON). (Ford Motor Company)

FORD TAUNUS The car, carrying Jaws (RICHARD KIEL) and a group of Stromberg's (CURT JURGENS) thugs, that chases Bond (ROGER MOORE) and Anya (BARBARA BACH) on a Sardinian highway in *The Spy Who Loved Me.* Using the Lotus Esprit's defense mechanisms, Bond lowers a back panel and sprays the windshield of the Taunus with a cement mixture that blinds the driver and forces the car over a cliff and into the roof of a peasant's house. *Note:* One of the thugs is British stuntman George Leech, who can be seen firing at Bond while hanging out of the Taunus's window.

FORDISE (or Four Dice) Q's (GEOFFREY BAYLDON) workshop assistant, portrayed by John Wells, in *Casino Royale.* He's assigned to prepare Evelyn Tremble (PETER SELLERS) for his Monte Carlo baccarat assignment as James Bond, Secret Agent 007. Tremble is thus outfitted with the latest in waistcoats, complete with one outlandish gadget after another. It's a good thing that airport security booths were not standard in 1967.

FORNOF, J. W. "CORKEY" (New Orleans, Louisiana, December 5, 1945–) Aerial stunt coordinator, pilot, engineer, and inventor who flew his Acrostar BD-5 mini-jet in *Octopussy* and then took over aerial action chores on *Licence to Kill.* On the latter film, Fornof coordinated Bond's (TIMOTHY DALTON) capture of Sanchez's (ROBERT DAVI) getaway plane, 007's water-skiing stunt behind the seaplane, and Pam Bouvier's (CAREY LOWELL) crop-duster high jinks. Fornof was originally hired to fly twin mini-jets in *Moonraker,* but the stunt sequence was canceled when the riverbed feeding Brazil's Angel Falls went dry. *See* ACROSTAR MINI-JET.

FORT KNOX, KENTUCKY A U.S. Army base protecting the gold repository of the United States, where, in 1964, $15 billion in gold bullion was stored. It is named after General Henry Knox, America's first Secretary of War.

In *Goldfinger,* the title character's plan is to detonate a small atomic bomb—supplied by the Red Chinese—in the repository, thereby effec-

The exterior of Fort Knox, built full size on the Pinewood Studios backlot for *Goldfinger.* (Ronnie Udell Collection)

The interior of Ken Adam's dazzling Fort Knox set. (Gert Frobe, Harold Sakata, and Sean Connery can be seen on the fourth floor at the vault door entrance. (Ronnie Udell Collection)

Goldfinger's enormously detailed map of Fort Knox and the surrounding countryside. The railroad line was a part of the original heist as depicted in Ian Fleming's novel. (Ronnie Udell Collection)

The golden arena of Fort Knox where James Bond (SEAN CONNERY) and Oddjob (HAROLD SAKATA) have a scheduled bout in *Goldfinger*. (Ronnie Udell Collection)

Goldfinger's heavy gold vault door was used in both interior and exterior sequences. (Ronnie Udell Collection)

tively eliminating the entire U.S. gold reserve for 58 years. Resultant economic chaos in the West will please the Chinese, and the value of Goldfinger's smuggled horde will increase tenfold.

Although director Guy Hamilton's film crew was allowed to film on the base, where his cameras caught the actions of hundreds of U.S. soldiers as they fell "unconscious," the crew was forbidden to film inside or near the U.S. gold repository. With the building and its vaults a key set in the film, production designer Ken Adam was asked to re-create the full-size exterior of the repository on the back lot at England's Pinewood Studios. It was built complete with a huge concrete driveway and iron fencing. Its interior was constructed inside a soundstage, where Adam stacked gold four stories high.

"The very nature of a gold repository is very dull," explained Adam. "You can't stack gold very high because of weight problems and questions of transportation. The ingots need to be stored in small chambers situated along narrow tunnels. And there's simply no drama in a series of little rooms.

"In my case, I stacked gold bars 40 feet high under a gigantic roof. I had a whole crew of men polishing the metalwork so that it would shine when we turned the lights on. And it was the perfect place to stage the final battle between Bond (SEAN CONNERY) and Oddjob (HAROLD SAKATA). It was like a golden arena, and Bond was able to use gold bars as weapons."

Film editor Peter Hunt, who marveled at Adam's creations, remembered the day the two of them were told they couldn't visit the interior of the real Fort Knox. "I told this nice American liaison from the Treasury Department that it was ridiculous not to let us take a look at the vault area," said Hunt. "After all, what were they afraid of, anyway? And he told me, 'Don't you understand, you all think that there is a lot of gold in there, but in actuality there is nothing in there at all. We can't let you know that.' Whether he was telling the truth or not, both Ken and I thought that would have been a great ending for the film. Goldfinger breaks into the world's largest bank and finds nothing."

44 The amount of points lost by Mr. Simmons (AUSTIN WILLIS) to a cheating Auric Goldfinger (GERT FROBE) in the first gin game of the day at the Fontainebleau Hotel in Miami Beach.

45 MINUTES, 30 SECONDS The amount of time left before the NATO bomber in *Thunderball* is scheduled to return to base. At this point, S.P.E.C.T.R.E. mercenary Angelo Palazzi (PAUL STASSINO), posing as NATO aerial observer François Derval, is asked to switch places with the copilot.

45,000 FEET Cruising altitude of the doomed NATO jet bomber in *Thunderball*. Hijacked by S.P.E.C.T.R.E. mercenary Angelo Palazzi (PAUL STASSINO), it will drop below radar and land in the Caribbean's Golden Grotto.

41,000 The number of U.S. Army troops guarding the gold repository (circa 1964) at Fort Knox, Kentucky, in *Goldfinger*. One of the gangsters who attends Goldfinger's (GERT FROBE) "hoods convention" mistakenly guesses 35,000.

FOR YOUR EYES ONLY (United Artists, 1981) ★ ★ ★ ½ The twelfth James Bond film, produced by Albert R. Broccoli. U.S. release date: June 26, 1981. U.S. film rentals: $27 million. Running time: 127 minutes.

Having followed the *Goldfinger* formula for so many years, and with *Moonraker* a spectacular hit, Broccoli reeled in the fantasy in his twelfth outing and returned to the serious spying that was once a hallmark of *From Russia with Love*. Richard Maibaum returned to write the screenplay—this time in collaboration with Michael G. Wilson—and John Glen, an editor and second-unit director, was given the directing reins. The result is another high point in the series—a fascinating spy adventure with plenty of mysterious characters, plot twists, romance, and the perfect Bond heroine in Melina Havelock.

The movie begins on a sour note with one of the series' most underwhelming teasers, capped by a bit of inane dialogue that was probably left over from *Moonraker*. But once Maurice Binder's dazzling titles fade, this film is off to a running start—first with the sinking of a camouflaged British spy ship, and then with the horrifying assassination of Melina's parents in Corfu Harbor. Intertwined in the plot to recover a top secret submarine attack-communicator is Bond's involvement in a cold-blooded feud between two Greek ex-partisans—Kristatos and Columbo.

There are no fantasy elements in *For Your Eyes Only*. Kristatos and Columbo are flesh-and-blood human beings who have very real reasons for hating one another. Hate and revenge—two very real human emotions—play important parts in the film. Melina is determined to avenge her parents at all costs. She's Greek, and she takes her logic from the legend of Electra, who avenged her loved ones.

Replacing the shuttle assault on Drax's space station in *Moonraker* is *For Your Eyes Only*'s pièce de résistance—a very real climb up the Meteora in Greece, where the evil Kristatos has sequestered himself in an old monastery. And assisting in that climb was stuntman Rick Sylvester, who had once skied off the Asgard Peak in the teaser for *The Spy Who Loved Me*.

High points: Carole Bouquet's meaty Melina Havelock, Julian Glover's Kristatos, and Topol's Columbo; the Meteora Climb; the underwater search for the *St. Georges* surveillance ship; the teaser's solemn beginning, which takes place in the cemetery—where Bond places flowers on Tracy's grave; and the comical ending of the film, which has Margaret Thatcher on the phone with Max, the parrot.

The monastery of Greece's Meteora—a key location in *For Your Eyes Only*. (Rick Sylvester)

FOR YOUR EYES ONLY CAST

James Bond	Roger Moore
Melina Havelock	Carole Bouquet
Milos Columbo	Topol
Bibi	Lynn-Holly Johnson
Aris Kristatos	Julian Glover
Countess Lisl	Cassandra Harris
Jacoba Brink	Jill Bennett
Emile Leopold Locque	Michael Gothard
Eric Kriegler	John Wyman
Timothy Havelock	Jack Hedley
Miss Moneypenny	Lois Maxwell
Q	Desmond Llewelyn
Minister of Defense	Geoffrey Keen
General Gogol	Walter Gotell
Tanner	James Villiers
Ferrara	John Moreno
Claus	Charles Dance
Karageorge	Paul Angelis
Iona Havelock	Toby Robins
Apostis	Jack Klaff
Santos	Alkis Kritikos
Nikos	Stag Theodore
Hector Gonzales	Stefan Kalipha
First Sea Lord	Graham Crowden
Vice Admiral	Noel Johnson
McGregor	William Hoyland
Bunky	Paul Brooke
Rublevitch	Eva Rueber-Staier
Vicar	Fred Bryant
Girl in Flower Shop	Robyn Young
Mantis Man	Graham Hawkes
Denis	John Wells
The Prime Minister	Janet Brown

Girl at Casino ....Max Vesterhalt
Gonzales's Pool Girls ..Lalla Dean, Evelyn Drogue, Laoura Hadzivageli, Koko, Chai Lee, Kim Mills, Tula, Vanya, Viva, Lizzie Warville, Alison Worth

FOR YOUR EYES ONLY CREW

Producer ....Albert R. Broccoli
Director ....John Glen
Screenplay by ....Richard Maibaum, Michael G. Wilson
Executive Producer ....Michael G. Wilson
Music by ....Bill Conti
Title Song Performed by ....Sheena Easton
Lyrics by ....Michael Leeson
Production Designer ....Peter Lamont
Associate Producer ....Tom Pevsner
Main Title Designed by ....Maurice Binder
Director of Photography ....Alan Hume
Editor.......................John Grover
Special Effects Supervisor ....Derek Meddings
Production Supervisor ....Bob Simmonds
Production Managers ...Mara Blasetti, Phil Kohler, Aspa Lambrou
Production Controller ......Reginald A. Barkshire
Production Accountant...........Douglas Noakes
Director of Publicity ....Charles Juroe
Assistant Director ....Anthony Waye
Camera Operator....................Alec Mills
Visual Effects Photography ....Paul Wilson
Continuity....................Elaine Schreyeck
Sound Mixer ....Derek Ball
Art Director ....John Fenner
Set Decorator ....Vernon Dixon
Action Sequences Arranged by......Bob Simmons
Driving Stunts Arranged by ....Remy Julienne
Second-Unit Direction and Photography ...Arthur Wooster
Underwater Photography ....Al Giddings
Ski Photography ....Willy Bogner, Jr.
Aerial Photography.................James Devis
Unit and Location Managers Vincent Winter, Peter Bennett, Michaelis Lambrinos, Redmond Morris, Umberto Sambuco
Second-Unit Assistant Director.....Gerry Gavigan
Second-Unit Continuity........Phyllis Townshend
Second Assistant Directors ....Terry Madden, Michael Zimbrich, Gareth Tandy, Tony Broccoli
London Contact ....Van Jones
Production Assistants ....Iris Rose, Sally Ball
Executive Producer's Secretary .....Johanna Brown
Casting by ..Maude Spector, Deborah McWilliams
Costume Designer ....Elizabeth Waller

Wardrobe Master..................Tiny Nicholls
Miss Bouquet's Wardrobe by ...Raemonde Rahvis, London
Ski Suits by ....Bogner
Additional Art Directors ..Michael Lamont, Mikes Karapiperis, Franco Fumagalli
Assistant Art Director ....Ernie Archer
Illustrator ....Dennis Rich
Scenic Artist ....Ernest Smith
Second-Unit Camera Operators ..Jack Lowin, John Morgan, Dewi Humphreys, Robert Kindred
Boom Operator ....Ken Nightingall
Makeup.............George Frost, Eric Allwright
Hairdressers ....Stephanie Kaye, Marsha Lewis
Special Effects......................John Evans
Stills.....................Keith Hampshire
Unit Publicist ....Brian Doyle
Construction Manager..........Michael Redding
Electrical Supervisor ....John Tythe
Camera Grip......................Chunky Huse
Property Master ....Brian Humphrey
Additional Editor ....Eric Boyd-Perkins
Assembly Editors ....Peter Davies, Derek Trigg
Dubbing Editors ..Colin Miller, Bill Trent, Vernon Messenger
Music Mixer......................John Richards
Rerecording Mixers..........Gordon McCallum, Ken Barker
Sound Effects ....Jean-Pierre Lelong
Marine Advisers ...David Halsey, Barry Goldsmith
Skating Scenes Staged by ....Brian Foley
Greek Wedding Scene ..The Bouas-Danilia Village, Corfu
Optical Effects............Michel François Films
Stunt Team ...Martin Grace, Pat Banta, Cyd Child, Jo Cote, John Eaves, Hans Hechenbichler, Michel Julienne, Wolfgang Junginger, George Leech, Wendy Leech, Gavin McKinney, Gareth Milne, Bernard Pascual, Frances Young
Aerial Team ......Marc Wolff, Albert Werry, John Crewdson, Andrew Von Preussen, Robin Browne, Czeslav Dyzma, Nigel Brendish
Ski Team ....Gerhard Fromm, Peter Rohe, George Ostler, Gerhard Huber, Christian Troschke, Wolfgang Kleinwaechter, Michael Ratajczak, Sabine Boueke, Victor Tourjansky, Verena Baldeo, Giovanni Debona
Underwater Team .....Ken Court, Walter Clayton, Charles Nicklin, Steve Bowerman, Arlette Greenfield, Randolph Johnson, Terry Kerby, Doug Laughlin, Jack Monestier, Richard Mula, Pete Romano, Moby Griffin, John Bremer
Climbing Team.................Rick Sylvester,

Herbert Raditschnig, Chester Brown, Bill Fox
Production Company . . . . Eon Productions
Distribution Company . . . . United Artists

FOR YOUR EYES ONLY COMPETITION

Competitive films in release when *For Your Eyes Only* opened in the United States on June 26, 1981:

Raiders of the Lost Ark

Superman II

The Great Muppet Caper

The Cannonball Run

Dragonslayer

Clash of the Titans

Outland

Nice Dreams

Stripes

History of the World—Part I

4 James Bond's (GEORGE LAZENBY) room mumber at Blofeld's (TELLY SAVALAS) allergy clinic in *On Her Majesty's Secret Service*. Bond is masquerading as London College of Arms heraldry expert Sir Hilary Bray. Although the room can be opened only from the outside, 007 short-circuits the electronic entry grid with a metal strip pulled from his ruler and shielded by the broken halves of a rubber eraser.

FOUR HOURS The amount of time Kamal Khan (LOUIS JOURDAN) and his bodyguard, Gobinda (KABIR BEDI), give themselves to reach safety when they preset the detonation time on the A-bomb, in *Octopussy*. Hidden in the base of a circus cannon, the bomb is timed to explode on a U.S. Air Force base in West Germany, where the Octopussy Circus is performing. Fortunately, Bond (ROGER MOORE) was present when they activated the bomb, and he manages to arrive in the nick of time to deactivate it.

482 POUNDS, 15 SHILLINGS, 9 PENCE Mata Bond's (JOANNA PETTET) cab fare from London to West Berlin in *Casino Royale*. Her irate cabdriver is actually Carlton Towers (BERNARD CRIBBENS) of the foreign service, who's sent to West Germany to keep an eye on Mata.

456 AND 457 The identification numbers on the two atomic bombs aboard a NATO jet bomber hijacked by S.P.E.C.T.R.E. in *Thunderball*. The bombs are MOS-type, with fuses in the white security box.

453 DEGREES BELOW ZERO FAHRENHEIT The temperature of the liquid helium in Francisco Scaramanga's (CHRISTOPHER LEE) solar energy plant in *The Man with the Golden Gun*. According to Scaramanga, absolute zero must be maintained in order to prevent what he refers to as "prompt criticality"—in other words, a major catastrophe. (Absolute zero is 459.69 degrees below zero Fahrenheit, or 273.16 degrees below zero centigrade). Mary Goodnight (BRITT EKLAND) knocks out Kron, the only security man in the plant, and dumps him into one of the solar vats. His body immediately begins to raise the temperature of the system, causing a dangerous overload that eventually triggers explosions that obliterate the entire plant.

410 MEGACYCLES The auto-gyro's, Little Nellie, radio frequency in *You Only Live Twice*.

439 According to Q (DESMOND LLEWELYN), in *For Your Eyes Only*, this is the number for St. Cyril's that's listed in the Greek geography book. Columbo (TOPOL), however, remembers the correct St. Cyril's—a monastery/hideaway that he and Kristatos (JULIAN GLOVER) once used during their days with the Greek resistance during World War II.

400 TINY TIME PILLS Ingredients of the deadly A-bomb tablet invented by Dr. Noah (WOODY ALLEN) in *Casino Royale*. It's designed to turn a human being into, literally, a walking atomic device. As each tiny time pill explodes within the body, it triggers a chain reaction that eventually leads to a full-scale nuclear explosion. *See* NOAH, DR.

FOUR MINUTES The amount of time on the counter when Mr. Ling (BURT KWOUK) activates the atomic device that's set to explode inside Fort Knox, in *Goldfinger*. The timer later stops at 007, even though Bond (SEAN CONNERY) quips, "Three more ticks and Mr. Goldfinger would've hit the jackpot" (*See* "THREE MORE TICKS. . . ."). It's also the amount of time that Bond (ROGER MOORE) has left to stop World War III when he enters the shattered command center of the *Liparus* supertanker in *The Spy Who Loved Me*.

During Bond's rush to change the trajectory of the soon-to-be-launched nuclear missiles, a technical blooper occurs in the dialogue regarding the time remaining. Only ten seconds after the *Liparus*'s skipper (SYDNEY TAFLER) says four minutes remain until the launch, Commander Carter (SHANE RIMMER) says only three minutes are left.

4132 KX License plate on the explosive-laden, remote control Wright's Dairies milk truck that chases Sir James Bond (DAVID NIVEN) in *Casino Royale*.

$4.9 MILLION The amount of drug loot stolen by James Bond (TIMOTHY DALTON) from one of drug runner Franz Sanchez's (ROBERT DAVI) seaplanes in *Licence to Kill*. The cash had just been loaded onto the plane by Sanchez's local U.S. distributor Milton Krest (ANTHONY ZERBE), whose underwater shipment of cocaine was also sabotaged by Bond.

To make matters worse, Bond later hides the money in the decompression chamber on Krest's *Wavekrest* research vessel, where it is discovered by Sanchez. Convinced that Krest is plotting against him, Sanchez throws him in the decompression chamber, where he super-inflates and explodes.

4.2 MILLIMETER The unusual caliber of Francisco Scaramanga's (CHRISTOPHER LEE) automatic pistol in *The Man with the Golden Gun*. Its bullets are custom manufactured by a Macao gunsmith named Lazar (MARNE MAITLAND).

FOUR POUNDS The amount of weight that James Bond (SEAN CONNERY) actually loses at the Shrublands health clinic in *Never Say Never Again*. Whether it's from a low-fat diet or from being chased around the lower level by the terrifying Lippe (PAT ROACH), no one can say.

14TH The day that Tanya (DANIELA BIANCHI) thinks Bond (SEAN CONNERY) is going to launch his raid on the Russian embassy in Istanbul in order to steal the Lektor decoding machine in *From Russia with Love*. Mistrusting this sexy defector, 007 actually attacks on the 13th instead.

14 The date where Bond's (GEORGE LAZENBY) thrown knife sticks in *On Her Majesty's Secret Service*. "But today is the 13th," Draco reminds him. Bond replies, "I'm superstitious." Another of screenwriter Richard Maibaum's references to moments from the previous Bond films, this one from *From Russia with Love*.

422 FLEMING ST. Address of the *Licence to Kill* production office during shooting in Key West, Florida, in July and August 1988.

423 Tracy's (DIANA RIGG) suite number at the Portuguese hotel/casino in *On Her Majesty's Secret Service*. Bond (GEORGE LAZENBY) awakens the following morning with Tracy gone and her account paid in full, thanks to two 10,000-franc chips she leaves for him.

FOX, EDWARD (London, April 13, 1937–) British actor who portrayed Bond's

Never Say Never Again's Edward Fox became the fourth actor to portray M, following Bernard Lee, John Huston, and Robert Brown. (Taliafilm)

(SEAN CONNERY) superior, M, as a hot-tempered, contemptuous bureaucrat in *Never Say Never Again*. The performance was a striking contrast to that of the actor who played Sean Connery's last superior—the fatherly Bernard Lee. But *Never Say Never Again* doesn't hesitate to portray the British Secret Service in a more contemporary era of tighter operational constraints and squeezed budgets. In the 1980s, in the eyes of the new M and, perhaps, the government, the 00 section has become more of an embarrassment than an asset. Once again, it's up to James Bond (SEAN CONNERY) to prove them wrong.

FRANCE The country chosen by Largo (KLAUS MARIA BRANDAUER) to demonstrate the Domination video game to James Bond (SEAN CONNERY) in *Never Say Never Again*. During this game Bond learns that the machine will give the losing player a powerful electrical shock. *See* DOMINATION.

FRANCISCO THE FEARLESS Circus daredevil, portrayed by veteran Bond stuntman Richard "Dicky" Graydon, who flies out of a cannon in *Octopussy*. It is within the base of this artillery that General Orlov (STEVEN BERKOFF) and Kamal Khan (LOUIS JOURDAN) have placed an atomic device that will be exploded on a U.S. Air Force base in West Germany. As the timer on the bomb counts down, Francisco and his cannon are rolled into the circus big top. However, his entrance is upstaged by James Bond's (ROGER MOORE). As the crowd watches, Bond disarms the A-bomb, after which Francisco looks out from the cannon's barrel and says, impatiently, "Now?"— one of the film's best laughs.

FRANCO James Bond's (ROGER MOORE) Venice gondolier in *Moonraker* who's knifed by one of Drax's hoodlums (CLAUDE CARLIEZ) during the canal chase.

FRANKS, PETER Tough British diamond smuggler, portrayed by actor/stuntman Joe Robinson in *Diamonds Are Forever*. Franks is an international courier for a diamond-smuggling syndicate that is rapidly being decimated by Ernst Stavro Blofeld (CHARLES GRAY). Cap-

tured by the British Secret Service on his way to Amsterdam for a pickup, Franks is replaced in the pipeline by James Bond (SEAN CONNERY), who assumes Franks's identity. He receives his credentials from Miss Moneypenny (LOIS MAXWELL) at the channel crossing.

Bond also benefits from a fantastic invention of Q—phony fingerprints that convince Tiffany Case (JILL ST. JOHN) that he's the genuine Franks. Unfortunately, Franks escapes from the British and arrives at Case's Amsterdam apartment, where he is killed by Bond in a vicious elevator fight. Switching billfolds with the dead man, 007 hands the wallet to Tiffany, who discovers James Bond's Playboy Club membership. As far as Tiffany is concerned, he's just killed James Bond.

FRAZIER Hugo Drax's (MICHEL LONSDALE) California chauffeur in *Moonraker*.

FRAZIER, PROFESSOR British solar energy expert in the Far East, portrayed by Gerald James in *The Man with the Golden Gun*.

FREE RADICALS A medical term, quoted by M (EDWARD FOX) in *Never Say Never Again*, referring to harmful toxins that can destroy the body and the brain. In Bond's (SEAN CONNERY) case, they're caused by too much red meat, white bread, and dry martinis. It is M's hope that a lengthy stay at the Shrublands health clinic will "purge" 007's body of any and all free radicals.

FRENCH JOCKEY CLUB Equestrian organization mentioned in *A View to a Kill*. Concerned that billionaire French industrialist Max Zorin (CHRISTOPHER WALKEN) may be involved in horse fixing, the club hires detective Aubergine (JEAN ROUGERIE) to look into the case.

FRIENDSHIP AIRPORT, BALTIMORE Destination of Goldfinger's (GERT FROBE) private jet, which leaves Switzerland with a tranquilized James Bond (SEAN CONNERY) on board. Having entered the States, the Lockheed Jetstar, piloted by Pussy Galore (HONOR BLACKMAN), will then travel to its final destination—Blue Grass Field, Kentucky.

FROBE, GERT (Zwickau, Saxony, Germany, February 25, 1913–September 4, 1988) (real name, Karl-Gerhard Frobe) Rotund German character actor who portrayed the title character in *Goldfinger*—the best villain in the entire series. Although his voice was later completely dubbed, Frobe's mannerisms were perfectly suited to the fabulously wealthy megalomaniac who is intent on exploding an atomic device inside Fort Knox, Kentucky—home of America's gold reserves.

Israel banned the release of *Goldfinger* in 1964 when it was discovered that Frobe had been a member of the Nazi party during World War II. However, after the ban, a Jewish man named Mario Blumenau came forward and told the world that Frobe had saved his and his mother's lives by hiding them during the war. The ban was lifted after Frobe also proved he had not been active in the party. *See* GOLDFINGER, AURIC.

FROLICH, HUBERT Swiss production liaison on *On Her Majesty's Secret Service* who, in the bar of the St. Moritz Hotel on a Sunday afternoon in December 1967, suggested that the production crew take a look at the new revolving restaurant being built atop the Schilthorn Mountain near Murren. Piz Gloria, as it was called, would become the stronghold of Ernst Stavro Blofeld (TELLY SAVALAS).

FROM A VIEW TO A KILL Original title of *A View to a Kill*. The change was made in May 1984, three months before shooting began.

FROM RUSSIA WITH LOVE (United Artists, 1963) ★ ★ ★ ★ The second James Bond film produced by Albert R. Broccoli and Harry Saltzman. U.S. opening: May 27, 1964. Budget: $2.2 million. U.S. box-office rentals: $9.9 million. Running time: 118 minutes.

A classic adventure film, *From Russia with Love* is the most serious film in the series, probably because it is the most serious of Ian Fleming's novels. With this book, Fleming attempted to upgrade his character and create an incredibly intricate blackmail and murder plot, involving the most dastardly group of villains ever assembled. In that novel's concluding scene, when Klebb kicks Bond with one of her poison-tipped shoe-knives, it looks like the end of 007. And it actually was.

Fleming was upset with the disappointing sales of the book at that time, and his intention was to kill off 007 once and for all. It was only through the intervention of American author Raymond Chandler, who was a big Bond fan, that Fleming was encouraged to revive Bond in his next book, *Dr. No*. Thus, *From Russia with Love* was grounded in a seriousness that was well preserved in Richard Maibaum's thoughtful adaptation.

Having scored well with location photography on *Dr. No*, the producers wisely decided to shoot much of *From Russia with Love* on location in Istanbul. Casting was particularly effective in this entry. Robert Shaw and Lotte Lenya respectively stole the picture as the blond ice-water-in-his-veins assassin, Red Grant, and his spymaster, Rosa Klebb. And the charming Pedro Armendariz—in his final film role—brought Kerim Bey to life.

Like many of Hitchcock's classics, which were inspirational to both Maibaum and returning director Terence Young, this Bond film has many memorable set pieces. There's the gypsy camp where Bond witnesses a particularly nasty girl fight and then has to fight off an invading army of Bulgar killers. There's the assassination of Krilencu, who attempts to exit his apartment through a movie billboard. There's Tanya's seduction of Bond in his Istanbul hotel room, filmed by a hidden movie crew. There's the fight on the train between Grant and Bond—probably the best fight ever choreographed on film—a fight that is seldom shown uncensored on television. And there's the famous helicopter and motorboat chase that concludes the film.

I doubt if today's younger audience will appreciate this film as much as I did back in the mid-1960s. It's not very funny, the gadgets are kept to a minimum, and four-letter words are absent. But it's still one of the best adventure films ever made.

While cinematographer Ted Moore, *left*, sets his camera position, Sean Connery and Daniela Bianchi prepare for their love scene in the bridal suite of an Istanbul hotel in *From Russia with Love*. (Rex Features Ltd./RDR Productions)

FROM RUSSIA WITH LOVE CAST

James Bond . . . . Sean Connery
Tatiana Romanova . . . . Daniela Bianchi
Kerim Bey . . . . Pedro Armendariz
Rosa Klebb . . . . Lotte Lenya
Red Grant . . . . Robert Shaw
M . . . . Bernard Lee
Sylvia Trench . . . . Eunice Gayson
Morzeny . . . . Walter Gotell
Vavra, the Gypsy Leader . . . . Francis de Wolff
Train Conductor . . . . George Pastell
Kerim's Girl . . . . Nadja Regin
Miss Moneypenny . . . . Lois Maxwell
Vida . . . . Aliza Gur
Zora . . . . Martine Beswick
Kronsteen . . . . Vladek Sheybal
Belly Dancer . . . . Leila
Bulgar Agent . . . . Hasan Ceylan
Krilencu . . . . Fred Haggerty

Rolls Chauffeur . . . . Neville Jason
Commissar Benz . . . . Peter Bayliss
Tempo . . . . Nushet Atear
Rhoda . . . . Peter Brayham
Major Boothroyd . . . . Desmond Llewelyn
Masseuse . . . . Jan Williams
McAdams . . . . Peter Madden
Nash . . . . Bill Hill

FROM RUSSIA WITH LOVE CREW

Producers . . . . . Albert R. Broccoli, Harry Saltzman
Director . . . . Terence Young
Screenplay by . . . . Richard Maibaum
Director of Photography . . . . Ted Moore, B.S.C.
Editor . . . . Peter Hunt
Production Manager . . . . Bill Hill
Art Director . . . . Syd Cain
Title Song Written by . . . . Lionel Bart
"From Russia with Love" Sung by . . . Matt Munro

"James Bond Theme" Written by . . Monty Norman
Orchestral Music Composed and Conducted
  by . . . . John Barry
Assistant Director . . . . David Anderson
Second-Unit Cameraman . . . . Robert Kindred
Camera Operator . . . . Johnny Winbolt
Continuity . . . . Kay Mander
Makeup . . . . Basil Newall, Paul Rabiger
Hairstylist . . . . Eileen Warwick
Location Manager . . . . Frank Ernst
Istanbul Production Assistant . . . . Ilham Filmer
Special Effects by . . . . John Stears
Assisted by . . . . Frank George
Stunt Work Arranged by . . . . Peter Perkins
Sound Recordists . . . . John W. Mitchell,
                                        C. LeMessurier
Assembly Editor . . . . Ben Rayner
Dubbing Editors . . . Norman Wanstall, Harry Miller
Costume Designer . . . . Jocelyn Rickards
Wardrobe Mistress . . . . Eileen Sullivan
Wardrobe Master . . . . Ernie Farrer
Assistant Art Director . . . . Michael White
Set Dresser . . . . Freda Pearson
Titles Designed by . . . . Robert Brownjohn
Assisted by . . . . Trevor Bond
Production Company . . . . Eon Productions
Distribution Company . . . . United Artists

British actress Fiona Fullerton portrayed Soviet KGB agent Pola Ivanova in *A View to a Kill.* (London Management)

FROM RUSSIA WITH LOVE COMPETITION

Competitive films in release when *From Russia with Love* opened in Los Angeles on May 27, 1964. *Note:* In L.A., *From Russia with Love* was featured on a double bill with *War Is Hell:*

How the West Was Won

Bridge on the River Kwai (reissue)

Rhino!

Dr. Strangelove

What a Way to Go!

Becket

Judgment at Nuremberg/Exodus (reissue)

South Pacific/Oklahoma (reissue)

FUGIWA, MATSU Japanese double agent in *Thunderball*, whose blackmail at the hands of S.P.E.C.T.R.E. is revealed at an organizational briefing in Paris. For their trouble, S.P.E.C.T.R.E. will receive 40 million yen—Fugiwa's entire fortune, according to S.P.E.C.T.R.E. Agent No. 7.

FULLERTON, FIONA British actress who portrayed Soviet KGB agent Pola Ivanova in *A View to a Kill.* Fullerton also portrayed Tatiana Romanova in screen tests with Timothy Dalton prior to *The Living Daylights* (they re-created the scene in *From Russia with Love* where Bond finds Tanya in his hotel room bed). *See* IVANOVA, POLA.

FUN HOUSE Francisco Scaramanga's (CHRISTOPHER LEE) training ground in *The Man with the Golden Gun.* The whole atmospheric maze—built inside his fabulous island home—comes complete with a shooting gallery where wooden dummies fire back with live ammunition, false doorways and exits, and a mirror maze that confuses his opponents. To help keep his eyesight and reflexes at their sharpest levels, Scaramanga invites the world's top guns to this maze, where they are at a distinct disadvantage.

While Scaramanga stalks his targets, tiny Nick Nack (HERVE VILLECHAIZE) operates the electronics that control the audio and visual elements of the fun house, which serve to further startle all visitors. Scaramanga's challenge: to reach his own golden gun before exposing himself to his opponent's firepower.

Rodney (MARC LAWRENCE), a slick syndicate hit man, is Scaramanga's first victim and Bond (ROGER MOORE) is nearly the second. A sign of Scaramanga's respect for 007 is a wooden figure of 007 that stands in the midst of the maze. In the final shoot-out, Bond impersonates that figure and wins a gun duel with his ultimate nemesis.

The fun house set was designed by Peter Murton and built at Pinewood Studios. Setting the moody stage for these indoor gun duels is John Barry's score—a definite plus in the film.

FURST, JOSEPH Actor who portrayed Professor-Dr. Metz, the world's leading authority on laser refraction, in *Diamonds Are Forever*. A renegade European scientist, Metz is in the employ of Ernst Stavro Blofeld (CHARLES GRAY).

G

GALORE, PUSSY Goldfinger's (GERT FROBE) personal jet pilot and fellow conspirator in Operation Grand Slam. She's portrayed by athletic British actress Honor Blackman in *Goldfinger*. Pussy is also the leader of a group of female aerial acrobats—Pussy Galore's Flying Circus. The circus, composed of five voluptuous blonds flying Commanche monoplanes, will spray the deadly Delta Nine nerve gas into the atmosphere over Fort Knox, immobilizing 41,000 U.S. Army troops that guard the gold repository.

In the Richard Maibaum/Paul Dehn screenplay, Pussy was no longer the lesbian gang

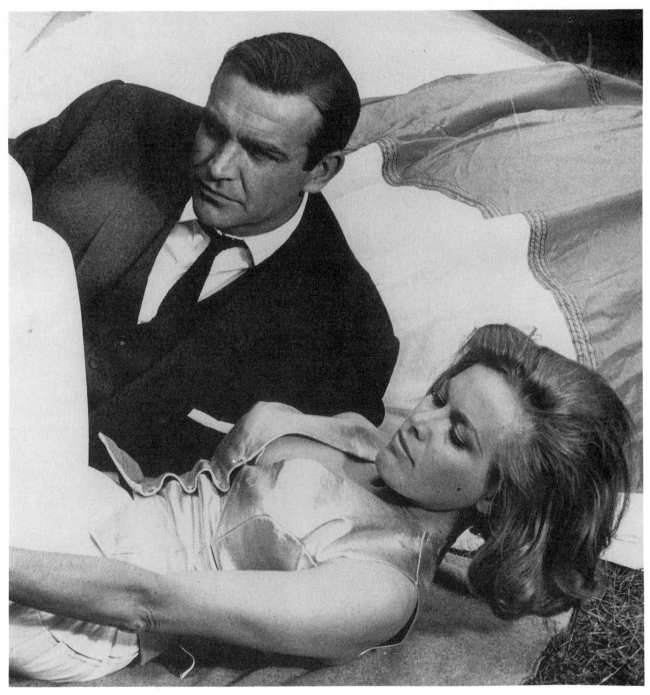

"This is no time to be rescued." Bond (SEAN CONNERY) and Pussy Galore (HONOR BLACKMAN) hit the silk in *Goldfinger*. (Rex Features Ltd./RDR Productions)

In *Goldfinger*, Pussy (HONOR BLACKMAN) and Bond (SEAN CONNERY) arrive in Kentucky, (actually Northolt Airport, London). (Rex Features Ltd./RDR Productions)

leader depicted in Ian Fleming's novel, but instead a resourceful female who prefers the company of her fellow pilot-acrobats. That is, until James Bond (SEAN CONNERY) arrives in bluegrass country.

Seduced in the hay of the Auric Stud barn, Pussy neutralizes the gas attack by switching the canisters at the last minute and alerting Washington to the planned assault on Fort Knox. With this information, Felix Leiter (CEC LINDER) is able to pull off a grand deception in which the entire base pretends to fall unconscious from the gas, only to awaken and begin a furious counterassault when Goldfinger's atomic device arrives.

Because of the sensitive nature of her name, the producers of *Goldfinger* were prepared to change it to Kitty Galore if the censors proved difficult. Eon Productions' publicity man, Tom Carlisle, solved the problem by granting an exclusive to a London newspaper if their photographer would snap a picture of Honor Blackman and Prince Philip at a charity ball and give it the caption "Pussy and the Prince." When the paper appeared the next day, no one objected, and the producers were emboldened to go ahead and use the name in the final cut of the film. Pussy was the first of a long line of James Bond females with patently sexual names.

GALSWORTHY, MARILYN Actress who portrayed Stromberg's (CURT JURGENS) luscious assistant in *The Spy Who Loved Me* and who becomes one of the film's early shark victims. She's the one responsible for selling the nuclear-submarine tracking system developed by Stromberg's scientists.

GAMMA GAS Poison gas employed by S.P.E.C.T.R.E. in *Thunderball* to murder NATO aerial observer François Derval (PAUL STASSINO) and the members of his nuclear bomber crew.

GARDEN OF REMEMBRANCE The final resting place for Peter Franks's (JOE ROBINSON) ashes in *Diamonds Are Forever*. Located at the Slumber Inc. funeral home in Las Vegas, the ashes are placed in a niche adorned by "restful chartreuse curtains and angel's breath gold trim."

GARLIC INCIDENT, THE A funny off-screen incident in *On Her Majesty's Secret Service* that involved actors George Lazenby and Diana Rigg. According to British tabloid accounts, the incident supposedly took place in the Pinewood commissary on a Wednesday afternoon prior to their first love scene. As Lazenby told it, midway through their lunch, Rigg called over to him and jokingly shouted, "Hey George, I'm having garlic with my pate; I hope you are too." Lazenby smiled and went back to his meal. The headlines the next day read, DIANA RIGG EATS GARLIC BEFORE KISS WITH GEORGE LAZENBY.

"The press kept feeding the fire to keep the story going," said Lazenby. "Contrary to the newspaper accounts, Diana and I didn't hate each other. But Diana did have a big ego (after all, she had been around for a while, and I was just an upstart). I'm sure she didn't like us being treated on the same level. Also, the press was very interested in me because I was new, while they had all done interviews with Diana before. Even Telly Savalas was affected. He kept saying, 'Why am I the best-kept secret on this picture?' "

GARRATT, DONNA (Santa Ana, California, November 17, 1942–   ) Acrobatic American stuntwoman and stunt arranger who portrayed Bambi in *Diamonds Are Forever*.

Stuntwoman Donna Garrett portrayed Bambi the bodyguard in *Diamonds Are Forever*. (Donna Garrett)

GASWORKS SUPERVISOR Bookish Trans Siberian Pipeline executive in *The Living Daylights*, portrayed by Peter Porteous (who was Lenkin, the jewel forger, in *Octopussy*), who is on duty at the Bratislava substation when defecting Russian General Georgi Koskov (JEROEN KRABBE) goes shooting through the pipeline in the internal scouring plug—the "pig." To distract him, voluptuous pipeline engineer Rosika Miklos (JULIE T. WALLACE) unzips her coveralls and buries the supervisor's nose in her cleavage.

The system goes haywire when Koskov's pig comes shooting through, but the supervisor's too involved with Rosika to realize a thing. Of course, when the pig is safely on its way to Austria, Rosika gets to her feet, zips up her coveralls, and yells at the supervisor, claiming she's not *that* type of girl.

GAVIN, JOHN (Los Angeles, California, April 8, 1928–   ) Handsome American actor and future diplomat who was actually signed to play James Bond in *Diamonds Are Forever*, but who lost the role to Sean Connery when film executive David Picker made the veteran 007 one final offer he couldn't refuse.

It's actually hard to believe that Eon Productions would hire an American to play James Bond. But Gavin isn't the only Yank to be seriously considered for the role. Throughout the years, names like Paul Newman, Steve McQueen, Burt Reynolds, James Brolin, even Jimmy Stewart were considered. Picture Jimmy Stewart as Bond with his slow, stuttering delivery: "My . . . My . . . My . . . n-n-name is B-B-Bond. J-J-James, Bond-d-d." *Note:* President Ronald Reagan appointed Gavin as the U.S. ambassador to Mexico in May 1981.

GAY, JOHN British actor who portrayed Hammond, M's (BERNARD LEE) butler, in *On Her Majesty's Secret Service*.

GAYSON, EUNICE (London, March 17, 1931–   ) British actress who portrayed Bond's fetching girlfriend, Sylvia Trench, in *Dr. No* and *From Russia with Love*. According to Gayson, her role was going to be a running bit in the series; however, when director Terence Young left the series during preproduction on

British actress Eunice Gayson portrayed society dame Sylvia Trench in *Dr. No* and *From Russia with Love*. (National Film Archive, London)

Goldfinger, her part was eliminated. It was to Sylvia Trench that Bond (SEAN CONNERY) uttered his first line of dialogue, "I admire your courage, Miss?"

G-BIHN Identification letters on the fin of Max Zorin's (CHRISTOPHER WALKEN) blimp in *A View to a Kill*.

GEE, PRUNELLA British actress who portrayed Shrublands physical therapist Patricia Fearing in *Never Say Never Again*. The role was originated by Molly Peters in *Thunderball* (1965).

GEIGER-COUNTER WATCH One of the gadgets supplied to 007 (SEAN CONNERY) by Q (DESMOND LLEWELYN) in *Thunderball*. The watch is used to detect any radioactivity near the false bottom of the *Disco Volante* yacht, a clue that could determine if the A-bombs are on board.

GENUINE FELIX LIGHTER, A Bond's (ROGER MOORE) reference to the hidden radio receiver in the cigarette lighter of Strutter's (LON SATTON) auto in *Live and Let Die*.

GEOLOGICAL CONFIGURATIONS OF THE EASTERN CARIBBEAN BY LYELL
A book, in John Strangways's laboratory, in which 007 finds a receipt from Dent Laboratories for the testing of ore samples in *Dr. No*. According to the receipt, Dent charged Strangways two pounds, 20 pence for the work.

GERMAN-CHINESE Dr. No's (JOSEPH WISEMAN) nationality. His father was a German missionary, and his mother, a Chinese girl from a good family.

GHETTO BLASTER One of Q's (DESMOND LLEWELYN) "toys," introduced in *The Living Daylights*. It's a portable radio equipped with a built-in rocket launcher—something he's "cooking up for the Americans."

GIBRALTAR British naval base that is the site of war games between the British Secret Service Double-O Section and the Special Air Service (S.A.S.) in *The Living Daylights* teaser. The mission calls for three skydiving double-O agents—002 (GLYN BAKER), 004 (FREDERICK WARDER), and 007 (TIMOTHY DALTON)—to penetrate the island's radar station, which is defended by S.A.S. troops. What they don't know is that an assassin working for arms dealer Brad Whitaker (JOE DON BAKER) and renegade Russian General Georgi Koskov (JEROEN KRABBE) has already penetrated the base security.

After 002 is captured by the S.A.S., the assassin kills 004 by cutting his climbing rope. Planting a tag that says "Smiert Spionam" ("Death to Spies") on his body, the assassin makes his escape in a stolen Land Rover. Having found 004's body and the body of a murdered S.A.S. soldier, Bond goes after their killer—eventually jumping on top of the Land Rover as it speeds down the mountainside. A vicious fight in the cab ensues until Bond gets the upper hand.

As the Land Rover smashes its way over a cliff, Bond instantly pulls the rip cord on his parachute and is shunted out of the quickly descending vehicle, which explodes as it hits the rocky shore. His parachute on fire, Bond lands carefully on the deck of a luxury yacht where Linda (KELL TYLER) is bemoaning the lack of good men in her life.

Introducing himself as "Bond. James Bond," 007 grabs the portable phone, takes the offered glass of wine, calls the office, and says he'll be back in an hour. Staring at Linda's inviting figure, he then corrects himself and says, "Make it two."

GIBSON British scientist/inventor who, in *The Man with the Golden Gun*, creates a solar cell that could solve the world's energy crisis. Considered 95 percent efficient, the cell—known as a "solex agitator"—can convert solar radiation into electricity on an industrial basis. Scaramanga (CHRISTOPHER LEE) is commissioned by ruthless industrialist Hai Fat (RICHARD LOO) to kill Gibson and steal the solex. Gibson is assassinated, but James Bond (ROGER MOORE) witnesses the event and eventually tracks Scaramanga to his island retreat.

GILBERT, LEWIS (London, March 6, 1920–) British film director, former actor, and documentary filmmaker. A Bond veteran, he directed *You Only Live Twice* (1967), *The Spy Who Loved Me* (1977), and *Moonraker* (1979). Having originally turned down *You Only Live Twice*, Gilbert was persuaded to accept the assignment when producer Albert R. Broccoli convinced him that a huge audience was waiting to see his work.

Said Gilbert, "When you make an ordinary film, you never know what your audience is going to be like. You have no idea. It may be 20 people or 20 million. But when you make a Bond, you know that whether the film is good or bad, there is going to be a huge audience waiting to see it. To me, that became an important challenge."

GILLESPIE, CHERRY Short, dark-haired beauty who portrayed Midge, an acrobatic smuggler, in *Octopussy*.

GIRL FIGHT The erotic fight to the death in rural Istanbul between two beautiful Gypsy girls

(MARTINE BESWICK and ALIZA GUR) who love the same man, in *From Russia with Love*.

One of the James Bond series's best moments takes place in art director Syd Cain's sprawling "Gypsy camp," which was built in an area of the studio called the "Pinewood paddock." Peopled with an assortment of exotic types, including 007 (SEAN CONNERY), Kerim Bey (PEDRO ARMENDARIZ), Vavra (FRANCIS DE WOLFF), and Leila the belly dancer, this sequence benefits strongly from John Barry's staccato theme music and the sexual energy that both girls brought to the battle.

Martine Beswick, who would go on to play 007's assistant, Paula Caplan, in *Thunderball* described the action: "We were like two wildcats, crashing about, crying out—all to the tune of Terence Young, who was terribly vocal. He was yelling all the time, saying things like, 'Kill her, Martine! Now hit her, get her foot, that's right, now turn over. Go, Aliza! Jump on her.'

"Stuntman Peter Perkins was doing the same thing. Both of them were very involved. And it was wonderful that they did that, because it gave us the impetus to make it real. We needed that impetus because it was cold out there at night, simply freezing, and all we had to wear were those torn scarfs and rags. It was like running around in our bloomers.

"But we didn't show a thing, and still it turned out to be a terribly erotic sequence. Just the sight of two women fighting like that at close quarters was a big turn-on to everybody on the set, including Sean Connery, who seemed to be having a ball."

GIRL IN PHILADELPHIA, THE The woman with whom James Bond (SEAN CONNERY) had his best sexual experience, as told to wicked S.P.E.C.T.R.E. assassin Fatima Blush (BARBARA CARRERA) in *Never Say Never Again*. This news is particularly galling to Fatima because she wants 007 to write down, for posterity, that their own tryst in Nassau was the best sex he had ever had.

GLD 376 Isthmus City license plate on South American drug runner Franz Sanchez's (ROBERT DAVI) getaway car in *Licence to Kill*.

GLEN, JOHN (Sunbury on Thames, England, May 15, 1932-   ) British film direc-

Handling second-unit chores on *The Spy Who Loved Me*, director John Glen prepares his cameras on Baffin Island's icy Asgard Peak, site of Rick Sylvester's incredible ski jump. (Rick Sylvester)

tor who joined the Bond series as a second-unit director and editor on *On Her Majesty's Secret Service*. He filmed the famous ski/parachute jump in *The Spy Who Loved Me* teaser and has directed five Bond films, starting with *For Your Eyes Only*.

After Glen worked for several years as a supervising editor and a director on various TV series, director Peter Hunt invited him to become the editor and second-unit director on *OHMSS*. Having a solid background in action-film editing and second-unit work, Glen still found it difficult to convince producer Cubby Broccoli that he should direct *For Your Eyes Only* in 1981. Glen eventually won the assignment and delivered a terrific 007 adventure.

Since then, he's fit the series like a well-worn glove. Unfortunately, Glen's directing expertise is only as good as the scripts he works from, and those have been inconsistent.

As to the longevity of the series, he told film journalist Craig Modderno in 1989: "Bond has never been corrupted and has always been a citizen above suspicion doing the right thing. In times of mixed morality and abuse of power by many of the people we admire, it's nice to know James Bond is still around to show what heroes are all about!"

Glen's 007 directing credits: *For Your Eyes Only, Octopussy, A View to a Kill, The Living Daylights, Licence to Kill*.

GLOVER, BRUCE (Chicago, May 2, 1932–
) American character actor who portrayed
the homosexual assassin Mr. Wint in *Diamonds
Are Forever*. Partnered with the bald Mr. Kidd
(PUTTER SMITH), Glover picks up the scorpion and kills the motorcycle-riding diamond
smuggler in an early scene. And in the film's
concluding scene, Glover ends up going over the
rail of a luxury liner with a time bomb attached
to his privates.

Initially, Glover was told that he was much
too "normal" for the part of Mr. Wint. As he
explained, casting director Billy Gordon was
going for a modern version of the Sydney
Greenstreet/Peter Lorre type of relationship.
"However," recalled Glover, "when they went
for the rather wild look of Putter Smith, they
suddenly decided they had had enough of that
kind of look and felt I was fine."

Interestingly, up until the first day of shooting, Glover wasn't sure which part he was going
to play. Thus, he decided not to memorize his
lines. It wasn't until the stuntman handed him a
scorpion in the middle of the Nevada desert on
the first day of shooting that he realized he was
to play Mr. Wint.

At first, Glover was concerned whether the
homosexual element of Mr. Wint and Mr.
Kidd's relationship was believable. "After all,"
he smiled, "I looked over at Putter's mouth and
realized that kissing that was an impossibility.
He was so wild looking. Eventually, I simply
decided that he was a giant teddy bear—my
plaything. There were really no sexual thoughts
at all. However, I was very possessive of him.
After we shot the hand-holding sequence, I
looked over at Putter and saw that he had
turned beet red, he was so embarrassed." *See*
WINT, MR.

GLOVER, JULIAN (1935–   ) British
character actor who portrayed well-tailored heroin smuggler and Soviet agent Aris Kristatos in
For Your Eyes Only. *See* KRISTATOS, ARIS.

British actor Julian Glover brought the art of Bond
villainy down to earth in *For Your Eyes Only* as
Kristatos, a KGB agent posing as the wealthy patron of a
spoiled ice skater (LYNN-HOLLY JOHNSON). (Jeremy
Conway)

Wish you were here.
Having a wonderful time.

BRUCE GLOVER
in   Diamonds are forever

The comical calling card used by actor Bruce Glover
after his Bond experience as Mr. Wint in *Diamonds Are
Forever*. (Bruce Glover Collection)

GOBINDA Kamal Khan's (LOUIS JOURDAN) giant East Indian bodyguard, portrayed by Kabir Bedi, in *Octopussy*. Unsmiling and unsympathetic, with hands that can crush dice cubes—reminiscent of Oddjob (HAROLD SAKATA) and the Slazenger One golf ball in *Goldfinger*—Gobinda still has that semi-Jaws quality of gaining the audience's respect even as he's trying to kill Bond.

One often wishes that Bond could someday assemble a group of his ex-enemies as an A-team commando force. Unfortunately, they're all dead. Gobinda would be particularly able. In *Octopussy*, his attempts on Bond become increasingly more difficult. First, there's the wild three-wheeler chase through Udaipur, followed by the raucous tiger hunt through the bush that surrounds the Monsoon Palace, then the train-hopping escapade in West Germany.

Finally, Kamal asks the ever-dutiful Gobinda to climb outside their twin-engined plane and battle Bond in midair. In a classic moment in the series, Gobinda sticks a blade in his mouth, summons up some Hindu resolve, and crawls outside the aircraft for one final confrontation. As they're maneuvering for position on the plane's fuselage, Bond is able to whip the radio antenna into Gobinda's face. Stunned, the big Indian loses his grip and falls to his death.

GOGOL, GENERAL ALEXIS Soviet senior KGB officer who is a running character in the James Bond series. Portrayed by actor Walter Gotell, who first appeared in *From Russia with Love* as Morzeny, the S.P.E.C.T.R.E. field commander, General Gogol was introduced as M's (BERNARD LEE) opposite number in *The Spy Who Loved Me*.

Pitted against freelance madman Karl Stromberg (CURT JURGENS), James Bond (ROGER MOORE) joins forces with a Russian KGB agent, Anya Amasova (BARBARA BACH). This alliance—a tip of the cap to detente—includes their respective bosses, M and Gogol, who operate offices in the underground chambers of an Egyptian tomb.

Portrayed as a humanistic Soviet military man, Gogol is definitely a new breed of Russian character in Western cinema. As the series evolves, he becomes even more sympathetic.

After a brief appearance in *Moonraker* and *For Your Eyes Only* (he arrives by helicopter, only to discover that the A.T.A.C. computer has been destroyed), Gogol returns in *Octopussy* as the counterpoint to fanatical General Orlov (STEVEN BERKOFF), who is ready to "create" a nuclear accident on a U.S. air force base in West Germany in order to force unilateral nuclear disarmament throughout Western Europe. Determined to avoid confrontation with the West, Gogol stands firmly against Orlov and eventually wins over the Russian premier. When Orlov's smuggling activities are exposed, Gogol launches the investigation to find and arrest the renegade Soviet general—which leads to the final confrontation on the train tracks near the West German border, where Orlov is machine-gunned by border guards.

Gogol returns in *A View to a Kill* to warn Max Zorin (CHRISTOPHER WALKEN) that his murderous activities are not sanctioned by the KGB. When Bond kills Zorin, Gogol is delighted to award 007 the Order of Lenin.

In *The Living Daylights*, Gogol appears in his newest guise—as a high-ranking foreign service bureaucrat who allows Kara Milovy (MARYAM D'ABO) to perform in Austria.

GOLDEN BULLET The trademark of assassin Francisco Scaramanga (CHRISTOPHER LEE) in *The Man with the Golden Gun*. These dumdum bullets are designed to flatten upon impact for maximum wounding effect. Scaramanga has them custom manufactured in Macao by a gunsmith named Lazar (MARNE MAITLAND), who also designed the fascinating weapon that shoots them.

Because of the type of security checks he often faces, Scaramanga must have a weapon that, when disassembled, doesn't look like a weapon. His golden gun thus converts to a ballpoint pen, a cuff link, a cigarette lighter, and cigarette case that he reveals just prior to the assassination of heavily guarded industrialist Hai Fat (RICHARD LOO). Scaramanga hides his bullet in his belt buckle.

At the beginning of *The Man with the Golden Gun*, one of the custom gold bullets, with an engraved 007, is sent to the British Secret Service. M (BERNARD LEE) points out that in the past an engraved bullet has been used by Scaramanga to terrify his intended victims.

Rather than go into hiding, Bond (ROGER MOORE) takes the initiative. First he journeys to Beirut to question the girlfriend of one of Scaramanga's unconfirmed kills—002, Bill Fairbanks. Saida, the belly dancer (CARMEN SAUTOY), keeps in her belly button, as a lucky charm, the golden bullet that killed Fairbanks.

During a fight with enemy agents, Bond bumps into Saida's stomach and swallows the bullet. Through x-rays, Q (DESMOND LLEWELYN), determines that the bullet weighs 20.003 grams and was fired from a 4.2-millimeter handgun—a caliber of weapon that supposedly doesn't exist. The content of the bullet is determined to be soft 23-karat gold with traces of nickel—elements that are hardly ever used in Europe but are more common in Southeast Asia.

This last clue takes Bond to Lazar, who is coerced into revealing how Scaramanga receives his shipment of bullets. Agent 007 then goes to a local casino, where he sees Scaramanga's woman, Andrea Anders (MAUD ADAMS), picking up the bullets. Later, in Bangkok, Bond discovers that it was Andrea who sent the bullet after all.

GOLDEN DRAGON COMPANY Oriental coin and jewelry shop in Hong Kong, in front of which James Bond (ROGER MOORE) observes Scaramanga's (CHRISTOPHER LEE) assassination of Gibson, the British solar energy expert, in *The Man with the Golden Gun.* Meanwhile, Scaramanga takes his shot from the second story of the same shop.

GOLDENEYE The nickname of author Ian Fleming's beachfront vacation home in Jamaica, where—between 1952 and 1964—he wrote his James Bond novels and short stories.

GOLDEN GATE BRIDGE San Francisco Bay landmark that is the location for the final confrontation between James Bond (ROGER MOORE) and Max Zorin (CHRISTOPHER WALKEN) in *A View to a Kill.*

Having stopped Zorin's plot to destroy Silicon Valley (See PROJECT MAIN STRIKE), Bond next faces Zorin himself. Zorin has captured Stacey Sutton (TANYA ROBERTS) and is making his escape in a getaway blimp. As the airship heads for San Francisco, Bond takes hold of one of the mooring lines, which transports him on a hair-raising excursion across the city's skyline.

Nearing the Golden Gate Bridge, Bond is able to tie his line around the uppermost cable on the bridge—a maneuver that effectively immobilizes the forward momentum of the blimp. As 007 gains his balance on one of the bridge's huge cables, Zorin comes after him with an axe. Fighting on the windswept surface is difficult, but Bond eventually gets the upper hand, and Zorin loses his grip, falling 700 feet to his death.

Seeing his "creation" dead, Dr. Mortner (WILLOUGHBY GRAY) lights a batch of dynamite and prepares to fling it at Bond. But 007 is quicker. He takes Zorin's axe and cuts the mooring cable. As the blimp suddenly shifts position, Mortner loses his balance and drops the dynamite, which explodes inside the blimp housing. While the remains of the blimp float gently to the water's surface, Bond and Stacey stand tall atop the bridge's highest rampart, with Bond breaking the ice with the comment, "There's never a cab when you need one."

GOLDEN GROTTO An area of the Caribbean Sea, not far from Nassau in the Bahamas, that is the habitat of an especially deadly species of shark in *Thunderball.* It's also the hiding place for Largo's (ADOLFO CELI) hijacked British nuclear bomber.

After a prolonged search of the Atlantic fails to find the bomber, Bond (SEAN CONNERY) and Felix Leiter (RIK VAN NUTTER) are about to turn for home, when their helicopter passes over an area that Leiter identifies as the Golden Grotto. Remembering that Largo's sharks are of the Golden Grotto variety, Bond realizes that they've found their prize at last.

GOLDEN GROTTO SHARKS Millionaire Emilio Largo's (ADOLFO CELI) unusual hobby, which he stores in one of his Palmyra estate's swimming pools, in *Thunderball.* He collects these big-game fish for various marine institutions, a fact he relates to James Bond (SEAN CONNERY) during the latter's social visit to Palmyra. It is this salient fact that helps 007 find the missing NATO bomber when Felix Leiter (RIK VAN NUTTER) maneuvers his helicopter over the actual Golden Grotto region of the Caribbean. In reality, the Golden Grotto sharks are tiger sharks.

After Bond finds the body of Paula Caplan

(MARTINE BESWICK), he gets into a fight with one of Largo's henchmen, and both men fall into the shark pool. It was a difficult sequence because 007 is caught in the pool without a diver's mask, thus prohibiting the use of a double. Reluctantly, Connery agreed to swim with the huge tiger sharks.

Said underwater cinematographer Lamar Boren, "Those sharks weren't drugged, nor were their jaws wired. They were the real thing, and Sean was depending on us to keep him out of trouble. But you really don't have to worry about sharks anyway, unless there's blood in the water or a lot of garbage. And in that pool, the sharks were very sluggish. They ended up ignoring Sean and just swimming around."

The same tiger sharks were later used in the eerie sequence where Bond finds the Vulcan bomber.

GOLDEN GUN Francisco Scaramanga's (CHRISTOPHER LEE) unusual weapon in *The Man with the Golden Gun*. Manufactured by Lazar (MARNE MAITLAND), a Portuguese gunsmith, it fires a 4.2-millimeter shell weighing 20.003 grams. The gun itself can be disassembled into such innocuous parts as a ballpoint pen, a cigarette lighter and case, and a cuff link. Plus, he keeps a bullet in his belt buckle.

The golden parts were totally inconspicuous and allowed Scaramanga freedom of movement through airport x-ray machines and physical searches, which allowed the assassin to kill with surprising ease, as shown in the film when he disposes of Hai Fat (RICHARD LOO) in the latter's dining room. The industrialist thought that Scaramanga was merely enjoying a smoke as he placed his lighter and case on the table. Little did Hai Fat know that a gun was being assembled under his nose and that a golden bullet would soon find its mark across the room.

GOLDFINGER (United Artists, 1964) ★ ★ ★ ★ The third James Bond film, produced by Albert R. Broccoli and Harry Saltzman. U.S. release date: December 25, 1964. Budget: $3.5 million. First box-office report: 64

theaters, 41 cities, less than two weeks in release, $2,906,328—a national record in its day. Total domestic film rentals: $23 million. Running time: 111 minutes.

Although *From Russia with Love* has a better story, *Goldfinger* is the best film in the James Bond series. It alone elevated the series to a level of pop entertainment that very few films achieve. *Goldfinger* was a worldwide phenomenon when it was released during Christmastime in 1964. It was so popular that many theaters stayed open 24 hours a day to accommodate the crowds. It was the first mega-hit film.

In the past, box-office winners established their records over a long period of time. *Goldfinger* rewrote the record book from its first day in release. No film had ever made as much money in as little time. Why? *Goldfinger* was a big fantasy story with three elements that have never quite been equaled.

First, it has Goldfinger himself, the best of all possible villains, with the most perfect of all schemes. He's going to explode an atomic device in Fort Knox, Kentucky. When all of America's gold is irradiated, the value of Goldfinger's gold will increase tenfold. He's also accompanied by Oddjob, a wicked Korean manservant who talks through a very lethal bowler.

Second, the film has the most alluring gallery of women ever seen in the series. The first two Bond films introduced a strong sexual chemistry between the very dashing Sean Connery and his women. *Goldfinger* exploited that quality by introducing its female characters in outrageous fashion.

Bonita, the flamenco dancer, is pulled from a soapy bathtub by Bond and later slugged in the mouth with an assassin's blackjack. Jill appears in black panties and bra, helping Goldfinger cheat at cards. Then she's clubbed by Oddjob, painted gold, and suffocated. Pussy Galore greets Bond on a private jet plane. Agent 007 can't believe it's her real name. The tires on Tilly's Mustang are shredded by Bond. She then joins him on a wild ride in his Aston Martin, only to lose her head to Oddjob.

Third, the film had the "excalibur sword" of the series—the Aston Martin DB-5 with modifications. No film prop, gadget, or item has ever been as idolized as the *Goldfinger* car. Remember, this was the mid-1960s, the era of the space race and the beginnings of super technol-

Pinewood Studios interior of the *Goldfinger* private jet where James Bond awakens to greet Pussy Galore. (Ronnie Udell Collection)

Pussy Galore (HONOR BLACKMAN) gets a taste of her own medicine, courtesy of Gentleman Jim Bond (SEAN CONNERY) in *Goldfinger*. (Express Newspapers, London)

Goldfinger takes Paris by storm in 1964. (Rex Features Ltd./RDR Productions)

"Shocking, positively shocking." Bond (SEAN CONNERY) surveys the battlefield in the *Goldfinger* teaser as Bonita (NADJA REGIN) begins to wonder whether show business is really worth it. Capungo (stuntman ALF JOINT) simmers in the tub. (Globe Photos)

ogy. For months, the Aston Martin was the talk on every school campus in the world. As a promotional prop, it was a veritable lightning rod.

From Russia with Love had introduced some memorable set pieces, but *Goldfinger* introduced legendary ones: the laser beam inching toward Bond's privates; the aerial gas attack on Fort Knox, which is neutralized by Pussy Galore; the fight between Bond and Oddjob in the vault room of Fort Knox; the Aston Martin car chase; and the golf match between Bond and Goldfinger, with a bar of gold as the stake. Add to that Shirley Bassey's arresting title song and the memorable teaser sequence where Bond removes a wet suit, only to reveal a perfectly dry, white tuxedo and carnation, and you have the best of all possible Bonds—and the blueprint for most of the films in the series.

GOLDFINGER CAST

James Bond . . . . .Sean Connery
Auric Goldfinger . . . . .Gert Frobe
Pussy Galore . . . . .Honor Blackman
Jill Masterson . . . . .Shirley Eaton
Tilly Masterson . . . . .Tania Mallet
Oddjob . . . . .Harold Sakata
M. . . . . .Bernard Lee
Major Boothroyd . . . . .Desmond Llewelyn
Mr. Solo . . . . .Martin Benson
Felix Leiter . . . . .Cec Linder
Mr. Simmons .Austin Willis
Miss Moneypenny . . . . .Lois Maxwell
Midnight . . . . .Bill Nagy
Capungo . . . . .Alf Joint
Old Lady Gatekeeper . . . . .Varley Thomas
Bonita . . . . .Nadja Regin
Sierra . . . . .Raymond Young
Colonel Smithers . . . . .Richard Vernon
Brunskill . . . . .Denis Cowles
Kisch . . . . .Michael Mellinger
Mr. Ling . . . . .Burt Kwouk
Strap . . . . .Hal Galili
Henchman . . . . .Lenny Rabin
Sydney . . . . .Tricia Muller
Dink . . . . .Margaret Nolan
Mei-Lei . . . . .Mei Ling

What really happened to the enemy Mercedes 190 that's caught in Bond's oil slick in *Goldfinger*. (John Stears Collection)

GOLDFINGER CREW

Producers .....Harry Saltzman, Albert R. Broccoli
Director ....Guy Hamilton
Screenplay by.......Richard Maibaum, Paul Dehn
Production Designer ....Ken Adam
Director of Photography ....Ted Moore, B.S.C.
Editor ....Peter Hunt
Production Manager................L. C. Rudkin
Art Director ....Peter Murton
"Goldfinger" Title Song Sung by ...Shirley Bassey
Title Song Lyrics by ....Leslie Bricusse,
                                Anthony Newley
Music Composed and Conducted by....John Barry
Assistant Director ....Frank Ernst
Camera Operator................Johnny Winbolt
Continuity ....Constance Willis
Makeup ....Paul Rabiger, Basil Newall
Action Sequences by ....Bob Simmons
Stuntman........................George Leech
Special Effects ....John Stears
Assisted by ....Frank George
Assembly Editor ....Ben Rayner
Dubbing Editors...Norman Wanstall, Harry Miller
Sound Recorders ......Dudley Messinger, Gordon
                                McCallum
Hairstylist ....Eileen Warwick
Wardrobe Supervisor...............Elsa Fennell
Wardrobe Mistress ....Eileen Sullivan
Wardrobe Master ....John Hilling
Assistant Art Directors ...Michael White, Maurice
                                Pelling
Set Dresser ....Freda Pearson
Titles Designed by ....Robert Brownjohn
Choreographer ....Selina Wylie
Production Company ....Eon Productions
Distribution Company ....United Artists

GOLDFINGER COMPETITION

Competitive films in release when *Goldfinger* opened in the United States on December 25, 1964:

Mary Poppins

The Americanization of Emily

How the West Was Won

Get Yourself a College Girl

Circus World

A Shot in the Dark

Goodbye Charlie

The Luck of Ginger Coffey

My Fair Lady

Cheyenne Autumn

Sex and the Single Girl

The T.A.M.I. Show (Teenage Awards Music International)

Emil and the Detectives

GOLDFINGER, AURIC The title character in the third James Bond film produced by Albert R. Broccoli and Harry Saltzman, and arguably the best villain in the entire series. Goldfinger was portrayed by German actor Gert Frobe, although his voice was entirely redubbed.

A British citizen, Goldfinger is a fabulously wealthy man with worldwide interests, including a country club and a metallurgical facility in England, a factory in Switzerland, and a stud farm in Kentucky, in addition to a fleet of cars, a private jet, and an army of Chinese and Korean servants. As Felix Leiter (CEC LINDER) puts it, he's a "big operator."

In the story, the Bank of England suspects that Goldfinger has been smuggling large amounts of gold bullion out of England. It's true, but it's all a smoke screen. His real caper—planned with the help of the Red Chinese—is to detonate an atomic bomb inside the gold repository at Fort Knox, Kentucky, where America's entire gold reserve ($15 billion) is stored. With the U.S. gold radioactive and useless for 58 years, economic chaos in the West will result, pleasing the Chinese and making Goldfinger's own supply of gold increase in value 10 times.

Why is Goldfinger the best villain in the series? Because he is one of the best-drawn characters, combining a realistic greed and obsession for gold with an outsized, almost fantasylike image. Like Dr. No and the villains in *From Russia with Love*, Goldfinger could easily be the perfect cartoon villain, but, thanks to a marvelous script (once again written by Richard Maibaum), he's also totally convincing in the role.

There's nothing "typical" about Goldfinger. First of all, Gert Frobe is perfectly cast in the role. He's an overweight man, but he's dressed smartly and expensively, and he has a certain lightness and grace to him. He's also supremely confident, self-assured, and resourceful. And even though Bond keeps thwarting him, nothing will shake his will to succeed.

That roly-poly panache doesn't disguise pure ruthlessness and evil, however. Only a twisted, demented megalomaniac would have Oddjob (HAROLD SAKATA) murder Jill Masterson (SHIRLEY EATON) by covering her body with gold paint or kill Mr. Solo (MARTIN BENSON) and crush the brand-new Lincoln Continental around him. Worse yet, Goldfinger plans to spray poison gas into the air and kill 41,000 American soldiers who guard the Fort Knox installation. This is not the type of man you want to have pointing a laser beam at you.

His fate: during a fight with Bond on his private jet, Goldfinger's golden gun goes off—shattering a window, depressurizing the cabin, and sucking the villain into the stratosphere.

Maibaum told me that at one point, while he was working on an early draft of *Diamonds Are Forever*, he considered bringing back Goldfinger's twin brother as the diamond-smuggler villain. It never happened. The villain instead became Blofeld.

GOLDFINGER'S TWIN BROTHER The original villain in an early draft of screenwriter Richard Maibaum's *Diamonds Are Forever* screenplay. Moving away from the serious approach of the previous film, *On Her Majesty's Secret Service*, Maibaum introduced the brother as a power-mad Swedish shipping magnate who houses a laser cannon in the hull of one of his fleet's supertankers. Plans were even made to find Gert Frobe and have him play the "twin." This story idea was later abandoned when producer Cubby Broccoli initiated the idea of Blofeld (CHARLES GRAY) impersonating a reclusive Howard Hughes-like billionaire (JIMMY DEAN). *See* CUBBY BROCCOLI'S DREAM.

GOLDFINGER THEME It's being whistled by the janitor, portrayed by Norman McGlen, when Bond (GEORGE LAZENBY) is brought to Draco's (GABRIELE FERZETTI) office in *On Her Majesty's Secret Service*—another of screenwriter Richard Maibaum's references to the rich 007 legacy.

GOLF MATCH One of the highlights of *Goldfinger*. Ordered to probe the activities of

Sean Connery's obsession with golf begins on the fairway at Stoke Poges in *Goldfinger*. Director Guy Hamilton can be seen to the right of Connery's hat brim. (Rex Features Ltd./RDR Productions)

In *Goldfinger*, the golf match took place on a quiet fairway with Bond, Goldfinger, Oddjob, and Hawker. In reality, an army of filmmakers were present to create a classic Bond scene. Cubby Broccoli can be seen at the far right. Director Guy Hamilton stands a few feet behind Connery. Gert Frobe is the man with the cap. (Rex Features Ltd./RDR Productions)

suspected gold smuggler Auric Goldfinger (GERT FROBE), and supplied with a bar of gold loaned to him by the Bank of England to use as bait, Bond (SEAN CONNERY) tricks Goldfinger into a high-stakes golf challenge match at an English golf club.

In a series where the action seldom slows down and where human beings and realistic situations are often replaced by cardboard characters and a comic-book sensibility, the golf match in *Goldfinger* stands out. Superbly directed at an easygoing pace by Guy Hamilton and tightly written by Richard Maibaum, who abbreviated Fleming's original 18-hole match to two holes, the simple battle of wills between Bond and Goldfinger is perfectly demonstrated on the beautifully serene fairways and putting greens of the club.

Bond is nattily dressed in sports shirt, V-neck sweater, and pants, while Goldfinger looks amazing in a pair of knickers ("plus fours"). It was one of the few times in the entire series where everyone caught their breath for a moment and settled down to some real intensity.

Bond's cleverness—later replaced in the series by his overdependence on Q Branch's hardware—is perfectly demonstrated on the golf links where, to thwart his cheating adversary, he "cheats him one better." This concept would be copied a decade later when screenwriter David Ward created a card game for *The Sting* (1973) between Paul Newman and Robert Shaw, in which Newman once again cheats better than his adversary. It was while taking golf lessons for this sequence in *Goldfinger* that Sean Connery developed a passion for the sport that continues today.

GONZALES, HECTOR Cuban hit man, portrayed by Stefan Kalipha, working for Aris Kristatos (JULIAN GLOVER) in *For Your Eyes Only*. Posing as a friendly seaplane pilot who brings Melina Havelock (CAROLE BOUQUET) back to her family's yacht in Corfu, Gonzales seemingly flies away, only to return to the yacht on a strafing run that kills both of Melina's parents. Seeking revenge in the best Greek tradition, Melina stalks Gonzales to a villa outside Madrid, where she puts a crossbow bolt in his back.

GOODHEAD, DR. HOLLY Tall and slinky American astrophysicist and undercover CIA agent portrayed by Lois Chiles in *Moonraker*. On loan to Drax Industries from NASA, Holly isn't too impressed with Bond (ROGER MOORE) from the start, since it was his government that lost the shuttle in the film's teaser. Gradually, they learn to respect one another, and eventually they track Drax's (MICHEL LONSDALE) secret operation to Rio de Janeiro and the jungle.

Captured by Drax, Holly and Bond are about to be roasted by a shuttle engine, when they escape through a ventilation shaft. Eventually, they steal aboard a shuttle and participate in the final assault on the radarproof space station. Their shuttle finally destroys the orchid-bearing nerve-gas pods that could depopulate the Earth.

Holly and Bond are assuming a tender position aboard their returning shuttle, when closed-circuit video reveals them to M (BERNARD LEE), Q (DESMOND LLEWELYN), and Freddie Gray (GEOFFREY KEEN). As to what they're doing, Q quips, "He's achieving reentry."

GOODNIGHT, MARY James Bond's (ROGER MOORE) Far Eastern liaison officer and in-between lover, portrayed by Swedish beauty Britt Ekland, in *The Man with the Golden Gun*. Having been assigned to staff intelligence for two years, Mary feels qualified to give Bond an assist on his present assignment. Unfortunately, the lovely British agent spends most of her time sleeping in closets, while Bond makes love to the mysterious Andrea Anders (MAUD ADAMS).

Although quite the bumbler, Goodnight's ability to get herself locked in the trunk of Scaramanga's (CHRISTOPHER LEE) flying car actually helps Bond track the dangerous assassin to his private island off the coast of China. There she is completely helpless to prevent the duel of the century—Walther PPK versus Golden Gun. When Scaramanga and his island are blown to smithereens, Bond and Goodnight escape in the villain's motor junk.

GOODTHIGHS, MISS GIOVANA Enemy agent, portrayed by Jacqueline Bisset, who slips mild-mannered Evelyn Tremble/James Bond (PETER SELLERS) a Mickey Finn in *Casino Royale*. She's later iced by Vesper Lynd (URSULA ANDRESS). *See* BISSET, JACQUELINE.

GOTELL, WALTER (1924–) British character actor who has risen in rank throughout the James Bond series, starting out as S.P.E.C.T.R.E. tactical chief Morzeny in *From Russia with Love*; promoted to KGB general as Gogol in *The Spy Who Loved Me, Moonraker, For Your Eyes Only, Octopussy,* and *A View to a Kill*; and then transferred to a high-ranking position in the Soviet diplomatic corps in *The Living Daylights*.

GOTHARD, MICHAEL (1939–1993) Actor who portrayed Emile Locque in *For Your Eyes Only. See* LOCQUE, EMILE LEOPOLD.

Actor Michael Gothard played Locque, the well-dressed killer, in *For Your Eyes Only.* (John Redway)

GRACE, MARTIN (Kilkenny, Ireland, 1942–) Top Irish stunt coordinator who was the action-sequence arranger on *A View to a Kill* and who had previously doubled Roger Moore on the previous four James Bond movies, *The Spy Who Loved Me, Moonraker, For Your Eyes Only,* and *Octopussy.*

During the train stunts for *Octopussy,* Grace was involved in an accidental collision that resulted in a broken pelvis and eight months of recuperation. On *A View to a Kill,* Grace supervised more than 100 British, French, Swiss, and American stuntmen.

The highlights of Grace's work were May Day's (GRACE JONES) jump from the Eiffel Tower (accomplished by American stuntman B. J. Worth); the chaotic flooding and dynamiting of the Main Strike Mine, which includes the machine-gunning of its mine workers; and the amazing fight between Bond (ROGER MOORE) and Max Zorin (CHRISTOPHER WALKEN) atop the Golden Gate Bridge (most of which was shot on a duplicated set at Pinewood Studios).

Grace described his first look at the real bridge: "Three people can fit in the elevator going up to the top of the Golden Gate Bridge, and one of them was the elevator operator. So, I went up with Karen Allen, the double for Tanya Roberts. When we arrived at the top—this is about 750 feet from the water—I got out and walked straight on and straight down the cables. I didn't hesitate.

"The cables are surrounded by a great big cylinder, which is about three feet wide. It's circular, which means that you only have about 18 inches at the top that you actually walk on; the rest is curving away from you. But there is a handrail at both sides. If you have people with you, if you give them confidence, you have no problems. If you don't give them confidence, you have problems.

"Roberts's double was actually a high-wire artist in her own right, but she had never been up that high. Doing a high-wire act, she was probably up about 40 feet. And 700 feet is quite higher, so the first reaction can be a little tricky. For her, the best thing that could happen was that I went up and walked down and pretended I was going to lunch. And then she was okay.

"So we established that, and then we came back to the studio, where we had a duplicate of the bridge's top section, and we actually did the real fight there with Roger, Chris, and Tanya. The highest point was about 50 feet from the ground, and we had a duplicate airship swinging from the top."

Grace also carefully coordinated the sequence in which Bond rides the blimp's mooring cable to the bridge. Said Grace, "When Bond's being carried to the bridge, he's wearing a harness. We had a wire running through the rope so that he was harnessed from the waist onto a little loop coming out of the wire; we also had a foot stirrup made for him so he could put his foot in it and rest.

"It almost sounds too easy, but the thing is, hanging from a helicopter for 15 minutes without those little aids—you couldn't do it. It's impossible to hang that long. There's a limit to how long even the strongest man can hold onto a hanging rope. . . . So, obviously, there must be these safety precautions."

GRAND SLAM TASK FORCE The code name given to the convoy of military vehicles that will assault Fort Knox in *Goldfinger.* Smuggled across the Mexican border by underworld confederates of Mr. Strap, portrayed by Hal Galili, the convoy consists of jeeps, trucks, and an ambulance equipped with Goldfinger's (GERT FROBE) laser. In the jargon of Operation Grand Slam, Goldfinger is the Grand Slam Task Force Leader.

GRANDFATHER M's (ROBERT BROWN) code name in his transmission to Q (DESMOND LLEWELYN) at the end of *A View to a Kill.* Q's trailer is parked outside Stacey Sutton's (TANYA ROBERTS) mansion, where he's controlling the motorized snooper that locates Bond (ROGER MOORE) and Stacey in her shower.

GRANT, DONALD "RED" Agent 007's cool and deadly adversary, portrayed by the late Robert Shaw, in *From Russia with Love.* A convicted murderer, the blond-haired Grant escaped from Dartmoor Prison in England in 1960 and was recruited by S.P.E.C.T.R.E. in 1962. According to their records, Grant has been diagnosed as a "homicidal paranoiac," which is considered superb material for their assassination training.

Working under the command of S.P.E.C.T.R.E. Agent No. 3 Rosa Klebb (LOTTE LENYA), and S.P.E.C.T.R.E. Agent No. 5 and head of planning Kronsteen (VLADEK SHEYBAL), Grant's mission is to kill James Bond (SEAN CONNERY) on the fabled Orient Express and capture a Lektor decoding machine that 007 has stolen from the Russian embassy in Istanbul.

Aiding S.P.E.C.T.R.E. without her knowledge is Russian cipher clerk Tatiana Romanova (DANIELA BIANCHI), who will seduce Bond in the bridal suite of an Istanbul hotel room while a S.P.E.C.T.R.E. motion-picture crew films their lovemaking from a sweaty *cabinet de voyeur* located behind a mirror above the bed.

To instigate Kronsteen's plan, Grant kills a Russian agent in Istanbul, which precipitates a bloody vendetta between Russian-trained Bulgar assassins and British-trained gypsies. During a frenzied battle at the Gypsy camp, Grant places himself in an aerie high above the battle and becomes Bond's "guardian angel," using his pistol to pick off one Bulgar who is about to stab 007.

Later, in the famous St. Sophia Mosque, Grant kills again, this time doing away with another Bulgar who is about to finger Tatiana Romanova as a traitor. Finally, after 007 has stolen the Lektor and escaped Istanbul with Romanova aboard the Orient Express, Grant kills Bond's friend Kerim Bey (PEDRO ARMENDARIZ) and Benz (PETER BAYLISS), the Russian agent tailing them.

Impersonating Captain Nash, a British agent based in Yugoslavia whom he has just murdered, Grant drugs Tanya and disarms Bond. He's about to kill 007, who sits defenseless on the floor of their railroad car, when greed gets the better of him. Having informed Grant of the presence of 50 gold sovereigns in his attaché case, Bond tricks his adversary into opening another case and searching for a similar cache—triggering a tear-gas cartridge that staggers the S.P.E.C.T.R.E. assassin.

Bond eventually stabs Grant with a flat-bladed throwing knife, also hidden in a secret compartment in his briefcase, and then garrotes him with his own "strangler's watch."

GRAY, CHARLES (Bournemouth, Hampshire, England, 1928–   ) (real name, Donald M. Gray) British character actor who portrayed grim-faced Dikko Henderson in *You Only Live Twice* and Ernst Stavro Blofeld in *Diamonds Are Forever*. The latter role was a much bigger one for Gray, who became the third actor to portray Blofeld on-screen (following Donald Pleasence and Telly Savalas).

Gray's Blofeld was certainly the most flamboyant of the series, but he's hardly threatening. Spouting philosophical bilge and strutting around in smart tunics, an expensive cigarette holder dangling from his lips, he's more an elegant cad than a true Bond villain. No wonder writers Tom Mankiewicz and Richard Maibaum stuffed him into the bathosub at the end of the film, rather than faced him off against the two-fisted 007 (SEAN CONNERY). Sean Connery versus Charles Gray? No contest.

Commented screenwriter Tom Mankiewicz,

British character actor Charles Gray portrayed humorless Dikko Henderson in *You Only Live Twice* and a wildly sophisticated Ernst Stavro Blofeld in *Diamonds Are Forever*. (London Management)

"It was wonderful to write this 'piss elegant' dialogue for Charles. You could give him lines like 'It's amusing watching the great powers flexing their muscles like so many impotent beach boys' because he could say them so well."

In *You Only Live Twice*, Gray's Dikko Henderson is a pained civil servant who's abandoned his occidental upbringing for the lifestyle of the Orient. Moments after greeting Bond, he's stabbed by one of Mr. Osato's (TERU SHIMADA) henchmen. *See* BLOFELD, ERNST STAVRO; HENDERSON, DIKKO.

GRAY, FREDERICK England's stalwart Minister of Defense, portrayed by actor Geoffrey Keen, who has become a running character in the James Bond series since *The Spy Who Loved Me*. Along with M, Q, and any other expert called into the case, Gray is part of the bureaucratic team that keeps tabs on Bond, provides him with innumerable dangerous assignments, and always greets his success with a mixture of surprise, envy, and disgust.

GRAY, WILLOUGHBY (1916–1993) British character actor who portrayed renegade Nazi scientist Dr. Carl Mortner in *A View to a Kill*. *See* MORTNER, DR. CARL.

Actor Willoughby Gray portrayed renegade Nazi scientist and steroid specialist Dr. Mortner in *A View to a Kill*. (Patrick Freeman)

GREEN FIGS, YOGURT, COFFEE, VERY BLACK James Bond's (SEAN CONNERY), uh, very appetizing breakfast selection made on the night he returns to the bridal suite from Krilencu's (FRED HAGGERTY) assassination in *From Russia with Love*. How about a prune danish, James?

GREEN SCRAMBLER The telephone line that M (BERNARD LEE) uses during his transatlantic conversation with Felix Leiter (CEC LINDER) of the CIA, in *Goldfinger*.

GREENE, SPARKY American stunt coordinator who was responsible for the incredible cargo-net fight in *The Living Daylights*. In that sequence, stuntman B. J. Worth doubled Bond (TIMOTHY DALTON), and Jake Lombard doubled Necros (ANDREAS WISNIEWSKI). Worth also doubled Grace Jones for the Eiffel Tower jump in *A View to a Kill*.

GRILLED SOLE The dinner order on the Orient Express for Bond (SEAN CONNERY), Tatiana (DANIELA BIANCHI), and Red Grant (ROBERT SHAW). Bond orders for Tatiana. Red Grant follows suit.

GRINDELWALD Swiss village, located two miles from Murren and Piz Gloria, which served as the location for the skating rink sequence in *On Her Majesty's Secret Service*. In that sequence, Bond (GEORGE LAZENBY), escaping from S.P.E.C.T.R.E. ski troops, is rescued by Tracy (DIANA RIGG), the woman he will marry.

Recalled director Peter Hunt, "The skating rink was melting as we shot on it. Some nights we had to wait and see if the temperature would drop below zero. We would wait until midnight or one o'clock in the morning and then ask, 'Is it freezing yet?' and we would be informed, 'No way.' So in the end, I just had to mark off certain areas and make sure the skaters didn't wander."

Adding visual interest to the skating sequences were Rudi and Gerda Johner, a skating duo who were given the center spotlight on the festive evening. Since Diana Rigg was incapable of skating with any degree of proficiency, the key sequence in the film where Tracy skates up to the bedraggled Bond was done with Miss Rigg's skating double. Hunt kept his camera panned on the double's legs as she skates up to Bond, and then he cut to a head shot of Miss Rigg in close-up.

GRUNTHER Tall, silent S.P.E.C.T.R.E. bodyguard featured as Irma Bunt's (ILSE STEP-PAT) assistant in *On Her Majesty's Secret Service* and portrayed by Yuri Borienko. He's the fellow who takes on Tracy (DIANA RIGG) in the climactic battle inside Piz Gloria, the only time ex-Avenger Rigg gets to show a semblance of her hand-to-hand combat skills.

G7W The call sign for MI-7 communications headquarters in London, as featured at the beginning of *Dr. No*.

GUEST, VAL (London, England, 1911–) British writer/director and occasional producer who codirected the 1967 *Casino Royale* spoof with John Huston, Joseph McGrath, Robert Parrish, and Ken Hughes.

GUINCHO BEACH A Portuguese beach that was the site of the opening fight sequence between Bond (GEORGE LAZENBY) and some Union Corse thugs in *On Her Majesty's Secret Service*. Shot in May 1969, the sequence was prepared carefully by the film's stunt coordinator, George Leech.

Remembered Leech, "It was one of the most enjoyable fights in the film, but it worried me at first. It looked okay in the script, but when we actually got down to that empty beach, we realized there weren't any props of any kind.

"I wondered how we could create a spectacular fight on a plain beach. So I got a few fishing boats lined up near the waterline, and these had some oars and nets lying around—props we could use. We were always looking for something different in the Bond fights, and this time I thought we would take the fight into the water, where just before sundown it would photograph well.

"So with the water, the boats, the nets, the oars, and a few anchors, we were able to work up a good fight. It wasn't easy. Terry Mountain, Takis Emmanuel, and I sat on that beach for days trying to plan the fight."

GUMBOLD, GEBRUDER Punctual Swiss lawyer, portrayed by James Bree, who represents the interests of Ernst Stavro Blofeld (TELLY SAVALAS) in *On Her Majesty's Secret Service*. Gumbold has been assisting the S.P.E.C.T.R.E. chieftain in his attempts to trace his bloodline through the London College of Arms.

Tipped off by Union Corse leader Marc Ange Draco (GABRIELE FERZETTI) that Gumbold might know the whereabouts of Blofeld, Bond (GEORGE LAZENBY) breaks into his fourth-floor office in Berne, Switzerland, and copies important documents that lead to College of Arms specialist Sir Hilary Bray (GEORGE BAKER), whose identity 007 assumes when he visits Blofeld's Piz Gloria stronghold.

GUR, ALIZA Actress who portrayed Vida, the smaller Gypsy who battles Zora (MARTINE BESWICK), in the girl fight in *From Russia with Love*.

GWENDOLINE An acrobatic member, portrayed by tall, blond Suzanne Jerome, of an East Indian cult of female smugglers in *Octopussy*. Along with Midge (CHERRY GILLESPIE), she's one of Octopussy's (MAUD ADAMS) primary assistants.

GYPSY CAMP, THE One of the most atmospheric sequences in the James Bond series, which takes place in *From Russia with Love*. Having tricked the Russians into following the wrong car, Kerim Bey (PEDRO ARMENDARIZ) takes James Bond (SEAN CONNERY) to visit his Gypsy friends on the outskirts of Istanbul.

An old friend of the family, Kerim Bey and Bond are allowed to stay, even though it is a bad night—two women in love with the same man must fight to the death. Bond and Kerim Bey are bidden to table, where they meet the Gypsy leader, Vavra (FRANCIS DE WOLFF), and a seductive belly dancer (LEILA). When the dance is over, the girl fight begins between Vida (ALIZA GUR) and Zora (MARTINE BESWICK).

Thanks to the perfect musical score provided by John Barry, the girl fight is a classic Bond sequence, pitting two voluptuous vixens in a clawing, strangling, pseudo-judo battle of wills. The fight is interrupted when Krilencu's (FRED HAGGERTY) Bulgar assassins attack the camp, precipitating a terrific battle sequence.

As Barry's music picks up the pace, 007 goes into action, saving Vavra's life and disposing of not a few Bulgars. Kerim Bey is wounded and unable to knock off his sworn enemy, Krilencu. S.P.E.C.T.R.E. assassin and 007's "guardian angel" Red Grant (ROBERT SHAW) is perched unseen in an aerie of the ruined citadel that surrounds the camp, picking off a knife-wielding Bulgar who is about to stab Bond.

The Gypsies, thanks to 007, eventually drive the Bulgars off, tending to their wounded and a captured Bulgar, who is tortured into revealing that Kerim Bey was the murder target on this night. For saving his life, Vavra makes Bond his son. Bond thanks Vavra for the honor and instead asks that the girl fight be stopped. Vavra asks 007 to choose the winner himself. It's a choice that Bond will take some offscreen time to make.

H

HADLEY M's (JOHN HUSTON) son, portrayed by British comedian Derek Nimmo, in *Casino Royale*. Joining Sir James Bond (DAVID NIVEN) after his father's untimely death in a mortar bomb barrage, Hadley helps 007 plot international strategy against the nefarious Dr. Noah (WOODY ALLEN). *See* NIMMO, DEREK.

HAGGERTY, FRED Actor who portrayed Krilencu, the Bulgar assassin in *From Russia with Love. See* KRILENCU.

HAI FAT Sinister Bangkok-based industrialist and the head of Hai Fat Enterprises, portrayed by Hawaiian-Chinese actor Richard Loo, in *The Man with the Golden Gun*. Determined to acquire a monopoly on solar-supplied energy, Hai Fat hires superassassin Francisco Scaramanga (CHRISTOPHER LEE) to kill Gibson, a British solar scientist, and steal the revolutionary solex agitator device.

When Bond (ROGER MOORE) tries to impersonate Scaramanga—complete with a third nipple—he's captured by Hai Fat's minions and brought to a karate school. Agent 007 holds his own with some formidable kick-boxers until he escapes. Meanwhile, Hai Fat is assassinated by Scaramanga, who steals the solex for himself.

HALEY'S LANDING The second reported destination of 007 (ROGER MOORE) during the wild motorboat chase in *Live and Let Die*. Louisiana police, led by comical J. W. Pepper (CLIFTON JAMES), first thought he was headed for the Irish Bayou.

HALL, LANI Smooth Latin songstress—and wife of music superstar Herb Alpert—whose title tune for *Never Say Never Again* was one of the film's highlights.

HAMA, MIE (1942–   ) Beautiful Japanese actress who portrayed Kissy, a Japanese Secret Service agent in *You Only Live Twice*

Songstress Lani Hall sang *Never Say Never Again*. (A&M Records)

Japanese media star Mie Hama, as she looks today. (Paul Sammon)

(1967) who "marries" Bond (SEAN CONNERY) on Ama Island. Although the Bond film was her most famous credit, Hama was also in *King Kong Versus Godzilla, What's Up, Tiger Lily?* (costarring her *You Only Live Twice* costar AKIKO WAKABAYASHI), and many other films. She later became a major media star in her native Japan—a kind of Japanese Jane Pauley.

HAMILTON British agent, on loan to the American CIA, who is assassinated in New Orleans in the *Live and Let Die* teaser. He's the unfortunate bystander who observes his own funeral procession.

HAMILTON AND MAXWELL Two of Felix Leiter's (NORMAN BURTON) CIA agents in *Diamonds Are Forever*.

HAMILTON, GUY (Paris, France, September 1922–   ) British film director who directed *Goldfinger* and went on to direct *Diamonds Are Forever, Live and Let Die,* and *The Man with the Golden Gun.*

Credit must be given to Hamilton for *Goldfinger*'s perfect balance of comic and serious elements. The deadly seriousness of *Dr. No* and *From Russia with Love* was gone, but the comedy of the future Bond films was still in check. Rumor has it, though, that there were some enormous script problems on *Goldfinger* and that at one point the movie was going to be shelved in favor of *Thunderball*. Fortunately, Richard Maibaum came to the rescue, and the film became the great box-office champion of 1964.

Hamilton would later direct Sean Connery's return to the 007 ranks in 1971's *Diamonds Are Forever*, as well as Roger Moore's debut as 007 in *Live and Let Die*.

Director Guy Hamilton takes a spin on one of the three-wheel cycles featured in *Diamonds Are Forever*. The moon buggy can be seen in the background. (Stephen Allen, Las Vegas News Bureau)

Director Guy Hamilton chats with a pre-golden Shirley Eaton during bedroom scenes in *Goldfinger*.
(National Film Archive, London)

Director Guy Hamilton offers some martial-arts advice to Roger Moore during kung-fu sequences filmed in Thailand on *The Man with the Golden Gun*. (Globe Photos)

HAMLISCH, MARVIN (New York City, June 2, 1944–   ) Academy Award–winning American composer who created the fanciful soundtrack score for *The Spy Who Loved Me* in 1977. Hamlisch's music perfectly sets up the incredible teaser in which James Bond skis off a Swiss mountaintop and parachutes to safety. Hamlisch's music for the chase sequence that featured the Lotus Esprit submarine car was also excellent.

HAMMOND M's (BERNARD LEE) butler, portrayed by John Gay, in *On Her Majesty's Secret Service*.

HANG GLIDER A method of airborne transportation used by James Bond (ROGER MOORE) in *Live and Let Die* and *Moonraker*. In actuality, Richard Maibaum was the first writer to put 007 in a hang glider. In one of the early drafts of *Diamonds Are Forever*, Bond uses a glider to find Marie, the woman who knows the whereabouts of Ernst Stavro Blofeld (in the final draft, Bond strangles her with her own bikini top until she gives him the information).

Screenwriter Tom Mankiewicz later used the same sequence in *Live and Let Die* when Bond (ROGER MOORE) hang glides his way from Quarrel, Jr.'s cabin cruiser to Solitaire's (JANE SEYMOUR) cliff-top sanctuary. In *Moonraker*, Bond (ROGER MOORE), piloting an armored motorboat in South America, is about to go over the falls, when he escapes in another hang glider that lands him gently in the jungle—not far from Hugo Drax's (MICHEL LONSDALE) secret rocket base.

HANLEY, JENNY Actress who portrayed the Italian allergy victim in *On Her Majesty's Secret Service*.

HANS Blofeld's (DONALD PLEASENCE) huge bodyguard, portrayed by Ronald Rich, in *You Only Live Twice*. During the climactic fight with Bond (SEAN CONNERY) inside Blofeld's living quarters, Hans is eaten alive when he falls into the piranha pool.

"HARD CURRENCY" A wad of bills worth 200,000 rupees that saves James Bond's (ROGER MOORE) life in *Octopussy*. Having taken Kamal Khan (LOUIS JOURDAN) for

that sum in a spirited backgammon game, Bond joins Vijay (VIJAY AMRITRAJ) in a three-wheeled scooter that is immediately chased by Kamal's bodyguard, Gobinda (KABIR BEDI), and his jeep-borne fanatics.

Fighting off the killers in a madcap chase through the crowded bazaars of Udaipur, India, Bond, at one point, is stabbed in the chest with a five-bladed knife. Fortunately, the blade catches on his wad of bills instead. Later in the chase, Bond further delays Gobinda's pursuit when he causes a riot by throwing the entire wad into the street.

HARDWICK, PAUL British actor who portrayed the Leonid Brezhnev look-alike in *Octopussy*.

HAREM GIRLS The beautiful companions of British agent-turned-desert-chieftain Sheik Hosein (EDWARD DE SOUZA) in *The Spy Who Loved Me*. They are portrayed by Felicity York, Dawn Rodriguez, Anika Pavel, and Jill Goodall.

HARGREAVES, ADMIRAL Flag Officer Submarines, portrayed by Robert Brown, in *The Spy Who Loved Me*. When a British nuclear submarine disappears, Hargreaves, Bond (ROGER MOORE), M (BERNARD LEE), Q (DESMOND LLEWELYN), and Freddie Gray (GEOFFREY KEEN)—the Minister of Defense—meet at a British base in Scotland to discuss a top secret submarine-tracking system that might have fallen into the wrong hands.

Hargreaves recognizes Bond from his previous service on the Ark Royal aircraft carrier, the first time in the series 007's naval career is mentioned. Hargreaves later joins the British Secret Service as the new M in *Octopussy*, a part he has played ever since. *See* BROWN, ROBERT.

HARI, MATA Famous World War I German spy, who, according to *Casino Royale*, was the great love of Sir James Bond's (DAVID NIVEN) life. After giving birth to their illegitimate child, Mata Bond (JOANNA PETTET), Mata Hari was lured across the Spanish border into France by 007, where she was captured and executed by the French. Her famous Dance and Spy School in West Berlin still stands, while the door to her boudoir has not been opened since 1916. *See* BOND, MATA.

HARRIER JUMP-JET British jet fighter, with a vertical takeoff, that carries defecting Russian General Georgi Koskov (JEROEN KRABBE) from Austria to England in *The Living Daylights*.

HARRIS, CASSANDRA Late Australian actress who was the wife of actor Pierce Brosnan. She portrayed Milos Columbo's (TOPOL) mistress, Countess Lisl Von Schlam, in *For Your Eyes Only*.

HARRIS, JULIUS W. American character actor who portrayed the chuckling Tee Hee in *Live and Let Die*. *See* TEE HEE.

HARRY AND THE ELEPHANT SHOES An amusing anecdote from the pre-production days of *The Man with the Golden Gun*. As related by screenwriter Tom Mankiewicz, "When *Golden Gun* was starting, producer Harry Saltzman went to Thailand. He wanted to have an elephant stampede in the picture. He told us that up in the Thai provinces, they use elephants for transport and work. He wondered whether Scaramanga could be working in the jungle, and when Bond arrives, they could chase each other on the backs of elephants.

"Director Guy Hamilton didn't like the idea. He'd seen it before in 10,000 Tarzan films. But Harry disregarded us. He went down and found a guy who worked with elephants, and he learned that the elephants had to wear shoes when they worked—actually, they wore coverings for their feet that protected them in rough areas such as stone quarries.

" 'This is fabulous,' Harry told me. 'I've never seen an elephant shoe before.' So Cubby is down in Southeast Asia watching over the filming, when some guy calls up and tells him that Eon's elephant shoes are ready. And Cubby says, 'What elephant shoes?'

"As it turned out, Harry had ordered something like 2,000 pairs of elephant shoes—even though there were no elephants in the script—which some guy had been working on for months. This guy still wanted his money." (Eon Productions still owns them, in fact.)

HARWOOD, JOHANNA Director Terence Young's resourceful script girl on *Dr. No* and *From Russia with Love*, who received co-credit on both films. According to Young, it was Harwood who suggested that they feature the stolen Goya portrait of Wellington for use in Dr. No's living room, a painting that everyone in England would recognize.

HATTON, JOHN Actor who portrayed the British Secret Service radio operator in London who loses contact with Commander John Strangways in Jamaica in *Dr. No*. Hatton's call sign was G7W London.

HAVELOCK, IONA The wife of archaeologist and British agent Timothy Havelock (JACK HEDLEY) and the mother of Melina Havelock (CAROLE BOUQUET), portrayed by actress Toby Robins in *For Your Eyes Only*. As part of Aris Kristatos's (JULIAN GLOVER) plan to acquire a British nuclear-submarine attack communicator, she and her husband are strafed and murdered by Cuban hit man Hector Gonzales (STEFAN KALIPHA).

HAVELOCK, MELINA Tall, statuesque, hauntingly beautiful half-Greek woman, portrayed by French actress Carole Bouquet, in *For Your Eyes Only*. The daughter of archaeologist Timothy Havelock (JACK HEDLEY) and Iona Havelock (TOBY ROBINS), Melina doesn't know that her father is secretly working for the British in an effort to salvage the sunken *St. Georges* surveillance ship.

When the Havelocks are killed by Cuban hit man Hector Gonzales (STEFAN KALIPHA), Melina exacts her own just revenge with a crossbow. Unfortunately, she also stumbles into a much bigger plot, involving 007 (ROGER MOORE) and a Soviet-British race to recover the A.T.A.C. device that was lost aboard the *St. Georges*.

Involved in the salvage operation—using her father's *Neptune* submarine—Melina and 007 are later captured and nearly flayed on a reef, in a scene right out of the *Live and Let Die* novel. Surviving, she joins 007 on the final mission to St. Cyril church atop Greece's famous Meteora cliffs.

HAVELOCK, TIMOTHY Melina Havelock's (CAROLE BOUQUET) archaeologist father, portrayed by Jack Hedley, in *For Your Eyes Only*. Secretly, he's working for the British in their attempt to salvage the sunken *St. Georges* surveillance ship. Unfortunately, Havelock and his wife Iona are strafed and murdered by Cuban hit man Hector Gonzales (STEFAN KALIPHA), who is working for Soviet agent Aris Kristatos (JULIAN GLOVER).

HAWAII Site of the space-tracking station that communicates with the *Jupiter 16* in *You Only Live Twice*. Manning that station are 007 veterans Ed Bishop (Klaus Hergersheimer, the radiation-shield checker in *Diamonds Are Forever*) and Shane Rimmer, the American submarine skipper in *The Spy Who Loved Me*.

HAWKER Bond's (SEAN CONNERY) feisty and all-knowing caddy in *Goldfinger*, portrayed by actor Gerry Duggan. *See* GOLF MATCH.

HAWKES, GRAHAM British actor who portrayed the underwater Mantis Man in *For Your Eyes Only*. *See* MANTIS.

HAWKINS DEA agent in Key West, portrayed by Grand L. Bush, who tells revenge-crazed James Bond (TIMOTHY DALTON) to forget about escaped drug runner Franz Sanchez (ROBERT DAVI) in *Licence to Kill*. The cáse is out of Bond's jurisdiction—a point seconded by M (ROBERT BROWN) during a heated confrontation at the Hemingway House, where Bond's double-0 status is revoked.

HAYWARD FAULT Earthquake-sensitive region of northern California that becomes a pawn in Max Zorin's (CHRISTOPHER WALKEN) plan to destroy Silicon Valley in *A View to a Kill*. *See* PROJECT MAIN STRIKE.

HEARSE Black Cadillac getaway vehicle for the three Jamaican murderers—the "three blind mice"—who assassinate John Strangways (TIM MOXON) in *Dr. No*. If you look closely at the side of the hearse when it's driven away from the murder site in the Queen's Club parking lot, you'll see the reflection of one of the film crew's arc lights.

The same hearse tries to run James Bond (SEAN CONNERY) off the road when he's on his way to Miss Taro's (ZENA MARSHALL) cottage in the Blue Mountains. Bond manages to stay on the highway, maneuvers his way under a construction vehicle, and watches as the hearse skids off the mountainside, goes over the cliff, and explodes.

HEART-SHAPED PENDANT What James Bond (ROGER MOORE) recovers from around the neck of a dead Agent 003 in *A View to a Kill*. It contains a new-generation microchip that British Intelligence has determined is impervious to magnetic pulse damage from a possible A-bomb blast in outer space. Ordinary microchips, on the other hand, could be rendered useless by such a calamity—for instance, shutting down every computer in Britain at a strategic moment.

HEATHROW London airport from which exiled Afghan prince Kamal Khan (LOUIS JOURDAN) departs for New Delhi, India, in *Octopussy*.

HEAT-SIGNATURE RECOGNITION A sophisticated electronic method of pinpointing the position of a submerged nuclear submarine by tracking its wake. This technique is explained by Q (DESMOND LLEWELYN) after the disappearance of the British nuclear submarine *Ranger* in *The Spy Who Loved Me*. Q compares it to using infrared satellite heat sensors to track the tail fire of nuclear missiles.

In the film, billionaire shipping magnate Karl Stromberg's (CURT JURGENS) scientific duo—Dr. Bechmann (CYRIL SHAPS) and Professor Markovitz (MILO SPERBER)—have developed a heat-signature recognition system that Stromberg uses to find and trap three nuclear submarines. However, Stromberg's system is betrayed by his secretary (MARILYN GALSWORTHY), who tries to make a fortune by selling it on the open market. This ploy eventually leads James Bond (ROGER MOORE) and KGB Major Anya Amasova (BARBARA BACH) to Stromberg's Atlantis hideaway off the coast of Sardinia.

"HE DISAGREED WITH SOMETHING THAT ATE HIM" Sign on a crumpled piece of paper that is stuffed into the mouth of Felix

Leiter (DAVID HEDISON) after the CIA man has been thrown to the sharks in *Licence to Kill*. It is actually a reference to an incident that occurs in author Ian Fleming's novel *Live and Let Die*. In *Licence to Kill*'s case, Leiter survives, but he loses his left leg below the knee.

HEDISON, DAVID (Providence, Rhode Island, May 20, 1929–   ) (real name, Ara Heditsian) Distinctive-voiced American character actor who is the only man to play CIA agent Felix Leiter twice—in *Live and Let Die* and *Li-*

David Hedison is the only actor to portray Felix Leiter in more than one 007 film. Whether he returns for a third time depends on whether his character remains in the CIA after his shark debacle in *Licence to Kill*. (Craig Wyckoff)

cence to Kill. In the latter film, Leiter is captured and mutilated by drug runner Franz Sanchez (ROBERT DAVI), who throws him to the sharks. This event sends James Bond (TIMOTHY DALTON) on a desperate, unauthorized mission of revenge. *See* LEITER, FELIX.

HEDLEY, JACK (1930–   ) British actor who portrayed Timothy Havelock, the marine archaeologist and Secret Service agent whose

brutal murder is avenged by his daughter, Melina (CAROLE BOUQUET), in *For Your Eyes Only*. *See* HAVELOCK, TIMOTHY.

HELLER South American drug lord Franz Sanchez's (ROBERT DAVI) head of security, portrayed by veteran American character actor Don Stroud, in *Licence to Kill*. Heller runs Sanchez's well-equipped private army in Isthmus City.

During an assault on the stronghold of some Hong Kong narcotics agents, Heller leads the full-scale attack in an armored vehicle. Having destroyed Milton Krest's (ANTHONY ZERBE) relationship with Sanchez, Bond continues his mind games on the Sanchez-Heller bond. Heller is ripe for a turnaround.

According to CIA undercover operative Pam Bouvier (CAREY LOWELL), Heller is going to try to return to the United States four Stinger missiles that were stolen from the Contra rebels. Unfortunately, he changes his mind when Bond (TIMOTHY DALTON) fails to kill Sanchez with the signature gun.

Later, at the Olimpatec Meditation Institute, Sanchez turns on Heller, who has the Stinger missiles in his possession. The security chief is then impaled on the blades of a runaway forklift.

HEMINGWAY HOUSE Key West, Florida, landmark where M (ROBERT BROWN) confronts revenge-crazed James Bond (TIMOTHY DALTON) in *Licence to Kill*. M's top agent has not reported for his next assignment in Istanbul. Worried that Bond will not back down after drug runners mutilate his CIA chum Felix Leiter (DAVID HEDISON) and murder Leiter's bride, Della Churchill (PRISCILLA BARNES), M realizes that the only way to stop 007 is to revoke his license to kill. That doesn't work either, as Bond defies his superior, fights off a couple of fellow British agents, and disappears.

Located at 907 Whitehead Street in Key West, the Hemingway House is where American author Ernest Hemingway spent the last 30 years of his life, until his death in 1961.

HEMPEL, ANOUSHKA Actress who portrayed the Australian allergy victim in *On Her Majesty's Secret Service*.

HENDERSON, DIKKO Bond's (SEAN CONNERY) fellow Secret Service operative in Tokyo, portrayed by Charles Gray, who would return to portray Ernst Stavro Blofeld in *Diamonds Are Forever*. Although British, Henderson has adopted many of the Japanese customs, including the kimono and an appropriately furnished apartment. Although his part is very brief, Henderson captures the spirit of the Dikko Henderson portrayed in the original Fleming novel.

How does Bond check Henderson's identity during their first meeting? He takes Henderson's cane and bashes his right leg, which turns out to be wooden. He lost it in Singapore in '42. Unfortunately, before we can get to know Henderson, he is knifed by one of Mr. Osato's (TERU SHIMADA) henchmen.

HENDRY, GLORIA (Jacksonville, Florida, 1949–   ) Actress and former Playboy bunny who portrayed the inept Rosie Carver in *Live and Let Die*. *See* CARVER, ROSIE.

HENRIQUES, SYLVANA Actress who portrayed the Jamaican allergy victim in *On Her Majesty's Secret Service*.

HERB ALPERT AND THE TIJUANA BRASS Colorful 1960s Latin pop group that provided the catchy instrumental theme for the *Casino Royale* spoof.

HERGERSHEIMER, KLAUS The innocent radiation-shield inspector, portrayed by Ed Bishop in *Diamonds Are Forever*. Attached to G Section, he's spent three years at Techtronics, a top secret division of Willard Whyte's global conglomerate specializing in satellite research and space exploration.

When Bond (SEAN CONNERY) sneaks into Techtronics, it is Hergersheimer whom he impersonates, gaining entrance to Professor-Dr. Metz's (JOSEPH FURST) lab. When the real Hergersheimer shows up, Metz sounds the alarm.

Live and Let Die's Gloria Hendry joined the author at the University of Southern California in 1982 for a salute to the TV version of "Casino Royale."

"HER PRICE IS FAR ABOVE RUBIES OR EVEN YOUR MILLION POUNDS" An old proverb quoted by James Bond (GEORGE LAZENBY) to Tracy Vicenzo (DIANA RIGG) on their wedding day in *On Her Majesty's Secret Service*.

HEY, VIRGINIA British actress who portrayed Rubavitch, Russian General Leonid Pushkin's (JOHN RHYS-DAVIES) girlfriend in *The Living Daylights*.

HIGH HEEL SHOES All that's left of S.P.E.C.T.R.E. assassin Fatima Blush (BARBARA CARRERA) after James Bond (SEAN CONNERY) disintegrates her with his rocket-firing fountain pen in *Never Say Never Again*. A definite steal from the Wicked Witch's demise in *The Wizard of Oz*—appropriate in this case because in every sense, Fatima Blush was a very wicked witch.

HILL, BILL The production manager on *From Russia with Love* who portrayed Captain Nash, the Yugoslavia-based British agent who is murdered by Red Grant (ROBERT SHAW) in the Zagreb train station rest room. Hill always joked about his brief nonspeaking part.

"It was totally preposterous, if you thought about it," said Hill. "Here I am, arriving in Zagreb station on this terribly important mission to assist a fellow agent, and after we trade the recognition signal, we're on our way to the bathroom. What were we supposed to be saying, anyway? 'Let's have a pee and then we'll board the train'?"

HIMEJI CASTLE Historic Japanese feudal castle that was used as the Ninja training grounds in *You Only Live Twice*.

HIP, LIEUTENANT Hong Kong police detective, portrayed by Soon-Taik Oh, who is James Bond's (ROGER MOORE) contact in *The Man with the Golden Gun*. They meet when Hip arrests Bond for the murder of Gibson, the British solar energy expert.

Hip later helps Bond escape from Hai Fat's (RICHARD LOO) estate. His friends are the swift-kicking young girls whose father runs a karate school. At the kick-boxing tournament, where Andrea Anders (MAUD ADAMS) is supposed to hand over the solex, Hip joins the

surveillance dressed in a peanut vendor's uniform.

HMS TENBY A British destroyer anchored in Gibraltar Harbor that in December 1966 served as the location for James Bond's (SEAN CONNERY) military "funeral" in *You Only Live Twice*. In the film, Gibraltar is playing Hong Kong Harbor.

When the body is dumped into the harbor, the film, in reality, cuts to the Bahamas, where underwater cinematographer Lamar Boren filmed the body floating to the ocean floor. Two skin divers then rescue it and bring it to a waiting British submarine. The actual interior of the sub was located in the east tunnel of Pinewood and was completed in mid-October 1966.

HOFFNER, FRAU Mata Hari's Prussian dance teacher and the current owner of West Berlin's Mata Hari Dance and Spy School in *Casino Royale*. She's portrayed by Anna Quayle.

HOGLEG Slang term for a sidearm, used by Willard Whyte (JIMMY DEAN) in *Diamonds Are Forever*. The message to leave his "hogleg" behind is given to James Bond (SEAN CONNERY) in the bathroom of Whyte's Las Vegas hotel suite. In actuality, it is Blofeld (CHARLES GRAY) who is speaking, thanks to an electronic device that allows him to perfectly imitate Whyte's voice.

HOLDEN, WILLIAM (O'Fallon, Illinois, April 17, 1918–October 16, 1981) (real name, William Franklin Beedle, Jr.) Superstar American leading man of the 1950s who portrayed acronym-obsessed CIA chief Ransome in *Casino Royale*. See RANSOME.

HOLDER, GEOFFREY (Port-of-Spain, Trinidad, 1930–   ) Tall (six feet, six inches), imposing actor/dancer/choreographer who portrayed the mystical Baron Samedi in *Live and Let Die*. Known more for his soft-drink commercials than his film roles, Holder was perfectly cast as Kananga's (YAPHET KOTTO) giant henchman, who may or not be a supernatural being.

HOMER A small electronic surveillance device designed to track friendly and enemy agents in *Goldfinger*. In order to follow Goldfinger

(GERT FROBE) to his Swiss base, Bond (SEAN CONNERY) plants one of the magnetic homers in the villain's Rolls-Royce. The signal is then received on an audiovisual panel built into the dashboard of 007's Aston Martin DB-5. Its range is 150 miles.

A smaller homer is standard field issue and is fitted into the heel of James Bond's shoe. This device allows the CIA to determine that Bond has been captured by Goldfinger and transported to the United States on a private jetliner headed for Friendship Airport, Baltimore.

In order to alert the CIA about Goldfinger's plan to detonate an A-bomb in Fort Knox, Bond removes the homer from his shoe and places it in the suit pocket of Mafioso Mr. Solo (MARTIN BENSON), who is supposedly headed to the local airport for a trip to New York. Unfortunately, when Oddjob (HAROLD SAKATA) murders Solo and completely crushes his Continental, the homer is destroyed, and Felix Leiter (CEC LINDER) is unable to receive the message.

In *The Man with the Golden Gun*, Bond (ROGER MOORE) employs a similiar audiovisual receiver in the cockpit of his seaplane when he tracks Mary Goodnight (BRITT EKLAND) to Scaramanga's (CHRISTOPHER LEE) remote island off the coast of China.

HOME SECRETARY High-level British official, portrayed by Roland Culver, with direct access to No. 10 Downing Street, in *Thunderball*. At the meeting of all double-0 agents, he plays the tape that reveals the S.P.E.C.T.R.E. extortion plot. Later, when time is running out, he begins plans to assemble the $280 million diamond ransom that will be used to retrieve the two missing atomic weapons.

HONDA ATC-90 Motorbike ridden by Dr. Tynan (DAVID DE KEYSER) to a South African desert rendezvous with Mr. Wint (BRUCE GLOVER) and Mr. Kidd (PUTTER SMITH) in *Diamonds Are Forever*. The smuggled diamonds he's carrying are stored in a secret compartment built into the motorbike's muffler.

HONG KONG Bustling Asian capital that figures in several Bond films. In *You Only Live Twice*, it's the location of Bond's (SEAN CON-

NERY) tryst with Ling (TSAI CHIN) and his faked assassination. In *Diamonds Are Forever*, it's the destination of Tiffany Case (JILL ST. JOHN) once she gets the diamonds from James Bond.

In *The Man with the Golden Gun*, British Secret Service headquarters in the Far East are located aboard the twisted wreckage of the *Queen Elizabeth I*, which caught fire and partially sank in Hong Kong Harbor.

HONG KONG–MACAO HYDROFOIL CO. LTD. Sea link between Hong Kong and Macao in *The Man with the Golden Gun*. While aboard one of this firm's hydrofoils, James Bond (ROGER MOORE) follows Francisco Scaramanga's girlfriend, Andrea Anders (MAUD ADAMS), to Hong Kong. At one point, the hydrofoil travels past the rusted hulk of the *Queen Elizabeth I* ocean liner, the interior of which has been transformed into British Secret Service Far East headquarters.

HOODS CONVENTION The nickname given to the group of gangsters who arrive at Auric Stud to collect their million dollars in *Goldfinger*. Gathered in the huge game room, they soon find themselves being lectured on the potential of Operation Grand Slam, Goldfinger's (GERT FROBE) plan to rob Fort Knox, Kentucky. They're also given a choice: each of the hoods can leave, if they like, with their $1 million, or they can participate in the robbery and come away with $10 million each.

Impressed by their host's plan, every hood agrees, except for Mafia kingpin Mr. Solo (MARTIN BENSON), who wants to leave with his $1 million in gold. What the hoods don't know is that Goldfinger has no intention of stealing the gold. He's instead going to irradiate it with an atomic bomb supplied by the Red Chinese.

They're also doomed men, because no sooner does Goldfinger leave the room to provide Solo with his gold than his assistant Kisch (MICHAEL MELLINGER) hermetically seals off the game room and sprays Delta Nine poison gas into the room, killing everyone.

HORSFALL, BERNARD Blond British actor who portrayed Campbell, 007's (GEORGE

LAZENBY) doomed Swiss contact in *On Her Majesty's Secret Service*.

HOSEIN, SHEIK British Secret Service agent, portrayed by British actor Edward de Souza, masquerading as a desert chieftain outside Cairo, in *The Spy Who Loved Me*. An old college chum of Bond (ROGER MOORE), Hosein provides 007 with his first contact on the road to retrieving the nuclear-submarine tracking system that is being peddled on the open market. He also offers Bond a bed and a bedmate for the night.

HOT AIR BALLOON Piloted by Q (DESMOND LLEWELYN), it's how James Bond (ROGER MOORE) arrives in the thick of the Monsoon Palace assault in *Octopussy*.

HOTEL CALA DI VOLPE Resort on the island of Sardinia that was featured in *The Spy Who Loved Me*. Part of the enormous Costa Smeralda real estate development financed by the Aga Khan, it served as James Bond's (ROGER MOORE) and Major Anya Amasova's (BARBARA BACH) hotel prior to their visit to Stromberg's (CURT JURGENS) Atlantis base.

HOTEL TROPICALE Evelyn Tremble/James Bond's (PETER SELLERS) Monte Carlo hotel in *Casino Royale*. It's where he meets Miss Goodthighs (JACQUELINE BISSET).

HOVERCRAFT Large channel-crossing passenger vessel that takes James Bond (SEAN CONNERY) from England to Holland in *Diamonds Are Forever*. It rides above the water on a current of air.

HOWARD, ARTHUR (1910–   ) British character actor and brother of Leslie Howard who portrayed Drax's (MICHEL LONSDALE) butler in *Moonraker*.

HOWDAH Name for the ornamental riding platforms used on Indian elephants during the tiger hunt in *Octopussy*. Trapped in the grass beneath Gobinda's (KABIR BEDI) elephant, James Bond (ROGER MOORE) unbuckles the strap holding his howdah in place. When Bond dashes into the brush, Gobinda tries to open fire, but the loosened howdah topples him to the ground.

HOWE, W. G. Corrupt California bureaucrat with the Division of Oil and Mines, portrayed by Daniel Benzali, who is on the payroll of psychotic industrialist Max Zorin (CHRISTOPHER WALKEN) in *A View to a Kill*.

When Bond (ROGER MOORE), masquerading as London *Financial Times* reporter James Stock, asks Howe about the potential danger of Zorin's pumping of seawater into his oil pipeline, Howe assures him that it's simply a method of testing the integrity of the pipeline for leaks. When geologist Stacey Sutton (TANYA ROBERTS) brings to Howe's attention the fact that Zorin may be pumping water into the unstable Hayward earthquake fault, he fires her.

Determined to prove their theory, Bond and Stacey break into Howe's office at City Hall and discover the details of Zorin's Project Main Strike. Unfortunately, the two are discovered by Zorin and his bodyguard, May Day (GRACE JONES).

When Howe arrives, Zorin details how he's going to frame Bond and Stacey for Howe's murder. Alarmed, Howe says, "But that means . . . ," after which Zorin shoots him.

Zorin's assistants, Jenny Flex (ALISON DOODY) and Pan Ho (PAPILLON SOO SOO), then spread gasoline in Howe's office and along the corridors. Zorin takes Bond and Stacey to an elevator, where they're trapped between floors when Scarpine (PATRICK BAUCHAU) kills the power. Zorin then starts a fire from which 007 and Stacey make a narrow escape. *See* PROJECT MAIN STRIKE.

HUDSON, TINA Curvaceous actress who portrayed Bianca, James Bond's (ROGER MOORE) Cuban assistant, in *Octopussy*. *See* BIANCA.

HUGHES, KEN (Liverpool, England, January 19, 1922–   ) British film director who codirected the 1967 *Casino Royale* spoof with John Huston, Val Guest, Robert Parrish, and Joseph McGrath. He was responsible for the surreal Mata Bond (JOANNA PETTET) sequence in West Berlin.

HUNGARY Native country of the United Nations diplomat who is speaking when a British agent is assassinated in the *Live and Let Die* teaser.

HUNT, PETER ROGER (London, England, March 11, 1928–   ) British film director and former editor who was intimately involved in the production of the first six James Bond films. As supervising editor on the first five films, second-unit director on *You Only Live Twice*, and director of *On Her Majesty's Secret Service*, Hunt contributed greatly to the visual style and pacing of the early Bond films.

Starting with *Dr. No*, Hunt and director Terence Young used a film editing technique comparable to television commercial cutting, which produced a very lean visual structure. For instance, if an actor walked out a doorway and headed for his car, Hunt would get him there as quickly as possible. The phrase "cut to the chase" aptly describes this type of editing style.

Said Young, "We used to cut in the middle of pans. There was no dissolving. You went straight into flash cuts. There were a lot of sound cuts and an enormous number of tracks and pans so that one always got the impression that something was moving on-screen. The result was that it was only on the way home that the husband turned to the wife and said, 'It was rather nonsense, wasn't it?' But people would qualify their criticism with, 'Look, you enjoyed it for a couple of hours, what else do you want?' "

The idea of keeping *Dr. No* moving at all times was a key to its success. Everyone, including producers Albert R. Broccoli and Harry Saltzman, was concerned that American audiences would not accept a Scottish actor as a leading man and hero. Consequently, much of *Dr. No*'s screen time is devoted to movement, action, and fights. Sean Connery has a minimum of dialogue in the first film.

Peter Hunt's pacing, combined with Terence Young's precise direction, Richard Maibaum's script, and John Barry's music initiated a new style in filmmaking—a style that was carried on by director and former editor John Glen, who worked for Hunt as a second-unit director/editor on *On Her Majesty's Secret Service*. Hunt's editing technique owes a debt to his early

schooling at the London College of Music, where he studied music theory and violin. His appreciation of timing in music would have a profound effect on his Bond film editing.

Hunt was also responsible for suggesting Sean Connery as a possible James Bond in 1961. At that time, Hunt was editing *On the Fiddle*, a British Abbott and Costello–like service comedy with comedian Alfie Lynch and Connery.

One night while having dinner at London's Polish Club with the film's producer, Benjamin Fisz, Hunt bumped into producer Harry Saltzman, who was then conducting the 007 casting search. Hunt suggested Connery for the part, and Saltzman eventually looked at some footage. He came to the same conclusion that Cubby Broccoli would have in Los Angeles while screening Walt Disney's *Darby O'Gill and the Little People*—that Sean Connery was their Bond.

Eager to make his directing debut, Hunt began to tire of the editing chores on the Bond films after the release of *Thunderball* in 1965. He agreed to return as editor and second-unit director on *You Only Live Twice* only if producers Broccoli and Saltzman would let him direct the next picture. The producers kept their part of the bargain, and Hunt was signed to direct the best of Ian Fleming's novels, *On Her Majesty's Secret Service*. Unfortunately, Sean Connery had left the series by then, so Hunt was forced to find his own Bond.

Australian model George Lazenby won the role in 1968. He proved capable and charismatic, but true fans will always wonder what would have happened if Sean Connery had played Bond one more time, especially in a film where he falls in love and gets married to Diana Rigg.

Ironically, considering the tight pacing he brought to the series, Hunt's directorial debut is the longest, at 140 minutes. However, OHMSS is also one of the most interesting films to watch. Determined to make an impact in his directorial debut, Hunt studied the original novel and worked closely with screenwriter Maibaum to create what is probably, along with *From Russia with Love*, the most accurate dramatization of an Ian Fleming work—down to the naval cannon in the driveway of M's home.

Pay particular attention to the opening sequence, which serves to introduce George Lazenby as Bond. The action sequences are quick and boisterous, particularly a fight in the surf in the film's teaser and a quick battle outside Marc Ange Draco's (GABRIELE FERZETTI) office in Portugal. *See* 140 MINUTES.

HUSTON, JOHN (Nevada, Missouri, August 5, 1906–1987)—Two-time Oscar-winning American director, writer, and actor; son of actor Walter Huston; and father of actress Angelica Huston. He portrayed M in *Casino Royale* and also codirected the film.

Huston's M, a low-key bureaucrat with an extremely bright red wig, is blown up in rural England when a barrage directed at Sir James Bond's (DAVID NIVEN) mansion by M himself falls short. Appropriately, considering the tone of this film, the only surviving body part is his wig. Huston directed himself and the Deborah Kerr sequence that takes place at a Scottish manor house. *See* M.

HYDROFOIL What the slow-moving *Disco Volante* yacht converts to in *Thunderball*. Leaving its "cocoon" behind to deal with a flotilla of Coast Guard warships, Emilio Largo (ADOLFO CELI) orders the hydrofoil to head for Miami with an A-bomb on board.

Having survived an underwater battle with S.P.E.C.T.R.E. frogmen, Bond (SEAN CONNERY) hitches a ride on one of the hydrofoil's jet skis and gains access to the bridge. There he gets into a furious fistfight with Largo and the hydrofoil skipper (stuntman HAROLD SANDERSON) while the hydrofoil goes out of control at 60 mph.

When Largo is speared by Domino (CLAUDINE AUGER), his body becomes wedged in the ship's steering gear, making it impossible to steer the craft away from an oncoming reef. At the last possible moment, Bond, Domino, and Kutze (GEORGE PRAVDA), the Polish nuclear expert, jump ship and escape the hydrofoil's obliteration. (Kutze had thrown the fuse to the A-bomb overboard, preventing a nuclear explosion.)

HYPER-INTENSIFIED MAGNETIC FIELD
A special feature of James Bond's (ROGER MOORE) watch in *Live and Let Die* that is very handy for attracting bullets or teaspoons.

I

"I ADMIRE YOUR COURAGE, MISS?" The first line of dialogue spoken by James Bond in the Albert R. Broccoli–produced 007 series. It is delivered by Sean Connery at a chemin de fer gaming table to actress Eunice Gayson, portraying playgirl Sylvia Trench. The location is the club Les Ambassadeurs in London. Gayson replies, "Trench. Sylvia Trench. Mr.?" to which Connery replies, "Bond. James Bond" while he is lighting his cigarette.

When director Terence Young first shot this sequence, Connery started his dialogue with the flick of his lighter, which caused a few chuckles among the crew. Young suggested that Connery flick his lighter sooner. Thus, when the camera would swing around to reveal Bond, he would be pictured in a swirl of cigarette smoke, there would be a beat, then one of the most famous lines in screen history would be uttered. The technique obviously worked.

ICE HOCKEY RINK Unusual battleground featured in *For Your Eyes Only*. Attacked on the indoor ice in Cortina by three stick-wielding, uniformed hockey players working for Soviet agent Aris Kristatos (JULIAN GLOVER), Bond manages to outplay all three. Each time a disabled player falls into his net, a goal alarm sounds. After a moment's combat, the score is Bond 3, Enemy Agents 0. Wayne Gretzky, eat your heart out.

ICEBERG-CAMOUFLAGED LAUNCH The unusual manner in which James Bond (ROGER MOORE) escapes from KGB ski troops in the teaser for *A View to a Kill*. The launch is piloted by fellow agent Kimberley Jones (MARY STAVIN). Like the escape pod from Atlantis in *The Spy Who Loved Me*, the seagoing vehicle becomes the perfect love nest for a long voyage—five days to Alaska.

IDENTIGRAPH 3-D visual identity computer employed by Q Branch in *For Your Eyes Only*. Bond (ROGER MOORE) uses the experimental model to identify Emile Leopold Locque (MICHAEL GOTHARD) as the man who paid off Cuban hit man Hector Gonzales (STEFAN KALIPHA) for murdering Timothy Havelock (JACK HEDLEY) and Iona Havelock (TOBY ROBINS). Once a composite of the suspect is created, the identigraph can tap into the photographic files of the French Surete, Interpol, the CIA, Mossad, and the West German police.

IGUANA Unusual lizard pet of drug runner Franz Sanchez (ROBERT DAVI) in *Licence to Kill*. It wears an expensive diamond collar that is coveted by Sanchez's girlfriend, Lupe Lamora (TALISA SOTO). In the end, thanks to James Bond's (TIMOTHY DALTON) efforts, Lupe wins the sparkler.

ILLYSTRIA A region of southwestern Yugoslavia that borders the Adriatic Sea. It is the jumping-off point for Bond (SEAN CONNERY) and Tanya's (DANIELA BIANCHI) motorboat trip to Venice in *From Russia with Love*.

"I LOVE YOU" The password between British Intelligence and Japanese S.I.S. in *You Only Live Twice*. Moneypenny (LOIS MAXWELL) gives it to Bond (SEAN CONNERY), who refuses to repeat it to her. Bond then gives it to Aki (AKIKO WAKABAYASHI), and later Tiger (TETSURO TAMBA) gives it to Bond.

IMMINENT Code name for a possible American nuclear attack against Russia in *You Only Live Twice*. Having lost one *Jupiter* space capsule to what they think is a Russian plot to control outer space, the U.S. government announces that if anything should happen to their second *Jupiter* capsule, they will launch an attack against Russia.

Little do they know that S.P.E.C.T.R.E., courtesy of their *Intruder* ship, is playing the Americans off against the Russians on behalf of the Red Chinese. Thanks to James Bond (SEAN CONNERY), who gets to the control panel in time and triggers the *Intruder*'s self-destruct mechanism, a nuclear nightmare is averted.

IMPELLER Internal rotating screw that is part of the pumping apparatus on Max Zorin's (CHRISTOPHER WALKEN) San Francisco Bay oil facility in *A View to a Kill*. Tipped off by a Bay area fisherman (BILL ACKRIDGE) who claims that his crab fishing is being ruined by Zorin's pumping activities, Bond (ROGER MOORE) takes an underwater swim to investigate.

Entering one of the pumping intake pipes, Bond is swimming toward the impeller when Zorin orders the system to be tested. Fighting against the current, which is rapidly pulling him toward the impeller's swirling blades, Bond takes his air tank and successfully jams it into the impeller, shutting down the system. Zorin's men retrieve the tank, which has been punctured by the blades, and reactivate the impeller motor.

When May Day (GRACE JONES) captures another underwater snooper, KGB agent Klotkoff (BOGDAN KOMINOWSKI), Zorin orders him thrown into the intake pipe where he's sliced to ribbons by the impeller.

IMPULSE CONDUCTOR CIRCUIT The area surrounding the detonation chamber of the nuclear missile that James Bond (ROGER MOORE) disassembles in *The Spy Who Loved Me*. The circuit is magnetic, and if Bond touches it with the detonator, the bomb will go off.

"IN, OUT, IN, OUT" Suggestive rowing commands uttered to the female oars handlers aboard the title character's barge in *Octopussy*.

INFERNO Spirited thoroughbred owned by Max Zorin (CHRISTOPHER WALKEN) in *A View to a Kill* and controlled by a microchip that has been surgically implanted in its leg. Given to Bond (ROGER MOORE) for a workout on Zorin's steeplechase course, the horse suddenly bolts and leads 007 on a frantic ride through the countryside, where Zorin's henchmen attempt to unseat him at every turn.

It's all part of Zorin's attempt to kill 007, now that he's been identified as a member of the British Secret Service. Bond somehow survives the wayward run, only to be knocked unconscious and thrown into the back of his Rolls-Royce, where he joins the dead Sir Godfrey Tibbett (PATRICK MACNEE). When the car is ditched in a lake, Bond escapes from the sinking automobile and survives underwater by sucking the air out of one of the Michelin tires.

INFRARED SUNGLASSES Card-cheating device used by Soviet masterspy Le Chiffre (ORSON WELLES) to win at baccarat, in *Casino Royale*. He's already ruined two Greeks and a maharaja when Evelyn Tremble/James Bond (PETER SELLERS) arrives at the table. When Vesper Lynd (URSULA ANDRESS) steals the sunglasses, Le Chiffre is vulnerable, and Tremble eventually beats him.

INTERNATIONAL AUCTION What Ernst Stavro Blofeld (CHARLES GRAY) plans to hold once his laser satellite is operational, in *Diamonds Are Forever*. With a space weapon capable of destroying any target on earth in his hands, Blofeld plans to sell nuclear supremacy to the highest bidder.

This plan is contrary to what Blofeld's principal scientist, Professor-Dr. Metz (JOSEPH FURST), has been told. He had been lured into S.P.E.C.T.R.E.'s employ after Blofeld guaranteed that total disarmament and peace for the world would be achieved once the satellite was operational. (You just can't trust Mr. Blofeld.) Fortunately, Bond (SEAN CONNERY) arrives to once again destroy S.P.E.C.T.R.E.'s plans for world domination.

INTERNATIONAL BROTHERHOOD FOR THE ASSISTANCE OF STATELESS PERSONS A legitimate philanthropic organization based in Paris that in actuality is a S.P.E.C.T.R.E. front, in *Thunderball*. Beneath its offices is the sleek, modern, stainless-steel headquarters of Ernst Stavro Blofeld.

INTERNATIONAL HOTEL Las Vegas hotel (now the Las Vegas Hilton) that figures prominently in the plot of *Diamonds Are Forever*.

INTERNATIONAL MOTHER'S HELP Social welfare organization, in the *Casino Royale* spoof, that is a cover for the Mata Hari Dance and Spy School in West Berlin. Located on the Feldmanstrasse, it supplies baby-sitters and au pair girls to some of the most important families in Europe. Inside, Frau Hoffner (ANNA QUAYLE) and Polo (RONNIE CORBETT) preserve the spy school that Mata Hari founded—a school that trains agents of all countries.

Las Vegas's International Hotel, *background*, doubled for the Whyte House in *Diamonds Are Forever*. It's also a short walk to the gas station where Tiffany Case (JILL ST. JOHN) distracts Dr. Metz so that Bond (SEAN CONNERY) can steal aboard his passenger van. (Stephen Allen, Las Vegas News Bureau)

INTRUDER The name given to the S.P.E.C.T.R.E. rocket in the *You Only Live Twice* script. It is also code-named *Bird One* on its final mission.

The instrument of Ernst Stavro Blofeld's (DONALD PLEASENCE) plan to aid the Red Chinese by igniting World War III between the United States and Russia, the *Intruder*'s mission is to literally swallow enemy space capsules. Equipped with an electronically operated snout that opens like the mouth of a whale, the *Intruder* performs well, capturing one Russian and one U.S. *Jupiter* spacecraft.

Having snatched the ships from their earthly orbit, the *Intruder* then returns to its secret rocket base, hidden inside the cone of a dormant Japanese volcano. Like the space shuttle, the *Intruder* has the ability to return to Earth under its own power.

On its third mission to capture a second *Jupiter* spacecraft, a hostile act which the Americans will be led to believe is precipitated by the Russians (the *Intruder* is this time decorated with the Red star insignia to further confuse the U.S. astronauts), James Bond (SEAN CONNERY) is able to break into Blofeld's rocket base and activate the self-destruct mechanism on the *Intruder* before it accomplishes its task.

The idea of playing the Russians and Amer-

S.P.E.C.T.R.E.'s Intruder rocket blasts off from Blofeld's secret rocket base in Japan. (UPI)

icans off against one another is typical of S.P.E.C.T.R.E., which initiated such a caper in *From Russia with Love*. Writer Richard Maibaum and director Lewis Gilbert, reteaming on *The Spy Who Loved Me*, went back to such a plot device in that film, only this time billionaire marine specialist Karl Stromberg (CURT JURGENS) replaced Blofeld as the megalomaniac who's intent on destroying the world for his own selfish gain. The supertanker of the film—the *Liparus*—was simply an updated, seaborne *Intruder* rocket, just as Little Nellie, the autogyro in *You Only Live Twice*, was an updated—albeit airborne—Aston Martin.

INVISIBLE EMPIRE What South American drug lord Franz Sanchez (ROBERT DAVI) dubs his growing cocaine operation in *Licence to Kill*. To buy into the expanding business, which already stretches from Chile to Alaska, international distributors are being offered franchises at $100 million per territory. As members of the cartel, they will pay $20 million per metric ton of cocaine.

The price and quality will be guaranteed by Sanchez for five years. Actually, the price and quality are guaranteed for only about 24 hours, since James Bond (TIMOTHY DALTON) and Pam Bouvier (CAREY LOWELL) put Sanchez out of business.

IONIAN SEA Body of water off the coast of Albania where the *St. Georges* surveillance ship is sunk in *For Your Eyes Only*. *See* ST. GEORGES.

IRISH BAYOU According to the Louisiana State Police, led by Sheriff J. W. Pepper (CLIFTON JAMES), this is James Bond's (ROGER MOORE) destination during the motorboat chase in *Live and Let Die*. This destination is later amended to Haley's Landing.

IRKUTSK Site of the Soviet rocket-tracking station in *You Only Live Twice* that follows the progress of a Russian spacecraft that is eventually hijacked by the S.P.E.C.T.R.E. *Intruder* rocket.

ISLAMABAD 225 KM, KARACHI 200 KM Signposts on the Pakistani roadway trav-

eled by Bond (TIMOTHY DALTON) and Kara (MARYAM D'ABO) after escaping from a doomed Russian transport plane in *The Living Daylights*. Bond knows a great restaurant in Karachi.

ISLAND IN THE BAHAMAS The retirement goal of Pussy Galore (HONOR BLACKMAN) in *Goldfinger*. She plans to buy it, put up a No Trespassing sign, and go back to nature. Whether that means she's going to start a female-only nudist colony, we'll never know.

ISTANBUL Headquarters for Station T-Turkey in *From Russia with Love*. It is in this city on the Bosphorus that S.P.E.C.T.R.E. initiates its plan to steal a Russian Lektor decoding machine and humiliate and murder James Bond (SEAN CONNERY).

Istanbul is also the site of James Bond's (TIMOTHY DALTON) next mission in *Licence to Kill*—which 007 turns down in favor of his assault on Franz Sanchez's (ROBERT DAVI) drug empire. The unlawful act on Bond's part forces M (ROBERT BROWN) to revoke his license to kill.

ISTHMUS CITY Fictional South American coastal city that is actually the cocaine capital of Franz Sanchez's (ROBERT DAVI) drug empire in *Licence to Kill*. Ruled by puppet President Hector Lopez (PEDRO ARMENDARIZ JR.), the city has been virtually bought by Sanchez, who owns the main hotel and the bank.

Many interior and exterior sequences in Isthmus City were actually filmed in Mexico City. The city's Main Post Office became the interior of the Banco de Isthmus, where Sanchez launders all of his drug loot. Bond's (TIMOTHY DALTON) hotel, El Presidente, was filmed inside Mexico City's Gran Hotel Ciudad de Mexico. Its exterior was shot outside the Biblioteca de la Banco de Mexico—the Library of the Bank of Mexico.

The exterior shots of Sanchez's office building were filmed outside the famous El Teatro de la Ciudad (Theater of the City). The casino where elegant blackjack dealer Lupe Lamora (TALISA SOTO) helps Bond meet Sanchez was filmed inside Mexico City's Casino Espagnol, a private club and ex-gambling house.

ITHACA'S COLT Full brother of Max Zorin's (CHRISTOPHER WALKEN) prize thoroughbred Pegasus in *A View to a Kill*. He's the main attraction at Zorin's French horse sale and is expected to bring in a minimum of $3 million.

IVAN AND BORIS KGB Major Anya Amasova's (BARBARA BACH) Cairo assistants in *The Spy Who Loved Me*. During a scuffle outside the tomb of Cheops, they're overmatched by James Bond (ROGER MOORE).

IVANOVA, POLA Soviet KGB agent and ex-ballerina, portrayed by Fiona Fullerton, who's sent to San Francisco to investigate Max Zorin's (CHRISTOPHER WALKEN) oil-pumping activities in *A View to a Kill*. While

Bond (ROGER MOORE) and her partner Klotkoff (BOGDAN KOMINOWSKI) are battling their way in and out of an intake pipe, Ivanova is conducting a tape-recorded surveillance of Zorin's conversation with his oil company chief, Bob Conley (MANNING REDWOOD).

Later, on the beach, Bond tackles Ivanova and realizes she's an old adversary who once tried to seduce him. Getting into her silver Corvette, both agents retire to a comfortable hot tub at the Nippon Relaxation Spa, where they renew their acquaintance, serenaded by a Tchaikovsky cassette provided by 007.

Leaving the spa, Ivanova takes what she thinks is her surveillance tape and joins her boss, General Gogol (WALTER GOTELL), for a quick getaway. What they soon realize is that 007 has stolen their tape.

J

JAMES BOND BRITISH FAN CLUB

President Graham Rye has revitalized this organization, and his quarterly publication *007* is well worth the membership fee. A newsletter is also published. Bond fans everywhere will enjoy hearing news and views from 007's homeland. Write to: The James Bond British Fan Club, P.O. Box 007, Addlestone, Weybridge, Surrey, England KT15 1DY.

JAMES BOND 007 FAN CLUB

Founded by native New Yorker Richard Schenkman, this is the oldest organization of 007 enthusiasts in the world. The club publishes a collectible quarterly magazine called *Bondage*, as well as a newsletter. I highly recommend membership in this club. Write to: The James Bond 007 Fan Club, P. O. Box 414, Bronxville, New York 10708 U.S.A.

JAMES BOND OF THE SECRET SERVICE

Early working title of a script by Kevin McClory, Len Deighton, and Sean Connery that was planned as a remake of *Thunderball* but was never produced. In 1965, McClory, while producing *Thunderball* in partnership with Albert R. Broccoli and Harry Saltzman, had signed an agreement that prevented him from producing another Bond film from the *Thunderball* source materials for 10 years.

Promptly in 1975, McClory announced *James Bond of the Secret Service*, which would feature the return of Sean Connery in the lead role. Now producing alone for United Artists and remembering the competition provided by Columbia Pictures's *Casino Royale* in 1967, Broccoli was not about to let a rival Bond into the marketplace without a fight.

A long legal battle with McClory soon began and it wasn't until 1982, when producer and top entertainment lawyer Jack Schwartzman entered the fray, that a *Thunderball* remake finally went before the cameras. Based on an entirely different script, it became *Never Say Never Again*. *Note:* During its conception, *James Bond*

of the Secret Service was also known as *Warhead*. *See* McCLORY, KEVIN.

JAMES BOND THEME

Credited to Monty Norman but actually composed by John Barry, it's the music Bond (ROGER MOORE) hears on Vijay's (VIJAY AMRITRAJ) snake-charmer flute when he arrives in New Delhi in *Octopussy*.

Although the Bond films have never taken themselves too seriously, the later films in the series have begun to take the art of "spoofing" oneself to an entirely different level. In *On Her Majesty's Secret Service*, the janitor in Marc Ange Draco's (GABRIELE FERZETTI) office is whistling the theme from *Goldfinger* when Bond (GEORGE LAZENBY) arrives. In *The Spy Who Loved Me*, when Bond (ROGER MOORE) and Anya (BARBARA BACH) abandon their ravaged cargo van and cross the desert on foot, the audience hears the theme from *Lawrence of Arabia*.

Touches like these—comical musical reminders—have become popular elements of many of the Bond films.

"JAMES BOND WILL RETURN IN *FOR YOUR EYES ONLY*"

Incorrect statement featured at the end of the credits to *The Spy Who Loved Me* in 1977. Actually, the next James Bond movie was *Moonraker*.

JAMES, CLIFTON

(Spokane, Washington, May 29, 1921–   ) Rotund American charac-

Burly Clifton James portrayed comical J. W. Pepper in *Live and Let Die* and *The Man with the Golden Gun*.

ter actor who portrayed bumbling Louisiana Sheriff J. W. Pepper in both *Live and Let Die* and *The Man with the Golden Gun.*

JAMES, GERALD British actor who portrayed Professor Frazier, a solar energy expert based in the Far East in *The Man with the Golden Gun.*

"JAMES, LOVE ALWAYS. DELLA & FELIX" Sentiment engraved on the back of the gold cigarette lighter given to James Bond (TIMOTHY DALTON) by Della (PRISCILLA BARNES) and Felix Leiter (DAVID HEDISON) after their wedding in *Licence to Kill.* Later, 007 uses that same lighter to ignite gasoline-drenched Franz Sanchez (ROBERT DAVI).

JANNI A tough S.P.E.C.T.R.E. henchman, portrayed by Michael Brennan, in *Thunderball.* He works for millionaire Emilio Largo (ADOLFO CELI).

JAPAN Location of the fifth James Bond film, *You Only Live Twice.* It also figures in a curious blooper. In the film, British Agent Henderson (CHARLES GRAY) asks Bond (SEAN CONNERY) if he's ever been to Japan. 007 says, "No, never." However, in *From Russia with Love,* Bond says, "Once when M and I were in Tokyo . . . ," which is on the tape recorder that records Tanya's Lektor data. So, Bond has been to Tokyo before.

Japan is also the third target selected in the Domination video-game battle between Maximillian Largo (KLAUS MARIA BRANDAUER) and James Bond (SEAN CONNERY) in *Never Say Never Again.* It's worth $16,000, and Largo wins. *See* DOMINATION.

JASMINE TEA Sir James Bond's (DAVID NIVEN) drink of choice in *Casino Royale.* Retired to private life, he's become something of a health nut.

JAWS Enormous, apparently invulnerable steel-toothed assassin portrayed by Richard Kiel in *The Spy Who Loved Me* and *Moonraker.* In *Spy,* Jaws is introduced in the employ of fanatical billionaire shipping magnate Karl Stromberg (CURT JURGENS). His mission is to retrieve a microfilm copy of the nuclear-submarine track-ing system that Stromberg is using to capture enemy subs.

Partnered initially with bald Sandor (MILTON REID), Jaws continues solo when Sandor is killed in Cairo. Huge but clumsy, Jaws battles Bond (ROGER MOORE), losing each contest, including the fight at the Egyptian tomb, where he's buried under a mountain of rubble; in the train compartment, where his steel teeth are electrocuted and he's tossed through the compartment window; on the Sardinian roadway, where his car goes off a cliff and into the roof of a peasant's house; and in Atlantis itself, where he's fastened to the plate of an electromagnet and thrown into the shark pen.

At first glance, the Jaws character seemed to take the Bond series across the thin line between fact and fantasy. Up until *The Spy Who Loved Me,* the films had prided themselves on flesh-and-blood heroes and villains. No matter how wild the story lines became, villains were eventually eliminated for good—except for Blofeld, who had a strange habit of reappearing in successive films—and peace was somehow restored to the world. Jaws was a character right out of the comic books—a killer on the loose who can't be stopped or killed, with a touch of Wile E. Coyote from the "Roadrunner" cartoons. Yet, in retrospect, Jaws was a very shrewd addition to the series.

By the mid-1970s, most of the people who had grown up with Bond were growing out of the core movie audience of 12- to 24-year-olds. In other words, they were no longer guaranteed ticket buyers. To woo the younger audience—the repeat buyers who would turn *Star Wars, E.T.,* and, later, *Batman* into mega-hits—producer Albert R. Broccoli needed to freshen up the series with new elements.

Fresh characters of the bigger-than-life variety were the answer, and Jaws was one of those characters. His appearances in *The Spy Who Loved Me* and *Moonraker* certainly helped the box-office sales of those two films. And although his character was a bit exaggerated compared with the very mortal Red Grant and Oddjob, he was extremely appealing to the new generation of Bond fans.

Capitalizing on the character's huge popularity, producer Albert R. Broccoli asked screenwriter Christopher Wood to revive Jaws as one of Drax's (MICHEL LONSDALE) assassins in *Moonraker*. In that film, Jaws appears in the amazing teaser sequence, where he throws James Bond (ROGER MOORE) out of an airplane without a parachute. Unfortunately, his own rip cord malfunctions, and Jaws lands on top of a huge circus tent, which, of course, collapses.

Later he masquerades as a Mardi Gras mummer in Rio, where he's whisked away by revelers before he can deal with Bond (ROGER MOORE). An amazing fight erupts between Bond, Holly Goodhead (LOIS CHILES), and Jaws atop two cable cars high above Rio Harbor. Once again, Jaws is revealed as huge but clumsy and surrounded by incompetence. As the two secret agents jump to safety, Jaws's cable car loses its braking capability and crashes into the wheelhouse. He survives, dusts himself off, and meets his first girlfriend, buxom Dolly (BLANCHE RAVALEC).

Later, all four characters become passengers on one of the shuttles carrying Drax's master race to his radar-proof space station. But Jaws soon realizes that he and his new girlfriend are not in Drax's mad scheme. At the last minute, he thus joins Bond in the furious assault on the space station. Victorious, Bond and Holly leave Jaws and Dolly to ride home with the U.S. space troopers. Opening a bottle of champagne, Jaws proposes a toast to Dolly, uttering his only dialogue of the series, "To us!"

J.B. The initials appearing on the coffin of S.P.E.C.T.R.E. agent Jacques Boitier at his Paris "funeral," which is attended by 007 (SEAN CONNERY) and his French contact (MITSOUKO), in *Thunderball*. As she remarks, they're also James Bond's initials.

JENKINS, RICHARD British assistant director who worked on both *Thunderball* and *Live and Let Die*.

JEROME, SUZANNE (1960–1986) Tall blond actress who portrayed Gwendoline, one of the acrobatic smugglers in *Octopussy*.

JET PUMP POWERBOATS The highspeed motorboats featured in *Live and Let Die* that use jet streams of water for propulsion. The engine on these unusual boats sucks in the water and pumps it out in a fast jet that propels the boat forward and provides rudder control. Without the jet stream, the boat has no steering—a dangerous fact that actor Roger Moore learned during location shooting in Louisiana.

Moore had been practicing some tight turns on a bayou waterway when his motor cut out, leaving him with no steering at 45 mph. Losing control, he smashed into a dock—an unfortunate accident that sent the new James Bond to the local doctor with a jammed leg, a fractured front tooth, and general bruising.

J.I.M. Specialized deep-sea diving equipment featured in *For Your Eyes Only* for salvage work at depths over 300 feet. In order to find the A.T.A.C. computer in the wreck of the *St. Georges* surveillance ship, Bond (ROGER MOORE) and Melina (CAROLE BOUQUET) don the J.I.M. devices for their dive. Using a breathing mixture of oxygen and helium, they have a total of eight minutes to spend at 584 feet, where the wreck lies.

JOE Dr. Tynan's (DAVID DE KEYSER) usual smuggling contact in *Diamonds Are Forever*. However, when he motorcycles out to meet Joe in the South African desert, Tynan instead meets Mr. Wint (BRUCE GLOVER) and Mr. Kidd (PUTTER SMITH), two killers working for Ernst Stavro Blofeld (CHARLES GRAY) who bump off the doctor with a deadly scorpion and steal his diamonds.

JOHNNY TRABER'S TROUPE A family of high-wire tightrope walkers from Germany. They performed under the big top during Jaws's (RICHARD KIEL) unexpected arrival in the *Moonraker* pretitle sequence.

JOHNSON, LYNN-HOLLY (Chicago, Illinois, December 13, 1958–) Blond American actress and former champion figure skater who portrayed sex-crazed Bibi Dahl in *For Your Eyes Only*. Although Johnson brought to the film her winsome good looks and some very American mannerisms, her comic interaction with 007 (ROGER MOORE) does appear to be a bit out of place in a movie that features one of the most sinister groups of enemy villains since *From Russia with Love*. See DAHL, BIBI.

JOINT, ALF British stuntman who portrayed Capungo, the Latino assassin who gets "fried" in the bathtub in the *Goldfinger* teaser.

JONAH SET, THE Nickname for the huge interior of the *Liparus* supertanker designed by Ken Adam and built on the 007 stage at Pinewood Studios for *The Spy Who Loved Me*. Since the plot involved a supertanker that swallows nuclear submarines, it was appropriate to name the set after the biblical whale that swallowed Jonah.

Originally, Adam planned to design his set within a traditional soundstage. If not at Pinewood, he would make use of another installation, perhaps a World War II dirigible hangar. Adam found a suitable hangar in England, but the expense of converting it into a soundstage with a huge water tank to accommodate the nuclear submarines was equal to that of constructing an entirely new stage at Pinewood. The cost of transporting crews back and forth between the studio and the hangar was also prohibitive.

Adam reasoned that the only way to do things right was to follow the example of *You Only Live Twice* and build the set right on the lot. Eon Productions thus entered the real estate business, investing in the "007 Stage," the biggest soundstage in the world.

Remembered Adam, "The stage was built to accommodate nuclear submarines that were five-eighths the size of real submarines. A real nuclear submarine is about 425 feet long. To accommodate that size of vessel would have required a set in excess of 600 feet. I couldn't go that long because the relationship of the men to the ships would have been awkward."

Adam constructed a model of the proposed set that was viewed with awe by the director and the screenwriters. The script called for a huge battle to take place within the tanker when Bond releases the three captive submarine crews, who then attempt to take over the tanker before enemy submarines can fire their nuclear missiles on Moscow and New York. The battle would rage over the entire dock area, along the catwalks, up staircases, and along the corridors where the prisoners break out of their brig and gather weapons in the tanker's arsenal. When the special effects team was finished, the interior of the *Liparus* would be set ablaze with dozens of fires and explosions.

In one of the early scripts, the supertanker is controlled from the bridge area, located on the surface of the tanker. In that script, Bond and his men battle to the surface and then attack the bridge along the deck of the ship. When Adam formulated the design for his interior set, it was decided to move the control room inside the tanker, where it would be attacked from the dock area. (Interestingly, the final control room strongly resembled Blofeld's communications center in Adam's volcano set for *You Only Live Twice*.)

"Much of the credit for the accuracy of the set and the swiftness in which it was constructed goes to the Pinewood construction crews, who were now used to the type of way-out set designs featured in a James Bond film," said Adam. "Over the years, they have organized themselves to cope with those sort of situations. I don't quite know what would happen if we tried to build such a set in another country. For one thing, the cost factor would be higher in Hollywood. The 007 Stage eventually cost about a half million dollars. For the biggest stage in the world, that isn't much. And it was built in four months."

Upon completion, the 007 Stage measured 374 feet long, 160 feet wide, and 53 feet high. It included an interior tank into which Adam placed his nuclear-submarine mock-ups. The stage was officially christened "No. 007" on December 5, 1976, in a ceremony attended by Britain's Prime Minister Harold Wilson.

Like his *You Only Live Twice* volcano set, the supertanker interior featured, in a very realistic setting, a working monorail, miles of steel-girder work, and a docking area. Submarines had replaced the space rocket, but the same unbelievable atmosphere prevailed. Here was movie design at its most impressive.

JONES, GRACE (Spanishtown, Jamaica, May 19, 1952–   ) Unusual-looking, wildly costumed actress, singer, and ex-model who portrayed May Day, Max Zorin's (CHRISTOPHER WALKEN) bodyguard/assassin/lover in *A View to a Kill*. Jones won the part

Grace Jones was a striking presence in *A View to a Kill*. (Anthony Tate Collection)

after her strong appearance in *Conan the Destroyer* (1984) as Zula, the fierce Amazonian warrior woman.

As is the case in many of the more recent Bond films, henchwoman May Day steals the scene from the "real" villain, her superior, Zorin. Quick as a cat and super strong, she ranks high among the rogues' gallery of Bond film henchmen.

As to her costuming and makeup, Jones explained, "The look for May Day was a collaboration between my personal designer, Azzedine Alaia; the film's costume designer, Emma Porteous; and me. I knew what I wanted.

"I think the film company liked some of my personal wardrobe, and several outfits were copied for the movie. The look is very striking. It bears a resemblance to something out of Walt Disney.

"May Day is a fantasy character, and the role allowed me to go as far as I wanted. When I first did my makeup, I was afraid director John Glen might think it was too strong. But he loved it and even said that I should add more color, more reds on the face. It was wonderful to be given a free hand."

Jones also performed some of her own stunts, which included keeping a tight hand on the reins of a spooked thoroughbred and climbing up the broken structural supports of a ruined mine shaft—with a long drop to the stage floor where it was filmed. *See* MAY DAY.

JONES, KIMBERLEY Beautiful blond British agent, portrayed by Mary Stavin, who pilots the camouflaged iceberg launch that helps James Bond (ROGER MOORE) escape from Siberia in the teaser for *A View to a Kill*.

JONES, MR. The alias used by a mysterious chauffeur, played by Reggie Carter, who arrives at Kingston Airport in a Chevrolet convertible to transport 007 (SEAN CONNERY) to his hotel in *Dr. No*. In actuality, he is one of Dr.

No's (JOSEPH WISEMAN) assassins, sent to kill Bond. Agent 007 easily gets the best of this bumbler, but before he can divulge any information, Mr. Jones bites down on a cyanide-flavored cigarette. His parting shot at Bond, "To hell with you."

JONES, MR. AND MRS. James Bond (SEAN CONNERY) and Tiffany Case's (JILL ST. JOHN) alias during their stay at the Whyte House's bridal suite in *Diamonds Are Forever*.

JONES, TOM (Pontypridd, South Wales, Great Britain, June 7, 1940–) Sexy Welsh pop superstar, nicknamed the Voice, who warbled the title song to *Thunderball* in 1965. Jones was fairly new to audiences when the fourth James Bond film was released that Christmas. The previous year, he had scored with his first chart-busting single, "It's Not Unusual" (Decca, 1965).

Tom Jones sang one of the most popular of all the James Bond songs: "Thunderball." (Tom Jones)

JORDAN, JOHNNY (April 12, 1925–May 16, 1969) British cameraman and aerial specialist who filmed action sequences on *You Only Live Twice* and *On Her Majesty's Secret Service*. During location shooting on *You Only Live Twice* in Japan, he was involved in a terrifying aerial collision.

Working with second-unit director Peter Hunt, Jordan was responsible for shooting the aerial battle sequence that pits Bond (SEAN CONNERY) and his tiny auto-gyro (LITTLE NELLIE) against four S.P.E.C.T.R.E. armed helicopters. Jordan would be filming from inside one of the speedy French Alouette copters, where a special Panavision camera was rigged to the helicopter's metal skid. Four Japanese stunt pilots would be flying the four S.P.E.C.T.R.E. choppers, while Wing Commander Ken Wallis, Little Nellie's inventor and the only person who could fly the auto-gyro with any degree of expertise, would be doubling Connery.

On the afternoon of September 22, 1966, Jordan was filming above the little village of Ebino, when the four enemy helicopters began their dive on Bond. Peter Hunt was on the ground observing the action from a jeep.

"Our problem," he remembered, "was that the helicopters were always getting too spread out. Our Japanese pilots were very nervous and wary of flying in too close a formation. We had radio communications with all the copters, and we were always yelling at them to close up so we could get them all in the same frame."

At two o'clock on that same afternoon, Jordan's Alouette was keeping pace with two black Hilliers, when one of the action helicopters struck an updraft, hurtling it toward the helpless camera ship. Before the pilot could react, Jordan's ship was struck by the Hillier's rotor blade, which sliced through the Alouette's skis and Johnny Jordan's extended leg. Hunt watched the whole disaster speechlessly.

"We were filming this close-order formation, when suddenly there was a terrible crash and the Alouette skidded on its side into a tree only a few yards from us," said Hunt. "The pilot was okay, but Johnny's foot was hanging by a thread. Typical of a cameraman's mentality, he had photographed his own foot when he got hit, hoping that it might be useful for the surgeons."

Ironically, Ebino was a health resort for tubercular and bone disease patients. There were a number of hospitals in the area, and one of them sent out an ambulance to rescue the injured aerial cameraman.

Said Hunt, "It just so happened that this hospital was one of Japan's finest bone centers, and they were doing operations that very day. The Japanese surgeons rushed him into an operating room and attempted to save his leg. At the time, there was only one artery going strong. It was hopeless."

But they were able to stop the loss of blood and preserve the leg until Jordan returned to England, where three months later it was amputated. The loss of Jordan completely demoralized the second-unit crew on *You Only Live Twice*, and Peter Hunt soon requested that they temporarily abandon the helicopter stunts and return to London at once.

"It was a disaster," he recalled. "We were pretty early in the helicopter shooting when

Two portraits of aerial camera specialist Johnny Jordan. The helicopter shot was taken during filming in Switzerland in 1968 on the set of *On Her Majesty's Secret Service*. (Judy Jordan Collection)

Jordan was hit, and we had finished only a couple of the establishing shots of the copters moving across the volcanos. We ended up doing the rest of the fight over Spain, above Torremolinos on the Costa del Sol, before Christmas—under those bright Spanish skies. We were lucky, because behind Torremolinos there are many volcanic mountains that perfectly matched our locations on Kyushu.'' Jordan's work was later completed by Tony Brown.

Equipped with an artificial limb, Jordan returned to the 007 series on *On Her Majesty's Secret Service*, working this time from a camera rig he designed himself, which hung down from the belly of a helicopter like a parachute harness. By using such a platform, Jordan drifted above the treetops with complete freedom of movement and 360 degrees of traverse.

He was responsible for some of the film's most beautiful aerial sequences, including the shots of Draco's (GABRIELE FERZETTI) phony Red Cross helicopters headed across Switzerland for their attack on Piz Gloria, and the aerial view of the hair-raising bobsled chase in which Bond has one last chance to eliminate Blofeld.

Johnny Jordan was killed in May 1969 when he was thrown from the fuselage of a B-25 bomber during the filming of *Catch-22*.

JOURDAN, LOUIS (Marseilles, France, June 18, 1920–) (real name, Louis Gendre) Smooth French leading man who portrayed exiled Afghan Prince Kamal Khan in *Octopussy*. Jourdan appears to be enjoying himself in one of his most unsympathetic roles in years. He's played a cad before (especially in *The Best of Everything* in 1959), but that's nothing compared with the seething evil he projects in *Octopussy*.

Thwarted at every turn by Bond (ROGER MOORE), Kamal Khan at one point takes his frustration out on his imprisoned guest by relishing a gourmet treat at the dinner table— stuffed sheep's head. Without blinking, he reaches in, plucks out the sheep's eyeball, and pops it in his mouth—certainly one of the most disgusting moments in James Bond film history, but most appropriate for the thoroughly despicable Kamal Khan. Interestingly, director Steven Spielberg took the gross-out element of *Octopussy*'s dinner table sequence a step further the

following year in *Indiana Jones and the Temple of Doom. See* KHAN, PRINCE KAMAL.

JUAREZ 1939 film on the life of Mexican revolutionary Benito Juarez (Paul Muni). Director William Dieterle's unusual introduction of Juarez was so memorable to *Dr. No*'s director Terence Young that he borrowed it for his introduction of 007 (SEAN CONNERY) in the first Bond feature. In *Juarez*, actor Paul Muni plays the whole first scene with his back to the camera and then turns around when someone asks him his name. "Juarez," he sneers.

For *Dr. No*, Young blocked James Bond's introduction in the Les Ambassadeurs gambling club in London the same way. His camera faces Sean Connery's back until the precisely worked out moment when Sylvia Trench (EUNICE GAYSON) addresses him, and then Bond is seen for the first time—lighting his cigarette, and announcing himself as "Bond . . . James Bond."

JULIENNE, REMY Top French auto-stunt coordinator whose frenetic car chases have become a standard in the James Bond series. Julienne began his Bond association on *For Your Eyes Only*, where he coordinated the Citroen Deux Cheveux chase and the motorbike fight in Cortina D'Ampezzo.

On *Octopussy*, his drivers took Bond (ROGER MOORE) on the wild chase through the German countryside to an American air force base. On *A View to a Kill*, in his native Paris, Julienne took a local imported car down concrete steps to the Seine River, then obliterated its windshield and eventually cut the car completely in half as Bond attempts to keep up with a parachuting May Day (GRACE JONES). Later in the same film, his auto daredevils were put to work in downtown San Francisco during Bond's hook-and-ladder chase. In Mexicali, Mexico, on *Licence to Kill*, Julienne was intimately involved in the Kenworth tractor-trailer stunts.

JULY 4, 1966 The first day of shooting on *You Only Live Twice*. Director Lewis Gilbert was filming the sequence in which Bond (SEAN CONNERY) is murdered in Ling's (TSAI CHIN) Hong Kong apartment. Joining the action that day in addition to Sean Connery and Tsai

Chin were six Chinese extras, actors Patrick Jordan and Anthony Ainley—who were portraying two British military police officers—and stuntman Bob Simmons, who, doubling Connery, gets thrown into the hideaway Murphy bed.

JULY 18, 1988 First day of shooting on *Licence to Kill*. Working in the Churubusco Studios in Mexico City, director John Glen filmed the interior of Lupe Lamora's (TALISA SOTO) love nest on Cray Cay in the Bahamas, where she and her lover (GERARDO MORENO) are surprised by Sanchez (ROBERT DAVI) and his men. A second location that day was the interior of Felix Leiter's (DAVID HEDISON) bedroom in Key West, where James Bond (TIMOTHY DALTON) finds the body of Leiter's bride, Della Churchill (PRISCILLA BARNES).

"JUMP UP JAMAICA" A fast-paced calypso dance song featured in *Dr. No* and sung by the Byron Lee Band at Puss-Feller's (LESTER PRENDERGAST) club in Jamaica.

JUNE 27, 1984 Date of a disastrous fire that destroyed the 007 Stage at Pinewood Studios and changed the production plans for the fourteenth James Bond film, *A View to a Kill*. Fed by exploding gas cylinders that had been used to fuel some camp fires on a large forest set for director Ridley Scott's fantasy film *Legend*, the blaze leveled the structure.

Despite costing more than one million pounds to rebuild the set, the disaster added little to the budget for *A View to a Kill*, although it did extend the film's shooting schedule for two to three weeks. The set for the abandoned Main Strike silver mine was actually constructed simultaneously with the laying of the roof on the new stage.

JUNKANOO Nassau's version of the New Orleans Mardi Gras, complete with elaborate

Remy Julienne's stunt team takes Melina Havelock's Citroen through its paces in *For Your Eyes Only*. (Rex Features Ltd./RDR Productions)

floats, marching bands, and a party-in-the-streets atmosphere—all of which becomes an elaborate backdrop to the action in *Thunderball*.

In the story, Bond (SEAN CONNERY) is captured by S.P.E.C.T.R.E. assassin Fiona Volpe (LUCIANA PALUZZI) and her thugs, who transport him in a car to Emilio Largo's (ADOLFO CELI) Palmyra estate. On the way, they're held up by the parade and a drunk who happens to put his bottle of liquor in the window near Volpe, who is lighting her cigarette. Bond kicks outward, and the liquor splashes on the flame, creating a momentary distraction that allows 007 to dive out of the car. Wounded in the ankle by a stray bullet, he limps his way through the parade and ends up in the bathroom at the Kiss Kiss Club, where a hasty tourniquet stops the bleeding.

Normally held on Boxing Day, December 26, the Nassau Junkanoo was held during Easter 1965 when Eon Productions offered to back the whole affair with cash prizes for the most elaborate costumes. For the sequence, 548 locals were hired, along with 55 European extras.

"The Junkanoo was a real parade," remembered Richard Jenkins, a third assistant director on *Thunderball*, who had worked with Terence Young on *The Amorous Adventures of Moll Flanders* the previous year. "Terence planned to film around the parade as it moved through downtown Nassau. He told us that whatever happened, we weren't to try to stop it, or move it backward. We just had to shoot around it, doing the best we could. We all told Terence that his advice was very sensible.

"The parade was something like two miles long, traveling around in a big circle, and there were 40 companies cosponsoring the event. To bring the whole thing to a halt might have caused a riot.

"As the parade moved through Nassau, there was this constant rhythm of 'whistle, whistle, boom, boom.' And for two nights, that was all we heard. The performers were wild, and when their paper costumes began to loosen up, they would take them off and heat them over flames to make them stiff again. Several times, our cameras picked up a crowd of people coming around a corner with nothing on.

"Well, this 'whistle, whistle, boom, boom' had been going on for six hours the second night, when Terence finally called out, 'I've got a headache; we must stop this parade for a little while.' And Terry Churcher, Robert Watts, and I just stood there, transfixed.

"There must have been 45,000 people watching the parade by then, and we were afraid to walk out there and stop the momentum. But we did it, and Terence was able to realign some cameras and continue shooting. I remember that later the same evening, Terence was sipping some champagne from a paper cup when he said, 'God, this is a rough location, my champagne is warm.' "

JUPITER 16 A manned U.S. spacecraft about to enter its fourth orbit of the Earth in the *You Only Live Twice* teaser. While one of its astronauts is on an EVA mission, the ship is attacked by the mysterious S.P.E.C.T.R.E. *Intruder*—a spacecraft capable of swallowing the U.S. capsule, which it does, severing one of the astronaut's lifelines and sending him into a deep-space grave.

Entombed inside the *Intruder*, the *Jupiter 16*, along with its remaining astronaut, is brought back to Earth inside the cone of a dormant Japanese volcano, which is now the secret rocket base of S.P.E.C.T.R.E. chief Ernst Stavro Blofeld (DONALD PLEASENCE). Although it isn't identified as such, the ship, piloted by two astronauts, is patterned after the *Gemini* spacecrafts that were prominent in the U.S. space program of the mid-1960s.

JURGENS, CURT (1916–1982) German character actor who portrayed billionaire shipping magnate and megalomaniac Karl Stromberg, the man with the webbed hands, in *The Spy Who Loved Me*.

German character actor Curt Jurgens portrayed Stromberg, a modern-day Neptune in *The Spy Who Loved Me*.

K

KALBA, MAX Egyptian black-market trader and the owner of Cairo's Mojaba nightclub in *The Spy Who Loved Me*, portrayed by veteran character actor Vernon Dobtcheff. Following a clue he finds on the dead body of Aziz Fekkesh (NADIM SAWALHA), Bond (ROGER MOORE) goes to the Mojaba Club to find Kalba and bid on a microfilm copy of a missing nuclear-submarine tracking system that he possesses.

Now competing for the microfilm with KGB Major Anya Amasova (BARBARA BACH), Bond is prepared to offer a higher bid, when Kalba is called to the phone. Instead of receiving a call, Kalba finds Jaws (RICHARD KIEL) waiting for him in the booth. He's "cut off," Jaws steals the film, Bond finds the body, Anya joins him, and both stow away in Jaws's phone utility truck.

In an early screen treatment of *The Spy Who Loved Me*, the meeting with Kalba at the swank nightclub featured a tense high-stakes game of backgammon in which Bond comes from behind to win 50,000 pounds from Kalba, who dies before he can pay up. Bond and Anya still go after Jaws, but this time they follow him in a sports car.

The desert sequence was much more elaborate, with the two agents fighting off marauding bands of Tuareg bandits, with Anya's pearl necklace providing them with mini hand grenades. The aborted backgammon game was later resurrected in *Octopussy*, when Bond battles the evil Kamal Khan (LOUIS JOURDAN).

KALIPHA, STEFAN Lean Middle Eastern actor who portrayed Cuban hit man Hector Gonzales, the phony seaplane pilot in *For Your Eyes Only*.

KAMEN, MICHAEL (New York City) London-based American film composer who scored *Licence to Kill*.

KANANGA, DR. (aka Mr. Big) The sinister foreign minister of mythical San Monique Island in *Live and Let Die*, portrayed by American actor Yaphet Kotto. While he poses as a mild-mannered third world diplomat, Kananga is actually a resourceful megalomaniacal drug smuggler who is about to corner the North American heroin market.

In America, he poses as Harlem drug czar Mr. Big. Kananga's plan is to cultivate two tons of San Monique heroin and sell it free of charge through his chain of Fillet of Soul nightclubs. Such a ploy would force his competitors out of business and double the number of addicts in the United States.

His entourage includes the mystical Baron Samedi (GEOFFREY HOLDER), who may or may not be a supernatural being; Whisper (EARL JOLLY BROWN) and Tee Hee (JULIUS HARRIS), his principal assassins; and Solitaire (JANE SEYMOUR), a fortune-teller whose tarot cards can predict the future of Kananga's evil deeds. Kananga is eventually killed in an underwater scuffle with James Bond (ROGER MOORE) when he is forced to swallow a "bitter pill." See BIG, MR.

KANANGA, ROSS An amiable part-Seminole Indian whose Jamaican crocodile farm became a principal location in *Live and Let Die*. Discovered on a location survey by Guy Hamilton, Syd Cain, and Tom Mankiewicz, Kananga's ranch contained nearly 1,400 crocodiles and alligators. Since Mankiewicz was on the survey, it is logical to think that Kananga the crocodile farmer lent his name to Kananga the drug smuggler.

KARAGEORGE One of Milos Columbo's (TOPOL) nimble Greek fighters, portrayed by Paul Angelis, in *For Your Eyes Only*. Karageorge joins Columbo, Bond (ROGER MOORE), and Melina Havelock (CAROLE BOUQUET) in the final assault on the St. Cyril monastery.

KARL-MARX-STADT East German city where Kamal Khan (LOUIS JOURDAN) and General Orlov (STEVEN BERKOFF) plant a nuclear device in a circus cannon in *Octopussy*. Using the traveling Octopussy Circus as a cover, Orlov and Kamal plan to detonate the bomb on a U.S. air force base across the border in Feldstadt, West Germany—an act that Orlov is certain will initiate unilateral nuclear disarmament along the border, opening the way for a massive Soviet invasion.

Unable to tap into a final briefing between Orlov and Kamal at the Monsoon Palace—because of the interference from Magda's (KRISTINA WAYBORN) blow-dryer—007 (ROGER MOORE) does hear the name Karl-Marx-Stadt and the reference to "one week." Escaping from Kamal's fortress, Bond makes it back to East Germany in time to destroy the insidious plan.

KASZNAR, KURT (Vienna, Austria, August 12, 1913–August 6, 1979) Portly Viennese character actor, usually in sinister roles, who portrayed KGB chief Smirnov in *Casino Royale*. See SMIRNOV.

KAWASAKI 900 Motorcycle featured in *The Spy Who Loved Me*. Equipped with a tele-guided explosive sidecar, its rider chases Bond's (ROGER MOORE) Lotus Esprit on a Sardinian mountain road. When the sidecar blows up a mattress truck instead of Bond, the motorcycle's rider is blinded by a shower of feathers and forced over a cliff to his death.

KEEL-HAULING How fiendish Aris Kristatos (JULIAN GLOVER) plans to torture and kill James Bond (ROGER MOORE) and Melina Havelock (CAROLE BOUQUET) in *For Your Eyes Only*. The procedure, taken from Ian Fleming's novel *Live and Let Die*, involves tying Bond and Melina together, tossing them over the side of a motor launch, and dragging their bodies over a razor-sharp reef.

The plot works until Bond and Melina dive under the water and use the reef to cut the towing rope. When they fail to surface, Kristatos mistakenly thinks they've become shark food and heads back to shore. Fortunately, Melina had left an air tank near one of her father's archaelogical excavations on the sea floor, which becomes a needed source of oxygen until Kristatos moves off.

KEEN, GEOFFREY (1916–   ) British character actor whose role as Freddie Gray, the Minister of Defense, has become a running character in the Bond series since *The Spy Who Loved Me*. See GRAY, FREDDIE.

KEMPF, RUTH American actress who portrayed Mrs. Bell, the terrified flying student whose training plane is commandeered by James Bond (ROGER MOORE) in *Live and Let Die*.

KENNEDY, MISS CIA agent Pam Bouvier's (CAREY LOWELL) cover name in Isthmus City in *Licence to Kill*. Joining forces with revenge-seeking James Bond (TIMOTHY DALTON), Pam arrives in town as his executive secretary—although she thinks that he should be *her* executive secretary. She undergoes a makeover and wardrobe change as well. See BOUVIER, PAM.

KENNISTON Assistant to the Home Secretary in *Thunderball*, portrayed by Reginald Beckwith, who bore an amazing resemblance to producer Harry Saltzman.

KENT British city that is the location for Goldfinger's (GERT FROBE) metallurgical facility in England, which we never visit in the film. According to Colonel Smithers (RICHARD VERNON) of the Bank of England, Goldfinger is a legitimate international jeweler who has authorization to run a modest metallurgical facility where gold can be melted down and recast.

KENTUCKY FRIED CHICKEN Colonel Sanders's famous poultry franchise, which is plainly visible on a Kentucky boulevard when Felix Leiter (CEC LINDER) tracks 007's homing signal in *Goldfinger*. Unfortunately, the signal isn't Bond's at all, but that of the unfortunate Mr. Solo (MARTIN BENSON), a Mafia ne'er-do-well who is murdered and crushed by Oddjob (HAROLD SAKATA) into the bodywork of a Lincoln Continental. Although this scene plays as Kentucky, it was actually shot in Miami, Florida.

KENWORTH W900B TRUCKS Huge 18-wheel American tanker trucks, four of which are featured in the exciting conclusion to *Licence to Kill*. Filled with a 31,600-pound mixture of cocaine and gasoline, each truck's drug cargo is worth more than $40 million. Headed down the highway from Franz Sanchez's (ROBERT DAVI) drug laboratories beneath the Olimpatec Meditation Institute, the cocaine convoy is virtually destroyed by James Bond (TIMOTHY DALTON)—with a super assist from CIA fly girl Pam Bouvier (CAREY LOWELL).

The incredible chase was orchestrated by second-unit director Arthur Wooster, 007 car chase veteran Remy Julienne, and special effects supervisor John Richardson, who spent seven weeks in the blazing desert mountains south of Mexicali, Mexico, near the California–Mexico border. Their primary road was a deserted section of the Rumorosa mountain pass—an isolated, accident-prone mountain highway. Onto this treacherous terrain came a convoy of vehicles, including three specially designed Kenworth trucks that were modified for stunt use; five older Kenworths, which were purchased and refurbished in Mexico; and a dozen tanker trailers, five of which were made out of wood for the explosion sequences.

KERIM BEY, ALI Head of Station T–Turkey and Bond's (SEAN CONNERY) right arm, portrayed by actor Pedro Armendariz, in *From Russia with Love*.

Kerim Bey is one of those wonderfully mysterious supporting characters in the tradition of Peter Lorre and Sydney Greenstreet that populate the best spy stories. His moments on-screen are unforgettable: the spying on the Russian consulate through a British periscope hidden in a Byzantine reservoir; an assignation with a ravishing brunette that is cut short by a limpet mine explosion; the murder of Krilencu; the evening at the Gypsy camp; and his expert movements on the Orient Express, where he helps Bond prepare for his escape across the border.

These moments painted well a character who expertly personified the mountain of Turkish pride and stamina that was Ian Fleming's Kerim Bey. As to his background, the only thing we ever learn is that Kerim Bey started out in the circus as a strongman who broke chains and bent bars for a living. His cover in Istanbul is that of a Persian rug salesman. In the film, he helps Bond escape Istanbul on the Orient Express, but he and Russian Agent Benz are murdered by Red Grant.

Interestingly, a key scene involving Kerim Bey was cut out of *From Russia with Love*, according to director Terence Young. It occurs just before Bond meets Tanya on the Bosphorus ferryboat. Young could not save the sequence in post-production for a very good reason.

Said Young, "We had a scene where everywhere Bond went he was followed by this Bulgar, the man with the big mustache, the black beret, and the Citroen. In the scene, Bond has to go onto the ferry to meet the girl, and he has to shake off the opposition.

"He's in a taxi being followed by the Bulgar, when Bond suddenly leans across in front of the taxi driver and pumps the brakes. The taxi comes screeching to a halt, the Bulgar piles in behind, and he, in turn, is struck by a third car. Out of car number one steps James Bond; out of car number two steps the Bulgarian, who's protesting that this is not protocol and that this is not the way we behave, that such an act is unfair and dishonest. And out of the third car steps Pedro Armendariz.

"We ended up shooting 10 takes. Pedro wanted an ash on the end of his cigar, and every time the Bulgarian expressed his shock, an ash would fall away from his cigar. On take 10, Pedro came out with his cigar with a long ash, and this Bulgarian turned on him, saying: 'You're the one responsible for this. This is an outrage. What am I going to do? Tell me, what am I going to do?' And Pedro took his cigar and tapped it, saying, 'My friend, this is life.'

"At that very moment, the big British embassy Rolls-Royce drove up, and Bond got in and drove away to his rendezvous with Tanya. With his car locked between bumpers, the Bulgarian could not follow 007 to the ferryboat. It was a perfect deception and certainly Armendariz's best scene.

"We were running the picture later. We had our final cut and our married print. United Artists had seen it and loved it. Everybody was happy. And my son, who was then age 12, came and saw the picture at a private showing a week before the film came out.

"When it came time for the sequence with Pedro, my son turned to me and said, 'Daddy, that man with the beret was already killed. Robert Shaw killed him in Saint Sophia Mosque behind the pillar.' And, of course, we all said, 'Yes, he did, didn't he?' So that was the end of that sequence.''

Young recalls that when he later found out that actor Pedro Armendariz was dying of cancer, he went to his hotel and tried to say something dignified and meaningful, but could only stare at the walls. Once more, Armendariz had a cigar in his mouth. He leaned across, looked Young right in the eye, tapped an ash on the carpet, and said, "That, my friend, is life." *See* ARMENDARIZ, PEDRO.

KERR, DEBORAH (Helensburg, Scotland, September 30, 1921–) (real name, Deborah Kerr-Trimmer) Scottish leading lady who portrayed the completely wacky Mimi, an enemy agent posing as M's (JOHN HUSTON) widow, in *Casino Royale*. Actually, it's very difficult to understand a word she says in the film as she prances around a Scottish manor house, dancing to bagpipes, spouting historical sayings, and referring constantly to the mystical piper who always comes to play once a McTarry dies (McTarry was M's real name). Definitely the most unusual performance of Kerr's illustrious career. *See* MIMI.

KERSHNER, IRVIN (Philadelphia, Pennsylvania, April 29, 1923–) American film director who helmed *Never Say Never Again* in 1983. Handicapped by an uneven script that was being rewritten as he filmed, and yet surrounded by one of the best casts ever assembled for a James Bond movie, Kershner's outing—the first serious Bond feature from an American filmmaker—was, in itself, uneven. When the film is forced to follow the guidelines of a *Thunderball* remake, it falls woefully short.

The hijacking of two cruise missiles, even

Director Irvin Kershner sizes up Sean Connery and Barbara Carrera during location activity in the Bahamas on *Never Say Never Again*. (Taliafilm)

with David Dryer's marvelous effects, was less than riveting and compares unfavorably to the Vulcan-bomber hijacking in the first film. In fact, the entire plot lacks a sense of worldwide alarm that was so prevalent in *Thunderball*.

Back in 1965, when Sean Connery walked into the enormous British Secret Service conference room to listen to a tape-recorded S.P.E.C.T.R.E. message, you knew that the fate of the planet was on the line. No such element is prevalent in *Never Say Never Again*.

What the new film does have is some wonderful performances that carry the film for a time. Certainly, the very presence of Connery made the whole project worthwhile. On-screen, his assuredness in the role is remarkable, considering it had been 20 years since his first outing, in *Dr. No*. The throwaway humor, the playfulness, the confident sexuality, the two-fisted machismo—all the elements that had made him a success in the first place were still present in good quantity. And his presence is felt from the very first punch he throws in the South American jungle. After all, that's a Connery punch!

Klaus Maria Brandauer's Maximillian Largo is the most interesting villain since Auric Goldfinger. Handsome, debonair, and fabulously wealthy, he's extremely sympathetic until he starts to lose his mistress, Domino (KIM BASINGER), to Bond. But even in Largo's most psychotic moments, Brandauer maintains a level of control that makes his performance extremely interesting and believable. His was a performance of dimension and resonance for which Kershner must be given strong credit.

Barbara Carrera's wild Fatima Blush was definitely the film's life force. Once she's killed, the film's final third begins to die on the vine. Without a ticking bomb (and there really is no time frame for *Never Say Never Again*'s cruise missile warhead to explode), a key element in any Bond film is the final confrontation between Bond and the villain. With Fatima Blush out of the way, there really is no confrontation. A pitifully weak underwater battle between Bond and Largo fails to generate much tension and is cut short when Largo is impaled on Domino's (KIM BASINGER) spear.

In all fairness to Kershner, the same problem faced Terence Young in *Thunderball* once Fiona Volpe (LUCIANA PALUZZI) is killed. That film's final third section was consumed by the underwater action, which was also too slow and, to some viewers, confusing.

KEY GEOLOGIC LOCK A natural rock formation located along the San Andreas Fault and beneath the Main Strike Mine in *A View to a Kill*. A kind of safety belt, it prevents all earthquake faults in the region from moving at once. In psychotic industrialist Max Zorin's (CHRISTOPHER WALKEN) twisted Project Main Strike, a huge bomb will be detonated above the lock, triggering a massive earthquake that will sink Silicon Valley underneath the waters of a newly formed lake. *See* PROJECT MAIN STRIKE.

KG 1881 The license plate on Manuela's (EMILY BOLTON) white M.G. sports car, which Bond (ROGER MOORE) spots in Rio traffic in *Moonraker*.

KHAN, PRINCE KAMAL Exiled Afghan prince portrayed with a strong touch of evil by Louis Jourdan in *Octopussy*. In league with fanatical Russian General Orlov (STEVEN BERKOFF), Kamal Khan is getting a treasure trove of Kremlin jewelry in return for his services in supplying the Octopussy Circus as a cover for Orlov's plan to detonate a nuclear device on a U.S. air force base in West Germany. Octopussy (MAUD ADAMS) is actually being kept in the dark about the bomb—she thinks it's a simple jewelry-smuggling operation.

Bond meets the suspicious Kamal Khan for the first time at Sotheby's, where he enters the bidding for a jeweled Fabergé Easter egg and boosts the price considerably. Following him to Udaipur, India, 007 enters a backgammon game against the cheating prince and wins 200,000 rupees. In order to retrieve the real Fabergé egg that Bond stole from the auction—by carefully switching its forgery for the real thing—Khan employs the seductive Magda (KRISTINA WAYBORN), who beds Bond and steals back the egg, which now contains a listening bug planted there by 007. Waving good-bye to the beautiful Swedish girl, 007 is knocked unconscious by Khan's bodyguard, Gobinda (KABIR BEDI). He wakes up in Kamal Khan's Monsoon Palace, where he is an imprisoned guest. When Orlov arrives for a final briefing, Bond attempts to listen in to their conversation, but Magda's blow-dryer jams the frequency. All he can hear is "Karl-Marx-Stadt."

Escaping from the palace, Bond becomes the prey in a festive tiger hunt, with Kamal Khan and Gobinda pursuing him atop elephants. Bond survives and eventually makes his way to Karl-Marx-Stadt, where he sees Kamal and Orlov planting a nuclear device in the base of the Octopussy Circus cannon. He then follows the train to Feldstadt and disarms the bomb, with only seconds to spare.

After Octopussy's army of acrobatic women storm the Monsoon Palace and defeat his garrison, Kamal Khan kidnaps Octopussy and attempts his own form of escape aboard a twin-engine light plane. Bond follows on horseback (à la Indiana Jones) and eventually gets aboard the plane after an amazing fight with Gobinda outside the plane. As Kamal Khan tries to land the disabled aircraft, Bond and Octopussy dive out of the plane, which crashes into a hillside, killing Kamal Khan. *See* JOURDAN, LOUIS.

KHOW-PING-KAN An unusually picturesque island off the coast of Thailand that was the location of Scaramanga's (CHRISTOPHER LEE) solar energy complex in *The Man with the Golden Gun*. In the story, the island is located off the coast of China and is protected from interlopers by Red Chinese troops who man a neighboring island surveillance outpost.

Scaramanga's home and solar station have been built by Hai Fat's (RICHARD LOO) Bangkok-based construction company. In addition to the solar energy complex with its liquid helium-filled basins, the home features an incredible animated "fun house" maze through which Scaramanga tracks his fully armed opponents.

KIDD, MR. Bookish, nearly bald, homosexual assassin, teamed with Mr. Wint (BRUCE GLOVER), in *Diamonds Are Forever* and portrayed by musician Putter Smith. Working for Ernst Stavro Blofeld (CHARLES GRAY), Kidd and Wint are eliminating the members of an international diamond-smuggling operation one by one—a confrontation that eventually brings them up against Bond (SEAN CONNERY), who is posing as a smuggler.

In the film's concluding scene aboard a lux-ury liner, Kidd, impersonating a waiter and about to attack Bond with flaming shish kebabs, is doused with wine and set afire. He then jumps overboard and is drowned.

In this last sequence, stuntman George Leech doubled Putter Smith. The sequence was done with the help of a very skillful special effects makeup department, which designed a mask made of fireproof rubber that was perfectly molded to the stuntman's features and that, on the outside, was the image of the bespectacled Smith. The mask also featured two copper gauze eyepieces through which Leech could see and a copper gauze plate over the mouth so that he could breathe. Protecting the rest of his body was an asbestos automobile racing suit.

"When I first tried out the mask," said Leech, "I put on an asbestos apron and put the fiery gel in front of the mask. I brought the flame closer and closer until it caught on and enveloped my entire face. The mask was loose so that the moment I noticed something wrong I could throw it away. But it worked fine in the test. If something had gone wrong in the actual take, I couldn't have gotten out of the suit. I'd have had to wait for someone to put the flame out with a handy fire extinguisher.

"When it came time to do the actual stunt, the effects man put so much of this liquid gel on me that I was really ablaze. He also threw in some aircraft dope, which is like gasoline. And I could smell that stuff, so I asked him what it was, and he said, 'It's only a little aircraft dope to give the flame some color.' And I told him, 'Get out of here with that stuff.'

"So here I was on fire, and I had to stagger around a little bit in front of the camera and then go to the edge of the boat set and supposedly jump over the edge onto a pad where a fireman stood by with an extinguisher. I told the fireman, before the scene, that as soon as I hit the pad, he was to put me out. So I hit the pad and I'm still lying there burning and nothing is happening. And I found this idiot waiting for the director to say 'cut.' Instead of having the extinguisher in his hand, he's got it a distance away. So he comes over and looks up at the director and looks down at me and then walks nonchalantly over and picks up the extinguisher and puts me out. The goon!

"By then, my hands were burning because

some of the gel had leaked down through my gloves. It took ages for them to heal. Although the gloves were made out of the same fireproof material as the mask, they had cracked under the extreme heat, and the liquid had simply trickled down onto my hands. The gloves turned out to be the Achilles' heel of the entire outfit.

"Before the scene had started, the assistant director had told me, 'First we'll set fire to you, and then we'll run the camera. . . .' And I had replied, 'No, first you'll run the camera, and when you've got the speed up, then you'll set fire to me.' Otherwise, they would have set the fire and I would have been waiting around while they got the right speed up. A guy would have appeared from nowhere and said, 'Does anyone want a chicken sandwich?' and all the while I'd be burning away. It's not a joke. I've seen it happen many times.

"Years ago, when I first came into the business, I relied on the assistants and the director. But they sometimes don't have all the answers, especially when it comes to stunt work. You end up having to watch out for yourself, because when your life's at stake, you can't rely on someone else to check the proper safety measures."

KIEL, RICHARD Seven-foot, two-inch-tall American character villain whose career was given a big boost in 1976 when producer Albert R. Broccoli signed him to play Jaws in *The Spy Who Loved Me* and *Moonraker*. Outfitted with cobalt steel incisors, Jaws was the perfect fantasy villain for a new generation of James Bond fans, even though some purists felt the character was straight out of the comic books. Appearing in two of the most successful films in the series guaranteed that Jaws became one of the great pop culture villains of the late 1970s.

KILLIFER, ED Traitorous Drug Enforcement Administration (DEA) operative, portrayed by Everett McGill, who takes a $2 million bribe to help convicted drug runner Franz Sanchez (ROBERT DAVI) escape from the United States in *Licence to Kill*. Killifer accomplishes his mission on the Seven Mile Bridge in the Florida Keys when he clubs the driver of the armored truck that's carrying Sanchez, grabs the wheel, and drives off the bridge into the ocean.

Underwater, Sanchez and Killifer are rescued by divers and a minisub from the *Wavekrest* research vessel. Not only does Killifer free a major international drug lord, but he inadvertently causes CIA agent Felix Leiter (DAVID HEDISON) to be thrown to the sharks, and his new bride, Della Churchill (PRISCILLA BARNES), to be murdered. Avenging his friends, Bond (TIMOTHY DALTON) throws Killifer to the sharks, along with his $2 million payoff.

KING ERISON COMBO The featured band at Nassau's Kiss Kiss Club in *Thunderball*.

KINSALE STREET A street in Kingston, Jamaica, that was the site of Commander John Strangways's (TIM MOXON) cottage in *Dr. No*.

KIREK, MILOW Actor who portrayed a nuclear physicist working for S.P.E.C.T.R.E. in *Never Say Never Again*.

KISCH One of Auric Goldfinger's (GERT FROBE) henchmen, portrayed by Michael Mellinger, who handcuffs James Bond (SEAN CONNERY) to the ticking A-bomb placed inside Fort Knox. When Goldfinger's troops are attacked by the surprisingly healthy U.S. Army garrison, Kisch is locked inside the vault with Bond and Oddjob (HAROLD SAKATA). When he threatens to disarm the bomb, Kisch is killed by the unreasonably loyal Oddjob, who tosses him off the top floor of the vault.

KISS KISS CLUB An outdoor nightclub in Nassau that becomes a temporary shelter for a wounded James Bond (SEAN CONNERY) in *Thunderball*. Chased by Fiona Volpe (LUCIANA PALUZZI) and her S.P.E.C.T.R.E. thugs, 007 takes a moment's rest in the club's bathroom, applies a tourniquet to his wounded ankle, and then mingles among the dancers. However, he's cornered again and soon finds himself in Fiona's arms on the dance floor, as a S.P.E.C.T.R.E. assassin prepares his silencer.

As the staccato bongo beat of the King Erison Combo reaches its zenith, Bond spots the assassin and whirls Fiona around just in time for her to take the bullet instead. Dragging her body over to a table, he tells the seated patrons that his partner needs a break because "she's just dead."

Originally, this location was referred to as the "Jump Jump Club." Actress Diane Hartford played the woman who briefly dances with Bond prior to Fiona's arrival.

KISSY Lovely Japanese Secret Service agent-turned-pearl-diver, portrayed by Mie Hama in *You Only Live Twice*. To improve the credibility of James Bond's (SEAN CONNERY) cover as an Ama Island boatman, she receives orders from S.I.S. chief Tiger Tanaka (TETSURO TAMBA) to become 007's bride in a mock ceremony. Backed by one of John Barry's most romantic musical sequences, they then row out to the pearl beds and blend in with the other Ama Island couples. Later they follow the trail of two dead islanders to the Rosaki Cave on the mainland, where they find lethal phosgene gas and a route to an extinct volcano—the site of Blofeld's (DONALD PLEASENCE) secret rocket base.

Although this character was created by Ian Fleming, who dubbed her "Kissy Suzuki" and her name is listed in the film's credits simply as "Kissy," in *You Only Live Twice* her name is never mentioned. She doesn't introduce herself, no one calls her name, and Bond never addresses her by name. If it were not for the end titles, she would be known as the unknown agent.

KITZMILLER, JOHN (1913–1965) Character actor who portrayed Quarrel, the Cayman Islander, in the first James Bond film, *Dr. No*. Director Terence Young first saw him in the 1946 Roberto Rossellini film *Paisa*. Kitzmiller had settled in Italy after completing his U.S. military service during World War II. *See* QUARREL.

A break in the action on *Dr. No* with, *left to right*, Cubby Broccoli, John Kitzmiller, Sean Connery, and Ursula Andress. (*Los Angeles Times*)

KLAFF, JACK British actor who portrayed Apostis, the henchman of Aris Kristatos (JULIAN GLOVER), in *For Your Eyes Only*. He is killed by Bond (ROGER MOORE) during a fight atop Greece's St. Cyril monastery.

KLEBB, COLONEL ROSA S.P.E.C.T.R.E. masterspy recruited from SMERSH in *From Russia with Love* and portrayed by Lotte Lenya. Code-named No. 3 in the S.P.E.C.T.R.E. hierarchy, she's ordered by Blofeld to execute Kronsteen's (VLADEK SHEYBAL) plan to humiliate James Bond (SEAN CONNERY) and steal a Russian Lektor decoding machine.

Klebb recruits top assassin Red Grant (ROBERT SHAW), whose fitness she tests with a knuckle duster to the abdomen. She also recruits beautiful Russian cipher clerk, Tatiana "Tanya" Romanova (DANIELA BIANCHI), who will seduce Bond in Istanbul.

After the plan fails, Klebb is nearly executed by Blofeld's assistant, Morzeny (WALTER GOTELL), who kills Kronsteen instead. Given one more chance to eliminate Bond, Klebb impersonates a Venetian hotel maid and is about to shoot Bond when Tanya distracts her.

Bond fights off Klebb, who attacks with poison-tipped daggers in her shoes, but 007 is saved when she's shot and killed by Tanya. "A horrible woman," sighs Romanova. Replies Bond, "She's had her kicks." *See* LENYA, LOTTE.

KLEIN, JORDAN (Miami, Florida, December 1, 1925–   ) Academy Award–winning underwater filmmaker, cameraman, inventor, and engineer who worked on *Thunderball*, *You Only Live Twice*, *Live and Let Die*, and *Never Say Never Again*. Klein's film career began in 1952 when he was hired by Barry and Enright Productions to produce a pilot for an underwater series called "20 Seconds to Zero." The pilot bombed, but Klein learned some valuable lessons about the filmmaking process.

Since 1954, when he shot underwater stills on *Creature from the Black Lagoon*, Klein has been involved on virtually every major film and television show that featured underwater sequences. His early association with the Ivan Tors Company on "Sea Hunt" and "Flipper" made him a natural selection to build all the underwater props for *Thunderball* in 1965.

His original assignment called for the manufacture of the underwater A-bomb carrier and six swift one-man scooters. The bomb carrier was designed by Ken Adam, who sent Klein a balsa-wood model. From that basic model, Klein designed the fully working carrier, which was equipped with a 12-HP motor.

It was completed in five weeks. "I didn't go home," he laughed. It took three 55-gallon drums of epoxy resin to create the finish on the carrier, which was built over a structure of steel and chicken wire. The bodywork was smoothed, appropriately, with Bondo.

In addition to his engineering skill, Klein was recruited to share filming chores with Lamar Boren. "I shot most of the inserts—little crabs on the ocean floor, dead divers, spear hits, etc. I also ended up on camera, running the bomb carrier," he said. "That's me in the cockpit. I had a gold Rolex, and you can see it."

Klein explained that the sequence in which the Vulcan bomber crash-lands in the Bahamas was shot in miniature off Rose Island. The miniature bomber was launched down a wire from a 150-foot tower. The full-size bomber shell was lowered into the water off Clifton Pier.

Klein's surprise on the film was the underwater backpack he designed for Bond (SEAN CONNERY). It was something he tinkered together over a weekend for the underwater battle sequence. The producers told him that if it wasn't ready for shooting at 8:30 A.M. Monday, it couldn't be used. Klein guaranteed its delivery, and it became a highlight of the shoot.

The pack was equipped with two spear guns, which were actually stainless-steel tubes with 12-gauge shotgun heads. The smokescreen was a yellow dye. The headlight never really worked, but since the battle was fought in daylight, it wasn't necessary. As for the pack's rocket motor, it was an effect. Connery's double, Frank Cousins, was actually pulled along by a piano wire attached to a high-speed motorboat.

On *You Only Live Twice*, Klein was once more teamed with Lamar Boren for the brief sequence in which British divers return the "corpse" of James Bond (SEAN CONNERY) to a nuclear submarine. Klein built a small section of the submarine, which was placed on the ocean floor off Nassau.

Although some of his shark footage appears in *Live and Let Die*, his next major 007 assignment was for *Never Say Never Again*, where he once again built a bomb carrier—this one designed to carry the S.P.E.C.T.R.E.-hijacked cruise missiles. In addition to the carrier, Klein built a huge section of the *Flying Saucer* yacht's hull, which was lowered into the water off Silver Springs, Florida. Unlike the *Disco Volante* in *Thunderball*, this time the underwater hatch was located on the side of the ship, rather than underneath it. It is through this side exit that the cruise missile carrier travels.

On both *Thunderball* and *Never Say Never Again*, Klein worked with huge 16-foot tiger sharks, which were drugged and worked like human extras. On the latter film, he was assigned the task of installing electronic sensors on the sharks' dorsal fins. The sensors are attracted to a homing device placed on Bond's scuba gear by the evil Fatima Blush (BARBARA CARRERA).

KLOTKOFF Russian KGB operative, portrayed by Bogdan Kominowski, in *A View to a Kill*. Klotkoff is with General Gogol (WALTER GOTELL) when the head of the KGB confronts Max Zorin (CHRISTOPHER WALKEN) at his French estate. It seems that Zorin no longer considers himself a KGB operative or under Gogol's command. To reinforce that point, Zorin's steroid-enhanced bodyguard, May Day (GRACE JONES), picks up Klotkoff and tosses him against a wall.

Klotkoff later participates in an underwater surveillance and demolition mission against Zorin's oil-pumping facility in San Francisco Bay. Captured by May Day, he's brought to Zorin, who orders him to disarm the limpet mine he placed. Klotkoff is then tossed into one of the station's intake pipes, where's he's sliced to ribbons by an impeller.

KNIGHT, GLADYS (Atlanta, Georgia, May 28, 1944–   ) Superstar singer and multiple-Grammy winner, who sang the title song in *Licence to Kill*.

Singer Gladys Knight with her fabled Pips.

KNIGHT TAKES BISHOP, CHECK Kronsteen's (VLADEK SHEYBAL) chess move that leads to the defeat of McAdams (PETER MADDEN), his Canadian opponent in *From Russia with Love*. McAdams follows with "King to Rook Two." Kronsteen then moves "Queen to King Four," after which McAdams capitulates.

KOHEN, MUHAMMAT A Turkish tour guide who portrayed himself during location sequences inside Istanbul's St. Sophia Mosque in *From Russia with Love*.

KOMINOWSKI, BOGDAN Actor who portrayed doomed KGB agent Klotkoff in *A View to a Kill*. See KLOTKOFF.

KOSKOV, GENERAL GEORGI Renegade Russian General, portrayed by handsome Dutch leading man Jeroen Krabbe (pronounced HER RUIN, CRAB BAY), who joins forces with arms dealer Brad Whitaker (JOE DON BAKER) to perpetrate a huge drug deal in *The Living Daylights*. Actually, the story begins a million miles away from anything resembling a drug deal.

Koskov is introduced in Bratislava, Czechoslovakia, as a defecting Russian general. Bond (TIMOTHY DALTON) is assigned to help him across the border into Austria, and during the operation, he foils the assassination attempt of a beautiful blond cellist named Kara Milovy (MARYAM D'ABO). Bond is unaware of the fact that Koskov is Milovy's patron/lover and that he planned the assassination attempt to make his defection appear genuine. Koskov is actually partnered with Whitaker in a huge drug deal.

Using a $50 million advance provided by the Russians for his latest high-tech weapons, Whitaker and Koskov plan to convert the money into diamonds and trade them to the drug-dealing Snow Leopard Brotherhood of Afghanistan for a cache of raw opium. They will then sell the drugs on the open market, making enough of a profit to have enough money left over to supply the Russians with their arms. All they need is time, but KGB chief General Leonid Pushkin (JOHN RHYS-DAVIES), already on the trail of Koskov—won't give it to them.

Arriving in England, Koskov is quartered at the heavily guarded Bladen safe house. There he quickly tells M (ROBERT BROWN), Minister of Defense, Freddie Gray (GEOFFREY KEEN), and Bond (TIMOTHY DALTON) that Pushkin is behind a fiendish plot called "Smiert Spionam," which is designed to kill off a number of British and American agents.

Soon after spilling this information, which compels M to order 007 to liquidate Pushkin, Koskov is liberated from the safe house by what appears to be a KGB agent named Necros (ANDREAS WISNIEWSKI). In actuality, Necros is working for Koskov and the rescue is another sham—designed to confuse both the British and the KGB.

Brought safely to Whitaker's house in Tangier, Koskov prepares to leave for Afghanistan and his drug deal. First, he informs Whitaker that Pushkin will be killed before Whitaker has to return the $50 million arms advance, but Whitaker's not convinced that the British will assassinate Pushkin. Koskov determines that another British agent must die before the British act.

Necros then goes to Vienna, where he kills Saunders (THOMAS WHEATLEY), the local head of the section. Determined to stop "Smiert Spionam," Bond arrives in Tangier to kill Pushkin, but instead joins forces with the KGB general to expose the Koskov/Whitaker plot. Pushkin dies in a "sham assassination" at the hands of Bond.

But 007 forgets about Kara, who is tricked by Koskov into thinking that Bond is a KGB agent. Drugged by Kara, Bond is shipped to Afghanistan on Koskov's transport plane. Kara soon learns that she followed the wrong man's advice. Still, they manage to escape from a Russian air base, and with the help of local Mujahedeen rebels, they're able to disrupt Koskov's drug deal, destroying a cargo plane full of raw opium in the process. Koskov unbelievably survives one of the most incredible head-on crashes with a twin-engine plane, but is later captured in Tangier by Pushkin. His probable destination: Siberia. See KRABBE, JEROEN.

KOTTO, YAPHET (New York City, November 15, 1937-   ) American character actor who portrayed the villainous alter egos Dr. Kananga/Mr. Big in *Live and Let Die*. See KANANGA, DR.; BIG, MR.

KOVACS, DR. European nuclear physicist, portrayed by Milow Kirek, who's working for S.P.E.C.T.R.E. in *Never Say Never Again*. Initially based on a fishing boat off the English coast, Kovacs supervises the electronic jamming that confuses the guidance system on the two cruise missiles hijacked by S.P.E.C.T.R.E.

Unbeknownst to the U.S. Air Force officers who are using them for a mid-Atlantic test, the missiles have been armed with W-80 nuclear warheads. Guided by Dr. Kovacs, they eventually make a soft landing in the Bahamas, where they're recovered by Largo's (KLAUS MARIA BRANDAUER) underwater troops.

KOZLOWSKI Chief of Security for the Russian embassy in Istanbul, he's seen briefly through Kerim Bey's (PEDRO ARMENDARIZ) periscope in the embassy conference room in *From Russia with Love*.

KRABBE, JEROEN (Holland, 1944–   ) (pronounced HER RUIN, CRAB BAY) Handsome Dutch leading man who portrayed renegade Russian General Georgi Koskov in *The Living Daylights*. Krabbe, a marvelous character actor, is actually too sympathetic as Koskov. He seems to spend most of the movie hugging his various associates, including Bond (TIMOTHY DALTON), several times. Although Russians are stereotyped as being very demonstrative, the hugging begins to obscure the fact that Koskov is supposed to be a villainous drug smuggler.

Sympathy for Koskov demonstrates one of the major problems with *The Living Daylights*: there's no real villain, at least not the kind you love to hate (à la Goldfinger or Blofeld). Koskov also survives the most incredible plane/car head-on collision ever seen in films. He walks away virtually unscathed. *See* KOSKOV, GENERAL GEORGI.

KREMLIN ART REPOSITORY Atmospheric Moscow storehouse for Soviet treasures where art forger Lenkin (PETER PORTEOUS) is carefully duplicating a cache of jewels for General Orlov (STEVEN BERKOFF) in *Octopussy*. General Gogol (WALTER GOTELL) eventually discovers the forgery operation, bringing Borchoi (GABOR VERNON), the curator of Leningrad's Hermitage, to identify Lenkin's work.

Picking up a duplicate of the Romanoff Star, Borchoi scrutinizes it with a magnifier and then drops it onto the floor, where he crushes it into a million pieces with his boot. Lenkin is then arrested, and Gogol pursues his investigation of Orlov.

KREST, MILTON Boozy drug runner portrayed by Anthony Zerbe, who's masquerading as the head of a marine genetic-engineering firm in *Licence to Kill*. The weak link in Franz Sanchez's (ROBERT DAVI) enormous South American cocaine empire, Krest becomes the first target of James Bond's (TIMOTHY DALTON) deadly scheme to avenge his mutilated CIA friend Felix Leiter (DAVID HEDISON), who was thrown into Krest's shark pen by Sanchez. Once Leiter is out of the way, Krest bears the brunt of Bond's fury, including repeated assaults on his Key West–based smuggling operation.

Eventually, Bond steals aboard the huge *Wavekrest* research vessel and sabotages a drug run, destroying the cocaine and stealing $5 million of Sanchez's money. That princely sum becomes the key to Bond's plot to discredit and destroy Krest in Sanchez's eyes. With CIA pilot and undercover operative Pam Bouvier (CAREY LOWELL) helping him, Bond plants the drug loot in the decompression chamber of the *Wavekrest*, where it's found by Sanchez and his men. Krest can't explain how it got there and pleads with Sanchez to believe in him, but the drug lord is now convinced that there's a traitor in his midst—thanks to Bond—and the cache of money proves who it is. Krest is then thrown into the decompression chamber, where he super-inflates and explodes.

KRIEGLER, ERIC Powerfully built East German biathlon champion and henchman of Soviet agent Aris Kristatos (JULIAN GLOVER) in *For Your Eyes Only*. He's portrayed by actor John Wyman. Bond (ROGER MOORE) first sees him when ice skater Bibi Dahl (LYNN-HOLLY JOHNSON) points him out during a biathlon competition in the snows of Cortina D'Ampezzo in the Italian Alps. Kriegler tries to kill Bond during a ski chase, but 007 escapes. Later, during the battle atop St. Cyril's in Greece, Bond pushes Kriegler through a window to his death.

KRILENCU Bulgar assassin, portrayed by Fred Haggerty, who has a personal vendetta against Kerim Bey (PEDRO ARMENDARIZ) in the first half of *From Russia with Love*. According to Kerim Bey, Krilencu has given Station T–Turkey trouble before, but he's stayed out of Istanbul for over a year.

Krilencu places the limpet mine on the outside wall of Kerim Bey's office. He also leads the Bulgar assault on the Gypsy camp in an effort to assassinate Kerim Bey. In return, Krilencu is himself gunned down by a wounded Kerim Bey, who uses 007's (SEAN CONNERY) AR-7 sniper's rifle to kill the Bulgar when he attempts to sneak out of a trapdoor in his Istanbul apartment—a door that exits out of the mouth of an Anita Ekberg billboard for *Call Me Bwana*.

KRISTATOS, ARIS Sinister millionaire tycoon who is working for the Russians in *For Your Eyes Only*. At first, he introduces himself to Bond (ROGER MOORE) in Cortina as an enthusiastic Anglophile who was a resistance fighter during World War II and who won the King's Medal for his gallantry.

In ski country, he is acting as patron to a young Olympic ice skater (LYNN-HOLLY JOHNSON). He even tells Bond to watch out for Milos Columbo (TOPOL), a man he claims is a drug smuggler, white slaver, and contract murderer.

In reality, Kristatos is a heroin smuggler and a top Russian agent charged with salvaging the A.T.A.C. device from the hulk of the sunken *St. Georges* surveillance vessel. On several occasions, his henchmen, Locque (MICHAEL GOTHARD) and Kriegler (JOHN WYMAN), try to kill Bond. Kristatos is also involved in a blood feud with Columbo, who was betrayed by Kristatos during World War II when the latter worked as a double agent for the Nazis.

Kristatos eventually retrieves the A.T.A.C. from Bond, tries to kill him and Melina Havelock (CAROLE BOUQUET) by keel-hauling the pair, and later retreats to his aerie atop the Meteora cliff in Greece. In the film's finale, Bond assaults the Meteora, and Columbo kills Kristatos.

KRON A maintenance and security chief who runs the solar energy plant on Scaramanga's

(CHRISTOPHER LEE) island, in *The Man with the Golden Gun*, portrayed by Sonny Caldinez. One of the interesting complaints about the movie was that production designer Peter Murton had created a huge solar energy complex, but Central Casting provided only one person to staff it. Was this decision reflective of Scaramanga's reputation as a harsh taskmaster? Or was it a tightening of the belt on the part of the producers? Somehow those purse strings opened in the next film, *The Spy Who Loved Me*, which had some of the largest set pieces ever created for a Bond movie. Some sources spell his name Kra.

KRONSTEEN S.P.E.C.T.R.E.'s director of planning, aka No. 5, in *From Russia with Love*. He's portrayed by actor Vladek Sheybal. Working under Blofeld, this sleepy-eyed nemesis plans S.P.E.C.T.R.E.'s revenge against James Bond for killing their operative, Dr. No.

Kronsteen is introduced in Venice as the Czechoslovakian chess master who won the International Grandmaster's championship over McAdams of Canada. He played the white pieces.

Kronsteen considers his plan to steal the Lektor decoding machine and humiliate Bond in the process a foolproof one. Why? Because he's anticipated every possible variation of countermove.

The fact that he treats life like a chess game probably is the cause of his demise. Chess pieces do not carry concealed knives in their shoes, but Morzeny (WALTER GOTELL) does. Kronsteen is stabbed and poisoned to death after his plan fails miserably on the Orient Express.

KUTUZOV Sophisticated Russian computer employed by fanatical General Orlov (STEVEN BERKOFF) in *Octopussy* to plan his attack against the West. *See* ORLOV'S COMMAND.

KUTZE, LADISLAV Polish nuclear expert, portrayed by George Pravda, who is working for S.P.E.C.T.R.E., in *Thunderball*. Assigned to Largo's (ADOLFO CELI) operation in Nassau, Kutze's job is to maintain the stolen nuclear weapons and prepare them for possible detonation.

Weak-hearted and intimidated, Kutze eventually saves Domino (CLAUDINE AUGER)

from Largo's fury and sabotages the final A-bomb that is on board the *Disco Volante*. When the yacht is about to crash into a reef, Bond (SEAN CONNERY), Domino, and Kutze jump ship, but Kutze is never seen again.

KWANG Dedicated Hong Kong narcotics officer, portrayed by Cary-Hiroyuki Tagawa, who is working undercover as one of Franz Sanchez's (ROBERT DAVI) Far Eastern drug distributors in *Licence to Kill*. Dressed in Ninja garb, Kwang disrupts Bond's (TIMOTHY DALTON) assassination attempt on Sanchez. Brought to a rural safe house outside Isthmus City, Bond is interrogated by Kwang and his attractive associate, Loti (DIANA LEE-HSU). He learns that they've been planning an undercover operation for years, and they're not about to let a rogue agent blow it.

Tied to a table, Bond is incapable of lending a hand when the safe house is attacked and Loti is killed by Sanchez's men. To avoid capture, a badly wounded Kwang takes cyanide. The fact that Bond is tied to the table is a boon when Sanchez arrives with his security chief, Heller (DON STROUD). It helps bolster Bond's cover as a sympathetic, unemployed British agent seeking security work.

KWOUK, BURT (Manchester, England, July 18, 1930–   ) (his name rhymes with "cluck") British actor of Chinese heritage who portrayed Mr. Ling, the Red Chinese specialist in nuclear fission, in *Goldfinger*. He also played

Burt Kwouk was the bespectacled Mr. Ling, the specialist in nuclear fission, in *Goldfinger*. He's better known as Inspector Clouseau's fanatical manservant, Kato, in the Pink Panther films. (London Management)

one of Ernst Stavro Blofeld's (DONALD PLEASENCE) space scientists in *You Only Live Twice* and one of the Chinese army officers who bids for compromising photos during a madcap auction in *Casino Royale*. Kwouk is probably best known as Kato, Inspector Clouseau's (PETER SELLERS) fanatical martial arts assistant, in the *Pink Panther* series. *See* LING, MR.

L

LABELLE, PATTI (October 4, 1944–) Superstar singer who sang the concluding track, "If You Asked Me To," in *Licence to Kill*.

LABINSKY, COUNTESS One of Hugo Drax's (MICHEL LONSDALE) drawing room ladies in *Moonraker*, portrayed by actress Catherine Serre. Together with Lady Victoria Devon, the women are listening to the billionaire industrialist's piano playing when Bond (ROGER MOORE) arrives. Later in the story, we discover that Labinsky and Devon are also two of Drax's master-race astronauts.

LACEY, MARGARET Actress who portrayed Mrs. Whistler, the teacher-turned-diamond-smuggler in *Diamonds Are Forever*.

LADY IN BAHAMAS How actress Valerie Leon is identified in the credits to *Never Say Never Again*. Although nameless, she's a sexy sport-fishing enthusiast who "hooks" Bond (SEAN CONNERY) in the Caribbean after 007 escapes from a group of radio-controlled man-eating sharks. Later in her bed, she and Bond discover that S.P.E.C.T.R.E. agent Fatima Blush (BARBARA CARRERA) has blown up Bond's hotel suite. *See* LEON, VALERIE.

LADY JAMES BOND British Secret Service agent known as "the detainer," portrayed by Daliah Lavi, who infiltrates the lair of Dr. Noah (WOODY ALLEN) in *Casino Royale*. Captured by Noah, Lady Bond worms her way into his confidence and eventually tricks him into drinking a glass of champagne that contains his atomic bomb pill. After 400 burps, Noah and every other prominent cast member in this farce is blown to bits. *See* LAVI, DALIAH.

LADY ROSE The name given to scholarship cellist Kara Milovy's (MARYAM D'ABO) Stradivarius cello in *The Living Daylights* (all Stradivarius cellos have names). Built by hand in 1724, it was sold at a New York auction for $150,000 to arms dealer Brad Whitaker (JOE DON BAKER), who gives it to renegade Russian General Georgi Koskov (JEROEN KRABBE) as a present for his protege/lover, Kara.

The cello also becomes a clue to Koskov's whereabouts. When Kara tells Bond (TIMOTHY DALTON) that the cello is called "Lady Rose," Bond's local contact, Saunders (THOMAS WHEATLEY), discovers that it was purchased by Whitaker at the New York auction. Since Whitaker is based in Tangier, Bond knows where to find Koskov. During their madcap escape from Czech border troops, Bond and Kara actually use the expensive cello as an ersatz ski pole, guiding their descent down a treacherous mountainside.

LAFITTE ROTHSCHILD 1959 Champagne ordered by French detective Achille Aubergine (JEAN ROUGERIE) during his Eiffel Tower lunch with James Bond (ROGER MOORE) in *A View to a Kill*.

LAKE MEAD Nevada resort that became the site of a wild boat chase in an early draft of Richard Maibaum's *Diamonds Are Forever* screenplay. Maibaum had discovered that each major hotel in Las Vegas maintained its own yacht on the lake for recreation and publicity purposes. Caesars Palace owned a Roman galley, the Riviera Hotel had a pirate frigate, etc.

In the film's conclusion, Bond tracks an escaping Blofeld to the lake and watches as the S.P.E.C.T.R.E. chieftain takes off in a high-powered boat. Bond jumps on a powerboat himself, but before he gives chase, he speaks through a loudspeaker, summoning the captions of all the colorful yachts to do their duty for Las Vegas and blockade Blofeld's escape route. With that, the whole flotilla gives chase, eventually cornering Blofeld above the awesome Hoover Dam. The Lake Mead boat chase was later abandoned in favor of the climactic battle aboard the oil-drilling platform.

LAKE TOPLIZ A lake located in the Salz-Kammergut region of Austria. Also, according to the Bank of England, the rumored location of a horde of Nazi gold secreted away at the end of World War II, one bar of which becomes the prize in a golf challenge match between 007 (SEAN CONNERY) and Auric Goldfinger (GERT FROBE).

218

LAKEFRONT AIRPORT Located outside New Orleans, it was the site of the wild chase between Bond (ROGER MOORE)—in his training Cessna—and Kananga's (YAPHET KOTTO) killers in *Live and Let Die*. Stunt coordinator Joie Chitwood organized the chase, which involved crashing cars into, over, and around airplanes. Chitwood's team even crashed the training Cessna through some partially closed hangar doors, which sheered off its wings.

LAMONT, PETER (November 12, 1929–) Three-time Oscar-nominated British production designer whose association with 007 dates back 25 years to a draftsman's assignment on *Goldfinger*. Hired on by art director Peter Murton, who would become production designer on *The Man with the Golden Gun*, Lamont moved steadily up

the art department pyramid, through *Thunderball* (chief draftsman), *You Only Live Twice* (set decorator), *On Her Majesty's Secret Service* (set decorator), *Diamonds Are Forever* (set decorator), *Live and Let Die* (co-art director), *The Man with the Golden Gun* (art director), and *The Spy Who Loved Me* (art director and Oscar nominee).

In 1981, Lamont was fortunate to be in the perfect position when fellow designer Ken Adam went to the United States to work on *Pennies from Heaven*. In need of a production designer, Cubby Broccoli did what he likes to do best: he promoted from within, giving Lamont his first shot at the top spot. And Lamont has been there ever since, designing the productions for *For Your Eyes Only*, *Octopussy*, *A View to a Kill*, *The Living Daylights*, *Licence to Kill*, and *Goldeneye*.

The art department team takes time out for dessert in Portugal on *On Her Majesty's Secret Service*. *Left to right*: Ronnie Quelch, buyer; Roy Dorman, draftsman; Peter Lamont, set decorator; and Ronnie Udell, construction supervisor. (Ronnie Udell Collection)

LAMORA, LUPE Hot-blooded South American drug runner's moll, portrayed by Talisa Soto in *Licence to Kill*. Her tryst with Alvarez (GERARDO MORENO), a local lothario, brings drug lord Franz Sanchez (ROBERT DAVI) to the Bahamas in the film's teaser sequence.

After Dario (BENICIO DEL TORO) literally cuts out the man's heart, Sanchez whips Lupe, throws her into a jeep, and attempts to make his escape. When DEA agents intercept the drug runner and his men, a shoot-out occurs, and Lupe is separated from her boyfriend. Bond (TIMOTHY DALTON) greets her momentarily while chasing after Sanchez.

Since there's no reason to hold Lupe—the authorities are unaware that she's Sanchez's girlfriend—she's released, which allows her to join Sanchez's local drug distributor, boozy Milton Krest (ANTHONY ZERBE), who will transport her back to Isthmus City aboard his research vessel, the *Wavekrest*. Bond sees Lupe again when he sneaks aboard the *Wavekrest*, and she begins to see him as another potential savior.

When Bond arrives in Isthmus City as a high-rolling gun for hire, he spends some time at Sanchez's casino, where Lupe is a rather elegant blackjack dealer. Once again, she sees the man who could free her from literal bondage.

As Bond worms his way into the confidence of Sanchez—part of his plan to infiltrate and destroy the drug runner's cocaine empire—he also finds himself prey to Lupe's seductive moves. Lupe eventually loses Bond to CIA agent Pam Bouvier (CAREY LOWELL), but she has her own happy ending as the new paramour of Isthmus City's President Hector Lopez (PEDRO ARMENDARIZ, JR.).

Talisa Soto and Timothy Dalton take some last-minute instructions from director John Glen during location filming in Key West on *Licence to Kill*.

LANE, TOMMY Actor who portrayed Adam, the speedy motorboat driver in *Live and Let Die*. Doused and blinded by gasoline, Lane loses a watery battle with Bond (ROGER MOORE) in an old navy shipyard.

"LARA'S THEME" The theme from the 1965 film *Dr. Zhivago*, which plays on Russian KGB Major Anya Amasova's (BARBARA BACH) bedroom music box/communicator in *The Spy Who Loved Me*.

LARGO, EMILIO S.P.E.C.T.R.E.'s ruthless one-eyed spymaster portrayed by Adolfo Celi in *Thunderball*. Posing as a wealthy Nassau businessman who collects predator fish for marine institutions, Largo is actually S.P.E.C.T.R.E. No. 2, in charge of the organization's NATO Project.

The ultimate international blackmail scheme, the plan calls for S.P.E.C.T.R.E. to hijack two NATO atomic bombs from an English jet bomber and then demand a ransom of $280 million. If their demands are not met, S.P.E.C.T.R.E. will destroy a major city in either England or the United States.

Largo, with a large amphibious organization under his command, maintains his field headquarters aboard the *Disco Volante*, a swift yacht that can also convert to a hydrofoil in emergency situations. His huge Palmyra estate is a few minutes from downtown Nassau.

Largo is no match against Bond (SEAN CONNERY). In quick order, he loses several games of baccarat; his mistress, Domino (CLAUDINE AUGER); his right arm, Vargas (PHILIP LOCKE); his fellow S.P.E.C.T.R.E. assassin, Fiona Volpe (LUCIANA PALUZZI);

Largo's (ADOLFO CELI) losing streak against Bond (SEAN CONNERY) begins at the baccarat table in Nassau. Perhaps there was a S.P.E.C.T.R.E. at his shoulder, after all. (Rex Features Ltd./RDR Productions)

most of his command; his atomic bombs; and finally, his prize yacht, which crashes into a reef. Largo, himself, is speared by Domino in the film's thrilling finale.

LARGO, MAXIMILLIAN Billionaire industrialist who is also a psychotic S.P.E.C.T.R.E. masterspy, portrayed by Klaus Maria Brandauer, in *Never Say Never Again*. Like Emilio Largo in *Thunderball*, Maximillian Largo is involved in a nuclear blackmail scheme involving two hijacked NATO nuclear weapons. He also has a beautiful mistress named Domino (KIM BASINGER).

Referred to as No.1 in the S.P.E.C.T.R.E. chain of command, Largo reports to Blofeld (MAX VON SYDOW), resides in the Bahamas, and travels aboard his huge oceangoing yacht, the *Flying Saucer*—the English translation of the Italian "Disco Volante" (*see DISCO VOLANTE*).

Born in Bucharest, Romania, in 1945, Largo has no criminal record or associations. His assets, worth $2.492 billion, include shipping, timber, and hotels.

When Captain Jack Petachi (GAVAN O'HERLIHY) helps arm two NATO cruise missiles with nuclear warheads, the weapons are directed to land in the Bahamas, where they're safely recovered by Largo's underwater troops. S.P.E.C.T.R.E.'s scheme is to demand a ransom equivalent to 25 percent of the annual oil purchases of each country in NATO (plus Japan), otherwise one of the stolen warheads will be detonated. The bombs themselves have been planted under the White House and in the Tears of Allah archaeological excavation, which marks the beginning of a huge Arabian oil field in the Middle East.

Bond (SEAN CONNERY) meets Largo and Domino in the South of France, where 007 survives a hair-raising video game called Domination, plus the assassination attempts of Largo's S.P.E.C.T.R.E. associate, Fatima Blush (BARBARA CARRERA).

Tracking Largo's yacht to his North African estate—Palmyra—Bond is captured and thrown into a medieval dungeon populated by bleached bones and hungry vultures. He escapes, rescues Domino from a group of sleazy Arab traders, boards a U.S. Navy submarine, and heads for one final confrontation with Largo in his Tears of Allah dig. Attempting to escape with the one remaining cruise missile, Largo meets the identical fate of his *Thunderball* alter ego—he's speared by the avenging Domino.

LA ROCHEFOUCAULD French writer/philosopher quoted by Ernst Stavro Blofeld (CHARLES GRAY) in *Diamonds Are Forever*. The quote, uttered to Bond (SEAN CONNERY) on the oil rig is, "As La Rochefoucauld once observed, Mr. Bond, 'Humility is the worst form of conceit.' " It is still one of cowriter Tom Mankiewicz's favorite lines of dialogue in the film.

LASER A popular weapon in the James Bond film series, first introduced as a torture device in *Goldfinger*. In that film, Bond (SEAN CONNERY) is captured and strapped to a solid gold table, where the laser beam begins to eat away at the metal and is headed for 007's privates. Fortunately, Bond saves his loins by uttering the magic words, "Operation Grand Slam," the very name of Goldfinger's (GERT FROBE) supposedly top secret plan to detonate a Red Chinese A-bomb inside Fort Knox. Bond is then shot with a tranquilizer dart and shipped to Kentucky.

Laser beams reappear in *Diamonds Are Forever* when it is revealed that Blofeld (CHARLES GRAY), posing as billionaire aircraft manufacturer and recluse Willard Whyte, is building a formidable pre-Star Wars space weapon that projects a deadly beam through a shield of diamonds (the first real-life laser beam was also projected through a diamond).

In *The Man with the Golden Gun*, Scaramanga (CHRISTOPHER LEE) uses a solar energy device to create a type of laser cannon, which he uses to obliterate Bond's (ROGER MOORE) seaplane. In *Moonraker*, Q Branch builds a laser rifle that American space troops employ against Hugo Drax's (MICHEL LONSDALE) space station. A similar laser is built into the nose of an American shuttle that Bond (ROGER MOORE) uses to destroy the deadly nerve-gas spheres that are headed for the earth's atmosphere.

In *Never Say Never Again*, Q (ALEC MCCOWEN) supplies Bond (SEAN CONNERY) with a tiny laser embedded in his wristwatch, which can cut through manacles.

LAST YEAR AT MARIENBAD Director Alain Resnais's art-house hit of 1962, which inspired director Terence Young's teaser in *From Russia with Love*. The Resnais film featured some incredibly beautiful night shots in a garden surrounded by Greek statues. Young duplicated this setting on the Pinewood back lot as S.P.E.C.T.R.E. assassin Red Grant (ROBERT SHAW) tracks down and murders the phony Bond.

LAS VEGAS Predominant location in the seventh James Bond film, *Diamonds Are Forever*. The film actually combines some of Las Vegas's classic landmarks, such as Fremont Street and the colorful Circus Circus Casino, with the incredible interior creations of production designer Ken Adam.

Recalled director Guy Hamilton, "We were location-hunting around Vegas and had already settled on the International Hotel for Blofeld's headquarters. But we still had to find the perfect suite for Bond. I asked Eddie Torres, who managed the Riviera Hotel where we were staying, if he could tell us where to find the most vulgar hotel suite in town. And Torres told us it was at Caesars Palace.

"We walked in and it was an enormous suite with a sunken living room and a mile-long bathroom. It was perfect. We really couldn't hope for anything nicer.

"But Ken Adam was furious. He said to me, 'I can do better vulgar than this.' I told him I didn't care if he could do better vulgar than this, that this was fine. But Ken persisted, saying, 'Guy, if you photograph this suite on the screen, everybody is going to think I designed it.' I finally gave in, and Ken built the suite at Pinewood.

"He also did a tremendous job on Blofeld's apartment. We had rented out some bungalows at Universal when we started the film, and Ken was there designing, and he showed me the sketch for the penthouse. I told him it was gorgeous, but there was one thing missing—the map of Willard Whyte's industrial holdings.

"It was a very important part of the story because an oil-rig model on the Baja, California, area of the map leads Bond to Blofeld's final bastion. And Ken replied, 'Bond is standing on the map.' And it was then that I noticed that the whole floor of Blofeld's living room was a huge map. It was simply fantastic."

LAUGHING WATER The nickname of the hideaway estate of Mrs. Minnie Simpson of Jamaica, a fan of Fleming's 007 novels. In 1962, its fabulously exotic beach simulated the hostile shore of Crab Key, home of Dr. No's impenetrable fortress.

LAUTERBRUNNEN Swiss village that was the site of the humorous stock-car rally in *On Her Majesty's Secret Service*. In the film, screenwriter Richard Maibaum continued the festive mood present in Grindelwald, where an escaping Bond (GEORGE LAZENBY) is rescued by a resourceful Tracy (DIANA RIGG), by creating the European Car Rally that is rudely interrupted when Tracy's Cougar and the big, lumbering S.P.E.C.T.R.E. Mercedes come smashing onto the racecourse. While the astonished crowd watches, the cars continue their game of cat and mouse, to the consternation of the rally drivers, whose little foreign compacts are being smashed around like toys.

The rally took place on an icy track in Lauterbrunnen, only two miles from Murren. There director Peter Hunt assigned racing specialist Anthony Squires to choreograph the race, which featured a number of spectacular crashes—one involving the S.P.E.C.T.R.E. Mercedes, which overturns and explodes. Shooting began at Lauterbrunnen on Sunday, February 2, 1969, and continued until ten o'clock that night, when heavy snows began to fall. On Friday, the 7th, George Lazenby, Diana Rigg, and Peter Hunt braved a blizzard at London Airport and left for Lauterbrunnen to do their close-ups in the race, with cameras mounted on the hood of Tracy's Cougar.

LAVI, DALIAH (Kibbutz Shavei-Zion, Israel, 1942–) Dark-haired Israeli beauty who played "the detainer," a Lady James Bond, in *Casino Royale*. *See* LADY JAMES BOND.

LAW, JOHN Scottish humorist and friend of Peter Sellers who was hired by producer Charles K. Feldman to cowrite the *Casino Royale* spoof in 1967 with Wolf Mankowitz and Michael Sayers.

LAWRENCE, MARC (New York City, February 17, 1910–) Tough-guy American character actor and former opera singer who portrayed Rodney, the syndicate hit man who becomes Scaramanga's (CHRISTOPHER LEE) first "fun house" victim, in *The Man with the Golden Gun*. Lawrence had previously portrayed one of the Las Vegas diamond syndicate hoods in *Diamonds Are Forever*. After Plenty O'Toole (LANA WOOD) is unceremoniously tossed out of a hotel room window, Lawrence utters the immortal line, "I didn't know there was a pool down there."

"LAWRENCE OF ARABIA" THEME Classic movie music that plays over Bond's (ROGER MOORE) and Anya's (BARBARA BACH) desert trek in *The Spy Who Loved Me*. Aside from the whistling janitor's use of the *Goldfinger* theme in *On Her Majesty's Secret Service*, this was the first time in the series that familiar music from other films began to seep into the action of a Bond movie. It would become particularly present in the next film, *Moonraker*, when themes from *The Magnificent Seven* and *Close Encounters of the Third Kind* are used.

LAZAR Portuguese gunsmith portrayed by Marne Maitland in *The Man with the Golden Gun*. Based in Macao, he specializes in weapons and munitions for anonymous gunmen, including Francisco Scaramanga (CHRISTOPHER LEE), for whom he makes a special golden dumdum bullet designed to flatten upon impact for maximum wounding effect. Bond (ROGER MOORE), on the trail of Scaramanga, finds clues in Beirut that lead him to Lazar, who is coerced into revealing how he supplies Scaramanga with his lethal ammunition.

LAZENBY, GEORGE (Goulburn, Australia, September 5, 1939–) Handsome Australian leading man who replaced Sean Connery as James Bond and appeared in one 007 movie, *On Her Majesty's Secret Service* in 1969. An Australian by birth and blood, he came to England in 1964 after a couple of successful years selling automobiles in his native country.

Taking photographer Chard Jenkins's advice, Lazenby became a top male model. He had gained some popularity on TV commercials for Big Fry Chocolates, where he was seen carrying crates of chocolate on his back to give to children, when producers Albert R. Broccoli and Harry Saltzman began their search for a new James Bond in 1968.

"I had no acting experience," Lazenby remembered years later. "I didn't even know any actors. They were in a different class altogether, especially the young ones. A lot of these guys couldn't even afford drinks, while I was making 500 and 600 pounds a week. But I was bored with modeling by then. There was no challenge in it."

Contacted by his agent, Maggie Abbott, Lazenby was sent to the 007 auditions. Lazenby already knew Albert R. Broccoli indirectly. They were both customers of Kurt's Barber Shop in Mayfair, and unbeknownst to Lazenby, Broccoli had once mentioned to Kurt that he thought the young model would someday make an excellent James Bond.

Broccoli often pointed to the way he walked, the fact that he had that same catlike grace that had once sold Broccoli on Sean Connery. He was a big man, yet he moved well. Figuring that the best thing to do was to keep his Australian accent under wraps, Lazenby walked in to the Audley Square offices of Eon Productions and pretended he was English.

Said Lazenby, "I walked right in and asked Harry Saltzman's assistant for an interview. He was on the phone with Harry that very moment. He put the phone down and asked me some quick questions."

Lazenby lied and told the assistant that he was a playboy who raced sports cars for a living. He also mentioned his acting experience in Germany and Australia. The assistant repeated the information to Saltzman, who granted Lazenby an interview. Lazenby was escorted down a wood-paneled hallway to Saltzman's office. He found Saltzman behind his desk, talking on the phone, his shoeless feet draped over the top of his desk.

Saltzman motioned Lazenby to a chair, but the nervous model instead walked over to a window and gazed out. Saltzman hung up the phone and looked over the newcomer. He was impressed.

"So, you want to be James Bond?" Saltz-

George Lazenby returns to the spotlight during The James Bond Weekend in Los Angeles (1981). Here he's interviewed by the author.

man asked. "Yes," Lazenby replied. "Well," Saltzman continued, "You'll have to first meet our director, Peter Hunt. He'll be here tomorrow at four o'clock. Can you make it?" Lazenby hedged, "No, I'm sorry, I have to go back to Paris for a job."

"I don't know why I said that," remembered Lazenby. "I was just getting nervous sitting in Harry's big, plush office. You could tell there was a Rolls-Royce sitting outside, with a chauffeur standing next to it. I'd never been in touch with this kind of person before. Also, I guess I was stalling because I knew that when I met the director, he was going to know right away that I couldn't act."

Lazenby agreed to stay in town for a fee of 500 pounds. He eventually met Hunt and tested with another nonprofessional, Australian singer Trisha Noble, and did quite well. He was asked to stay in London for further testing on a retainer of 150 pounds a week.

By April 1968, Broccoli and Saltzman had narrowed the field down to five actors. Besides Lazenby, they were considering John Richardson, who had recently starred alongside Raquel Welch in *One Million Years B.C.*, and who was romantically linked with former Bond girl Martine Beswick; and three young English actors, Anthony Rogers, Robert Campbell, and Hans de Vries. All five were being tested individually on the Pinewood stages, along with the many young women who were also testing for parts in *On Her Majesty's Secret Service*. Lazenby's ability with his fists eventually won him the part after a test fight worked spectacularly well.

For the test, stunt coordinator George Leech picked a sequence from the film where Bond is surprised by a would-be assassin in the bedroom of a hotel on the Portuguese coast. Leech asked former wrestler Yuri Borienko to double the villain, a Union Corse gunman.

Remembered Leech, "Yuri Borienko didn't have a lot of experience in film fighting, and Lazenby had virtually none at all. I had to instruct both of them in the basic mechanics. Yuri certainly didn't have to learn to fight, but he did have to learn how to react for the cameras. Lazenby was good physically, so he could learn how to punch easily enough. His main problem was learning not to flinch when a punch came his way."

Progress was slow at first. The overly energetic Lazenby got carried away several times and actually bloodied Borienko's nose. The latter, a good-natured man, took the action in stride. For his diligence, Borienko was rewarded with a major part—that of Blofeld's (TELLY SAVALAS) assistant, Grunther—in the new film.

After three weeks of tough rehearsal, Hunt set up his cameras on Pinewood's Stage B and began shooting the final cut of the test fight. In its finished form, the fight lasted two minutes and was so realistic that Hunt later regretted that he couldn't use it as a real sequence. (In the film, Lazenby would fight the same battle with actor Irvin Allen.)

Convinced that Connery was definitely gone from the series, producers Broccoli and Saltzman agreed that of the five candidates, Lazenby was the perfect replacement. And after viewing the test-fight footage, United Artists in New York was inclined to agree. Negotiations were immediately halted with a number of other stars, and plans were finalized to go with George Lazenby when shooting began that fall.

Lazenby's appearance as Connery's replacement was, on the whole, a good one. Although he lacked the polish of a more experienced actor, he was very convincing as James Bond. And while his acting came up short in some key emotional sequences, especially the low-key ending to the film when his bride, Tracy (DIANA RIGG), is murdered by Blofeld (TELLY SAVALAS), his catlike grace worked amazingly well in the film's action sequences. Lazenby could be a very physical actor, and director Peter Hunt played to this strength.

Unfortunately, besieged by worldwide press interest, and under the pressure of replacing one of the world's most popular sex symbols, Lazenby began to crack. His relationship with director Peter Hunt also disintegrated when Hunt preferred to leave Lazenby on his own most of the time. Hunt later termed such a "hands-off" policy as part of his strategy of getting a performance from a nonprofessional, especially in the film's romantic sequences when Bond falls in love with Tracy.

"I wanted that feeling of isolation," said Hunt. "That is Bond. He's a loner. George wasn't experienced enough to interpret this feeling of utter emptiness, especially the loss Bond feels when Tracy is killed. In that sequence, I didn't want him bright and alert. I wanted him beaten down and angry. I thus left him entirely alone that day, hoping that he would get angry at me and then show some of that feeling in the scene."

The strained relationship between actor and director soon spread to other parts of the production, creating a long-running controversy that was picked up and fueled by the British press. The press was particularly eager to exploit an apparent rift between Lazenby and Diana Rigg, especially when the latter announced she was going to eat garlic prior to a key love sequence (*see* GARLIC INCIDENT, THE).

Lazenby later acknowledged that he was the cause of the eventual collapse of his relationship with Hunt and the producers. "It was definitely an ego thing on my part," said Lazenby. "The result was that I did virtually the whole film without a director, and if you look at the call sheet, you'll find that I did almost every scene in one take. I was practically a one-take man. If I made a goof, the crew would shoot the scene from another angle, and if that was good, that was what they would print. So I never really got warmed up in any of my scenes."

Lazenby's comments agree with those of the London critics, who later claimed that his version of Bond was a mere shell of Connery's. Hunt, though, had kinder words for Lazenby: "Apart from one or two moments of frustration brought about by his own feelings about his performance in the film, which we worked out, I had no problem with George. In fact, I had fewer problems with him during the shooting than I've had with more established stars. And he did everything in the film very well. It was only during the latter part of the production, when he became involved in quarrels and questions about his contract, that he became difficult. Eventually, he began to hate the film and, in consequence, me as well."

Hunt continually advised Lazenby to keep a low profile and to wait until the film was released; then his strengths could be acknowledged. But others advised Lazenby to take advantage of his new image.

Said Hunt, "Things would have turned out differently if he had been more sensible and not gone rushing around behaving in such a ridiculous way, saying all sorts of unpleasant things about people. Whether they were true didn't really matter; he was still making a spectacle of himself.

"The public will latch onto these things when they hear them, and you've got to be a pretty experienced person to be able to deal with the press. You have to be able to turn those quotes around so they don't become a knife in the back. George wasn't capable of doing that, and the result was that he got an incredible amount of bad publicity—a fact that probably damaged his career after OHMSS.

"As a young man who had never done a film before, he was still good, and he came through in the role. And you had to be a pretty mean critic to find no talent in him. And I knew that if he went on to make other Bond films, he would have grown into the role, as Roger Moore did.

George Lazenby showed in 1981 that he still had that 007 form.

"Unfortunately, George didn't have the experience at the time to realize this, and he was badly advised by others. I had too much on my plate to stand by him, to take him on as a friend and confidant. It was a long shooting schedule, and on such a shoot, you expect anyone at certain moments to have outbursts and periods of anxiety. He was under a tremendous amount of pressure.

"For six years, the world had identified the character of James Bond with Sean Connery. The phenomenon of Bond had reached its peak under Connery's lead. To many, there could be no other James Bond."

Lazenby's relationship with Hunt and the producers jeopardized his opportunity to return in the next Bond movie, *Diamonds Are Forever*. During a publicity tour for *OHMSS*, he even refused to shave off a beard he had grown during his vacation.

In 1980, Lazenby said, "Right now I could do it. I could sign a contract to do the Bond pictures for seven years. In those days, I couldn't because I was too immature for it. I felt as if I was doing them a favor. After all, I used to think, 'I had a better life before I met you guys.' So I had this chip on my shoulder, and my attitude was entirely wrong. I wasn't looking toward the future.

"Also, in the beginning, I thought I was the only one with an ego. Now I know that everyone on a movie set has one. You have to tread very lightly through the vines. This was something I didn't understand originally, because I was moving around so much. I never stayed in one place long enough to wear out my welcome.

"In those days it also took something like 24 hours for me to learn a page of dialogue. Today it would take me maybe 20 minutes. And that takes a lot of pressure off. At least you have your lines and you feel a lot more secure with them."

After *On Her Majesty's Secret Service*, the word was out that Lazenby was unmanageable, and for a few years he found it impossible to get film work. He later went to Hong Kong, where he worked with Bruce Lee until that actor's untimely death. Lazenby's appearance in a number of low-budget Kung Fu films tided him through the early seventies, after which he went to the United States to play more serious roles.

LAZLY, GENERAL Director of Soviet Military Intelligence in Istanbul. He's seen briefly through Kerim Bey's periscope in the conference room of the Russian embassy in *From Russia with Love*.

LEE, BERNARD (London, January 10, 1908–January 17, 1981) British character actor who portrayed M, Bond's no-nonsense, retired-admiral-turned-Secret-Service-superior in the first 11 James Bond movies. Like the Q character, M's serious demeanor is in direct contrast to 007's frivolous, cavalier attitude toward bureaucratic authority and the "stiff-upper-lip" British mentality.

In *Dr. No*, Bond and M's relationship is appropriately established in the early morning hours, when Bond arrives in M's very conservative, leather-upholstered office after gambling at Les Ambassadeurs. After assigning his top operative to a missing-persons case in Jamaica, M, ever efficient, orders Bond to turn in his handgun, which he declares to be unsafe. This short interplay, written by Richard Maibaum, perfectly establishes Bond as an individual always intent on breaking the rules, even to the point of stealing his own gun back from his boss—a comic touch that perfectly caps the sequence.

Bond and M's relationship is resumed in *From Russia with Love*, once again in M's office. The comic touch this time comes later in the

Bernard Lee, M, found the military uniform and bearing a comfortable element in his many film roles. (National Film Archive, London)

film, when M, Moneypenny, and a half-dozen Secret Service chiefs are listening to an audio-tape, supplied by 007, in which Tatiana Romanova (DANIELA BIANCHI) describes in detail the Russian Lektor decoding machine.

The seriousness of this audio briefing is broken when Romanova starts to get very personal with Bond, eventually pleading with him to constantly make love to her in England. M's embarrassment in front of Miss Moneypenny may be one of the comic high points of the whole series.

Lee established himself as the perfect authority figure, such as in the huge "conference room" sequence in *Thunderball*, where every double-0 operative in Europe learns of S.P.E.C.T.R.E.'s blackmail plot. Eventually, M would leave the staid confines of his London office, and the films' art directors would start to give him the most unusual forward bases.

In *You Only Live Twice*, he would take command from inside a submarine anchored in Hong Kong Harbor—a site M would return to in *The Man with the Golden Gun*; only this time, the location would be inside the half-sunken, burned-out *Queen Elizabeth I* luxury liner.

In *The Spy Who Loved Me*, his advance base was inside an Egyptian tomb, where, for the first time, he was teamed up with his opposite number in the KGB, General Gogol (WALTER GOTELL). M's low-key displeasure with Bond, always at the forefront of their relationship, is demonstrated aboard the British warship that recovers the Stromberg escape capsule containing Bond (ROGER MOORE) and Anya (BARBARA BACH). Peering inside the window, M spots the nude couple in a typical embrace and offers a final, suitably exasperated "James!"

LEE, CHRISTOPHER (London, May 27, 1922–   ) Tall, sinister British character actor and veteran of countless horror films who joined the James Bond series as Francisco Scaramanga, the title character in *The Man with the Golden Gun*. The part was an about-face for Lee, who was used to playing the dark and horrifying side of every possible villain, but who, in *Golden Gun*, was given the opportunity to portray Scaramanga as a sexy, extremely suave, and sophisticated man-about-town assassin who sleeps

The other side of horror superstar Christopher Lee. This happy pose reflects the likable approach he brought to the character of Francisco Scaramanga in *The Man with the Golden Gun*. (National Film Archive, London)

with Andrea Anders (MAUD ADAMS), sunbathes on his private beach, and liquidates his employer's enemies for $1 million a shot.

In fact, Lee is so likable in the role that some critics of the film pointed out that it was hard to accept him as Bond's deadly nemesis. After all, a man who wears jogging suits and tells stories about his pet elephant dying at the hands of an evil handler can't be all bad.

Commented Lee, "All villains should be slightly sympathetic. You should never play them 100 percent heavy. You should always play them with sympathy, sadness, loneliness, amusement, wit, charm, elegance, style, or glamour. These traits make the character much more interesting. And in the role of Scaramanga, all of these qualities were able to come into play. He wasn't just a thug. Instead of playing him with no redeeming qualities at all, with no charm, I was able to play him as an educated, articulate man who killed because he liked money and women and because he simply enjoyed killing."

In a 1974 interview with *Cinefantastique*'s

Chris Knight, Lee pointed out that director Guy Hamilton was the real force behind the new Scaramanga. "Guy Hamilton," recalled Lee, "got something out of me in this picture which I've never been able to show on the screen. In his own words, he got the spook out of me. He got the Dracula out of me. Because, obviously, I can become very menacing, rather heavy, if I'm not careful, even with ordinary lines because I've done it so often. But on this picture, Guy got me to do Scaramanga in such a light way that you can hardly believe this man is as lethal as he is. He got me to smile and even made me laugh, something which, I admit, I haven't found very easy to do as an actor."

Christopher Lee was destined to appear in the Bond series. He was the cousin of author Ian Fleming (Lee's stepfather, Harcourt Rose, was Fleming's uncle), and he was probably the inspiration for Fleming's Dr. No character. *See* SCARAMANGA, FRANCISCO.

LEE, CHUCK James Bond's (ROGER MOORE) likable San Francisco CIA contact, portrayed by David Yip, in *A View to a Kill*. Lee briefs Bond on Max Zorin's (CHRISTOPHER WALKEN) local activities, including his oil-pumping operation on San Francisco Bay. He also introduces 007 to O'Rourke (BILL ACKRIDGE), a disgruntled fisherman who claims that Zorin's pumping has ruined one of the best crab-fishing patches in the bay.

This information is enough to send Bond on an underwater visit to Zorin's pumping station that night, where 007 finds himself competing with Russian KGB agent Pola Ivanova (FIONA FULLERTON). Ivanova has captured some key dialogue between Zorin and Bob Conley (MANNING REDWOOD) on a tape-recorded cassette, which Bond eventually steals from her after a steamy hot-tub encounter.

After Bond saves the life of geologist Stacey Sutton (TANYA ROBERTS), who is being pressured by Zorin into giving up her father's shares in Sutton Oil, Lee joins his British Secret Service contact at Sutton's house. There he's strangled by May Day (GRACE JONES).

LEECH, GEORGE (December 6, 1921–) Top British stuntman and stunt coordina-

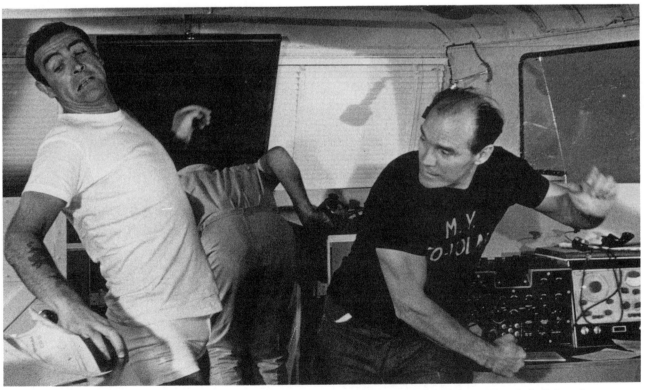

Stuntman George Leech takes a swing at Sean Connery during the hydrofoil cabin fight in *Thunderball*. Leech was involved with the Bond series from the beginning and was the stunt arranger for *On Her Majesty's Secret Service*. He retired in 1986 after forty years in the business. (Rex Features Ltd./RDR Productions)

tor who worked closely with stunt arranger Bob Simmons on many of the early Bond films, including *Goldfinger, Thunderball, You Only Live Twice, On Her Majesty's Secret Service, Diamonds Are Forever*, and *The Spy Who Loved Me*.

LEECH, WENDY British stuntwoman, and the daughter of Bond stunt veteran George Leech, who portrayed the kidnapped millionairess in the war game featured in the teaser for *Never Say Never Again*. Brainwashed by fanatical revolutionaries, she stabs James Bond (SEAN CONNERY) in the arm with a phony knife after he rescues her.

LEE-HSU, DIANA Beautiful Chinese actress and ex-*Playboy* magazine playmate who portrayed Loti, a Hong Kong narcotics agent masquerading as the girlfriend of one of Franz Sanchez's (ROBERT DAVI) drug distributors in *Licence to Kill. See* LOTI.

LEFTY O'DOUL BRIDGE Located on Third Street at China Basin in San Francisco, this drawbridge is featured in the comical hook-and-ladder truck chase in *A View to a Kill*.

LE GRANDE Deuxième Bureau chief and ex-vice officer portrayed by Charles Boyer in *Casino Royale*. Le Grande—accompanied by M (JOHN HUSTON), Ransome (WILLIAM HOLDEN), and Smirnov (KURT KASZNAR)—comes to a rural English manor house to plead with Sir James Bond (DAVID NIVEN) to accept one last desperate mission. Sir James notes that Le Grande still carries a selection of deadly poisons hidden in each of his fly buttons. *See* BOYER, CHARLES.

LEILA The extremely sexy and beautiful Gypsy belly dancer in *From Russia with Love*.

LEITER, CLARENCE British agent, portrayed by Michael Pate, who joins James Bond (BARRY NELSON) on a mission against Soviet masterspy Le Chiffre (PETER LORRE) in the TV film "Casino Royale" (1954). In essence, Leiter is a British version of Fleming's original American CIA agent Felix Leiter—a logical move, since writers Antony Ellis and Charles Bennet had created an American James Bond.

As an agent of Station S of the British Secret Service—specialists on the Soviet Union—working with the French Deuxième Bureau and American Combined Intelligence, Leiter's mission is to supply Bond with 26 million francs in order for him to bankrupt a Soviet masterspy named Le Chiffre (PETER LORRE) at the baccarat table in Monte Carlo. Le Chiffre is the chief Soviet agent in the area. He's been illegally betting Soviet funds at the baccarat table and has already lost heavily. If Bond can win his remaining 26 million francs, in effect bankrupting him, the Soviet government will send out their own assassination team to get rid of Le Chiffre. The embarrassment will be a major victory for Allied Intelligence. *See* PATE, MICHAEL.

LEITER, FELIX Bond's long-time friend and compatriot in the U.S. Central Intelligence Agency, usually a second banana who represents U.S. interests on Bond's various operations. He's been portrayed by many different actors, who employed a number of approaches to the character.

The first Felix Leiter was actually Australian actor Michael Pate, who portrayed him in the CBS-TV film "Casino Royale" in 1954. In this film, he's identified as Clarence Leiter, an agent with British Intelligence who briefs Bond about Le Chiffre's card-playing activities.

Broccoli and Saltzman hired Jack Lord to play Leiter in *Dr. No*. The tropical climate must have agreed with him, because he went on to spend most of his acting career in Hawaii as American detective Steve McGarrett in the "Hawaii Five-0" television series.

Lord's Leiter was followed by Canadian Cec Linder (*Goldfinger*), who was the quintessential 1960s businessman-type Leiter; Rik Van Nutter, the lanky, prematurely gray beach boy Leiter (*Thunderball*); Norman Burton, another businessman-type (*Diamonds Are Forever*); David Hedison, the New England–debonair Leiter (*Live and Let Die* and *Licence to Kill*); Bernie Casey, the black Leiter (*Never Say Never Again*); and John Terry, probably the youngest Leiter ever, who looked like a kid just off the southern California beaches (*The Living Daylights*).

In the case of Hedison's return in *Licence to Kill*, Leiter becomes the key to the plot when,

Felix Leiter (BERNIE CASEY) prepares to open fire with a submachine gun during the assault on the Tears of Allah excavation in *Never Say Never Again*. (Taliafilm)

on his wedding day to Della Churchill (PRIS-CILLA BARNES), he's thrown into a shark pool by ruthless drug runner Franz Sanchez (ROBERT DAVI). Leiter's mutilation—he loses his left leg below the knee—and Della's murder prompt James Bond (TIMOTHY DALTON) to break away from the British Secret Service and stage his own revenge scheme.

One other note about *Licence*: Bond finds Leiter barely alive, with a scrap of paper stuffed in his mouth with the saying "He disagreed with something that ate him." This scene was actually taken from author Ian Fleming's novel *Live and Let Die*.

LEKTOR DECODING MACHINE The prize in *From Russia with Love*. Referred to as a Spektor in Ian Fleming's original novel (the screenwriters changed it to Lektor because they were now using the S.P.E.C.T.R.E. organization as the villain in the film), it was based on an actual decoding machine used during World War II—the famous Enigma decoder, which helped win the war when Britain's Ultra organization broke the German diplomatic code in 1939.

The truth about Ultra, the Enigma de-coder, and Ian Fleming's part in its activities wasn't revealed until 1975, when British war-time secrets were first declassified. Sir William Stevenson, the head of Ultra and a close friend of Fleming, revealed the secrets of Fleming's own contribution in a book titled *A Man Called Intrepid*. This concise history of British Intelligence activities would later explain a great deal of the source material upon which Fleming based his James Bond novels, including the Spektor/Lektor decoder of *From Russia with Love*.

Technical details: The decoder weighs 10 kilograms and is carried in a brown case like a typewriter. It has self-calibrating and manual capabilities, with a built-in compensator. There are 24 symbol and 16 code keys on its key-board. Inside, the mechanism includes a light and perforated copper disks.

In the film, M states that the British Secret Service has been attempting to get a Russian Lektor for years. Now, according to their sta-tion contact in Istanbul—Ali Kerim Bey (PEDRO ARMENDARIZ)—a Russian embassy cipher clerk named Tatiana Romanova (DAN-IELA BIANCHI) will steal the Lektor if James Bond (SEAN CONNERY) will come to Istanbul and help her defect. All of this, of course, is an intricate S.P.E.C.T.R.E. trap.

The Lektor is first seen in the communications room of the Russian embassy in Istanbul, where it is captured by Bond when the building is dynamited by Kerim Bey. Bond carries it aboard the Orient Express and eventually brings it to Venice, where it is nearly stolen back by Rosa Klebb (LOTTE LENYA) before she is killed by Romanova.

LENKIN General Orlov's (STEVEN BERKOFF) expert jewelry forger, portrayed by Peter Porteous, in *Octopussy*. Working out of the atmospheric Kremlin Art Repository, Lenkin pleads with Orlov to retrieve an original Fabergé egg stolen from the repository and illegally placed on the auction block in Britain. Lenkin needs the egg because an unscheduled inventory of all art objects will soon take place.

Meanwhile, General Gogol (WALTER GOTELL) has been investigating General Orlov and has traced his illegal activities to Lenkin. Arriving at the repository one night with Borchoi (GABOR VERNON), the curator of Le-

ningrad's Hermitage Museum, Orlov hands the priceless Romanoff Star to Borchoi. He scrutinizes it and then smashes it onto the floor, where it breaks into its obviously glass fragments. Lenkin is then arrested by KGB agents.

LENTIL DELIGHT, DANDELION SALAD, AND GOAT'S CHEESE The dietary surprise that sexy physical therapist Patricia Fearing (PRUNELLA GEE) brings to James Bond's (SEAN CONNERY) room at Shrublands in *Never Say Never Again*. Bond counters admirably with Beluga caviar, quail eggs, fois gras, and vodka.

LENYA, LOTTE (1900–1981) (real name, Karoline Blaumauer) Austrian character actress, better known internationally as the performer of her husband's, Kurt Weill, famous song repertoire, who portrayed one of the best villains in the James Bond series—S.P.E.C.T.R.E. Agent No. 3, Rosa Klebb, ex-head of operations for SMERSH, in *From Russia with Love*. It's hard to picture the woman who portrayed Klebb as an internationally respected singer/entertainer, but

A party on the Chess Match set in *From Russia with Love*. Guests include, *left to right*, Daniela Bianchi, Ian Fleming, Lois Maxwell, Lotte Lenya, and Sean Connery. (National Film Archive, London)

it's true. The part of Klebb was apparently a romp for her, and her comfort in the role is evident.

Lenya is every inch the character of Rosa Klebb. Her military outfits and bearing, her whiplike screaming voice, her knuckle-duster to Grant's (ROBERT SHAW) abdomen, and her terror in Blofeld's presence are riveting. At one point, Tatiana Romanova (DANIELA BIANCHI) balks at an espionage assignment, asking Klebb what the punishment will be if she refuses. Klebb turns to her and replies straightforwardly, "Then you will not leave this room alive." When Tanya says she will then perform the assignment, the film gets one of its best laughs.

LEON, VALERIE British actress who portrayed the Sardinian hotel receptionist in *The Spy Who Loved Me* and the sexy Nassau deep-sea fishing enthusiast who "hooks" Bond (SEAN CONNERY) in *Never Say Never Again.*

LES AMBASSADEURS A gaming club in London frequented by James Bond. Here Sean

Valerie Leon spends some strategic time in bed with Sean Connery in *Never Say Never Again.* (Taliafilm)

Connery was introduced as James Bond in *Dr. No.*

LES BEATLES Words scribbled on the wall of a French outdoor men's rest room in the teaser for the *Casino Royale* spoof (1967). These words are literally the first thing one sees on-screen. The camera widens to reveal James Bond, aka Evelyn Tremble (PETER SELLERS), in Monte Carlo waiting for French Special Police Detective Mathis (DUNCAN MACRAE).

LEWARS, MARGARET Jamaican actress who portrayed the shapely and deadly freelance photographer who is determined to photograph Bond (SEAN CONNERY) in *Dr. No.* She had recently won the title of Miss Jamaica of 1961.

LEYLAND R. T. The make of the double-decker bus that was transported to Jamaica in 1972 to perform stunt chores in *Live and Let Die.* Fresh off of London's Bakersee Route 19, it was driven by London bus-driving instructor Maurice Patchett.

The Leyland was equipped with a standard 98-hp engine, a 35-gallon gasoline tank, and a coat of grayish-green paint simulating the colors of fictional San Monique Transport. It was impossible to notice that a team of metal workers had actually sawed off the top half of the bus body, placed it on metal rollers, and reattached it to the lower body so that when Patchett hit the low-level trestle bridge, the upper half would easily come smashing off. *See* PATCHETT, MAURICE.

L'HEURE BLEU Tracy's (DIANA RIGG) perfume in *On Her Majesty's Secret Service.*

LH 450 Lufthansa Airlines flight from Amsterdam to Los Angeles that carries James Bond (SEAN CONNERY), Tiffany Case (JILL ST. JOHN), Mr. Wint (BRUCE GLOVER), Mr. Kidd (PUTTER SMITH), and the body of Peter Franks (JOE ROBINSON), along with a 50,000-carat diamond cache tucked up Franks's alimentary canal, in *Diamonds Are Forever.*

LICENCE REVOKED Original title of *Licence to Kill.* The question of whether or not the public would understand the definition of the word "revoked" was probably behind the change. Silly, isn't it, but a title can play a substantial part in a film's marketing effectiveness.

LICENCE TO KILL (United Artists, 1989) ★ ★ ½ The 16th James Bond film produced by Albert R. Broccoli, and the first to feature a title that is not based on an Ian Fleming novel. U.S. film debut: July 14, 1989. Running time: 135 minutes.

Timothy Dalton returns as James Bond in *Licence to Kill*, the first Bond film to receive a Restricted (R) rating code for excessive violence. Unfortunately, the added violence featured in the film was unnecessary. It would have been one thing if Bond and Sanchez were involved in an incredibly violent fight (à la *From Russia with Love*), but the violent episodes affect other characters.

Felix Leiter is thrown to the sharks and loses a leg, Milton Krest's head inflates and explodes in a decompression chamber, Carey Lowell takes a bullet in the back (she survives, courtesy of a Kevlar vest), and Bond nearly falls into a bag shredder that claims the knife-wielding Dario. This is a 007 adventure that plays like an expensive episode of "Miami Vice." What the film needed wasn't excessive violence but a fresh story line.

In the most serious Bond movie since *From Russia with Love*, writer Michael G. Wilson, working from Richard Maibaum's outline (Maibaum, due to the Writers Guild of America strike, was unable to write the script), eliminated some of the very elements that have contributed to the longevity of the series—namely, the biting humor, fascinating locations, and a grandiose scheme perpetrated by a fantasy villain.

Robert Davi's Franz Sanchez is a suitably ruthless drug runner who has the heart cut out of the man found cheating with his girlfriend, Lupe, but his international drug dealing is a bore. International audiences could find a similar train of events on the front pages of their daily newspapers.

The film was also a claustrophobic Bond considering its limited globe-trotting. Audiences used to the series's outrageous locations were disappointed by the uninteresting trips to Key West and Isthmus City.

The movie starts out with a good twist when Bond's longtime friend Felix Leiter is thrown to the sharks by Sanchez. Forsaking M and the Secret Service, Bond becomes a rogue agent seeking revenge at all costs—a great plot device, and one almost used by Bond in *On Her Majesty's Secret Service*, which also involved a bride being murdered on her wedding day. Unfortunately, once 007 arrives in Isthmus City, the movie loses all of its tension and impact.

Bond's assassination attempt on Sanchez's life is stopped by a group of Hong Kong narcotics agents. Bond is too easily accepted into Sanchez's inner circle as a friend and security adviser, and he's able to slowly turn the drug kingpin against his confederates.

There's too much talk and not enough action. Even the tanker-trailer chase—despite some amazing stunt work—is a lackluster climax. And the expected one-on-one encounter between Bond and Sanchez is over much too quickly.

Highlights: Dalton, who is once again serious and on target, although he should have been lightened up a bit. Audiences who spend two or more hours with Bond need to laugh once in a while. Thankfully, Q, in his largest role in the series, is on hand to provide some crucial comic relief. Carey Lowell is a delightful Pam Bouvier, a resourceful, beautiful CIA pilot and undercover operative who helps Bond at every turn—the best Bond girl in years. Her introduction in the Barrelhead Bar in Bimini is a classic. Benicio del Toro's Dario is also an excellent villain.

LICENCE TO KILL CAST

James Bond	Timothy Dalton
Pam Bouvier	Carey Lowell
Franz Sanchez	Robert Davi
Lupe Lamora	Talisa Soto
Milton Krest	Anthony Zerbe
Sharkey	Frank McRae
Killifer	Everett McGill

Timothy Dalton prepares to leave Key West for Istanbul during airport scenes in *Licence to Kill*. (Erik Hollander)

Professor Joe Butcher . . . . Wayne Newton
Dario . . . . Benicio Del Toro
Truman-Lodge . . . . Anthony Starke
President Hector Lopez . . . . . Pedro Armendariz, Jr.
Q . . . . Desmond Llewelyn
Felix Leiter . . . . David Hedison
Della Churchill . . . . Priscilla Barnes
M . . . . Robert Brown
Miss Moneypenny . . . . Caroline Bliss
Heller . . . . Don Stroud
Hawkins . . . . Grand L. Bush
Kwang . . . . Cary-Hiroyuki Tagawa
Perez . . . . Alexander Bracho
Braun . . . . Guy de Saint Cyr
Mullens . . . . Rafer Johnson
Loti . . . . Diana Lee-Hsu
Fallon . . . . Christopher Neame
Stripper . . . . Jeannine Bisignano
Montelongo . . . . Claudio Brook
Consuelo . . . . Cynthia Fallon
Rasmussen . . . . Enrique Novi

Oriental . . . . Isami Kawawo
Doctor . . . . George Belanger
Wavekrest Captain . . . . Roger Cudney
Chief Chemist . . . . Honorato Magaloni
Pit Boss . . . . Jorge Russek
Bellboy . . . . Sergio Corona
Ninja . . . . Stuart Kwan
Tanker Driver . . . . Jose Abdala
Ticket Agent . . . . Teresa Blake
Della's Uncle . . . . Samuel Benjamin Lancaster
Casino Manager . . . . Juan Peliaz
Coast Guard Radio Operator . . . . Mark Kelty
Hotel Assistant Manager . . . . Umberto Elizondo
Sanchez's Driver . . . . Fidel Carriga
Barrelhead Waitress . . . . Edna Bolkan
Clive . . . . Eddie Enderfield
Warehouse Guards . . . Jeff Moldovan, Carl Ciarfalio

LICENCE TO KILL CREW
Producers . . Albert R. Broccoli, Michael G. Wilson
Director . . . . John Glen

Screenplay by . . . . .Michael G. Wilson, Richard Maibaum

Associate Producers. . . . . .Tom Pevsner, Barbara Broccoli

Production Design by . . . . .Peter Lamont

Director of Photography . . . . .Alec Mills

Special Visual Effects . . . . .John Richardson

Main Title Song Sung by. . . . . .Gladys Knight

End Title Song Sung by . . . . .Patti LaBelle

Original Score Composed and Conducted by . . . . .Michael Kamen

Second Unit Directed and Photographed by . . . . . . Arthur Wooster

Costume Designer . . . . .Jodie Tillen

Main Title Designed by . . . . .Maurice Binder

Casting . . . . .Jane Jenkins, Janet Hirshenson

Production Supervisor . . . . .Anthony Waye

Underwater Scenes Directed and Photographed by . . . . .Ramon Bravo

Production Accountant. . . . . .Douglas Noakes

Stunt Coordinator . . . . .Paul Weston

Driving Stunts Arranger . . . . .Remy Julienne

Aerial Stunt Supervisor . . . . .Corkey Fornof

Director of Marketing . . . . .Charles Juroe

Production Supervisor (Mexico) . . . . .Hector Lopez

Production Manager. . . . . .Philip Kohler

Unit Manager . . . . .Iris Rose

Assistant Directors. . . . . . .Miguel Gil, Miguel Lima

Camera Operator . . . . .Michael Frift

Sound Recordist . . . . .Edward Tise

Continuity . . . . .June Randall

Electrical Supervisor . . . . .John Tythe

Art Director. . . . . .Michael Lamont

Set Decorator . . . . .Michael Ford

Construction Manager . . . . .Tony Graysmark

Makeup Supervisors . .George Frost, Naomi Dunne

Hairdressing Supervisor. . . . . .Tricia Cameron

Editor. . . . . .John Grover

Sound Editor . . . . .Vernon Messenger

Production Manager. . . . . .Efren Flores

Production Manager (Mexicali) . . . . .Crispin Reece

Location Manager (Mexicali) . . . . . . .Laura Aguilar

Production Coordinator . . . . .Loolee Deleon

Production Coordinator (Mexicali) Georgina Heath

Second Assistant Director. . . . . .Callum McDougall

Production Assistants . . .Ignacio Cervantes, Marcia Perskie, Gerardo Barrera, Monica Greene

Production Secretary . . . . .Ileana Franco

Casting (Mexico). . . . . .Claudia Becker

Accountants . . . . .Jane Meagher, Rosa Maria Gomez

Assistant Accountant . . . . .Andrew Noakes

Assembly Editor . . . . .Matthew Glen

Editor (Mexico). . . . . .Carlos Puente

Sound Editors . . . . .Peter Musgrave, Mark Auguste

Music Editor .Andrew Glen

Assistant Editors . .John Nuth, Wayne Smith, Ross Adams, Richard Fettes, Mark Mostyn, Rob Green

Additional Sound Effects . . . . . . .Jean-Pierre Lelong

Rerecording Mixers . . . . .Graham Hartstone, John Hayward

Music Mixer .Dick Lewzey

Music Programming . . . . .Stephen McLaughlin

Music Performed by London National Philharmonic Orchestra

Art Director . . . . .Dennis Bosher

Assistant Art Directors . . . . .Neil Lamont, Richard Holland, Andrew Ackland-Snow, Hector Romero

Sketch Artist .Roger Deer

Graphics . . . . .Robert Walker

Sculptor . . . . .Daniel Miller

Scenic Artist . . . . .Gilly Noyes-Court

Camera Focus . . . . .Frank Elliott

Second Cameras (Mexico) Donald Bryant, Tim Ross

Camera Grip. . . . . .Chunky Huse

Boom Operator . . . . .Martin Trevis

Costume Supervisors . . . .Barbara Scott, Hugo Pena

Wardrobe Master (Mexicali). . .Enrique Villavencio

Makeup . . . . .Norma Webb

Special Effects Supervisors (Mexico) . . . .Laurencio Cordero, Sergio Jara

Special Effects (First Unit). . . . . .Neil Corbould

Special Effects Technicians . . .Peter Pickering, Clive Beard, Nick Finlayson

Director of Publicity . . . . .Saul Cooper

Stills Photographer . . . . .Keith Hamshere

Production Buyer . . . . .Ron Quelch

Property Master . . . . .Bert Hearn

Standby Propman. . . . . .Bernard Hearn

Armourers . . . . .Harris Bierman, Tony Didio

Transport Manager. . . . . .Arthur Dunne

Transport Captain (Mexico) . . . . . . .Mauro Venegas

London Contact. . . . . .Amanda Schofield

Los Angeles Contact. . . . . .Linda Brown

Second Unit

First Assistant Directors . .Terry Madden, Sebastian Silva

Second Assistant Director . . . . .Marcia Gay

Continuity. . . . . .Sue Field

Camera Operator . . . . .Malcolm Macintosh

Camera Focus . . . . .Michael Evans

Camera Grip . . . . .Ken Atherfold

Stills Photographer . . . . .George Whitear

Special Effects Supervisor ....Chris Corbould
Special Effects Technicians ...Andy Williams, Paul Whybrow
Makeup/Hair ....Di Holt
Standby Propman................Rodney Pincott

Florida
Production Supervisor ....Ned Kopp
Production Coordinator ....Patricia Madiedo
Location Manager.................Colette Hailey
Location Accountant...............Jack Descent
Second Camera ....John Elton
Art Director........................Ken Court
Set Decorators ...Richard Helfritz, Fredrick Weiler
Special Effects Coordinator ......Larry Cavanaugh
Electrical Supervisor ....Norman Zuckerman
Key Grip ....Eddie Knott III
Costume Supervisor ....Robert Chase
Marine Coordinator ....Lorentz Hills
Transport Coordinator................Joyce Lark
Stunt Team Supervisors....Gerardo Moreno, Marc Boyle, Art Malesci
Stunt Team ....Simon Crane, Jake Lombard, Steve Dent, David Reinhardt, Mark Bahr, Julian Bucio, Javier Lambert, Mauricio Martinez, Alex Edlin
Driving Team .....Gilbert Bataille, Jo Cote, Didier Brule, Jean-Claude Houbart, Dominique Julienne
Aerial Cameraman.................Phil Pastuhov
Parachute Stunt Coordinator.........B. J. Worth
Camera Helicopter ....French Aircraft Agency
Helicopter Pilot ....Ken Calman
U.S. Coast Guard Technical Advisor ..Commander John McElwain
U.S. Coast Guard Helicopter Pilots ....Lt. Commander Randy Meade III, Lt. Neil Hughes, Lt. Commander R. Allen
Underwater Coordinator ....Rita Sheese
Underwater Location Managers.....Nicole Kolin, Tony Broccoli
Underwater Camera Assistant.........Pepe Flores
Underwater Special Effects..........Daniel Dark
Divers ...Emilio Magana, Juan Dario Corona, Alex Arnold, Jorge Cardenas, Manuel Cardenas
Special Consultants to the Producers.......Sparky Greene, Jillian Palenthorpe
Camera Equipment ......Tratafilms (Mexico City), Cine Video Tech (Miami)
Film Stock ....Kodak Mexicana
Lighting and Transport ....Servicios Filmicos
Travel ....Travel Shop International, The Travel Company
Freight........Jose Vasquez A., Vital International Freight Services, Renown Freight

Catering by ....Alimentacion Filmica Especializada
Medical Services ....Lifestar International
Weapons by ....Stembridge Gun Rentals Inc.
Gun Holsters by.............Galco International
Animals Supplied by ....Carlos Renero
Jewelry ....Sheila Goldfinger
Production Company ....Eon Productions
Distribution Company ....United Artists

LICENCE TO KILL COMPETITION
Competitive films in release when *Licence to Kill* opened in Los Angeles on July 14, 1989:
Batman
Lethal Weapon 2
Indiana Jones and the Last Crusade
Star Trek V: The Final Frontier
Honey, I Shrunk the Kids
Dead Poets Society
Ghostbusters II
The Karate Kid, Part III
Great Balls of Fire!
Peter Pan (reissue)
UHF
Weekend at Bernie's
When Harry Met Sally
Do the Right Thing

LIECIER, DULICE Actress who portrayed Ava, a CIA agent working for Felix Leiter (JOHN TERRY) in Tangier in *The Living Daylights*.

LILY, SISTER One of Dr. No's (JOSEPH WISEMAN) extremely efficient secretary/receptionists on Crab Key. She's portrayed by actress Yvonne Shima.

LIMPET MINE An explosive device attached to the wall of Kerim Bey's (PEDRO ARMENDARIZ) office by Bulgarian agent Krilencu (FRED HAGGERTY) in *From Russia with Love*. Thanks to the lovemaking pleas of his girlfriend (NADJA REGIN), Kerim Bey retires to a settee and is saved from the blast.

LINCOLN LOUNGE A nightclub at Las Vegas's Whyte House Hotel in *Diamonds Are Forever*. It's where comedian and syndicate member Shady Tree (LEONARD BARR) and his Acorns are performing their act.

LINDA Jet-setter bathing beauty, portrayed by shapely Kell Tyler in *The Living Daylights* teaser, who, while speaking to her friend Margo, bemoans the scarcity of real men until James Bond (TIMOTHY DALTON) "drops" onto her yacht.

LINDER, CEC (pronounced CEESE, short for Cecil) (Galicia, Poland, March 10, 1921-) (real name, Cecil Yekuthial Lindner) Canadian character actor of Polish heritage who portrayed Felix Leiter in *Goldfinger*. Always dapper in a business suit and fedora, Linder's Leiter is also a very businesslike, by-the-rules kind of guy, who nonetheless knows how 007 (SEAN CONNERY) operates.

In many ways he's probably the quintessential CIA man of the Kennedy era, perhaps paralleling the business-suited FBI agents that were seen trudging through a mucky Mississippi swamp in the Gene Hackman-Willem Dafoe film *Mississippi Burning* (1988). More apt to make a phone call than use his fists, Leiter keeps track of Bond when he's captured by Goldfinger (GERT FROBE), and it is Linder's Leiter who calls the shots during the U.S. Army's counterattack on Goldfinger's Operation Grand Slam against Fort Knox.

Linder was actually chosen to play Mr. Simmons, the cardplayer, but at the last minute he was given the part of Leiter—a casting switch that didn't please Austin Willis, who ended up playing Simmons. "He had a right to be upset," remembered Linder. "He got a few days on the picture, but I ended up with 12 weeks."

Linder and Willis were the only two actors sent to Florida for the U.S. shoot. Guy Hamilton's crew shot at the Fontainebleau pool, where producer Harry Saltzman loaned Linder his fedora for his introductory walk-by. They filmed the chase between Leiter and Oddjob, which concluded at a wrecking yard and featured a double for Harold Sakata, and they shot a brief sequence on the highway, where Leiter gets the word from his partner that Bond's signal is moving. Everything else was shot in England, including the incredible assault on Fort Knox, which was built full-size on the back lot.

After his CIA role in *Goldfinger*, Canadian actor Cec Linder found comfort in other military roles. (Cec Linder Collection)

Linder, unfortunately, was not asked to play Leiter on the next film, *Thunderball*. (He was replaced by Rik Van Nutter.) "I guess they wanted a younger guy," he recalled, "someone who could fight sharks and that kind of thing." *See* LEITER, FELIX; FONTAINEBLEAU.

LINDSTROM, PIA Daughter of Ingrid Bergman and a prominent New York City television film critic who was tested to play the part of Russian cipher clerk Tatiana Romanova in *From Russia with Love*. Director Terence Young claimed that she tested terrifically. Unfortunately, she was photographed against a backdrop of black satin sheets, which gave her a distinct five-o'clock shadow—an effect that killed her chances of becoming the sexy spy.

LING James Bond's (SEAN CONNERY) delectable Chinese girlfriend, portrayed by actress Tsai Chin, at the beginning of *You Only Live Twice*. After she gives 007 "the very best duck," she pushes a button that swings her hide-a-bed, along with Bond, into the wall and then allows two machine-gunning thugs into her apartment. After they're done spraying the bed, it looks like 007 is dead. We know better.

LING, MR. Red Chinese specialist in nuclear fission, portrayed by Burt Kwouk, in *Goldfinger*. Ling's government is providing Goldfinger (GERT FROBE) with an atomic device that will be detonated inside the American gold repository at Fort Knox, irradiating the gold for 58 years. The trade-off: economic chaos in the West for the Chinese plus a tenfold increase in the value of Goldfinger's own smuggled gold cache.

When the Americans counterattack, Goldfinger, wearing an American officer's uniform, shoots Ling in front of an advancing column of U.S. Infantry. Convinced that he's one of them, the Americans move on and are promptly mowed down by Goldfinger.

LING PO The servant of sinister Bangkok-based industrialist Hai Fat (RICHARD LOO) in *The Man with the Golden Gun*.

Lovely Pia Lindstrom was in the running for the Tatiana Romanova part in *From Russia with Love* in 1963.

LIPARUS A supertanker that is the pride of Karl Stromberg's (CURT JURGENS) fleet and the pawn in his scheme to destroy the world in *The Spy Who Loved Me*. The second largest tanker in the world at over a million tons—behind the Soviet *Karl Marx*—it is equipped with enormous bow doors that can swing open and swallow nuclear submarines whole. Hence, it isn't surprising that the 007 Stage interior of the *Liparus* at Pinewood Studios was dubbed the "*Jonah* Set,"—after the biblical whale that swallowed Jonah.

In the film, after noticing a model of the *Liparus* at Stromberg's Atlantis laboratory, Bond (ROGER MOORE) and Anya (BARBARA BACH) check up on the supertanker's history and discover that since it was fitted out nine months before, it has never once been in port (obviously, Stromberg's hiding something—probably those suspicious bow doors). Inside the *Liparus* is a fascinating miniharbor with docking space for three submarines, a monorail, an armored control room, and a virtual army of sailors and deckhands, some of whom will eventually gain control of two of the captured submarines.

After Stromberg takes captured Major Anya Amasova (BARBARA BACH) back to his Atlantis base and two subs exit the tanker, Bond (ROGER MOORE) makes his move. Stealing a ride in a monorail car, he clubs a guard (in a scene that is practically identical to one in *You Only Live Twice* inside Blofeld's volcano rocket base) and frees the three captured submarine crews.

Breaking into the armory, Bond and the escaping submariners outfit themselves with machine guns and hand grenades and launch an all-out assault on the *Liparus* crew. The following battle sequence is one of the most impressive ever seen in the Bond series.

Despite heavy casualties and the loss of the British submarine's commander (BRYAN MARSHALL), 007's men succeed in breaking into the control room. Using a ship's computer, Bond sends new attack coordinates to the two enemy submarines so that when they launch their nuclear missiles, they will destroy each other instead. On fire from numerous internal explosions caused by the pitched battle, the *Liparus* eventually sinks, but not before the last sub, the USS *Wayne*—with Bond aboard—escapes.

The concept of a supertanker swallowing a nuclear submarine was not farfetched, especially when the last scene in the film introduced a real British naval vessel with the capability of flooding its cargo area to receive the Atlantis escape pod.

LIPPE Huge S.P.E.C.T.R.E. assassin portrayed by Pat Roach in *Never Say Never Again*.

Makeup personnel go to all lengths to get the job done. In this case, Pat Roach undergoes some last-minute touching up prior to Lippe's fight sequence at Shrublands in *Never Say Never Again*. (Taliafilm)

Unlike the well-groomed Count Lippe character portrayed by Guy Doleman in *Thunderball*, *Never Say Never Again*'s Lippe is a simple killing machine who practically destroys the lower level of the Shrublands health clinic in his attempts to kill Bond (SEAN CONNERY).

Aside from his pure strength, his most terrifying weapon is a razor-sharp metallic belt that can cut through metal like a knife through butter. Eventually cornered in a specimen storage room, Bond manages to stun Lippe by flinging a beaker full of yellow liquid in his face. Losing his balance, the giant falls against a rack of glass laboratory instruments and is impaled upon them. As Lippe falls to the floor with a glass tube sticking out of his back, Bond looks at the beaker and realizes that it was 007's own urine that did the job.

LIPPE, COUNT Sinister S.P.E.C.T.R.E. agent, portrayed by Guy Doleman, who engages in an unsuccessful game of cat and mouse with Bond (SEAN CONNERY) at the Shrublands health clinic in *Thunderball*. Working with S.P.E.C.T.R.E. assassin Fiona Volpe (LUCIANA PALUZZI), Lippe is assigned the task of getting a plastic surgery–aided duplicate of aerial observer François Derval (PAUL STASSINO) onto a nuclear-equipped NATO bomber. Unfortunately, when Derval is murdered, Bond finds the bandage-wrapped body at Shrublands and begins to investigate.

Lippe's involvement isn't helped when 007 notices a telltale Tong sign tatooed to his wrist. And the entire S.P.E.C.T.R.E. scheme to hijack the bomber is later jeopardized when Lippe tries unsuccessfully to kill Bond by sabotaging his motorized traction table. For his bumbling, S.P.E.C.T.R.E. No. 1, Ernst Stavro Blofeld, orders Lippe assassinated—a job that is accomplished on the highway by a rocket-firing, motorcycle-riding Volpe.

LIQUOR FOR THREE According to Felix Leiter (CEC LINDER), this is Bond's (SEAN CONNERY) drink allotment on the special government plane en route to the White House at the end of *Goldfinger*.

LITTLE FINGER ON BOND'S RIGHT HAND The target of Tee Hee's (JULIUS HARRIS) snipping claw if Solitaire (JANE

SEYMOUR) fails to give Kananga (YAPHET KOTTO) the correct answers during an interrogation scene in *Live and Let Die*. Solitaire passes the test, and Bond's pinkie is saved. When Bond (ROGER MOORE) leaves the room, Kananga reveals that Solitaire actually failed the test—proof that she has lost her power.

LITTLE NELLIE (official name, Beagle-Wallis Auto-gyro Type WA-116, military serial number XR 943, civil registration G-ARZB) The amazing portable auto-gyro (minihelicopter) designed by Wing Commander Kenneth H. Wallis and flown by James Bond (SEAN CONNERY) in *You Only Live Twice*.

Transported to Tokyo by Q (DESMOND LLEWELYN) in four suitcases, it contains an arsenal of weapons, including two machine guns, fixed to 100 yards; two rocket launchers, forward firing on either side, with incendiary and high-explosive capability; heat-seeking air-to-air missiles; two flame guns firing astern, range of 80 yards; two smoke ejectors; and aerial mines. Bond takes his new toy on a reconnaissance of Japan's volcano country and runs into four S.P.E.C.T.R.E. helicopters that are no match for Nellie's deadly charms.

During the filming of this unique battle sequence, ace cameraman Johnny Jordan lost a leg in a terrifying helicopter collision. Caught in a severe updraft, one of the S.P.E.C.T.R.E. helicopters slammed into Jordan's camera ship, severing his leg. The fact that the torn limb fell into the backyard of a Japanese medical facility was at first considered a great piece of luck, but, unfortunately, surgeons were unable to reattach the leg to Jordan, who nevertheless returned to film ski sequences in *On Her Majesty's Secret Service* (*see* JORDAN, JOHNNY).

As to who discovered Wallis and his in-

Sean Connery takes Little Nellie through her paces before the magical blue screen in *You Only Live Twice*. The skies above Japan's volcano country will be matted in at a later date. (Rex Features Ltd./RDR Productions)

credible minihelicopter, credit must be split between production designer Ken Adam, who heard a radio interview with Wallis, and producer Harry Saltzman, who saw the auto-gyro in an aviation magazine. During filming in Japan from August through October 1966, Wing Commander Wallis doubled Sean Connery. Close-ups of Connery were later shot on the special effects stage at Pinewood against a blue screen. The tiny helicopter flew 85 sorties over Japan, for a total of 46 hours in the air. It was an incredibly versatile flying machine, capable of a speed range of 14 to 130 mph.

According to journalist Robin Harbour, who interviewed Wallis for a 1988 article in *007* magazine, the official publication of The James Bond British Fan Club, Nellie weighed 250 pounds and could lift twice its own weight. Its range was 170 miles, and it could remain in the air two and a half hours with a fuel consumption of 17 liters per hour. Because it is against the law to fire guns—even phony ones—in midair over Japan, the Bond crew eventually completed the battle sequences in Spain near Torremolinos.

LITTLE VALENTINE Ruthless drug lord Franz Sanchez's (ROBERT DAVI) euphemism for the heart that Dario (BENICIO DEL TORO) cuts out of Lupe's (TALISA SOTO) lover's (GERARDO MORENO) body in *Licence to Kill*. Even though it wasn't shown on screen, the act was another gratuitously violent reference that was uncommon for a James Bond movie.

LIVE AND LET DIE (United Artists, 1973) ★ ★ ½ The eighth James Bond film produced by Albert R. Broccoli and Harry Saltzman. U.S. release date: June 27, 1973. U.S. film rentals: $16 million. Running time: 121 minutes.

Continuing their series in 1972 with yet another James Bond—their third Bond in three films—producers Broccoli and Saltzman hired Roger Moore to play 007 in their eighth film.

Witty screenwriter Tom Mankiewicz, who had collaborated with Richard Maibaum on *Diamonds Are Forever*, returned as the sole writer on *Live and Let Die*. Mankiewicz's wit perfectly matched Moore's own approach to the character. A new era was about to begin.

Before he became James Bond on screen, Moore was a successful television actor who was respected for his work in such series as "Maverick," "The Persuaders," and, especially, "The Saint." He was hero material with a very light touch. Broccoli and Saltzman had considered him in 1962, but Moore was termed too "pretty boy" in those days. A decade later, he had matured, and—considering that the series was going in the *Goldfinger* direction with outlandish plots, plenty of sexy women, and unbelievable stunts the rule—Moore was considered perfect 007 material.

Live and Let Die plays like a DC comic book. Its plot is superfluous (something about drug smuggling that is never properly explained or dealt with), its characters are fantasy types (Whisper, Baron Samedi, Tee Hee), and its direction is uninspired. It does, however, have some good motorboat action-sequences, a mysterious heroine in Jane Seymour's Solitaire, and a slam-bang title tune from Paul and Linda McCartney.

LIVE AND LET DIE CAST

James Bond	Roger Moore
Dr. Kananga/Mr. Big	Yaphet Kotto
Solitaire	Jane Seymour
Sheriff J. W. Pepper	Clifton James
Tee Hee	Julius Harris
Baron Samedi	Geoffrey Holder
Felix Leiter	David Hedison
Rosie Carver	Gloria Hendry
M	Bernard Lee
Miss Moneypenny	Lois Maxwell
Adam	Tommy Lane
Whisper	Earl Jolly Brown
Quarrel, Jr.	Roy Stewart
Strutter	Lon Satton
Cab Driver No. 1	Arnold Williams
Mrs. Bell	Ruth Kempf
Charlie	Joie Chitwood
Miss Caruso	Madeline Smith
Dambala	Michael Ebbin
Sales Girl	Kube Chaza
Singer	B. J. Arnau

Bond (ROGER MOORE) and Solitaire (JANE SEYMOUR) make their escape from a voodoo ritual in *Live and Let Die*. (UPI)

LIVE AND LET DIE CREW

Producers .....Albert R. Broccoli, Harry Saltzman
Director ....Guy Hamilton
Screenplay by ....Tom Mankiewicz
Music by ....George Martin
Title Song Composed by................Paul and
Linda McCartney
Title Song Sung by ....Paul McCartney and Wings
Director of Photography ....Ted Moore, B.S.C.
Production Supervisor ....Claude Hudson
Assistant Director ....Derek Cracknell
Location Manager ....Bernard Hanson
Main Titles Designed by ....Maurice Binder
Supervising Art Director ....Syd Cain
Co-Art Directors ....Bob Laing, Peter Lamont

Special Effects ....Derek Meddings
Optical Effects...................Charles Staffell
Editors ....Bert Bates,
Raymond Poulton, John Shirley
Choreographer ....Geoffrey Holder
Costume Designer ....Julie Harris
Casting Director ....Weston Drury, Jr.
Stunts Coordinated by ...Bob Simmons, Jerry Co-
meaux, Ross Kananga, Bill Bennot, Eddie Smith,
Joie Chitwood

United States Crew
Production Managers ....Stephen F. Kesten,
Steven P. Skloot
Assistant Director ....Alan Hopkins

Roger Moore takes time out to pose with the "white pimpmobile," license plate: 347–NDG. (National Film Archive, London)

Unit Manager . . . . Michael Rauch
Location Coordinator . . . . Jack Weis
Art Director . . . . Stephen Hendrickson
Camera Operators . . . . George Bouillet,
Warren Rothenberger
Shark Scenes by . . . . William Grefe
The James Bond Theme by . . . . Monty Norman
Production Company . . . . Eon Productions
Distribution Company . . . . United Artists

LIVE AND LET DIE COMPETITION

Competitive films in release when *Live and Let Die* opened in Los Angeles on June 27, 1973:

The Man Who Loved Cat Dancing

The Friends of Eddie Coyle

A Touch of Class

Blume in Love

Battle for the Planet of the Apes

The Last of Sheila

Shaft in Africa

O Lucky Man!

The Harrad Experiment

The Aristocats/Song of the South (reissue)

Cahill—U.S. Marshal

Scarecrow

Billy Jack

LIVERPOOL Actual hometown of Milos Columbo's (TOPOL) mistress Lisl Von Schlam (CASSANDRA HARRIS) in *For Your Eyes Only*. In Corfu, she's posing as an Austrian countess.

LIVING DAYLIGHTS, THE (United Artists, 1987) ★ ★ ★ The 15th James Bond film produced by Albert R. Broccoli. U.S. release date: July 31, 1987. U.S. film rentals: $28 million. Running time: 130 minutes.

Cheers for Timothy Dalton, who makes a stunning debut as James Bond in *The Living Daylights*! For those of us who grew up on Sean Connery's interpretation of 007, the Roger Moore era was a disappointment, largely because the films were just too funny, the action sequences were not believable, and somehow Roger was just too nice to be a secret agent with a license to kill. Timothy Dalton brings back the danger in Bond. You're never quite sure what he's going to do, and that makes his character intriguing.

Sometimes Bond can and should be a bastard. When the chips are down and the free world's at stake, the rule book is thrown out the window. He's an agent with a license to kill, and if there's killing to be done, he should be doing it.

Notice that Roger Moore was never involved in an assassination or a cold-blooded murder. The audience would never have accepted him as that kind of agent. Instead, and very shrewdly, the producers chose to make him a likable hero who saves the world every two years with charm, intelligence, and great dialogue.

The Living Daylights works because Dalton is excellent in the role. He's done his homework, which is surprising, since he was a last-minute choice after Pierce Brosnan proved unavailable. It's also a very romantic film thanks to the casting of Maryam d'Abo, who makes a very fetching Kara Milovy.

Unfortunately, the problem with *The Living Daylights* is its dearth of strong villains. General Georgi Koskov is too lovable to be dangerous (he hugs practically everyone he meets), and Brad Whitaker is denied enough screen time to develop any true malice. He's a gunrunner who

Czechoslovakian border guards attempt to stop James Bond in *The Living Daylights*. (AP/Wide World Photos)

James Bond's missile-firing Aston Martin turns a Czech roadblock into an inferno in *The Living Daylights*.
(AP/Wide World Photos)

likes to play with army figures. Big deal.

The only truly villainous character in the film is Necros, played effectively by Andreas Wisniewski. But he's not on-screen long enough to make any true impact, and even he has his sympathetic moments. The plot is another throwaway that would take an MIT graduate to figure out. Just as you're starting to figure out why Koskov and Whitaker are partners, the plot switches to a big drug deal in Afghanistan—talk about sharp left turns!

Highlights: The great teaser on Gibraltar. John Barry's warmly romantic score. Maryam d'Abo. Art Malik's Kamran Shah. Caroline Bliss's new Moneypenny.

THE LIVING DAYLIGHTS CAST

James Bond . . . . Timothy Dalton
Kara Milovy . . . . Maryam d'Abo
General Georgi Koskov . . . . Jeroen Krabbe
Brad Whitaker . . . . Joe Don Baker
General Leonid Pushkin . . . . John Rhys-Davies
Kamran Shah . . . . Art Malik
Necros . . . . Andreas Wisniewski
Saunders . . . . Thomas Wheatley
Q . . . . Desmond Llewelyn
M . . . . Robert Brown
Minister of Defense . . . . Geoffrey Keen
General Gogol . . . . Walter Gotell
Miss Moneypenny . . . . Caroline Bliss
Felix Leiter . . . . John Terry
Rubavitch . . . . Virginia Hey
Colonel Feyador . . . . John Bowe
Rosika Miklos . . . . Julie T. Wallace
Linda . . . . Kell Tyler
Liz . . . . Catherine Rabett
Ava . . . . Dulice Liecier
Chief of Security, Tangier . . . . Nadim Sawalha
Koskov's KGB Minder . . . . Alan Talbot
Imposter . . . . Carl Rigg
Chief of the Snow Leopard Brotherhood . . . .
Tony Cyrus
Achmed . . . . Atik Mohamed
Kamran's Men . . . . Michael Moor, Sumar Khan
Jailer . . . . Ken Sharrock
Gasworks Supervisor . . . . Peter Porteous
Male Secretary, Bladen . . . . Antony Carrick
004 . . . . Frederick Warder
002 . . . . Glyn Baker
Sergeant Stagg . . . . Derek Hoxby
Butler, Bladen . . . . Bill Weston
Trade Center Toastmaster . . . . Richard Cubison

Concierge, Vienna Hotel . . . . Heinz Winter
Lavatory Attendant . . . . Leslie French
The Girls . . . Odette Benatar, Femi Gardiner, Mayte Sanchez, Dianna Casale, Patricia Keefer, Cela Savannah, Waris Walsh, Sharon Devlin, Ruddy Rodriguez, Karen Seeberg, Karen Williams

THE LIVING DAYLIGHTS CREW

Producers . . Albert R. Broccoli, Michael G. Wilson
Director . . . . John Glen
Screenplay by . . . . Richard Maibaum,
Michael G. Wilson
Associate Producers . . . . Tom Pevsner,
Barbara Broccoli
Music by . . . . John Barry
Production Designer . . . . Peter Lamont
Director of Photography . . . . Alec Mills
Title Song Sung by . . . . a-ha
Main Title Designer . . . . Maurice Binder
Action-Sequence Supervisor . . . . Paul Weston
Second-Unit Director and Cameraman . . . . . Arthur Wooster
Vehicle Stunt Coordinator . . . . Remy Julienne
Special Effects Supervisor . . . . John Richardson
Editor . . . . John Grover, Peter Davies
Location Managers . . . Nick Daubeny, John Bernard, Arie Bohrer, Stefan Zucher, Driss Gaidi
Moroccan Production Liaison . . . . . . Zakaria Alaoui
Gibraltar Production Liaison . . . . Joseph Viale
Second-Unit Assistant Director . . . . . Terry Madden
Second-Unit Continuity . . . . Jean Bourne
Additional Assistant Directors . . . .
Callum McDougall, Crispin Reece, Nick Heckstall-Smith, Terry Blyther, Urs Egger, Ahmed Hatimi, Mohamed Hassini
Assistant Accountant . . . . Allan Davies
Location Accountants . . . . Jane Meagher, Christl Kirchner
Location Transport Managers . . Arno Esterez, Andy Grosch
Production Coordinators . . . . Pam Parker, Janine Lodge, Daniela Stibitz, Ihsanne Khalafaoui, Brenda Ramos, Dawn Severdia, May Capsakis
Secretary to Mr. Broccoli . . . . Sandra Frieze
Secretary to Mr. Wilson . . . . Joanna Brown
Secretary to Mr. Juroe . . . . Amanda Schofield
Location Production Secretaries . . . .
Sophie Koekenhoff, Hind Hanif, Sonja Beutura
U.S. Contacts . . . . Mary Stellar, Rina Banta
Additional Art Directors . . . . Michael Lamont, Ken Court, Fred Hole, Bert Davey, Thomas Riccabona, Peter Manhard
Assistant Art Directors . . James Morahan, Ted Am-

brose, Dennis Rosher

Assistant Set Decorators ...Jillie Brown, Christoph Kanter

Additional Construction Managers.............. Ken Pattenden, Alfred Dobsak

Property Master ....Bert Hearn

Production Buyers ....Sid Palmer, Peter Palmer

Sketch Artist ....Roger Deer

Chief Sculptor ....Fred Evans

Scenic Artist ....Jacqueline Stears

Model Photography ....Leslie Dear

Additional Photography ....Phil Pastuhov, Tom Sanders

Second-Unit Camera Operator . Malcolm Macintosh

Additional Camera Operators ..Michael Anderson, Fred Waugh, Peter Rohe

Focus ....Frank Elliott, Michael Evans, Nicholas Wilson, Dan McKinny, Horst Becker

Camera Grips ......Chunky Huse, Ken Atherfold, Richard Haw

Video Effects Supervisor.........Richard Hewitt

Front Projection ....Roy Moores

Boom Operator ....Ken Nightingall

Additional Sound Recorders ......Brian Marshall, Roby Guever

Music Editor ....Alan Killick

Sound Editors..............Vernon Messenger, Derek Holding, Peter Musgrave

Assistant Editors ....Matthew Glen, John Nuth, Wayne Smith

Assistant Sound Editors...William Barringer, Ross Adams, Robert Gavin, Mark Mostyn

Additional Sound Effects ....Jean-Pierre Lelong

Orchestrations ....Nicholas Raine

Music Mixer ....Dick Lewzey

Rerecording Mixers ....Graham Hartstone, John Hayward

Costume Supervisor ....Tiny Nicholls

Costumes Made by ....Bermans and Nathans

Second-Unit Wardrobe Master ....Don Mothersill

Makeup ....Naomi Dunne, Eric Allwright, Edwin Erfmann

Hairdressers ....Helen Lennox, Barbara Sutton

Horses Provided by ....La Societe R.E.H.A.

Aerial Liaison.....................Marc Wolff

Safety Climber ....Hamish MacInnes

Special Effects.....Chris Corbould, Joss Williams, Brian Smithies, Ken Morris, Willy Neuner

Armourer ....Simon Atherton

Model-Maker ....Terence Reed

Unit Publicist....................Geoff Freeman

Stills ....Keith Hampshire, George Whitear

Publicity Assistant.................Rebecca West

Travel and Transport ..Renown Freight, The Travel Company, D & D International Locations, Location Facilities

Location Catering ..Rafael Hosteleria International, The Location Caterers

CIA Boat.....................Spectral Marine

Military Dioramas...........Little Lead Soldiers

Floral Arrangements .....Kenneth Turner Flowers

Hats..........................David Shilling

Swimwear ....Gottex

Whitaker's Villa ...*Forbes* magazine, Palais El Mendoub, Tangier

Stunt Team ......Doug Robinson, Michel Julienne, Nick Wilkinson, Simon Crane, Elaine Ford, Roy Alon, Del Baker, Jason White

Horse Stunts ....Brian Bowes, Graeme Crowther, Jorge Casares, Steve Dent, Nick Gillard, Joaquin Olias, Miguel Pedregosa, Jose Maria Serrano

Aerial Stunts ....Jake Brake, Garry Carter, Jake Lombard, Dan O'Brien

Driving Stunts..............Christian Bonnichon, Jo Cote, Jean-Claude Houbard, Dominique Julienne, Jean-Claude Justice, Jean-Jacques Villain, Brigitte Magnin

Snow Stunts...........John Falkiner, Ida Huber, Rene Seiler, Herman Sporer

Production Company ....Eon Productions

Distribution Company ....United Artists

THE LIVING DAYLIGHTS COMPETITION

Competitive films in release when *The Living Daylights* opened in Los Angeles on July 31, 1987:

Summer School

The Lost Boys

Snow White and the Seven Dwarfs (reissue)

Maid to Order

Innerspace

Robocop

The Witches of Eastwick

Roxanne

Beverly Hills Cop II

The Untouchables

Dragnet

Jaws—the Revenge

La Bamba

Hellraiser

Stakeout

Adventures in Babysitting

Superman IV: The Quest for Peace

LIZ Blond CIA operative, portrayed by Catherine Rabett, who's working for Felix Leiter (JOHN TERRY) in Tangier, in *The Living Daylights.* Along with her colleague Ava (Dulice Liecier), she helps James Bond (TIMOTHY DALTON) escape from local police after he "assassinates" General Pushkin (JOHN RHYS-DAVIES).

LLEWELYN, DESMOND (Newport, Wales, 1913–) Tall, silver-haired British character actor who has effectively portrayed Q (aka Major Boothroyd), the long-suffering Secret Service equipment officer, in practically all the James Bond movies.

After actor Peter Burton briefly introduced the Major Boothroyd character in *Dr. No,* Llewelyn took over the role in *From Russia with Love,* where he introduced the trick briefcase. He has appeared in every James Bond film produced by United Artists, except for *Live and Let Die.*

A perfect foil to 007's frivolous nature, especially in the Connery Bonds, Llewelyn has been one of the series's most enduring characters.

LOCHGILPHEAD Hilly, rock-strewn region in Scotland that was the location for the helicopter chase in *From Russia with Love.* Piloting the S.P.E.C.T.R.E. chopper that day was Royal Air Force Captain John Crewdson.

LOCKE, PHILIP Lean British character actor of stage, screen, and television who portrayed Vargas, the sullen S.P.E.C.T.R.E. assassin in *Thunderball.* Vargas is speared by 007 (SEAN CONNERY) on Love Beach.

LOCKHEED JETSTAR Goldfinger's (GERT FROBE) private jet, piloted by Miss Pussy Galore (HONOR BLACKMAN), which transports a tranquilized James Bond (SEAN CONNERY) from Switzerland to Friendship Airport, Baltimore. The stewardess on the flight is Mai Li (MAI LING), and the copilot is Sydney.

LOCQUE, EMILE LEOPOLD Aris Kristatos's (JULIAN GLOVER) murderous henchman, portrayed by Michael Gothard, in *For Your Eyes Only.* James Bond (ROGER MOORE) first sees him at Gonzales's (STEFAN KALIPHA) villa outside Madrid—with the payoff money for the Havelock murders.

Tracking him to Cortina D'Ampezzo in the Italian Alps, Bond learns from Kristatos that Locque is actually working for Columbo (TOPOL). He's wrong, but Bond doesn't learn that until Locque murders Bond's Italian contact, Ferrara (JOHN MORENO), and Columbo's mistress, Lisl (CASSANDRA HARRIS). The truth comes out when Columbo captures Bond and brings him to his fishing boat.

That night, during a raid on Kristatos's drug-smuggling operation in Albania, Bond sees Locque at Kristatos's side. Attempting to escape by car, Locque finds himself looking down the barrel of Bond's Walther PPK. He's wounded, and his car goes out of control and nearly falls over a cliff. Bond sees him wedged precariously on the edge. He takes a white dove pin that Locque had left on Ferrara's body—the symbol of Columbo, left to confuse Bond—throws it at the killer, and then kicks his car off the cliff.

LO FAT Hai Fat's business partner in one of screenwriter Tom Mankiewicz's early drafts for *The Man with the Golden Gun.* The character was later axed from the script.

LOG CABIN GIRL Gorgeous Austrian blond, portrayed by British actress Sue Vanner, who betrays Bond (ROGER MOORE) to the KGB in *The Spy Who Loved Me* teaser.

British actor Philip Locke "got the point" in *Thunderball.* (Jeremy Conway Ltd.)

LOMBARD, JAKE Stuntman who doubled Necros (ANDREAS WISNIEWSKI) during the hair-raising cargo-net battle in *The Living Daylights.*

LONSDALE, MICHEL (Paris, 1931–   ) Polished French actor who portrayed billionaire industrialist Hugo Drax with a strong touch of dry wit and sarcasm in *Moonraker.*

LOO, RICHARD (Hawaii, 1903–1983) Hawaiian-Chinese character actor who made a career of playing fanatical Japanese soldiers in a series of American propaganda films of the World War II era and who later portrayed sinister industrialist Hai Fat in *The Man with the Golden Gun. See* HAI FAT.

"LOOKING FOR SOMETHING SPECIAL?" The first phrase of the CIA-British Secret Service recognition code, uttered by CIA agent Chuck Lee (DAVID YIP) to James Bond (ROGER MOORE) on Fisherman's Wharf in San Francisco in *A View to a Kill.* Bond answers with, "Yes, soft-shell crabs," to which Lee responds, "I have some in the back."

LOPEZ, PRESIDENT HECTOR The puppet president of Isthmus City, a fictional South American drug capital in *Licence to Kill,* portrayed by Pedro Armendariz, Jr. Lopez, in effect, works for drug lord Franz Sanchez (ROBERT DAVI), who, for all intents and purposes, owns Isthmus City.

When Lopez complains that his paycheck has been cut, Sanchez wonders why he was so quiet when the DEA was arresting him in the Bahamas. Sanchez also reminds Lopez that he's only president for life. In the end, thanks to James Bond (TIMOTHY DALTON), Lopez is rid of Sanchez, and he has a new decoration on his arm—Sanchez's girlfriend, Lupe Lamora (TALISA SOTO).

LORD, JACK (New York City, December 30, 1928–) (real name, John Joseph Ryan) American tough-guy actor who was the first to portray CIA agent Felix Leiter when the character made its debut in *Dr. No* in 1962. Unlike some of the later Leiters, who were given comic support from the screenwriters almost to the

Actor Jack Lord, circa 1955. Seven years later, he would play Felix Leiter in *Dr. No.* (Goodman Publicity)

point of high camp, Lord's CIA man was strictly no-nonsense. From *Dr. No,* Lord went on to portray another serious detective in the tropics, Steve McGarrett in the fabulously successful and long-running television series "Hawaii Five-0."

LORRE, PETER (Rosenberg, Carpathia, Hungary, June 26, 1904–March 23, 1964) (real name, Laszlo Loewenstein) Hungarian character actor who portrayed the first James Bond villain, Le Chiffre, in the live-television film "Casino Royale" in 1954. Lorre's nemesis is an Americanized James Bond portrayed by Barry Nelson. *See* CHIFFRE, LE.

Sinister Peter Lorre won the part of the first Bond villain—Le Chiffre in the TV film "Casino Royale". (Twentieth Century–Fox)

LOTI Stunning Hong Kong narcotics agent, portrayed by ex-*Playboy* magazine playmate Diana Lee-Hsu, who is working undercover as the girlfriend of one of Franz Sanchez's (ROBERT DAVI) Far Eastern drug distributors in *Licence to Kill.*

Loti and her associate Kwang (CARY-HIROYUKI TAGAWA) are about to break a major case against Sanchez, when James Bond (TIMOTHY DALTON), working as a rogue agent, disrupts their plan by attempting to assassinate the drug lord. Dressed in Ninja outfits, Kwang and Loti disarm Bond and bring him to their safe house, where he's strapped to a table. Unfortunately, Sanchez's private army soon attacks, and both Loti and Kwang are killed.

LOTUS ESPRIT SUBMARINE CAR James Bond's (ROGER MOORE) fabulous trick sports car featured in *The Spy Who Loved Me* and *For Your Eyes Only.* Nicknamed Wet Nellie, a homage to the weapon-laden auto-gyro in *You Only Live Twice,* the Lotus was still another example of how the Bond team—even in the late 1970s—could rise to the occasion and top the effects of their previous films.

Motorized by Perry Oceanographics of Miami, the submarine car, which was referred to as Esther Williams in an early draft of the screenplay, was actually the product of two geniuses—production designer Ken Adam and special effects supervisor Derek Meddings.

Remembered Meddings, "When we decided to turn a sports car into a submarine, Ken Adam came to me with the suggestion that we

An enemy torpedo nearly ends Wet Nellie's career. (Don Griffin, Perry Oceanographics)

Modified shells of the Lotus Esprit arrive in Miami for underwater conversion in *The Spy Who Loved Me.* (Don Griffin, Perry Oceanographics)

Rear view of the Lotus Esprit wet submersible built by Perry Oceanographics in Florida for *The Spy Who Loved Me.* (Don Griffin, Perry Oceanographics)

The Lotus submarine car with its trail of bubbles from divers inside. The special effects department had considered rebreather units that do not emit bubbles, but they were scrubbed. (Don Griffin, Perry Oceanographics)

Roger Moore and Barbara Bach pose with James Bond's car, the Lotus Esprit from *The Spy Who Loved Me*.
(Express Newspapers, London)

use the shell of the new Lotus Esprit. Neither of us knew anything about the aquadynamics of underwater driving, but we went ahead with the Lotus because it was the most beautiful car we could find in England—it had to be an English car, of course.

"The car was then given to us in shell form from the Lotus factory. We had five or six of the shells, and into each we built a special operating effect. First, to give the car the underwater streamlined effect, we had to create wheels that could disappear inside the body, and wheel arches that came down and filled in the space. We then built louvers that would go into place over the windshield, to create the impression of strengthening the glass against underwater pressure.

"Only one car was equipped to work underwater. It had an engine, and you could drive it underwater like an airplane. When it turned, it would bank, and it would dive and climb. Two men were assigned to drive it.

"The special modifications, such as the sur-face-to-air missile launcher, the underwater rockets, and the mine-laying panel, were all constructed and perfected in the Pinewood special effects shop."

When the Pinewood unit had finished with its modifications, Meddings transported the shell of the Lotus over to Miami and to Perry Oceanographics, a unique underwater engineering firm that built submarines and underwater scooters for the U.S. Navy. They were the final authority on Wet Nellie's seaworthiness.

Said Ken Adam, who returned to the Bond series after a five-year layoff, "We went over to Miami, showed them the designs on our car, and asked them if they could motorize it and create a 'wet submersible.' Instead of having two ordinary people inside a dry car, the plan was to go with two skin divers driving the vehicle. They would be wearing breathing apparatuses, but because of the louvers over the front windscreen, you wouldn't be able to see these devices clearly.

"We didn't want a dry submersible. When

you build something that has an air compartment, you have problems with ballast. You're faced with the problem of continually pumping ballast in and out of the car, and that was something we wanted to avoid.

"The Perry people looked at our designs and said they could motorize the car. They also gave us the idea of having our divers use a rebreather unit that didn't leave a telltale trail of bubbles. However, we ended up going back to regular Aqua-lungs, not only because they were much safer, but we realized that without any bubbles coming from the car, we were sacrificing a degree of realism. With the bubbles trailing the car from the Aqua-lungs, we had a much more realistic picture of a car moving underwater. The last thing we wanted was the audience to get the impression we were using a model car in a studio tank."

The underwater sequences with the motorized Lotus Esprit were filmed in the crystal-clear waters of the Bahamas by veteran underwater cinematographer Lamar Boren, who was also returning to the Bond films after a long absence.

LOTUS FORMULA 3 Race car driven by Evelyn Tremble/James Bond (PETER SELLERS) in *Casino Royale*. Although introduced as a formidable driving machine, the Lotus never makes it to the road because Tremble/Bond is immediately captured by Le Chiffre (ORSON WELLES). What could have been an exciting chase sequence never materializes.

"LOUISIANA—THE SPORTSMAN'S PARADISE, WELCOMES YOU" Sign on a billboard behind which Sheriff J. W. Pepper (CLIFTON JAMES) waits for speeders in *Live and Let Die*.

LOVE BEACH Name given to the Nassau beach location, in *Thunderball*, where James Bond (SEAN CONNERY) uses his teeth to pull the poisonous egg spines out of Domino's (CLAUDINE AUGER) foot. It's also where Vargas (PHILIP LOCKE) "gets the point."

LOVE NESTS Possible future residences discussed by James Bond (GEORGE LAZENBY) and Teresa "Tracy" Vicenzo (DIANA RIGG) in *On Her Majesty's Secret Service*. After 007 pro-

poses to Tracy in a snow-bound barn in Switzerland, the pair discuss their ideal love nests. These include homes on Vocatia Avenue, Cannon Ridge, Cambridge, Wales; Belgrave Square, London; the Via Veneto, Rome; Paris; and Monaco. Unfortunately, the couple never moves into any of these residences, for Tracy is murdered by Blofeld (TELLY SAVALAS) at the film's conclusion.

LOVERS, THE A tarot card featured in the deck of the mysterious Solitaire (JANE SEYMOUR) in *Live and Let Die*. It symbolizes the potential of romance and love between two strangers.

In order to trick her into sleeping with him and thus switching allegiances, James Bond (ROGER MOORE) brings a phony deck of tarot cards to Solitaire's sanctuary on San Monique Island. When asked to pick a card, Solitaire picks the Lovers, unaware that the deck consists entirely of Lovers cards. Convinced that she is destined to lose her virginity and her power to Bond, Solitaire gives in. You'd think that a seer of her power would know such things.

LOWELL, CAREY (New York, February 11, 1961–   ) Tall, beautiful American actress and ex–cover girl who portrayed CIA undercover operative Pam Bouvier in *Licence to Kill*. Lowell is the highlight of the film—a fresh-faced, intelligent, gutsy agent counterpart who lends Bond (TIMOTHY DALTON) a resourceful hand against South American drug kingpin Franz Sanchez (ROBERT DAVI).

In many ways, she perfectly represented the new action-woman of the '80s—à la Sigourney Weaver in *Aliens*—who can handle herself just as well as a man and whose qualities enhance a dangerous situation rather than compound it. *See* BOUVIER, PAM.

LOW-GRADE IRON PYRITES What Professor R. J. Dent (ANTHONY DAWSON) incorrectly calls the radioactive ore samples discovered by John Strangways (TIM MOXON) in *Dr. No*.

LOW-SCAN CH RADAR Dr. No's (JOSEPH WISEMAN) surveillance and detection apparatus on Crab Key. It's discovered by a U.S. reconnaissance plane sent over the island by Felix Leiter (JACK LORD).

LOX Abbreviation for "liquid oxygen," a rocket propellant featured in *You Only Live Twice*. At first, Japanese Secret Service Chief Tiger Tanaka (TETSURO TAMBA) thinks that the lox shipment identified on an invoiced order for naval stores is smoked salmon. Bond (SEAN CONNERY) correctly identifies it as rocket fuel.

LOYALTY A key word in drug lord Franz Sanchez's (ROBERT DAVI) vocabulary in *Licence to Kill*. He says it's more important to him than money. In his effort to destroy Sanchez and his operation, Bond (TIMOTHY DALTON) uses the loyalty question to undermine the drug lord's trust in his key employees—namely, Milton Krest (ANTHONY ZERBE) and Heller (DON STROUD).

LUFTHANSA German airline that flies James Bond (SEAN CONNERY), Tiffany Case (JILL ST. JOHN), Mr. Wint (BRUCE GLOVER), and Mr. Kidd (PUTTER SMITH) from Amsterdam to Los Angeles in *Diamonds Are Forever*. The short interior airliner sequence was actually filmed at the Frankfurt Airport.

Carey Lowell and Timothy Dalton attend the London premiere of *Licence to Kill* in 1989. (Express Newspapers, London)

British pop singer, Lulu. (Alfa)

British actress Joanna Lumley played one of the allergy victims in *On Her Majesty's Secret Service*. (ICM)

LULU (Glasgow, Scotland, November 3, 1948–) (real name, Marie McDonald McLaughlin Lawrie) Multitalented Scottish pop singer, actress, and media star who sang the bouncy title song to *The Man with the Golden Gun* in 1974. Prior to her Bond experience, Lulu had scored with the international hit song "To Sir with Love," which she sang in the popular 1967 film.

LUMLEY, JOANNA Actress, and future star of "The New Avengers" television series, who portrayed the English allergy victim in *On Her Majesty's Secret Service*.

LUNDGREN, DOLPH (Stockholm, Sweden, 1959–) Swedish super-hunk who appears briefly in *A View to a Kill* as Venz, the KGB agent. *See* VENZ.

LUNDIGAN, WILLIAM (Syracuse, New York, June 12, 1914–December 21, 1975) Impressive-voiced American actor and ex-radio announcer who was hosting the CBS Climax Mystery Theater on the night of October 21, 1954, when Ian Fleming's "Casino Royale" made its debut as a live, one-hour television show. Lundigan was the first person to introduce the world of Ian Fleming's James Bond to the public via the mass media.

He appeared on-screen while holding a French baccarat shoe, the significance of which he explains in his opening remarks: "Good evening. This doesn't look dangerous, does it? But it's killed plenty of men and women. It's made beggars of many and millionaires of a few, mighty few.

"In French gambling casinos, this is called a shoe. It holds the cards for baccarat—king of gambling games—and its purpose is to make sure that no one can pull any funny business, like dealing from the bottom. The game to be played tonight is for the highest stakes of all. A man is going to wager his life. Climax presents 'Casino Royale,' from the bestseller by Ian Fleming. It stars Barry Nelson, Peter Lorre, and Linda Christian. And now, 'Casino Royale.' "

LYND, VESPER Blond seductress and double agent, portrayed by Ursula Andress, in *Casino Royale*. Introduced as a wealthy black-

After her auspicious debut in *Dr. No,* Ursula Andress returned to the world of 007 as seductress Vesper Lynd in the *Casino Royale* spoof.

market trader who owes millions in back taxes to the British government, Lynd is employed by Sir James Bond (DAVID NIVEN) to seduce mild-mannered baccarat expert Evelyn Tremble (PETER SELLERS) into accepting a challenge to play against Soviet masterspy Le Chiffre (ORSON WELLES) in Monte Carlo.

Lynd lures poor Tremble into her boudoir, where they frolic to the moody sounds of Dusty Springfield's "The Look of Love." She has an apricot birthmark on her hip and a stolen statue of Lord Nelson in her living room. Lynd, however, is not what she appears to be.

When Tremble is captured by Le Chiffre in Monte Carlo, Vesper arrives to machine-gun a battalion of bagpipe players, but she also shoots Tremble. Like everyone else in the cast, she's blown to bits when Dr. Noah's (WOODY ALLEN) A-bomb pill explodes in the film's climactic scene. *See* ANDRESS, URSULA.

M

M   James Bond's crusty superior and the head of the British Secret Service. His full name was Admiral Sir Miles Messervey, K.C.M.G.

Venerable British actor Bernard Lee became the first M, in *Dr. No* in 1962, and played him in every United Artists Bond movie until his death in 1981. As portrayed by Lee, M was a conservative, almost fatherly, figure who put up with 007's increasingly outrageous behavior because he knew that Bond was his best agent and the only man he could trust on the most dangerous assignments.

M's office, disguised as Universal Exports in London, was always the starting point for Bond—a temporary haven where 007 traded double entendres with Miss Moneypenny (LOIS MAXWELL) and received his careful briefing from M. Today, there is something very nostalgic about that office—the leather double-door entry with the red and green warning lights; the warm, leathery, naval decor of the room, with its ship models, paintings, and assorted bric-a-brac—typical for a retired navy man; and the quiet, low-key M himself—smoking his pipe, ready to send 007 out on one more impossible mission.

When Roger Moore took over the role in 1973, Bond's relationship with M lost quite a bit of its subtlety. The sour interplay between M and Q (DESMOND LLEWELYN) in *The Man with the Golden Gun* was a definite low point. For Bernard Lee, however, the parts became a bit more mobile—with M and his secretary visiting Bond on locations in Egypt and the Far East.

When Lee died before filming began on *For Your Eyes Only*, producer Albert R. Broccoli's interim choice as Bond's superior was actor James Villiers, who portrayed Secret Service Chief of Staff Tanner. Robert Brown, who had earlier been introduced as Admiral Hargreaves in *The Spy Who Loved Me*, took over as the official new M in *Octopussy* and has portrayed him ever since in very much the same manner as Lee.

By contrast, Edward Fox played M as a contemptuous bureaucrat in *Never Say Never Again* for producer Jack Schwartzman, and John Huston—wearing an incredible bright red wig—played him in the outrageous *Casino Royale* spoof in 1967. In that film, one assumes that M dies in a barrage destined for Sir James Bond's (DAVID NIVEN) country house; however, his death is never explained—one of the enormous plot holes in the film.

Bernard Lee established the character of M in 1962 and played him for nearly two decades. (National Film Archive, London)

M'S HOUSE   It's featured for the only time in *On Her Majesty's Secret Service*, when Bond (GEORGE LAZENBY) arrives to inform M (BERNARD LEE) about Blofeld's (TELLY SAVALAS) attempts to trace his bloodline through the London College of Arms. Thanks to director Peter Hunt's desire to perfectly capture the mood, spirit, and essence of the original Ian Fleming novel, M's house is detailed down to the antique naval cannon that sits in the middle of M's driveway, and the appearance of Hammond (JOHN GAY), M's butler.

MACADAMS The bespectacled Canadian chess opponent of Kronsteen (VLADEK SHEY-BAL), portrayed by actor Peter Madden in *From Russia with Love*. MacAdams played the black pieces and lost the game. *See* MADDEN, PETER.

MAYBELLE J. W. Pepper's (CLIFTON JAMES) wife, who's introduced in Thailand in *The Man with the Golden Gun*.

MCCALLUM, GORDON K. (1918–1988) Academy Award–winning motion-picture sound engineer who worked on many James Bond movies. McCallum was chief dubbing mixer for Pinewood Studios when he retired in 1984 after 45 years in the movie industry and after earning more than 300 feature credits, several of which won him Oscar nominations.

MCCARTNEY, PAUL (Liverpool, England, June 18, 1942–   ) International superstar singer/composer and ex-Beatle who, with his group Wings, composed and performed the title song for *Live and Let Die* in 1973. Ironically, producers Albert R. Broccoli and Harry Saltzman had the opportunity to produce the Beatles' first movie in 1962, but they passed.

Ex-Beatle Paul McCartney's title tune was a highlight of *Live and Let Die*.

MCCLORY, KEVIN (1926–   ) Dapper, resourceful, and fabulously wealthy Irish film producer and director who was the first to collaborate with author Ian Fleming on a film script featuring his James Bond character. The collaboration would later turn sour and initiate one of the great legal battles in film history, as well as an important chapter in the history of the James Bond films.

Introduced to Fleming by Ivar Bryce in 1959, shortly after he had directed the film *The Boy and the Bridge*, McClory suggested that instead of using one of Fleming's previous Bond novels as the basis for a script, an entirely new adventure should be written that would feature plot and production values geared to a film audience. McClory also hoped that Bryce's film company, Xanadu Productions, could benefit from the British Eady Subsidy Plan and thus have the majority of its production costs underwritten. Since McClory was also eager to film a story with underwater elements, the company could shoot in the lush Bahamas, which were part of the British Commonwealth and within Eady Subsidy boundaries.

Much was made of McClory's experience in 1955 and 1956 when he worked with producer Michael Todd on *Around the World in 80 Days*, the colorful adventure that had reaped huge profits with its travelogue backgrounds and action-packed vignettes. Such a cosmopolitan portrait of the world could fit in with a James Bond story, McClory reasoned. He also felt that Bond should be placed in a plot that involved international backgrounds.

Eventually, McClory, Fleming, and British screenwriter Jack Whittingham collaborated on a film script titled *Latitude 78 West*, a story that introduced S.P.E.C.T.R.E. and its plan to hijack two atomic bombs from the NATO powers. When, in 1960, Ivar Bryce withdrew as a possible financial backer, and McClory was unable to secure additional funds, Fleming left for his annual vacation in Jamaica, where he innocently wrote a novel based on his film story.

He called it *Thunderball*—based on the NATO code name for the recovery of the stolen A-bombs.

No sooner did McClory read an advance copy than he and Whittingham petitioned the high court of London for an injunction to hold up publication. In their legal plea, they claimed that Fleming had infringed on their joint copyright by publishing a book based on the script without their approval.

The *Thunderball* infringement case, which dragged on for three years, was eventually a major victory for McClory, who won film and television rights to *Thunderball* and all of its variations (Fleming, Whittingham, and McClory had written 10 different versions of the story during their collaboration, and the rights to each of these was now McClory's property). Additionally, future published copies of Fleming's *Thunderball* would have to include the credit "Based on a film treatment by Kevin McClory, Jack Whittingham, and Ian Fleming."

While McClory was fighting for his rights, producers Albert R. Broccoli and Harry Saltzman had, in 1961, acquired film rights to all the other James Bond novels. When McClory won the *Thunderball* case in 1963, Broccoli and Saltzman had already produced the first two films in the series, *Dr. No* and *From Russia with Love*, and actor Sean Connery was on the threshold of becoming an international sensation as 007. Their success proved to be an immediate roadblock for McClory, who could not interest any financial backer in competing with the Broccoli–Saltzman team.

Eventually, McClory went to Broccoli and Saltzman and proposed a merger. He would sell them the screen rights to *Thunderball* for a producer credit and a percentage of the profits. Why did Broccoli and Saltzman make the deal? "We didn't want anyone else to make *Thunderball*," said Broccoli. "We had the feeling that if anyone else came in and made their own Bond film, it would have been bad for our series. After *Goldfinger*, we naturally felt that we knew more about Bond than anyone else.

"And this fact was certainly proven two years later when my dear friend Charlie K. Feldman finally made *Casino Royale*. The making of that film, which everybody thought we made, ended up costing us a lot of customers. The public thought we had slipped. Early on, I could sense that happening with *Thunderball*. So I went ahead and made the deal with McClory to insure that the best of Fleming's stories could be our film."

McClory couldn't have been more delighted. Not only was his film about to be produced with Sean Connery in the lead role, but it was getting out at the most auspicious time—the virtual height of worldwide Bond fever. With 20 percent of the film's profits written into his contract, what more could he ask for? There was one more thing.

McClory included in his contract a promise that he would wait 10 years before he would produce another film based on the various *Thunderball* stories. The thought of another *Thunderball* didn't bother Broccoli and Saltzman enough to challenge that paragraph. *Thunderball* was produced, it became the biggest hit in the series, and McClory deposited loads of profits in his bank account.

But, promptly 10 years later, he announced a new James Bond project titled *James Bond of the Secret Service*. Once again, Broccoli—now alone, having bought out Saltzman's share in Eon Productions—was not about to let a rival 007 production get off the ground. Legal armies began to assemble.

McClory declared that he alone owned the rights to S.P.E.C.T.R.E. and that Broccoli could not use the organization in his latest 007 film, *The Spy Who Loved Me*. Broccoli, in turn, stonewalled McClory's project, claiming McClory had no rights to make additional James Bond movies from the original *Thunderball* stories. Outgunned, McClory stepped back. However, Broccoli did order screenwriter Richard Maibaum to remove any vestige of S.P.E.C.T.R.E. from *The Spy Who Loved Me*.

Between 1975 and 1981, McClory would occasionally announce *James Bond of the Secret Service*—or its alternate title, *Warhead*—as a viable project, but nothing came of it until he was introduced to entertainment-lawyer-turned-film producer Jack Schwartzman. Schwartzman, a former Lorimar production executive, was the perfect collaborator for McClory. A legal whiz, Schwartzman knew full well that McClory had the rights to do what he wanted to do; he just needed to present his case properly with some solid financial muscle behind him to face off against Broccoli's legal army.

With Warner Brothers's help, Schwartzman (who is married to actress Talia Shire) allied himself with McClory, and the road to a *Thunderball* remake was paved. McClory would later take executive producer credit on the film, which was titled *Never Say Never Again*, and which brought Sean Connery back to the role he had made famous.

Released in 1983, *Never Say Never Again* was just what Broccoli feared—a competitive Bond film. Nevertheless, both *Never Say Never Again* and Broccoli's 1983 entry *Octopussy* were major international successes.

Kevin McClory, based in Nassau, maintains his interest in *Thunderball* and the S.P.E.C.T.R.E. organization, and as recently as July 1989 announced a new James Bond film headed for production. It's titled *Warhead 8*. Whether he can mount a costly 007 film on his own remains to be seen.

MCCOWEN, ALEC (Tunbridge Wells, England, May 26, 1925–) British character ac-

Algernon (ALEC MCCOWEN), the Q equivalent in *Never Say Never Again*. (Taliafilm)

tor who portrayed dry-witted, sinus-plagued Algernon ("Algy"), the equipment officer, in *Never Say Never Again*. See ALGERNON.

MACCRAE, DUNCAN Actor who portrayed Mathis, an inspector with the French Special Police, who escorts Evelyn Tremble/James Bond (PETER SELLERS) to the Monte Carlo casino in *Casino Royale*. MacCrae actually speaks the film's first line of dialogue to Sellers: "Mr. Bond?"

MCGILL, EVERETT (Miami Beach, Florida, 1945–) Rugged American character actor who portrayed Killifer, the DEA agent who

Actor Everett McGill, the quintessential American villain, was well cast as traitorous Killifer in *Licence to Kill*.

accepts a $2 million bribe to free convicted drug lord Franz Sanchez (ROBERT DAVI) in *Licence to Kill*. See KILLIFER.

MCGRATH, JOSEPH (1930–) Scottish feature and television comedy director who codirected the 1967 *Casino Royale* spoof with Val Guest, John Huston, Robert Parrish, and Ken Hughes. McGrath's responsibility was the Peter Sellers sequence, where Sellers is seduced by Ursula Andress to the tune of Dusty Springfield's "The Look of Love."

MCLAREN, JOHN Actor who portrayed the Brigadier, an American infantry officer who leads the counterassault against Goldfinger (GERT FROBE) at Fort Knox.

MACNEE, PATRICK (London, February 1922–   ) Dapper British actor and longtime veteran of "The Avengers" television series who joined James Bond (ROGER MOORE) as fellow agent and horse expert Sir Godfrey Tibbett in *A View to a Kill*. Working undercover as Bond's chauffeur, Macnee provides much of the film's early comic relief as he stumbles around with 007's luggage and resents Bond's condescending remarks—appropriate, since they're both trying to trick Max Zorin's (CHRISTOPHER WALKEN) security team. *See* TIBBETT, SIR GODFREY.

MCRAE, FRANK (Memphis, Tennessee) American character actor and former professional football player who portrayed Sharkey, Felix Leiter's (DAVID HEDISON) fisherman friend, in *Licence to Kill*. *See* SHARKEY.

MCTARRY M's (JOHN HUSTON) real name in *Casino Royale*. He owns a huge manor house in Scotland that is taken over by enemy agents of Dr. Noah (WOODY ALLEN). Led by Mimi (DEBORAH KERR), who is impersonating the widow McTarry, their mission is to de-

Classy British actor Patrick MacNee and his favorite costar Diana Rigg. Both would play key characters in the Bond series. (National Film Archive, London)

stroy Sir James Bond's (DAVID NIVEN) celibate image.

MCTARRY, LADY FIONA M's (JOHN HUSTON) widow in *Casino Royale*, impersonated by Dr. Noah's (WOODY ALLEN) agent, Mimi (DEBORAH KERR). Along with her legion of female agents, Mimi moves into the McTarry Manor in Scotland and prepares to seduce Sir James Bond (DAVID NIVEN). *Note:* We never discover what happened to the original Lady Fiona, or why Bond is lured to McTarry Manor in the first place.

MADAGASCAR BLACK SCORPION The species of scorpion wielded by Mr. Wint (BRUCE GLOVER) in *Diamonds Are Forever*. He uses one to kill the unfortunate South African dentist/smuggler.

For this sequence, which was shot in the desert outside Las Vegas, Glover was shown a selection of 25 scorpions, including the large Madagascar variety and its smaller, yet more deadly, California cousins. Fortunately, the little buggers were without their stingers, which had been conveniently clipped.

MADDEN, PETER (1904-1976) Thin British character actor who portrayed MacAdams, the bespectacled Canadian chess master who opposes Kronsteen (VLADEK SHEYBAL) and loses a tournament game at the beginning of *From Russia with Love*.

MADRID The location in Spain of Cuban hit man Hector Gonzales's (STEFAN KALIPHA) villa in *For Your Eyes Only*. James Bond (ROGER MOORE) goes there to investigate the death of marine archaeologist and British agent Timothy Havelock (JACK HEDLEY). And Melina Havelock (CAROLE BOUQUET), with crossbow in hand, goes there seeking revenge for her parents' brutal murder.

At Gonzales's pool, Bond gets his first look at Locque (MICHAEL GOTHARD), one of Aris Kristatos's (JULIAN GLOVER) agents, before Melina puts a crossbow bolt in Gonzales's back. When 007's Lotus Esprit self-destructs, Bond and Melina escape in her Citroen Deux Cheveux.

Madrid is also the site of a British agent's assassination in *Casino Royale*. As reported to

Sir James Bond (DAVID NIVEN) by Hadley (DEREK NIMMO), he was burned in a blazing bordello.

MAGDA Circus performer, seasoned pickpocket, and all-around Girl Friday, portrayed by Swedish actress Kristina Wayborn, in *Octopussy*. Octopussy's (MAUD ADAMS) second-in-command and Kamal Khan's (LOUIS JOURDAN) assistant/mistress, Magda first meets Bond (ROGER MOORE) briefly in London at the Sotheby's auction. They're reunited in the casino in Udaipur, India, and they eventually spend a passionate night in 007's hotel suite until Magda steals Bond's genuine Fabergé egg.

Magda's name is actually mentioned only once in the film—when Kamal formally introduces her to Bond at the Monsoon Palace dinner. On the East German border, she helps Octopussy prepare documents for the border guards, then performs magic tricks in the circus procession through Feldstadt. She even picks the U.S. air force base commander's wallet. Returning to Udaipur after 007 disarms the A-bomb, the swift-kicking Magda leads her fellow acrobats in the successful assault on Kamal's Monsoon Palace.

MAGINOT LINE A string of fortifications stretching along the French-German frontier that were completely outflanked by Hitler's armored blitzkrieg through the low countries in the summer of 1940.

During the winter of 1967-68, producer Harry Saltzman and production designer Syd Cain toured the line searching for a possible redoubt for Ernst Stavro Blofeld in *On Her Majesty's Secret Service*. Accompanied by a group of French officials, they were given a complete tour of a key position southeast of Metz.

Saltzman and Cain trudged along miles of concrete tunnels, viewing the facilities that were designed to support a huge French army in static defense. After five and a half hours of walking among huge gun emplacements, underground airfields, and railroads, Saltzman turned to Cain and asked, "What do you think?" Replied Cain, "I think we can build all of this in the studio."

In actuality, Eon Productions was spared that chore when the unit discovered the marvelous mountaintop restaurant above Murren, Switzerland, which eventually became Piz Gloria, Blofeld's (TELLY SAVALAS) allergy research center in the film.

"MAGNIFICENT SEVEN" THE THEME
(aka "The Marlboro Theme") Classic theme music from the 1960 United Artists western that is played underneath a sequence in *Moonraker* in which James Bond (ROGER MOORE) appears as a mounted gaucho in a Brazilian jungle village.

MAIBAUM, RICHARD (New York City, May 26, 1909–1991) American screenwriter who has either written or cowritten every Albert R. Broccoli–produced James Bond movie, except for *You Only Live Twice, Live and Let Die,* and *Moonraker.* Maibaum was an honored New York playwright by the time he began his screenwriting career in the 1930s. Prior to the Bond films, he had worked for Broccoli and his first producing partner, Irving Allen, on a number of offshore adventure films, including *Paratrooper, Hell Below Zero,* and *Zarak.* But it was with the 007 character that Maibaum found the perfect writer's medium.

It's not surprising that Broccoli chose an American to be the first to dramatize Bond for the big screen. Broccoli's contention all along, even as he and Saltzman were selling the series to United Artists, was that Bond had to possess the qualities that would appeal to an American audience. He had to be a ballsy, sexy, two-fisted adventurer in the Raymond Chandler/Mickey Spillane style. Maibaum knew that character well.

He also brought to the screen stories an element that was not a part of Ian Fleming's novels—humor. Maibaum brightened the dark action of the series with a clever line or two—often coming at the end of a particularly hair-raising stunt or set piece. Thus, having been taken to the edge of their seats, audiences were suddenly allowed to release their tension through laughter. It was an unbeatable combination, especially when the lines were delivered by the sly and sexy Sean Connery.

Another Maibaum element was the films' approach to sex. In the early 1960s, the Bond movies may not have initiated the sexual revolution that was coming, but they certainly guided it along with their enthusiastic depiction of Bond's sexual appetite. Although the casting

Screenwriter Richard Maibaum with actor Claude Rains, on the set of *Song of Surrender,* (which Maibaum wrote and produced) in 1949. (Richard Maibaum Collection)

department helped out by supplying a never-ending troupe of voluptuous leading ladies, Maibaum perfectly captured the playful antics of Bond in a series of teasing love scenes that conveyed everything and showed nothing.

That the early Bond movies could flawlessly go from danger to humor to sex and back again was due to Maibaum's screenwriting skills. But, the trend-setting writing of the early films began to unravel as the guard changed.

During the Roger Moore era, the Bond films, though still exciting and wonderfully inventive, lost the early charm that had made them the critical darlings of the mid-1960s. They became triumphs of engineering rather than story-telling. Big doesn't necessarily mean better, and the bigger the Bond films became, the less interesting they were—with exceptions, of course.

Having surrendered the writing chores on *Moonraker* to Christopher Wood, who created the silliest, yet one of the most successful films in the series, Maibaum returned on *For Your Eyes Only* to, in his own words, "pull the balloon down." Working from two Fleming short stories, "Risico" and "For Your Eyes Only," he anchored the story in a fascinating blood feud, reminiscent of *From Russia with Love,* between two Greek ex-partisans.

The only scene in the entire film that speaks falsely is the ridiculous encounter between Bond (ROGER MOORE) and the Blofeld look-alike who offers Bond a "stainless-steel delicatessen" in London if Bond will let him go. Maibaum still maintains that the line was not in his final shooting script, and I believe him. As to who wrote that silly line, which virtually destroyed the credibility of the teaser, one must look in a certain actor's corner.

Starting with *For Your Eyes Only*, Maibaum began a collaboration with production executive Michael G. Wilson, which continued throughout the 1980s and into the 1990s. A lawyer, engineer, and member of the Broccoli family (he's Cubby's stepson), Wilson had 25 years of experience as a Bond fan and contributor when he took pen in hand to join Maibaum on the scripts. Maibaum, who has been something of a lone-wolf writer in his career, told Cubby Broccoli that he was perfectly willing to work with Wilson. The result on *For Your Eyes Only* was, to quote Humphrey Bogart in *Casablanca*, the "beginning of a beautiful friendship."

"I think *For Your Eyes Only* turned out pretty well," said Maibaum, "except for the teaser, which was one of the worst in terms of audience reaction. I particularly liked Carole Bouquet, who played Melina. She was cool and beautiful, and she could hold her own alongside Bond. And the villains were very believable."

For the next film, *Octopussy*, Maibaum once again worked with Wilson. And George MacDonald Fraser, who wrote *The Flashman* novels, also contributed a script draft. "We started with two elements," Maibaum remembered, "Fleming's *Octopussy* novella and a short story called "The Property of a Lady." That proved to be the springboard for the story.

"George came on and worked on a draft and came up with a lot of the elements dealing with the Fabergé eggs. He worked with Michael, then I was brought back to do the shooting script. We had a devil of a time coming up with

Screenwriter Richard Maibaum, circa 1965. His Bond scripts were always written on a manual typewriter.
(Marc Sharratt, Richard Maibaum Collection)

a story about Octopussy, but it helped when we discovered that there actually is an organization in Japan composed entirely of women—a kind of female Mafia. And since we had once considered India as a location, it became the basis of this den of female thieves led by a woman named Octopussy."

Recently, the guard has changed again, and Maibaum finds himself working with still another James Bond—Timothy Dalton. "We knew we had to get a younger man. Roger was maturing, and the film audiences were getting younger. It was time for a change," said Maibaum. In actuality, *The Living Daylights* script was written with Roger Moore in mind rather than Dalton, who was a last-minute choice.

That film was followed by *Licence to Kill*, which was a disappointment in the United States. On that project, Maibaum was unable to write the screenplay due to the Writers Guild strike in 1988. Faced with fan reaction that the film was too serious, that there wasn't enough humor, and that the story seemed bland, Maibaum pointed to the villain's caper as a key problem.

"There was very little fantasy about *Licence to Kill*," he said. "The villain's caper was bland when you compare it to destroying Fort Knox or the food supply of the world. And Bond shouldn't be so damn funereal. There should have been more humor."

As to the long-term success of the series, Maibaum points a finger in Cubby Broccoli's direction, claiming that he's the number-one 007 fan in the series. "He's a big kid, really," Maibaum said. "His enthusiasm and excitement about James Bond propel us. The series would never have reached this point without him."

MAIN STRIKE Abandoned northern California silver mine purchased by Max Zorin (CHRISTOPHER WALKEN) in *A View to a Kill*. It becomes the nucleus of Project Main Strike, Zorin's plot to destroy Silicon Valley by creating a massive earthquake.

Situated above the San Andreas Fault, Main Strike becomes a safe deposit for a mountain of high explosives planted beneath its principal shaft. Zorin intends to detonate the explosives, thereby creating enough force to not only trip the San Andreas Fault, but to carry on to the nearby Hayward Fault as well. The twin killer quakes, timed to strike at the height of spring tide, will bury Silicon Valley under a massive lake. *See* PROJECT MAIN STRIKE.

MAITLAND, MARNE British character actor, a longtime resident of Italy, who portrayed Lazar, the Portuguese gunsmith in *The Man with the Golden Gun* who manufactures Francisco Scaramanga's (CHRISTOPHER LEE) golden bullets. *See* LAZAR.

Actor Marne Maitland played the Portuguese gunsmith in *The Man with the Golden Gun.*
(Marmont Management Ltd.)

MALIK, ART (Pakistan, 1952–) Handsome Pakistani actor, raised in England, who portrayed Kamran Shah, a Mujahedeen rebel leader who helps James Bond (TIMOTHY DALTON) in *The Living Daylights*. *See* SHAH, KAMRAN.

Art Malik played the well-educated Mujahedeen leader in *The Living Daylights.*
(Caroline Dawson)

MALLET, TANIA Striking British actress who portrayed revenge-seeking Tilly Masterson in *Goldfinger*. *See* MASTERSON, TILLY.

"MAN COMES . . . , A" The first line of dialogue spoken by Solitaire (JANE SEYMOUR) in *Live and Let Die*. It's a narration sequence that accompanies James Bond's (ROGER MOORE) flight to New York from London. Using her mystical tarot cards, plus her own power as a seer, Solitaire is able to identify a potential threat to Dr. Kananga (YAPHET KOTTO), the sinister island diplomat/drug smuggler.

MAN IN THE COFFIN, THE One of Hugo Drax's (MICHEL LONSDALE) assassins, portrayed by stuntman Claude Carliez, in *Moonraker*. Hidden in the coffin of a gondola hearse, he takes out Bond's (ROGER MOORE) gondolier with a throwing knife, but is, in turn, killed by 007.

MANKIEWICZ, TOM (Los Angeles, June 1, 1942–   ) American screenwriter who cowrote *Diamonds Are Forever* and *The Man with the Golden Gun* with Richard Maibaum. Mankiewicz also received solo credit on *Live and Let Die*.

Known for his wit and tongue-in-cheek approach to story-telling—later well suited to the *Superman* films he wrote—Mankiewicz was just what the James Bond series needed in the early to mid-1970s. Bond was slowly and inexorably moving away from the serious approach of the first few Sean Connery films.

After the relative box-office failure of the very serious *On Her Majesty's Secret Service*, the future films in the 007 series were destined to become globe-trotting extravaganzas with fantastic villains, incredible production design, and a light touch that would easily accommodate the strengths of actor Roger Moore, who took over the role in 1973. Even Sean Connery's return in *Diamonds Are Forever* in 1971 was a fantastic romp, with elements of pure whimsy.

In the past, Sean Connery had balanced an enormous amount of serious spying with a few throwaway witticisms to lighten the load. In *Diamonds*, the pendulum swung the other way, with a few moments of spying arrayed against predominantly outlandish situations.

In 1967, Mankiewicz wrote his first film, a surfing movie titled *The Sweet Ride*, which

Witty screenwriter Tom Mankiewicz. (Richard Schenkman)

starred a young Jacqueline Bisset. After some abortive work on Broadway, Bond beckoned young Mankiewicz. "It turned out that Dick Maibaum had done a draft on *Diamonds* and was through with it," recalled Mankiewicz. "Cubby and Harry were thus looking for a young American writer—because this Bond took place largely in the United States—who had been around and also could write English dialogue. David Picker, who had seen my Broadway musical 'Georgy Girl', recommended me for the job."

On a crisp fall morning in 1970, Mankiewicz arrived at Cubby Broccoli's mansion on Hillcrest Drive in Beverly Hills and was greeted by the producer and director Guy Hamilton, who had just flown over from England. Within moments, the young screenwriter was signed to a two-week contract guaranteeing him $1,250 a week.

After two weeks, Mankiewicz turned in the first 40 pages of his script and was put on an indefinite retainer. For the next six months, he was completely engrossed in the world of James Bond. His relationship with 007 would continue for three more years.

MANKOWITZ, WOLF (London, November 7, 1924–   ) British screenwriter, playwright, and novelist who, as an early collaborator of screenwriter Richard Maibaum on *Dr. No*, was partially responsible for giving the "Dr. No" moniker to the villain's monkey—a plot element that did not endear either writer to producer Cubby Broccoli. Mankowitz left the project after completing the first draft and did not receive screen credit in the final film.

Mankowitz's wit was better appreciated five years later when he cowrote the *Casino Royale* spoof for producers Charles K. Feldman and Jerry Bresler. *Casino Royale* was also his fourth association with director Val Guest, who codirected the film with John Huston, Robert Parrish, Joseph McGrath, and Ken Hughes.

MANTIS Sophisticated deep-sea diving suit worn by a henchman of Kristatos (JULIAN GLOVER) in *For Your Eyes Only*. The Mantis Man was portrayed by actor Graham Hawkes.

Ordered to intercept Bond (ROGER MOORE) and Melina (CAROLE BOUQUET) as they dive on the *St. Georges* wreck in search of the missing A.T.A.C. computer, the Mantis Man breaks into the *St. Georges*'s communications room and gives 007 plenty of trouble until Bond takes the self-destruct mechanism from the A.T.A.C. and attaches it to the Mantis. As Bond and Melina paddle back to their *Neptune* submarine, the Mantis is blown to kingdom come.

MANUELA Gorgeous British Secret Service agent based in Rio de Janeiro (Station VH) and portrayed by Emily Bolton in *Moonraker*. Standing outside the Carlos & Wilmsberg import/export warehouse while Bond (ROGER MOORE) searches inside, Manuela is nearly killed by Jaws (RICHARD KIEL), but is saved by 007 at the last possible moment.

MAN WITH THE GOLDEN GUN, THE (United Artists, 1974) ★ The ninth James Bond film produced by Albert R. Broccoli and Harry Saltzman. U.S. release date: December 19, 1974. U.S. film rentals: $9.4 million. Running time: 125 minutes.

This film is a turkey. Nonetheless, you have to give the producers credit for recovering from this disaster and producing one of the best films in the series, *The Spy Who Loved Me*. Is this the same Guy Hamilton who directed *Goldfinger*? Obviously not, because *The Man with the Golden Gun* is about as subtle as an elephant stampede—which would have been included in the film had Harry Saltzman been given his way.

The biggest problem with the film is that the key villain, Scaramanga, portrayed by Christopher Lee, is much too sympathetic. Actually, the part was a respite for Lee, who had been enslaved to the horror genre for years. Portrayed as a dashing million-dollars-a-shot assassin with a great-looking girlfriend, an incredible island house, and a sleek wardrobe, Scaramanga was light-years away from Lee's usual fright-filled Dracula, Frankenstein, and fiend-on-the-loose roles.

At one point in the story, Scaramanga even tells Bond a tragic tale of how his pet elephant was brutally killed in the circus, and how he turned to a life of crime by bumping off the elephant's murderer. This type of side story shows the similarities between Bond and Scaramanga and how they should have been fighting on the same side.

Another problem is that there is no clear motivation for destroying Scaramanga, aside from the fact that he's stolen a prize solar energy device. Thus, the final confrontation in the maze has very little tension.

There are other problems with this film. M and Q are reduced to a couple of insufferable magpies. Bond's Far Eastern secretary, Mary Goodnight, who was such a fine character in the books, is reduced to a buffoon in Britt Ekland's hands. And the action sequences all lack credibility. When Sheriff J. W. Pepper returns to the story, you know the film's in trouble. Also, one

of the movie's most innovative stunts—the 360-degree car jump in Thailand—is ruined by slow-motion photography and a kazoolike musical sound effect.

High points: Herve Villechaize as Nick Nack, a perfect Bond henchman (a kind of miniature Oddjob), those incredible prehistoric islands off the coast of Thailand, and Lulu's title track. A file-and-forget-it Bond adventure.

THE MAN WITH THE GOLDEN GUN CAST

James Bond . . . . .Roger Moore
Francisco Scaramanga . . . . .Christopher Lee
Mary Goodnight . . . . .Britt Ekland
Andrea Anders . . . . .Maud Adams
Nick Nack . . . . .Herve Villechaize
Sheriff J. W. Pepper . . . . .Clifton James
Hip . . . . .Soon-Taik Oh

James Bond (ROGER MOORE) and J. W. Pepper (CLIFTON JAMES) are about to discover that Scaramanga has given them the slip in *The Man with the Golden Gun*. Geez, you'd think a Louisiana sheriff would be used to firearms by now. (Rex Features Ltd./RDR Productions)

Hai Fat.........................Richard Loo
Rodney.........................Marc Lawrence
M..............................Bernard Lee
Q..............................Desmond Llewelyn
Miss Moneypenny ....Lois Maxwell
Lazar ....Marne Maitland
Colthorpe ....James Cossins
Chula ....Chan Yiu Lam
Saida ....Carmen Sautoy
Frazier ....Gerald James
Naval Lieutenant ....Michael Osborne
Communications Officer ....Michael Fleming

THE MAN WITH THE GOLDEN GUN CREW

Producers .....Albert R. Broccoli, Harry Saltzman
Director ....Guy Hamilton
Screenplay by ....Richard Maibaum,
 Tom Mankiewicz
Music by.......................John Barry
Title Song Sung by ....Lulu
Lyrics by......................Don Black
Associate Producer ....Charles Orme
Production Supervisor ....Claude Hudson
Assistant Director ....Derek Cracknell
Location Manager (Thailand)......Frank Ernst
Location Manager (Hong Kong) .....Eric Rattray
Directors of Photography..........Ted Moore,
 Oswald Morris
Camera Operator ....Bob Kindred
Sound Mixer ....Gordon Everett
Production Designer ....Peter Murton
Art Directors .....John Graysmark, Peter Lamont
Construction Manager (Studio) .....Leon Davis
Construction Manager (Location).Michael Redding
Supervising Editor ....John Shirley
Editor.........................Ray Poulton
Makeup ....Paul Engelen
Hairdressers ......Mike Jones, Elaine Bowerbank
Wardrobe Supervisor ....Elsa Fennell
Continuity ....Elaine Schreyeck
Special Effects ....John Stears
Production Company ....Eon Productions
Distribution Company ....United Artists

THE MAN WITH THE GOLDEN GUN COMPETITION

Competitive films in release when *The Man with the Golden Gun* opened in Los Angeles on December 19, 1974:

Steppenwolf
The Towering Inferno
Lenny
The Godfather Part II
The Front Page
The Island At the Top of the World
Young Frankenstein
Airport 1975

MARCH 19, 1964 Sean Connery's first day of shooting on *Goldfinger*. He reported to Stage D at Pinewood Studios, which was set up as the El Scorpio Nightclub in South America. A crowd of 50 men and women, all playing South American locals, were being rehearsed by choreographer Selina Wylie, while three dummy musicians, their music piped in electronically, were portraying a typical flamenco trio on a small stage in the center of the room. Nearby, shapely actress Nadja Regin was practicing her sexy dancing.

MARCH 30, 1962 Day on which principal photography was concluded on *Dr. No*.

MARGO The woman whom bored jet-setter Linda (KELL TYLER) is speaking to on the portable telephone when James Bond (TIMOTHY DALTON) "drops" onto her yacht for an impromptu visit in *The Living Daylights* teaser.

MARIE Bikini-clad French jet-setter featured in *Diamonds Are Forever*, portrayed by Denise Perrier, who may or may not have significant information on the whereabouts of Ernst Stavro Blofeld (CHARLES GRAY). Tipped off by a fez-wearing blackjack player, Bond (SEAN CONNERY) confronts her on a beach in the Antibes, rips off her top, and nearly strangles her with it until he gets the information that he needs.

Bond's obsession with Blofeld's whereabouts is justified—the head of S.P.E.C.T.R.E. murdered his wife (DIANA RIGG) in the previous film, *On Her Majesty's Secret Service*. Bond's ruthlessness with Marie is a throwback to the methods he used in *Dr. No*, where he pumped two shots into Professor Dent (ANTHONY DAWSON).

MARK 46 Type of nonnuclear torpedo used by the USS *Wayne* to destroy the bow doors of the supertanker *Liparus* in *The Spy Who Loved Me*. Commander Carter (SHANE RIMMER) also uses them to sink Karl Stromberg's (CURT JURGENS) Atlantis research facility.

MARKOVITZ, PROFESSOR Nuclear physicist portrayed by Milo Sperber in *The Spy Who Loved Me* who, with his partner, Dr. Bechmann (CYRIL SHAPS), is murdered after developing a nuclear-submarine tracking system for fanatical billionaire shipping magnate Karl Stromberg (CURT JURGENS). Method of assassination: their helicopter is blown out of the sky near Sardinia. *See* SPERBER, MILO.

MARSHALL, BRYAN British actor who portrayed Captain Talbot of the nuclear submarine HMS *Ranger* in *The Spy Who Loved Me*. *See* TALBOT, CAPTAIN.

MARSHALL, MICHAEL Actor who portrayed Colonel Scott, the American officer in charge of U.S. space forces in *Moonraker*. *See* SCOTT, COLONEL.

MARSHALL, ZENA (1925–) British leading lady with French ancestry who portrayed the seductive half-Chinese agent Miss Taro in *Dr. No*. Her appearance fresh from the bath, wrapped in a towel in the hallway of her Blue Mountain cottage, was certainly one of the film's high points. *See* TARO, MISS.

MARTIN, GEORGE British superstar music-producer/arranger who produced the Beatles music until 1969 and later scored *Live and Let Die* in 1973.

MASSAGE What Bond (SEAN CONNERY), disguised as a masseur, gives Domino (KIM BASINGER) in one of *Never Say Never Again*'s best scenes. The brief sequence is highly erotic as 007 attempts to question the mistress of Maximillian Largo (KLAUS MARIA BRANDAUER) as she lies naked under a towel in the massage room of a Nice health club.

At one point, she tells him "lower," and he begins to knead her behind. When the real masseuse shows up, 007 beats a hasty exit, and Domino learns that she's been duped. The smile on her face indicates that it wasn't an entirely uncomfortable experience.

MA 7-1 Identification number for the American rocket scheduled to orbit the moon at the

Sultry Zena Marshall, popular in sophisticated British dramas of the 1950s, would don Asian makeup as Miss Taro in *Dr. No*. (National Film Archive, London)

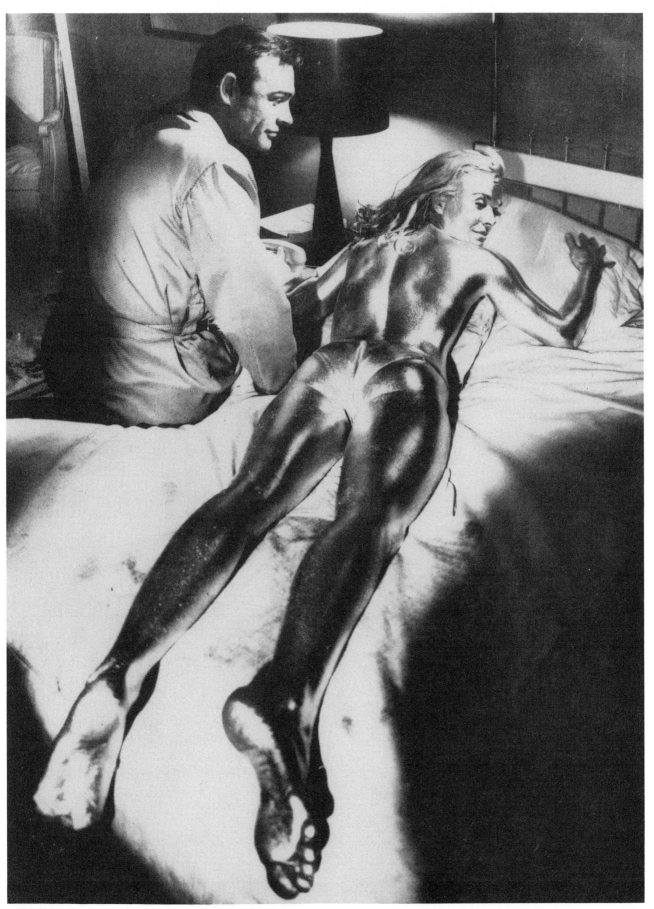

Come on, Jill. You're supposed to be dead! A behind-the-scenes shot from *Goldfinger*. (Express Newspapers, London)

conclusion of *Dr. No.* It is being directed from Mercury Control at Cape Canaveral.

MASTERSON, JILL Auric Goldfinger's (GERT FROBE) seductive Girl Friday in Miami Beach, portrayed by blond actress Shirley Eaton. Bond (SEAN CONNERY) finds Masterson in Goldfinger's suite at the Fontainebleau Hotel, helping her boss cheat at gin with Mr. Simmons (AUSTIN WILLIS). Equipped with a radio transmitter and a pair of high-powered binoculars, she is spying on Simmons's hand and communicating the results to her boss via a receiver camouflaged as Goldfinger's hearing aid.

Dressed in black bra and panties and lying sexily prone on a chaise longue, she is surprised by Bond, who then forces Goldfinger to start losing to Simmons; otherwise he'll report the scam to the Miami Beach Police. Masterson, of course, falls in with Bond, and they go directly to his bedroom in the same hotel.

By switching allegiances, Masterson pays the ultimate penalty—death by skin suffocation—when her entire body is painted gold by Oddjob (HAROLD SAKATA), Goldfinger's mute Korean manservant. Bond later finds out that such a death is not uncommon among cabaret dancers. To prevent such a demise, a small patch of skin must be left bare at the base of the spine so that the skin can breathe—a safety measure that was not performed in Miss Masterson's case. *See* EATON, SHIRLEY.

MASTERSON, TILLY Golden girl Jill Masterson's (SHIRLEY EATON) revenge-seeking sister, portrayed by Tania Mallet, in *Goldfinger.* Determined to kill Goldfinger (GERT FROBE), who had Oddjob (HAROLD SAKATA) murder Jill in Miami Beach, Tilly follows him to Switzerland, where on two occasions she tries to shoot him with a high-powered hunting rifle. Bond (SEAN CONNERY) intercepts her and shreds the tires on her 1964 Mustang convertible. They later join forces in a spectacular car chase. Unfortunately, Tilly runs afoul of Oddjob's razor-sharp bowler and is killed.

MATA HARI DANCE AND SPY SCHOOL Fictional spy school, located on Feldmanstrasse in West Berlin, founded by the famous World War I spy and featured in *Casino Royale.* Its cover is International Mother's Help, which supplies baby-sitters and au pair girls to the best families in Europe. According to its present owner, Frau Hoffner (ANNA QUAYLE), it's the only truly international school of espionage in the world with no political prejudices.

Mata Bond (JOANNA PETTET) is sent there by her father, Sir James Bond (DAVID NIVEN), to learn all she can about Le Chiffre's (ORSON WELLES) organization. Through the diminutive Polo (RONNIE CORBETT), she learns about an auction of compromising military photographs being held to raise currency for Le Chiffre's betting activities in Monte Carlo. *See* BOND, MATA.

MATHIS Officer with the French Special Police, portrayed by Duncan MacCrae, who escorts James Bond/Evelyn Tremble (PETER SELLERS) to the Monte Carlo casino in *Casino Royale.*

MATHIS, VALERIE French double agent with the Deuxième Bureau, portrayed by Linda Christian, who helps James Bond (BARRY NELSON) in the TV film "Casino Royale." An ex-lover of Bond, Mathis at first appears to be working for Soviet masterspy Le Chiffre (PETER LORRE). In reality, she is a Deuxième Bureau agent assigned to support Bond's efforts to bankrupt Le Chiffre at the baccarat table in Monte Carlo.

At a key moment in the game when Bond is wiped out, he suddenly receives an envelope with 35 million francs. The money is from Mathis, and it's enough to keep Bond, who eventually bankrupts Le Chiffre, in the game. Bond then discovers that Mathis is really a French agent who gave him the money and that she's been captured by the Soviet agent. Unless Bond gives Le Chiffre a check for the winnings—87 million francs—Mathis will be killed.

Bond returns to his hotel room, where he finds Mathis, but she's followed by Le Chiffre and his two thugs. Tied up in the bathroom, Bond is tortured by Le Chiffre (one of the thugs uses a pliers on his toes) in full view of Mathis. She can't take it and eventually reveals that she saw Bond using a screwdriver earlier. Le Chiffre finds the check for 87 million francs hidden in the number plate on Bond's door. While he's searching the room, Bond breaks free and kills Le Chiffre and one of the thugs.

Mathis gets her name from Fleming's Rene

Mathis character, who was also an agent with the Deuxième Bureau. *See* CHRISTIAN, LINDA.

MATSU Island situated on the route between Kobe and Shanghai in *You Only Live Twice*. It is pictured in the coastline photo stolen by Bond (SEAN CONNERY) from Osato's (TERU SHIMADA) safe.

MAX The Havelock family parrot and pistachio lover in *For Your Eyes Only*. Quite the talker, Max leads James Bond (ROGER MOORE) and Melina Havelock (CAROLE BOUQUET) to Kristatos's (JULIAN GLOVER) aerie at St. Cyril's. Max also has a comical and potentially scandalous conversation with Margaret Thatcher (JANET BROWN) at the film's conclusion.

MAXIE Plenty O'Toole's (LANA WOOD) Las Vegas boyfriend, portrayed by Ed Call, in *Diamonds Are Forever*. When he's busted at the crap table, Plenty transfers her allegiance to high-rolling James Bond (SEAN CONNERY).

MAXWELL, LOIS (Kitchener, Ontario, Canada, February 14, 1927-) Canadian leading lady who had a brief Hollywood career (1946–1948) before settling in England, where she portrayed M's secretary, Miss Moneypenny, in 14 James Bond films. During one of his frequent visits to the set of *Dr. No* in 1962, Ian Fleming said to Maxwell, "You know, Miss Maxwell, when I visualized Miss Moneypenny in the James Bond stories, I saw her as a tall, distinguished-looking woman with the most kissable lips in the world. You, my dear, are exactly the woman I visualized." *See* MONEYPENNY, MISS.

MAXWELL, PAUL Bond's (SEAN CONNERY) British agent contact in Venice in *From Russia with Love*. Bond is speaking with him on the phone when he spots S.P.E.C.T.R.E. Agent No. 3, Rosa Klebb (LOTTE LENYA), trying to steal the Lektor decoder from his hotel room.

MAY DAY Max Zorin's (CHRISTOPHER WALKEN) steroid-enhanced, super-bodyguard/lover/assassin, portrayed by singer Grace

Jones, in *A View to a Kill*. Wildly costumed and sporting the most unusual hairdos, May Day is one of Bond's (ROGER MOORE) most formidable opponents. 007 first sees her alongside Zorin at the British racetrack, Ascot, where she's costumed like a character out of *Alice in Wonderland*—a soldier of the Red Queen, no doubt!

At the Eiffel Tower Restaurant, she's in costume again, this time impersonating a nightclub puppeteer who assassinates Bond's French contact, Aubergine (JEAN ROUGERIE). Chased up the tower, with Bond blazing away at her with his Walther, May Day stops at the edge of one of the girders, hesitates for a split second, then jumps off the landmark, apparently to her doom. But a parachute opens (just like for Bond on the Asgard in *The Spy Who Loved Me* teaser), and she makes a soft landing aboard a wedding-party barge on the river Seine.

At an elegant horse show at Zorin's sumptuous French estate, May Day keeps a calculated eye on Bond's suspicious activities. After a night's investigation into Zorin's secret steroid research area—where he's increasing the stamina of his racehorses through illegal surgery—Bond finds himself unable to return to his bedroom before Zorin and May Day check his room. Instead, he slips under the covers in May Day's suite, prompting an amorous night with the Amazonian assassin. But May Day quickly turns murderous, disposing of Bond's fellow agent, Sir Godfrey Tibbett (PATRICK MAC-NEE), and helping Zorin dispose of Bond as well (although he survives the sinking of his Rolls-Royce by sucking the air out of one of the car's Michelin tires).

In San Francisco, May Day takes a backseat to Zorin, who's preparing his Project Main Strike. However, when Zorin orders his abandoned silver mine flooded, he doesn't forewarn his bodyguard, May Day, who is nearly killed with the rest of the miners.

Betrayed and double-crossed, May Day joins forces with Bond, helping him remove a huge bomb from a bed of high explosives that could cause a major earthquake in northern California. Hustling it onto a railroad handcar, May Day remains with the bomb so that she can keep a faulty hand brake in place. It turns out to be a noble, yet suicidal act, as the car explodes safely outside the mine. Her last words to Bond: "Get Zorin for me!"

"MAY THE PEACE OF ALLAH DESCEND UPON THIS MAGNIFICENT ABODE AND ALLOW A POOR TRAVELER TO ENTER" The first phrase of the British Secret Service recognition code between James Bond (ROGER MOORE) and Sheik Hosein (EDWARD DE SOUZA) in *The Spy Who Loved Me*. Hosein is to respond with, "And may the hospitality of these miserable quarters be sufficient to your honored needs."

MAY 3, 1985 Date on the $5 million check written by Max Zorin (CHRISTOPHER WALKEN) to Stacey Sutton (TANYA ROBERTS) for her shares of Sutton Oil in *A View to a Kill*. Stacey later tears up the check.

MAY 27, 8:00 P.M. GREENWICH MEAN TIME The precise date and time that the diamond ransom must be delivered to S.P.E.C.T.R.E. in *Thunderball*. *See* MERGUI ARCHIPELAGO.

MECHANICAL ALLIGATOR Reminiscent of the phony seagull from *Goldfinger*, the alligator is another form of camouflage that allows Bond (ROGER MOORE) to approach Octopussy's (MAUD ADAMS) island at night without being seen.

MEDDINGS, DEREK British special effects supervisor who joined the Bond team on *Live and Let Die* and *The Man with the Golden Gun* and later contributed extraordinary effects work to *The Spy Who Loved Me* and *Moonraker*. While working on *Fear Is the Key*, an Alistair MacLean adventure film, Meddings got his first Bond assignment. "On *Fear Is the Key*, I was supervising all of the effects on the picture, the floor effects—explosions, etc.—as well as the model effects," said Meddings. "It involved work with a crashing airplane, a bathyscaphe, and underwater sequences. And it was a very

Having arrived in the Bahamas in specially built crates, two of FX expert Derek Meddings's miniature nuclear submarines await sea trials on *The Spy Who Loved Me*. (Don Griffin, Perry Oceanographics)

successful picture. Syd Cain was the production designer, and when he was assigned by Cubby Broccoli to *Live and Let Die*, Syd asked me to come along and work on the film's special effects.''

Meddings's principal contribution to *Live and Let Die* was the explosion of Kananga's (YAPHET KOTTO) poppy fields on mythical San Monique—a terrific fiery effect that was done completely in miniature on a Pinewood effects stage. The producers were so pleased with the sequence that they offered Meddings an assignment on *The Man with the Golden Gun*, where he used his explosive expertise to expunge Scaramanga's (CHRISTOPHER LEE) solar reactor.

The model work that Meddings conceived on *The Spy Who Loved Me* qualifies as some of the best in the series, especially some terrific aerial shots of the *Liparus* supertanker swallowing the American nuclear submarine. In that particular sequence, both ships are beautifully realistic, appearing to cruise on a sparkling sea as if they were being photographed from 20,000 feet up.

"When we went on location in Nassau to look for a place to film the model sequences," he recalled, "we found a place called Coral Harbor, which was ideal because it was right on the ocean and had these canals that led out to the sea where we could prepare our models. We wanted to be near the ocean because of its unlimited scope. With the sea, you don't have to go around wondering whether the camera is going to catch a bit of the studio tank or whether the lighting is realistic or whether the water looks like real water. And since we were dealing with a 63-foot-long tanker, we needed a vast work area. The ocean next to Coral Harbor was perfect.

"One day, when we were planning the capture of the submarine and were looking for the right angles, I spotted a huge cement tower that was part of a nearby deserted hotel complex overlooking the ocean like a lighthouse. It had a staircase leading up to its concrete observation tower and had long since been abandoned.

"I went up there on an impulse to see what our tanker model would look like from that height and discovered a great shot. I knew that if we picked the right day, we would have a lovely, sparkling ocean, and it would look as if we were shooting the ships from an airplane. And that's exactly what happened.''

In addition to the submarine miniatures that were filmed entering and leaving the tanker, Meddings was also working with a miniature Atlantis, which, in the script, is destroyed by torpedoes; and the little four-foot version of Bond's Lotus submarine car, which appears in the brief sequence in which Bond (ROGER MOORE) drives up to the window of Atlantis to peer through a glass viewing port.

"MEDIUM DRY VODKA MARTINI, MIXED, NOT STIRRED" Technically, Bond's first drink, brought to him by room service during his stay in Jamaica on the *Dr. No* assignment. "Mixed" would later be changed to "shaken," creating the classic 007 cocktail.

MEI-LEI The golden-clad stewardess, portrayed by actress Mei Ling, on Auric Goldfinger's (GERT FROBE) private jet. She informs 007 (SEAN CONNERY) that his black attaché case did not survive the trip; it was "damaged when examined, so sorry."

MEI LING Actress who portrayed private-jet stewardess Mei-Lei in *Goldfinger*. In terms of character names, this is about as close as you can get to playing yourself. Other sources spell her name Mai Ling. *See* MEI-LEI.

MELLINGER, MICHAEL (Kochel, Bavaria, May 30, 1929–   ) German character actor of stage and screen, and a longtime resident of Britain, who portrayed Kisch, an associate of

Michael Mellinger today. He was Kisch, the luckless member of Operation Grand Slam who is tossed off the top of Fort Knox by Oddjob in *Goldfinger*. (L'Epine Smith)

Goldfinger (GERT FROBE) who locks Bond's (SEAN CONNERY) wrist to the A-bomb in Fort Knox. *See* KISCH.

MERGUI ARCHIPELAGO An island group off the coast of Burma where NATO will drop S.P.E.C.T.R.E.'s $280 million diamond ransom in *Thunderball*. According to Blofeld's precise instructions, the cache will be delivered at 2000 hours on May 27, Greenwich mean time, at latitude 20 degrees north, longitude 60 degrees east.

After verifying that the contents are the flawless blue-white diamonds weighing between three and eight carats, S.P.E.C.T.R.E. will alert NATO on radio frequency 16.23 megacycles as to the location of the missing atomic bombs.

METAL-DETECTING RAKE Where else would you find a metal detector disguised as a garden rake but in a Bond movie—in this case, *The Living Daylights*. The rake protects the entrance to the Bladen safe house in rural England, where "defecting" General Koskov is being kept.

METZ, PROFESSOR-DR. Blofeld's fussy laser specialist, portrayed by Joseph Furst, in *Diamonds Are Forever*. Another in a long series of renegade European scientists employed by S.P.E.C.T.R.E. to help blackmail the world, Metz has designed a laser satellite powered by a huge diamond solar shield. A bit of a pacifist, he hopes that the world will meet Blofeld's demands this time.

Unfortunately, on the oil rig at the film's conclusion, the S.P.E.C.T.R.E. chief has his typical bout of last-minute rage and insanity, and orders the satellite to open fire anyway. Fortunately, Bond (SEAN CONNERY) and attacking CIA helicopters sabotage the controls, and the satellite is rendered harmless.

"MEXICAN SCREW-OFF" James Bond's (ROGER MOORE) quip when he shoves the outboard screw of a Thai motor pan into the path of Hai Fat's (RICHARD LOO) thugs in *The Man with the Golden Gun*.

MEYER, TONY AND DAVID Twin actors who portrayed Mischka and Grischka, the

David Meyer played one of the evil knife-throwing twins in *Octopussy*. Both were highlights of the film. (Lou Coulson)

knife-throwing assassins in *Octopussy*. *See* MISCHKA AND GRISCHKA.

MGM LION Famous motion-picture studio logo that appeared at the beginning of *Octopussy*. It reflected the merger of MGM and United Artists. Since then, the companies have split apart and combined several times. Even though the lion was featured, it was almost immediately followed by the United Artists logo, which is a staple of the series.

MIAMI BEACH Site of James Bond's (SEAN CONNERY) first meeting with Auric Goldfinger (GERT FROBE) at the Fontainebleau Hotel. Also the target of a S.P.E.C.T.R.E.-hijacked A-bomb in *Thunderball*.

MICHELIN The manufacturer of the Rolls-Royce tire that Bond (ROGER MOORE) uses as a makeshift air supply in *A View to a Kill*.

MICROCHIP Essential computer part manufactured by Max Zorin (CHRISTOPHER WALKEN) in *A View to a Kill* and the key to the film's plot. Referred to technically as a silicon integrated circuit, the microchip is an essential part of all modern computers.

British Intelligence fears that the magnetic-pulse damage caused by a nuclear bomb being exploded in space by the Russians could render all microchips useless. That's why they're so interested in a chip retrieved by Bond (ROGER MOORE) from the body of 003, who stole it from the Russians in Siberia. It's impervious to micropulse damage.

Reasoning that Max Zorin might be supplying this new generation of chips to the Russians, M (ROBERT BROWN) orders Bond to look into Zorin's activities. His first stop is a British racetrack where horse-fancier Zorin's own thoroughbred, Pegasus, easily wins a stakes race.

Later, in France, Bond and fellow agent Sir Godfrey Tibbett (PATRICK MACNEE) discover that Zorin has been using steroids and a surgically implanted microchip to augment the racing ability of his horses. However, like Goldfinger's (GERT FROBE) gold-smuggling activities in the third James Bond movie, Zorin's microchip dealings with the Russians and his horseracing activities are mere smoke screens for a much bigger scheme—Project Main Strike.

In order to monopolize the world's supply of microchips, Zorin plans to utterly destroy northern California's Silicon Valley—the high-technology capital of the world, where 80 percent of the planet's microchips are manufactured. His plan calls for using his oil wells on the California coast to pump seawater into the Hayward Fault, a major earthquake zone. Simultaneously, he's going to explode a bomb near another primary earthquake fault. The resulting double earthquake will turn Silicon Valley into a huge lake.

Like the "hoods convention" in *Goldfinger*, Zorin calls together a group of his world microchip distributors and offers them an opportunity to join the scheme and his new microchip cartel. The price: $100 million a franchise. One disgruntled Taiwanese tycoon (ANTHONY CHIN) becomes a latter-day Mr. Solo (MARTIN BENSON). Instead of being crushed inside a Continental limousine, the tycoon is tossed out the exit door by May Day (GRACE JONES). This exit, though, is 5,000 feet up—in Zorin's blimp.

MICRO-MINI UZI 9-mm, 32-round submachine gun used by South American drug runner Franz Sanchez (ROBERT DAVI) and his thugs in *Licence to Kill*.

MIDGE Short, dark-haired acrobatic smuggler, portrayed by Cherry Gillespie, in *Octopussy*. Like Gwendoline (SUZANNE JE-

ROME), she's one of Octopussy's (MAUD ADAMS) primary assistants.

MIDNIGHT Time of the second U.S. space launch in *You Only Live Twice*. If the Soviet Union tampers with this rocket, the United States says World War III could be imminent. Midnight is also the appointed time for Kananga's (YAPHET KOTTO) poppy fields to be destroyed by incendiary time bombs planted by Quarrel, Jr. (ROY STEWART), in *Live and Let Die*.

MIDNIGHT, MR. American gangster portrayed by Bill Nagy, whose organization helps Auric Goldfinger (GERT FROBE) smuggle Delta Nine nerve-gas canisters across the Canadian border. Ironically, that same gas later kills Midnight and the rest of the "hoods convention" assembled in the Auric Stud game room.

MIKLOS, ROSIKA Voluptuous Czechoslovakian gasworks employee and British agent, portrayed by Julie T. Wallace, in *The Living Daylights*. To help spirit defecting Russian General Georgi Koskov (JEROEN KRABBE) through the pipes into Austria, Miklos and Bond (TIMOTHY DALTON) lower their charge into the "pig"—a pipe-cleaning scouring plug that has been modified to carry a human being. She then instructs Bond to fire the pig into the pipeline when the pressure reaches 100 pounds.

To distract the gasworks supervisor (PETER PORTEOUS, who played Lenkin, the jewel forger in *Octopussy*), Rosika enters his office, unzips her coveralls and plunges his nose into her cleavage. When the pressure hits 100, Bond zaps Koskov into the pipeline, creating a lot of noise, none of which is heard by the thoroughly distracted gasworks supervisor. Score one for Miklos.

MILES M's (BERNARD LEE) first name, mentioned by KGB General Gogol (WALTER GOTELL) in *The Spy Who Loved Me*. It's the first time in the series that M's first name is used.

MILLER'S BRIDGE Site of a police river-block, in *Live and Let Die*, designed to halt the progress of a desperate motorboat chase between James Bond (ROGER MOORE) and a gang of Kananga's (YAPHET KOTTO) henchmen. The river block fails as both Bond and Adam (TOMMY LANE) bust through.

MILOVY, KARA Beautiful, wide-eyed Czechoslovakian cellist, portrayed by Maryam d'Abo, who falls in love with James Bond (TIMOTHY DALTON) in *The Living Daylights*. Taking the cue from Ian Fleming's original short story, Kara is introduced as a Soviet sniper, supposedly assigned to liquidate defecting Russian General Georgi Koskov (JEROEN KRABBE). In reality, she's an innocent dupe who impersonates a sniper to help her lover/patron Koskov convince British Intelligence that his defection is genuine.

Staring at her stunning features through the cross hairs of his sniper's rifle, Bond—on a mission to kill any potential assassin— hesitates and shoots the rifle out of Kara's hands instead. After Koskov is whisked away to England and to safety—only to be quickly recaptured by

what the British are supposed to think is a KGB operation—Bond returns to Bratislava to find Kara and question her. Mesmerized by her beauty during an afternoon concert, 007 follows her and discovers that she's being shadowed by the KGB (they're suspicious of her supposed involvement with a defector).

Posing as a friend of the missing Koskov, Bond helps Kara escape from Bratislava into Austria—after a wild ride in his Aston Martin. Having never been out of her native Czechoslovakia, Vienna is a treat for Kara, who dreams of performing at the city's famous concert hall. Bond buy her a beautiful evening gown—"on Georgi's money"—and enjoys touring the city with her, including a romantic interlude on a Ferris wheel, where they kiss for the first time. They finally track Koskov to Tangier, where Bond joins forces with KGB General Pushkin (JOHN RHYS-DAVIES), who is also suspicious of Koskov's involvement with sinister arms dealer Brad Whitaker (JOE DON BAKER).

When Georgi persuades Kara that Bond is a KGB agent, she mistakenly helps drug 007. Be-

Maryam d'Abo shined in *The Living Daylights* as Czechoslovakian cellist Kara Milovy. (Jeremy Conway)

fore losing consciousness, Bond explains that he was the one who shot the gun out of her hand in Bratislava—a fact that wins her back to his side. However, before they act, they're imprisoned on a Russian transport plane headed for Afghanistan, where Koskov plans to hand 007 over to a local Soviet air force base commander. He charges Bond with the murder of Pushkin, whose death was actually faked by 007 in Tangier to convince Koskov that his cover as a Russian agent on special assignment is clean.

Bond and Kara escape into the wilderness with the help of a fellow prisoner, Mujahedeen leader Kamran Shah (ART MALIK). They soon discover that Koskov, in league with Whitaker, is using $50 million in Soviet funds earmarked for arms purchases to buy raw opium in Afghanistan.

This "quick killing" is disrupted by 007, who, with Kamran Shah's help, launches an attack on the Russian base. When 007 steals the opium-laden Russian transport, Kara joins him by driving her jeep into the open belly of the cargo plane. And when Bond enters the cargo bay for an incredible fight to the death with Necros (ANDREAS WISNIEWSKI), Kara takes the controls. Disposing of Necros, Bond repeats the maneuver he performed in the film's teaser—pulling the rip cord on the jeep in the cargo bay seconds before the out-of-gas transport crashes into a mountainside.

After a return trip to Tangier, where Bond eliminates Whitaker and helps Pushkin capture Koskov, Kara returns to Austria and to a triumphant concert that is observed by M (ROBERT BROWN), General Gogol (WALTER GOTELL), and Kamran Shah and his men. But where is James Bond? Kara is heartbroken that he didn't show up for her concert debut. However, when she returns to her dressing room, she finds him waiting there, with champagne and a passionate embrace. *See* D'ABO, MARYAM.

MIMI Agent of Dr. Noah (WOODY ALLEN), portrayed wildly by Deborah Kerr, who impersonates M's widow in an attempt to seduce Sir James Bond (DAVID NIVEN), in *Casino Royale*. One of the problems with *Casino Royale* is that you have absolutely no idea why James Bond is journeying to the McTarry residence. Obviously, M (John Huston) is dead, but we do not know how he died and what happened to the real Widow McTarry.

In any case, Bond arrives and meets Mimi and her legion of beautiful girls, all of whom are assigned the task of destroying 007's celibate image. They fail, and Mimi actually falls in love with Bond before taking her nun's vows and retiring to a convent for life. She appears later in Sir James's office in full nun's garb. *See* KERR, DEBORAH.

MINIATURE VERY PISTOL A signaling device supplied to Bond (SEAN CONNERY) by Q (DESMOND LLEWELYN) in *Thunderball*. Trapped in an underwater cave/grotto, 007 uses the pistol to signal Felix Leiter (RIK VAN NUTTER) and a Coast Guard rescue helicopter. *Note:* The Very pistol was invented by an American naval officer, Edward W. Very, whose "Very lights" were a common signaling device among U.S. warships.

MINT JULEP The favorite drink of Goldfinger (GERT FROBE) on his Auric Stud property in Kentucky. When offered the same drink, Bond (SEAN CONNERY) instructs the waiter, "Sour mash, but not too sweet."

MIRAMONTE James Bond's (ROGER MOORE) hotel in Cortina D'Ampezzo in *For Your Eyes Only*. Returning to his room, he finds youthful ice skater Bibi Dahl (LYNN-HOLLY JOHNSON) waiting in his bed. Gracefully, he tells her to put on her clothes and he'll buy her an ice cream.

MISCHKA AND GRISCHKA Formidable twin assassins, and circus knife-throwing experts employed by Kamal Khan (LOUIS JOURDAN) in *Octopussy* and portrayed by Tony and David Meyer. The twins are a throwback to the serious killers of the early Bond films (*Dr. No*, *From Russia with Love*), bringing with them a realistic element of danger.

They're introduced in the film's most atmospheric scene—their night chase through an East German forest in pursuit of clown-suited 009 (ANDY BRADFORD). Everything recalls the moody Renaissance Garden exterior in *From*

Russia with Love: the proximity of the border, the stillness of the forest, 009's nervousness, the catlike grace of the twins. Even the bursting of one of 009's balloons recalls the snapping of a twig by Red Grant (ROBERT SHAW).

Caught by one of the twin killers, 009 is wounded, but he manages to karate-chop the twin to his knees. Running toward a bridge, 009 climbs quickly up the girder but takes a well-aimed knife in his upper back. Stunned, he falls into a flood-control basin. 009 survives long enough to drop a Fabergé egg at the feet of the British ambassador. The twins return to the circus.

When Bond (ROGER MOORE) arrives in East Germany, he observes General Orlov (STEVEN BERKOFF) and Kamal replacing a cache of stolen Russian jewels with an atomic device. When Orlov and Kamal leave the railroad car where the device is hidden in the base of the circus cannon, they leave Mischka on guard. Bond enters the train car and is temporarily blinded by Mischka's blowtorch. Diving for cover, he barely survives a series of throwing knives, then hits a lever that drops the cannon barrel on Mischka's head, killing him.

Changing clothes with the dead man, Bond heads for the bomb-carrying train in General Orlov's Mercedes. Later, disguised in a gorilla suit, Bond is in the bomb compartment when the train crosses the West German border. Spied by Gobinda (KABIR BEDI) and the remaining twin, Grischka, 007 heads for the roof of the train and is immediately involved in fierce hand-to-hand combat atop the various cars. While grappling with Grischka, 007 is thrown completely off the train and into the forest.

Unarmed and facing a deadly set of throwing knives, Bond retreats to a forest cabin where the revenge-crazed twin pins 007 against a door with his knives. Grischka comes in for the kill, sneering, "For my brother!," but he is tripped up by Bond, who kills him with one of his own knives. 007 gets in the last word: "That's for 009."

MISS GALAXY International beauty pageant won by Lupe Lamora (TALISA SOTO) in *Licence to Kill*. It was supposedly fixed by her lover, drug runner Franz Sanchez (ROBERT DAVI).

"MISSING DUEL, THE" A sequence in *The Man with the Golden Gun* that ended up on the cutting-room floor. It involved the tail end of the beach duel that pits Bond's (ROGER MOORE) Walther against Scaramanga's (CHRISTOPHER LEE) golden automatic.

Lee explained the missing sequence: "In the duel, they cut out a great deal of footage that they felt would hold up the pace of the picture. As you recall, Bond turns around, and Scaramanga is gone. The next time you see me, I'm coming around the corner of the 'fun house.' That was the way the final film came out.

"The way we shot it originally, you could see by the expression on my face that I wasn't going to play by the rules of the duel. So, as Bond is walking away from me, I dive out of the frame and just disappear. I had cheated, which presents an interesting psychological point, because if Scaramanga really thought he was the best assassin in the world, what was he doing cheating?

"Bond realizes I'm hiding in the rocks, and we have a long conversation, shouting at each other. Bond is 30 or 40 yards away, also hiding behind some rocks. It's all very cat-and-mouse.

"Bond tries to flush me out by flinging a thermos of petrol in the air and exploding it above my head. We actually shot that, and it does appear in the trailer. I dodge the thermos, and we end up in the 'fun house.' But in the cutting room, they decided that two men standing behind rocks shouting at each other didn't work. And they were probably right. It was too conventional."

MITCHELL, BILLY J. Actor who portrayed Captain Pederson, the commander of the American nuclear submarine that is shadowing Maximillian Largo's (KLAUS MARIA BRANDAUER) *Flying Saucer* yacht in *Never Say Never Again*.

MITSOUKO (real name, Maryse Guy Mitsouko) Japanese actress who portrayed James Bond's (SEAN CONNERY) French contact in the *Thunderball* teaser.

MODIFIED B-17 A converted Coast Guard bomber that helps rescue 007 (SEAN CONNERY) and Domino (CLAUDINE AUGER) in

A French Secret Service agent (MITSOUKO) joins Bond (SEAN CONNERY) at what appears to be the funeral of Jacques Boitier in *Thunderball*. We know better. (Rex Features Ltd./RDR Productions)

Thunderball. Having obliterated the *Disco Volante* yacht on the nearby reef, 007 and Domino climb from the water into a life raft dropped by the B-17, inflate its signal balloon, and then strap themselves to a harness connected to the balloon's cable.

The B-17—equipped with a V-shaped, metal catcher on its nose— then snags the balloon, which lifts Bond and Domino skyward into the rescue plane. It's not the most dignified form of rescue but nonetheless provides a rousing conclusion to what is probably the most popular James Bond film of all time—in number of tickets sold in the United States.

MOJABA CLUB Cairo nightclub run by black-market trader Max Kalba (VERNON DOBTCHEFF) in *The Spy Who Loved Me*. James Bond (ROGER MOORE) and KGB Major Anya Amasova (BARBARA BACH) go there to find a nuclear-submarine tracking system, a microfilm copy of which is being peddled on the open market. Unfortunately, just as he's about to auction off the film, Kalba is called to a phone booth and murdered by Jaws (RICHARD KIEL), who steals the film and disappears into the desert.

M-1026-A License plate of Melina Havelock's (CAROLE BOUQUET) Citroen Deux Cheveux in *For Your Eyes Only*. When Bond's (ROGER MOORE) Lotus Esprit self-destructs, he's forced to escape with Melina in the clunky French compact, which somehow survives a jarring car chase with enemy agents.

Pamela Salem took on the Moneypenny role in *Never Say Never Again*. No doubt the producers said, "Get a Lois Maxwell type." (Taliafilm)

MONEYPENNY, MISS

M's (BERNARD LEE, ROBERT BROWN) efficient, love-starved secretary and one of 007's most ardent admirers, portrayed solidly by Canadian actress Lois Maxwell in the first 14 James Bond films released by United Artists. She's also the only character in the entire series that has been featured in every film (M was not featured in *For Your Eyes Only*; Q was not featured in *Live and Let Die*).

Starting with her introduction in *Dr. No* in 1962, Moneypenny's blatantly sexual repartee with Bond before and after a briefing with M became a staple in the series. Like M and Q (DESMOND LLEWELYN), her character was less comedic in the early films, as was her relationship with Bond. The new Moneypennys, Pamela Salem in *Never Say Never Again* and

A youthful Lois Maxwell during her Warner Brothers' contract days in the 1940s.

The customary repartee between Bond (SEAN CONNERY) and Miss Moneypenny (LOIS MAXWELL). The intercom will interrupt this in about five seconds. (Rex Features Ltd./RDR Productions)

Caroline Bliss in *The Living Daylights* and *Licence to Kill*, have been less than memorable follow-ups to Maxwell.

MONEYPENNY'S DAUGHTER Sir James Bond's (DAVID NIVEN) secretary, portrayed by Barbara Bouchet, in *Casino Royale*. The new Miss Moneypenny was working for the late M (JOHN HUSTON), whose job Bond has assumed. Having failed to seduce Bond after all those years, her mother took her nun's vows and left the service. The new Miss Moneypenny helps Bond select an A.F.S.D. (Anti-Female Spy Device) that will neutralize a rash of agent assassinations. The successful candidate is supposed to be immune to seduction.

Lining up a group of candidates, Moneypenny proceeds to kiss them, until she discovers Cooper (TERENCE COOPER), whom she deems worthy of further investigation. Actually, the A.F.S.D. turns out to be Evelyn Tremble (PETER SELLERS), a mild-mannered card expert, who is sent to Monte Carlo to bankrupt a Soviet masterspy named Le Chiffre (ORSON WELLES)—a mission that has absolutely nothing to do with the rash of agent assassinations.

MONLAUR, YVONNE Parisian actress who was considered for the part of "Domino" in *Thunderball*, but lost out to former Miss France Claudine Auger.

MONSOON PALACE The fortress home of exiled Afghan Prince Kamal Khan (LOUIS JOURDAN) in *Octopussy*. Located in the mountains above Udaipur, India, it's garrisoned by hardy mountain troops that are loyal to Kamal.

Captured in Udaipur, Bond (ROGER MOORE) is brought to the palace and kept locked in his room until Kamal invites him to a perfectly awful dinner that features "stuffed sheep's head'' as the main entree. When renegade Russian General Orlov (STEVEN BERKOFF) arrives for a final briefing, Bond manages to listen in on their conversation, thanks to a bug planted in the tiny carriage inside a phony jeweled Fabergé Easter egg. Unfortunately, due to interference from Magda's (KRISTINA WAYBORN) blow-dryer, all that Bond hears is ''Karl-Marx-Stadt'' and ''one week.''

Hiding in a meat freezer that also contains the bodies of some of Kamal's previous dinner guests, Bond impersonates a corpse and is carried out the next morning for burial. Coming to life, he knocks aside his guards and goes off into the bush, only to be chased and eventually surrounded by Kamal's tiger hunters. Unfastening the belt on Gobinda's (KABIR BEDI) howdah, which knocks the huge bodyguard to the ground, Bond finds an escape route that carries him to the river and eventual safety.

After their A-bomb plot in West Germany fails, Kamal and Gobinda return to the Monsoon Palace and plot their own escape. Outside, their palace is about to be invaded by Octopussy (MAUD ADAMS) and her troupe of acrobats. The athletic women eventually overwhelm the garrison with Bond and Q's (DESMOND LLEWELYN) help, but Kamal and Gobinda—with a kidnapped Octopussy—escape and head for the airstrip.

MOON BUGGY NO. 1 Bond's (SEAN CONNERY) comical getaway vehicle from Techtronics, in *Diamonds Are Forever*. Designed for travel on the lunar surface, the moon buggy is hijacked by Bond, who finds it perfect for smashing through walls and gates and navigating across the Nevada desert.

An American stuntman, doubling Sean Connery, crashes the moon buggy through the wall of Willard Whyte's Techtronics plant outside Las Vegas in *Diamonds Are Forever*. (Stephen Allen, Las Vegas News Bureau)

Guy Hamilton's film crew catches the moon buggy in action during location shooting at the Johns Manville gypsum plant outside Las Vegas in *Diamonds Are Forever*. (Stephen Allen, Las Vegas News Bureau)

MOONRAKER (United Artists, 1979) ★ The 11th James Bond film produced by Albert R. Broccoli. U.S. release date: June 29, 1979. U.S. film rentals: $34 million. Budget: $30 million. Running time: 126 minutes.

Although Broccoli was correct in following the *Goldfinger* formula after the success of *Diamonds Are Forever* in 1971, *Moonraker*'s story line was much too fantastic, even for a Bond film. Building upon the momentum created by

The Spy Who Loved Me in 1977 and backed by an inspired marketing campaign, *Moonraker* nonetheless was a huge financial success and the biggest money-maker in Bond history up till then. It's still a member of the 007 turkey class, though.

Aside from sending Bond into outer space, where no double-0 agent should ever go, *Moonraker* returned to *The Man with the Golden Gun* style of action without credibility. Except for the wild parachute jump in the teaser, the action sequences are just plain stupid, including the unbelievably dumb moment when Bond glides through Venice's St. Mark's Square while riding a gondola-hovercraft. Even a pigeon did a double take. Interestingly, what could have been a great action sequence in the film—Bond flying a mini-jet behind Angel Falls in Brazil—was eliminated from the shooting script when the river dried up.

Jaws returns in *Moonraker* and adds some tension to the film, but his Wile E. Coyote heroics are not as flavorful as they were in *Spy*. Lois Chiles is a cocky Bond heroine, but she's an ice machine in the charisma department. Michel Lonsdale spends much of the film mumbling about Bond's ability to survive numerous assassination attempts. One of those is actually the film's most effective sequence—the centrifuge trainer mishap.

High points: John Barry's score and Corinne Clery's death scene in the forest, where she becomes lunch for Drax's Dobermans—a scene that found its way into the film's teaser trailer.

MOONRAKER CAST

James Bond	Roger Moore
Holly Goodhead	Lois Chiles
Hugo Drax	Michel Lonsdale
Jaws	Richard Kiel
Corinne Dufour	Corinne Clery
M	Bernard Lee
Q	Desmond Llewelyn
Miss Moneypenny	Lois Maxwell
Frederick Gray	Geoffrey Keen
Manuela	Emily Bolton
Chang	Toshiro Suga
Dolly	Blanche Ravalec
Private Jet Pilot	Jean Pierre Castaldi
Private Jet Hostess	Leila Shenna
General Gogol	Walter Gotell
Cavendish	Arthur Howard
Blonde Beauty/Drax Girl	Irka Bochenko
Colonel Scott	Michael Marshall
Mission-Control Director	Douglas Lambert
Consumptive Italian	Alfie Bass
Museum Guide/Drax Girl	Anne Lonnberg
U.S. Shuttle Captain	Brian Keith
Captain Boeing 747	George Birt
R.A.F. Officer	Kim Fortune
Launch Technician No. 1	Chris Dillinger
Launch Technician No. 2	Georges Beller
Sky Divers	Johnny Traber's Troupe
Russian Girl	Lizzie Warville
Drax's Girls	Chichinou Kaeppler,

Francoise Gayat, Catherine Serre, Christina Hui, Nicaise Jean-Louis, Beatrice Libert

MOONRAKER CREW

Producer	Albert R. Broccoli
Director	Lewis Gilbert
Screenplay by	Christopher Wood
Associate Producer	William P. Cartlidge
Executive Producer	Michael G. Wilson
Music by	John Barry
Title Song Performed by	Shirley Bassey
Lyrics by	Hal David
Production Designer	Ken Adam
Director of Photography	Jean Tournier
Film Editor	John Glen
Visual Effects Supervisor	Derek Meddings
Production Manager (France)	Jean-Pierre Spiri-Mercanton
Production Manager (U.K.)	Terence Churcher
Location Manager (Brazil)	Frank Ernst
Location Manager (Italy)	Philippe Modave
Location Manager (Florida)	John Comfort
Unit Manager (France)	Robert Saussier
Unit Manager (U.K.)	Chris Kenny
Second Unit Directors	Ernie Day, John Glen
First Assistant Director	Michel Cheyko
Casting Directors	Margot Capelier, Budge Drury
Stunt Arranger	Bob Simmons
Art Directors	Max Douy, Charles Bishop
Visual Effects Art Director	Peter Lamont
Visual Effects Cameraman	Paul Wilson
Optical Effects Cameraman	Robin Browne
Set Decorator	Peter Howitt
Second Unit Cameraman	Jacques Renoir
Camera Operators	Alex Mills, Michel Deloire, John Morgan
Continuity	Elaine Schreyeck
Costume Designer	Jacques Fonteray
Production Controller	Reg Barkshire
Production Accountant	Brian Bailey
Main Titles Designed by	Maurice Binder
Assembly Editor	John Grover
Dubbing Editor	Allan Sones
Dubbing Mixer	Gordon K. McCallum
Sound Mixer	Daniel Brisseau
Script Editor	Vernon Harris
Space Consultant	Eric Burgess
Wardrobe Master	Jean Zay
Special Effects	John Evans, John Richardson
Makeup Artists	Monique Archambault, Paul Engelen
Hairdressers	Pierre Vade, Mike Jones
Stills Cameraman	Patrick Morin
Unit Publicists	Steve Swan, Gilles Durieux

Production Company . . . . .Eon Productions
Distribution Company . . . . .United Artists

MOONRAKER COMPETITION

Competitive films in release when *Moonraker* opened in Los Angeles on June 29, 1979:

Rocky II

The Muppet Movie

Alien

Prophecy

The Main Event

Escape from Alcatraz

Nightwing

Bloodline

The In-Laws

Game of Death

Soldier of Orange

Manhattan

The Champ

Lost and Found

MOONRAKER The name given to the U.S. space shuttle, on loan to the British, that is hijacked off a Royal Air Force 747 airliner in the *Moonraker* teaser. The name is also used generically to describe each ship in Hugo Drax's (MICHEL LONSDALE) shuttle fleet (Moonraker No. 1, Moonraker No. 2, etc.). Drax later admits to Bond (ROGER MOORE) that the Moonraker was hijacked to replace another shuttle that developed a fault during assembly.

MOONRAKER NO. 5 One of the shuttles in Hugo Drax's (MICHEL LONSDALE) space fleet in *Moonraker*. Captured by Drax, Bond (ROGER MOORE) and Dr. Holly Goodhead (LOIS CHILES) are locked in a concrete chamber located beneath the engine exhausts of Moonraker No. 5. When that shuttle blasts off, both agents will be incinerated.

Fortunately, Bond and Holly avert their own execution by escaping through a ventilation shaft. Once the battle inside Drax's radarproof space station is won, Bond and Holly steal the Moonraker No. 5, and its nose-mounted laser cannon, to destroy the toxic-gas cylinders that could destroy human life on Earth.

MOONRAKER NO. 6 Another shuttle in Hugo Drax's space fleet in *Moonraker*, it carries James Bond (ROGER MOORE) and Dr. Holly Goodhead (LOIS CHILES), who stow away for a trip to the radarproof Drax space station.

MOORE, ROGER (London, October 14, 1927-   ) Dashing British actor who won the part of James Bond in *Live and Let Die* in 1973 and started his own dynasty that would last 12 years and seven films. Producers Broccoli and Saltzman had first considered Moore during the initial 007 casting search back in 1962, but he was considered too much of a ''pretty boy'' to play Bond. He was also portraying ''The Saint'' on television and was thus unavailable to Eon Productions.

When Connery left the Bond series after *Diamonds Are Forever*, the producers returned to Moore, and this time he was available and perfect for the role. The ''Moore Dynasty,'' as it should be called, took an even more fantastic approach to the original Fleming stories than did the Connery films. Globe-trotting adventure was the key, along with tongue-in-cheek action and repartee. Gone was the cruel sensuality of Connery epitomized by *Dr. No* and *From Russia with Love*.

While Moore was hardly the aristocratic snob that some critics claimed was closer to Fleming's original concept of Bond (another falsehood), he did bring a different tone to the character. His was a more outwardly self-assured, confident, and polished 007.

Screenwriter Tom Mankiewicz, who would be involved in three of the Moore films, put it more succinctly. Said Mankiewicz, ''When Sean Connery used to walk into a bar, your immediate feeling was 'uh oh, there's going to be trouble.' Sean can look like a bastard, especially when he's angry.

''Roger, on the other hand, looks like your typical nice-guy secret agent. There is no way that he can look evil. He is much more the Etonian dropout that Fleming once conjured, and in the Moore Bond films, we had to play to those strengths. While Sean could just look at somebody and they would back away, Roger has to come on with a line like, 'Excuse me, haven't we met?'

''Sean, of course, could just be nasty, and the audience loved him for it. He could sit at a table with a girl, and he could lean over the table

A youthful Roger Moore visits Anne Francis at MGM in the mid-1950s. (Rex Features Ltd./RDR Productions)

and kiss her and then stick a knife into her under the table, saying to a nearby waiter, 'Excuse me, but I have nothing with which to cut my meat,' and the audience would go along with it. They would take that from Sean because he had that glint in his eye—that touch of the lorry driver in him—even though he was always the quintessential good guy inside. Audiences wouldn't take that kind of stunt from Roger.

"Roger, however, can have much more fun in a sophisticated setting. For instance, in the

original script for *The Man with the Golden Gun*, Roger was pretending to be an ornithologist, which is really a conceit, because James Bond is named after an ornithologist. So Bond is at this party in Bangkok, and an ambassador comments to him, 'I understand you're doing a book on ornithology,' to which Roger replies, 'Yes, sir,' and the man says, 'What is it called?' and Roger looks at the ambassador's beautiful wife, a Thai girl, and responds, 'Birds of the Far East.'

"Now, Roger can say 'Birds of the Far East'

Rough and tumble action on "The Persuaders" television series with Tony Curtis would prepare Roger Moore for the rigors of 007 duty.

in a much more refined way than Sean ever could. Roger is a good comedian, and he can play direct comedy much better than Sean. Sean's strong point was not playing comedy at all. If he had played the comedy in the Bond films, it would have looked phony."

One of Moore's first scenes is a perfect example of the new order described by Mankiewicz. In *Live and Let Die*, Bond follows Kananga (YAPHET KOTTO) to a nightclub in Harlem, where he's easily disarmed and captured by his enemies. He politely introduces himself to Solitaire (JANE SEYMOUR), and they engage in a stoic repartee until Kananga, who, unbeknownst to Bond, is masquerading as Harlem drug kingpin Mr. Big, marks him for immediate execution. Outside, Bond manages to distract and disable his two executioners, and he makes it out of Harlem with the help of a resourceful CIA man, Strutter (LON SATTON).

Given the same set of circumstances, Sean

Connery would have probably approached the nightclub after dark, where he could camouflage his intentions more easily. Inside the club, he would have punched out a few people before surrendering to Mr. Big's minions. The introduction to Solitaire would have been less polite, and Bond wouldn't have taken so easily to the prospect of execution. And the fight with the two executioners would probably have been along the order of his confrontation with Red Grant in *From Russia with Love*.

Critics generally agree that Roger Moore finally grew into the James Bond role with *The Spy Who Loved Me*, a film that many fans consider his best Bond. There is no question that the film was a cut above his previous two efforts and even contained some subtle dramatic moments that surprised both the fans and the critics. The most impressive of these occurs in Bond's and Anya's (BARBARA BACH) Sardinian hotel suite after a hair-raising chase se-

The suave antics of Simon Templar on "The Saint" would prepare Roger Moore well for his involvement with the luscious ladies of the 007 series.

quence in which Bond eludes a combined assault by enemy motorcyclists, cars, and helicopters by taking his specially equipped Lotus Esprit into the Mediterranean, where it becomes an instant submarine.

Bond is lighting a cigar with a special lighter, which Anya admires. When she ask him where he got it, he tells her it came from Berngarten in Austria, where he had done some skiing. This information startles Anya, whose lover, a Russian agent, was recently killed in Berngarten on a mission (his mission was to kill James Bond). She shows him a picture of her lover, and Bond replies that he does not know the face. However, when Anya states that he was killed while on a mission, Bond confesses that he probably killed him during a high-speed ski chase. Anya turns cold and informs Bond that when their mission is over, she will kill him. She then walks away. It is one of Roger Moore's best scenes in years. It's warmly reminiscent of the early Connery Bonds, when drama was ever present, even amid the fun. The look on Moore's face during the sequence, his mannerisms, the whole feel of the moment seem to come from another film entirely. Director Lewis Gilbert later agreed that Moore had taken his character to a new level of honesty, a factor that contributed to the success of the on-screen relationship between Bond and Anya.

By ordering their screenwriters to play to Moore's strengths, Broccoli and Saltzman were nonetheless retreating from their original concept of Bond as a "ballsy Englishman" in the Mickey Spillane/Mike Hammer tradition of American detectives. Moore, in essence, was not the physically imposing actor that Connery was. However, his pure likability and comfort with witty lines and tongue-in-cheek action was to become a strong asset in the mid-1970s, when the tenor of the films themselves changed.

Those films emphasized a huge circuslike canvas that won them millions of new fans, turning Moore into an internationally famous movie star. They were brighter, funnier films that didn't hesitate to spoof themselves. It is unlikely that the serious Connery films of the early 1960s would have worked as well in America a decade later. The post-Vietnam, post-Watergate audience was looking for escapist fun, and nothing provided it more successfully than the Bond movies.

Prior to the arrival of a new generation of science-fiction and fantasy heroes in the late 1970s (from *Superman*, *Star Wars*, and *Star Trek*), Roger Moore's James Bond was probably the most popular pop hero on the planet. And throughout the early 1980s, he maintained that rank in the face of increasing competition. His retirement in 1985, after the release of his seventh film, *A View to a Kill*, was due primarily to age and the need the producers felt to enliven the series with a fresher face.

One factor that has contributed to the problems of Moore's replacement, Timothy Dalton (at least, in U.S. domestic box office sales), is that he's not a star of Roger Moore's caliber. He's an excellent actor, yes, but probably not a true audience draw. The international popularity of Roger Moore's seven Bond adventures cannot be overemphasized. With his presence on the poster, Moore revived the series's fortunes and brought the films to new heights.

Roger Moore strikes a pose in Paris during *A View to a Kill*. (Express Newspapers, London)

MOORE, TED (Cape Province, South Africa, August 7, 1914–1987) (real name, Frank Edward Moore) Academy Award–winning South African cinematographer who photographed seven of the first nine James Bond movies.

MORENO, GERARDO Stunt supervisor who portrayed Alvarez, Lupe Lamora's (TALISA SOTO) unfortunate lover in the *Licence to Kill* teaser. His heart becomes drug runner Franz Sanchez's (ROBERT DAVI) Little Valentine. *See* ALVAREZ.

MORENO, JOHN Actor who portrayed Luigi Ferrara, James Bond's (ROGER MOORE) Secret Service contact in northern Italy in *For Your Eyes Only*.

MORGAN'S HARBOR Located in Kingston, Jamaica, it is the location in *Dr. No* where Bond (SEAN CONNERY) first meets Quarrel (JOHN KITZMILLER).

British cinematographer Ted Moore, one of the unsung heroes of the early James Bond movies. (Mignon Moore Collection)

MORGANTHAU III, HENRY American multimillionaire producer who in 1956 collaborated with Ian Fleming on the idea for a television series titled "Commander Jamaica." When the concept failed to interest NBC, Fleming took the story idea and wrote his sixth James Bond novel, *Dr. No*.

MORTNER, DR. CARL Renegade Nazi scientist, portrayed by Willoughby Gray, hired by Max Zorin (CHRISTOPHER WALKEN) as a horse-breeding consultant in *A View to a Kill*. In actuality, Mortner is Hans Glaub, a renowned German specialist in the development of steroids.

During World War II, in an attempt to enhance intelligence in newborns, Glaub experimented with steroid injections in pregnant concentration-camp inmates. Virtually all children were aborted, but a handful were born with incredible IQs. The only side effect was that they all turned out to be psychotics. One of those children was Max Zorin.

After World War II, the Russians grabbed Mortner before he could be arrested and tried for his war crimes. He was set up to develop steroids for Soviet athletes. British Intelligence lost track of him around 1970.

In Zorin's employ, Mortner has been using his steroid knowledge on racehorses. By surgically implanting microchips and a small supply of natural horse steroids in the animals' legs, Mortner can overcome their fatigue on the racecourse. Zorin's prize thoroughbred, Pegasus, demonstrates that ability in a race observed by James Bond (ROGER MOORE) and Sir Godfrey Tibbett (PATRICK MACNEE).

After Bond successfully averts Zorin's plot to destroy Silicon Valley by triggering a huge earthquake, Mortner joins Zorin and Scarpine (PATRICK BAUCHAU) in the getaway blimp. During an amazing fight atop the Golden Gate Bridge, Mortner is blown to bits when a batch of dynamite headed 007's way explodes prematurely.

MORTON, CHARLES The alias James Bond (ROGER MOORE) uses while traveling to East Germany in *Octopussy*. Passing through Checkpoint Charlie, he poses as a manufacturer's representative from Leeds who's visiting furniture factories in the East.

MORZENY The S.P.E.C.T.R.E. operations chief, portrayed by actor Walter Gotell in *From Russia with Love*, who is first seen at the beginning of the movie when he congratulates Grant (ROBERT SHAW) on his murder of the phony James Bond. Later, he escorts Rosa Klebb (LOTTE LENYA) around S.P.E.C.T.R.E. Island's training area, and he eventually leads the motorboat attack on Bond (SEAN CONNERY) and Tanya (DANIELA BIANCHI). He also kills S.P.E.C.T.R.E. master-planner Kronsteen (VLADEK SHEYBAL) with a kick from his poisoned shoe knife.

Morzeny is killed in the motorboat battle with Bond when his flotilla is obliterated in a gasoline fire ignited by 007's flare pistol. Gotell returns in later films as General Gogol, a continuing character in the James Bond series who later jumps from the espionage to the diplomatic side of the KGB. *See* GOTELL, WALTER.

MOSES, ALBERT (1937–) East Indian character actor who portrayed the Egyptian bartender in *The Spy Who Loved Me* and Sadruddin, Head of Section I in New Delhi, in *Octopussy*.

MOSSBERG "ROGUE" SHOTGUN Formidable pump-action weapon employed by CIA undercover agent Pam Bouvier (CAREY LOWELL) during a wild brawl in Bimini's Barrelhead Bar in *Licence to Kill*. Eventually, she uses the gun to blow out a section of barroom wall, through which she escapes with Bond (TIMOTHY DALTON).

MOTORIZED TRACTION TABLE Also known as "the rack," this device is used by qualified physical therapists to stretch a patient's spine. In *Thunderball*, Bond (SEAN CONNERY), recovering at the Shrublands health clinic, is strapped to the table by Patricia Fearing (MOLLY PETERS). Turning on the mechanism, she excuses herself for 15 minutes, during which time S.P.E.C.T.R.E. agent Count Lippe (GUY DOLEMAN) enters the room and trips the lever to the highest danger level.

Bond is saved from assassination when Fearing returns in time to turn off the machine. Quipping, "I must be six inches taller," Bond staggers into the steam room, taking Fearing in with him for additional recuperative value.

MOUTON ROTHSCHILD 1955 The wine selected by S.P.E.C.T.R.E. assassins Mr. Wint (BRUCE GLOVER) and Mr. Kidd (PUTTER SMITH) when they bring dinner to James Bond (SEAN CONNERY) and Tiffany Case (JILL ST. JOHN) in *Diamonds Are Forever*.

Sniffing Wint's potent aftershave and remembering the scent from a previous encounter, Bond decides to test Wint's wine knowledge. He tastes the Mouton and terms it excellent. But he tells the "waiter" that for such an elaborate meal, a claret wine would have been more suitable.

Wint falls for the ploy and says that the liner's cellar is poorly stocked with clarets. Bond blows Wint's cover by explaining that Mouton *is* a claret. In the ensuing fight, Bond is about to be strangled by Wint while Kidd attacks with two flaming shish kebabs. Agent 007 then douses Kidd with the Mouton, turning him into a Roman candle. Wint is dispatched with a bombe surprise attached to his trousers.

MOXON, TIM Actor who portrayed British Secret Service agent Commander John Strangways in *Dr. No*.

MULLER, TRICIA Blond British actress who portrayed Sydney, Pussy Galore's copilot and a member of her "Flying Circus," in *Goldfinger*.

MUNGER, SIR DONALD Extremely knowledgeable diamond broker portrayed by British actor Laurence Naismith in *Diamonds Are Forever*. Like Colonel Smithers (RICHARD VERNON) of the Bank of England in *Goldfinger*, it is Munger's job to brief Bond (SEAN CONNERY) and M (BERNARD LEE) on a plague of smuggling—in this case, diamond smuggling—that is crippling British mining in South Africa.

Like Fleming, Munger communicates a great deal of information on the peculiarities of African diamond mining while narrating documentarylike footage of a typical mining operation. Apparently, though, the dialogue in Richard Maibaum and Tom Mankiewicz's script was not sufficiently long to cover the scope of the minidocumentary on diamond mining. Thus, if you listen carefully, you'll notice that the following phrase is repeated in order to stretch out the narration: ". . . even though the industry prides itself on the loyalty and devotion of its workers."

MUNRO, CAROLINE British actress, and a favorite of fantasy-film fans, who portrayed Stromberg's (CURT JURGENS) assistant and

Actress Caroline Munro portrayed Naomi, the winsome helicopter pilot, in *The Spy Who Loved Me*. (Roberto Tuma, Dennis Selinger)

helicopter pilot in *The Spy Who Loved Me*. The cat-and-mouse game between Bond's (ROGER MOORE) trick Lotus submarine car and Naomi's Jet Ranger helicopter is one of the film's highlights, capped delightfully by her knowing wink in the heat of battle. *See* NAOMI.

MURREN A small picturesque village in Switzerland, located beneath the Schilthorn Peak, that became a principal location in *On Her Majesty's Secret Service* in 1968. It was atop the Schilthorn that a revolving restaurant, dubbed

Piz Gloria, was constructed. It, too, became a location in the film, along with the fully functional cable car/funicular that connected the restaurant to Murren.

Murren proved to be an excellent location for other reasons. Not only were there excellent ski runs nearby, but it was a good location for the unit to construct a workable bobsled run, which was completed, prior to shooting, on the site of an older run that had been closed since 1937.

MURTON, PETER   A native Londoner and Bond veteran who was the production designer on *The Man with the Golden Gun*. Murton began his career as a draftsman, moved up the ranks to art director, and worked with Ken Adam on several pre-Bond films. The pair worked together in 1963 on *Dr. Strangelove*, and Adam asked Murton to join him on *Goldfinger*.

MUTUAL DISARMAMENT TALKS Subject of a heated debate between diplomatic General Gogol (WALTER GOTELL) and hard-line fanatic General Orlov (STEVEN BERKOFF) before a tribunal of Soviet leaders in *Octopussy*. Gogol feels that NATO proposals do not compromise the defensive alignment of the Soviet Eastern Bloc. Orlov is in favor of a massive military invasion of the West.

When Gogol mentions the possibility of nuclear retaliation, Orlov sneers at his comment, claiming that the Western democracies are decadent and incapable of defending themselves against a superior military force. The Soviet premier (PAUL HARDWICK, a Leonid Brezhnev look-alike) enters the debate on Gogol's side, ending the discussion. He predicts that global socialism will be achieved peaceably.

"MY LITTLE OCTOPUSSY"   How Magda (KRISTINA WAYBORN) describes the octopus tattoo she has on her buttocks in *Octopussy*. It's the symbol of the legendary Octopus Cult that Octopussy (MAUD ADAMS) has revived on her island off the coast of Udaipur.

N

NABILA Enormous 300-foot oceangoing yacht owned by billionaire Adnan Khashoggi in 1982, which became Maximillian Largo's (KLAUS MARIA BRANDAUER) *Flying Saucer* in *Never Say Never Again*. Khashoggi eventually sold the *Nabila* to Donald Trump, who renamed it the *Trump Princess*. *See* FLYING SAUCER.

NAISMITH, LAURENCE (1908–   ) (real name, Lawrence Johnson) British character actor who portrayed Sir Donald Munger, the diamond broker in *Diamonds Are Forever*.

Behind the scenes on the *Nabila* yacht during *Never Say Never Again*. Director Irvin Kershner is the man in the white hat. Producer Jack Schwartzman is at far right. (Taliafilm)

Adnon Khashoggi's *Nabila* yacht, which became the "Flying Saucer" in *Never Say Never Again*. (Taliafilm)

Distinguished British character actor Lawrence Naismith portrayed broker Sir Donald Munger in *Diamonds Are Forever*. (National Film Archive, London)

NANCY Lovely German allergy patient, portrayed by Catherine Von Schell, who resides at Piz Gloria, in *On Her Majesty's Secret Service*.

She's allergic to potatoes. Nancy becomes enamored with Bond (GEORGE LAZENBY, posing as heraldry expert Sir Hilary Bray) at dinner and later sneaks into his room after he returns from a romp with Ruby (ANGELA SCOULAR).

NAOMI Billionaire shipping magnate Karl Stromberg's (CURT JURGENS) luscious assistant and helicopter pilot, portrayed by Caroline Munro, in *The Spy Who Loved Me*. When Bond (ROGER MOORE) and Anya (BARBARA BACH) arrive in Sardinia for a visit with Stromberg, stunning, bikini-clad Naomi meets them at their hotel dock for a short motorboat trip to Atlantis—Stromberg's amphibious laboratory. Her obvious interest in 007 doesn't agree with Anya at all, but a potential cat fight is averted when Bond returns from his abbreviated visit with Stromberg.

The advantages of playing the world's most famous secret agent, *left to right*, Caroline Munro, Roger Moore, and Barbara Bach. (Rex Features Ltd./RDR Productions)

Later, when the pair escape from killer motorcycles and cars, their final hurdle is Naomi herself, flying a machine-gun–equipped Jet Ranger helicopter that sticks to Bond's trick Lotus like glue—until he drives into the ocean and converts to submarine-car status.

One of the film's clever touches is Naomi winking at Bond while she's trying to kill him. Hovering over the ocean, Naomi is unfortunately a ripe target for a subsurface-to-air missile that obliterates her and her chopper. One of the most sympathetic of all of James Bond's adversaries, Naomi nevertheless took her paycheck from Stromberg—a fact that qualifies her for liquidation. *See* MUNRO, CAROLINE.

NAPOLEON'S EMPRESS The original owner of a priceless statuette that Maximillian Largo (KLAUS MARIA BRANDAUER) hands to Domino (KIM BASINGER) in *Never Say Never Again*. Now aware that he was responsible for her brother Jack's (GAVAN O'HERLIHY) death, Domino wants nothing to do with Largo, let alone his priceless gifts. Hounded by the psychotic billionaire, she tries to give him back the statue, but it drops and breaks into a thousand pieces. Largo laughs and sends Domino to be auctioned off to Arab traders.

NASH, CAPTAIN The unfortunate Yugoslavia-based British agent, portrayed by *From Russia with Love*'s production manager, Bill Hill, who is murdered by Red Grant (ROBERT SHAW) in the rest room of the Zagreb train station. Grant then assumes his identity, stealing his wallet, hat, and briefcase. The masquerade works, and Bond is tricked into thinking that S.P.E.C.T.R.E.'s deadliest assassin is a helpful Brit.

NATO PROJECT The code name for S.P.E.C.T.R.E.'s scheme, in *Thunderball*, to steal two atomic bombs from a NATO bomber and then blackmail the North Atlantic Treaty powers to the tune of $280 million.

The plan involves substituting an exact duplicate for NATO aerial observer François Derval (PAUL STASSINO), who will then hijack a bomber to the Bahamas with two atomic weapons on board. There, off Nassau, using a small army of underwater troops, S.P.E.C.T.R.E. Agent No. 2, Emilio Largo (ADOLFO CELI), will hide the bombs until NATO pays the money. If something goes wrong, Largo has orders to destroy Miami, Florida, with one of the bombs.

The NATO bomber can be seen undergoing construction during location filming in Nassau on *Thunderball* in 1965. (Ronnie Udell Collection)

NEAME, CHRISTOPHER British actor who portrayed Fallon, the Secret Service operative and ally of Hong Kong narcotics agent Kwang (CARY-HIROYUKI TAGAWA), who identifies Bond (TIMOTHY DALTON) as a rogue agent in *Licence to Kill*.

NECROS Formidable blond assassin (in the Red Grant mold) employed by renegade Russian General Georgi Koskov (JEROEN KRABBE) in *The Living Daylights* and portrayed by Andreas Wisniewski. Necros's first mission is to spirit Koskov away from the Bladen safe house in England, where the defector is being interrogated by British Intelligence.

Impersonating a milkman he strangled, Necros breaks into the house, kills a British agent during a boisterous fight in the kitchen, and grabs Koskov, who's quickly taken to a waiting Red Cross helicopter—actually, more of Koskov's men. In order to further convince the British that the KGB is behind a plot called "Smiert Spionam" ("Death to Spies"), Necros is sent to Vienna where he kills local Section Chief Saunders (THOMAS WHEATLEY).

Necros is at the trade convention in Tangier when Bond (TIMOTHY DALTON) "assassinates" KGB Chief General Pushkin (JOHN RHYS-DAVIES). It's a fake killing that's planned to expose Koskov's real plot involving a huge diamonds-for-opium swap with the Snow Leopard Brotherhood of Afghanistan.

Drugged and shipped to Afghanistan on a Russian military transport, Bond escapes, joins forces with the Mujahedeen rebels, and participates in an attack on the Soviet air base where Koskov's transport is being loaded with the opium cache. Bond hijacks the transport and takes off with Necros on board.

Leaving the flying to cellist Kara Milovy (MARYAM D'ABO), who inadvertently opens the cargo hold in midair, Bond and Necros engage in an incredible fight while hanging onto the netting that holds the opium bundles in place. Bond eventually gets the upper hand, and Necros falls to his death.

NELSON, BARRY (Oakland, California, April 16, 1920–) (real name, Robert Nielsen) Likable American stage and screen actor who portrayed 007 in the very first James Bond outing, "Casino Royale," a one-hour, live television dramatization that was broadcast on the CBS Climax Mystery Theater on October 21, 1954. Little more than a year after Ian Fleming had published his first Bond novel, and long before any semblance of a 007 following had been established in the United States, Barry Nelson's Bond was introduced as an American agent fighting against Russian operatives in

Yankee Barry Nelson won the part of James Bond in the TV version of "Casino Royale" in 1954. His nickname: "Card Sense Jimmy Bond."

Monte Carlo. Not only did 007 debut in the States as a Yank counterspy, but he was given an outrageous nickname—Card Sense Jimmy Bond—by a British agent named Clarence Leiter (MICHAEL PATE).

In essence, Bond in 1954 was simply an international version of such standard American gumshoes as Sam Spade, Philip Marlowe, and the heroes of Mickey Spillane's pulp thrillers. Although Bond gets to dally with a beautiful and mysterious woman (LINDA CHRISTIAN) and match wits with a vicious Soviet spymaster (PETER LORRE)—plot elements that would become trademarks of the future film series—Barry Nelson's 1954 version of 007 was pretty much a low-budget Bond, whose turf was a CBS soundstage in Los Angeles.

NENE VALLEY RAILWAY British railroad yard and station that was the location for Bond's (ROGER MOORE) chaotic escape from Karl-Marx-Stadt in *Octopussy*. Augmented by Peter Lamont's art department, the British station was equipped with German fences and East/West German crossing points.

NEPTUNE Marine archaeologist and British agent Timothy Havelock's (JACK HEDLEY) two-man submarine in *For Your Eyes Only*. Bond (ROGER MOORE) and Melina Havelock (CAROLE BOUQUET) use the sub to find the wreck of the *St. Georges* surveillance ship off the coast of Albania.

NEVER SAY NEVER AGAIN
(Warner Brothers, 1983) ★ ★ ★ A remake of the novel *Thunderball*, this Bond film was produced by Jack Schwartzman. U.S. release date: October 7, 1983. Budget: $36 million. U.S. film rentals: $28 million. Running time: 137 minutes.

It's long, we've seen most of the action before in *Thunderball*, it has the worst musical score in the series, and the climax is boring, but *Never Say Never Again* is a Sean Connery Bond movie, and when he's on screen, the movie works. Fortunately, he's on screen a lot.

Interestingly, Connery looks better in this film than he did 13 years previously in *Diamonds Are Forever*. He's lean, tanned, and quick on his feet. And he can still deliver those throwaway lines with aplomb. Fatima Blush waterskis up to him in Nassau and apologizes, "I've

Sean Connery and Kim Basinger listen to some last-minute instructions prior to their escape from Palmyra in *Never Say Never Again*. (Taliafilm)

made you all wet." Bond replies, "Yes, but my martini is still dry." Only Connery could get away with a line like that.

Producer Schwartzman also surrounded Sean with the best of all possible casts, including Klaus Maria Brandauer as Largo, Kim Basinger as Domino, and Barbara Carrera as Fatima Blush. What the film lacks is action. Aside from the war-game teaser sequence, the overblown battle with Lippe at Shrublands (will the filmmakers ever do justice to Shrublands?), and a brief motorcycle chase, this Bond movie is a talky one—with characters grinning and growling at one another without much physical interplay.

With Connery in the role, it's also a sexy Bond—helped immensely by Kim Basinger and Valerie Leon, who's into sports fishing. Carrera's wicked Fatima Blush is a performance right out of *The Wizard of Oz*. She's so good in the role that we miss her after Bond blows her back over the rainbow.

The final third of *Never Say Never Again* is bland. The ticking clock that rang true in *Thunderball* is curiously missing from this film. You know Bond and Leiter have to recover the A-bomb from the Tears of Allah excavation, but you don't get the impression that they have to hurry.

High points: Carrera's Fatima Blush, the Domination video game, Basinger's dancing, the health-club sequence where 007 gives Domino a rubdown, the tango. Low points: Edward Fox's shrill M and Michel Legrand's nonscore.

Sean Connery and Barbara Carrera on location in the Bahamas. (Taliafilm)

James Bond (SEAN CONNERY), Domino (KIM BASINGER), and North African bandits—all chummy for the requisite publicity photo. (Taliafilm)

NEVER SAY NEVER AGAIN CAST

James Bond . . . . Sean Connery
Maximillian Largo . . . . Klaus Maria Brandauer
Ernst Stavro Blofeld . . . . Max von Sydow
Fatima Blush . . . . Barbara Carrera
Domino Petachi . . . . Kim Basinger
Felix Leiter . . . . Bernie Casey
Algernon . . . . Alec McCowen
M . . . . Edward Fox
Miss Moneypenny . . . . Pamela Salem
Lippe . . . . Pat Roach
Patricia . . . . Prunella Gee
Nigel Small-Fawcett . . . . Rowan Atkinson
Captain Jack Petachi . . . . Gavan O'Herlihy
Lady in the Bahamas . . . . Valerie Leon
Nicole—Agent 326 . . . . Saskia Cohen Tanugi
Captain Pederson . . . . Billy J. Mitchell
Girl Hostage . . . . Wendy Leech
Lord Alpert . . . . Anthony Sharp
U.S. Air Force General . . . . Manning Redwood
Dr. Kovac . . . . Milow Kirek

NEVER SAY NEVER AGAIN CREW

Producer . . . . Jack Schwartzman
Executive Producer . . . . Kevin McClory
Director . . . . Irvin Kershner
Screenplay by . . . . Lorenzo Semple, Jr.
Based on an Original Story by . . . . Kevin McClory,
　　　　　　　　　　Jack Whittingham, Ian Fleming
Associate Producer . . . . Michael Dryhurst
Director of Photography . . . .
　　　　　　　　　　　　Douglas Slocombe, B.S.C.
Production Designers . . . . Philip Harrison,
　　　　　　　　　　　　　　　　　　Stephen Grimes
Supervising Film Editor . . . . Robert Lawrence
Title Song Sung by . . . . Lani Hall
Title Song Music by . . . . Michel Legrand
Title Song Lyrics by . . . Alan and Marilyn Bergman
Music by . . . . Michel Legrand
Second-Unit Director . . . . Michael Moore
Underwater Sequence Directed by . Ricou Browning
First Assistant Director . . . . David Tomblin
Consultant to the Producer . . . .
　　　　　　　　　　　　Talia Shire Schwartzman
Costume Designer . . . . Charles Knode
Casting Maggie Cartier, Mike Fenton, Jane Feinberg
Optical Effects by . . . . Apogee Inc., Los Angeles
Supervisor of Special Visual Effects . . David Dryer
Production Controller . . . . Jack Smith
Production Supervisor . . . . Alex De Grunwald
Special Effects Supervisor . . . . Ian Wingrove
Supervising Art Director . . . . Les Dilley

Art Directors . . . . Michael White, Roy Stannard
Set Decorator . . . . Peter Howitt
Property Master . . . . Peter Hancock
Construction Manager . . . . Bill Welch
Second-Unit Director of Photography . . . .
　　　　　　　　　　　　　　　Paul Beeson, B.S.C.
Aerial Photography . . . . Peter Allwork, B.S.C.
Production Manager (U.K.) . . . . John Davis
Production Coordinator . . . . Gladys Pearce
Script Supervisor . . . . Pamela Mann Francis
Production Accountant . . . . Paul Tucker
Film Editor . . . . Ian Crafford
Additional Editing . . . . . . Peter Musgrave, G.B.F.E.
Dubbing Editors . . Norman Wanstall, John Poyner,
　　　　　　　　　　　　　　　　　　　G.B.F.E.
Music Editor . . . . Valerie Lesser
Assistant Directors . . . David Tomblin, Roy Button,
　　　　　　　Carlos Gil, Greg Dark, Steve Harding
Production Manager (Bahamas) . . . . Malcolm Christopher
Production Manager (France) . . . . Jean-Pierre Avice
Production Managers (Spain) . . . Arnold Ross, Apolinar Rabinal
Camera Operators . . . . Chic Waterson,
　　　　　　　　　　　　　　　　　　　Wally Byatt
Focus Pullers . . . . Robin Vidgeon, Keith Blake
Assistant Art Directors . Don Dossett, George Djurkovic, John Wood
Property Buyer . . . . John Lanzer
Chief Makeup Artist . . . . Robin Grantham
Makeup and Hairdressing for Mr. Connery . . . Ilona Herman
Chief Hairdresser . . . . Stephanie Kaye
Hairdresser . . . . Sue Love
Wardrobe Supervisor . . . . Ron Beck
Assistant to Mr. Kershner . . . . Anne Marie Stein
Associate to Mr. Schwartzman . . . . . Julian Plowden
Assistants to Mr. Schwartzman . Yvonne McGeeney,
　　　　　　　　　　　　　　　　　Anne Schwebel
Merchandising Coordinator . . . . Jeff Freedman
Production Assistants . . . .
　　　Linda Rabin, Jill Bender, Beatrice Geffriaud
Second-Unit Manager . . . . Evzen Kolar
Location Consultant . . . . Anne Glanfield
Special Effects Technicians . . . . David Beavis, David
　　Harris, David Watkins, Trevor Neighbor, Roger
　　　　　　　　　　　　Nicholls, Branwell McClory
Electronics Graphics Supervisor . . . Rob Dickenson
Assistant Electronics Graphics . . . . Ira Coleman
Stunt Coordinators . . Glen Randall, Vic Armstrong
Motorcycle Stunts by . . . . Mike Runyard
Stunts . . . . Roy Alon, Dickie Beer,

Marc Boyle, Edward Garcia, Frank Henson, Billy Horrigan, Wendy Leech

Underwater Consultant . . . . Scott Carpenter

Director of Photography for Underwater Sequences . . . . Bob Steadman

Underwater Camera Operators . . . . . . Jordan Klein, Mike Ferris

Underwater Gaffer . . . . Montie Taylor

Divemaster . . . . Gavin McKinney

Boatmaster . . . . "Moby" Griffin

Sound Recorder . . . . Simon Kaye

Sound Mixer . . . . David Allen

Sound Boom . . . . David Sutton

Sound Maintenance . . . . Taffy Haines

Tango à la Bond under the watchful eye of a choreographer. (Taliafilm)

Assistant Film Editors .... Wally Nelson, Johnathan Nuth, Nicholas Moore, Bill Barringer, Annie Negro
Dubbing Mixer .... Bill Rowe
Dubbing Assistant .... Ray Merrin
Music Mixer .... Keith Grant
Unit Publicist .... Sara Keene
Stills Photographer .... Bob Penn
Standby Crew ..... Robert Betts, George Gibbons, Stephen Hargreaves, Allan Williams, Joe Dipple, Robert Hill
Camera Grip .... Brian Osborne
Electrical Gaffer .... Martin Evans
Best Boy .... Ray Meehan
Optical Special Effects Production Supervisor .... Robert R. Shepherd
Optical Supervisor .... Roger Dorney
Chief Optical Camera Operator .... Douglas Smith
Technical Adviser .... Guy Alimo
Production Company .... Taliafilm
Distribution Company.......... Warner Brothers

NEVER SAY NEVER AGAIN COMPETITION

Competitive films in release when *Never Say Never Again* opened in Los Angeles on October 7, 1983:

Romantic Comedy

Rumble Fish

The Ballad of Gregorio Cortez

Brainstorm

Stuck on You!

Revenge of the Ninja

Educating Rita

The Big Chill

Eddie and the Cruisers

The Lonely Lady

Rear Window (reissue)

Cross Creek

NEW ORLEANS Louisiana city and gateway to the bayou country that is an important location in *Live and Let Die.* The second of three British agents is murdered here in the film's teaser.

Standing across the street from the Fillet of Soul nightclub, a suspected drug hangout in New Orlean's French Quarter, British agent Hamilton observes a funeral procession moving slowly down the street to a solemn beat. Little does he know that it's his own funeral that he's watching. After a seemingly innocuous man stabs him in the back, the funeral procession stops, places the coffin over his body, and removes it to a much livelier beat.

The same exact assassination method is repeated later in the film when the unfortunate CIA man, Harold Strutter (LON SATTON), is also murdered in front of the Fillet of Soul.

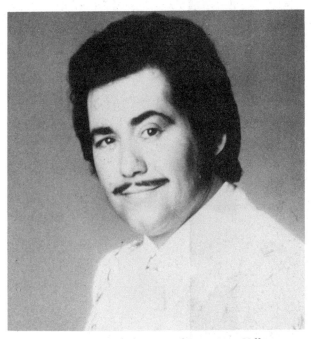
Wayne Newton joined the cast of *Licence to Kill* as a sleazy preacher, Professor Joe Butcher. (Las Vegas Hilton)

NEWTON, WAYNE (Roanoke, Virginia, April 3, 1942–) Las Vegas superstar singer, entertainer, and recording artist who portrayed lecherous televangelist Joe Butcher in *Licence to Kill.* In what could have been a distraction, Newton is well cast as the "sincere" religious peddler who is actually a front for Franz Sanchez's (ROBERT DAVI) cocaine empire. *Note: Licence to Kill* was incorrectly identified in the film's press kit as Newton's motion picture debut. *See* BUTCHER, JOE.

NEW YORK CITY Mafioso Mr. Solo's (MARTIN BENSON) destination when he leaves the Kentucky stud farm in *Goldfinger.* Unfortunately, he never makes it there.

NEW YORK CITY AND MOSCOW Twin targets of megalomaniac Karl Stromberg's (CURT JURGENS) planned nuclear attack in

The Spy Who Loved Me. His vehicles of destruction are two captured British and Russian nuclear submarines that have been redesignated Stromberg No. 1 and Stromberg No. 2.

N5VH Identification number on the Apollo Airways turboprop, in the *Moonraker* teaser, from which 007 (ROGER MOORE) has his parachuting adventure with Jaws (RICHARD KIEL).

N54743 Identification number on the light Cessna monoplane flown by drug runner Franz Sanchez (ROBERT DAVI) in the *Licence to Kill* teaser. Chased by James Bond (TIMOTHY DALTON), who catches up to him in a Coast Guard jet helicopter, Sanchez's plane is literally hooked by 007, who fastens the chopper's winch to the aircraft's tail section. With the plane in tow, Bond returns the drug runner to DEA authorities in the Bahamas.

NICE City on the French Riviera that is the destination of Largo's (KLAUS MARIA BRANDAUER) yacht, the *Flying Saucer*, when it leaves Nassau in *Never Say Never Again.*

NICK NACK Scaramanga's (CHRISTOPHER LEE) diminutive servant, portrayed by French actor and "Fantasy Island" veteran Herve Villechaize, in *The Man with the Golden Gun.* Nick Nack perfectly proves that you don't have to be seven feet tall to give James Bond (ROGER MOORE) big trouble.

Villechaize was actually a throwback to the mysterious character actors of the 1930s—Sydney Greenstreet, Peter Lorre, John Carradine—who brought their distinctive personalities to their roles. In *Golden Gun,* Nick Nack is fascinating to watch in his tiny waiter's outfit, delivering tabasco sauce to the sunbathing Scaramanga and Andrea (MAUD ADAMS), or munching peanuts behind Bond at the kickboxing match.

He's also quick on his feet as he plays with the controls that operate the "fun house" on Scaramanga Island or as he is chased around Bond's stateroom on the Chinese junk. Eventually, the pesky little villain is netted and strung up in the junk's rigging, proving another adage, that what goes up—even if it doesn't go up very far— must eventually come down.

NICOLE (aka Agent 326) James Bond's (SEAN CONNERY) Secret Service contact in the South of France in *Never Say Never Again,* portrayed by actress Saskia Cohen Tanugi. She's later murdered by S.P.E.C.T.R.E. assassin Fatima Blush (BARBARA CARRERA), who strangles Nicole and stuffs her in Bond's water bed.

NIMMO, DEREK (1931–   ) British comedian and dialect specialist, primarily on television, who portrayed Hadley, M's (JOHN HUSTON) son in *Casino Royale.* See HADLEY.

NIMPHALIS POLYCLURIS One of M's (BERNARD LEE) mounted butterflies that Bond (GEORGE LAZENBY) correctly identifies in *On Her Majesty's Secret Service.*

NINA British pop singer whose tune "Do You Know How Christmas Trees Are Grown?" is featured in the sixth James Bond film, *On Her Majesty's Secret Service.*

9:40 P.M. WEDNESDAY, AUGUST 3 Time set aside in Aziz Fekkesh's (NADIM SAWALHA) pocket calendar to meet Max Kalba (VERNON DOBTCHEFF) at the Mojaba Club, in *The Spy Who Loved Me.* Bond (ROGER MOORE) finds the clue on the body of Fekkesh, who is a victim of Jaws's (RICHARD KIEL) handiwork. Bond makes the appointment himself, only to discover that KGB Major Anya Amasova (BARBARA BACH) is already bidding on the stolen nuclear-submarine tracking system.

9:41 A.M. The time at which Max Zorin (CHRISTOPHER WALKEN) plans to initiate Project Main Strike by blowing up a mountain of explosives above northern California's San Andreas Fault, in *A View to a Kill.* With the Hayward Fault already unstable from the seawater being pumped into it by Zorin's oil wells, the explosion will destroy a key geologic lock in the region, tripping both faults at once and burying Silicon Valley under a huge lake. See PROJECT MAIN STRIKE.

945 SET The enabling code for space shuttle Moonraker No. 5's nose-mounted laser cannon.

Ford's 1971 Mustang Fastback seen here with the custom hood was featured in *Diamonds Are Forever*. (Ford Motor Company)

9'6" The clearance on a low-level bridge navigated by James Bond's (ROGER MOORE) double-decker bus in *Live and Let Die*. Agent 007 clears the bridge, but the collision sheers off the bus's top level, which is left on the roadway. A trailing police car collides with it and ends up in a swamp. In actuality, the bus was driven by London bus instructor Maurice Patchett. *See* PATCHETT, MAURICE.

936 YEARS The amount of time that South American drug lord Franz Sanchez (ROBERT DAVI) will serve if he's convicted in the U.S courts in *Licence to Kill*. The question of his conviction is academic, since he's sprung from protective custody by traitorous DEA agent Killifer (EVERETT MCGILL).

1985 JAMES BOND FILM VIEWER POLL Conducted by studio researchers in 1985, before the release of *A View to a Kill*, it was announced that in the United States, 100 percent of filmgoers polled had seen at least one James Bond movie; 88 percent had seen *Goldfinger*—the most well-attended Bond film; and approximately 1.5 billion people worldwide had seen a Bond movie.

1940 Year in which the gold bar, featured as the prize in *Goldfinger*'s golf match, was smelted at the Weisling Foundry in Essen, Germany. It was part of a smelt of 600 ingots that were lost in 1944 near the end of World War II, but are now rumored to be lying at the bottom of Lake Topliz in Austria's Salz-Kammergut region.

1971 MUSTANG A red hardtop, with California license plate CA52H6, driven by James Bond (SEAN CONNERY) and Tiffany Case (JILL ST. JOHN) in *Diamonds Are Forever*. The car figures in the hilarious chase down Fremont Street between Bond and the Las Vegas Police Department, ending up in a parking lot behind the Mint Hotel (actually, the back lot at Universal Pictures).

In the final moment, Bond appears to be stopped at a narrow alley, but he manages to prop the car up on two wheels and navigate the alleyway, eluding the police. If you look carefully at this sequence, you'll notice a blooper. Bond drives into the narrow alley on his right tires (with the left side of the car up in the air), but he exits on his left tires (with the right side of the car up in the air).

1916 The last time Mata Hari visited her dance and spy school in West Berlin, as revealed by Polo (RONNIE CORBETT) to Mata Bond (JOANNA PETTET) in *Casino Royale*. She was executed by a French firing squad soon after. Mata Bond is her illegitimate daughter, a product of her liaison with Sir James Bond (DAVID NIVEN).

1965 ROLEX OYSTER PERPETUAL
Evelyn Tremble's (PETER SELLERS) wristwatch in *Casino Royale*. It's equipped with a date indicator and log table around the outer band. Since Tremble is assuming the name James Bond and a dangerous assignment in Monte Carlo, he's given a new watch—a two-way TV communicator that operates on Channel 6. This mechanism is based on the watch of an American comic-strip character, presumably Dick Tracy.

1964 LINCOLN CONTINENTAL Driven by Oddjob (HAROLD SAKATA) in *Goldfinger*, this is the car that is supposed to take Mafia kingpin Mr. Solo (MARTIN BENSON) and his million dollars in gold to the airport. Instead, Solo is killed, and the car is completely crushed at an auto-wrecking yard. If you look closely as the car is being lifted into the auto compactor, you'll notice that the engine is missing.

1964 ½ FORD MUSTANG CONVERTIBLE Tilly Masterson's (TANIA MALLET) cream-colored sports car with red upholstery in *Goldfinger*. After her failed assassination attempt against Goldfinger (GERT FROBE) on a Swiss mountain highway, Tilly is chased by 007 (SEAN CONNERY), who shreds her tires with his trick Aston Martin. The Mustang, the first of its model line to be featured in a major motion picture, was also the first of many Ford Motor cars to appear in the James Bond series.

1965 FORD THUNDERBIRD The car in which Emilio Largo (ADOLFO CELI) arrives at S.P.E.C.T.R.E. headquarters in Paris, in *Thunderball*. He parks illegally in front of the building and almost gets a parking ticket, until the police officer recognizes him.

1965 LINCOLN CONTINENTAL LIMOUSINE Vehicle that escorts the widow (ROSE ALBA) of "deceased" S.P.E.C.T.R.E. agent Jacques Boitier (BOB SIMMONS) to her chateau, in the *Thunderball* teaser.

1965 MUSTANG Fiona Volpe's (LUCIANA PALUZZI) sports car in *Thunderball*. It's a

A 1965 Lincoln Continental. The limousine version of this model was featured in the *Thunderball* teaser. A convertible version is later driven to Palmyra by James Bond (SEAN CONNERY). The 1964 model, which was essentially the same car, was crushed in *Goldfinger*. (Ford Motor Company)

The first Mustang ever featured in a movie debuted in *Goldfinger* in 1964. It was Tilly Masterson's car. Fiona Volpe drove a 1965 Mustang, essentially the same car, in Nassau in *Thunderball*. (Ford Motor Company)

light blue model with a white top. When 007 (SEAN CONNERY) leaves the water after his underwater escapade underneath the docked *Disco Volante*, he hitches a ride with Volpe in this car.

1965 SILVER LINCOLN CONTINENTAL The luxury car, with a white landau top, that James Bond (SEAN CONNERY) drives to Emilio Largo's (ADOLFO CELI) Palmyra estate, in *Thunderball*.

1969 MERCURY COUGAR The car of Contessa Teresa "Tracy" de Vicenzo (DIANA RIGG), daughter of Marc Ange Draco (GABRIELE FERZETTI), head of the Union Corse crime syndicate, in *On Her Majesty's Secret Service*. It's a red convertible, license plate 2318 TT7S.

1934 MOUTON ROTHSCHILD A wine that 007 (ROGER MOORE) remarks is very similar to the one offered to him by Scaramanga (CHRISTOPHER LEE) in *The Man with the Golden Gun*.

98.4 DEGREES The correct temperature for serving saki, as revealed in *You Only Live Twice*.

95 Bond's (SEAN CONNERY) geiger reading when he enters Dr. No's (JOSEPH WISEMAN) decontamination center on Crab Key, in *Dr. No*.

90 SECONDS The amount of time left before the A-bomb explodes in *Octopussy*—computed from the time Bond approaches the base commander (BRUCE BOA) in the circus tent. Note that there's a technical blooper: if you apply the stopwatch, it's closer to 70 seconds.

NINGPO A Japanese freighter, owned by Osato Chemical and bound from Shanghai to Kobe, Japan, a microphoto of which is stolen by James Bond (SEAN CONNERY) out of Osato's (TERU SHIMADA) Tokyo safe in *You Only Live Twice*. By enlarging the photo, Bond and Tanaka (TETSURO TAMBA) discover Ama pearl divers in the background, which establishes the position of the freighter near their island.

Later at the Kobe docks, Bond finds the *Ningpo* loading liquid oxygen (LOX) contain-

ers—a rocket propellant that could be fueling the secret S.P.E.C.T.R.E. *Intruder* spaceship.

NINJAS Stealthy Japanese warriors featured in *You Only Live Twice*. Skilled in the practice of concealment and surprise, the commandolike Ninjas are trained by Tiger Tanaka (TETSURO TAMBA) at the famous Himeji Castle, and they participate in the climactic attack on S.P.E.C.T.R.E.'s secret rocket base.

Like ants, 100 of their number swarm into the crater of the extinct volcano, avoid the machine-gun-fire of Blofeld's (DONALD PLEASENCE) automated guns, tie their ropes to the roof superstructure, and glide to the concrete floor like mountaineers. Led by Bond (SEAN CONNERY) and Tiger, they eventually overwhelm the S.P.E.C.T.R.E. garrison and destroy the base.

To film this sequence inside production designer Ken Adam's enormous rocket-base set, practically every stuntman in England was summoned to Pinewood Studios and trained under the guidance of Bob Simmons and George Leech. Rappeling from the roof of the volcano base was a particularly dangerous stunt. Several of the men were required to ride down with one hand and fire a submachine gun with the other. Their progress on the rope would be controlled by a mountaineering device, actually a piece of rubber hose that was squeezed to break their fall. Once a stuntman hit the ground, he had to move off quickly, because a comrade was coming down right behind him.

You Only Live Twice, recalled Leech, "was one of the most difficult experiences of my life. There were too many headaches, especially in getting more than 100 stuntmen ready for the battle sequences.

"The worst thing was having to tell certain men that they weren't needed for the rope sequences. When the master shots were completed, we needed only 40 men, and neither Bob nor I wanted to tell anyone to go home. Needless to say, the rejected ones weren't too happy, especially when the pay on the close-up stunts was very good.

"For the battle sequences, we used a number of new techniques to give the action a spectacular feel. About 12 of our best men were used on the trampoline. It was an interesting form of trampolining. It wasn't your expertise in tumbles and perfect somersaults that mattered. You just had to look as if you were being blown up—no pointed toes or classic positions. You went off screaming, with your arms and legs flailing every which way. You landed into a made-up bed about 20 feet away. The special effects team timed their real explosions to your jump."

NIPPON RELAXATION SPA Public bathhouse where Bond (ROGER MOORE) and KGB agent Pola Ivanova (FIONA FULLERTON) renew their acquaintance in *A View to a Kill*. Recovering from their underwater surveillance of Max Zorin's (CHRISTOPHER WALKEN) oil-pumping facility in San Francisco Bay, Bond and Ivanova relax in a Jacuzzi, serenaded by a Tchaikovsky cassette provided by 007. *See* IVANOVA, POLA.

NIVEN, DAVID (Kirriemuir, Scotland, March 1, 1909–1983) (real name, James David Graham Niven) Urbane, quintessential British actor who was perfectly cast as retired Sir James

Likable David Niven portrayed Sir James Bond in the *Casino Royale* spoof in 1967. Niven was better in the *Pink Panther*.

Bond in the *Casino Royale* spoof. Surrounded by ineptitude and forced by international events to accept one final mission, Sir James is a throwback to the hell-for-leather adventure heroes of World War I and the 1920s—roughly paralleling Niven's own career as a top studio actor in countless films of sophisticated wit and derringdo. *See* BOND, SIR JAMES.

NOAH, DR. Supervillain of *Casino Royale*, born on April Fools' Day, and portrayed by Woody Allen. In reality, he's Sir James Bond's (DAVID NIVEN) bumbling nephew Jimmy Bond—the son of Bond's sister, Nelly—a British agent who was originally assigned to operations in the Caribbean, where he was immediately captured and nearly put to death.

As Dr. Noah, head of a powerful criminal organization made up entirely of beautiful women, he plans a twofold assault on mankind. First, he plans to assassinate every prominent world leader. His army of perfectly conceived robot duplicates will then take over their positions and report directly to him. Second, he's going to unleash the deadly "Dr. Noah's bacillus"—a germ-warfare weapon that makes all women beautiful and destroys all men over 4'6".

Having failed to assassinate Sir James Bond on a number of occasions, Dr. Noah kidnaps his daughter, Mata Bond (JOANNA PETTET), with a huge flying saucer that takes her to his secret base near Monte Carlo. Meanwhile, Noah is busy torturing one of the female James Bonds (DALIAH LAVI). Boasting of his many weapons, he reveals to her an atomic bomb disguised in tablet form, which itself contains 400 tiny time pills. As each one explodes, it sets off a chain reaction that eventually leads to a nuclear explosion.

Feigning desire for and fascination with Noah, the lady James Bond accompanies him to his robot command center, where she manages to drop the A-bomb tablet in his champagne. Noah drinks heartily, swallowing his own bomb. Four hundred burps later, he explodes, taking virtually every member of the *Casino Royale* cast with him. *See* ALLEN, WOODY.

NO, DR. James Bond's (SEAN CONNERY) archenemy, portrayed by Joseph Wiseman, in the first James Bond movie. The son of a German missionary and a Chinese girl from a good family, No joined the Tong Society—a Chinese version of the Mafia—and escaped to America with $10 million of their money. Turned away by both the U.S. and Red Chinese scientific communities, No became a leading agent for S.P.E.C.T.R.E, the Special Executor for Counter-intelligence, Terrorism, Revenge, and Extortion.

Fleming based Dr. No on the title character in author Sax Rohmer's *Fu Manchu* stories, as well as on the screen characters portrayed by British character actor Christopher Lee, who was actually Ian Fleming's cousin. When both Lee and Fleming's friend Noel Coward turned down the role, it went to Wiseman.

In the book, Fleming described Dr. No as an immense worm, clutching objects with his hooks and glaring at people with jet-black eyes. The character was so grotesque that screenwriters Richard Maibaum and Wolf Mankowitz, in their first-draft script, actually gave the name Dr. No to a monkey who sat on the villain's shoulder.

This bit of nonsense enraged producer Cubby Broccoli, who was determined to make a serious spy story. Mankowitz would later leave the project, and Maibaum would finish the script, toning down Fleming's Dr. No.

Helped by the makeup department and some exquisite Nehru jackets, Wiseman was also equipped with a pair of plastic hands, the result of what he calls an unfortunate accident and a deformity that proves to be his undoing in the final battle with Bond above the reactor pool.

NO EARLOBES A physical characteristic of the de Bleuchamp, a royal family that Ernst Stavro Blofeld (TELLY SAVALAS) lays claim to in *On Her Majesty's Secret Service*.

When Bond (GEORGE LAZENBY), masquerading as heraldry expert Sir Hilary Bray, arrives at Piz Gloria—Blofeld's Swiss mountain allergy clinic—the S.P.E.C.T.R.E. chief immediately shows off the fact that he too does not have earlobes. Bond notes the fact, but he insists that Blofeld accompany him on a trip to the de Bleuchamp ancestral home in Augsburg. Only there will he be able to draw on the final evidence needed to confirm Blofeld's de Bleuchamp claim.

"NO JOY ON EITHER" Phrase uttered by a British Secret Service communications operative, in *Dr. No*, when he informs his superior that he is not receiving transmissions from Jamaica on either the main or the emergency frequencies. "Joy" referred to radio messages during the early 1960s.

NOLAN, MARGARET British ingenue who portrayed Dink, the masseuse, in *Goldfinger*. Although her scene was brief, it did not prevent her from appearing topless in an issue of *Playboy* magazine that followed the release of the film.

NORRIS, KEN Actor and Roger Moore look-alike who portrayed mustachioed South American army officer Colonel Luis Toro in the *Octopussy* teaser. *See* TORO, COLONEL LUIS.

NORTH BY NORTHWEST (MGM, 1959) Alfred Hitchcock's classic suspense film, which inspired the helicopter chase in Richard Maibaum's *From Russia with Love* script. In the Hitchcock film, Cary Grant, portraying Manhattan advertising executive Roger Thornhill, is lured into the deserted flatlands of Prairie Stop, Illinois, by enemy agents who chase him in a crop-dusting plane equipped with a machine gun. The cat-and-mouse game ends when the crop duster slams into a tanker truck and explodes.

In screenwriter Maibaum's sequence in *From Russia with Love*, which was not in the original Ian Fleming novel, the crop-duster plane in *North by Northwest* becomes a deadly S.P.E.C.T.R.E. helicopter carrying two black-suited, grenade-equipped killers. After they straddle Bond's Chevrolet stake-truck with grenades, 007 (SEAN CONNERY) takes off on foot across the Yugoslavian foothills.

In a manner similar to the Hitchcock film, the chopper plays with Bond before the villains prepare to do him in with a hand grenade. Fortunately, 007 has his folding sniper's rifle with him, and he manages to shoot one of the killers, who promptly drops the grenade and blows the chopper to pieces.

The classic chase scene from *North by Northwest* that inspired screenwriter Richard Maibaum's helicopter chase in *From Russia with Love*.

Excellent special effects work by John Stears enhances this scene, as does Bond's closing throwaway line, "I'd say one of their aircraft was missing." Like the crop-dusting chase in *North by Northwest*, this helicopter cat-and-mouse chase sequence became a favorite scene in the film and one that was prominently displayed in all of the film's coming-attractions.

NORTHOLT British airfield outside London that simulated Blue Grass Field, Kentucky, in *Goldfinger*. Formerly London's main airport, the field was also used in *Octopussy* to simulate a South American air force base.

NORTH, VIRGINIA Dark-haired actress who portrayed Olympe, Marc Ange Draco's girl, in *On Her Majesty's Secret Service*.

"NOT IMMINENT" The code phrase that stops a possible American nuclear attack against Russia in *You Only Live Twice*. Bond's (SEAN CONNERY) success in triggering the self-destruct mechanism on the S.P.E.C.T.R.E. *Intruder* rocket, five seconds before it envelops a U.S. *Jupiter* spacecraft, preserves the human race from a nuclear nightmare.

NOVEMBER 6, 1973 The first day of shooting on *The Man with the Golden Gun*. Director Guy Hamilton and a skeleton crew motored out to Hong Kong Harbor to film the wreck of the *Queen Elizabeth I* ocean liner. For this early sequence, actor Mike Lovatt doubled Roger Moore, who wasn't due in Hong Kong until the following April.

N77029 Aircraft identification number on a training plane commandeered by James Bond (ROGER MOORE) in *Live and Let Die*. It belongs to the Bleeker Flying School. Chased by Mr. Big's (YAPHET KOTTO) thugs, Bond steals the plane along with its terrified student copilot, Mrs. Bell (RUTH KEMPF).

N6964N Identification number on the drug-running Cessna 185 seaplane that is commandeered by James Bond (TIMOTHY DALTON) in *Licence to Kill*. Escaping underwater from the *Wavekrest* research vessel after he's sabotaged a major drug deal, Bond shoots a harpoon into the skid of the seaplane, and as the plane takes off, 007 suddenly becomes a water skier.

Gradually, he makes his way aboard the plane; wins a fight with the pilot, who's tossed out; and takes over. In addition to commandeering an escape vehicle, he's now saddled with $5 million in drug loot—a cache he will soon put to good use in Isthmus City.

NUMBER FIVE PARKING LOT Where Bond's (SEAN CONNERY) Sunbeam sports car is parked in the Kingston hotel in *Dr. No*.

NUMBER 48 Lot number of the green Imperial gold egg auctioned at Sotheby's gallery in London, in *Octopussy*. Known as the Coronation

Egg and designed by Carl Fabergé in 1897, the egg is enameled in translucent green, enclosed by a gold laurel-leaf trellis, and set with blue sapphires and four-petaled gold flowers with diamonds. *See* FABERGE EGGS.

NUMBER ONE The code number for S.P.E.C.T.R.E. Chief Ernst Stavro Blofeld in *From Russia with Love* and *Thunderball*. It's also the S.P.E.C.T.R.E. code number for Maximil-lian Largo (KLAUS MARIA BRANDAUER) in *Never Say Never Again*.

NUMBER ELEVEN Helga Brandt's (KARIN DOR) S.P.E.C.T.R.E. code number in *You Only Live Twice*.

NUMBER TWELVE Fatima Blush's (BARBARA CARRERA) S.P.E.C.T.R.E. code number in *Never Say Never Again*.

O

OBEAH (aka "the second sight") A supernatural power that Solitaire (JANE SEYMOUR) possesses in *Live and Let Die*. With her tarot cards, it allows her to predict the future for her boss, Dr. Kananga (YAPHET KOTTO), a sinister island-diplomat-turned-drug-smuggler.

OCEAN LINER The method by which James Bond (SEAN CONNERY) and Tiffany Case (JILL ST. JOHN) return to Europe in *Diamonds Are Forever*. Thankful billionaire Willard Whyte (JIMMY DEAN) tells 007 that if he's having a good time, just let Whyte know, and he'll have the captain sail the ship around in circles. Unfortunately, appearing in a porthole are S.P.E.C.T.R.E. assassins Mr. Wint (BRUCE GLOVER) and Mr. Kidd (PUTTER SMITH), who are ready to liquidate 007 once and for all.

For the short sequence in which the assassins appear in that porthole, the *Diamonds* crew actually journeyed to the English seacoast to film aboard a real luxury liner. The actual interiors of the ship were filmed on a soundstage at Pinewood Studios, where designer Ken Adam created Bond's luxurious shipboard suite.

OCTOBER 6, 1962 The night of the *Dr. No* world premiere at the Pavilion Theater in London.

OCTOBER 21, 1968 The first day of shooting on *On Her Majesty's Secret Service*. The location was the mountaintop Piz Gloria restaurant in Switzerland, where filming began at 7:45 A.M. with new 007 George Lazenby and 10 gorgeous women.

OCTOPUSSY (United Artists, 1983) ★ ★ ★ ½ The 13th James Bond film pro-

duced by Albert R. Broccoli. U.S. release date: June 10, 1983. U.S. film rentals: $34 million. Running time: 130 minutes.

Building on the Bond revival engineered by *The Spy Who Loved Me*, *Octopussy* was financially the most successful film in the Bond series—thus far, of course. Thanks to a risqué title, another inspired marketing campaign, and an interesting blend of *Goldfinger* glitz and *From Russia with Love* intrigue, it's an excellent entry that keeps up the momentum despite an excessive length.

This time, Bond finds himself in the midst of a cold-war plot by a fanatical Russian general who plans to explode a nuclear bomb on a U.S. air force base in West Germany and force unilateral disarmament in Western Europe. Aiding and abetting his scheme is a female smuggler named Octopussy and her sleazy partner, exiled Afghan Prince Kamal Khan.

Comfortably directed by John Glen, the film is filled with memorable set pieces that keep the plot moving, such as the mini-jet teaser, 009's murder in East Germany, and Bond's attempts to disarm the A-bomb while dressed as a circus clown. Like *For Your Eyes Only*, the film is filled with mysterious characters and henchmen, including Kamal Khan's deadly twin assassins, portrayed effectively by the Meyer twins, and Kabir Bedi's awesome Gobinda.

Low points: Maud Adams's Octopussy serves little purpose in the plot and takes a backseat to Kamal Khan's treachery. Kristina Wayborn's Magda actually steals the film out from under her. Although the sequences in India are suitably exotic, the chase through the streets of Udaipur is too silly and features another double-taking animal—this time, a camel. But once the film gets to Germany, it takes off and builds incredible drama inside the circus tent, where Bond disarms the bomb.

Many fans were concerned when prerelease publicity stills were published, revealing Bond in a clown getup. As it turns out, the disguise is perfect for Bond as he penetrates the American air force base in time to rescue thousands from a nuclear nightmare.

High points: Steven Berkoff's strutting General Orlov, the John Barry score, and Rita Coolidge's title song.

Maud Adams and Roger Moore take a stroll during the making of *Octopussy* in 1982. (Rex Features Ltd./RDR Productions)

The Girls of *Octopussy. From left, back row,* Suzanne Jerome, Carolyn Seaward, Mary Stavin, Camella Thomas, Tina Robinson, Carole Ashby, and Janine Andrews. *Front row, from left,* Lynda Knight, Joni Flynn, Safira, Alison Worth, and Cherry Gillespie. (AP/Wide World Photos)

OCTOPUSSY CAST

James Bond	Roger Moore
Octopussy	Maud Adams
Kamal Khan	Louis Jourdan
Magda	Kristina Wayborn
Gobinda	Kabir Bedi
General Orlov	Steven Berkoff
Mischka (Twin No. 1)	David Meyer
Grischka (Twin No. 2)	Anthony Meyer
Q	Desmond Llewelyn
M	Robert Brown
Miss Moneypenny	Lois Maxwell
Penelope Smallbone	Michaela Clavell
General Gogol	Walter Gotell
Vijay	Vijay Amritraj
Sadruddin	Albert Moses
Minister of Defense	Geoffrey Keen
Jim Fanning	Douglas Wilmer
009	Andy Bradford
Auctioneer	Philip Voss
U.S. General	Bruce Boa
U.S. Aide	Richard Parmentier
Soviet Chairman	Paul Hardwick
Gwendoline	Suzanne Jerome
Midge	Cherry Gillespie
Kamp	Dermot Crowley
Lenkin	Peter Porteous
Rublevitch	Eva Rueber-Staier
Smithers	Jeremy Bullock
Bianca	Tina Hudson
Thug with Yo-Yo	William Derrick
Major Clive	Stuart Saunders
British Ambassador	Patrick Barr
Borchoi	Gabor Vernon
Karl	Hugo Bower
Colonel Toro	Ken Norris
Mufti	Tony Arjuna
Bubi	Gertan Klauber
Schatzl	Brenda Cowling
Gas-Pump Attendant	David Grahame

South American V.I.P. . . . . .Brian Coburn
South American Officer . . . . .Michael Halpie
Circus Ringmaster . . . . .Roberto Germains
Francisco the Fearless . . . . .Richard Graydon
Circus Performers . . . . .The Hassani Troupe,
   The Flying Cherokees, Carol and Josef Richter,
   Vera and Shirley Fossett, Barrie Winship
Octopussy Girls . . . . .Mary Stavin,
   Carolyn Seaward, Carole Ashby, Cheryl Anne,
   Jani-Z, Julie Martin, Joni Flynn, Julie Barth, Kathy
   Davies, Helene Hunt, Gillian De Terville, Safira
   Afzal, Louise King, Tina Robinson, Alison
   Worth, Janine Andrews, Lynda Knight
Gymnasts . . . . .Suzanne Dando (supervisor), Teresa
   Craddock, Kirsten Harrison, Christine Cullers,
   Lisa Jackman, Jane Aldridge, Christine Gibson,
   Sumisha Hassani Tracy Llewellyn, Ruth Flynn
Thugs . . . . .Ravinder Singh Reyett,
   Gurdial Sira, Michael Moor, Sven Surtees, Peter
   Edmund, Ray Charles, Talib Johnny

OCTOPUSSY CREW

Producer .Albert R. Broccoli
Executive Producer . . . . .Michael G. Wilson
Director . . . . .John Glen
Screenplay by . .George MacDonald Fraser, Richard
   Maibaum, Michael G. Wilson
Director of Photography . . . . .Alan Hume
Camera Operator . . . . .Alec Mills
Production Designer . . . . .Peter Lamont
Music by . . . . .John Barry
"All Time High" Sung by . . . . .Rita Coolidge
Lyrics by . . . . .Tim Rice
Associate Producer . . . . .Tom Pevsner
Editor . . . . .John Grover
Main Title Designer . . . . .Maurice Binder
Second-Unit Director and Cameraman . . . . .Arthur
   Wooster
Vehicle Stunt Coordinator . . . . .Remy Julienne
Special Effects Supervisor . . . . .John Richardson
Indian Production Adviser . . . . . .Shama Habibullah
Location Managers . . .Peter Bennett, Rashid Abassi
Second-Unit Assistant Director . . . . .Gerry Gavigan
Additional Assistant Directors . . . . . . .Baba Shaikh,
   Don French
Second-Unit Continuity . . . . .Doreen Soan,
   Penny Daniels
Second Assistant Directors .Terry Madden, Michael
   Zimbrich, Andrew Warren, Tony Broccoli
Location Accountants . .Jane Meagher, Marge Row-
   land, Ursula Schlieper
Production Assistants . . . . .Iris Rose, Joyce Turner,
   Sheila Barnes, May Capsakis, Mohini Banerji
Executive Assistant . . . . .Barbara Broccoli

Production Secretaries .Mary Stellar, Joanna Brown,
   Eleanor Chaudhuri
U.S. Casting .Jane Jenkins
Model Effects Supervisor . . . . .Brian Smithies
Model Photography . . . . .Leslie Dear
Additional Photography .Jimmy Devis, Bob Collins
Second-Unit Camera Operators . .Malcolm Vinson,
   David Nowell, Jack Lowin
Front Projection . . . . .Charles Staffell
Costume Supervisor . . . . .Tiny Nicholls
Costumes Made by . . . . .Bermans and Nathans
Additional Art Directors . . . .Michael Lamont, Ken
   Court, Ram Yedekar, Jan Schlubach
Set Dresser (India) . . . . .Crispian Sallis
Assistant Art Directors . . . . .Ernie Archer,
   Jim Morahan, Fred Hole
Production Buyer . . . . .Ron Quelch
Scenic Artists . . . . .Ernest Smith, Jacqueline Stears
Boom Operator . . . . .Ken Nightingall
Makeup . . . . .Peter-Robb King, Eric Allwright
Hairdresser . . . . .Jeanette Freeman
Second-Unit Effects Supervisor . . . . .John Evans
Unit Publicist . . . . .Geoff Freeman
Stills . . . . .Frank Connor, George Whitear
Construction Manager . . . . .Michael Redding
Electrical Supervisor . . . . .John Tythe
Camera Grips . . . . . .Chunky Huse, Colin Manning
Property Master . . . . .David Jordan
Stunt Engineers . . . . . . .Dave Bickers, Dan Peterson
Boatmaster .Michael Turk
Big Top by . . . . .Supertents
Catering by . . . . .The Location Caterers Ltd.
Helicopters . . . . .Management Aviation Ltd.
Travel and Transport . .Renown Freight, The Travel
   Company, D & D International Locations
Sound Effects . . . . .Jean Pierre Lelong
Dubbing Editors .Derek Holding, Michael Hopkins
Music Mixer .John Richards
Rerecording Mixers . . . . .Gordon McCallum,
   Ken Barker
Stunt Supervisors . . . . .Martin Grace,
   Paul Weston, Bill Burton
Stunt Team . . . . .Dorothy Ford, Clive Curtis,
   Del Baker, Pat Banta, Bill Weston, Rocky Taylor,
   Jim Dowdall, Wayne Michaels, Nick Hobbs,
   Jazzer Jeyes, Christopher Webb, Malcolm Weaver
Aerial Team Director . . . . .Philip Wrestler
Coordinator . . . . .Clay Lacy
Beach 18 . . . . .B. J. Worth, Rande Deluca,
   Jake Lombard, Joe Taylor
Acrostar Mini-Jet . . . . .Corkey Fornof, Rick Holley
Production Company . . . . .Eon Productions
Distribution Company . . . . .United Artists

Northolt Aerodrome outside London is transformed into a South American air-force base and horse trial in *Octopussy*. (Royal Air Force, Northolt)

OCTOPUSSY COMPETITION

Competitive films in release when *Octopussy* opened in Los Angeles on June 10, 1983:

Trading Places

WarGames

Return of the Jedi

Psycho II

Blue Thunder

Flashdance

Breathless

The Man with Two Brains

Spacehunter: Adventures in the Forbidden Zone

OCTOPUSSY The title character in the 13th James Bond film, produced by Albert R. Broccoli and released in 1983. As portrayed by Maud Adams, the only leading lady ever to play two different Bond characters (she was also Andrea Anders in *The Man with the Golden Gun*), Octopussy is the fabulously wealthy and resourceful leader of the Octopus Cult, a sect of acrobatic lady smugglers who live on a secluded island in the middle of Lake Pichola off the coast of Udaipur, India.

Octopussy is the daughter of Major Dexter Smythe, an ex-British army officer and Secret Service agent who stole a cache of Chinese gold from North Korea and, in so doing, murdered his guide. Twenty years later, James Bond (ROGER MOORE) traced Smythe to Sri Lanka and gave him 24 hours to clear up his affairs before Bond brought him back to London for trial. Rather than face the disgrace of a court-martial, Smythe committed suicide. Before he died, Smythe had become a leading authority on octopi. His pet name for his only daughter was "Octopussy."

When Octopussy's father's gold ran out, the people of Hong Kong who helped dispose of it offered Octopussy a commission to smuggle some diamonds. Developing a talent for such illegal activities, she revived the old Octopus Cult and populated its ranks with a group of attractive young women who were searching for a spiritual discipline. As her wealth increased, Octopussy diversified into shipping, hotels, carnivals, and circuses.

As the film begins, Octopussy's circus is performing in East Germany. She's now partnered with Kamal Khan (LOUIS JOURDAN) in a scheme to smuggle Russian jewels out of the Soviet Union. What she doesn't know is that Kamal Khan and his partner, fanatical General Orlov (STEVEN BERKOFF), are using her circus to gain access to a U.S. Air Force base, where they plan to detonate an atomic bomb.

In Udaipur, Octopussy meets James Bond, who arrives on her island disguised as an alligator. Surprisingly, she is grateful to him for giving her father the opportunity to avoid a scandalous court-martial. Spending the night, 007 saves Octopussy's life when a group of kill-crazy fanatics hired by Kamal break into her house. When Octopussy last sees Bond, he's grappling with a killer in the alligator-infested waters that surround her island home. After the fight is over, the water is still, and Octopussy assumes that her lover is dead. But Bond is very much alive.

He goes to Karl-Marx-Stadt, East Germany, where he sees Kamal and Orlov planting the A-bomb in the Octopussy Circus cannon. Later, on the U.S. Air Force base at Feldstadt, West Germany, 007 shows up in clown makeup and garb and tries to convince the base commander that a bomb is about to go off. Octopussy, Magda (KRISTINA WAYBORN), the commander (BRUCE BOA), and his aide (RICHARD PARMENTIER) think he's crazy, until Bond produces the Romanoff Star—a Soviet treasure he stole from Kamal's cache—which startles Octopussy.

As Bond desperately tries to break into the casing that holds the bomb in the base of a circus cannon, a fight breaks out between the air force security troops and the circus performers. Bond is eventually wrestled to a stop. Octopussy then steals a pistol from one of the MPs and shoots open the lock on the bomb casing, revealing the nuclear device. The stunned base commander orders his MPs to release Bond and he quickly deactivates the bomb.

Outraged that Kamal would consider murdering thousands of innocent people, including her entire cult, Octopussy returns to India and confronts Kamal at his Monsoon Palace. While his garrison is being overrun by her acrobatic assault team, Kamal and his bodyguard, Gobinda (KABIR BEDI), disarm Octopussy, knock her unconscious, and escape via horseback into the bush. Bond, having arrived with Q (DESMOND LLEWELYN) by hot-air balloon, follows closely behind, tracking Kamal to his airstrip.

The final confrontation occurs on board Kamal's twin-engine plane. To Octopussy's as-

tonishment, Bond appears outside the aircraft, holding onto the fuselage. When 007 begins to disable the plane, Kamal sends Gobinda outside to kill him. He fails, Bond enters the plane to rescue Octopussy, and both go diving out as the plane crashes into a mountainside. *See* ADAMS, MAUD.

OCTOPUSSY'S BED Shaped like a giant octopus, it was designed by Peter Lamont for *Octopussy.* Said Lamont, "The bed was made from polystyrene, and once we approved the shape, the whole thing was strengthened with wire mesh and linen soaked in plaster, primed, sealed, and covered in red ochre. It was then rubbed down to give the impression of wood." Octopussy (MAUD ADAMS) and James Bond (ROGER MOORE) are relaxing on this unusual bed when the buzz saw yo-yo man strikes.

OCTOPUSSY'S GIRLS The gorgeous female inhabitants of Udaipur, India's "floating palace" in *Octopussy.* They are portrayed, in alphabetical order, by Safira Afzal, Janine Andrews, Cheryl Anne, Carole Ashby, Julie Barth, Kathy Davies, Marie Elise, Joni Flynn, Helene Hunt, Louise King, Lynda Knight, Julie Martin, Tina Robinson, Carolyn Seaward, Mary Stavin, Gillian De Terville, Alison Worth, and Jani-Z. Mary Stavin would return to play Kimberley Jones, the iceberg-launch skipper, in the teaser for *A View to a Kill.*

OCTOPUSSY'S GYMNASTS Athletic actresses and stuntwomen who joined forces with the Octopussy girls for the climactic assault on the Monsoon Palace in *Octopussy.* In alphabetical order, they were portrayed by Jane Aldridge, Teresa Craddock, Christine Cullers, Suzanne Dando, Ruth Flynn, Christine Gibson, Kirsten Harrison, Sumisha Hassani, Lisa Jackman, and Tracy Llewellyn.

ODDJOB The prototypical villain's henchman, as portrayed by Japanese actor Harold Sakata in *Goldfinger.* A Korean by birth, and mute, the powerfully built Oddjob works for Auric Goldfinger (GERT FROBE) as his bodyguard/chauffeur/assassin and sometime caddy. His trademark weapon is a bowler hat equipped with a razor-sharp steel brim, which in his hands becomes a sort of lethal Frisbee™.

Dressed impeccably in formal suits, with a perpetually wicked smile across his face, he's a formidable presence who nearly destroys Bond (SEAN CONNERY) in the climactic fight inside glittering Fort Knox. Oddjob's roots as an unemotional, unstoppable adversary probably date back to Mary Shelley's *Frankenstein*. Predating the karate/kung fu genre by a full decade, Oddjob was one of a series of Asian supervillains who are quite popular in the internationally driven 007 series. *See* SAKATA, HAROLD.

08952 Government license plate on the armored truck that carries notorious drug runner Franz Sanchez (ROBERT DAVI) to Quantico, Virginia, in *Licence to Kill*. Sabotaged by traitorous DEA agent Killifer (EVERETT MCGILL), the truck never makes it to its destination.

057429 Identification number on S.P.E.C.T.R.E. agent Helga Brandt's (KARIN DOR) monoplane in *You Only Live Twice*. Trapped in the plane after she disables the controls and jumps out, Bond (SEAN CONNERY) breaks the wooden slat that pins his hands and manages to crash-land the plane, escaping before it explodes in a ball of flames.

OH CULT VOODOO SHOP A Kananga (YAPHET KOTTO) front in *Live and Let Die*. Located at 33 East 65th Street in New York City, it's one block from the headquarters of Kananga's San Monique diplomatic mission. It's where James Bond (ROGER MOORE) finds Whisper's (EARL JOLLY BROWN) white Cadillac "pimpmobile." And it is from the Oh Cult garage that Bond tails Kananga and his entourage to Harlem.

OH DEATH, WHERE IS THY STING A LING A LING? Shelved Bondlike World War I film adventure from United Artists that was British author Roald Dahl's only screenwriting experience prior to accepting the assignment to write *You Only Live Twice* in 1966.

It was the story of a huge German zeppelin fortress located on a lake on the Swiss/German border, and the British Flying Corps' plan to destroy it. Since the British lacked the range to bomb the factory from their bases in France, they instead dismantled their bombers and transported them under haywagons across Western Europe. Once they crossed into Swiss territory, the planes were reassembled for the final bombing run.

The wild caper of *You Only Live Twice*, with Blofeld's (DONALD PLEASENCE) rocket base hidden inside a dormant volcano and Bond (SEAN CONNERY) disguised as a Japanese who leads Ninja warriors in an all-out assault, owes more than a nod to this early film project from short-story master Dahl.

O'HERLIHY, GAVAN Irish-American character actor who portrayed U.S. Air Force officer Captain Jack Petachi in *Never Say Never Again*. Perfectly cast as the nervous traitor who falls under the spell of vicious S.P.E.C.T.R.E. assassin Fatima Blush (BARBARA CARRERA), O'Herlihy's Petachi is a whimpering bundle of nerves forced into increasingly dangerous activity to save his sister Domino's (KIM BASINGER) life. *See* PETACHI, CAPTAIN JACK.

OHMSS Acronym for *On Her Majesty's Secret Service*, the title of the sixth James Bond film, produced by Albert R. Broccoli and Harry Saltzman. The initials also appear on the cover of the dossier provided to all double-0 agents involved in the *Thunderball* mission.

OH, SOON-TAIK Asian actor who portrayed resourceful Hong Kong police detective and British Secret Service contact Lieutenant Hip in *The Man with the Golden Gun*.

OIL-RIG BATTLE The pièce de résistance in *Diamonds Are Forever*, in which CIA helicopters raid Blofeld's (CHARLES GRAY) oil-rig command post in the Gulf of Baja. Aboard the rig, Blofeld commands an orbiting laser satellite, powered by a huge diamond solar shield, that can wipe out any target on earth.

As he waits for the Western powers to provide a huge ransom—otherwise, Washington, D.C., will be destroyed—Bond (SEAN CONNERY) arrives innocently inside a giant inflatable ball that has been dropped into the ocean near the oil rig. His mission is to somehow enter Blofeld's control room and substitute a phony command cassette for the one being used to guide the satellite.

Why would Blofeld allow him anywhere

near the navigation apparatus for the satellite? Because Bond villains notoriously reveal their plans to 007 before they kill him. It's an unspoken rule.

Bond achieves his mission, but, unfortunately, Tiffany Case (JILL ST. JOHN) misinterprets his subterfuge and actually puts the real cassette back into play. By then, the CIA helicopters have launched their attack on the oil rig, which Blofeld has turned into a fortress with anti-aircraft cannon, machine guns, and armor plating. The sudden attack—initiated by Bond, who thought the phony cassette was working—actually confuses Blofeld and his missile expert Professor-Dr. Metz (JOSEPH FURST). Thanks to some direct hits, the command center is blown apart, and the satellite's laser cannon is neutralized.

Bond, meanwhile, has found Blofeld trying to escape in his bathosub. Knocking out a crane operator, Bond assumes control of the winching mechanism and begins to have some torturous fun with the S.P.E.C.T.R.E. chieftain. Lifting the sub out of the water, he eventually slams it into the control room, supposedly killing Blofeld—although he returns briefly in a wheelchair in the For Your Eyes Only teaser.

The oil-rig battle was filmed aboard a studio-customized oil rig that was rented and placed off the coast of southern California, near Oceanside. The rig itself was a portable, floatable device built around a bargelike structure with enormous retractable sea legs. The crew was based in Oceanside at the Bridge Motel. Each morning, helicopters would transport the cast, director, and immediate production staff to the rig, while boats carried the extras and technical crew.

At a nearby dirt airfield, the picture helicopters were being prepared for their assault on the rig. Each chopper was outfitted with rocket-firing apparatus, including metal tubes filled with electrically activated power charges that simulated the "whoosh" of the air-to-ground rockets, and small strobe lights that simulated the fire of machine guns.

During one sequence that doesn't appear in the finished film, the helicopters dropped demolition-carrying frogmen into the water around the rig to prepare for the rig's final destruction. According to Robert Short, who ob-

served some of the oil-rig sequence in 1971, the frogmen sequence explains their presence on the film's final release poster.

OLD ALBERT Huge crocodile featured in *Live and Let Die*. It's responsible for taking Tee Hee's (JULIUS HARRIS) right arm.

OLD MAN The irritating catchphrase used by Red Grant (ROBERT SHAW) when he addresses Bond (SEAN CONNERY) on the Orient Express in *From Russia with Love*.

OLIMPATEC MEDITATION INSTITUTE (OMI) Oddly shaped, surreal religious retreat that is the home of televangelist Joe Butcher (WAYNE NEWTON) in *Licence to Kill*. Located outside fictional Isthmus City, it's also the nerve center of drug runner Franz Sanchez's (ROBERT DAVI) cocaine laboratories, where the drug is being dissolved in gasoline.

From this unusual location, the tanker-truck convoy begins its ride to the ocean. In reality, the OMI complex, much of which is cone-shaped—hence, the film's reference to "cone power"—belongs to the very religious Otomi people of Toluca, Mexico, who erected the modernist edifice in 1980 as a meeting place.

OLIN MARK VI The brand of skis used by James Bond (ROGER MOORE) during his escape from KGB agent Eric Kriegler (JOHN WYMAN) and his men in *For Your Eyes Only*.

OLYMPE Marc Ange Draco's (GABRIELE FERZETTI) girl, portrayed by actress Virginia North, in *On Her Majesty's Secret Service*. Bond (GEORGE LAZENBY) meets her at Draco's private bullring in Portugal.

OLYMPIA BRASS BAND Name that appears on the sash of the bandleader during the New Orleans funeral procession in *Live and Let Die*. The band and the procession are part of Kananga's (YAPHET KOTTO) drug-smuggling operation.

OLYMPIC AIRLINES 11:00 P.M. FLIGHT James Bond's (ROGER MOORE) airline flight from Madrid to Athens after his escapade in

Spain with revenge-seeking Melina Havelock (CAROLE BOUQUET) in *For Your Eyes Only*.

100,000 POUNDS Baccarat expert Evelyn Tremble/James Bond's (PETER SELLERS) stake in his game against Soviet masterspy Le Chiffre (ORSON WELLES) in *Casino Royale*. It's supplied to him by the British Secret Service. If Tremble can bankrupt Le Chiffre, the Russian will be assassinated by his own KGB.

$115,200 Insured value of the jewelry worn by Lupe Lamora (TALISA SOTO) in *Licence to Kill*. The antique chokers, bracelets, and rings were supplied to the production by a Los Angeles collector/dealer. Her name: Sheila Goldfinger.

150,000 POUNDS Starting bid on the jeweled Fabergé egg at Sotheby's, in *Octopussy*. Kamal Khan (LOUIS JOURDAN) is the eventual high bidder at 500,000 pounds. *See FABERGE EGGS.*

140 MINUTES The controversial running time of *On Her Majesty's Secret Service*, clearly the longest Bond movie in the series. Editor John Glen had cut nearly 40 minutes of footage before he settled on the 140-minute cut, the length of which was kept a close secret from producers Broccoli and Saltzman.

"Eventually," said director Peter Hunt, "I did have to tell them, and Harry was furious. I think they had told United Artists that the final print would be less than two hours long. Of course, with a longer running time, UA couldn't get in as many screenings.

"So there was this big song and dance about how long the film was and that it had to be cut. I was eventually saved from a major edit on the film by George Pinches, the booking manager of the Rank Organization, who came to see the film in the little theater at Audley Square. Harry and Cubby told him to come and see them after the film.

"When it was over, George was very complimentary about the film's potential. Before anyone could say a word, I said to him, 'George, do you think I should cut the film anywhere? Is it too long?' And he said, 'Long? Long? How long have I been here, an hour and a half?' And

I told him that he had been in the theater for almost two and a half hours. He told us not to touch a foot. This, of course, was said right in front of the producers, which ended any controversy over whether the film was going to be re-edited."

The running time, however, did create a problem when the film was prepared for its U.S. television debut. Because it was considered too long for the standard two-hour time slot, ABC, without consulting Eon Productions or Peter Hunt, decided to edit the film for a two-night run.

Instead of cutting sequences, which had been a hallmark of earlier Bond telecasts, the network actually added footage by running sequences twice, once at the beginning of Part Two, with a phony Bond narrator, and then in their proper position at the film's conclusion. Thus, the film's second part would begin with the narrator commenting on Bond's icy predicament by saying, "I bet you wonder how I got into this situation." It was a silly touch that angered fans throughout the United States.

Since then, ABC has chosen simply to run the film in a longer time slot. Since the Bond films of the 1980s have also been close to or over two hours long, guaranteeing an appropriate time slot for a Bond telecast is no longer a problem. After all, the Bond films have always been a ratings leader for the network.

145 Identification number on the New York City taxicab, in *Live and Let Die*, that picks up Bond (ROGER MOORE) in front of the Oh Cult Voodoo Shop and transports him to Harlem.

100-KILOTON YIELD The explosive force of the A-bomb planted on a U.S. Air Force at Feldstadt, in *Octopussy*. According to a Russian A-bomb expert, the effect is similar to an American medium-yield bomb.

Since satellite intelligence will rule out a launch from Russia, renegade Russian General Orlov (STEVEN BERKOFF) is convinced that the explosion will be treated like a nuclear "accident." Western Europe then will demand unilateral nuclear disarmament, opening the borders to a massive Soviet invasion of the West planned by Orlov.

$100 MILLION The amount that each international distributor will pay drug lord Franz Sanchez (ROBERT DAVI) for a cocaine franchise in *Licence to Kill*. After putting up that amount, they'll be given the opportunity to purchase metric tons of cocaine at $20 million per ton. Quality and price will be guaranteed for five years.

$100 MILLION IN GOLD BULLION The amount of money in *You Only Live Twice* that Blofeld (DONALD PLEASENCE) expects to receive from the Red Chinese in return for igniting World War III between Russia and the United States. The money is to be deposited in the S.P.E.C.T.R.E. account in Buenos Aires.

$100,000 In *Thunderball*, the amount of S.P.E.C.T.R.E. mercenary Angelo Palazzi's (PAUL STASSINO) original fee for undergoing two years of plastic surgery to become an exact duplicate of NATO aerial observer François Derval. He demands a raise to $250,000 before he will hijack a NATO bomber with nuclear bombs on board.

100,000 RUPEES The stake in the rigged backgammon game with Kamal Khan (LOUIS JOURDAN) when James Bond (ROGER MOORE) takes over Major Clive's (STUART SAUNDERS) position, in *Octopussy*. *See* BACKGAMMON GAME.

124 Auction lot number of Kara Milovy's (MARYAM D'ABO) Lady Rose Stradivarius cello in *The Living Daylights*. It was sold for $150,000 in New York to arms dealer Brad Whitaker (JOE DON BAKER), who gave it to his partner, renegade Russian General Georgi Koskov (JEROEN KRABBE). It becomes Koskov's gift to his protege/lover, Kara. *See* LADY ROSE.

120 MILES The altitude of the second U.S. *Jupiter* spacecraft when it is about to be captured by S.P.E.C.T.R.E. in *You Only Live Twice*.

$1 MILLION The cost of building the 10-inch-thick glass facade outside Dr. No's (JOSEPH WISEMAN) underground living quarters. Convex in design, the glass magnifies the fish and marine life on the ocean floor. Minnows pretending they're whales, perhaps? Also the amount of money that Goldfinger (GERT FROBE) promised to each of the criminal organizations supplying vital equipment to his Operation Grand Slam, in *Goldfinger*.

$1.25 MILLION Sean Connery's salary on *Diamonds Are Forever*. To entice him back into the 007 role, United Artists's production executive, David Picker, also agreed to finance two films of Connery's choice. Other elements of the unprecedented offer included a percentage of the film's profits and a provision that if the film went over its 18-week shooting schedule, Connery would get an extra $10,000 a week.

The enormous length of the Bond production schedules had always irritated Connery, who did not like to spend so much of his time devoted to one project. *Diamonds Are Forever* was finished on schedule, sparing UA the extra cash outlay for its star.

ONE MILLION FRANCS The bank at the baccarat table in the TV film "Casino Royale" when James Bond (BARRY NELSON) wins his first hand with a nine versus the bank's "baccarat," or zero. It's also the bank when Le Chiffre (PETER LORRE) wins his first hand on the following night—with a nine versus a player's seven.

ONE MILLION POUNDS STERLING The dowry offered to James Bond (GEORGE LAZENBY) by Marc Ange Draco (GABRIELE FERZETTI) if he will marry his daughter, Tracy (DIANA RIGG), in *On Her Majesty's Secret Service*. When 007 ties the knot at the film's conclusion, Draco offers him the check, but Bond declines the money.

ONE MINUTE AND 56 SECONDS Total amount of screen time completed on the first day of shooting on *Dr. No*, which took place at the Palisadoes Airport in Kingston, Jamaica, on January 16, 1962.

ONE MINUTE AND 52 SECONDS The amount of time it takes S.P.E.C.T.R.E. assassin Red Grant (ROBERT SHAW) to track and strangle the phony James Bond (SEAN CONNERY) in the *From Russia with Love* teaser.

ONE MINUTE AND 47 SECONDS The amount of time it takes James Bond (SEAN CONNERY) to complete an unusually realistic training mission in the South American jungle in *Never Say Never Again*. To top it off, he gets stabbed in the arm by the very woman he rescues (stuntwoman WENDY LEECH).

10134 AND 10135 Serial numbers of the cruise missiles hijacked by S.P.E.C.T.R.E. in *Never Say Never Again*.

$1,000 The amount of money paid to author Ian Fleming by CBS in 1954 for television rights to "Casino Royale." The one-hour dramatization, starring Barry Nelson as James Bond, was telecast live at 8:30 P.M. on October 21, 1954, as the third entry on the network's Climax Mystery Theater, an anthology series hosted by actor William Lundigan.

ON HER MAJESTY'S SECRET SERVICE (United Artists, 1969) ★ ★ ★ ★
The sixth James Bond film produced by Albert R. Broccoli and Harry Saltzman. U.S. release date: December 18, 1969. U.S. film rentals: $9.1 million. Running time: 140 minutes.

A truly epic James Bond film with a story to match. Had Sean Connery the patience to remain for one more film, OHMSS would have been his best. After the mind-numbing experience of *You Only Live Twice*, OHMSS brings 007 down to earth in one of the series's most human stories, in which 007 finally meets his female match, falls in love, and gets married.

Ex-model George Lazenby was no Sean Connery, but thanks to the careful direction of Peter Hunt and the fabulous script by Richard Maibaum, he comes across extremely well. Lazenby brought his own form of charisma to the role. He was handsome, light on his feet, and believable.

One can only wonder what would have happened if the part had not gone to his head. Had he not quit the series after one film, there is every reason to believe that he would have established himself in the role of Bond. He had the potential. He could play the droll humor, he had the two-fisted machismo, his dialogue delivery was good. OHMSS was his training ground for a continuing part that, unfortunately, never materialized.

Having edited the first four films and shot second unit on *You Only Live Twice*, Peter Hunt finally won his directing spurs on OHMSS. Presented with one of Fleming's best books, Hunt worked carefully with Maibaum to create one of the most carefully produced Bond films. Once again, the set pieces are legendary, but they do not deflect the story line as they did in *You Only Live Twice*.

Lazenby's introduction is another classic, which takes place on the beach in Portugal with Bond rescuing Tracy from the surf. The fistfight in the water with a Draco henchman is a perfect example of Hunt's rapid-fire directing style. The Bond series has benefited strongly when its editors have been given the opportunity to direct. Peter Hunt, like John Glen, knew where to place his cameras for maximum effect.

Like *From Russia with Love*, and *For Your Eyes Only*, OHMSS is filled with mysterious characters and realistic action. Blofeld's plot involves germ warfare—a very earthbound caper—and his stronghold this time is a converted Swiss allergy clinic, not a volcano rocket base. The film is loaded with action—ski chases, bobsled chases, car chases, helicopter attacks, fights in the surf, fights in the hotel, fights in the office. Like *Dr. No*, the producers wanted to keep the focus in this film on movement, distracting the audience from noticing that a new Bond was on duty. They succeeded.

Diana Rigg was an inspired bit of casting. She was a star in America, thanks to her Emma Peel role in the ever-popular "The Avengers" series, and audiences were ready to accept her as Bond's potential mate. Telly Savalas's Blofeld was fair. A European actor along the lines of Adolfo Celi would have been better. Gabriele Ferzetti was excellent as Marc Ange Draco, the mafioso who joins forces with Bond to rescue his daughter, Tracy. And John Barry outdid himself with one of the series's best musical scores, including his rousing title instrumental.

"Suspended Animation"—In the Alps (1968), on *On Her Majesty's Secret Service*'s ace aerial cameraman Johnny Jordan films action sequences from an unusual parachute harness. (Judy Jordan Collection)

ON HER MAJESTY'S SECRET SERVICE CAST

James Bond	George Lazenby
Tracy	Diana Rigg
Ernst Stavro Blofeld	Telly Savalas
Irma Bunt	Ilse Steppat
Marc Ange Draco	Gabriele Ferzetti
Grunther	Yuri Borienko
Campbell	Bernard Horsfall
Sir Hilary Bray, Baronet	George Baker
M	Bernard Lee
Q	Desmond Llewelyn
Miss Moneypenny	Lois Maxwell
Ruby Bartlett	Angela Scoular
Nancy	Catherine Von Schell
Olympe	Virginia North

Piz Gloria Girls

American Girl	Dani Sheridan
Scandinavian Girl	Julie Ege
English Girl	Joanna Lumley
Chinese Girl	Mona Chong
Australian Girl	Anoushka Hempel
German Girl	Ingrid Black
Italian Girl	Jenny Hanley
Indian Girl	Zara
Jamaican Girl	Sylvana Henriques
Israeli Girl	Helena Ronee

Draco's Men

Toussaint	Geoffrey Cheshire
Che Che	Irvin Allen
Raphael	Terry Mountain
Klett	Bill Morgan
Driver	Richard Graydon

Blofeld's Men

Felsen	Les Crawford
Braun	George Cooper

Driver . . . . .Reg Harding
Gumpold (Swiss Lawyer) . . . . .James Bree
Manuel (Portuguese Hotel Manager) . .Brian Worth
Janitor (Who Whistles "Goldfinger") . . . . .Norman McGlen
Hall Porter .Dudley Jones
Draco's Helicopter Pilot . . . . .John Crewdson
Piz Gloria Receptionist . . . . .Josef Vasa

At the Casino
American Guest. . . . . .Bessie Love
Greek Tycoon .Steve Plytas
Chef de Jeu . . . . .Robert Rietty
American Guest. . . . . .Elliott Sullivan
Chef de Jeu Hussier . . . . .Martin Leyder

ON HER MAJESTY'S SECRET SERVICE CREW

Producers . . . . .Albert R. Broccoli, Harry Saltzman
Director . . . . .Peter Hunt
Screenplay by . . . . .Richard Maibaum
Associate Producer . . . . .Stanley Sopel
Production Supervisor . . . . .David Middlemas
Production Secretary . . . . .Golda Offenheim
First Assistant Director . . . . .Frank Ernst
Continuity . . . . .Joan Davis
Director of Photography . . . . .Michael Reed
Camera Operator . . . . .Alec Mills
Camera Focus . . . . .Ron Drinkwater
Film Editor . . . . .John Glen
Sound Mixers . . .John Mitchell, Gordon McCallum
Production Designer . . . . .Syd Cain
Art Director . . . . .Bob Laing
Set Dresser . . . . .Peter Lamont
Construction Manager . . . . .Ronnie Udell
Costume Designer . . . . .Marjory Cornelius
Wardrobe Supervisor . . . . .Jackie Cummins
Wardrobe Master . . . . .John Brady
Makeup Artists . . . . .Basil Newall, Paul Rabiger
Hairstylist . . . . .Eileen Warwick
Head Special Effects . . . . .John Stears
Second-Unit Director . . . . .John Glen
Dialogue Coach . . . . .Job Stewart
Assembly Editor . . . . .Robert Richardson
Stunt Arranger . . . . .George Leech
Second-Unit Cameramen . .Egil Woxholt, Roy Ford
Aerial Cameraman . . . . .Johnny Jordan
Ski Cameramen . . . . .Willy Bogner Jr., Alex Barbey
Dubbing Editors . . . . .Nicholas Stevenson, Harry Miller
Stock-Car Sequence Director . . . . .Anthony Squire
Additional Dialogue. . . . . .Simon Raven
Music Composed and Conducted by . . . .John Barry

"We Have All the Time in the World" Sung by . . . . .Louis Armstrong
Lyrics by . . . . .Hal David
Main Title Design by . . . . .Maurice Binder
Production Company . . . . .Eon Productions
Distribution Company . . . . .United Artists

ON HER MAJESTY'S SECRET SERVICE COMPETITION

Competitive films in release when *On Her Majesty's Secret Service* opened in Los Angeles on December 18, 1969 (*Note*: It was billed as a double feature with *Kill a Dragon*):

Topaz
2001: A Space Odyssey
Hello, Dolly!
They Shoot Horses, Don't They?
The Arrangement
Sweet Charity
Cactus Flower
Anne of the Thousand Days
John and Mary
Doctor Doolittle/Planet of the Apes (reissue)

092765491 Code number on James Bond's (ROGER MOORE) reprogramming message to pirate nuclear-submarine Stromberg No. 1, in *The Spy Who Loved Me*. The message adjusts the trajectory of the sub's Polaris missile so that it will destroy Stromberg No. 2.

002 (aka Bill Fairbanks) British Secret Service agent, mentioned in *The Man with the Golden Gun*, who was supposedly assassinated by Francisco Scaramanga (CHRISTOPHER LEE) in a Beirut cabaret in 1969, although the bullet was never recovered. Saida (CARMEN SAUTOY), the belly dancer and Fairbanks's ex-girlfriend, now wears the bullet as a charm in her belly button.

A different 002 (GLYN BAKER) participates in Ministry of Defense war games on Gibraltar in *The Living Daylights* teaser. Skydiving onto the island, he's quickly captured by an S.A.S. defender.

003 British Secret Service agent found dead by James Bond (ROGER MOORE) in the snows of Siberia, in *A View to a Kill*. Inside a heart-shaped pendant around the dead agent's neck, 007 finds a microchip that 003 stole from the

Russians. According to Q (DESMOND LLEW-ELYN) this chip is part of a new breed, developed by Zorin Industries, that is totally impervious to magnetic-pulse damage from a possible A-bomb detonated in outer space.

004 Double-0 agent, portrayed by Frederick Warder in *The Living Daylights*, who is assassinated on Gibraltar during Ministry of Defense war games. The killer, working for arms dealer Brad Whitaker (JOE DON BAKER) and renegade Russian General Georgi Koskov (JEROEN KRABBE), leaves a tag on 004's body; it reads, "Smiert Spionam" (Russian for "Death to Spies"). *See* GIBRALTAR.

005 Time left on the countdown panel when James Bond (SEAN CONNERY) triggers the S.P.E.C.T.R.E. *Intruder* rocket's self-destruct mechanism in *You Only Live Twice*. If Bond fails, the counter goes to zero, and the *Intruder*—disguised as a Russian ship—envelops a U.S. *Jupiter* space capsule, initiating an American nu-

clear attack against the Soviet Union and World War III.

000131 Number on the personal check for $5 million that Max Zorin (CHRISTOPHER WALKEN) offers Stacey Sutton (TANYA ROBERTS) for her shares of Sutton Oil in *A View to a Kill*. Stacey later tears up the check.

007 James Bond's code prefix. "00" refers to his "license to kill," granted by the British government and given to a very select group of Her Majesty's agents. It is also the appropriate number that appears on the countdown panel when a scientist deactivates the A-bomb in *Goldfinger*.

007 STAGE Enormous soundstage constructed on the Pinewood Studios lot in 1976 and first utilized for Ken Adam's gargantuan "Jonah" set in *The Spy Who Loved Me*. The soundstage was partially destroyed in 1985 during the filming of Ridley Scott's *Legend*; however, it was rebuilt the same year for *A View to a Kill*. *See* JONAH SET, THE.

A fire engulfs the 007 stage at Pinewood during the making of director Ridley Scott's *Legend*.

008 Bond's (SEAN CONNERY) replacement in case he fails on the *Goldfinger* mission. It's also his replacement if he fails to assassinate Russian General Leonid Pushkin (JOHN RHYS-DAVIES) in *The Living Daylights*. According to M (ROBERT BROWN), 008 can be easily recalled from his assignment in Hong Kong if Bond finds the death of Pushkin distasteful. *See* PUSHKIN, GENERAL LEONID.

009 British Secret Service agent, portrayed by stuntman Andy Bradford in *Octopussy*, who attempts to steal a counterfeit Fabergé egg from Octopussy's (MAUD ADAMS) circus in East Berlin. Disguised in clown's garb, and chased into the woods near the circus by twin killers Mischka and Grischka (TONY AND DAVID MEYER), 009 is climbing a bridge to freedom when a knife finds its mark in his back. He then falls into a flood-control basin.

Later, at a well-attended party at the residence of the British ambassador to East Berlin, 009 staggers onto the grounds with the knife still imbedded in his back, smashes through a window into the ambassador's office, falls to the floor, and dies—the captured egg rolling across the floor.

O-RH POSITIVE The blood type of John Strangways's secretary, who is murdered by Dr. No's assassins. Her blood patch is found on the floor of Strangways's communications room by Bond and Officer Duff of the Kingston Police.

OPERATION BEDLAM The British Secret Service code name for the Blofeld search, as featured in *On Her Majesty's Secret Service*. The worldwide hunt for the missing head of S.P.E.C.T.R.E., last seen disappearing into the interior of his volcano rocket base in *You Only Live Twice*, is led by his most ardent foe—James Bond (GEORGE LAZENBY).

OPERATION GRAND SLAM The code name for Goldfinger's (GERT FROBE) plan to detonate a Red Chinese atomic bomb in Fort Knox, a plan he has spent 15 years of his life developing. With America's entire gold reserve radioactive for 58 years, economic chaos in the West will result, and Goldfinger's own gold will increase in value tenfold.

Thanks to screenwriters Richard Maibaum and Paul Dehn, this plot was a major improvement over the story in Ian Fleming's original novel, in which an attempt to actually steal the gold is made by Goldfinger and his team of organized-crime bosses. In the movie, Grand Slam has two tactical elements—the Grand Slam Task Force, which will break into Fort Knox and detonate the bomb, and Champagne Section, a flight of private planes that will spray the deadly Delta Nine nerve gas over the Fort Knox military reservation, eliminating the 41,000 American troops stationed there. The air-support mission is code-named Operation Rockabye Baby.

OPERATION PASSOVER The CIA's plan to give smuggler Tiffany Case (JILL ST. JOHN) a cache of diamonds at the Circus Circus Casino in *Diamonds Are Forever*. Once she has the diamonds, Felix Leiter (NORMAN BURTON) plans to tail her to the next stop on the smuggling pipeline.

Despite the net of CIA men, Tiffany gives them the slip when she sneaks out the back exit of the Zambora transformation show. Fortunately, Bond (SEAN CONNERY) finds Tiffany at her desert house, where Plenty O'Toole (LANA WOOD) has been drowned. Tiffany then helps Bond track the diamonds to an airport locker, where Burt Saxby (BRUCE CABOT) picks them up and later gives them to Professor-Dr. Metz (JOSEPH FURST) in a gas station.

When Tiffany distracts Metz, Bond sneaks into the back of his van and takes a trip out to Willard Whyte's (JIMMY DEAN) Techtronics installation, where Blofeld (CHARLES GRAY), posing as Whyte, has supervised the construction of a laser satellite capable of blackmailing the world.

OPERATION ROCKABYE BABY The code name for Goldfinger's (GERT FROBE) plan to spray Delta Nine nerve gas into the atmosphere above the Fort Knox U.S. Army installation. Five voluptuous female members of Pussy Galore's (HONOR BLACKMAN) Flying Circus will accomplish the mission in Piper Cherokee monoplanes. Their flight moniker is Champagne Section.

The women of this flight and Pussy Galore have no idea that Delta Nine nerve gas is fatal and that Operation Rockabye Baby will put 41,000 troops to sleep permanently. Fortunately, Pussy comes to her senses about Goldfinger's real motives and switches the gas canisters at the last minute.

OPERATION TROVE James Bond's (ROGER MOORE) mission, in *Octopussy*, to discover who's selling a priceless Fabergé egg, a fake of which was stolen by 009 (ANDY BRADFORD) in East Berlin before he was murdered. *See* FABERGE EGGS.

OPERATION UNDERTOW James Bond's (ROGER MOORE) mission, in *For Your Eyes Only*, to recover the A.T.A.C. (Automatic Targeting Attack Communicator) from the sunken hulk of the *St. Georges* surveillance ship.

ORCHIDAE NIGRA The scientific name for a highly toxic jungle plant (the black orchid) from which billionaire industrialist and madman Hugo Drax (MICHEL LONSDALE) has developed a nerve gas that could destroy all human, but not animal, life, in *Moonraker*. According to Q (DESMOND LLEWELYN), who briefs Bond at a Brazilian jungle village, the plant was thought to have been extinct but was brought back from Brazil's Tipperapi River by a missionary. Archaeological reports indicate that long-term exposure to the orchid's pollen caused sterility to the race of people who built the ancient city in the Amazon, which is now Drax's space-shuttle launch site.

ORDER OF LENIN Prestigious Soviet medal awarded to James Bond (ROGER MOORE) for liquidating Max Zorin (CHRISTOPHER WALKEN) and ending his nefarious plot to monopolize the world's supply of microchips, in *A View to a Kill*. According to General Gogol (WALTER GOTELL), 007 is the first-ever non-Soviet citizen to receive such a decoration.

ORIENT EXPRESS The famous passenger train that is the location for a good portion of *From Russia with Love*. Although its schedule has changed many times since its first trip on October 4, 1883, the Simplon Orient Express originally left Istanbul and traveled through Thessalonika, Belgrade, Venice, and Lausanne, until it eventually arrived in Paris four days and five nights later.

In *From Russia with Love*, Bond (SEAN CONNERY); Kerim Bey (PEDRO ARMENDARIZ), the head of the British Secret Service in Turkey; and defecting Soviet cipher clerk Tatiana "Tanya" Romanova (DANIELA BIANCHI) board the train in Istanbul after blowing up the Russian embassy and stealing the Lektor decoding machine. Unfortunately, two enemy agents follow them onto the train: Benz (PETER BAYLISS), a Russian security agent, and Red Grant (ROBERT SHAW), a ruthless S.P.E.C.T.R.E. assassin who, by following master planner Kronsteen's (VLADEK SHEYBAL) scheme, is intent on murdering Bond, Romanova, Kerim Bey, and Benz, as well as stealing back the Lektor decoder.

Trains have always provided a perfect setting for mysteries, and the Orient Express doesn't disappoint. Terence Young's direction is masterful, considering that the entire sequence was shot on a stationary soundstage at Pinewood Studios. You believe you are on the actual Orient Express headed for exotic points west.

On the train, with Kerim Bey's help, Bond and Tanya prepare their escape near the Bulgarian frontier, where they will leave the train and catch a chartered plane to Athens and then a jet to London. Kerim Bey even corners Benz and decides to keep him company until his friends get across the border with the stolen decoder. But Grant steps in and destroys the plan's chances for success by killing Kerim Bey, Benz, and Nash (BILL HILL), the latter a British agent in Zagreb whose identity he assumes.

Thanks to editor Peter Hunt, much of the following sequences are intercut with scenes of the Orient Express making its way across the Balkans at night—a map superimposed over the action, showing the train's position. John Barry's moody score takes on the character of the Orient Express itself—penetrating, relentless, full throttle.

The train stops in Belgrade, and Bond informs one of Kerim Bey's sons about the fate of his father. Agent 007 asks for help from M (BERNARD LEE), who must send an agent to the next stop—Zagreb. In Zagreb, help comes from local agent Nash, who unfortunately, becomes Grant's next victim—in the station rest room—and the S.P.E.C.T.R.E. agent's perfect cover.

All of these sequences have a great reality and vitality about them, thanks to the no-nonsense acting of Sean Connery and Robert Shaw. First of all, both actors look good—tall, muscled, well dressed, and ready for action. The train has an ominous, unfriendly air about it; the stations, equally so.

It is good to have friends nearby at times like this, Bond learns too late. Worming his way into 007's confidence, Grant (as Nash) drugs Tanya and knocks Bond unconscious, trapping 007 in what becomes one of the James Bond series's most threatening situations. Disarmed and on his knees, Bond finds himself looking down the long barrel of Grant's silenced automatic.

Listen to the dialogue in this sequence, and you will hear the gems of screenwriter Richard Maibaum. Bond is going to die; there's no way he's going to survive the ruthless Grant, who has murdered everyone in sight thus far in the movie. Fortunately, Grant's greed and the trick briefcase save the day See BRIEFCASE.

Staggered by the tear-gas cartridge, Grant loses the initiative and is jumped by Bond. One of the best fights in cinema history begins, filmed expertly by Terence Young, and later edited to a knife's edge by Peter Hunt, who added a free camera to catch much of the action that spilled across two compartments.

The men trade incredible punch after punch after punch, until Grant pulls out his "strangler's watch" and nearly kills Bond, who has also reached for a gadget—the throwing knife hidden in the briefcase. He finally stabs Grant in the arm. Staggered by the blow, Grant drops his guard and allows Bond to strangle him with his own watch.

With the barely conscious Tanya and the Lektor decoder in tow, Bond exits the train as it makes its own unscheduled stop for what was supposed to be Grant's escape route. A S.P.E.C.T.R.E. agent (PETER BRAYHAM) has stalled his Chevrolet truck on the tracks, a ploy that will stop the train long enough for Grant to make good his own escape. Unfortunately for the agent, it is Bond who commandeers his vehicle and escapes.

ORLOV, GENERAL Fanatical Russian general portrayed by Steven Berkoff in *Octopussy*. Determined to convince the detente-conscious Soviet leadership that a successful military invasion of Western Europe is still possible, Orlov plans to detonate a nuclear weapon on an American air force base in Feldstadt, West Germany. Such an "accident," Orlov claims, will force unilateral disarmament, emptying the borders of a nuclear deterrent and allowing Soviet tank and infantry armies to cross at will.

To accomplish this task, Orlov makes a pact with an Afghan devil named Kamal Khan (LOUIS JOURDAN), whose associate Octopussy (MAUD ADAMS) owns an international circus that can gain access to the American base. In return, Orlov is offering a treasure trove of jewels stolen from the Kremlin Art Repository and replaced with duplicates forged by his expert, Lenkin (PETER PORTEOUS). One of these forgeries, a jeweled Fabergé Easter egg, is stolen from East Berlin by 009 (ANDY BRADFORD). When it ends up in the hands of the British Secret Service, Bond (ROGER MOORE) is sent on Operation Trove to find the egg's real owner.

Orlov is first seen by Bond when the general arrives by Soviet helicopter at Kamal Khan's Monsoon Palace in the mountains above Udaipur. Having escaped from his room, where he is being held prisoner, 007 tries to listen in on the Orlov/Kamal Khan conversation, but lovely Magda's (KRISTINA WAYBORN) blow-dryer interferes with the bug that Bond has placed in the fake jeweled egg. All he hears is "one week" and "Karl-Marx-Stadt."

Orlov is confronted by Bond in Karl-Marx-Stadt, East Germany (where Octopussy's circus is performing), but the general escapes when his Soviet guards attack. Now pursued by General Gogol (WALTER GOTELL), who has discovered Orlov's forged jewelry operation, Orlov makes it to the West German border. But when he crosses illegally, he's gunned down by East German border guards. Gogol stands over him, branding him a thief and a disgrace to his uniform. With his dying gasp, Orlov says, "Yes, but tomorrow I will be a hero of the Soviet Union."

ORLOV'S COMMAND Russian military units under the direct command of General Orlov (STEVEN BERKOFF) in *Octopussy*. They compose 31 divisions, including 11 tank divisions and five tank divisions in Czechoslovakia. They are supported on the western border of Russia by an additional 60 divisions, including 22 tank divisions, thus giving Orlov a ten-to-one advantage over U.S./NATO forces in Western Europe.

Based on a plan he has devised on the new Kutuzov computer, Orlov feels that a lightening thrust with 10 armored divisions from the north, supported by another five through Czechoslovakia, can achieve total victory in the West within five days against any possible defense. General Gogol (WALTER GOTELL) informs the Soviet leadership that any such foolhardy invasion would almost assuredly be met by nuclear weapons. What Gogol doesn't know is that Orlov is planning to eliminate that deterrent.

O'ROURKE, MR. Disgruntled San Francisco Bay crab fisherman, portrayed by Bill Ackridge, in *A View to a Kill*. O'Rourke tells Bond (ROGER MOORE), who's posing as a reporter for the London *Financial Times*, that Max Zorin's (CHRISTOPHER WALKEN) oil-pumping station is responsible for ruining one of the best crab patches in the bay.

"What happened to the crabs?" Bond asks. "They just disappeared," O'Rourke replies. What Bond doesn't know is that Zorin's station is pumping seawater into the unstable Hayward earthquake fault—the first stage of Zorin's Project Main Strike, a plan to destroy Silicon Valley, California. *See* PROJECT MAIN STRIKE.

OSATO CHEMICAL AND ENGINEERING COMPANY, LTD. A S.P.E.C.T.R.E. front managed by Mr. Osato (TERU SHIMADA), in *You Only Live Twice*. Osato is a multifaceted company with manufacturing, pharmaceutical, and shipping interests. The company's liquid oxygen product (LOX) is being used by Blofeld (DONALD PLEASENCE) as a propellant for the S.P.E.C.T.R.E. *Intruder* rocket ship. His shipping line, based in Kobe, is transporting the LOX to the rocket base.

Bond (SEAN CONNERY) breaks into Osato Chemical when he follows Henderson's (CHARLES GRAY) assassin to the corporate headquarters building in Tokyo. Later 007 returns to the company, posing as Mr. Fisher, the manager of Empire Chemicals.

OSATO, MR. Japanese industrialist and S.P.E.C.T.R.E. agent, portrayed by character actor Teru Shimada, in *You Only Live Twice*. The president of the Osato Chemical and Engineering Company Ltd., a S.P.E.C.T.R.E. front, Osato manufactures liquid oxygen, which Blofeld (DONALD PLEASENCE) uses as a propellant for his *Intruder* spaceship. The liquid oxygen (identified by the abbreviation LOX) is transported by freighter from the docks at Kobe. Osato's assistant is the luscious Helga Brandt (KARIN DOR).

Following Henderson's (CHARLES GRAY) assassin, Bond (SEAN CONNERY) breaks into Osato's safe and gains his first clue—a receipt for a simple order for naval stores that includes 50 containers of LOX. Unable to assassinate Bond, Osato eventually retires to the rocket base, where he's killed by Blofeld during the final battle with Tanaka's Ninjas.

06 Identification number on the Soviet helicopter that brings General Orlov (STEVEN BERKOFF) to Kamal Khan's Monsoon Palace in *Octopussy*.

03 4285 219 The new target coordinates sent by James Bond (ROGER MOORE) to pirate nuclear-submarine Stromberg No. 1 in *The Spy Who Loved Me*. They will adjust the trajectory of a Polaris missile so that it will destroy the other pirate submarine, Stromberg No. 2.

O'TOOLE, PETER (Connemara, Ireland, August 2, 1932–   ) Superstar Irish actor who had a cameo role in *Casino Royale* as a bespectacled bagpipe player who confronts Evelyn Tremble/James Bond (PETER SELLERS).

O'TOOLE, PLENTY Voluptuous Las Vegas floozy, portrayed by Lana Wood, in *Diamonds Are Forever*. When James Bond (SEAN CONNERY) arrives in the Whyte House casino, she dumps her boyfriend, Maxie (ED CALL), who's broke, and hooks up with the well-heeled Bond. After introducing herself, Bond replies, "Named after your father, perhaps."

Following a successful night at the tables,

Plenty O'Toole (LANA WOOD) is given a quick exit in *Diamonds Are Forever*. The two goons are doubles and Plenty is actually a dummy. (Stephen Allen, Las Vegas News Bureau)

after which he gives his new girlfriend a sizable bonus, Bond and Plenty arrive at 007's hotel suite, only to be greeted by three diamond syndicate hoods, two of whom literally throw poor Plenty out the window. When she lands in a swimming pool, one of the hoods (MARC LAWRENCE) replies, "I didn't know there was a pool there." Bond is then free to find Tiffany Case (JILL ST. JOHN) waiting for him in bed.

In a scene that was later cut from the final film, Plenty actually returns to the hotel suite and finds Tiffany Case's purse, along with the address of her house in Las Vegas. Later, she goes there to join Bond, but is drowned instead. The hotel suite sequence was cut, so audiences never really knew how Plenty got to Tiffany's house.

"OUR MAN IN HONG KONG" How the British representative to the UN Security Council refers to James Bond (SEAN CONNERY) at the beginning of *You Only Live Twice*.

OXFORD College alma mater of Kamran Shah (ART MALIK), the handsome leader of the Mujahedeen rebels, in *The Living Daylights*.

P

P Code reference to Q's opposite number in the KGB. It's mentioned in an early draft of the screenplay for *The Spy Who Loved Me*, but it was discarded in the final draft.

PA JA MA The name of undercover CIA agent Sharkey's (FRANK MCRAE) fishing boat in *Licence to Kill*.

PAINT PELLETS "Ammunition" supplied to Special Air Service (S.A.S.) defenders on Gibraltar during the war game with the Double-0 Section in *The Living Daylights* teaser. Their guns have little effect on an assassin (CARL RIGG) who's working for arms dealer Brad Whitaker (JOE DON BAKER) and renegade Russian General Georgi Koskov (JEROEN KRABBE). He's firing live ammunition. *See* GIBRALTAR.

PALAZZI, ANGELO A S.P.E.C.T.R.E. mercenary, portrayed by Paul Stassino, who for $100,000 undergoes plastic surgery to become an exact duplicate of NATO aerial observer Major François Derval in *Thunderball*. After disposing of Derval with a blast of deadly gamma gas, Palazzi informs his S.P.E.C.T.R.E. coconspirators Fiona Volpe (LUCIANA PALUZZI) and Count Lippe (GUY DOLEMAN) that his payment must be increased to $250,000 or he will not hijack an A-bomb–equipped NATO bomber to the Bahamas. They agree, and he succeeds in gaining entrance to a NATO air base by posing as Derval.

Aboard the Vulcan bomber, he murders his fellow crew members by inserting the gamma gas into their oxygen system, takes control of the plane, and lands it in the water near the yacht of S.P.E.C.T.R.E. spymaster Emilio Largo (ADOLFO CELI). Its landing gear lowered, the plane gently floats to the sea floor of the Golden Grotto, a section of the Caribbean that is home to a deadly species of shark. When his seat belt becomes stuck, Angelo seeks the help of Largo, who has arrived in scuba gear.

But instead of rescuing the mercenary, Largo takes his knife and cuts Palazzi's oxygen hose. Trapped by the malfunctioning seat belt, he drowns in the cockpit of the downed bomber.

When this sequence was shot in the water off Nassau's Clifton Pier, diver Courtney Brown, a member of the Ivan Tors crew, was doubling actor Paul Stassino. According to diving specialist and underwater cameraman/engineer Jordan Klein, Brown's actual air hose was supposed to be cut in the sequence, with the diver relying on a "bale-out" bottle of air for sustenance once the shot was completed. However, during the sequence, Brown dropped his bale-out bottle and nearly drowned before diving assistants brought him to the surface and took him to the hospital. Recovering from this accident, Brown went back to work for the climactic underwater battle, only to be injured when an explosive charge simulating one of Bond's (SEAN CONNERY) spear-gun hits ignited under his wet suit, causing a severe burn.

PALISADOES AIRPORT The Caribbean airport that services the island of Jamaica. It served as the film series's first location on the morning of January 16, 1962, when James Bond, portrayed by Sean Connery, arrived in Jamaica aboard Pan American Flight 323, in *Dr. No*.

PALMYRA Emilio Largo's (ADOLFO CELI) huge seaside Nassau estate in *Thunderball*. In 1965 it was the summer home of the Nicholas Sullivans of Philadelphia. In one of its two swimming pools, Largo keeps his deadly Golden Grotto sharks (actually tiger sharks).

Palmyra is also the name of Maximillian Largo's (KLAUS MARIA BRANDAUER) North African fortress/estate in *Never Say Never Again*. Traveling there from southern France as a guest on Largo's *Flying Saucer* yacht, Bond is later captured and shackled to the wall of a medieval dungeon filled with bleached bones and vultures. He breaks his bonds, thanks to his laser-equipped watch, steals a horse, and rescues Domino (KIM BASINGER) from a group of sleazy Arab traders. Chased across the ramparts of the fortress, Bond, Domino, and the horse dive into the Mediterranean as an American nuclear submarine blasts the Arabs with its deck cannon.

Italian bombshell Luciana Paluzzi scored in *Thunderball* as S.P.E.C.T.R.E. assassin Fiona Volpe.

PALUZZI, LUCIANA (Rome, June 10, 1939–) Red-headed Italian leading lady who portrayed S.P.E.C.T.R.E. assassin Fiona Volpe in *Thunderball*. Luciana's introduction while wearing a sheer negligee in Derval's (PAUL STASSINO) bedroom was definitely an early highlight of the film. She's the perfect example of the type of woman the producers liked to cast as a ruthless villain in the early 007 thrillers— European, large-breasted, and very sexy. Definitely one of the better female characters in the series. *See* VOLPE, FIONA.

PANAMA The registry of the *Disco Volante* yacht in *Thunderball*. It's written on the ship's stern.

PAN AMERICAN FLIGHT 1 The identification number of 007's (SEAN CONNERY) flight from London to Istanbul in *From Russia with Love*.

PAN AMERICAN FLIGHT 323 The flight identification number of 007's airliner from New York to Jamaica in *Dr. No*. In the late 1950s and early 1960s, it was common for transatlantic flights to stop in New York before the jaunt to the islands. Today, direct flights— London to Jamaica—are available.

PAN HO One of Max Zorin's (CHRISTOPHER WALKEN) assistants, portrayed by actress Papillon Soo Soo, in *A View to a Kill*. Along with Jenny Flex (ALISON DOODY), Pan Ho is killed in the flood in the Main Strike Mine.

PARATROOPER (aka *The Red Beret*) 1954 Alan Ladd wartime adventure film, directed by Terence Young and written by Richard Maibaum, which influenced the motorboat chase written by Maibaum in *From Russia with Love*. In *Paratrooper*, Ladd's unit of soldiers is trapped in a mine field. To escape, one of the soldiers skips a bazooka rocket across the ground, touching off a path of lethal mines.

For *From Russia with Love*, Maibaum merely changed the location of the sequence to the sea. Bond (SEAN CONNERY) dumps his speedboat's punctured gasoline drums overboard, watches them float among the S.P.E.C.T.R.E. boats, and then skillfully fires a flare at the gasoline. The skipping effect of the flare rocket ignites the gas, engulfing the enemy flotilla. This was also the first film produced in Europe by Albert R. Broccoli and his partner Irving Allen.

PARIS, FRANCE Location of headquarters of S.P.E.C.T.R.E. in *Thunderball*. It's also where May Day (GRACE JONES) skydives off the Eiffel Tower in *A View to a Kill*.

PARKS, TRINA American actress who portrayed the very acrobatic Thumper in *Diamonds Are Forever*.

PARMENTIER, RICHARD Actor who portrayed the enthusiastic aide to the U.S. Air Force general (BRUCE BOA) in *Octopussy*.

PARRISH, ROBERT (Columbus, Georgia, January 4, 1916–) American film director who codirected the 1967 *Casino Royale* spoof with

John Huston, Val Guest, Ken Hughes, and Joseph McGrath.

PASO EL DIABLO (Devil Pass) Rendezvous point for drug runner Franz Sanchez (ROBERT DAVI) and his cocaine tanker convoy in *Licence to Kill*—a sequence that was shot at the isolated Rumorosa Pass, south of Mexicali, Mexico. *See* KENWORTH W900B TRUCKS.

PASTELL, GEORGE Actor who portrayed the resourceful train conductor on the Orient Express in *From Russia with Love.*

London bus driver Maurice Patchett was hired by Eon Productions to drive the stunt bus in *Live and Let Die*. Here he shares a free moment with the man he doubled—Roger Moore. (Express Newspapers, London)

"Mr. Somerset, Mr. Somerset!" Actor George Pastell portrayed the train conductor on the Orient Express in *From Russia with Love.* (National Film Archive, London)

PATCHETT, MAURICE London double-decker bus-driver instructor who was hired by Eon Productions in 1972 to be a stunt driver in *Live and Let Die*. With five weeks leave from his job and double pay, Patchett and an R. T. Leyland double-decker bus, fresh off London Bakersee Route 19, were transported to Jamaica, where they performed in the hair-raising chase between Bond (ROGER MOORE) and drug

smuggler Kananga's (YAPHET KOTTO) henchmen riding in cars and motorcycles.

Patchett expertly skidded the bus on a small rural highway, forcing the motorcycles and cars off the road. He also drove the double-decker under a trestle bridge, shearing off its precut top deck. The fact that he bore a slight resemblance to Roger Moore helped Patchett win the job from 24 other instructors.

PATE, MICHAEL (Sydney, Australia, 1920–) Australian character actor who portrayed Clarence Leiter, a British agent who assists an American James Bond (BARRY NELSON) in the 1954 live television film "Casino Royale." *See* LEITER, CLARENCE.

PEAK OF SPRING TIDE The time at which Max Zorin (CHRISTOPHER WALKEN) plans to initiate Project Main Strike in *A View to a Kill*. Zorin's deadly plot will trigger a huge earthquake that will bury Silicon Valley, California, underneath a massive newly formed lake. The high tide will guarantee a maximum amount of flooding in the region.

PEDERSON, CAPTAIN U.S. naval officer, portrayed by Billy J. Mitchell, who commands the nuclear submarine that shadows Maximillian Largo's (KLAUS MARIA BRANDAUER) *Flying Saucer* yacht in *Never Say Never Again*.

PEGASUS Thoroughbred racehorse owned by Max Zorin (CHRISTOPHER WALKEN) in *A View to a Kill*. After observing his victory at an English stakes race, Bond (ROGER MOORE) joins fellow agent Sir Godfrey Tibbett (PATRICK MACNEE) at Zorin's horse sale in France.

Posing as horse breeder James St. John-Smythe, 007 discovers that Zorin has been injecting steroids into Pegasus, the amount of which is being determined by a microchip surgically implanted in his leg. The natural horse steroids are designed to overcome the leg fatigue that occurs in a race.

PENDIK, BAY OF A body of water off the coast of Turkey and near the Greek border that was the original location for the motorboat chase in *From Russia with Love*. Bad weather, unserviceable boats, and an inexperienced group of local production assistants forced the move to Scotland, where filming was completed off the coastal town of Crinan.

PENFOLD HEARTS The brand of golf ball used by James Bond (SEAN CONNERY) during his high-stakes challenge match with Goldfinger (GERT FROBE).

PENNY Bond's (SEAN CONNERY) nickname for Miss Moneypenny (LOIS MAXWELL) aboard the British submarine in *You Only Live Twice*. It's the only time he uses it in the entire series.

Decked out in Royal Navy whites, Moneypenny looks smart and extremely attractive. The repartee reflects their comfort with one another, plus the audience's familiarity with their characters at this point in the 007 series.

PEPPER, SHERIFF J. W. Bumbling Louisiana lawman, portrayed by American character actor Clifton James in both *Live and Let Die* and *The Man with the Golden Gun*. A caricature of the tough-talking Southern peace officer, Pepper was introduced in *Live and Let Die* as an outraged policeman who can't seem to halt a hair-raising motorboat chase between Bond (ROGER MOORE) and Kananga's (YAPHET KOTTO) water-borne henchmen.

Having stopped Adam (TOMMY LANE) for speeding, Pepper is about to make his first arrest, when motorboats start flying over the highway. One of them crashes into his police car. Adam escapes, and Pepper joins the chase, eventually catching up to 007 when the agent introduces himself to local authorities as a "secret agent." Pepper is incredulous. "A secret agent?" he screams. "On whose side?"

A popular element of the movie, the producers brought Pepper back in the next 007 film, *The Man with the Golden Gun*. This time, Pepper, vacationing in Thailand with his wife, thinks he sees Bond motoring down a causeway. "Nah," he thinks.

In the film's most outrageous sequence, Pepper is admiring a new red AMC Hornet in a Bangkok showroom, when Bond suddenly jumps into the car and drives it through a plate-glass window. Bond does a double take when he sees Pepper, but he's in too much of a hurry chasing Scaramanga (CHRISTOPHER LEE) to think about it. Aware of Bond's true identity, Pepper gets into the spirit of the chase to the point where he even flashes his Louisiana State Police ID to an approaching troop of angry Thai police officers, who handcuff him instead.

And Pepper is in the passenger seat when Bond and his Hornet perform the famous 360-degree jump over the collapsed Thai River bridge. *See* JAMES, CLIFTON.

PEREZ One of drug runner Franz Sanchez's (ROBERT DAVI) henchmen, portrayed by Mexican actor Alexander Bracho, in *Licence to Kill*. Perez is one of the men who helps throw captured CIA agent Felix Leiter (DAVID HEDISON) into the shark pool.

PERKINS, PETER British stunt coordinator on *From Russia with Love*, who was responsible for choreographing the famous fight between Bond (SEAN CONNERY) and Red Grant (ROBERT SHAW) on the Orient Express. In that sequence, Bob Simmons, who would replace Perkins as stunt coordinator on later films in the series, doubled Connery, while Jack Cooper doubled Shaw.

PERINGE French antimatter specialist who, after defecting to the Russians, was assassinated by S.P.E.C.T.R.E.—an affair mentioned at an organizational briefing in *Thunderball*. According to S.P.E.C.T.R.E. Agent No. 10, the "hit" was worth three million francs, paid by the Special Department of the Quai D'Orsay (French Secret Service).

PETACHI, CAPTAIN JACK Traitorous U.S. Air Force officer, portrayed by Gavan O'Herlihy, and brother of Largo's mistress, Domino (KIM BASINGER), in *Never Say Never Again*. Attached to the ground staff of a cruise missile base in England, Petachi is bribed by S.P.E.C.T.R.E. and forced to undergo an unusual corneal implant operation that will give him the same right eye-print as the president of the United States. With that capability, he can pass a top-level security check and arm two cruise missiles with nuclear warheads.

Petachi is assigned to "cruel mistress" Fatima Blush (BARBARA CARRERA). His addiction to heroin and her sexual demands gradually turn him into a nervous, pathetic human being. When Petachi sneaks a cigarette in his room at the Shrublands health clinic—an act that supposedly clouds his special vision—Blush beats him up, then offers him a significant drug dose if he'll practice the security maneuver that will eventually arm the missiles. Bond (SEAN CONNERY) observes this scuffle and begins to suspect Petachi.

Later, while searching Petachi's room, 007 finds a book of matches with the Largo (KLAUS MARIA BRANDAUER) emblem on the cover, a clue that leads him to Largo's home base in the Bahamas. Petachi completes his bomb-arming mission and drives off the base. Blush arrives to congratulate him but tosses a snake into his car instead. Losing control, Petachi slams head-on into a building and dies in the collision. *See* O'HERLIHY, GAVAN.

PETACHI, DOMINO Maximillian Largo's (KLAUS MARIA BRANDAUER) pampered mistress, portrayed by Kim Basinger, in *Never Say Never Again*. She's also the sister of U.S.

Air Force Captain Jack Petachi (GAVAN O'HERLIHY), who has defected to S.P.E.C.T.R.E.

Secretly terrified of Largo's increasingly bizarre behavior, Domino is ripe for a new lover, when she meets Bond (SEAN CONNERY) at a health spa in the south of France. The encounter—one of the film's best moments—occurs when 007 impersonates a masseur and gives Domino an especially arousing massage. They continue their repartee at Largo's charity ball, where Bond beats Largo at his own game of Domination. Bond's "prize" is one dance with Domino.

During a rather conspicuous tango, Domino learns from 007 that Largo is responsible for her brother's death. Later, during a visit aboard the *Flying Saucer* yacht, Bond further humiliates Largo by kissing Domino tenderly in the ship's gym, which has a two-way mirror leading to Largo's control room.

The psychotic S.P.E.C.T.R.E. masterspy retaliates later by throwing Bond in a North African prison cell and selling Domino to Arab traders. Bond escapes—thanks to his laser watch—steals a horse, and rescues Domino from the Arabs. Joining 007 aboard a U.S. nuclear sub, Domino eventually dives into the Tears of Allah archaeological dig and exacts her own revenge on Largo with a CO_2 spear gun. *See* BASINGER, KIM.

PETERS, MOLLY British actress who portrayed Patricia Fearing, the randy physical therapist in *Thunderball*.

PETTET, JOANNA (London, November 16, 1944–) British-born American actress who portrayed Mata Bond, the illegitimate daughter of Sir James Bond (DAVID NIVEN) in *Casino Royale*. *See* BOND, MATA.

PHANTOM 337 The model of Rolls-Royce owned by Auric Goldfinger (GERT FROBE) and driven by his servant, Oddjob (HAROLD SAKATA). In order to smuggle his gold out of England, Goldfinger cleverly replaces his car's bodywork with an 18-carat gold facsimile fabricated in his metallurgical plant in Kent, England, and later melted back into gold bars in Switzerland.

This is the car into which 007 (SEAN

CONNERY) places a homer—an electronic signaling device supplied by Q Branch that transmits the Rolls's position to a receiver in Bond's Aston Martin, thus allowing 007 to tail the sinister gold smuggler to his Swiss factory.

PHASE 4 A delicate part of the plastic surgery operation planned by Ernst Stavro Blofeld (CHARLES GRAY) in *Diamonds Are Forever* to create a duplicate of himself. This phase deals specifically with the nose. Bond (SEAN CONNERY) breaks into Blofeld's South American facility and kills what he thinks is the genuine Blofeld. Unfortunately, it's just one of many Blofelds that the real S.P.E.C.T.R.E. chief has already duplicated.

PHONY FINGERPRINTS An ingenious invention of Q's (DESMOND LLEWELYN) featured in *Diamonds Are Forever*. Convinced that a diamond-smuggling syndicate has elaborate methods of confirming the identity of their couriers, Q provides James Bond (SEAN CONNERY) with a set of phony fingerprints, which 007 wears to Amsterdam when he takes on the identity of smuggler Peter Franks (JOE ROBINSON).

Sure enough, when he arrives at the apartment of fellow smuggler Tiffany Case (JILL ST. JOHN), she takes his drinking glass, dusts it for fingerprints, and then compares them to those of the real Peter Franks. They match, and Bond's cover is left intact.

PHONY HORSE-TRAILER The hiding place for James Bond's (ROGER MOORE) mini-jet plane in the *Octopussy* teaser. It's the perfect cover for Bond, who, with his assistant Bianca (TINA HUDSON), is operating at an equestrian event outside the walls of a secret South American air force base.

Once Bond deals with some local paratroopers, he jumps into Bianca's car, disconnects the trailer, bids her good-bye, and goes back to the trailer, which, as we discover, also contains a phony horse's hindquarters. He then climbs into the jet and takes off.

PHONY MANTA RAY Giant underwater costume worn by James Bond (TIMOTHY DALTON) in *Licence to Kill*. A throwback to the phony seagull on the diving mask in *Goldfinger*, the manta-ray disguise helps Bond sneak aboard the *Wavekrest* research vessel, where he proceeds to sabotage a major drug deal.

PHOSGENE GAS Lethal gas released into Japan's Rosaki Cave by Blofeld (DONALD PLEASENCE), in *You Only Live Twice*, to discourage curiosity seekers. According to the story that Kissy (MIE HAMA) relates to Bond (SEAN CONNERY), two Ama Islanders were exploring the cave when they were mysteriously killed. Later, when Bond and Kissy follow their route, they find the gas that killed the islanders—fortunately, they dive into the water before the gas can take effect.

PHUKET A city in Thailand that is the jumping-off point for a trip to the unusual islands featured in *The Man with the Golden Gun*. On a location trip in the vicinity in 1974, the recon team discovered a chain of tiny islands so extraordinary in appearance that production designer Peter Murton thought they had crossed the time barrier and were back in the prehistoric age.

Covered with jungle foliage, shaped like overturned boulders, and appearing from the air like a series of giant stepping stones, each island was a photographer's delight. One of these strange pieces of Asian geography was to become the Scaramanga (CHRISTOPHER LEE) Island. In the Thai geography book, it was called Khow-Ping-Kan, and it featured a lovely sandy beach fronting a grotto that would later accommodate James Bond's (ROGER MOORE) seaplane, as well as be the site of the beach duel between Bond and Scaramanga.

In the background were smaller, unusually shaped islands that lent the entire scene a sense of exotic mystique far removed from anything the crew, let alone film audiences, had ever imagined. Ironically, the remote chain of islands was not far from the Mergui Archipelago (just up the coast about 100 miles), which in *Thunderball* was designated as S.P.E.C.T.R.E.'s drop zone for the diamond ransom.

PHUYUCK Barely digestible 1974 vintage Thai champagne served in 007's (ROGER MOORE) Bangkok hotel room in *The Man with the Golden Gun*. It probably compares well with the Siamese vodka that Bond (SEAN CONNERY) guzzles in *You Only Live Twice*.

PICKETT'S CHARGE Confederate maneuver during the Battle of Gettysburg that is incorrectly plotted on Brad Whitaker's (JOE DON BAKER) diorama in *The Living Daylights*. According to 007 (TIMOTHY DALTON), who has returned to Whitaker's home in Tangier to kill the arms dealer, Pickett's Charge took place up Cemetery Ridge, not Little Round Top, as Whitaker has it. Whitaker claims he's fighting the battle the way he wants.

PIG A scouring plug designed to clean the interior of a natural-gas pipeline that is used as defecting Russian General Georgi Koskov's (JEROEN KRABBE) escape route from Bratislava, Czechoslovakia, in *The Living Daylights*. This pig has been modified to carry a human being.

PILATUS AIRCRAFT FACTORY Location outsider Lucerne, Switzerland, that was used by the *Goldfinger* crew to film the exterior of Auric Enterprises. Once Bond (SEAN CONNERY) penetrated the compound, the sequences were shot on the Pinewood Studios lot, along with the incredible automobile chase involving 007's trick Aston Martin.

PINDER Bond's (SEAN CONNERY) Nassau contact, portrayed by actor Earl Cameron, in *Thunderball*. See CAMERON, EARL.

PIPER CHEROKEES The five single-engine monoplanes flown by the voluptuous blonde pilots of Pussy Galore's (HONOR BLACKMAN) Flying Circus in *Goldfinger*. The aerial element of Auric Goldfinger's (GERT FROBE) Operation Grand Slam, their mission is to immobilize Fort Knox by spraying Delta Nine nerve gas into the atmosphere above the base.

PIRANHA FISH Blofeld's (DONALD PLEASENCE) nasty pets in *You Only Live Twice*. They later consume S.P.E.C.T.R.E. agents Helga Brandt (KARIN DOR) and Hans (RONALD RICH).

PISTACHIO NUTS The favorite food of both Max, the parrot, and Columbo (TOPOL), the smuggler, in *For Your Eyes Only*.

PITON GUN The helpful gadget/weapon that Bond (SEAN CONNERY) uses to gain entrance to Willard Whyte's (JIMMY DEAN) secretive suite at the Whyte House Hotel in *Diamonds Are Forever*. It fires a mountaineering device that allows 007 to swing over to a bathroom window. Inside the suite, he uses the same gun to strike a Blofeld (CHARLES GRAY) duplicate in the forehead.

PIZ GLORIA A revolving mountaintop restaurant in Switzerland that became the location for Ernst Stavro Blofeld's (TELLY SAVALAS) Alpine redoubt in *On Her Majesty's Secret Service*. Suggested by Swiss production liaison Hubert Frolich, the facility that had been constructed atop the Schilthorn Mountain was nearly identical to the fictional fortress described in Ian Fleming's novel.

Construction of the revolving restaurant began in 1961 with the help of helicopters, which transported the building materials to the top of the Schilthorn. By Christmas 1967, the structure was completed, as was the cable-car run to the village of Murren below. Everything was brand-new, and plans were being made to furnish the restaurant's interior, when the James Bond crew arrived.

A complicated series of negotiations began the following spring to secure the location for filming. Eon Productions agreed to furnish the interior of the restaurant, as well as construct, next to the main building, a helicopter landing pad that could be used for rescue missions. In return, the filmmakers were given permission to film throughout the five-story mountaintop complex.

Production designer Syd Cain would be in charge of the operation that would eventually transform the bleak restaurant into Blofeld's exotic allergy institute. It was not an expensive task, costing only 60,000 pounds, compared with the nearly 300,000 needed for Blofeld's rocket base in *You Only Live Twice*. The principal cost went to the construction of the heliport, which was accomplished by the Swiss government, working to Cain's designs.

PLEASENCE, DONALD (Workshop, England, October 5, 1919–1995) British character actor who was the first to portray S.P.E.C.T.R.E. chief Ernst Stavro Blofeld on-camera, in 1967's *You Only Live Twice*. Thanks to a makeup department scar, he was suitably evil-looking, but his slight form and demeanor never matched the attributes of the enormously villainous character featured in the original Fleming novels. *See* BLOFELD, ERNST STAVRO.

PLAYDELL-SMITH, PRINCIPAL SECRETARY British foreign service officer in charge in Jamaica and portrayed by Louis Blaazer in *Dr. No*. He helps Bond conduct his investigation into the mysterious deaths of Commander Strangways (TIM MOXON) and his secretary.

PLIERS Crude torture device used by an associate of Soviet masterspy Le Chiffre (PETER LORRE) on captured James Bond's (BARRY NELSON) toes in the TV film "Casino Royale." Le Chiffre needs to know what Bond has done with the check for 87 million francs in baccarat winnings—a sum that the Russian must return immediately to Soviet coffers.

POHLMANN, ERIC (1913–) Viennese character actor who dubbed the voice for Ernst Stavro Blofeld in *From Russia with Love* and *Thunderball*.

POLARIS SUBMARINE PENS, NEW LONDON A projected nuclear target if American authorities attempt to locate Goldfinger's (GERT FROBE) atomic device and interfere with his plan to explode it inside Fort Knox. Other potential targets are Cape Kennedy and somewhere near the White House.

POLAROID CAMERA Equipped with a laser, it's another one of the deadly gadgets that Q (DESMOND LLEWELYN) brings to Isthmus City in *Licence to Kill*. It's also capable of taking x-ray pictures.

POLO Diminutive assistant, portrayed by Ronnie Corbett, at the Mata Hari Dance and Spy School in *Casino Royale*. Because his exterior pacemaker is constantly malfunctioning, Polo is in a continual state of anxiety. He has a great fondness for Mata Hari, whom he served, and a newfound fascination with Mata Bond (JOANNA PETTET), her illegitimate daughter.

Flirting with Polo, which drives his pacemaker crazy, Mata Bond is able to get key information out of him. This information leads her to disrupt an auction of compromising photos organized to raise funds for Le Chiffre (ORSON WELLES).

PORTEOUS, PETER British character actor who portrayed Lenkin, the nervous jewelry forger, in *Octopussy*. He returned to play the bookish gasworks supervisor, in *The Living Daylights*, whose nose is buried in Rosika Miklos's (JULIE T. WALLACE) cleavage when defecting General Georgi Koskov (JEROEN KRABBE) escapes Czechoslovakia in the "pig." *See* LENKIN; PIG.

PORT ROYAL ROAD A main highway out of Kingston, Jamaica, that is a location in *Dr. No*. To get to Miss Taro's (ZENA MARSHALL) cottage in the Blue Mountains, Bond (SEAN CONNERY) travels along the Port Royal Road and turns onto the Windward Road, which he follows until he gets to the cement factory. He then turns left and follows the road up the hill and down the other side. Two miles farther on, he will come to 2171 Magenta Drive, which is on the left.

"POSITIVE MENTAL ATTITUDE, FOOD, SHARED BODILY WARMTH" The three survival lessons that KGB Major Anya Amasova (BARBARA BACH) learned in her Siberian survival course. She explains them to James Bond (ROGER MOORE) while aboard an Egyptian sailing vessel in *The Spy Who Loved Me*.

POTEMKIN A Russian nuclear submarine swallowed by the *Liparus* supertanker in *The Spy Who Loved Me*. Its Soviet crew replaced by enemy submariners, the sub becomes a pawn in Karl Stromberg's (CURT JURGENS) plot to destroy the world. Fortunately, Bond (ROGER MOORE) short-circuits the plot, and the *Potemkin* is blown apart before it can accomplish its mission.

POTTER, COLONEL An ex-Indian army officer who is one of John Strangways's bridge cronies at the Queen's Club in Jamaica in *Dr. No.*

PPW 306R Licence plate of 007's (ROGER MOORE) modified white Lotus submarine car in *The Spy Who Loved Me*.

PRATA CAFE Meeting place in Vienna where Bond (TIMOTHY DALTON) hopes to receive important travel documents from Austrian Section Chief Saunders (THOMAS WHEATLEY) in *The Living Daylights*. The papers will help cellist Kara Milovy (MARYAM D'ABO) travel to Tangier to rendezvous with her patron/lover Georgi Koskov (JEROEN KRABBE).

Saunders comes through with the documents, but he's murdered by Necros (ANDREAS WISNIEWSKI). The killing convinces Bond that 007's next target must be KGB chief General Leonid Pushkin (JOHN RHYS-DAVIES). *See* PUSHKIN, GENERAL LEONID.

PRAVDA, GEORGE (1919–1985) Actor who portrayed Polish nuclear expert Ladislav Kutze in *Thunderball*. *See* KUTZE, LADISLAV.

PRENDERGAST, LESTER Jamaican actor who portrayed nightclub owner and ex-alligator wrestler Puss-Feller in *Dr. No*.

PRINCE WILLIAM ALEXANDER Name on the side of an Amsterdam sightseeing boat that passes the body of Mrs. Whistler (MARGARET LACEY), which authorities are retrieving from the canal in *Diamonds Are Forever*.

PRITCHARD, GROUP CAPTAIN Bond's (SEAN CONNERY) air force liaison to Station C-Canada in *Thunderball*. He's portrayed by Leonard Sachs. Agent 007's transfer to the Bahamas later takes him out of Pritchard's jurisdiction.

PRIVATE JET HOSTESS James Bond's (ROGER MOORE) love interest, who turns out to be an enemy assassin, in the *Moonraker* teaser. She's portrayed by Leila Shenna. Pointing a gun at 007 while her partner, the pilot (JEAN-PIERRE CASTALDI), shoots out the controls, the pair parachute out of the disabled plane, leaving Bond behind. Bond, parachuteless, is then tossed out of the plane by Jaws (RICHARD KIEL), which initiates an outrageous midair fight between the pilot, 007, and the steel-toothed killer.

PROJECT MAIN STRIKE Code name for psychotic billionaire industrialist Max Zorin's (CHRISTOPHER WALKEN) plan to monopolize the world's microchip supply by destroying Silicon Valley, California, in *A View to a Kill*. The plot involves triggering a huge earthquake in the region—a cataclysmic event that will bury the high-technology capital of the United States underneath the waters of an enormous lake.

Two separate activities will precipitate the disaster. First, Zorin orders his coastal oil rigs to start pumping seawater into the extremely unstable Hayward earthquake fault. Second, and most importantly, his minions have taken over the abandoned Main Strike silver mine, which sits atop the San Andreas Fault, where a massive explosion is planned.

According to geologist Stacey Sutton (TANYA ROBERTS), who explains Zorin's plan to Bond (ROGER MOORE) when they break into his headquarters at the mine and view an animated model of the region, the Main Strike Mine also sits above the key geological lock between the Hayward and San Andreas faults. Any explosion that occurs at Main Strike will move both faults together, triggering the massive quake that Zorin is counting on. The explosion, planned to coincide with the spring tide, is set to occur at 9:41 A.M., only one hour away.

Attempting to escape, Bond and Stacey are identified and chased into the mine shaft by May Day (GRACE JONES), Jenny Flex (ALISON DOODY), and Pan Ho (PAPILLON SOO SOO). Double-crossing his bodyguard, assistants, and all of the miners, Zorin orders the mine shaft flooded. Stacey barely escapes to the surface. The rush of water kills Jenny Flex and Pan Ho, however, and carries Bond and May Day deeper into the mine.

Realizing that she's been double-crossed, May Day helps Bond raise Zorin's triggering bomb, which sits atop a massive pile of explosives. Unable to deactivate it because it's been

Special effects technicians prepare Zorin's bomb in *A View to a Kill*, while Grace Jones operates the faulty handbrake. (Amberle Chalk Pit Museum)

Special effects department handiwork: the dummy Grace Jones stands atop Zorin's bomb. (Amberle Chalk Pit Museum)

booby-trapped, 007 and May Day place the bomb on a railroad handcar. As the seconds tick down, May Day jumps on the car and keeps a faulty hand brake from stopping the car's momentum. The handcar arrives safely outside the mine, and the bomb detonates, blowing May Day to bits.

When Stacey is captured by Zorin and taken skyward in his blimp, Bond comes to her rescue by hanging onto one of the mooring lines. Transported across the skyline of San Francisco, where he somehow avoids being crumpled by several skyscrapers, Bond manages to wrap the mooring line firmly around one of the top girders of the Golden Gate Bridge, immobilizing the blimp.

A final battle takes place on the girder as Bond is attacked by an axe-carrying Zorin and a dynamite-wielding Dr. Mortner (WILLOUGHBY GRAY). Zorin fails, falling off the bridge to his death, and Mortner drops the dy-

namite before he can throw it at 007. The blimp explodes and falls into San Francisco Bay.

"PROPERTY OF A LADY, THE" Reference in the Sotheby's auction catalog, in *Octopussy*, to the anonymous owner of a priceless Fabergé Easter egg. Arriving at the auction gallery, Bond (ROGER MOORE) at first thinks the "lady" might be Magda (KRISTINA WAYBORN), the comely assistant of exiled Afghan Prince Kamal Khan (LOUIS JOURDAN).

PR 23 The identification number on Quarrel's (JOHN KITZMILLER) sailboat, which transports 007 (SEAN CONNERY) to Crab Key, in *Dr. No*.

PUSHKIN, GENERAL LEONID General Gogol's (WALTER GOTELL) replacement as the head of the Soviet KGB, portrayed masterfully by character actor John Rhys-Davies, in *The Living Daylights*. Actually, Pushkin finds himself snared in a drug-smuggling plot hatched by arms dealer Brad Whitaker (JOE DON BAKER) and renegade Russian General Georgi Koskov (JEROEN KRABBE). Pushkin knows Whitaker because he's given him a $50 million advance for a huge shipment of new-age weapons to be used against Mujahedeen rebels in Afghanistan.

Pushkin later arrives in Tangier to kill the deal when he suspects that Whitaker is involved with Koskov. Whitaker must return the money in two days, or he will be put out of business permanently.

When Koskov defects to the West with the help of James Bond (TIMOTHY DALTON), Pushkin arrests his girlfriend, Kara Milovy (MARYAM D'ABO), who claims she doesn't know anything about his whereabouts. When Koskov is recaptured by the KGB, Pushkin is even more suspicious, since he didn't order the mission.

During his short stay at the Bladen safe house in England, Koskov fingers Pushkin as the mastermind of "Smiert Spionam," a Soviet assault on the British Secret Service that has already begun with the death of 004 (FREDERICK WARDER) on Gibraltar. Believing Koskov, M (ROBERT BROWN) then orders Bond to assassinate Pushkin in Tangier, where the Russian is heading a trade delegation.

Equally suspicious of Koskov, Bond doesn't kill Pushkin but instead teams up with him in a counterplot to expose the operation being planned by Koskov and Whitaker. Bond's sniper attack is faked to make everyone, including Koskov, believe that Pushkin is out of the way.

Since Pushkin is the only one who suspects that Koskov wasn't recaptured by the KGB, Koskov now feels free to go to Afghanistan as a Soviet general and trade the $50 million arms advance—now converted into diamonds—for a huge opium cache. Bond foils that operation and returns to Tangier to kill Whitaker. Pushkin then arrests Koskov for numerous crimes against the state. He's to be shipped back to Mother Russia in the diplomatic bag. *See* RHYS-DAVIES, JOHN.

PUSS-FELLER The owner of a popular nightclub on the beach in Kingston, Jamaica, that bears his name. He's portrayed by Lester Prendergast in *Dr. No*. Puss-Feller is also a friend of Quarrel, who used to wrestle alligators for a living. First appearing as an enemy of Bond, Puss-Feller joins forces with 007 when Felix Leiter explains that they're working on the same side.

PUSSY Name that appears on the eating bowl of Stacey Sutton's (TANYA ROBERTS) cat in *A View to a Kill*.

Q

Q British Secret Service code initial for Major Boothroyd, the equipment officer. *See* BOOTH-ROYD, MAJOR.

Q (DESMOND LLEWELYN) lectures Bond (SEAN CONNERY) on Little Nellie's "charms" in *You Only Live Twice*. (Rex Features Ltd./RDR Productions)

A Q Branch jet-boosted motorcycle from *Never Say Never Again*. (Taliafilm)

QUANTICO U.S. Marine installation in Virginia that is the ultimate destination of the DEA convoy carrying drug lord Franz Sanchez (ROBERT DAVI) in *Licence to Kill*. Thanks to DEA agent Killifer's (EVERETT MCGILL) treachery, the convoy never makes it.

QUARREL James Bond's (SEAN CONNERY) Cayman Islander associate, portrayed by

John Kitzmiller, in *Dr. No*. One of the truly fun characters in the Bond series—and a throwback to another era when wide-eyed black sidekicks such as Eddie "Rochester" Anderson and Willie Best were common—Quarrel is of a tougher breed. (Rochester would never have talked out of the side of his mouth with a cigarette hanging from it.)

A Cayman Island fisherman, Quarrel is working for CIA agent Felix Leiter (JACK LORD) when Bond (SEAN CONNERY) meets him on the beach in Kingston. Quarrel's seamanship, plus a belly of rum, gets 007 to Crab Key in a small sailboat. However, the trusty fisherman pays with his life when he's burned to death in the swamps by the flamethrower in Dr. No's "dragon." Note that all of Quarrel's scenes in Kingston have a strong reality to them, no doubt due to Kitzmiller, a perfect casting choice. *See* KITZMILLER, JOHN.

QUARREL, JR. The son of Quarrel (JOHN KITZMILLER), featured in *Live and Let Die* and portrayed by Roy Stewart. Like his father, Quarrel, Jr., runs a fishing-boat charter service and works undercover for the CIA. Rather than Jamaica, his turf is the mythical island of San Monique (ironically, filmed in Jamaica).

Quarrel, Jr., helps Bond (ROGER MOORE) by piloting him out to the "Kananga woman's" (JANE SEYMOUR) sanctuary, where Bond's hang glider is turned loose. Later, Bond and Quarrel, Jr., swim from this same fishing boat toward the San Monique mainland, where they will place demolitions in Kananga's poppy fields.

QUARTERBACK The CIA code for Felix Leiter (NORMAN BURTON) during Operation Passover at Las Vegas's Circus Circus Casino in *Diamonds Are Forever*.

QUARTER TURN CLOCKWISE According to a Russian officer's careful instructions, it's the way you activate the A-bomb in *Octopussy*.

QUAYLE, ANNA (Birmingham, England, October 6, 1937–) British comedienne who portrayed Frau Hoffner, the strict owner of West Berlin's Mata Hari Dance and Spy School, in *Casino Royale*. See HOFFNER, FRAU.

QUEEN ELIZABETH I British ocean liner that caught fire and partially sank under mysterious circumstances in Hong Kong Harbor in 1971. In *The Man with the Golden Gun*, the interior of the liner has been transformed into British Secret Service Far East headquarters.

QUEEN OF CUPS A tarot card in *Live and Let Die* that becomes an important clue to CIA agent Rosie Carver's (GLORIA HENDRY) true identity. According to the rules of tarot, a Queen of Cups shown in the upside-down position means a deceitful, perverse woman; a liar; or a cheat. Supplied to Bond (ROGER MOORE) by Solitaire (JANE SEYMOUR), it helps him determine that Rosie is not a CIA operative at all, but one of Kananga's (YAPHET KOTTO) agents.

QUEEN'S CLUB The aristocratic-looking men's club in Kingston, Jamaica, where Commander John Strangways (TIM MOXON) plays bridge each day with his local cronies—Principal Secretary Playdell-Smith (LOUIS BLAAZER), Professor R. J. Dent (ANTHONY DAWSON), and Colonel Potter.

QUIST One of Largo's (ADOLFO CELI) henchmen, portrayed by Bill Cummings, in *Thunderball*. He bumbles an assassination attempt on Bond (SEAN CONNERY) in 007's Nassau hotel room. Disarmed by 007, he's sent back to Largo with the catchphrase "the little fish I throw back into the sea." Largo takes him literally and throws poor little Quist to his sharks.

R

RABETT, CATHERINE British actress who portrayed Liz, the CIA agent working in Tangier for Felix Leiter (JOHN TERRY), in *The Living Daylights.*

RADIOACTIVE LINT This Q-Branch invention featured in *OHMSS* is a tracking device that is planted in the clothes of an enemy agent. In actuality, this was an inside joke in the film that abandoned, for the time being, the use of gadgets as a standard Bondian prop. For *OHMSS*, Bond (GEORGE LAZENBY) once again relies on his wits rather than his toys to destroy the enemy.

RADIO-CONTROLLED SHARKS Man-eaters employed by S.P.E.C.T.R.E. assassin Fatima Blush (BARBARA CARRERA) to kill James Bond (SEAN CONNERY) in *Never Say Never Again.* The sharks have been equipped with an electronic receiver that homes in on a transmitting device that Blush places on Bond's scuba equipment. Agent 007 discovers the ruse in time and tricks the sharks into following the homer into an undersea wreck.

RAFT, GEORGE (New York City, September 27, 1895–November 24, 1980) Distinctive-voiced, tough-guy actor who had a cameo role in *Casino Royale.* He's the gangster-type who's tossing a coin at the bar of a Monte Carlo casino while a huge brawl goes on all around him.

RAIN-COOLED TAITTINGER Dr. Noah's (WOODY ALLEN) champagne of choice in *Casino Royale.* Pouring drinks for himself and Lady James Bond (DALIAH LAVI), Noah turns his back, allowing her to drop the A-bomb tablet into his glass. He then proceeds to swallow the tiny nuclear device. Four hundred burps later, he explodes.

RAJDAMNERN STADIUM Bangkok, Thailand, location of the kick-boxing match observed by James Bond (ROGER MOORE) in *The Man with the Golden Gun.* It's where 007 meets Scaramanga (CHRISTOPHER LEE) for the first time.

RAMIREZ, MR. The owner of the heroin installations destroyed by Bond (SEAN CONNERY) in the *Goldfinger* teaser. Ramirez was using the drugs, smuggled in heroin-flavored bananas, to finance revolutions.

RAMJET FLIGHT BRAVO X-RAY The identification code of the NATO bomber hijacked by S.P.E.C.T.R.E. in *Thunderball.* It's on a NATO training flight with nuclear bombs on board.

RANGER, HMS A British nuclear submarine captured by the *Liparus* supertanker in *The Spy Who Loved Me.* Captain Talbot (BRYAN MARSHALL) and his crew are imprisoned, along with the crews of two other submarines—one American, one Russian—until Bond (ROGER MOORE) engineers their mass escape.

Unfortunately, while the escapees are trying to gain entry to the control room, the *Ranger* and the Russian sub *Potemkin* are sent on an attack mission, with a crew of enemy submariners. Their mission is to launch two nuclear missiles and precipitate World War III.

Fortunately, Bond gains entry to the *Liparus* control room. With the help of the skipper of the USS *Wayne* (SHANE RIMMER), he reprograms the trajectory of the two enemy missiles so that they destroy the two submarines instead.

RANSOME Acronym-obsessed CIA chief, portrayed by William Holden, who joins his British, French, and Soviet counterparts in trying to persuade Sir James Bond (DAVID NIVEN) to accept one more desperate mission, in *Casino Royale.* Sir James notes with disgust that Ransome has a trick carnation that spits cyanide.

Bond knew him when he was a junior cipher clerk. Ransome refers to his promotion as going from J.C.C. Class G, S.I.C. to S.C.C.T., CIA Washington, D.C. Quite a mouthful. Ransome leads an unusual American force of cowboys and Indian paratroopers against the forces of Dr. Noah (WOODY ALLEN) in the outrageous Monte Carlo brawl that concludes the film. *See* HOLDEN, WILLIAM.

RATOFF, GREGORY (1897–1960) Russian actor/director who purchased the feature-film rights to *Casino Royale* from Ian Fleming for $6,000 in the mid-1950s. He would later sell the rights to American producer Charles K. Feldman, who produced *Casino Royale* as a spoof in 1967.

RATS Prominent and ferocious denizens of the 1,600-year-old underground Byzantine cistern featured in *From Russia with Love*. A horde of these creatures chases Bond (SEAN CONNERY), Tanya (DANIELA BIANCHI), and Kerim Bey (PEDRO ARMENDARIZ).

Filming this sequence in England was a problem for producers Harry Saltzman and Cubby Broccoli, because the law forbade the use of wild rats in film productions. Explained production designer Syd Cain, "We're not allowed to use wild rats in England, because if someone is bitten, we can have real trouble. We tried to use tame white rats that were dipped in cocoa to give them the proper color, but after we fixed our stage lights and dressed the set, they became terribly drowsy and wouldn't cooperate.

"Did you ever try to get a mouse to run? Here we were all standing around waiting for something to happen, and all they would do was lick chocolate coating off each other's bodies. So that was a bloody failure.

"We ended up going to Madrid, where you can film anything, and we hired a Spanish rat catcher who trapped 200 of the little beggars. We then hired out a garage and built a tiny part of the Byzantine cistern there. Director Terence Young shot the rats coming down the tunnel, with a plate of glass in front of the camera protecting us from the rats. In the end, everybody was on chairs, even Cubby, who came down to watch. Why? Because all of the rats escaped and nobody wanted to be bitten."

RAVALEC, BLANCHE Comical buxom blond who portrayed Jaws's (RICHARD KIEL) girlfriend in *Moonraker*.

RAVISHING GIRL Kerim Bey's (PEDRO ARMENDARIZ) girlfriend in *From Russia with Love*. She's portrayed by actress Nadja Regin, who returns to play Bonita, the fiery flamenco dancer in the *Goldfinger* teaser.

Identified in the *From Russia with Love* credits simply as the "ravishing girl," Regin is memorable for her cooing to Kerim Bey, "Ali Kerim Bey, Ali Kerim Bey"—an enticing ploy that saves his life when Krilencu's (FRED HAGGERTY) limpet mine obliterates his desk and most of his office.

REBREATHER A tiny pocket-sized Aqualung supplied to James Bond (SEAN CONNERY) by Q (DESMOND LLEWELYN) in *Thunderball*. It holds four minutes of air, and Bond makes good use of it in Largo's (ADOLFO CELI) shark-infested pool.

After filming was completed, *Thunderball*'s art director, Peter Lamont, received a call from a commander in the British Royal Navy who was having difficulty with a design of his own for a rebreather and wanted the scoop on the film's unit. Lamont disappointed the naval officer by explaining that it was only a prop. It was not the first time that the military had become intrigued with a James Bond gadget, only to find out it was a dose of movie magic.

RED James Bond's (SEAN CONNERY) color in the Domination game featured in *Never Say Never Again*. Largo (KLAUS MARIA BRANDAUER) played blue. *See* DOMINATION.

RED CHIANTI The wine ordered by Red Grant (ROBERT SHAW) on the Orient Express in *From Russia with Love*. Since Grant, posing as Captain Nash, has ordered the grilled sole as his dinner entree, this choice of wine immediately makes Bond (SEAN CONNERY) suspicious. Anyone knows that when you order fish, you order a white wine to go with it.

RED CROSS MERCY FLIGHT The cover for the Union Corse dawn helicopter assault on Ernst Stavro Blofeld's (TELLY SAVALAS) Alpine fortress in *On Her Majesty's Secret Service*. James Bond (GEORGE LAZENBY), Marc Ange Draco (GABRIELE FERZETTI), and his men claim to be carrying blood plasma and emergency equipment to Traffego to aid victims of the Italian flood disaster.

RED CROSS PARCELS How renegade General Georgi Koskov (JEROEN KRABBE) camouflages the cache of raw opium he buys from the Snow Leopard Brotherhood of Afghanistan in *The Living Daylights*. Unfortunately, Bond (TIMOTHY DALTON) hijacks the transport full of opium and jettisons the entire cargo.

RED DRAGON OF MACAO One of the notorious Chinese Tong societies, a criminal organization whose symbol is featured on a tattoo that appears on the wrist of S.P.E.C.T.R.E. agent Count Lippe (GUY DOLEMAN) in *Thunderball*. The tell-tale Tong sign is enough to raise the suspicions of James Bond (SEAN CONNERY), who is spending some R & R time at rural England's Shrublands health clinic.

REDWOOD, MANNING (New York City, February 16) American actor who portrayed oil

American actor Manning Redwood costarred as oil man Bob Conley in *A View to a Kill*. (Manning Redwood)

executive Bob Conley in *A View to a Kill*. He also portrayed U.S. Air Force General Miller in *Never Say Never Again*.

REGIN, NADJA Actress who appeared in two James Bond films, first as the "ravishing" girlfriend of Kerim Bey (PEDRO ARMENDARIZ) in *From Russia with Love*, then as Bonita, the fiery flamenco dancer in the *Goldfinger* teaser. *See* RAVISHING GIRL; BONITA.

REID, MILTON (1917–   ) A professional wrestler and actor with over 100 film credits, Reid portrayed one of Dr. No's (JOSEPH WISEMAN) guards in the first Bond film

and came back in *The Spy Who Loved Me* to play Sandor, the assassin. In the 1967 *Casino Royale* spoof, he played one of Mata Bond's (JOANNA PETTET) Indian attendants. *See* SANDOR.

REMOTE-CONTROL AIRWAYS A euphemism for Ernst Stavro Blofeld's helicopter, which operates on remote when its pilot is killed in the *For Your Eyes Only* teaser. What Bond (ROGER MOORE) thinks is going to be an urgent trip to London becomes, in Blofeld's hands, a ride of terror.

Somehow, 007 is able to break out of the rear section of the helicopter, enter the cockpit, rip out the remote-pilot switching, and take control. He then chases the bald-pated, wheelchair-bound Telly Savalas look-alike and impales his wheelchair on the chopper's skid.

The last we see of Blofeld, he's being unceremoniously dumped into a giant industrial chimney, a fate from which he won't return this time—although, technically speaking, Jack Schwartzman brought him back in the guise of Max von Sydow, in *Never Say Never Again*, for the rival Bond company.

Actress Nadja Regin takes time out to showcase her charms. She appeared in both *From Russia with Love* and *Goldfinger*. (National Film Archive, London)

Production designer Syd Cain and director Terence Young return in September 1989 to the Renaissance Garden exterior in *From Russia with Love*—actually the gardens behind the administration building of Pinewood Studios.

RENAISSANCE GARDEN An atmospheric standing location on the Pinewood Studios lot that was the background for the first teaser sequence of the series, in *From Russia with Love*. Tracked by S.P.E.C.T.R.E. assassin Red Grant, the phony 007 with the Sean Connery mask tiptoes his way through an evocative setting of finely manicured bushes and trees, walkways, fountains, and statuary.

Director Terence Young, filming his second James Bond film, based the mood of this sequence on a similar setting used in the Alain Resnais film *Last Year at Marienbad* (French, 1962). The Bond sequence began shooting on the night of April 12, 1963.

RENOIR, CLAUDE (Paris, France, December 6, 1914–September 5, 1993) Cinematographer on *The Spy Who Loved Me*, who is the grandson of the famous Impressionist painter, Pierre-Auguste Renoir, and nephew of film director Jean Renoir. Prior to *The Spy Who Loved Me*, Renoir was the cinematographer on two other Lewis Gilbert productions—*The Adventurers* (1970) and *Paul and Michelle* (1974).

RENTALS The percentage of the motion-picture ticket price that is returned to the studio—generally computed at between 40 and 50 percent of the box-office gross. Not surprisingly, the Bond movies have all placed on the list of the most successful films of all time.

The following list is based on U.S. domestic rentals only. Historically, the Bond movies have accrued about a third of their total world gross in the U.S. marketplace. Foreign revenue has thus played a vital factor in the continuing success of the series.

RENTAL FIGURES FOR BOND FILMS

Dr. No	$6,434,801
From Russia with Love	$9,924,279
Goldfinger	$22,997,706
Thunderball	$28,621,434
You Only Live Twice	$19,388,692
Casino Royale (the feature)	$10,200,000
On Her Majesty's Secret Service	$9,117,167
Diamonds Are Forever	$19,726,829
Live and Let Die	$15,925,283
The Man with the Golden Gun	$9,440,863
The Spy Who Loved Me	$24,364,501
Moonraker	$33,924,008
For Your Eyes Only	$26,577,736
Octopussy	$34,031,196
Never Say Never Again	$28,200,000
A View to a Kill	$25,316,185
The Living Daylights	$27,878,804
Licence to Kill	$16,662,000

REST OF THE WORLD, THE Final target selected in the Domination video-game battle between James Bond (SEAN CONNERY) and Maximillian Largo (KLAUS MARIA BRANDAUER) in *Never Say Never Again*. It's worth $325,000, and this time Bond wins. Taking into account his previous losses, his total winnings are $267,000. Charitably, 007 tells Largo he'll forgo his winnings in return for one dance with Domino (KIM BASINGER).

RHH 409 New York license plate of Mr. Big's (YAPHET KOTTO) brown Cadillac in *Live and Let Die*. Agent 007 (ROGER MOORE) tails this car to Harlem.

RHYS-DAVIES, JOHN British character actor who portrayed KGB General Pushkin in *The Living Daylights*. Having gained international popularity in *Raiders of the Lost Ark*—where he shined as Indiana Jones's Egyptian friend, Sallah—Rhys-Davies became the perfect choice for Pushkin, the new head of the KGB.

As such, he plays an honorable man who nonetheless faces a quick execution at the hands of Bond (TIMOTHY DALTON) unless he can prove himself blameless for "Smiert Spionam"—a fiendish war against the British Secret Service that has already killed 004 (FREDERICK WARDER). *See* PUSHKIN, GENERAL LEONID.

RIGG, CARL British actor who portrayed the assassin who infiltrates a British Secret Service war game on Gibraltar in the teaser for *The Living Daylights*.

RIGG, DIANA (Doncaster, England, July 20, 1938–) Sexy, athletic British actress who jumped from TV's "The Avengers" to the role of Tracy de Vicenzo in *On Her Majesty's Secret Service*. Unlike her female predecessors, Tracy has a serious love affair with Bond (GEORGE LAZENBY). And, to the astonishment of his fans, 007 eventually proposes marriage to her. In the film's conclusion, Bond and Tracy are married, but she is soon murdered by Ernst Stavro Blofeld (TELLY SAVALAS).

For the first time, the producers felt that the company should go with an established actress, someone who could work well with the fledgling Lazenby (an ex-model turned actor) and increase the power of the film's romantic scenes. Rigg fulfilled that requirement nicely. Not only did she look the part (three seasons on "The Avengers" had kept her in excellent shape), but she was a first-rate actress who rose to the occasion of playing the future Mrs. James Bond.

Her best scenes? Probably her arrival in Murren to rescue 007, who is being hunted down by Blofeld's S.P.E.C.T.R.E. goons. Skating up to Bond at the rink, she falls into his arms, senses the danger that surrounds him, and then offers to help him escape in her red Cougar. Her driving ability and, later, her prowess on skis make her the consummate 007 mate. She even gets a chance to show off some of her hand-to-hand combat skills during a fight with Grunther (YURI BORIENKO) at Piz Gloria.

Her much-publicized feud with Lazenby during the filming was more the product of tabloid imaginings than hard fact. *See* TRACY.

RIMMER, SHANE An actor who never seems to play the same character twice in the James Bond series. In *You Only Live Twice*, he's one of the space-tracking technicians. In *Diamonds Are Forever*, he's Willard Whyte's (JIMMY DEAN) right-hand man. And in *The Spy Who Loved Me*, he has his biggest role, as the skipper of the American nuclear submarine captured by Stromberg (CURT JURGENS).

RISBOURG, DOMINIQUE French singer/performer who appears in *A View to a Kill* with her cabaret act Dominique and the Enchanted Papillon, a show that combines singing with dozens of animated butterflies. *See* DOMINIQUE AND THE ENCHANTED PAPILLON.

ROACH, PAT Six-foot, six-inch British character actor who portrayed Lippe, the S.P.E.C.T.R.E. assassin who attacks Bond (SEAN CONNERY) at Shrublands in *Never Say Never Again*. *See* LIPPE.

ROBERTS, TANYA (New York City, October 15, 1955–) American actress and former

Pat Roach brought Lippe to life in *Never Say Never Again*. (Peter Charlesworth Ltd.)

What Tanya Roberts is doing underneath that coat is anyone's guess. Roger Moore, minus his mole, appears happy. (Rex Features Ltd./RDR Productions)

costar of "Charlie's Angels" who portrayed geologist and oil heiress Stacey Sutton in *A View to a Kill*. Roberts has the honor of being one of the most conservatively portrayed Bond women in the entire series.

Costumed mostly in long gowns, formal business attire, and mine-shaft coveralls, Roberts' shapely figure remained hidden throughout most of the film, making her the least sexy of 007's many playmates. If you discount a brief liaison with Pola Ivanova (FIONA FULLERTON) in a hot tub, *A View to a Kill* is a surprisingly tame romantic entry in the series, perhaps presaging the safe-sex Bond films of the late 1980s. *See* SUTTON, STACEY.

ROBINSON, JOE Stuntman/actor who portrayed tough diamond smuggler Peter Franks in *Diamonds Are Forever*. In a vicious Amsterdam elevator fight, Franks battles James Bond (SEAN CONNERY) and loses—a claustrophobic sequence that was one of the film's highlights.

ROBINS, TOBY Actress who portrayed Melina Havelock's (CAROLE BOUQUET) mother, Iona, in *For Your Eyes Only*. Both Iona and her husband, Timothy (JACK HEDLEY), are strafed and murdered by a Cuban hit man

named Gonzales (STEFAN KALIPHA), who is working for Russian agent Aris Kristatos (JULIAN GLOVER).

ROCK SALT What Stacey Sutton's (TANYA ROBERTS) shotgun is loaded with in *A View to a Kill*. Bond (ROGER MOORE) uses it to good effect against a squad of Zorin's (CHRISTOPHER WALKEN) goons sent to pressure Stacey into dropping her lawsuit and accepting Zorin's $5 million payoff.

RODNEY Syndicate hit man, portrayed by tough-guy character actor Marc Lawrence, in *The Man with the Golden Gun*. He is Scaramanga's (CHRISTOPHER LEE) first victim in the "fun house" maze.

ROMANOFF STAR (aka Romanov Star) Jewelry treasure that is among the many priceless items stolen by General Orlov (STEVEN BERKOFF) from the Kremlin Art Repository, in *Octopussy*, and replaced by forgeries designed by Lenkin (PETER PORTEOUS). The horde is being used by Orlov and his partner, Kamal Khan (LOUIS JOURDAN), to finance a scheme to explode an atomic bomb on a U.S. Air Force base in West Germany. The forgery is later ex-

Stuntman Joe Robinson loses a fight with a fire extinguisher in *Diamonds Are Forever*. (Express Newspapers, London)

posed by General Gogol's (WALTER GO-TELL) consultant, Borchoi (GABOR VERNON), from Leningrad's Hermitage Museum.

In the meantime, James Bond (ROGER MOORE) steals the real Romanoff Star when he comes across the jewelry that Kamal has hidden aboard a circus-train car in East Germany—a duplicate car, with the A-bomb hidden in the base of the circus cannon, has been attached to Octopussy's (MAUD ADAMS) train. By showing her the star, 007 is able to convince Octopussy that she's been double-crossed by Kamal.

ROMANOVA, CORPORAL OF STATE SECURITY TATIANA "TANYA" One of James Bond's sexiest women, she was portrayed by Italian beauty queen Daniela Bianchi in *From Russia with Love*. She becomes the innocent pawn in a deadly assassination and extortion plan concocted by S.P.E.C.T.R.E.

Stationed in Istanbul, and assigned to the Russian embassy's cryptographic section, where she works directly with the Lektor decoding machine, Romanova is a Corporal of State Security in the Russian army. Her friends call her "Tanya." She was originally stationed in Moscow, where she worked with the English decoding crew and where she first saw Colonel Klebb (LOTTE LENYA), whom she believes is still working for the Russians. Earlier in her life, she was a ballet student who was disqualified for growing one inch over regulation height.

Prior to meeting 007 in Istanbul, Tanya has had three lovers. Although Klebb orders her to seduce Bond in an Istanbul hotel suite—where, unbeknownst to her, the lovemaking will be filmed by a S.P.E.C.T.R.E. camera crew hiding in the cabinet de voyeur—she eventually falls in love with him.

Tanya joins Bond on the Orient Express with the Lektor decoding machine she has helped steal. Drugged by Red Grant, she survives the flight on the train and the ensuing battles with S.P.E.C.T.R.E. assassins in helicopters and speedboats. She eventually saves Bond's life in Venice by shooting Rosa Klebb.

Screenwriter Richard Maibaum revived her character in an early draft of *The Spy Who Loved Me*, but she was eventually replaced by Russian spy Triple X in the final script.

ROME AFFAIR A successful mission, mentioned by M (BERNARD LEE) in *Live and Let Die*, that James Bond (ROGER MOORE) completes just before he begins his new assignment. M passes on the congratulations of the Italian Secret Service, plus their puzzlement over the disappearance of their agent Miss Caruso (MADELINE SMITH). In actuality, Miss Caruso has fallen in love with Bond and is hiding in his closet.

RONEE, HELENA Actress who portrayed the Israeli allergy victim in *On Her Majesty's Secret Service*.

ROOM 602 Andrea Anders's (MAUD ADAMS) room at Hong Kong's Peninsula Hotel, in *The Man with the Golden Gun*.

ROOM 32 Bond's (SEAN CONNERY) first hotel room in Istanbul in *From Russia with Love*. When he discovers that it's covered with listening devices, he demands another room, claiming that the "bed's too small."

ROSAKI A huge cave on the Japanese mainland located across the sea from Ama Island in *You Only Live Twice*. When two Ama Islanders are found dead in their boat, James Bond (SEAN CONNERY) and his "wife," Kissy (MIE HAMA), investigate and discover deadly phosgene gas in the cave. Diving into the water, they eventually find their way to an extinct volcano, which is the site of Blofeld's (DONALD PLEASENCE) secret rocket base.

ROSE, SISTER One of Dr. No's (JOSEPH WISEMAN) extremely efficient secretaries/receptionists on Crab Key. She's portrayed by actress Michele Mok.

ROUGERIE, JEAN French actor who portrayed detective Achille Aubergine, who's assassinated by May Day (GRACE JONES) on the Eiffel Tower in *A View to a Kill*. See AUBERGINE, ACHILLE.

ROWSELL, JANETTE English actress with a wiggly walk who portrayed the maid at the Fontainebleau Hotel, in *Goldfinger*. She "helps"

James Bond (SEAN CONNERY) gain access to Goldfinger's (GERT FROBE) suite.

ROYAL BELUGA The caviar ordered by Bond (GEORGE LAZENBY) for Tracy (DIANA RIGG) and himself at the casino in *On Her Majesty's Secret Service*. It comes from "north of the Caspian."

ROYAL JELLY A gourmet treat of Sir James Bond (DAVID NIVEN) in *Casino Royale*. According to M (JOHN HUSTON), it helps the retired 007 cleanse his intestines. Gee, I wonder if they serve this at Shrublands?

RSD 522 Fictional Isthmus City license plate of the Rolls-Royce driven by Q (DESMOND LLEWELYN) in *Licence to Kill*. Working undercover for a change, the equipment officer is masquerading as James Bond's (TIMOTHY DALTON) chauffeur.

RUBAVITCH KGB General Leonid Pushkin's (JOHN RHYS-DAVIES) girlfriend, portrayed by Virginia Hey, in *The Living Daylights*. Accompanying him to Tangier, Rubavitch is in the hotel room when Pushkin discovers that he's about to be assassinated by James Bond (TIMOTHY DALTON). Pushkin eventually convinces 007 not to kill him, and they join forces to expose the plot of renegade Russian General Georgi Koskov (JEROEN KRABBE).

As their first act, Pushkin is assassinated by Bond, a scam that stuns an already shaken Rubavitch. She is further stunned when Pushkin rises from his gurney and removes the phony blood packs from under his uniform.

(Note: Rubavitch is not to be confused with General Alexis Gogol's lady friend, Rublevitch.)

RUBLEVITCH General Alexis Gogol's (WALTER GOTELL) very sexy assistant, portrayed by Eva Rueber-Staier, who is introduced in *The Spy Who Loved Me* and who also appears in *For Your Eyes Only* and *Octopussy*.

RUDI, MR. French journalist based in Dieppe who will break the Le Chiffre (PETER LORRE) scandal once British agent Clarence

Leiter (MICHAEL PATE) gives him the word in the TV film "Casino Royale." His phone number is 432.

RUEBER-STAIER, EVA German actress who portrayed Rublevitch, General Alexis Gogol's (WALTER GOTELL) assistant in *The Spy Who Loved Me*, *For Your Eyes Only*, and *Octopussy*.

RUM COLLINS The mixed drink ordered by James Bond (SEAN CONNERY) at Emilio Largo's (ADOLFO CELI) Palmyra estate in *Thunderball*.

RUNNING TIMES *Dr. No* and *Goldfinger* share honors as the shortest Bond features, at 111 minutes. *On Her Majesty's Secret Service* is the longest at 140.

RUNNING TIMES FOR BOND FILMS

Film	Length
Dr. No	111 Minutes
From Russia with Love	118 Minutes
Goldfinger	111 Minutes
Thunderball	129 Minutes
You Only Live Twice	116 Minutes
Casino Royale	130 Minutes
On Her Majesty's Secret Service	140 Minutes
Diamonds Are Forever	119 Minutes
Live and Let Die	121 Minutes
The Man with the Golden Gun	125 Minutes
The Spy Who Loved Me	125 Minutes
Moonraker	126 Minutes
For Your Eyes Only	127 Minutes
Octopussy	130 Minutes
Never Say Never Again	137 Minutes
A View to a Kill	131 Minutes
The Living Daylights	130 Minutes
Licence to Kill	135 Minutes

RUSSHON, CHARLES JOSEPH ANTHONY "RUSH" (March 23, 1911–June 26, 1982) Retired U.S. Air Force lieutenant colonel who was a key production liaison on five James Bond films.

Russhon's involvement with Eon Productions began in 1963 on *From Russia with Love* when he secured some U.S. military aid during location shooting in Turkey. The following year, he was instrumental in securing permission from

Military liaison Charles Russhon portrayed an American general during the Double-0 briefing in *Thunderball*. (Claire Russhon Collection)

Charles Russhon, who inspired Milt Caniff's Charlie Vanilla character in "Steve Canyon," offers Sean Connery an appropriate ice-cream cone during filming on *Thunderball*. (Claire Russhon Collection)

the U.S. Army and four other government agencies for the *Goldfinger* production crew to film in and around Fort Knox, Kentucky—where Pussy Galore's Flying Circus puts the garrison

to sleep. His relationship with President John F. Kennedy's press secretary, Pierre Salinger, helped cement the deal (it also helped that Kennedy was a huge Bond fan).

As an inside joke and a nod to Russhon, the film crew put up a sign on one of the Fort Knox airplane hangars saying "Welcome, General Russhon," which can be seen during the air-raid sequence. In addition to opening the doors to the base, Russhon contacted the Piper Aircraft Company and secured free use of a group of Commanche monoplanes for the film.

On the next film, *Thunderball*, Russhon received $92,000 worth of free underwater gear from AMF. He also contacted the U.S. Coast Guard, which participated in the final assault on Largo's (ADOLFO CELI) S.P.E.C.T.R.E. flotilla, and the U.S. Air Force Aqua-para team, which jumped—free of charge—for the film.

Russhon makes an appearance in *Thunderball* as a U.S. Air Force officer who's present when the Home Secretary (EDWARD UNDER-DOWN) briefs the Double-0 Section in Lon-

Resourceful Charles Russhon started his career in radio. Here he's covering the Winter Olympics at Lake Placid, New York, for NBC in 1932. He's standing in front of President-to-be Franklin D. Roosevelt. (Claire Russhon Collection)

don. On *You Only .Live Twice*, Russhon once again served as military liaison in Japan, his old stomping grounds. He joined the film crew for the initial reconnaissance, helped secure key transportation, and was a tremendous help on the logistically complicated shoot. He was even instrumental in working out a deal that brought Sony products into the film.

After a six-year absence, Russhon returned to the Eon Productions banner on *Live and Let Die* and helped secure key cooperation with the New York Police Department during location shooting in Manhattan.

RVC 435H The license plate on smuggler Peter Franks's (JOE ROBINSON) sports car in *Diamonds Are Forever*. When Franks is detained by British immigration while on his way to Amsterdam, Bond (SEAN CONNERY) steals both his car and his identity.

RYDER, HONEY Voluptuous island girl portrayed by Ursula Andress in *Dr. No*. In the Fleming novel, she was referred to as Honeychile Ryder.

The only child of a marine zoologist, Honey grew up all over the world, anywhere where her father could find sea life to study—the Philippines, Bali, Hawaii. Her school is the encyclopedia she has been reading since childhood—she's up to *T* when she meets Bond.

Although her father has been reported drowned off Crab Key, Honey believes that he was actually murdered by Dr. No's (JOSEPH WISEMAN) henchmen. After being orphaned, she stayed on in Kingston, Jamaica, until her kindly landlord turned lecherous and raped her. For revenge, Honey placed a female black widow spider under his mosquito netting. Bitten, he took an entire week to die, a fact that 007 finds unsettling.

Like a female Tarzan, Honey knows Crab Key intimately, and she helps guide Bond (SEAN CONNERY) and Quarrel (JOHN KITZMILLER) through the swamps until they reach Dr. No's fortress. *See* ANDRESS, URSULA.

S

SACHS, LEONARD (1908–1990) British actor who portrayed Group Captain Pritchard, Bond's (SEAN CONNERY) Royal Air Force liaison to Station C–Canada, in *Thunderball*.

SADOYANAMA Japanese sumo wrestler and James Bond's (SEAN CONNERY) first Tokyo contact in *You Only Live Twice*. Agent 007 meets Sadoyanama in the stadium locker room, and the immense wrestler gives him a special reserved seat that will put him adjacent to his next contact, Aki (AKIKO WAKABAYASHI).

SADRUDDIN British Secret Service agent and head of Station I in Udaipur, India, in *Octopussy*. He's portrayed by Albert Moses, who played a bartender in *The Spy Who Loved Me*.

SAIDA Lebanese belly dancer portrayed by Carmen Sautoy in *The Man with the Golden Gun*. She's the ex-girlfriend of Bill Fairbanks (002), who was allegedly assassinated by Francisco Scaramanga (CHRISTOPHER LEE) in Beirut in 1969, although the bullet was never recovered. Saida actually wears the bullet as a lucky charm in her belly button.

James Bond (ROGER MOORE), on the trail of the mysterious Scaramanga, tracks the bullet to Saida and eventually swallows it during a fistfight in her dressing room with enemy agents. From x-rays of Bond's stomach, Q

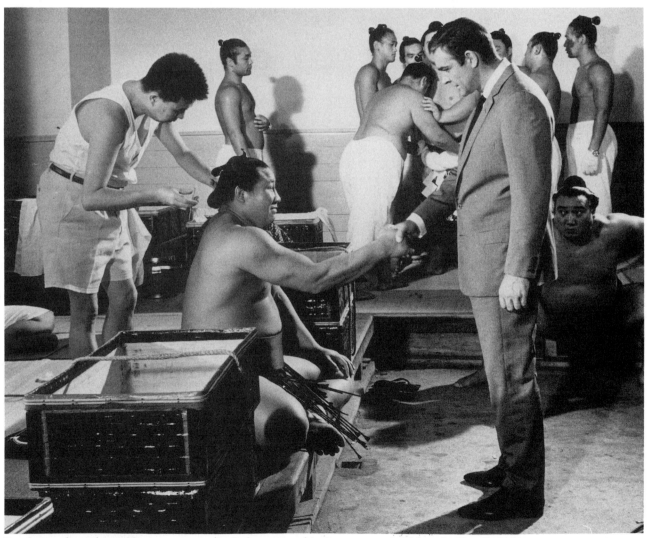

Bond introduces himself to sumo wrestler Sadoyanama, his first contact in Tokyo in *You Only Live Twice*. (Rex Features Ltd./RDR Productions)

(DESMOND LLEWELYN) determines the bullet's origins—clues that lead 007 to Macao and to Lazar, the gunsmith (MARNE MAITLAND).

ST. ANNA CATHEDRAL AT KIRSCHE

The real location of the de Bleuchamp family tombs, as revealed by Ernst Stavro Blofeld (TELLY SAVALAS) in *On Her Majesty's Secret Service*. Based on incorrect information supplied to him by heraldry expert Sir Hilary Bray (GEORGE BAKER), James Bond (GEORGE LAZENBY), impersonating Bray, tells Blofeld that the de Bleuchamp tombs are in the city of Augsburg. This faux pas, plus his bed-hopping escapades with Blofeld's allergy patients, help blow 007's cover at Piz Gloria.

ST. CYRIL'S Monastery/fortress atop the steep Meteora cliffs in Greece, featured in *For Your Eyes Only*. It's a personal retreat for Russian agent and heroin smuggler Aris Kristatos (JULIAN GLOVER). Bond's (ROGER MOORE) friend and compatriot Milos Columbo (TOPOL) explains that the abandoned monastery used to be a favorite hiding place for the Greek resistance during World War II.

Tipped off by Max, the parrot—who keeps uttering the name St. Cyril's—Bond, Melina Havelock (CAROLE BOUQUET), Columbo, and his men—all disguised as monks—assault the fortress and overwhelm Kristatos's garrison. They steal back the A.T.A.C. computer, which 007 destroys before it falls into Russian hands.

For this sequence, which was filmed against the wishes of the local clergy—who even hung laundry over their buildings to disrupt the filming—stuntman Rick Sylvester, veteran of *The Spy Who Loved Me* ski jump, doubled James Bond during his precarious climb to the top of the Meteora Cliff.

ST. GEORGES A British electronic surveillance and communications ship disguised as a Greek fishing trawler in *For Your Eyes Only*. On board is A.T.A.C. (Automatic Targeting Attack Communicator), a sophisticated electronic device that uses an ultra-low frequency-coded transmission to order nuclear submarines to launch their ballistic missiles.

When the *St. Georges* is sunk by a mine that gets caught in her fishing nets—placed there by

Soviet agent Aris Kristatos (JULIAN GLOVER)—technicians are unable to trigger the A.T.A.C. self-destruct mechanism. Thus, a race begins between the Russians and the British Secret Service to recover the A.T.A.C. from its watery grave off the coast of Albania.

ST. JOHN, JILL (Los Angeles, California, August 19, 1940–) (real name, Jill Oppenheim) Redheaded American actress and wife of actor Robert Wagner who portrayed diamond smuggler Tiffany Case in *Diamonds Are Forever*. As a favor to attorney Sidney Korshak, who was setting up location deals in Las Vegas, producer

One reason Jill St. John won the part of Tiffany Case in *Diamonds Are Forever*. (National Film Archive, London)

Albert R. Broccoli had first considered her for the part of Plenty O'Toole. However, director Guy Hamilton termed her too much of an actress for Plenty.

After she won the role, British columnist Peter Evans wrote, "Jill St. John for Tiffany Case was an oddly appealing idea, even if she did lack the charisma of a Faye Dunaway or the intellectual sensuality of a Jane Fonda. As Mrs. Lance Reventlow, she was once heiress-in-law to the F. W. Woolworth millions. Now one husband (singer Jack Jones) and many admirers later (including Frank Sinatra and Henry Kissinger), she is the richest, wildest dilettante since Nell Gwynn was dabbling in the orange business. . . . Also she had a lot going for her, including a price tag considerably more modest than her social aspirations."

On Hamilton's urgings, Broccoli signed Jill St. John to play Tiffany Case, and, as it turned out, she was excellent in the role. She had the versatility to be cool and detached when Bond (SEAN CONNERY) first meets her in Amsterdam; then comically frightened when she accompanies Bond on the madcap car chase through downtown Las Vegas; and finally downright cocky when she creates the diversion in the Las Vegas gas station that allows Bond to sneak into Professor-Dr. Metz's (JOSEPH FURST) utility van, headed for Blofeld's (CHARLES GRAY) missile installation.

ST. JOHN-SMYTHE, JAMES James Bond's (ROGER MOORE) cover at Max Zorin's (CHRISTOPHER WALKEN) horse sale in *A View to a Kill*. Allied with Sir Godfrey Tibbett (PATRICK MACNEE), who is also working undercover as Bond's chauffeur, 007 poses as a wealthy, yet novice horse breeder who is looking to improve the quality of his inherited stables in England.

After both agents discover a secret underground installation where Zorin is surgically implanting microchips and steroids into the legs of his racehorses, Bond is identified by Zorin and marked for execution. May Day (GRACE JONES) strangles Tibbett, and then Bond is taken for a ride on a dangerous stallion and later knocked unconscious. Awakening next to his dead friend in a rapidly sinking Rolls-Royce, Bond escapes out the door and survives underwater by sucking the air out of one of the tires.

ST. MARY'S STAR OF THE SEA CATHOLIC CHURCH Known as the second oldest church in the United States, this Key West, Florida, landmark was the site of the Felix Leiter (DAVID HEDISON)–Della Churchill (PRISCILLA BARNES) wedding in *Licence to Kill*.

ST. SOPHIA MOSQUE An Istanbul landmark, originally built as a church by the Roman emperor Justinian in the fourth century A.D. In *From Russia with Love*, it becomes the drop-off point for a map of the Russian embassy that is hidden in Tanya's (DANIELA BIANCHI) compact and left for Bond (SEAN CONNERY) at the foot of one of the mosque's columns.

The plan is nearly foiled when a Bulgar agent working for the Russians (HASAN CEYLAN) intercepts the compact, but he, in turn, is murdered by Red Grant (ROBERT SHAW), who is also lurking in the mosque. Bond is thus able to retrieve the stolen plans, crediting the Bulgar's death not to Grant, but to Istanbul's reputation for being a tough town.

SAKATA, HAROLD (1920–1982) (wrestling name, Tosh Togo) Powerfully built Japanese actor who portrayed Goldfinger's (GERT FROBE) mute henchman, Oddjob, who is electrocuted by Bond (SEAN CONNERY) during the climactic fight inside Fort Knox.

SALEM, PAMELA British actress who portrayed Miss Moneypenny in *Never Say Never Again*.

Pamela Salem portrayed the other Moneypenny in *Never Say Never Again*. (Taliafilm)

SALZKAMMERGUT A region in Austria, mentioned by Colonel Smithers (RICHARD VERNON) in *Goldfinger*, that is the location of Lake Topliz, the rumored site of a World War II Nazi gold horde, one bar of which has been recovered and will be used as bait by James Bond (SEAN CONNERY) in the golf challenge match with Auric Goldfinger (GERT FROBE).

SALTZMAN, HARRY (St. John, New Brunswick, Canada, October 27, 1915–September 27, 1994) Energetic Canadian producer, a longtime resident of England, who coproduced the first nine James Bond films with Albert R. "Cubby" Broccoli. An English journalist once described Saltzman as a "tiny, tubby man with a larger than life attitude." This description aptly fits the man who started his show-business career in vaudeville in 1928.

When Saltzman was only two years old, his family left Sherbrooke, Quebec, and moved to New York City. Harry attended elementary school in New York and soon developed a passion for vaudeville. He would wander out to Long Island, where promoters were rehearsing their acts, and simply hang around, hoping that someone would break him into the business. His first break came when he was hired as a reporter for a local entertainment sheet called *Zit's Weekly*.

Saltzman was soon looking for vaudeville talent on his own. With a bankroll, he purchased a franchise on one of the New York stages and began booking his own acts. By 1930, he was one of the most successful promoters on the East Coast vaudeville circuit, clearing up to $600 a week in the boom world of 1930s vaudeville. Prepping his acts in Philadelphia and Washington, D.C., he would bring the new talent into New York City and collect a sizable profit. Two years later, he moved to Paris and applied his savvy to the French music hall scene. He even managed a traveling circus.

When World War II broke out in Europe,

While he has his shoes shined in Istanbul, producer Harry Saltzman chats with writer Richard Maibaum during location filming on *From Russia with Love*. (Richard Maibaum Collection)

Saltzman joined the Royal Canadian Air Force as a flyer. He was given a medical discharge, though, early in the war, and he returned to New York City to manage the Henry Miller Theater. In 1942, he enlisted in the psychological warfare division of the Office of Strategic Services (O.S.S.) and spent the rest of the war in Europe. He continued booking entertainment after World War II, which led him directly into television. His most successful production, "Captain Gallant and the Foreign Legion," was filmed on location in North Africa and became a very popular program in America. His film career began in England in 1956 when he formed Woodfall Productions with playwright John Osborne and director Tony Richardson. Their partnership lasted three years and produced three of England's most critically acclaimed films of the era: *Look Back in Anger* (1959), which starred Richard Burton as an angry young man fighting the establishment in the fifties; *The Entertainer* (1960), a brilliant study of an actor on the skids, with Laurence Olivier in the title role; and *Saturday Night and Sunday Morning* (1960), which brought instant stardom to young Albert Finney.

His lawyer, Brian Lewis, introduced Saltzman to Ian Fleming. The fateful meeting between Fleming and Saltzman took place at noon on a winter's day in 1960 at Les Ambassadeurs, a fashionable club in London's West End. Ironically, Brian Lewis was also Fleming's lawyer, and he had advised Fleming to make a film deal soon, otherwise the trust value of his books would have to be based on the 1954 sale of *Casino Royale* to Gregory Ratoff for $6,000.

At Les Ambassadeurs, Saltzman began to discuss the films he had made at Woodfall with Tony Richardson and John Osborne. Fleming confessed that he didn't go to movies and that the only film he had seen recently, *The Boy and the Bridge*, had led him to a chaotic impasse with Kevin McClory (*see* MCCLORY, KEVIN).

Fleming came to the point and asked Saltzman what he could offer for the seven outstanding Bond books. Harry said that he could scrape together $50,000 for a six-month option, and if the project was picked up by a major studio, he would try to get Fleming $100,000 a picture, plus a percentage. The deal appealed to Fleming, who needed the option money to pay hospital bills. He suggested that Saltzman get in touch with his film agent, Bob Fenn of MCA, and work out the deal on paper.

Saltzman tried for five months to sell the studios on the idea of a series of James Bond movies. He encountered the same problems as Fleming: the studios would not touch the project without the commitment of a major star, and a major star would not commit himself to more than a couple of films. The frustration continued until one day in June 1961, with only 28 days left on his option, Saltzman received a call from his writer friend Wolf Mankowitz, who wanted to introduce him to another film producer, Albert R. "Cubby" Broccoli. Saltzman acknowledged the name and agreed to the meeting.

Although he had never met Broccoli, he knew of the latter's successful track record with coproducer Irving Allen in a series of films for Columbia Pictures. He thought it would be interesting to see what Broccoli would offer for the Bonds. Broccoli was very interested. Two years before, he had tried to interest his partner, Irving Allen, in the Bond books, but Allen wasn't interested. (Ironically, Allen would go on to produce the Dean Martin *Matt Helm* movies.)

Although no two producers could be more different in background, style, and approach to the film business, both had one solid point in common—they knew in their hearts that the Bond books were perfect escapist movie fare. Agreeing to venture forth as a team (with a 50-50 split), and calling their company Eon Productions (EON stands for "Everything or Nothing"), Saltzman and Broccoli were able to make a deal with United Artists—after Columbia Pictures turned them down—for a series of Bond movies.

While the Bond movies would become Broccoli's sole interest in the film business, Saltzman whistled a different tune. Almost from the beginning, he had other obsessions, other interests. He was a gambler, and when a table cooled off, Saltzman was ready to move on to new action. No sooner was Bond off and running than Saltzman was already searching for new projects. In effect, he was back to selling vaudeville acts, except now they appeared on celluloid and moved at twenty-four frames per second.

Harry and Jacqueline Saltzman attend a Bond premiere in London. Actress Edie Adams joins the party with an unidentified man. (National Film Archive, London)

Early in the Bond history, he acquired the rights to thriller writer Len Deighton's Harry Palmer stories, hired Michael Caine to play Palmer, and produced the three films away from the Eon banner. He also literally spent years on a huge World War II film titled *The Battle of Britain*, which Guy Hamilton directed in 1969. Actually, the only time Broccoli and Saltzman combined their efforts on a non-Bond project was the Bob Hope comedy *Call Me Bwana*, which bombed in 1963 (although its billboard pops up in a strategic spot in *From Russia with Love*).

Saltzman's outside interests began to interfere with his dedication to the Bond series; they also began to have an adverse effect on his fi-

nancial condition. A sudden reversal in the fortunes of Technicolor in the mid-1970s eventually forced him to sell his share in Eon Productions to United Artists. *The Man with the Golden Gun* was his last Bond movie.

SAMEDI, BARON One of Kananga's (YAPHET KOTTO) giant henchmen, portrayed by dancer/choreographer Geoffrey Holder, in *Live and Let Die*. Like some practical joker from Henry VIII's time, Samedi, at six feet, six inches, is an extension of Kananga's power in voodoo country.

Holder plays the role on two distinct imaginative levels. At times, he is simply one of Mr. Big's (YAPHET KOTTO) associates—an extremely conspicuous presence, but a mortal one. This emphasis changes in several key sequences when Holder seems literally to become Baron Samedi, who in the mythology of voodoo is the god of cemeteries and the chief of the legion of the dead who cannot die. It is Samedi who officiates over a sacrificial rite on San Monique in which Solitaire (JANE SEYMOUR) is nearly murdered by snake-bearing fanatics.

Holder—with his huge, powerful laugh and lithesome dancer movements—is nearly the symbol of the entire film. It thus is most fitting that he is the last character we see—riding the front of Bond's homeward-bound train, laughing as usual and warning us that the supernatural cannot be dismissed so lightly. Little does 007 know who is sitting on the front of the train. The appearance of Holder in the film's last scene was actually an afterthought. The producers felt strongly that having killed off practically all the black villains, it was important to end the film without a clear victory for Bond. With Samedi riding the end titles, the producers were giving their film a dose of equality that they hoped would help to not alienate the many black fans who would see the new film.

In *Live and Let Die*, you never quite know whether Samedi is real or a supernatural figure. At Bond's hotel, he's merely a dancing, laughing character in an elaborate floor show. In a very atmospheric moment in the hinterlands of San Monique, he's a moody panpipe player, greeting Bond (ROGER MOORE) and Solitaire (JANE SEYMOUR) and wishing them a good day. In the climactic fight to save Solitaire from voodoo fanatics, Bond finds Samedi to be a very mortal opponent who gets thrown into a coffin full of snakes. Samedi, by the way, is French for "Saturday."

SAN ANDREAS LAKE Northern California body of water that is situated above the Main Strike Mine in *A View to a Kill*. When Max Zorin (CHRISTOPHER WALKEN) orders his mine shaft flooded prior to the detonation of a tremendous bomb, the waters of the lake literally disappear into the mine, creating a completely dry lake bed above.

SANCHEZ, FRANZ Ruthless, murderous South American drug lord portrayed excellently by Robert Davi in *Licence to Kill*. Having

maimed Felix Leiter (DAVID HEDISON) and killed his bride, Della (PRISCILLA BARNES)—a particular sore point, since 007 lost his own wife on her wedding day—Sanchez becomes the target of revenge-seeking James Bond (TIMOTHY DALTON).

However, this time 007 won't be working for the British Secret Service. Ordered to forget the sordid fate of his best friends and report for a new mission in Istanbul, Bond defies M (ROBERT BROWN) and goes after Sanchez on his own—becoming a rogue agent. Sanchez is no easy target. Ensconced in Isthmus City, a South American drug capital that he practically owns, Sanchez is surrounded by a private army that keeps potential assassins at arm's length.

Having escaped from the Drug Enforcement Administration in Key West when he bribed a local agent (EVERETT MCGILL), Sanchez has returned to Isthmus City and his huge drug organization, which uses Reverend Joe Butcher's (WAYNE NEWTON) phony religious program as a means of communicating with Sanchez's American drug distributors. His chief American distributor is Milton Krest (ANTHONY ZERBE), who runs Wavekrest Marine Research in Key West.

Sanchez is in the midst of completing an enormous worldwide cocaine deal, with individual franchisees coughing up $100 million each for their territorial exclusivity. His lab technicians have also determined that by diluting the cocaine in gasoline, they can make it invisible to customs surveillance. The first shipment will soon be transported to the harbor in four huge tanker trucks.

Since Bond knows that the drug lord values loyalty above everything else, his plan is to infiltrate Sanchez's organization and sow the seeds of mistrust among his key associates. Krest is quickly identified as the American focal point of Sanchez's operation. After a minor skirmish in Sanchez's marine installation—where Killifer, the bribed DEA agent, is fed to the sharks—Bond steals aboard Krest's yacht and sabotages a substantial drug deal. He then takes off in a seaplane with millions of dollars in cash.

Joining forces with CIA pilot and undercover operative Pam Bouvier (CAREY LOWELL), Bond arrives in Isthmus City disguised as a high-rolling mercenary whose services are for sale. There he renews an acquaintance with San-

Actor Robert Davi proved to be an excellent choice for the role of drug runner Franz Sanchez in *Licence to Kill*. (Dick Delson)

chez's girlfriend, Lupe Lamora (TALISA SOTO), whom he met in Key West. Agent 007 eventually introduces himself to the drug dealer, but no relationship of consequence develops until Bond is captured by two Ninja-like Hong Kong narcotics agents (CARY-HIROYUKI TAGAWA, DIANA LEE-HSU) who disrupt 007's own assassination attempt.

Captured and tied to a table, Bond is being interrogated, when Sanchez's Security Chief Heller (DON STROUD) launches a major attack on their stronghold, killing everyone and rescuing Bond. Convinced that 007 was trying to help him, Sanchez befriends Bond and invites him to his house. Now in his enemy's good graces, 007 is free to plan his "mind warfare."

Krest is eliminated when Bond plants the money, which Krest claims was stolen by an unknown thief, in the decompression chamber of the *Wavekrest* yacht. Observing this double-cross at first hand, Sanchez orders Krest thrown into the chamber, where he super-inflates—à la Dr. Kananga in *Live and Let Die*—and explodes.

Bond is also able to turn Sanchez against Heller, thanks to information supplied by Pam.

However, 007's final assault on the huge drug operation based at Butcher's Olimpatec Meditation Institute is derailed when he's recognized by Dario (BENICIO DEL TORO), one of Sanchez's killers. Nearly decapitated in a cocaine-bundle shredder, Bond recovers. And with Pam's help, he manages to single-handedly disrupt the tanker-truck convoy—blowing up a fortune in gasoline-saturated cocaine.

Bond is then forced off the road and into the dirt, where he faces a machete-wielding Sanchez. Agent 007 takes the engraved gold lighter given to him by Felix and Della, and ignites the gasoline that has splattered his enemy's clothes. Sanchez flares up like a Roman candle.

SANDERSON, HAROLD British stuntman who portrayed the hydrofoil captain in *Thunderball*.

SANDERS, TOM (Jackson, Wyoming, December 13, 1953–) American aerial cameraman who filmed the incredible cargo-net fight in *The Living Daylights*. Flying over the desert near Palm Springs, California, which was simulating Afghanistan, Sanders, with a movie camera affixed to his helmet, crawled out on the plane's cargo ramp and filmed the incredible fight between Bond (TIMOTHY DALTON) and Necros (ANDREAS WISNIEWSKI).

SANDOR Bald, muscle-bound assassin portrayed by Milton Reid in *The Spy Who Loved Me*. Working for billionaire shipping magnate Karl Stromberg (CURT JURGENS) and teamed with fellow assassin Jaws (RICHARD KIEL), Sandor tries to kill Bond (ROGER MOORE) at Aziz Fekkesh's (NADIM SAWALHA) apartment in Cairo. The bullet misses the mark, and a fight, which Sandor loses, breaks out on the apartment roof. Before he falls to his death, Sandor tells 007 that Fekkesh can be found at the pyramids. *See* REID, MILTON.

SAN FRANCISCO CITY HALL Bay Area landmark that became a principal location in *A View to a Kill*. It's where Division of Oil and Mines official W. G. Howe (DANIEL BENZALI) has his office. Howe is actually on the payroll of psychotic billionaire industrialist Max

Zorin (CHRISTOPHER WALKEN), who is about to unleash a killer earthquake that will sink Silicon Valley into the sea. (*See* HOWE, W. G.)

When director John Glen's production crew filmed on the grounds of City Hall, relations with the city and Mayor Diane Feinstein were so good that the special effects team was given permission to set controlled fires on the building's premises. The fires emanated from fitted gas jets that were placed on the balcony of City Hall. Asbetos shielding was carefully placed to protect the building itself.

SAN MONIQUE Mythical and mystical Caribbean island represented at the United Nations by the mysterious diplomat Dr. Kananga (YAPHET KOTTO), in *Live and Let Die*. A nest of voodoo worshipers, San Monique is also the base of operations for a huge heroin-smuggling operation run by Kananga, who also masquerades as powerful Harlem crime kingpin Mr. Big.

The British Secret Service's involvement with Kananga begins when three British agents are murdered in New York, New Orleans, and San Monique. Following the trail of the murders, James Bond (ROGER MOORE) eventually sees through Kananga and discovers that he's about to corner the United States illegal drug market by unleashing a huge heroin shipment on the U.S. mainland—a shipment that will be delivered free of charge and distributed through a chain of Fillet of Soul nightclubs. Bond tracks the drugs to San Monique and eventually obliterates both Kananga and his poppy fields.

SAN MONIQUE TRANSPORT Sign on the side of a double-decker bus that Bond (ROGER MOORE) commandeers in *Live and Let Die*. See PATCHETT, MAURICE.

SAN PIETRO AIRPORT The Rio de Janeiro headquarters of Drax Air Freight in *Moonraker*. Bond (ROGER MOORE) and Dr. Holly Goodhead (LOIS CHILES) observe that a steady stream of Drax Air Freight planes is leaving San Pietro for destinations unknown, indicating that a Drax caper could be imminent.

SAN SOUCI The *Dr. No* crew's hotel in Ocho Rios, Jamaica, that served as the exterior

location of Miss Taro's (ZENA MARSHALL) cottage in the Blue Mountains. It is also the location for Bond's (ROGER MOORE) hotel and Baron Samedi's (GEOFFREY HOLDER) nightclub floor-show in *Live and Let Die*.

SANTA MAVRA Fiendish Russian agent Aris Kristatos's (JULIAN GLOVER) motorboat, in *For Your Eyes Only*, that attempts to keel-haul Bond (ROGER MOORE) and Melina Havelock (CAROLE BOUQUET). See KEEL-HAULING.

SARDADREAH Sardinian mattress manufacturer advertised on the back of the tractor-trailer truck blown up by an errant bomb fired from a motorcycle sidecar in *The Spy Who Loved Me*. The resultant storm of feathers blinds the enemy motorcyclist, forcing him over a cliff.

SARDINIAN HOTEL RECEPTIONIST The sexy lady, portrayed by the very beautiful Valerie Leon, who brings Bond (ROGER MOORE) a "message" in *The Spy Who Loved Me*. See LEON, VALERIE.

S.A.S. Acronym for the Special Air Service, an elite British commando team that's similar to the U.S. Delta Force. In Ministry of Defense war games, the S.A.S. is assigned the mission of defending a top secret radar station on Gibraltar against three double-0 agents in *The Living Daylights* teaser. Unfortunately, an enemy agent penetrates their security and kills 004 (FREDERICK WARDER) and several S.A.S. men before Bond (TIMOTHY DALTON) exacts revenge.

SATELLITE 7 Docking point on Hugo Drax's (MICHEL LONSDALE) space station for shuttle-borne American spacetroopers under the command of Colonel Scott (MICHAEL MARSHALL).

SATTON, LON American actor who portrayed Harold Strutter, the CIA agent in *Live and Let Die*. See STRUTTER, HAROLD.

SAUNDERS By-the-book British Secret Service section chief in Austria, portrayed by Thomas Wheatley in *The Living Daylights*. Responsible for aiding the defection of Russian General Georgi Koskov (JEROEN KRABBE) from Bratislava, Czechoslovakia, Saunders is upset when Bond (TIMOTHY DALTON) fails to kill a female KGB sniper (MARYAM D'ABO) who has Koskov in her sights. Bond merely shoots the gun out of her hands, then helps Koskov to a local substation of the Trans Siberian Pipeline, where he's whisked through the pipes into Austria.

Returning to Bratislava, Bond later learns that the girl he saved was not a KGB sniper but the girlfriend of Koskov. Her name is Kara Milovy, and Bond determines that she might be able to lead him to Koskov, who has been mysteriously rescued from his hideout in the English countryside.

Meeting Bond and Kara in Vienna, Saunders secures special travel papers and identification for Kara. He also discovers that her cello was purchased at auction in New York by notorious arms dealer Brad Whitaker (JOE DON BAKER), who is based in Tangier. Bond resolves to take Kara to North Africa. Saunders, however, is murdered by Necros (ANDREAS WISNIEWSKI), an assassin working for Koskov.

SAUNDERS, STUART British character actor who portrayed Major Clive, Kamal Khan's (LOUIS JOURDAN) partner in *Octopussy*'s rigged backgammon game. *See* CLIVE, MAJOR; BACKGAMMON GAME.

SAUTOY, CARMEN Actress who portrayed Saida, the Lebanese belly dancer with the golden bullet charm, in *The Man with the Golden Gun*. *See* SAIDA.

SAVALAS, TELLY (Garden City, New York, January 21, 1925–January 22, 1994) (real name, Aristotle Savalas) Bald American character actor of Greek extraction who portrayed Ernst Stavro Blofeld in *On Her Majesty's Secret Service*. He's also internationally known as New York City detective Theo Kojak on the hit CBS-Television series "Kojak." *See* BLOFELD, ERNST STAVRO.

SAVILE ROW A famous street in London known for its expensive men's tailors, where 007 is fitted for his suits.

SAWALHA, NADIM Egyptian actor who portrayed Aziz Fekkesh, the black-market trader, in *The Spy Who Loved Me*, and Tangier's chief of security in *The Living Daylights*. *See* FEKKESH, AZIZ.

SAXBY, BURT Tough casino boss at the Whyte House Hotel, in *Diamonds Are Forever*, who is secretly working for Ernst Stavro Blofeld (Charles Gray). Portrayed by character actor Bruce Cabot, Saxby is a no-nonsense hoodlum who continually fails to get the real diamonds back from Bond (SEAN CONNERY).

When Blofeld vacates the Whyte House, Saxby tries to assassinate his ex-boss, Willard Whyte (JIMMY DEAN). His sharpshooting is not very sharp, and he's killed by CIA agents who, along with 007, liberate Whyte from his desert home. When Whyte hears that Saxby was the sniper, he yells, "Burt Saxby? Tell him, he's fired!"

It is also Saxby's voice that Bond imitates during a conversation with Blofeld—the imitation aided by Q's voice simulator. *See* CABOT, BRUCE.

SAYERS, MICHAEL Thriller writer who was hired by producer Charles K. Feldman to cowrite the *Casino Royale* spoof in 1967 with Wolf Mankowitz and John Law.

SCARAMANGA, FRANCISCO The world's most expensive assassin—$1 million a kill—and the title character in *The Man with the Golden Gun*. He's portrayed by top British character actor Christopher Lee.

According to British Secret Service files, Scaramanga was born in the circus. His father was a ringmaster, and by the time Francisco was 10, he was a fabulous trick shot. His life of crime began innocently enough. His only friend in the circus was a huge African bull elephant who went berserk one day from his handler's mistreatment. When the handler emptied his gun into the elephant's eye, Scaramanga emptied his stage pistol into the handler.

A local gunman by the age of 15, Scaramanga was eventually recruited by the KGB, who trained him in Europe and made him another overworked and underpaid assassin. He went independent in the late 1950s. His current price is indeed $1 million a hit. No photographs of him exist, but he is known to have one anatomical abnormality—a third nipple, or supercilious papilla, which in some cultures is considered a sign of invulnerability and great sexual prowess.

For his assassinations, Scaramanga always uses a golden bullet, fired from the golden gun of the title. In the film, Scaramanga is working for a ruthless industrialist named Hai Fat (RICHARD LOO), who is determined to steal a priceless solar energy component called a "solex agitator"—the key to harnessing the sun as a top fuel alternative. Aware of the solex's value, Scaramanga eventually kills Hai Fat and steals the solex for himself.

Meanwhile, his path crosses that of 007 when Scaramanga's luscious girlfriend, Andrea Anders (MAUD ADAMS), sends Bond (ROGER MOORE) a golden bullet with an engraved 007 upon it. It is Anders's hope that Bond will rescue her from her life as Scaramanga's love slave.

Bond arrives in Asia hoping somehow to find Scaramanga and simultaneously guard a top solar energy expert. But he is unable to protect his charge from Scaramanga's bullet, and the solex is lost. Thanks to a homing device inside Scaramanga's flying car, Bond is able to eventually track the killer to his weird prehistoric island, where the classic duel between the Walther PPK and the golden gun takes place. Fortunately, Bond wins that duel inside Scaramanga's strange "fun house" maze.

As conceived by screenwriters Richard Maibaum and Tom Mankiewicz, the battle of wits and the eventual duel between Bond and Scaramanga was the classic good-versus-evil confrontation, similar to the Alan Ladd/Jack Palance fight in *Shane*. Unfortunately, the problem in *The Man with the Golden Gun* is that Christopher Lee plays Scaramanga too sympathetically. You never get the feeling of menace that Lee has projected countless times in the many horror classics that made him a star.

In this film, it's very difficult to hate a villain who dresses casually in sports clothes, speaks politely and respectfully, and at one time in his life loved a pet bull elephant enough to kill his mistreating trainer. There's no question that Christopher Lee was comfortable in the role (after years in one *Dracula* and *Frankenstein* film after another, Scaramanga was a pleasant change for Lee), but he was a little bit too comfortable to give the film the dramatic bite it

needed. In the Bond series, when villains are too sympathetic—as in *The Man with the Golden Gun* and *The Living Daylights*—dramatic tension is greatly diminished. *See* LEE, CHRISTOPHER.

SCARAMANGA'S ISLAND Incredibly shaped, breathtakingly beautiful prehistoric island located off the coast of China, in *The Man with the Golden Gun*. It's in Red Chinese waters and is protected by communist observation posts.

Scaramanga's (CHRISTOPHER LEE) fabulous house is located on the island, along with the solar energy plant built by Hai Fat's (RICHARD LOO) construction company. The house contains a "fun house" maze, which Scaramanga uses to keep his marksman's eye in shape. It also has a solar cannon, which later obliterates James Bond's (ROGER MOORE) seaplane.

Outside is a beautiful inlet and beach where Scaramanga sunbathes with his lady, Andrea Anders (MAUD ADAMS). The same beach is later used for the duel between Bond and Scaramanga.

A solar energy panel is built into a large rock mass adjacent to Scaramanga's house. It serves to fuel the solar cannon and every other electrical device on the island.

The actual island is called Khow-Ping-Kan and is located off the coast of Thailand, near Phuket. Filming was completed there in April 1974.

SCARECROWS Voodoo warning figures that guard Dr. Kananga's (YAPHET KOTTO) precious poppy fields in *Live and Let Die*. Some are equipped with surveillance cameras; others, with firearms activated by booby traps. One of the traps kills double agent Rosie Carver (GLORIA HENDRY).

SCARPINE Max Zorin's (CHRISTOPHER WALKEN) head of security, portrayed by Patrick Bauchau, in *A View to a Kill*. Introduced to Bond (ROGER MOORE) at Zorin's horse sale in France, Scarpine carefully monitors 007's activities during the course of the sale.

Later, at the Main Strike Mine near San Francisco, Scarpine joins his boss in machine-gunning the defenseless miners who have prepared the shaft for a cataclysmic explosion. Scarpine himself is blown to bits atop the Golden Gate Bridge when a batch of dynamite headed for James Bond detonates in Zorin's blimp.

SCHILTHORN Swiss mountain peak, located above Murren, that was the location of Piz Gloria in *On Her Majesty's Secret Service*. *See* PIZ GLORIA.

SCHWARTZMAN, JACK (New York City, July 22, 1932–   ) American producer and former entertainment lawyer who produced *Never Say Never Again* in 1983. Only a tenacious motion-picture industry veteran like Schwartzman could have successfully accomplished the seemingly impossible task of turning Kevin McClory's oft-postponed, legally mired *Thunderball* remake into a workable project. Not only was the project an enormous creative challenge, but Schwartzman faced a potentially costly legal battle with Eon Productions and producer Albert R. Broccoli.

By 1981 Broccoli and a huge legal team had been fighting McClory for six years. They were determined to wipe out the earnings potential of any rival Bond movies that hit the marketplace. Broccoli had been "burned" once before, in 1967, when producer Charles K. Feldman's 007 spoof *Casino Royale* hit the screen in the same season as *You Only Live Twice*. As Broccoli put it, many people thought that his company had produced the dreadful *Casino Royale*, thus contributing to a disappointing box-office return on the fifth official Bond movie. Broccoli wasn't about to let that happen again without a fight.

McClory was no stranger to legal battles. He had won the film rights to *Thunderball* in 1963 after a three-year court case against co-author Ian Fleming. Joining forces with Broccoli and Saltzman in 1965, McClory produced *Thunderball* and signed an agreement to wait 10 years before tackling, in any future films, other elements of the *Thunderball* story materials he owned.

Promptly in 1975, he announced a new variation on *Thunderball*, titled *James Bond of the Secret Service*. At one point, thriller writer Len Deighton and Sean Connery were working on the screenplay, whose title was later changed to *Warhead*. But McClory couldn't interest a studio in backing the project.

Enter Jack Schwartzman, a former production executive at Lorimar and an entertainment legal whiz who had known about McClory's project when it was first presented to and rejected by Lorimar. One year after Schwartzman left Lorimar to start his own company, Taliafilm (named after his wife, actress Talia Shire), he was contacted by an old friend, New York investment banker Philip Mengel, who happened to be McClory's financial adviser. Mengel wondered whether Schwartzman was interested in meeting with his client. Schwartzman was. He felt that Lorimar had made a mistake in rejecting the proposed Bond film.

Despite the legal entanglements, the prospect of Sean Connery returning to the part he had created 20 years before was too good an opportunity to pass up. Schwartzman met with McClory and read through his materials, but the *Warhead* screenplay didn't appeal to him. Instead, he persuaded McClory and Mengel to allow him to option the rights to the project and proceed with an entirely new screenplay.

Never Say Never Again was born as a remake, not of the 1965 *Thunderball* film, but of the *Thunderball* novel. Schwartzman's plan was to go back to elements of Ian Fleming's original book to fashion a story that also involved a nuclear blackmail scheme on the part of S.P.E.C.T.R.E. The story would also be updated to include the technology of the 1980s—B-1 bombers, cruise missiles, talking computers, and video games.

The first writer on the project was actually one of Schwartzman's associates at Lorimar, Julian Plowden. Plowden took a crack at the material, then recommended his friend, writer Lorenzo Semple, Jr., for the job. Semple wrote the shooting script, although writers Dick Clement and Ian Le Frenais were called up to add some comic elements to the final story and bridge some key scenes. They also wrote the opening war-game sequence, and they introduced the bumbling character Nigel Small-Fawcett (ROWAN ATKINSON) from the British foreign office in Nassau.

Schwartzman also received some help from his brother-in-law Francis Ford Coppola, who became a major contributor to the project. Coppola, however, was never considered for the job of director. That position went straight to Irvin

Producer Jack Schwartzman with actor Klaus Maria Brandauer during location shooting on *Never Say Never Again* in 1982. (Taliafilm)

Kershner, who had recently completed the second "Star Wars" film, *The Empire Strikes Back.*

With a finished script in hand and Sean Connery set to return as Bond—for $3 million, not the $5 million reported in the press—Schwartzman started casting the other roles. Having attended a prerelease screening of *I, the Jury,* a 1982 Mickey Spillane mystery that starred Armand Assante, Schwartzman selected costar Barbara Carrera to portray wicked Fatima Blush, the S.P.E.C.T.R.E. assassin. Director Irvin Kershner, who was then serving on the Academy Award committee for foreign film selection, found Klaus Maria Brandauer—who would play Maximillian Largo—in the critically acclaimed Hungarian film *Mephisto.* For the part of Domino, Talia Shire suggested the actress wife of her own makeup man, Ron Britton—Kim Basinger, who had just appeared in the TV

remake of *From Here to Eternity.*

Despite a tremendous cast and an incredibly commercial property, the making of *Never Say Never Again* was something of a nightmare for Schwartzman. Weather problems delayed expensive underwater shooting in the Bahamas and, according to Schwartzman, Kershner's indecisiveness caused further delays and confusion, particularly in the art department. And the budget mushroomed to $36 million.

"It was the first film I produced on my own," Schwartzman remembered. "And I totally underestimated what I was getting into. There were substantial cost overruns—all of which came out of my own pocket—so, in effect, I paid the price of my own shortcomings."

Had he been given the job to do all over again, Schwartzman admitted that he would have made the same picture, but he would have spent the money more efficiently. He also would have developed better relationships with his team. He further would have jettisoned Michel Legrand's musical score and hired a different composer. Schwartzman's original choice was up-and-comer James Horner, who has since become one of America's leading composers. Unfortunately, Sean Connery rejected Horner and chose Legrand instead.

Despite being the new producer on the block, Schwartzman was totally immersed in *Never Say Never Again* and contributed many creative elements. His business relationship with the brother of Arab billionaire Adnan Khashoggi helped secure the use of the huge *Nabila* yacht for 10 days of shooting. It was also Schwartzman's idea to use a video game for the casino confrontation between Largo and Bond.

"Warner Brothers had given us 100 Atari video arcade games for the casino sequence," he remembered. "It was logical for these very wealthy French charity guests. to be playing video games. And I thought it would be terrific for Bond to play Largo on video. By now, baccarat and chemin de fer were passé in Bond movies; we wanted to update what Fleming had originally conceived." That sequence, built around the game of Domination, is actually a highlight of the film.

While Schwartzman was busy shuttling between the film's many locations in France and the Bahamas, he was expecting legal trouble from producer Albert R. Broccoli. All was quiet until the film was about to open worldwide. Eon Productions then petitioned the high court of London to stop the release of *Never Say Never Again*. This time, however, Broccoli's legal team failed. By waiting until the film was finished, they undercut any chance of stopping the rival Bond. The judge simply asked, "Why did you wait until now?" With a $36 million film at stake, the law was not about to stop Jack Schwartzman.

Despite all the problems, Warner Brothers acquired U.S. distribution rights to the film and released it in 1983 during the Columbus Day holiday, October 7–10. Opening weekend gross for the four days was an astounding $10,958,157. The film would go on to gross more than $100 million worldwide, making it one of the most successful Bond movies of all time.

SCHWEIZERHOF HOTEL Elegant Swiss hotel, located in Berne, that served as the exterior of Gumpold's (JAMES BREE) office building in *On Her Majesty's Secret Service*.

SCOTCH AND WATER The first cocktail ever ordered by a dramatized James Bond. It occurs in the 1954 TV film "Casino Royale." Bond (BARRY NELSON) is seated in the bar of the Monte Carlo casino with British agent Clarence Leiter (MICHAEL PATE), who orders a Scotch and soda for himself.

SCOTT, COLONEL Officer in charge of the U.S. space forces in *Moonraker*. He's portrayed by Michael Marshall. Transported in their only remaining shuttle, Scott and his laser-equipped space troopers are unable to find Hugo Drax's (MICHEL LONSDALE) radarproof space station until Bond (ROGER MOORE) and Dr. Goodhead (LOIS CHILES) disable the station's "cloaking" device. Their target's position identified, Scott and his men dock their shuttle and participate in a hell-for-leather EVA space battle with Drax's men. Victorious, the space troopers then invade and eventually destroy the station itself.

One of *Moonraker*'s weakest links is the EVA battle. Although the quality of the special effects is fair, the battle involving the laser-rifle-equipped troops is boring. Like many battle sequences in countless adventure films, you can't tell the heroes from the villains. It's simply another huge set piece that was done in much better fashion in *Thunderball* and *The Spy Who Loved Me*. In attempting to compete with the successful "Star Wars" films of the late 1970s, the *Moonraker* producers forgot the sense of realism that George Lucas brought to his space epics.

SCOULAR, ANGELA Lovely British actress who portrayed plucky Ruby Bartlett, one of the allergy patients in *On Her Majesty's Secret Service*. Ruby becomes Bond's (GEORGE LAZENBY) first conquest when she writes her room number in lipstick on 007's inner thigh. Scoular also portrayed Agent Buttercup who

Actress Angela Scoular portrayed lipstick-writing Ruby Bartlett in *On Her Majesty's Secret Service*. (Vernon Conway)

takes a bath with Sir James Bond (DAVID NIVEN) in the *Casino Royale* spoof (1967). *See* BARTLETT, RUBY; BUTTERCUP.

SEA TULIPS A species of plant life that does not grow above the 200-foot level. Honey Ryder (URSULA ANDRESS) discovers them on the sea floor outside the window of Dr. No's underground living quarters.

SECRETARY GENERAL, PAN ISLAND UNITY CONFERENCE The diplomat that Kananga (YAPHET KOTTO) is writing to when he fools a CIA surveillance team with a phony tape-recorded dictation session in *Live and Let Die*. While the CIA listens to the "speech," Kananga and his entourage sneak out the back way of their embassy.

SECTION 473 Hong Kong law cited by Lieutenant Hip (SOON-TAIK OH) when he arrests James Bond (ROGER MOORE) for murdering Gibson, the solar energy expert, in *The Man with the Golden Gun*. Bond explains that it was Francisco Scaramanga (CHRISTOPHER LEE) who did the shooting.

SECTION 26, PARAGRAPH 5 Rule from the British Secret Service manual quoted by Austrian Section Chief Saunders (THOMAS WHEATLEY) to Bond (TIMOTHY DALTON) in *The Living Daylights*. It states that information can be related from agent to agent on "only a need-to-know basis." Thus, Saunders won't tell Bond how he plans to help defecting Russian General Georgi Koskov (JEROEN KRABBE) escape Bratislava, Czechoslovakia, to the West.

When Bond takes charge, removing Koskov from the boot and placing him in the passenger seat of a getaway vehicle, Saunders asks him where he intends to go. In reply, Bond quotes Section 26, Paragraph 5. He who lives by the rules . . .

SELLERS, PETER (Southsea, England, September 8, 1925–July 24, 1980) British superstar comedian who played mild-mannered baccarat expert Evelyn Tremble in *Casino Royale*. Recruited into the British Secret Service, Tremble is given the name James Bond and sent to Monte Carlo to challenge Soviet masterspy Le Chiffre (ORSON WELLES) to a game of baccarat.

Sandwiched between Sellers's various performances as bumbling French detective Inspector Jacques Clouseau (his most famous role), the part of Tremble is not as dependent on physical comedy and gives Sellers an opportunity to exercise his genius-level comedic skills by portraying a suave British agent. There are even touches of serious tension at the gaming table—although it's difficult to mention anything serious about *Casino Royale*, except that it had serious problems.

SEMPLE, JR., LORENZO American screenwriter, and veteran of the "Batman" television series, who penned *Never Say Never Again*.

SENTINEL Remote-controlled submersible owned by Milton Krest (ANTHONY ZERBE) in *Licence to Kill* and used to transport illegal drugs underwater. Its cocaine cargo is sabotaged by Bond (TIMOTHY DALTON). The *Sentinel*'s real name was the *Reef Hunter*, a sister sub to Perry Oceanographics's two-man *Shark Hunter II*, which was also featured in the film.

SEPTEMBER 27, 1982 The first day of shooting on *Never Say Never Again*. The location was Nice, France.

SEVEN DAYS The amount of time James Bond (SEAN CONNERY) has until S.P.E.C.T.R.E. plans to explode one of its hijacked nuclear cruise missiles in *Never Say Never Again*.

SEVEN FATHOMS The depth of the channel off the Arabian coast where Maximillian Largo's (KLAUS MARIA BRANDAUER) *Flying Saucer* yacht is anchored in the concluding sequences of *Never Say Never Again*. The depth is too shallow for the American nuclear sub that is shadowing it.

SEVEN-MILE BRIDGE Causeway in the Florida Keys where traitorous DEA agent Killifer (EVERETT MCGILL) hijacks an armored truck carrying notorious drug runner Franz Sanchez (ROBERT DAVI) in *Licence to Kill*. Driving off the bridge into the water, Killifer and Sanchez are rescued by scuba divers who work for local cocaine distributor Milton Krest (ANTHONY ZERBE).

7:00 A.M. The departure time of 007's (SEAN CONNERY) flight to Jamaica, in *Dr. No*, giving him three hours and 22 minutes from the time he leaves M's (BERNARD LEE) office to get ready. It's time enough, at least, for a quick tryst with Sylvia Trench (EUNICE GAYSON).

SEVEN TIMES AT SIX O'CLOCK The number of times that London's famous Big Ben tower clock is ordered to strike in *Thunderball*. According to S.P.E.C.T.R.E.'s demands, such a signal will indicate that Great Britain and America accept the organization's extortion terms. According to a BBC broadcast heard in Pinder's (EARL CAMERON) warehouse in Nassau, the last time such an unusual occurrence took place was in 1898 during a violent electrical storm.

728 The hotel room of a voluptuous deep-sea fishing enthusiast (VALERIE LEON) who makes love to James Bond (SEAN CONNERY) in *Never Say Never Again*. It's where 007 is enjoying himself when S.P.E.C.T.R.E. assassin Fatima Blush (BARBARA CARRERA) targets his own room (No. 623) for destruction.

SEYMOUR, JANE (Hillingdon, England, February 15, 1951–   ) (real name, Joyce Frankenberg) Lovely British actress, and the heroine of many films and miniseries, who portrayed the mystical Solitaire in *Live and Let Die*. On the set, Roger Moore called her "Baby Bernhardt," a reference to the famous actress Sarah Bernhardt.

Producers Albert R. Broccoli and Harry Saltzman had originally spotted her in a popular British television series titled, "The Onedin Line," a drama about the British shipping industry in the 1870s. She was an intelligent actress—unfortunately, too intelligent for the Mankiewicz script. The producers wanted Seymour to play a psychic sex object who could escape the clutches of Dr. Kananga (YAPHET KOTTO) by tugging at Roger Moore's coattails.

To fight such a one-dimensional characterization, she presented director Guy Hamilton with an interpretation that showed forcefulness and sheer bravado, delivered in a straightforward tone of voice cultivated during her years on the British stage and in radio. After a few weeks, the producers were threatening to resync all of Seymour's lines unless she became less Shakespearean in her delivery and more breathlessly sexy. Once they succeeded in altering her performance, they also began to make her up like a living doll.

"In one sequence," she recalled, "when I'm introduced at Mr. Big's headquarters in Harlem, they covered me with glitter and false eyelashes, and they gave me an exotic hairdo. That was their way of bringing in the occult.

"I was far more interested in the voodoo element in the story because I had actually attended a ceremony in Jamaica with Geoffrey Holder, who knew a great deal about the supernatural. The Solitaire character could have been much more interesting if this voodoo element was brought out. After all, she was respected by everyone as having the power of second sight, as did her mother before her, and she lived all alone in that house on the cliff. It had fascinating possibilities. Unfortunately, all I was given were breathlessly sexy lines and tons of eye makeup.''

Despite her frustrations with the character, Seymour had the time of her life on the film, taking her acting career to literally impossible heights. Not one to perform readily at extreme heights, she nonetheless consented to be hoisted over the center of a Pinewood Studios soundstage, above a pool filled with sharks. Terrified of gunshots, she was forced to undergo a strafing attack. Frightened of snakes, she was asked to stand perfectly still while someone shoved a fanged reptile right in her face. A nervous passenger, she actually sat calmly in the back of the imported double-decker bus while London busdriver Maurice Patchett rammed it under the low-clearance trestle bridge. To her credit, ''Baby Bernhardt'' survived it all without a scratch. *See* SOLITAIRE.

SHAH, KAMRAN Handsome, Oxford-educated Afghan Mujahedeen rebel leader, portrayed by Art Malik, in *The Living Daylights*. Rescued from a Soviet air force base, where he's convinced the Russians that he's a harmless idiot, Shah escorts Bond (TIMOTHY DALTON) and Kara (MARYAM D'ABO) to his fortress home. There he cleans himself up, cuts his hair and beard, and introduces himself as a Mujahedeen leader—in actuality, the deputy commander of the eastern district.

Rather than join Bond on an attack against the base, Shah invites 007 and Kara to accompany the Mujahedeen and their associates, the Snow Leopard Brotherhood, on a mission the next day. Bond knows that time is running out and that renegade Russian General Georgi Koskov (JEROEN KRABBE) will be escaping soon, yet he has no choice but to join Shah's convoy of horses and camels. To his surprise, the mission is to escort the Snow Leopard Brotherhood to a desert rendezvous with Koskov's armored convoy, where a huge amount of raw opium will be traded for diamonds.

Going in alone, Bond buries himself in the back of the opium-carrying truck and returns to the base. Kara goes after him on horseback, and soon Shah is leading the attack on the base. During the battle, which goes well for the Mujahedeen, Bond hijacks a Russian transport plane that has been loaded with the opium.

Bond disposes of Necros (ANDREAS WISNIEWSKI) and then helps Shah win his battle against the Russians by obliterating a bridge crowded with Soviet armored vehicles. As the transport dips its wings in salute, Shah and his warriors cheer their aerial benefactor.

Later, Shah and some of his warriors pay a surprise visit to Vienna to see Kara's concert debut in the West. Unfortunately, they're delayed at the airport—for obvious reasons—and they miss the performance. However, they still get a chance to pay their enthusiastic respects.

SHAPS, CYRIL British actor who portrayed doomed nuclear physicist Dr. Bechmann in *The Spy Who Loved Me. See* BECHMANN, DR.

SHARKEY Gentle fisherman and friend of Felix Leiter (DAVID HEDISON), portrayed by Frank McRae in *Licence to Kill*, who helps James Bond (TIMOTHY DALTON) track down the men who threw their friend to the sharks in Key West. Sharkey and Bond first infiltrate Milton Krest's (ANTHONY ZERBE) marine research warehouse, where Bond throws an assailant into a live bait tank.

Later, Bond is able to sneak aboard Krest's yacht, but Sharkey is captured, killed, and suspended between two dead sharks. The glee of the kill doesn't last long for one of the murderers, who is impaled on a CO_2 spear fired by Bond.

SHARK GUN Dr. Kananga's (YAPHET KOTTO) weapon in *Live and Let Die*. It fires compressed gas pellets, one of which Bond (ROGER MOORE) stuffs in Kananga's mouth in the climactic underwater fight scene. Detonated, the bullet causes the drug smuggler to super-inflate, rise to the ceiling, and explode.

SHARK HUNTER II Sleek, bright yellow, two-man submersible, built by Perry Oceanographics of Florida and used in two James Bond films—*The Spy Who Loved Me* and *Licence to Kill*. In *Spy*, the *Shark Hunter* emerges from Atlantis to participate in an attack on 007's (ROGER MOORE) Lotus submarine car. It's eventually disabled by an underwater mine deposited on the ocean floor by Bond.

In *Licence*, the *Shark Hunter II* is used to

Ace underwater cinematographer Lamar Boren instructs the crew of the *Shark Hunter II* minisub during filming in the Bahamas on *The Spy Who Loved Me*. (Don Griffin, Perry Oceanographics)

Perry Oceanographics' Shark Hunter II minisub appears in both *The Spy Who Loved Me* and *Licence to Kill*. (Don Griffin, Perry Oceanographics)

rescue drug runner Franz Sanchez (ROBERT DAVI) from a DEA van that is driven into the sea by Killifer (EVERETT MCGILL). The *Shark Hunter* was originally built in 1975.

SHARP, ANTHONY British character actor who portrayed Lord Alpert, the foreign minister in *Never Say Never Again*.

SHARROCK, KEN Muscular British actor who portrayed the sadistic jailer on the Russian air force base in *The Living Daylights*. Bond (TIMOTHY DALTON) uses his trick key-ring finder to disorient the jailer with stun gas, then throws him into a jail cell, practically breaking his arm in the process.

SHAW, MAXWELL British actor who portrayed the foreman of signals in the communications room of the British Secret Service in London, in *Dr. No*. He is asked to contact M (BERNARD LEE) when communication is broken with Commander John Strangways (TIM MOXON) in Jamaica.

SHAW, ROBERT (Lancashire, England, August 9, 1927–1978) This underrated British actor portrayed ruthless S.P.E.C.T.R.E. assassin Red Grant, one of 007's deadliest adversaries, in *From Russia with Love*. With his dyed-blond crew cut, a Charles Atlas physique, and feigning a definite psychotic edge, Shaw was brilliant in his role. Grant's confrontation with Bond (SEAN CONNERY) on the Orient Express is a

The many faces of Robert Shaw. (Paramount Pictures)

masterful scene. The setup, the dialogue, and the eventual fight are perhaps the best material in the entire series.

After 007 insults him by asking from which lunatic asylum he's escaped, Grant reaches over and slaps Bond hard across the face. "Don't make it tough on yourself, old man," he sneers. This is one moment in the series where you seriously wonder whether Bond is finished. He's on his knees in a small train compartment, looking down the barrel of a silenced automatic in the hands of a psychopath, who has strict orders from S.P.E.C.T.R.E. And there are no friends in sight. Even the staunchest critic might wonder how 007 is going to get out of this one. Working the talcum-powder/tear-gas cartridge into the story, screenwriter Richard Maibaum definitely improved upon the original novel, in which Bond's cigarette case deflects the assassin's bullet. *See* GRANT, DONALD "RED."

SHENNA, LEILA Exotic actress who portrayed the private-jet-hostess-turned-enemy-assassin in the *Moonraker* teaser.

SHEPRIDGE, JOHNNY A London talent agent and former employee of Darryl Zanuck and Charles K. Feldman who is credited with sending Ursula Andress's famous "wet T-shirt" photograph to Cubby Broccoli in January 1962. The eye-catching pic won Andress the Honey Ryder part in *Dr. No.* Shepridge's nickname was Ghoulash.

SHERIDAN, DANI Actress who portrayed the American allergy victim in *On Her Majesty's Secret Service.*

SHEYBAL, VLADEK (1928–   ) Sleepy-eyed Polish character actor who portrayed S.P.E.C.T.R.E. master planner and chess wizard Kronsteen in *From Russia with Love.* Having

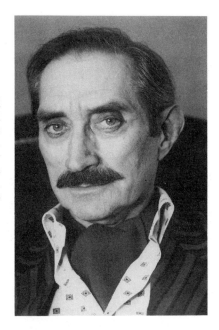

Sleepy-eyed Vladek Sheybal was memorable as S.P.E.C.T.R.E. master planner Kronsteen in *From Russia with Love.* (C.C.A.)

never seen a James Bond movie before, a number of people thought Kronsteen was Bond when this film was released in 1963. After all, he's introduced in an intense chess match, he looks like a foreign agent and dresses in dapper fashion, and he's summoned to a luxurious yacht anchored in the harbor in Venice. However, when he starts talking, you soon realize that this is another in a long series of Bond villains.

Sheybal was perfectly cast in the role as the man who treats espionage as a chess game. For his trouble, he gets a poisoned dagger in the leg from Morzeny (WALTER GOTELL). When it comes to killing Bond, there are no second chances in S.P.E.C.T.R.E.

Sheybal also played Le Chiffre's (ORSON WELLES) associate and auctioneer in *Casino Royale.* Sent to Mata Hari's dancing and spy school in West Berlin to auction off compromising photographs and state secrets to representatives of the United States, China, the Soviet Union, and Great Britain, Sheybal's character finds his scheme short-circuited by Mata Bond (JOANNA PETTET). She steals the box of transparencies, throws it in the nearest toilet, and escapes. Sheybal's character immediately calls Le Chiffre in Monte Carlo and relates the bad news. For his trouble, his phone booth is dynamited, opening a huge hole in the Berlin Wall—through which stream a number of refugees and their baby carriages.

SHIANIVAS HOTEL Bond's (ROGER MOORE) typically lavish hotel in Udaipur, India, in *Octopussy.* He's in Room 27. It's connected to Kamal Khan's (LOUIS JOURDAN) casino, where 007 challenges the exiled Afghan prince to a spirited game of backgammon.

It's also the arena of seduction for lithesome Magda (KRISTINA WAYBORN), who dines with Bond, then joins him for a night of passion in his hotel room. Sequestered in bed and drinking from a "loving cup," Bond notices the tiny octopus tattoo on Magda's buttock. "That's my little octopussy," she explains, prompting one of Roger Moore's patented double takes.

At dawn, Magda dresses, steals the Fabergé egg, kisses 007 good-bye, and makes her way to the balcony, where she ties off her wraparound sari and glides to the pavement. Bond waves good-bye to Kamal, who is waiting for her, then returns to his bedroom, only to be knocked unconscious by Gobinda (KABIR BEDI). What Kamal doesn't know is that 007 has planted a tiny listening bug inside the egg.

SHIMADA, TERU Well-known Japanese character actor who portrayed the ruthless industrialist and S.P.E.C.T.R.E. agent Mr. Osato in *You Only Live Twice.*

SHIMA, YVONNE Japanese actress who portrayed Sister Lily, one of Dr. No's well-mannered secretary/receptionists.

Japanese actor Teru Shimada portrayed Tokyo industrialist Mr. Osato in *You Only Live Twice.* (Columbia Pictures Corp.)

"SHOCKING, POSITIVELY SHOCK-ING" Bond's (SEAN CONNERY) famous retort after he throws an electric heater into Bonita's (NADJA REGIN) bathtub, which electrocutes Capungo (ALF JOINT), the assassin in the *Goldfinger* teaser. Staring down at the fried killer and then at a groggy Bonita, who has been smacked in the mouth, 007 dons his white dinner jacket and offers the perfect lead-in to Shirley Bassey's smashing title song.

SHOE KNIVES Retractable weapons dipped in a lethal nerve poison and imbedded in the shoes of S.P.E.C.T.R.E. agents Rosa Klebb (LOTTE LENYA) and Morzeny (WALTER GOTELL) in *From Russia with Love*. Morzeny kills Kronsteen (VLADEK SHEYBAL) with his, and Klebb attempts to kill Bond (SEAN CONNERY) with hers. Fortunately, she is shot dead by Tanya (DANIELA BIANCHI) before Bond can be stabbed.

Interestingly, in the Fleming book, Klebb comes after Bond with poisoned knitting needles. After she's disarmed, Bond's friend Rene Mathis escorts her out, but she manages to kick Bond with the poisoned shoe knife. Bond falls to the ground, and that's how the novel ends—giving rise to the theory that Fleming actually had 007 killed off in *From Russia with Love*, an act that could have ended the series in 1957. Since Fleming was very frustrated at that time over below-average book sales and the failure of any movie deal to transpire, the theory does hold some water.

SHOLOMIR, JACK (Rustenburg, South Africa, 1931–1988) South African stuntman who appeared in more than 30 motion pictures, including three James Bonds films. Specializing in car stunts, he worked on *From Russia with Love*, *Diamonds Are Forever*, and *Octopussy*.

SHOWER In *From Russia with Love*, before Bond (SEAN CONNERY) enters the bridal suite—where he meets a nude Tatiana Romanova (DANIELA BIANCHI)—he turns on his shower. The only thing is, he never turns it off. Considering Turkish water bills, he probably owes that hotel a considerable sum.

James Bond arrives at Shrublands in *Never Say Never Again*. The look this time was closer to Fleming's original concept. (Taliafilm)

SHRUBLANDS A pricey health clinic in rural England that is a principal location in the early scenes of *Thunderball* and *Never Say Never Again*. In *Thunderball*, Bond (SEAN CONNERY) goes to Shrublands to recover from wounds suffered in his fight with S.P.E.C.T.R.E. agent Jacques Boitier (BOB SIMMONS). There he meets the very suspicious Count Lippe (GUY DOLEMAN), who happens to have a tell-tale Tong sign tattooed to his wrist. That, plus the appearance of the mysteriously bandaged Mr. Angelo (PAUL STASSINO), starts 007 on an investigation that leads to an incredible nuclear blackmail scheme.

In the novel, Shrublands is patterned after Ian Fleming's own experiences in the spring of 1956 when he was a recuperating patient at Enton Hall, a large, well-maintained Victorian mansion in the heart of the Surrey stockbroker's belt. Production designer Ken Adam and production manager David Middlemas had visited Enton Hall and had found it to be old, run down, and highly uncinematic—hardly a proper exterior for a James Bond film. They were looking for something a bit more streamlined and modern. Returning from Surrey, they discovered a converted hotel not far from Pinewood Studios. With its concrete driveways and well-trimmed hedgerows, it became the perfect Shrublands.

Shrublands returns, as a more dignified old-style English manor house, in *Never Say Never Again*. This time Bond (SEAN CONNERY) has been sent to the health clinic to "purge" his body of free-radical toxins caused by too much white bread and red meat, and too many dry martinis. While suffering through "lentil delight" and goat's cheese, Bond smuggles in his own cuisine—Beluga caviar, quail's eggs, fois gras from Strasbourg, and vodka—a meal that seduces the very willing nurse, Patricia Fearing (PRUNELLA GEE).

During his stay, Bond also observes the suspicious activities of S.P.E.C.T.R.E. agent Fatima Blush (BARBARA CARRERA), who's masquerading as a private-duty nurse with a fearful corneal transplant patient named Jack Petachi (GAVAN O'HERLIHY). While there, Bond also battles another S.P.E.C.T.R.E. agent, a giant named Lippe (PAT ROACH), who comes after him with a razor-sharp belt. In an extremely violent encounter that practically destroys half the health clinic, Bond kills the S.P.E.C.T.R.E. assassin, first stunning him with a vial of 007's own urine, and then impaling him on a group of glass laboratory instruments.

SIAMESE FIGHTING FISH A species of deadly fish introduced at the beginning of *From Russia with Love* as Blofeld's pets. In the tank that sits behind Blofeld's desk, two Siamese fighting fish are locked in combat. In the next tank, a third fish watches, ready to pounce on the exhausted winner. Blofeld equates this tactic with the impending S.P.E.C.T.R.E. plan to outwit the Russians and the British by stealing a Soviet Lektor decoding machine and murdering James Bond.

SIAMESE VODKA Bond's (SEAN CONNERY) drink choice while pilfering Mr. Osato's (TERU SHIMADA) safe in *You Only Live Twice*. From the look on his face, it's pretty awful stuff.

SIBERIA Ice-bound region in the Soviet Union where James Bond (ROGER MOORE) finds the dead body of 003, in *A View to a Kill*. Recovering a microchip stolen from the Russians, Bond prepares to return to a camouflaged minilaunch piloted by fellow agent Kimberley Jones (MARY STAVIN). Complicating his escape, however, is an attack by a sizable number of armed Russian KGB agents, supported by a heavily armed helicopter.

When one of his skis is struck by machine-gun fire, Bond latches onto a Soviet Skidoo snowmobile, which is blasted apart by the helicopter. Agent 007 then takes one of the runners and literally surfs down a glacier—to the tune of the Beach Boys classic "California Girls" performed by Gideon Park. As for the helicopter, Bond fires a red flare into its cockpit, sending the out-of-control chopper into a snow peak, where it disintegrates.

SIDEY, HUGH American journalist and political columnist for *Time* magazine who while writing for *Life* magazine in 1963 noted that Ian Fleming's *From Russia with Love* novel was on President John F. Kennedy's reading list. The fact that the president of the United States had time to read about the adventures of 007 be-

Veteran columnist Hugh Sidey, who revealed in a 1961 article that *From Russia with Love* was on President John F. Kennedy's reading list. It was a publicity bonanza for the Bond books and the future movie series. (Hugh Sidey)

came a huge publicity windfall for the James Bond novels.

With that impetus from the White House, paperback publishers began to spread Ian Fleming's literary work across the American continent, and sales began to rise spectacularly. Bond was no longer being consumed solely by air travelers who browsed the shelves of airport book arcades. He was now entering the provinces of American youth, from grade-school to college age—the veritable "meat" of the huge box-office pool that would soon contribute to the success of the James Bond movies in America.

SIERRA James Bond's (SEAN CONNERY) South American contact, portrayed by Raymond Young, in the *Goldfinger* teaser. He's the one who tells Bond not to stick around after Mr. Ramirez's heroin operation is destroyed. Catching a plane to "Meeammi" is a better idea.

SIGNATURE GUN Custom-built sniper's rifle supplied to James Bond (TIMOTHY DALTON) by Q (DESMOND LLEWELYN) in *Licence to Kill*. Made up of seemingly innocuous Hasselblad camera parts, the gun fires .220-caliber, high-velocity shells and is equipped with a right-hand optical palm-reader programmed to Bond's hand print. Once programmed, only James Bond can fire the weapon.

It also has a Bushnell infrared gun sight. Unfortunately, Bond is captured by Hong Kong narcotics agents before he can put the signature gun to good use against drug runner Franz Sanchez (ROBERT DAVI).

SILICON VALLEY Located south of San Francisco, it's the heartland of high-technology electronics development in the United States and the microchip capital of the world (80 percent of the world's supply is produced there). It's also the target of psychotic industrialist Max Zorin's (CHRISTOPHER WALKEN) Project Main Strike in *A View to a Kill*.

Determined to monopolize the world's supply of microchips, Zorin plans to destroy Silicon Valley by detonating two powerful earthquakes in the region—twin seismic killers that will bury more than 250 companies beneath the waves of a giant lake. *See* PROJECT MAIN STRIKE.

SIMMONS, BOB (Fulham, England, March 31, 1933–1988) Top British stunt coordinator and stuntman who not only doubled Sean Connery and Roger Moore, but was responsible for the action sequences in many James Bond films. In a sense, Simmons put the fist into Cubby Broccoli's "two-fisted" approach to Ian Fleming's secret agent.

From the very beginning, the stunt sequences in the James Bond series were hard-hitting, fast-moving, and surprisingly realistic. With Sean Connery throwing the punches, it was no surprise that the films began to appeal to action-hungry fans, especially in America.

Having Peter Hunt in the cutting room was also a great boon to the series. With a musical background and a keen knowledge of television commercial editing, Hunt cut the action sequences to a razor's sharpness. There thus was no fat in Simmons's fights.

Simmons's first assignment for Cubby Broccoli was on *The Red Beret* in 1954. Simmons told Richard Schenkman of *Bondage* magazine in 1980, "After doing one third of the picture, Cubby told me he'd employ me on all of his pictures. They used to bring over a stunt arranger from America, but after I'd worked on *The Red Beret*, they didn't bring him over any more. I got the job.

"I was always looking for a better way . . . I admired the American way of working. It's terribly professional, and that's what I've always tried to push into the people who work for me. I knew damn well if it hadn't been for the Americans we wouldn't be in the film industry today.

"I used to see people doing fight sequences in bars and they could never do it in one take because it wasn't rehearsed. I started choreographing fight sequences so you could repeat every movement. You could tell the director where to put the camera, because you knew where the action was going to be.

"I used to work with Sean very carefully. Sean used to say, 'What do I do and what do you do for me?' Generally, I used to do a master shot. I'd have the whole fight planned. We'd go right through it and film it with a double. We would then shoot Sean for the necessary inserts. But we'd do the whole thing as a master shot first, with doubles, because as (director) Raoul Walsh always said to me when I was a kid, 'If the action's good enough, it can be a monkey in top hat and spats.'

"As the film was progressing, I'd say to Sean, 'I want you to come and look at this sequence; I'll show you something.' He'd come out and say, 'Okay, let's work on it.' Sean would be in the studio sometimes until ten o'clock at night; we'd stay there on the set with just the house lights on, when everybody else had gone—just the nightwatchman was there. Sean was so keen, so good."

According to director Terence Young, the handsome Simmons was actually considered as a candidate to play James Bond in *Dr. No*. When Connery won the role, Simmons, appropriately, became his stunt double and *Dr. No*'s stunt arranger.

And in key fight sequences throughout the series, it's often Simmons versus Connery in the key fights—including the fight with Mr. Jones, the chauffeur in *Dr. No*, and the vicious clash with Jacques Boitier in the *Thunderball* teaser. In the climactic fight with Dr. No (JOSEPH WISEMAN) in the reactor room, Simmons doubled Connery, while George Leech doubled Wiseman.

In *From Russia with Love*, Simmons doubled Connery in the train compartment fight. In *Goldfinger*, Simmons doubled actor Michael Mellinger, who, as Kisch, is thrown off the top of Fort Knox by Oddjob (HAROLD SAKATA). In *Thunderball*, Simmons drove Count Lippe's (GUY DOLEMAN) car when it was struck by rockets from Fiona Volpe's (LUCIANA PALUZZI) motorcycle.

SIMMONS, MR. Goldfinger's (GERT FROBE) gin pigeon in Miami Beach. He's portrayed by dapper Austin Willis. Simmons is being systematically cheated by Goldfinger, who uses his Girl Friday, Jill Masterson (SHIRLEY EATON), to spy on Willis's hand with binoculars. Goldfinger gets the information through a radio transmitter disguised as a hearing aid.

Before Bond (SEAN CONNERY) ferrets out the scam, Willis has lost $10,000. However, when 007 informs Goldfinger that the jig is up, the golden villain proceeds to lose back $15,000.

SIMON, CARLY (New York City, June 25, 1945–   ) Soulful pop singer who sang one of the best James Bond title songs, "Nobody Does It Better," from *The Spy Who Loved Me*.

Carly Simon, whose soulful title track, "Nobody Does It Better," was a highlight of *The Spy Who Loved Me*. (Epic Records)

380

SINATRA, NANCY (Jersey City, New Jersey, June 8, 1940–   ) American pop singer of the '60s and the daughter of Frank Sinatra. She sang the memorable title song to *You Only Live Twice* in 1967. Nancy recorded the song in London with John Barry conducting the London Philharmonic.

"That was a scary experience," she recalled. "John, whose music I just treasure, wrote the song, and lyricist Leslie Bricusse was an old friend of mine. Cubby Broccoli had known my father and mother for years, ever since I was born. And the London Philharmonic played on the session. Real pressure."

SINGAPORE TRACKING STATION A British installation that picks up faint echoes of a spacecraft landing somewhere near the Sea of Japan, in *You Only Live Twice*. The signal is the only clue to the disappearance of the U.S. *Jupiter 16* spacecraft.

SIRKECI STATION Istanbul's principal train station, which is featured during night sequences in *From Russia with Love*. It also doubled stations in Belgrade and Zagreb.

"SIT DOWN" Dr. No's (JOSEPH WISEMAN) first words of dialogue, spoken ominously and in an amplified tone to Professor R. J. Dent (ANTHONY DAWSON) in a waiting room inside Dr. No's fortress on Crab Key.

"SITTTTT" James Bond's (ROGER MOORE) command to a ferocious Bengal tiger he meets during his escape from Kamal Khan's (LOUIS JOURDAN) Monsoon Palace in *Octopussy*. It's actually a reference to the famous animal training techniques of England's Barbara Wodehouse. And it works!

SIX The number of trips from England to the European mainland that Goldfinger (GERT FROBE) makes each year, traveling in a Rolls-Royce Phantom 337. The car's bodywork is solid 18-carat gold—the very gold that Goldfinger is smuggling out of England.

It's also the number on the detonator that 007 (ROGER MOORE) removes from the nuclear missile he disassembles in *The Spy Who Loved Me*.

6574 Identification number on the Coast Guard helicopter—a French Aerospatiale model—that carries James Bond (TIMOTHY DALTON), Felix Leiter (DAVID HEDISON), and Sharkey (FRANK MCRAE) to Cray Cay in the *Licence to Kill* teaser. The same helicopter later helps 007 chase and disable Franz Sanchez's (ROBERT DAVI) private plane.

SIX HOURS The amount of time that Emilio Largo's (ADOLFO CELI) *Disco Volante* yacht was out of Nassau Harbor on the night of the A-bomb hijacking in *Thunderball*.

SIX MONTHS The amount of time Bond (SEAN CONNERY) spent in the hospital when his Beretta jammed, prior to the start of *Dr. No*. It's also the amount of time that has passed since Sylvia Trench has last seen 007, in *From Russia with Love*.

67444 Phone number advertised on the top of Jamaican cab No. 26, which drops 007 (SEAN CONNERY) off in front of his hotel in *Dr. No*.

16 The number of Polaris nuclear missiles on board the HMS *Ranger*, a submarine captured by the *Liparus* supertanker in *The Spy Who Loved Me*. One of these missiles is later fired by Stromberg's (CURT JURGENS) crew of fanatics, but Bond (ROGER MOORE) manages to reprogram the coordinates of their target and the missile destroys another hijacked submarine, the *Potemkin*, instead.

16 AGENTS French Deuxième Bureau casualties, inflicted by female agents of Dr. Noah (WOODY ALLEN), in *Casino Royale*.

16 HOURS The train travel time between New Orleans and New York in *Live and Let Die*. Solitaire (JANE SEYMOUR) and James Bond (ROGER MOORE) do not plan to catch up on their reading.

16TH CENTURY According to Max Zorin (CHRISTOPHER WALKEN) in *A View to a Kill*, it's the age of his beautiful French estate and stables—supposedly built by a duke who thought he'd be reincarnated as a horse. The story's correct—France's Chateau Chantilly, where the film was shot, was indeed constructed by an aristocratic horse fancier. But it dates back only to the 18th century.

6:32 P.M. The time of the Orient Express's arrival in Belgrade, Yugoslavia, in *From Russia with Love.*

$6,000 Actress Ursula Andress's salary for *Dr. No*—$1,000 a week for six weeks' work.

623 James Bond's (SEAN CONNERY) hotel room number in Nassau in *Never Say Never Again.* The room is destroyed by a bomb planted by S.P.E.C.T.R.E. assassin Fatima Blush (BARBARA CARRERA). Fortunately, Bond has chosen to join his deep-sea fishing girlfriend (VALERIE LEON) in her bed instead of his own.

65 French agent Valerie Mathis's (LINDA CHRISTIAN) Monte Carlo hotel room number in the TV film "Casino Royale."

SLAZENGER ONE The brand of golf ball used by Goldfinger (GERT FROBE) during a high-stakes challenge match with James Bond (SEAN CONNERY).

SLAZENGER SEVEN The brand of golf ball found by James Bond (SEAN CONNERY) during a golf match with Goldfinger (GERT FROBE). Goldfinger also plays a Slazenger, but it's a Slazenger One. Bond plays a Penfold Hearts.

When his adversary decides to make up for a bad lie by having his caddy, Oddjob (HAROLD SAKATA), illegally drop a new ball on the main fairway, Bond decides to use the Slazenger Seven for his own cheating ploy. Pulling his Penfold Hearts and Goldfinger's Slazenger One from the cup, Bond substitutes the Slazenger Seven for the Slazenger One, which Goldfinger promptly bangs onto the next fairway.

Losing the final hole on purpose by blowing his last putt, Bond goes to the cup and announces that poor Goldfinger has been playing the wrong ball. Since strict rules of golf are in force, he must lose both the hole and the match.

"SLOW BOAT FROM CHINA, A" What Mary Goodnight (BRITT EKLAND) calls the eight-hour junk ride from Scaramanga's Island to Hong Kong in *The Man with the Golden Gun.*

SLUMBER INC. The Las Vegas mortuary run by Morton Slumber (DAVID BAUER) in *Diamonds Are Forever.* It's actually a cover for an international diamond-smuggling syndicate.

Arriving in Los Angeles, Bond (SEAN CONNERY), carrying a 50,000-carat diamond cache—in the body of Peter Franks—is greeted by a hearse and three goons from the syndicate. They transport him to the desert mortuary—which was actually one of the offices of the Las Vegas Visitors Bureau—where 007 meets Slumber. At Slumber Inc., James Bond has one of his most terrifying brushes with death.

Knocked out by assassins Mr. Wint (BRUCE GLOVER) and Mr. Kidd (PUTTER SMITH), he's tossed into a coffin and placed in the mortuary's crematorium. In a frighteningly claustrophobic sequence, Bond fights to get out of the coffin, which is engulfed by flames. Fortunately, Slumber and Shady Tree (LEONARD BARR) discover that the diamonds Bond has brought are phonies, and they retrieve him from the crematorium just in time.

SMALLBONE, PENELOPE Miss Moneypenny's (LOIS MAXWELL) new assistant, introduced in *Octopussy* and portrayed by Michaela Clavell. *See* CLAVELL, MICHAELA.

SMALL-FAWCETT, NIGEL Idiotic foreign service officer, with an amazing upper-class accent, who's attached to the British embassy in Nassau and portrayed by Rowan Atkinson. He attempts to help Bond (SEAN CONNERY) in *Never Say Never Again.* Small-Fawcett first meets Bond in Nassau Harbor, providing 007 with some useful information on the activities of billionaire philanthropist Maximillian Largo (KLAUS MARIA BRANDAUER). By yelling Bond's name across the harbor, he, of course, eliminates any sense of secrecy about 007's visit.

He also has the habit of communicating with 007 at the wrong time. For instance, a phone call disturbs Bond while he's making love in the Bahamas to his lady friend (VALERIE

LEON). And at the film's conclusion, Small-Fawcett stumbles into the pool where 007 and Domino (KIM BASINGER) are relaxing.

The character of Small-Fawcett was created by uncredited comedy writers Dick Clement and Ian Le Frenais, who were hired by producer Jack Schwartzman to add humor to Lorenzo Semple, Jr.'s original screenplay.

"SMIERT SPIONAM" (Russian for "Death to Spies") According to defecting Russian General Georgi Koskov (JEROEN KRABBE) in *The Living Daylights*, it's the code name of a sinister KGB plot to kill American and British spies throughout the world. A tag with that phrase on it has already been found on the body of murdered British agent 004 (FREDERICK WARDER) in Gibraltar.

In reality, though, the phrase has nothing to do with the KGB. It's a plot hatched by Koskov and his partner, arms dealer Brad Whitaker (JOE DON BAKER), to get British Intelligence to assassinate KGB chief Leonid Pushkin (JOHN RHYS-DAVIES). With Pushkin—a man who strongly suspects that Koskov is up to no good—out of the way, Koskov can then fly to Afghanistan and use local Soviet military personnel to consummate a huge diamonds-for-opium deal with the Afghan Snow Leopard Brotherhood.

To further convince the British and 007 that "Smiert Spionam" is indeed a Russian plot, Koskov's agent, Necros (ANDREAS WISNIEWSKI), kills British Secret Service Austrian Section Chief Saunders (THOMAS WHEATLEY) and once again leaves the "Smiert Spionam" sign near the body—printed on a balloon. When cornered by Bond (TIMOTHY DALTON) in Tangier, Pushkin denies that "Smiert Spionam" exists. He refers to it as a Beria operation in Stalin's time that was deactivated 20 years earlier. Bond believes him, and eventually they both go after Koskov and Whitaker.

SMIRNOV KGB chief and former labor camp inspector portrayed by Kurt Kasznar in *Casino Royale*. Smirnov accompanies M (JOHN HUSTON), Ransome (WILLIAM HOLDEN), and Le Grand (CHARLES BOYER) to an English country manor house to persuade Sir James Bond (DAVID NIVEN) to accept one last dangerous assignment.

Smirnov was originally assigned to Icon 988 G.P.U. in the Siberian Sector. Sir James notes that Smirnov has a noisy, clanging armory concealed in his boots.

SMITH AND WESSON The make of the .45-caliber automatic owned by Professor R. J. Dent (ANTHONY DAWSON) in *Dr. No*. Equipped with a silencer, it has a six-shot magazine that Dent expels into what he thinks are the sleeping forms of Bond (SEAN CONNERY) and Miss Taro (ZENA MARSHALL), only to discover that it is a ruse and that Bond is seated right behind him.

The same gun, albeit a golden one, is carried by Pussy Galore (HONOR BLACKMAN) inside Goldfinger's (GERT FROBE) private jet. When she points it at Bond, 007 explains to her that it's extremely dangerous to fire guns in planes because the bullet will probably pass through him and puncture the plane's fuselage, creating rapid decompression. Goldfinger also carries the golden gun and later makes that mistake in the fight with Bond inside the presidential jet.

SMITH, EDDIE American stuntman who manned the motorboat that takes out the wedding cake in *Live and Let Die*.

SMITHERS Q's (DESMOND LLEWELYN) assistant in New Delhi. He's portrayed in *Octopussy* by Jeremy Bullock.

SMITHERS, COLONEL Bank of England executive, portrayed by Richard Vernon, who briefs Bond (SEAN CONNERY) and M (BERNARD LEE) on the activities of Auric Goldfinger. Smithers loans Bond a bar of gold worth 5,000 pounds, which will be used as bait in the celebrated golf challenge.

SMITH, MADELINE Actress who portrayed Miss Caruso, the Italian Secret Service agent whom Bond (ROGER MOORE) beds at the beginning of *Live and Let Die*. She was the first in a long line of 007 conquests during the Moore years.

SMITH, PUTTER Nearly bald musician who portrayed the bookish, homosexual assassin Mr. Kidd in *Diamonds Are Forever*. A bass fiddler with the Thelonious Monk Band, Smith was discovered in a Los Angeles nightclub by director Guy Hamilton, who felt that his wild look was perfect for Kidd. *See* MR. KIDD.

SMYTHE, MAJOR DEXTER Ex-British army officer and Secret Service agent who is the father of Octopussy (MAUD ADAMS) in the 13th James Bond movie. During the Korean War, Smythe stole a cache of Chinese gold from the North Koreans, murdered his guide, and disappeared, later settling in Sri Lanka, where his daughter was born. Becoming an authority on octopi, Smythe gave his daughter the unusual nickname Octopussy.

In the film, James Bond (ROGER MOORE) recalls that, 20 years later, he went to Sri Lanka to give Smythe 24 hours to clean up his affairs before he was brought back to London for a military court-martial. Given such an opportunity, Smythe decided to commit suicide rather than face the humiliation of a murder trial. Upon meeting the adult Octopussy, Bond learns that his daughter holds no grudge; on the contrary, she respects 007 for giving her father "an honorable alternative."

SNOOPER A doglike robot mounted on wheels and developed by Q (DESMOND LLEWELYN) in *A View to a Kill*. Introduced in M's (ROBERT BROWN) office as the "prototype of a highly sophisticated robot surveillance machine," the snooper returns at the story's conclusion to find James Bond (ROGER MOORE) showering with Stacey Sutton (TANYA ROBERTS).

SNOW LEOPARD BROTHERHOOD Afghan drug wholesalers, featured in *The Living Daylights*, who are rumored to be the biggest opium dealers in the Golden Crescent. Dealing with renegade Russian General Georgi Koskov (JEROEN KRABBE) and his partner, arms dealer Brad Whitaker (JOE DON BAKER), the Brotherhood is about to be involved in a huge raw-opium-for-diamonds swap. Unfortunately for Koskov and Whitaker, James Bond (TIMOTHY DALTON) hijacks the transport carrying the illegal drugs and jettisons the entire load into the stratosphere.

SOLAR POWER An alternative energy system that is strongly featured in the Richard Maibaum/Tom Mankiewicz script for *The Man with the Golden Gun*. Introduced by Maibaum, it replaced a running duel-type story between James Bond and $1 million-a-shot assassin Francisco Scaramanga that was the center of Mankiewicz's early drafts.

Said Maibaum, "As usual, we were looking for a world threat, and in the end it came down to either solar power or weather control. Harry Saltzman felt that weather control was not a good idea. He felt that it would just be a lot of special effects and stock footage showing hurricanes and tropical storms. He was right at the time. However, today, when special effects are a standard part of every science-fiction film, it is interesting to think about what the reaction might be to the weather-control idea."

SOLAR-POWERED LASER CANNON A weapon used by Scaramanga (CHRISTOPHER LEE) to destroy James Bond's (ROGER MOORE) seaplane in *The Man with the Golden Gun*.

SOLERO The sherry being served at dinner to diamond broker Sir Donald Munger (LAURENCE NAISMITH), James Bond (SEAN CONNERY), and M (BERNARD LEE) in *Diamonds Are Forever*. When Bond identifies it as a '51, M counters that sherries do not have years. Bond replies that he was referring to the original vintage on which this sherry is based—1851.

SOLEX AGITATOR A technological wonder introduced in *The Man with the Golden Gun*, it's a solar cell that can convert solar radiation into electricity with 95 percent efficiency. The British have it, a sinister industrialist named Hai Fat (RICHARD LOO) wants it, assassin Francisco Scaramanga (CHRISTOPHER LEE) kills for it, and James Bond (ROGER MOORE) rescues it from oblivion.

As in many other James Bond films, the solex and its emphasis on the effectiveness of solar energy were elements pulled directly from the headlines of contemporary newspapers. The year *The Man with the Golden Gun* was released—1974—will be remembered in America as the year of the oil crisis, when many people waited in long lines for gasoline.

The solar energy movement was given a boost by the oil crisis, and the folks at Eon Productions seized upon that opportunity to steal the concept for part of their story from actual headlines—a practice they would repeat in films such as *Moonraker* (the space-shuttle missions) and *Licence to Kill* (the worldwide drug war).

SOLITAIRE The mystical mistress of the tarot cards, portrayed by lovely Jane Seymour, in *Live and Let Die*. Like her mother and grandmother before her, Solitaire has the supernatural power of the obeah—the "second sight." Because of this gift, she's a virtual slave to Kananga's (YAPHET KOTTO) will. It is from the amazingly accurate predictions of her cards that Kananga wages his campaign to corner the North American heroin market.

Her mother lost the power when she lost her virginity, and Solitaire faces that same fate when she meets James Bond (ROGER MOORE), who is not a strong believer in the occult (he tricks her into bed by using a fake deck of tarot cards—all of which depict the "Lovers" symbol). Deprived of her power, Solitaire falls in love with Bond and eventually helps him destroy Kananga's island empire.

In an early draft of the *Live and Let Die* script, writer Tom Mankiewicz departed from Ian Fleming's original description of the beautiful white fortune-teller by introducing her as a black girl. Said Mankiewicz, "This was at a time when *Shaft* had come out and there was a whole new wave of black exploitation films that were making a lot of money. So I thought that this time out, if we do *Live and Let Die*, Bond could get into bed with a black girl; in our case, Solitaire, who was of Haitian origin.

"Everybody said 'great,' and David Picker of United Artists went along with us. So, in my early script, Solitaire became this beautiful black girl. And the little black agent, Rosie Carver, was originally written as a white girl. At the last minute, however, United Artists changed their mind. In their defense, I saw that they were very nervous about having a new

James Bond and were unwilling to try something different when it came to a Bond girl.

"If Sean Connery had come back for this one, we wouldn't have had any problems. But in the back of UA's mind was the Lazenby affair, where the public didn't readily accept a new Bond right off, and they were very wary about Roger Moore's chances. He wasn't by any means a sure thing.

"Picker told me that although he liked the idea of a black Solitaire and felt it would work in progressive cities like New York and London, he felt that when the film was distributed in the places where the Bond movies had done very well—the so-called hinterlands—there would be a lot of people who didn't want Bond championing the cause of civil rights. Picker said that the decision was simply a matter of economic fact and that the studio wasn't making an *On the Waterfront* but a commercial James Bond film. 'And frankly,' Picker told me, 'with Roger, we're scared.'

"Of course, nobody bothered to tell me about the decision. I found out when suddenly I heard the studio execs mentioning Catherine Deneuve to play Solitaire, which I thought was pretty funny considering I had written her as being black.

"I thought Jane Seymour was badly miscast as Solitaire. I think a much flashier girl should have been used, especially in Roger's first Bond film. Jane was so sweet and adorable looking that when Roger got into bed with her, it didn't work at all. It almost looked as if she was being taken advantage of. She's the type of girl you want to bring home to your mother, as opposed to a Bond girl who really knows her way around."

"SOLO" The original title of "The Man from U.N.C.L.E." television series, named after one of its principal characters, Napoleon Solo, whose name was penned by Ian Fleming. Threatened with a lawsuit by Eon Productions, which was using the character name Solo in their *Goldfinger* film, producer Norman Felton changed the TV series's name.

Compounding the issue at the time was the fact that Ian Fleming was also fighting a lawsuit against Kevin McClory over the rights to *Thunderball*. Sensing the possibility of a rival Bond in that corner, producers Albert R. Broccoli and Harry Saltzman were ready to protect any element of their series from possible imitators, including the men from U.N.C.L.E.

SOLO, MR. Mafia kingpin featured in *Goldfinger* and portrayed by actor Martin Benson. In exchange for $1 million in gold, Solo arranges for the Red Chinese A-bomb to be smuggled into the United States. Later, he is the only hood not to fall in with Operation Grand Slam. Electing to leave with his gold, he says good-bye to Goldfinger (GERT FROBE) and Bond (SEAN CONNERY) and is driven to the airport by Oddjob (HAROLD SAKATA), who instead kills him with a silenced pistol.

Solo's body and the entire Lincoln Continental in which he is riding are then crushed into a convenient lump of metal at a wrecking yard and returned to Auric Stud in the flatbed of a Ford Ranchero driven by Oddjob. In a nod to his host's previous remark, Bond quips, "As you said, he had a pressing engagement."

SOMERSET, MR. AND MRS. DAVID James Bond (SEAN CONNERY) and Tatiana Romanova's (DANIELA BIANCHI) cover names on the Orient Express in *From Russia with Love*. According to her passport, Romanova's first name is Caroline. Bond's cover says that he's a businessman returning to his home in Derbyshire. And, no, they don't have any children, not even one little boy.

SOO SOO, PAPILLON Actress who portrayed Pan Ho, one of Max Zorin's (CHRISTOPHER WALKEN) assistants, in *A View to a Kill*.

SOTHEBY'S AUCTIONEER Well-tailored employee of the famous London auction house, portrayed by Philip Voss in *Octopussy*, who sells Kamal Khan (LOUIS JOURDAN) a jeweled Fabergé Easter egg for a half-million pounds.

SOTO, TALISA (Brooklyn, New York, March 27, 1967–) (real name, Miriam

Talisa Soto joins Timothy Dalton and Caroline Bliss during a break from shooting on *Licence to Kill*.
(Express Newspapers, London)

Soto) Sultry actress and cover-girl model of Puerto Rican descent who portrayed drug runner's moll Lupe Lamora in *Licence to Kill*.

Although she looks great in the role and has a directness befitting a mobster's girlfriend, Lamora's problem in the film is the unbelievable manner in which she switches allegiances. Although it's obvious that her relationship with Sanchez (ROBERT DAVI) is a nightmare, the writers should have given her a little more time to develop a believable approach to seeking Bond (TIMOTHY DALTON) out. The key scene, where she shows up in Bond's hotel room to plead for his love, for instance, plays laughably.

Part of the problem is that 007's attentions are divided in the film, with CIA agent Pam Bouvier (CAREY LOWELL) eventually winning his heart—although even their romantic tryst on the motorboat comes too quickly to be believed.

In a similar plot element in *Live and Let Die*, Bond (ROGER MOORE) was able to steal Solitaire (JANE SEYMOUR) away from Kananga (YAPHET KOTTO). However, Solitaire was Bond's only focus in the film, thus writer Tom Mankiewicz gave the relationship time to develop. In *Licence to Kill*, time is not on Lupe Lamora's side. *See* LAMORA, LUPE.

SOUVENIRS The items that James Bond (GEORGE LAZENBY) removes from his desk when he resigns from the British Secret Service in *On Her Majesty's Secret Service*. They include Honey Ryder's (URSULA ANDRESS) knife from *Dr. No*, Red Grant's (ROBERT SHAW) strangler watch from the film *From Russia with Love*, and the miniature rebreather from *Thunderball*. Director Peter Hunt introduced these elements while John Barry played the signature theme over each item. They were yet another of screenwriter Richard Maibaum's references to the rich 007 history that was taking a turn with the introduction of a new James Bond.

SOVIET CHAIRMAN Leonid Brezhnev look-alike, portrayed by Paul Hardwick in *Octopussy*, who referees the heated argument between generals Gogol (WALTER GOTELL) and Orlov (STEVEN BERKOFF) during a party conference on the NATO/Eastern Bloc mutual disarmament talks. Gogol recommends that the leadership accept the proposals because they do not compromise the Russian defensive position. Orlov, on the other hand, advocates a lightning-like military invasion of the West through East Germany and Czechoslovakia. *See* ORLOV, GENERAL; ORLOV'S COMMAND.

SPAIN The second country chosen in Maximillian Largo's (KLAUS MARIA BRANDAUER) Domination video-game battle with James Bond (SEAN CONNERY) in *Never Say Never Again*. It's worth $9,000, and Largo wins. *See* DOMINATION.

S.P.E.C.T.R.E. The Special Executor for Counter-Intelligence, Terrorism, Revenge, and Extortion, a huge, multidenominational criminal organization headed by Ernst Stavro Blofeld, and 007's principal adversary in seven Bond films.

S.P.E.C.T.R.E.'s screen history dates back to 1958, when producer Kevin McClory attempted to bring Fleming's James Bond character to the screen. An assistant director on Mike Todd's epic film *Around the World in 80 Days*, McClory had acquired the reputation of a wunderkind filmmaker and was eager to transfer the 007 films to the screen.

Rather than use any of the Fleming novels that had been written to that date, McClory decided to create a new film story involving an international caper that could use many different locations, not unlike his then-recent experience on *Around the World in 80 Days*. In the early drafts of this story—conceived by McClory, Fleming, and screenwriter Jack Whittingham—the Mafia were the principal villains. Gradually, the Mafia was discarded and Fleming conceived of S.P.E.C.T.R.E., which first stood for Special Executive for Terrorism, Revolution, and Espionage.

In Fleming's own mythology, S.P.E.C.T.R.E. was an immensely powerful, privately owned organization manned by ex-members of SMERSH, the Gestapo, the Mafia, and the Black Tong of Peking. The organization struck a chord and became Bond's adversary in the story by McClory, Fleming, and Whittingham titled *Latitude 78 West*, which was named after a spot in the mid-Atlantic where S.P.E.C.T.R.E. hides two A-bombs it has hijacked from NATO.

When McClory could not convince a major studio to finance the project, Fleming went ahead and used the story elements in a novel titled *Thunderball*—the code name of Bond's mission to find the missing bombs. Claiming infringement on their collaboration, McClory and Whittingham later sued Fleming in the high court of London and won after a grueling three-year battle. As a result, McClory and Whittingham were given the screen rights to Fleming's *Thunderball* novel and co-credit on future editions of the popular book.

With these rights, and the inability to mount a film on his own, McClory would later make a deal with Albert R. Broccoli and Harry Saltzman to produce *Thunderball* in 1965 as part of their already thriving series of Bond movies. McClory also agreed to wait 10 years before he would produce another Bond movie based on the original *Thunderball* property.

Prior to the suit, producers Broccoli and Saltzman had used S.P.E.C.T.R.E. as the villain in both *Dr. No* (1962) and *From Russia with Love* (1963), even though the organization was not featured in either of those original Fleming novels. Originally, Dr. No worked for the Russians, as did Rosa Klebb and Red Grant in *From Russia with Love*. Considering the Cold War in the early 1960s, the producers decided—rightfully so—to avoid using the Soviets as cliché villains of the time. S.P.E.C.T.R.E. thus became the perfect umbrella organization for the type of fantastic schemes pulled off by the Fleming-esque villains. After *Thunderball* (1965), Blofeld and S.P.E.C.T.R.E. returned in *You Only Live Twice* (1967), *On Her Majesty's Secret Service* (1969), and *Diamonds Are Forever* (1971).

McClory resurfaced in 1975 with plans to bring a project called *James Bond of the Secret Service* to the screen. Also known as *Warhead*, this new 007 project was based on the original *Thunderball* materials created by Fleming, Whittingham, and McClory in 1958. Burned once before by the release of a rival Bond movie—Charles K. Feldman's *Casino Royale* in 1967—producer Albert R. Broccoli was determined to stop McClory. A running battle began between the two producers, culminating in a number of lawsuits that stalled the McClory project.

Interestingly, early drafts of the 1977 Broccoli-produced Bond entry, *The Spy Who Loved Me*, contained references to S.P.E.C.T.R.E., which had now been updated to include members of the Bader-Meinhof Gang, the Japanese Red Army, and other modern terrorist organizations. Faced with a McClory suit about the unauthorized use of S.P.E.C.T.R.E., Broccoli had his screenwriters remove these references from *The Spy Who Loved Me*, and villain Karl Stromberg (CURT JURGENS) became just another billionaire megalomaniac. Even the normally black-suited S.P.E.C.T.R.E. henchmen were given red uniforms in Stromberg's private army. Broccoli would also introduce a Blofeld lookalike in *For Your Eyes Only* (1981), but the character was not identified as Blofeld.

Sensing that McClory was within his rights to create a rival Bond, producer Jack Schwartzman would later enter the fray and produce the last James Bond movie, to date, to feature S.P.E.C.T.R.E. and Blofeld—1983's *Never Say Never Again*, which many people refer to as the *Thunderball* remake. In that film, actor Max von Sydow portrayed Ernst Stavro Blofeld.

Still based in Paris, the organization is now heavily involved in the arms business with extensive operations in the Middle East and Central America. To provoke insurgency and revolution, armaments and missles are indescriminately supplied to rebels and government forces—a typical S.P.E.C.T.R.E. tactic. In regard to future S.P.E.C.T.R.E.-related Bond movies, producer Kevin McClory has surfaced from time to time with plans to create another 007 project. The latest McClory–Bond project is *Warhead 8*, announced in 1989.

S.P.E.C.T.R.E. ISLAND The training ground for assassin Donald "Red" Grant (ROBERT SHAW) in *From Russia with Love*. Under the supervision of Morzeny (WALTER GOTELL), the island is the setting for the teaser sequence in which Grant tracks the phony Bond through the Renaissance Garden.

Later in the story, we see Grant sunbathing, while a bosomy masseuse (JAN WILLIAMS) works his deltoids. Klebb (LOTTE LENYA) meets Grant on the island and tests his fitness with a knuckle-duster to the abdomen. She also views the S.P.E.C.T.R.E. training facilities, where agents perform feats of marksmanship, karate, and other acts of mayhem, using live targets.

In reality, S.P.E.C.T.R.E. Island is located

on the Pinewood Studios lot. The main building is actually the studio's administration building.

SPERBER, MILO British actor who portrayed bookish Professor Markovitz, the doomed physicist in *The Spy Who Loved Me*. Along with his partner, Dr. Bechmann (CYRIL SHAPS), the professor is murdered after developing a nuclear-submarine tracking system for billionaire shipping magnate Karl Stromberg (CURT JURGENS).

"SPIRAL JUMP, THE" An amazing 360-degree automobile jump that is a highlight of *The Man with the Golden Gun*. Designed by Jay Milligan, a member of stuntman Joie Chitwood's daredevil team, the stunt involved a car being sent up a ramp, turned entirely around in the air, and landing upright on another ramp.

Milligan had worked out the stunt with the help of a Cornell University computer. Speed, car specifications, the length of the jump, and wind resistance were programmed into the computer's brain, and out came the mathematical specifications for the jump. From this information, Milligan knew that he needed a set speed, a specially designed car, and takeoff and landing ramps designed to give the car the proper lift and turn so that it could land easily on all four tires.

When *The Man with the Golden Gun* went into preproduction, Milligan was hired by the producers to do the stunt in Bangkok. Eon Productions purchased a two-year option on the stunt, which prohibited Milligan and any other stunt driver from performing it in public. The stunt was something that had to be kept as secretive as possible. The producers were always nervous about quickie television productions stealing their material as well as their stunts.

In Bangkok, production designer Peter Murton supervised the construction of specially designed takeoff and landing ramps over a Thai klong. The ramps were skillfully disguised as a fallen bridge.

In the story, Bond (ROGER MOORE), attempting to overtake Scaramanga's (CHRISTOPHER LEE) car, has to cross the canal in a hurry. With no bridge in sight, resourceful 007 spies the fallen bridge, backs up his car and rams it forward over the fallen timbers. In the process, Bond does the 360-degree jump and lands perfectly on the other side.

For a stunt that lasted all of fifteen seconds in the film, the producers spent a small fortune to build the fake bridge and the approach road, and to pay the salaries of Milligan's driving team. The cars themselves were provided by American Motors Corporation, which was keenly aware that an appearance in a Bond film could easily boost the sales of its new product line.

Although an AMC Hornet couldn't compete with Aston Martin in the styling department, it met Milligan's specifications perfectly. A team of engineers redesigned the car's chassis, placed the steering column in the center of the car, cut down the body in certain places and widened it in others, and monkeyed around with certain weight factors that could affect the eventual jump.

By June 1974, the Hornet was ready to jump the klong. Christopher Lee was one of hundreds of spectators who lined the canal on that summery day. "It was done right after lunch by Bumps Willard, one of Milligan's drivers," remembered Lee. "There were cranes and ambulances standing by should Willard end up in the water, and director Guy Hamilton had set up a number of cameras to catch the stunt from different angles.

"And then it just happened. The Hornet threw up a little dust, revved up its engine, and then hit the launch ramp. Before you knew it, it had flown across the canal, turned perfectly around and landed upright on four tires. He made it look easy.

"The stunt was so perfect that there was talk about doing it again. Some people worried that if it did look too easy, an audience might think it was faked. Any such talk was soon quashed, however, considering the added expense as well as the danger of putting Willard back in the car."

Interestingly, in the original script, screenwriter Richard Maibaum wanted Bond to do the stunt twice. Agent 007 jumps the klong and makes it to the other side, only to discover that Scaramanga is still on the opposite side of the klong. It was one Maibaum idea that was immediately dumped.

In the final film, Hamilton presents the

jump in slow motion, and it works very well, especially when Sheriff J. W. Pepper (CLIFTON JAMES) takes a look at Bond and realizes what he's about to do. However, the drama of the stunt—one of the Bond series's greatest moments—was cinematically ruined when a kazoo whistle was added to the soundtrack, a careless mistake.

SPY WHO LOVED ME, THE
(United Artists, 1977) ★ ★ ★ ½ The 10th James Bond film released by UA and the first produced solo by Albert R. Broccoli. (Harry Saltzman had sold his share of Eon Productions in 1975.) U.S. release date: August 3, 1977. Budget: $13.5 million. U.S. film rental: $24.4 million. Running time: 125 minutes.

This film single-handedly revived the sagging Bond series in the mid-1970s. Lavishly produced and featuring a Roger Moore who had grown comfortable in the role, *The Spy Who Loved Me* was the best Bond film since *Goldfinger*. For a new generation of young viewers—fans who would soon be rooting for Indiana Jones, Superman, and E.T.—*The Spy Who Loved Me* was a spectacular adventure with a way-out plot involving a submarine-swallowing supertanker, a steel-toothed assassin named Jaws, and a resourceful and beautiful Russian agent named Anya Amasova.

Returning to the elements that had contributed to *Goldfinger*'s success, producer Albert R. Broccoli gave production designer Ken Adam a free hand to design the spectacular *Jonah* Set, which duplicated the interior of the *Liparus*

Agent 007 and Major Amasova are all dressed up with no place to go in *The Spy Who Loved Me*. (Robert Penn/Camera Press, Globe Photos)

tanker. Meanwhile, Derek Meddings and Perry Oceanographics were designing the mid-1970s equivalent of the Aston Martin—the Lotus Esprit submarine car.

Like *Thunderball*, *The Spy Who Loved Me* introduced a sense of worldwide alarm that sends Bond on one of his most dangerous assignments, this time allied to a Soviet KGB agent who matches him play for play. And although there is a fantasy element about Karl Stromberg and his plot to blow up the world, it was big fantasy that appealed strongly to the young audiences of the day. Producer Albert R. Broccoli had carefully updated his saga of 007, and the huge success of *The Spy Who Loved Me* guaranteed the series's longevity.

High points: the submarine car, Barbara Bach, Derek Meddings's special effects, Carly Simon's title song. Low points: Jaws's invulnerability. Although the Jaws character contributed greatly to the film's success, compelling the producers to bring him back for *Moonraker*, the inclusion of an impervious assassin gave the story too much of a comic-book flavor. Jaws became Wile E. Coyote to Bond's Road Runner.

THE SPY WHO LOVED ME CAST

James Bond	Roger Moore
Major Anya Amasova	Barbara Bach
Karl Stromberg	Curt Jurgens
Jaws	Richard Kiel
Naomi	Caroline Munro
General Gogol	Walter Gotell
Minister of Defense	Geoffrey Keen
M	Bernard Lee
Q	Desmond Llewelyn
Miss Moneypenny	Lois Maxwell
Captain Benson	George Baker
Sergei Barsov	Michael Billington
Felicca	Olga Bisera
Sheik Hosein	Edward de Souza
Max Kalba	Vernon Dobtcheff
Hotel Receptionist	Valerie Leon
Liparus Captain	Sydney Tafler
Fekkesh	Nadim Sawalha
Log Cabin Girl	Sue Vanner
Rublevitch	Eva Rueber-Staier
Admiral Hargreaves	Robert Brown
Stromberg's Assistant	Marilyn Galsworthy
Sandor	Milton Reid

Bechmann	Cyril Shaps
Markovitz	Milo Sperber
Barman	Albert Moses
Cairo Club Waiter	Rafiq Anwar
Arab Beauties	Felicity York, Dawn Rodrigues, Anika Pavel, Jill Goodall
Arab Band	The Egyptian Folklore Group
USS *Wayne* Captain	Shane Rimmer
USS *Wayne* Crew	Bob Sherman, Doyle Richmond, Murray Salem, John Truscott, Peter Whitman, Ray Hassett, Vincent Marzello, Nicholas Campbell, Ray Evans, Anthony Forrest, Garrick Hagon, Ray Jewers, George Mallaby, Christopher Muncke, Anthony Pullen, Robert Sheedy, Don Staiton, Eric Stine, Stephen Temperley, Dean Warwick
HMS *Ranger* Captain	Bryan Marshall
HMS *Ranger* Crew	Michael Howarth, Kim Fortune, Barry Andrews, Kevin McNally, Jeremy Bulloch, Sean Bury, John Sarbutt, David Auker, Dennis Blanch, Keith Buckley, Jonathan Bury, Nick Ellsworth, Tom Gerrard, Kazol Michalski, Keith Morris, John Salthouse
Stromberg Crew	George Roubicek, Lenny Rabin, Irvin Allen, Yasher Adem, Peter Ensor

THE SPY WHO LOVED ME CREW

Producer	Albert R. Broccoli
Director	Lewis Gilbert
Screenplay by	Christopher Wood, Richard Maibaum
Associate Producer	William P. Cartlidge
"Nobody Does It Better" Performed by	Carly Simon
Lyrics by	Carole Bayer Sager
Composed by	Marvin Hamlisch
Song Produced by	Richard Perry
Music by	Marvin Hamlisch
Production Designer	Ken Adam
Main Title Designer	Maurice Binder
Editor	John Glen
Director of Photography	Claude Renoir
Production Manager	David Middlemas
Assistant Director	Ariel Levy
Assistant Director (Second Unit)	Chris Kenny
Location Manager (Egypt)	Frank Ernst
Location Manager (Bahamas)	Golda Offenheim
Production Coordinator (Canada)	Rene Dupont
Naval Adviser	Richard Kennan
Underwater Cameraman	Lamar Boren
Ski Sequence Photographed and Supervised by	Willy Bogner, Jr.
Special Assistant to Producer	Michael Wilson

Production Controller ......Reginald A. Barkshire
Art Director ....Peter Lamont
Assistant Art Director ....Ernie Archer
Production Accountant ....Brian Bailey
Production Assistant ....Marguerite Green
Casting Directors ..Maude Spector, Weston Drury, Jr.
Construction Manager...........Michael Redding
Camera Operator.....................Alec Mills
Continuity ....June Randall
Assembly Editor ....Alan Strachan
Dubbing Editor ....Allan Sones
Assistant Editor ....John Grover
Sound Recorder ....Gordon Everett
Dubbing Mixer ....Gordon K. McCallum
Makeup........................Paul Engelen
Hairdressing....................Barbara Ritchie
Fashion Consultant ....Ronald Paterson
Wardrobe Supervisor.........Rosemary Burrows
Script Editor ....Vernon Harris
Second-Unit Directors......Ernest Day, John Glen
Action Arranger ....Bob Simmons
Ski Jump Performed by ....Rick Sylvester
Special Visual Effects............Derek Meddings
Special Optical Effects ....Alan Maley
Special Effects (Studio)..............John Evans
James Bond Theme Written by ....Monty Norman
Music Recorded at ...The Music Center, Wembley

THE SPY WHO LOVED ME COMPETITION
Competitive films in release when *The Spy Who Loved Me* opened in Los Angeles on August 3, 1977:
Star Wars
MacArthur
The Deep
The Last Remake of Beau Geste
Sinbad and the Eye of the Tiger
The Island of Dr. Moreauu
Greased Lightning
Sorcerer
Smokey and the Bandit
New York, New York
One on One

SPY WHO LOVED ME, THE SCRIPT WARS
The series of editorial events in 1976 that led to a final shooting script for the 10th James Bond film, *The Spy Who Loved Me*. Because it is an unusual work told through the eyes of a young Englishwoman who meets 007 only in the last few chapters, *The Spy Who Loved Me* is one novel that Ian Fleming never wanted to be sold as a film project.

Running out of 007 titles in 1976, however, producer Albert R. Broccoli went to the Fleming estate and requested permission to use the title only. After a visit to Russia, Broccoli saw that an entirely new story could be built around a Russian agent who falls in love with James Bond.

The first writer on the project was a New York City comic-book writer and author named Cary Bates, who was recommended by Roald Dahl. Bates's script was actually an adaptation of Fleming's *Moonraker* novel, which was also being considered as a possible title. Bates had taken the Hugo Drax character and given him a S.P.E.C.T.R.E. association with a huge underground base on Loch Ness in Scotland. The story concerned a S.P.E.C.T.R.E. plot to hijack a nuclear submarine and Bond's attempt to foil the plot with the help of Russian agent Tatiana Romanova, the girl in *From Russia with Love*. It was an interesting script, but Broccoli was hesitant to go with it.

Instead, he hired novelist Ronald Hardy to start fresh. Ironically, Hardy also developed a story about nuclear submarines, this time featuring a sophisticated electronic tracking device that allows the villain to pinpoint and capture enemy submarines. If the script didn't impress Broccoli, the tracking device encouraged him to explore the idea further with another screenwriter, Anthony Barwick.

Barwick took the tracking device and gave it to a villain named Zodiak, whose henchmen included the sinister triplets Tic, Tac, and Toe. If the Western powers failed to surrender their art treasures, Zodiak intended to destroy fleets of nuclear submarines with his long-range torpedoes. Barwick left the project and was followed, in order, by Derek Marlowe; Sterling Silliphant; John Landis; and Anthony Burgess, the author of *A Clockwork Orange*, who developed the most outrageous of all the scripts—an undisguised parody of the world of James Bond.

Guy Hamilton was assigned to direct his fourth James Bond film in a row when Richard Maibaum was brought in to work on the script. In the early part of 1976, Maibaum decided to keep the S.P.E.C.T.R.E. influence but get rid of the typical Blofeld-type old guard. He introduced a young cadre of international terrorists—members of the Red Brigade, the Bader-Meinhof Gang, the Black September Organization, and the Japanese Red Army who have come together to form the new S.P.E.C.T.R.E. They aren't interested in blackmail or extortion. They're simply intent on destroying humanity by capturing a nuclear submarine and wiping out the world's oil fields. In the script's opening scenes, these young villains burst into S.P.E.C.T.R.E. headquarters and assassinate the old guard. They then put their plan into operation.

Maibaum was finishing up his script with some location scouting in Budapest, Hungary, when Guy Hamilton suddenly left the project to join *Superman*—the huge Warner Brothers film then in pre-production at Pinewood Studios (Hamilton was later replaced on *Superman* by Richard Donner). Lewis Gilbert was Broccoli's new choice for director, and he brought with him another writer, Christopher Wood, who began reworking Maibaum's draft.

Broccoli had liked Maibaum's script, but he felt that the young S.P.E.C.T.R.E. hoodlums were too political. Wood eliminated the terrorist group and instead brought back a Blofeld-type character named Stavros who is a shipping magnate with a huge supertanker. The supertanker is equipped with a special bow that allows it to open up and swallow nuclear submarines.

The tanker idea was Maibaum's, dating back to 1970 and to the *Diamonds Are Forever* script, which had Blofeld commandeer a huge tanker as a firing platform for his laser cannon. In the final Wood draft, S.P.E.C.T.R.E. uses the special tracking system to capture a Russian and a British submarine. Bond and a Russian agent named Major Anya Amasova (Maibaum's creation) are sent to Cairo to find a S.P.E.C.T.R.E. traitor who is putting the tracking system on the open market. Each agent thinks the other is behind the hijacking. They play a game of spy versus spy in Cairo, until it is revealed that a third party has been playing them off against each other—a typical S.P.E.C.T.R.E. ploy reminiscent of *From Russia with Love*. Bond and Anya join forces and eventually trace the tracking system to Stavros's base off the coast of Sardinia.

Leafing through the 15 drafts of *The Spy Who Loved Me* offers a textbook look at script construction. For Bond fans, the material is priceless, for it allows the reader to see how typical Bondian situations are created. For instance, Stavros's chief henchman went through several changes until he became the Jaws character, a giant of a killer with cobalt-steel teeth—played very effectively by Richard Kiel in the final film.

In the early scripts, there was an obsession with twins. In his *Moonraker* treatment, Cary Bates created a fearsome twosome named Pluto and Plato who work for Hugo Drax. Pluto is a chain smoker; Plato, an alcoholic. In the Anthony Barwick treatment, Zodiak is protected by three albino brothers named Tic, Tac, and Toe, all of whom are killed by 007.

However fascinating the idea of look-alike bodyguards might be, it was a casting director's nightmare—although twins would later be featured strongly in *Octopussy*. The writers eventually settled on Jaws, who became a one-man, indestructible army and who would survive to return in the next Bond film, *Moonraker*.

Shortly before production began on *The Spy Who Loved Me* in 1976, one last problem arose to haunt the shooting script. Kevin McClory, the Irish film producer who owned the film rights to *Thunderball*, and who was planning a new version of *Thunderball* titled *James Bond of the Secret Service*, suddenly filed an injunction to hold up production of *The Spy Who Loved Me*. In what was to become another long and complicated legal battle, McClory claimed that the final Broccoli script was unusually similar to McClory's own Bond project, which he had cowritten with thriller author Len Deighton and Sean Connery.

The McClory script had been written in 1975, 10 years after McClory had signed an agreement with Broccoli and Saltzman stating that after *Thunderball*, he would wait a full decade before producing another Bond film. Whether or not McClory had the rights to do another project beyond a remake of his original *Thunderball*, which would appear in 1983 as *Never Say Never Again*, he was still interested in Broccoli's *The Spy Who Loved Me* script.

The McClory/Deighton/Connery script, variously referred to as *James Bond of the Secret Service* and *Warhead*, also featured a spiderlike underwater headquarters, a shark pond, and a S.P.E.C.T.R.E. plot to destroy the world. Perhaps fearing the possibility of a legal battle with McClory—who, according to the favorable decision in the 1963 case with Ian Fleming, had sole film rights to S.P.E.C.T.R.E.—Broccoli eventually told screenwriter Christopher Wood to remove all traces of S.P.E.C.T.R.E. from the final shooting script of *The Spy Who Loved Me*. Stavros thus suddenly became billionaire shipping magnate Karl Stromberg, who alone plans to destroy the world. Any reference to his S.P.E.C.T.R.E. contacts was eliminated, and even his supertanker security troops wear red rather than S.P.E.C.T.R.E.'s black uniforms.

Such a transformation did not appease McClory. But there was little chance that he could stop Broccoli and *The Spy Who Loved Me* from filming. Rather than pay Broccoli's legal fees in a long, abortive case, McClory chose instead to withdraw his writ of injunction while he planned his own production. McClory and the possibility that Sean Connery would indeed return to play the part of James Bond would be a constant thorn in the side of Broccoli and United Artists, who, though quite satisfied with the public's acceptance of Roger Moore, were naturally concerned about the return of Connery in a rival camp.

SR 4785 The license plate on Kamal Khan's (LOUIS JOURDAN) brown Mercedes sedan in *Octopussy*. It's the car that takes Kamal and his bodyguard, Gobinda (KABIR BEDI), off the U.S. Air Force base at Feldstadt, West Germany where an A-bomb is set to explode at 3:45 P.M.

STAGE D Pinewood Studios soundstage where production designer Ken Adam created the Fontainebleau Hotel cabana area where Dink (MARGARET NOLAN) massages James Bond (SEAN CONNERY) in *Goldfinger*. Designed to match exteriors shot on location in Miami Beach, the set was also used for close-ups of the gin game between Goldfinger (GERT FROBE) and Mr. Simmons (AUSTIN WILLIS), as well as Felix Leiter's (CEC LINDER) arrival.

Fifty-five extras were on hand for the shooting, which took place on Friday, April 24th, and Saturday, April 25, 1964. Bunty Phillips and Richard Mills handled makeup chores, while Stella Rivers was the hairstylist.

STANWELL Location, outside London, of a storage-tank complex that simulated the South American holdings of Mr. Ramirez in the *Goldfinger* teaser. Inside one of the tanks (actually a Ken Adam–designed set at Pinewood), James Bond (SEAN CONNERY) places his demolition charges.

STARKE, ANTHONY (Chicago, Illinois, 1963–   ) American actor who portrayed financial wizard William Truman-Lodge in *Licence to Kill*. See TRUMAN-LODGE, WILLIAM.

STARK, GRAHAM (1922–   ) British comedy actor, and veteran of the *Pink Panther* films, who portrayed the Monte Carlo cashier who greets baccarat expert Evelyn Tremble (PETER SELLERS) in *Casino Royale*.

STAR OF SOUTH AFRICA DIAMOND One of the famous diamonds viewed by Bond (SEAN CONNERY) and M (BERNARD LEE) at the showroom of a London diamond syndicate in *Diamonds Are Forever*. According to M, the Star of South Africa is 83.5 carats, rough, and 47.5 carats, cut.

STASSINO, PAUL Italian actor who portrayed dashing NATO aerial observer Major François Derval in *Thunderball*. He also portrayed Derval's plastic surgery–aided duplicate—S.P.E.C.T.R.E. mercenary Angelo Palazzi, who, while posing as the NATO observer, hijacks a bomber to the Caribbean with nuclear bombs on board.

STATION C-CANADA Where M (BERNARD LEE) first assigns Bond (SEAN CONNERY) in *Thunderball*, until 007 requests a transfer to Nassau in the Bahamas.

STAVIN, MARY British actress who portrayed gorgeous Kimberley Jones, a Secret Service colleague of James Bond (ROGER MOORE), who pilots the camouflaged iceberg launch in the teaser for *A View to a Kill*. A former Miss World, Stavin also portrayed one of the Octopussy girls in the 13th James Bond movie. See JONES, KIMBERLEY.

STEAK PIZ GLORIA James Bond's (GEORGE LAZENBY) initial dinner entree at Blofeld's (TELLY SAVALAS) Swiss mountain hideaway in *On Her Majesty's Secret Service.* Agent 007, posing as heraldry expert Sir Hilary Bray and dressed remarkably in a Scottish kilt, eats with a group of gorgeous international allergy patients who are very curious about his profession. He then proceeds to bore them with a two-hour lecture on the ins and outs of British heraldry, history, and the definitions of titles and ranks.

Seated next to Bond is Ruby Bartlett (AN-GELA SCOULAR), who, unable to tell 007 where she is staying in the allergy institute, pulls up the skirt of his kilt and writes her room number (No. 8) in lipstick on his inner thigh. Asked by a very suspicious Irma Bunt (ILSE STEPPAT) if there is something wrong, Bond excuses himself from the table because of "a slight stiffness."

STEARS, JOHN (Uxbridge, Middlesex, England, August 25, 1934–   ) Oscar-winning British special effects expert who worked on the first six James Bond movies. Stears created and

Special effects expert John Stears hard at work in his lab at Pinewood Studios. One of the underwater sleds stands against the back wall, along with the Bell Rocket Belt. (John Stears Collection)

Special effects expert John Stears with another one of his prizes—Scaramanga's flying car from *The Man with the Golden Gun*. (John Stears Collection)

Special effects supervisor John Stears adds some last-minute touches to Fiona's rocket-firing cycle in *Thunderball*. (John Stears Collection)

destroyed the miniature bauxite mine for *Dr. No*; blew up the S.P.E.C.T.R.E. helicopter and speedboats in *From Russia with Love*; flew the private and presidential jets in *Goldfinger*; and destroyed the *Disco Volante* hydrofoil and cocoon in *Thunderball*, for which he won his first Oscar.

On *You Only Live Twice*, with its outer-space sequences and helicopter chases, he would be kept particularly busy. And that space experience would be advantageous later in his career when he was called on to create the special effects for George Lucas's *Star Wars*, for which he won his second Oscar for special effects. Stears also worked on *On Her Majesty's Secret Service*. His crew throughout his Bond association included Frank George (engineer and effects), Jimmy Snow (floor effects and engineer), Burt Luxford (engineer), Joe Fitt (prop man and effects), and Charlie Dodds (effects rigger).

STEPPAT, ILSE   (1917–1970) German character actress who portrayed Frau Irma Bunt, Blofeld's (TELLY SAVALAS) personal secretary, in *On Her Majesty's Secret Service*. A belligerent woman who would have made a great Gestapo chief, it is Bunt who machine-guns 007's bride, Tracy (DIANA RIGG), to death in the film's tragic ending.

STERLING, MR. AND MRS. ROBERT James Bond (ROGER MOORE) and KGB Major Anya Amasova's (BARBARA BACH) cover while visiting billionaire shipping magnate Karl Stromberg (CURT JURGENS) at his Atlantis facility off Sardinia in *The Spy Who Loved Me*.

STEWART, ROY Actor who portrayed Quarrel, Jr., the man who shares James Bond's hairbrush, in *Live and Let Die*.

STINGER MISSILES Deadly projectiles stolen from the Contra rebels by drug runner Franz Sanchez (ROBERT DAVI) in *Licence to Kill*. If Sanchez is assassinated, his chief of security, Heller (DON STROUD), has indicated that he will help return the missiles to the U.S. government.

However, when Bond (TIMOTHY DALTON) fails to kill Sanchez with his signature rifle, Heller changes his mind. The Stingers are used ineffectively against Bond in the wild tanker-truck chase.

"STIRRED, NOT SHAKEN?" If you're a Bond purist, you'll consider this to be one of the great bloopers of the series. Arriving at Henderson's (CHARLES GRAY) Japanese-furnished apartment in Tokyo in *You Only Live Twice*, Bond (SEAN CONNERY) is offered a martini. Henderson asks, "Stirred, not shaken?" And Bond, without batting an eye, says it's fine, apparently forgetting his long history of martinis—shaken, not stirred.

Either this was one of those little inside jokes that filmmakers sometimes play on audiences ("we know it's wrong, but we're having some fun with you"), or actor Charles Gray just blew the drink order and nobody felt like getting it right.

STOCK, JAMES James Bond's (ROGER MOORE) cover in San Francisco in *A View to a Kill*. Posing as a reporter with the London *Financial Times*, Bond is granted an interview with W. G. Howe, a local official with the Division of Oil and Mines who is actually on the payroll of Zorin Industries. *See* HOWE, W. G.

STOKE POGES An English country club where director Guy Hamilton filmed the golf match in *Goldfinger*.

STRANGLER WATCH The principal weapon of S.P.E.C.T.R.E. assassin Red Grant (ROBERT SHAW) in *From Russia with Love*. The watch features a retractable, thin-wire garrote, which is used to strangle an adversary. With such a weapon, Grant disposes of the phony James Bond (SEAN CONNERY) in the teaser and nearly kills the real 007 on the Orient Express, until Bond turns the watch on its keeper.

STRANGWAYS, COMMANDER JOHN British Secret Service agent, portrayed by Tim Moxon, who is the head of station in Jamaica in *Dr. No*. With the help of a local Cayman Island fisherman named Quarrel (JOHN KITZMILLER), Strangways has been gathering telltale ore samples on a nearby island called Crab Key.

For his investigative work, Strangways and his new secretary are ruthlessly gunned down by Dr. No's (JOSEPH WISEMAN) assassins. Strangways has the honor of being the first casualty in the United Artists 007 series.

STRAP, MR. American gangster portrayed by Hal Galili in *Goldfinger*. Strap's contribution to Goldfinger's (GERT FROBE) Operation Grand Slam is a convoy of military vehicles that are smuggled across the Rio Grande from Mexico. Along with the other gangsters who attend Goldfinger's "hoods convention," Strap is murdered by the deadly Delta Nine nerve gas.

STRICT RULES OF GOLF The conditions under which Bond (SEAN CONNERY) and Goldfinger (GERT FROBE) undertake a high-stakes golf challenge match at an English country club. Although the terms are suggested by Goldfinger, it is the clever 007 who takes advantage of them.

When Goldfinger tries to make up for his bad lie by having his caddy, Oddjob (HAROLD SAKATA), plant a phony ball on the fairway and then calling it his own, 007 finds an alternative ball and tricks Goldfinger into playing it on his final tee shot. Bond loses the match on purpose, goes to the cup, and announces that Goldfinger has "accidentally" played the wrong ball somewhere on the course. Since strict rules of golf are in force, Bond is sorry to say that Goldfinger has lost the hole and the match.

STROMBERG, KARL Billionaire shipping magnate and megalomaniac ocean lover portrayed by Curt Jurgens in *The Spy Who Loved Me*, Stromberg is planning for a futuristic undersea kingdom by first destroying the rest of the planet with nuclear weapons.

Based off the coast of Sardinia on a huge man-made amphibious structure called Atlantis, Stromberg commands a fleet of ships, including his prize the *Liparus*—an enormous supertanker that is secretly capturing British, American, and Soviet nuclear submarines. To destroy the world, Stromberg plans to refit the submarines with his own crews and then launch their missiles on specified targets in the United States and Russia.

Bond (ROGER MOORE) tracks Stromberg down when 007 and his erstwhile partner KGB Major Anya Amasova (BARBARA BACH) discover the Stromberg shipping-line logo while searching through a roll of microfilm containing a facsimile of a nuclear-sub tracking system that Stromberg's scientists have engineered. Surviving assassination attempts by Stromberg's two killers—Jaws (RICHARD KIEL) and Sandor (MILTON REID)—and his assistant Naomi (CAROLINE MUNRO), Bond eventually short-circuits the evil plan, obliterates the *Liparus* and Atlantis, and kills Stromberg with some well-aimed slugs from his Walther.

One of Stromberg's unusual traits is that he doesn't shake hands, probably because he doesn't want anybody to be shocked that his hands are webbed like duck's feet. *See* JURGENS, CURT.

STROMBERG MARINE RESEARCH LABORATORY (aka Atlantis) A huge spiderlike amphibious structure located off the coast of Sardinia, in *The Spy Who Loved Me*, that is the centerpiece of billionaire shipping magnate Karl Stromberg's (CURT JURGENS) planned undersea kingdom—a "city beneath the sea." It's a combined residence/laboratory/operational base for Stromberg's legal and illegal activities. In addition to shark pens, aquariums, and a functional heliport, the lab also contains a cocktail-glass–shaped escape pod that is used by Bond (ROGER MOORE) and Anya (BARBARA BACH).

STROMBERG NO. 1 AND STROMBERG NO. 2 Redesignation of the British and Russian nuclear submarines captured by Stromberg's (CURT JURGENS) *Liparus* supertanker in *The Spy Who Loved Me*. Operated by enemy submariners, the two vessels are sent into the mid-Atlantic on a mission to launch two *Polaris* missiles and initiate World War III.

However, before they can launch their missiles, Bond (ROGER MOORE), using the *Liparus*'s command computer, alters their planned trajectory so that instead of destroying a major city in the United States and Russia, they blow up Stromberg No. 1 and No. 2. How neat can you get?

STROMBERG'S ASSISTANT A well-dressed beauty, portrayed by Marilyn Galsworthy, who works for megalomaniac shipping magnate Karl Stromberg (CURT JURGENS) in *The Spy Who Loved Me*. She's thrown into the shark pen when it's discovered that she's the one responsible for selling the nuclear-submarine tracking system on the open market.

STROUD, DON (Hawaii, 1937–) Veteran American character actor who portrayed Heller, South American drug runner Franz Sanchez's (ROBERT DAVI) chief of security, in *Licence to Kill. See* HELLER.

STRUTTER, HAROLD Resourceful CIA operative portrayed by actor Lon Satton in *Live and Let Die*. Strutter follows Bond into Harlem and helps him escape from Mr. Big's (YAPHET KOTTO) assassins. Later in the story, while on surveillance across the street from the Fillet of Soul restaurant in New Orleans, he becomes another victim of the funeral parade that killed Hamilton, the British agent in the film's teaser.

STUFFED SHEEP'S HEAD The perfectly awful entree served by Kamal Khan (LOUIS JOURDAN) to James Bond (ROGER MOORE) at the Monsoon Palace in *Octopussy*. At one point, Kamal actually plucks out one of the sheep's eyeballs and pops it into his mouth. A similar gourmet "dining" experience is featured in Steven Spielberg's *Indiana Jones and the Temple of Doom*, which was released the following year.

SUGA, TOSHIRO Japanese actor who portrayed the very lethal Chang, Drax's (MICHEL LONSDALE) bodyguard, in *Moonraker. See* CHANG.

SUMO WRESTLING MATCH A Tokyo sporting event where James Bond (SEAN CONNERY) meets Japanese Secret Service agent Aki (AKIKO WAKABAYASHI) in *You Only Live Twice*. He gives her the appropriate password: "I love you."

SUNDAY The day on which Goldfinger (GERT FROBE) unleashes Operation Grand Slam against Fort Knox, Kentucky. *See* OPERATION GRAND SLAM.

SUPER SHOT The name given to the shooting gallery section of Francisco Scaramanga's (CHRISTOPHER LEE) "fun house" maze in

The Man with the Golden Gun. Both Rodney (MARC LAWRENCE) and Bond (ROGER MOORE) match their considerable shooting skills against this attraction.

SUTTON OIL Stacey Sutton's (TANYA ROBERTS) family oil company in *A View to a Kill.* It was taken over in a rigged proxy fight by psychotic industrialist Max Zorin (CHRISTOPHER WALKEN), who is using the San Francisco Bay oil wells to pump seawater into the unstable Hayward Fault.

SUTTON, STACEY Beautiful blond geologist and oil heiress, portrayed by Tanya Roberts, who battles Max Zorin (CHRISTOPHER WALKEN) in *A View to a Kill.* Since she's in financial trouble, Stacey works as a geologist for the State of California, Division of Oil and Mines. However, there was a time when she was fabulously wealthy. Stacey's grandfather started Sutton Oil in the San Francisco Bay area, where oil is pumped out of the unstable Hayward Fault.

As the first step in Project Main Strike, a plot to destroy northern California's Silicon Valley by triggering a massive earthquake, Zorin has taken control of Sutton Oil in a rigged proxy fight. To stop her lawsuit and keep her mouth shut, Zorin offers Stacey a sum of $5 million. The check is written by Zorin at his annual horse show in France and given to Stacey—all of which is observed by James Bond (ROGER MOORE), who's peering through the tinted window with trick sunglasses.

Later, 007 slips into Zorin's office and photocopies the Sutton check, making note of the huge sum. Posing as a journalist with the London *Financial Times,* Bond eventually sneaks into Stacey's mansion, in time to thwart a gang of Zorin's toughs who have been sent to pressure her into cashing the check and backing down.

Ever the gentleman, Bond offers to cook her dinner and stand guard that night. In the morning, the region is jolted by a minor earthquake whose epicenter is the Hayward Fault. When Bond explains that Zorin has been pumping seawater into her father's oil wells, Stacey is startled—she claims that a major earthquake could be imminent. However, when she tries to warn her boss, W. G. Howe (DANIEL BEN-

ZALI), she's fired. (She doesn't know that Howe is on Zorin's payroll.)

That night, Bond and Stacey break into Howe's office, but before they can steal the plans for Project Main Strike, they're captured by Zorin and his bodyguard, May Day (GRACE JONES). Howe arrives and is promptly murdered by Zorin, who plans to frame Stacey and Bond for the crime.

As his assistants pour gasoline into the office and hallways, Zorin places his captives in an elevator, which becomes stuck between floors when the power is cut. Zorin then tosses a Molotov cocktail into the elevator shaft, which explodes above Bond and Stacey. With the building on fire all around them, they barely escape and steal a fire department hook-and-ladder truck, leading the San Francisco police on a wild chase through the streets.

Arriving at the supposedly abandoned Main Strike silver mine, Bond and Stacey are surprised at the amount of activity there. They soon discover that Zorin is placing huge amounts of explosives under the mine shaft, the triggering of which will create the massive earthquake he needs to destroy Silicon Valley.

Chased into the mine shaft by May Day, Stacey escapes to the surface. However, when Zorin orders the shaft flooded, Bond and May Day are washed deeper into the mine. Double-crossed by Zorin, May Day helps Bond remove the triggering bomb from a literal mountain of high explosives. May Day mounts the bomb on a railway handcar, keeps a faulty hand brake in place, and safely takes the bomb out of the mine shaft. Once outside, she's obliterated in the bomb's explosion.

Zorin, now commanding his blimp, moves in and then scoops up Stacey. Bond follows by jumping onto one of the blimp's mooring lines, precipitating a hair-raising ride through the sky-scraper canyons of San Francisco. Above the Golden Gate Bridge, 007 manages to wrap the line around one of the bridge supports, which stalls the blimp.

A final battle takes place above the Golden Gate's highest girder as, first, axe-wielding Zorin and then dynamite-throwing Dr. Mortner (WILLOUGHBY GRAY) try to deal with Bond. Both fail. Zorin slips and falls to his death, while Mortner drops the batch of dynamite destined for Bond and is blown to bits in the blimp. Bond and Stacey retire to her shower where Q's (DESMOND LLEWELYN) automated snooper finds them in total bliss.

SWADLEY Headquarters in England of the 63rd Tactical Air Command, a U.S. Air Force cruise missile unit featured in *Never Say Never Again*. Captain Jack Petachi (GAVAN O'HER-LIHY) is a staff communications officer on the base and a traitor who has gone over to S.P.E.C.T.R.E. Having undergone an unusual corneal implant operation, Petachi now has the exact eyeprint of the president of the United States, which allows him to pass a top-level security procedure and arm two cruise missiles with nuclear warheads. *See* PETACHI, CAPTAIN JACK.

SWAT Acronym for Special Weapons and Tactics—an elite Florida police commando unit that is assigned to escort an armored truck carrying drug runner Franz Sanchez (ROBERT DAVI) to Quantico, Virginia, in *Licence to Kill*. When traitorous DEA agent Killifer (EVER-ETT MCGILL) drives the truck into the water off Seven-Mile Bridge, the SWAT members, despite their numbers and firepower, are left helpless.

SWEETMAN, CAPTAIN CYRIL Pilot of the recon helicopter carrying director Terence Young and assistant art director Michael White, which, on Saturday, July 6, 1963, was involved in an accident during a location survey off the coastal town of Crinan, Scotland, on *From Russia with Love*. There were only minor injuries.

SYDNEY Pussy Galore's (HONOR BLACK-MAN) copilot, portrayed by Tricia Muller, on Goldfinger's (GERT FROBE) private jet. She's also the leading member of Pussy Galore's Flying Circus, the aerial acrobatic team committed to Operation Rockabye Baby.

SYLVESTER, RICK Top American stuntman who in July 1976 performed the incredible ski/parachute jump off Baffin Island's Asgard Peak for *The Spy Who Loved Me* teaser. For his services, Sylvester received $30,000 (*See* AS-GARD JUMP, THE). He later returned to perform a mountain-climbing stunt off Greece's Meteora cliffs in *For Your Eyes Only*.

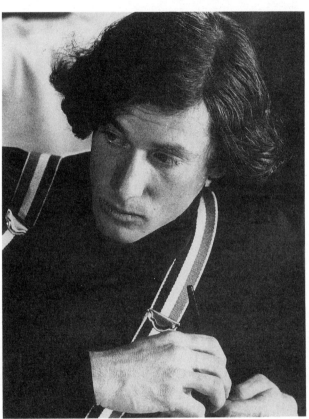

Ski jumper Rick Sylvester, who for $30,000 jumped off Baffin Island's 3,000-foot Asgard Peak and parachuted to safety in *The Spy Who Loved Me*. (Henry Diltz, Rick Sylvester)

SYNTHETIC TURPENTINE Phony label on Osato Chemical canisters in *You Only Live Twice*. They really contain liquid oxygen (LOX), a rocket propellant destined for Blofeld's (DONALD PLEASENCE) secret volcano base.

T

TAFLER, SYDNEY (1916–1979) British character actor who portrayed the captain of the supertanker *Liparus* in *The Spy Who Loved Me*.

Veteran British actor Sidney Tafler portrayed the captain of the *Liparus* supertanker in *The Spy Who Loved Me*. (National Film Archive, London)

TAGAWA, CARY-HIROYUKI Japanese actor who portrayed Kwang, a Hong Kong narcotics agent masquerading as one of Franz Sanchez's (ROBERT DAVI) Far Eastern drug distributors in *Licence to Kill*. See KWANG.

TAIWANESE TYCOON The only microchip distributor who doesn't want to ante up $100 million to become part of Max Zorin's (CHRISTOPHER WALKEN) Project Main Strike, in *A View to a Kill*. Portrayed by Anthony Chin, his reward, like Mr. Solo's (MARTIN BENSON) in *Goldfinger*, is a quick death—in this case, an unscheduled exit from Zorin's blimp.

TALBOT, CAPTAIN (aka Commander Talbot) The captain, portrayed by British actor Bryan Marshall, of the British nuclear submarine *Ranger* in *The Spy Who Loved Me*. When the *Ranger* is swallowed by the *Liparus* supertanker, Talbot and his men are taken prisoner by Stromberg's (CURT JURGENS) well-armed crew.

They're later joined by two other sub crews—one American (from the USS *Wayne*), and one Russian (from the *Potemkin*). Freed by Bond (ROGER MOORE), Talbot leads his men against the tanker's defenses, but he is killed in an abortive assault on the impregnable control room.

TALMADGE, RICHARD (1896–) (real name, Ricardo Metzetti) American stuntman and stunt coordinator who supervised the madcap casino fight sequence that concludes the 1967 *Casino Royale* spoof.

TAMBA, TETSURO (Tokyo, Japan, July 17, 1922–) (real name, Shozaburo Tanba) Handsome Japanese actor who portrayed Tiger Tanaka, the head of the Japanese Secret Service, in *You Only Live Twice*.

TANAKA, TIGER Japanese Secret Service (S.I.S.) chief, portrayed realistically by Tetsuro Tamba, in *You Only Live Twice*. A Japanese version of Bond's (SEAN CONNERY) friend Kerim Bey (PEDRO ARMENDARIZ) in *From Russia with Love*, Tiger is a resourceful spymaster who maintains his seclusion in an underground office complex in Tokyo, connected to a private train line.

Assigned to help Bond track a missing American spacecraft, Tanaka introduces him to many aspects of the Japanese culture, including sophisticated electronics, bathing girls, Ninja warriors, pearl divers, and, finally, a sham marriage to Kissy (MIE HAMA), one of the most beautiful women in the 007 series. With his Ninjas, Tanaka leads the final attack on Blofeld's (DONALD PLEASENCE) secret rocket base. See TAMBA, TETSURO.

TANGIER North African city where arms dealer Brad Whitaker (JOE DON BAKER) maintains his base of operations in *The Living Daylights*. It's where Bond (TIMOTHY DALTON) fakes an assassination of KGB Chief General Leonid Pushkin (JOHN RHYS-DAVIES)—a ploy to reveal Whitaker and renegade Russian General Koskov's (JEROEN KRABBE) real plot. It works, although Bond is drugged when he's captured and placed aboard a military air transport headed for Afghanistan and a major diamonds-for-opium deal.

TANGO An elaborate, stylized dance performed by Bond (SEAN CONNERY) and Domino (KIM BASINGER) at Largo's (KLAUS MARIA BRANDAUER) charity ball in *Never Say Never Again*. It's Bond's prize for beating Largo in the Domination video game.

During the dance, Bond has his first opportunity to tell Domino that Largo was responsible for her brother Jack's (GAVAN O'HERLIHY) death. Watching from the sidelines, Largo, in turn, tells Fatima Blush (BARBARA CARRERA) that she has his permission to try to assassinate Bond one more time.

TANGO ZEBRA British Secret Service emergency code used by James Bond (SEAN CONNERY) to contact his headquarters from the communications room of the *Flying Saucer* yacht in *Never Say Never Again*.

TANNER British Secret Service chief of staff, portrayed by James Villiers, in *For Your Eyes Only*. A temporary replacement for M, Tanner is Bond's (ROGER MOORE) superior on the mission to find the missing A.T.A.C. device.

Villiers replaced Bernard Lee, who died shortly before the start of production on *For Your Eyes Only*. Tanner, in turn, was replaced by M (ROBERT BROWN) on the next film, *Octopussy*.

TANUGI, SASKIA COHEN Actress who portrayed Nicole, James Bond's (SEAN CONNERY) Secret Service contact in the South of France, in *Never Say Never Again*. *See* NICOLE.

TARANTULA Huge spider used unsuccessfully by Professor Dent (ANTHONY DAWSON) to assassinate James Bond (SEAN CONNERY) in *Dr. No*. Sweating out the insect's agonizingly slow crawl up his body, Bond waits for it to momentarily rest on a pillow, then dives off the bed, grabs his shoe, and pounds the

A break between takes for Sean Connery, a very cool looking Akiko Wakabayashi, and Tetsuro Tamba.
(Rex Features Ltd./RDR Productions)

spider to pulp. Traumatized by the event, 007 staggers into the bathroom and shuts the door—providing one of the film's best laughs.

Pulled along by a string, the tarantula, nicknamed Rosie, actually crawled on the body of stuntman Bob Simmons. If you watch the sequence closely, a sheet of glass separates Bond from the tarantula in the final close-up, creating an effect similar to the one in *Raiders of the Lost Ark* where Indiana Jones finds himself staring at a deadly asp. In Fleming's original novel, the tarantula was actually a deadly giant centipede.

TARO, MISS British diplomat Playdell-Smith's (LOUIS BLAAZER) sexy secretary, portrayed by actress Zena Marshall, in *Dr. No*. Actually one of Dr. No's (JOSEPH WISEMAN) spies, Miss Taro is ordered to lure Bond (SEAN CONNERY) to her cottage in the Blue Mountains on 2171 Magenta Drive. On the road, assassins in a black hearse will then run 007 off the road.

However, the assassins are killed instead when, trying to avoid road-construction machinery, their car goes off a cliff. When her doorbell rings, Miss Taro is thus very surprised to greet Bond. Ordered via telephone to stall him, she consents to a tryst.

Zena Marshall was the quintessential enemy agent—voluptuous, as Broccoli and Saltzman required; deadly; and expendable—although instead of facing death, she is arrested by Duff's Jamaican police.

TAROT CARDS The mystical tools of Solitaire (JANE SEYMOUR) in *Live and Let Die*. A

Playtime in Miss Taro's bedroom during shooting on *Dr. No* in 1962, with Sean Connery and Zena Marshall. (Rex Features Ltd./RDR Productions)

virgin with the power of the obeah (the "second sight"), Solitaire uses the cards expertly to predict the future.

At first enslaved to Kananga (YAPHET KOTTO), Solitaire eventually sleeps with Bond (ROGER MOORE), switches allegiances, and loses her power. Later, she uses the cards to alert Bond to various dangers. For instance, when Bond meets an attractive CIA operative named Rosie Carver (GLORIA HENDRY), he also finds the Queen of Cups tarot card in the upside-down position. According to the rules of tarot, this means a deceitful, perverse woman; a liar; or a cheat. The card helps Bond realize that Carver is working for Kananga.

To help Bond rescue Solitaire on San Monique, three cards are left for him in the Fillet of Soul nightclub in New Orleans. They are the High Priestess (a reference to Solitaire herself), Death (meaning "great danger"), and the Moon (perhaps meaning "come only after dark").

The tarot cards for *Live and Let Die* were beautifully painted for the movie by Scottish artist Fergus Hall, and they are featured prominently in the film's advertising campaign. Interestingly, the 007 logo was featured on the back side of each tarot card. Even though the card backs were never featured in close-up in the film, you can plainly see the logo on the special cards that were sold to the public in a boxed tarot set after the film's release in 1973. If you look closely enough, though, you can see the 007 logo on the film cards as well.

"TART'S HANDKERCHIEF" The phrase that James Bond (SEAN CONNERY) uses to

Having tricked Mr. Wint (BRUCE GLOVER) into revealing his poor knowledge of wines, Bond (SEAN CONNERY) then sniffs the killer's after-shave, which still smells like a "tart's handkerchief." (T. Ockersen, Bruce Glover Collection)

describe the scent of Mr. Wint's (BRUCE GLOVER) aftershave, in *Diamonds Are Forever*. Rendered unconscious by knockout gas that staggers him in the Whyte House elevator, Bond is thrown into the trunk of Mr. Wint and Mr. Kidd's (PUTTER SMITH) car and taken to a construction site, where he is placed in a concrete pipe that is later buried in the ground.

In the morning, Bond finds himself underground inside a flood-control pipeline. His only companion is a mouse. Speaking to the mouse, Bond indicates that one of them smells like a "tart's handkerchief."

The smell becomes a factor in the film's final scene, when Wint and Kidd, posing as waiters on a luxury liner, enter Bond's suite. Agent 007 recognizes the smell, confuses Wint with a bit of wine knowledge, and kills both of them in spectacular fashion.

TARZAN'S YELL The call of the famous ape-man, imitated expertly by James Bond (ROGER MOORE) during his vine-swinging escape from Kamal Khan's (LOUIS JOURDAN) army of trackers in *Octopussy*. Practically unknown in the early films of the series, this comical reference to another film's signature theme became a common element in the Roger Moore Bond movies (e.g., the "Lawrence of Arabia" theme in *The Spy Who Loved Me* and the "Close Encounters of the Third Kind" and "The Magnificent Seven" themes in *Moonraker*).

TAURUS PT-99 A 9mm, 16-round Brazilian copy of the Italian Beretta handgun used by James Bond (TIMOTHY DALTON) in the *Licence to Kill* teaser. What's 007 doing with a Beretta—a gun that was outlawed by M in *Dr. No*? It's on loan from a DEA agent. Remember, Bond was on his way to Felix Leiter's (DAVID HEDISON) wedding and chose not to bring his Walther PPK with him.

TCHAIKOVSKY CASSETTE What Bond (ROGER MOORE) uses to serenade Pola Ivanova (FIONA FULLERTON) during their hot-tub lovemaking in *A View to a Kill*. Getting up from the tub to place the cassette in the machine, Bond also takes time to steal the surveillance tape she has made of Max Zorin's (CHRISTOPHER WALKEN) conversation atop his oil-pumping station in San Francisco Bay.

TEARS OF ALLAH Romantic code name for the S.P.E.C.T.R.E. nuclear hijacking operation in *Never Say Never Again*. It's also part of the inscription on the back of the priceless pendant that Maximillian Largo (KLAUS MARIA BRANDAUER) gives to Domino (KIM BASINGER). It reads: "The prophet wept for the baroness of the desert, and his tears made a well."

The surface of the pendant is actually a map, with the diamond marking the spot where a huge Middle Eastern oil field begins—and where S.P.E.C.T.R.E. places the second atomic bomb for possible detonation. The warhead itself is placed in a huge underground archaeological dig that is also called the Tears of Allah.

Transported to the mainland by XT-7B flying platforms, Bond (SEAN CONNERY) and Leiter (BERNIE CASEY) don their wet suits and enter a well that leads into an underwater passageway that takes them into the dig itself. Backed by divers from a U.S. nuclear submarine, Bond and Leiter launch an attack against Largo's S.P.E.C.T.R.E. forces.

Submachine guns open fire, bombs are thrown, the dig is staggered by an earthquake, and Bond chases Largo into the water, where they battle for control of the bomb. Largo's about to kill 007, when he's impaled on the spear of his mistress, Domino. The S.P.E.C.T.R.E. forces surrender, and, thanks to James Bond, the world is once again free from a nuclear nightmare.

TEASER A film term for a pre-titles sequence—what has become a hallmark of the United Artists James Bond series. Pre-titles sequences were not unprecedented. One of the first I can remember was shown in the bio-pic of Rommel *The Desert Fox*, in which a commando raid on Rommel's headquarters in North Africa is depicted.

Teaser sequences can get a film off to a rousing start, and that's exactly why they're used in the Bond movies. Technically, there is no pre-titles sequence in *Dr. No*, but the assassination of Strangways is very much like a teaser for the movie. Using an assassination as a teaser would later be perfected in *Live and Let Die*, in which three British agents are murdered.

The first true Bond teaser takes place in *From Russia with Love*, when Grant (ROBERT SHAW) stalks the phony Bond (SEAN CONNERY) in pre-titles. In *Goldfinger*, the quintessential teaser opened with Bond's arrival on the beach in South America wearing a fake seagull atop his diving mask. His fight in Bonita's (NADJA REGIN) dressing room with Capungo (ALF JOINT) was particularly vicious, culminating with Capungo being thrown into the bathtub along with an electric heater that electrocutes him. Agent 007's classic comment, "Shocking, positively shocking," serves to perfectly introduce the beginning of Shirley Bassey's title song.

Thunderball begins solemnly at a funeral during which Bond discovers that the corpse, a supposedly deceased S.P.E.C.T.R.E. agent, is instead very much alive and disguised as his grieving widow. After a gruesome fight in which Bond eventually breaks the "widow's" neck, 007 steals away in a one-man Bell rocket jet-pack, ushering in the era of the supergadgets. Bond then arrives back at his Aston Martin, which sprays three villains with water—the perfect prelude to Tom Jones's *Thunderball* theme song.

In *You Only Live Twice*, Bond is "assassinated" in Hong Kong in the teaser. In *On Her Majesty's Secret Service*, the teaser serves to introduce a new Bond, ex-model-turned-actor George Lazenby, who defeats a gang of hoods on the beach in southern France only to see his damsel in distress (DIANA RIGG) drive away without saying a word—something that definitely didn't happen to the other guy.

In the *Diamonds Are Forever* teaser, a revenge-minded Bond (SEAN CONNERY) tracks Blofeld (CHARLES GRAY) from Tokyo to Cairo and eventually attempts to bury him in boiling mud. In the very stylized teaser for *The Man with the Golden Gun*, Scaramanga (CHRISTOPHER LEE) assassinates a tough Mafia hit man (MARC LAWRENCE) in the fabulous "fun house" set.

Of all the teasers, however, the one for *The Spy Who Loved Me* is the best. Simply explained, ski-borne 007 (ROGER MOORE) shakes his enemy pursuers by jumping off an Austrian mountain peak and parachuting to safety, but the way in which the sequence is shot and the actual location that was chosen make this the daredevil sequence of all time. Even the sky-diving teaser in *Moonraker*, which was in itself wonderfully inventive, doesn't match that for *Spy*.

The more recent teasers have been fair to poor. *For Your Eyes Only* boasts the first teaser sequence to actually get the film off to the wrong start, with Bond (ROGER MOORE) playing footsy with a Blofeld look-alike while trying to get out of a disabled helicopter. The bit in which he unceremoniously dumps Blofeld into a smokestack while Blofeld tries to bribe Bond with the offer of a "stainless-steel delicatessen" was probably a low point among the Bond teasers.

Octopussy introduces 007's mini-jet in a rousing battle between Bond (ROGER MOORE) and a Latin American dictator's private army. *A View to a Kill* takes the teaser sequence back to familiar ground with a ski chase with, of all things, a Beach Boys song sound track. *The Living Daylights* teaser dazzles viewers with a war-game battle on the Rock of Gibraltar while simultaneously introducing yet another 007 (TIMOTHY DALTON).

In *Licence to Kill*, Bond and Felix Leiter (DAVID HEDISON) are on their way to Leiter's wedding, when they're suddenly ordered to capture a major drug kingpin (ROBERT DAVI). Hopping aboard a Coast Guard helicopter, Bond eventually chases and literally lassos the crook's private plane, towing it back to the base in very Bondian fashion.

One of the most interesting teasers was planned for *Never Say Never Again* but was never shot. As it stands, the film opens on a training exercise in the South American jungle—shot in the Bahamas—where James Bond (SEAN CONNERY) is introduced. This sequence is a teaser, although it takes place after the credits roll.

Originally, the film opened at a spectacular medieval pageant and tournament. Horses ridden by 15th-century knights are charging at one another in a thrilling competition. The lances they use are wooden and nonlethal. However, one of the knights suddenly picks up a lance that has a hidden metal-bladed tip. During the next competition, the metal lance kills one of the contestants.

Up until this point, the movie appears to be taking place 600 years ago. After the knight is killed, however, one of the other knights doffs his helmet, and we see that it's James Bond (SEAN CONNERY). Bond jumps on his horse and chases after the murderous knight. As Bond's horse clears a fence, we're suddenly in the middle of a huge parking lot. He spies the killer—a woman—climbing into a sports car and takes off after her.

In a thrilling steeplechase across the parking lot, with Bond jumping car after car, the escaping assassin is caught and killed. This teaser could have been one of the best in the series; unfortunately, it was deemed too expensive and was dropped from the final shooting script.

The Bond teasers are the perfect embodiments of the "Harry Houdini Syndrome"—that is, the ongoing battle for the Bond series to come up with more dangerous and death-defying stunts. The fact that, for the most part, the teasers have been rip-roaring fun is a great credit to the Bond producers, who have probably the best track record in film history when it comes to quality.

TECHTRONICS A Las Vegas–based division of Willard Whyte's (JIMMY DEAN) global conglomerate, specializing in satellite research and space exploration.

Having kidnapped Whyte, Ernst Stavro Blofeld (CHARLES GRAY) poses as the reclusive billionaire and uses Techtronics to develop a laser satellite powered by diamonds. Bond (SEAN CONNERY) breaks into the laboratory while impersonating Klaus Hergersheimer (ED BISHOP), the radiation-shield inspector, and steals a moon buggy to make good his escape.

The sequences at Techtronics were filmed at the Johns Manville gypsum plant outside Las Vegas.

TEE HEE Mr. Big's (YAPHET KOTTO) chuckling associate, portrayed by character actor Julius Harris, in *Live and Let Die*. Literally the drug kingpin's right-hand man (he has a grasping hook for a right hand), Tee Hee lost his real hand in a fight with Old Albert, a Louisiana crocodile.

In a climactic battle with Bond (ROGER MOORE) aboard a train destined for New York City, Tee Hee has the upper hand, until 007 manages to grab a scissors and snip the wires controlling his hook. Unable to remove himself from a precarious position, Tee Hee is literally kicked out of the train window. A similar train compartment fight between James Bond and Jaws (RICHARD KIEL) was featured in *The Spy Who Loved Me*.

TELEPHONE SERVICE Sign on the Egyptian utility van driven by Jaws (RICHARD KIEL) in *The Spy Who Loved Me*. It's also used by Bond (ROGER MOORE) and Anya (BARBARA BACH) during their chaotic escape from the desert ruins where Jaws has ripped the van virtually to shreds. The van eventually breaks down, and our heroes are forced to walk— guided by the soulful strains of the "Lawrence of Arabia" theme.

10 According to fanatical General Orlov (STEVEN BERKOFF) in *Octopussy*, this is the maximum number of American and West German armored divisions that can be deployed against any Russian invasion of Western Europe. Against this force, Orlov claims he has 91 total divisions available, including 33 tank divisions.

10 KILOS The weight of the Lektor decoding machine, in *From Russia with Love*, in its brown case, as described on tape by Russian cipher clerk Tatiana Romanova (DANIELA BIANCHI) to James Bond (SEAN CONNERY).

$10 MILLION Drug runner Franz Sanchez's (ROBERT DAVI) daily cash surplus from cocaine sales in *Licence to Kill*. The money is laundered through his own Banco de Isthmus and then wired to the U.S. Federal Reserve bank in Florida, where, he jokes, he's personally helping the U.S. trade deficit.

$10,958,157 Four-day box-office total for *Never Say Never Again* when it opened on Columbus Day weekend, October 7–10, 1983. At the time, it was the largest fall opening in motion-picture history.

$10,000 Mr. Simmons's (AUSTIN WILLIS) gin losses to Goldfinger (GERT FROBE) in Miami Beach.

$10,000 CREDIT WITH A $2,000 LIMIT Bond's (SEAN CONNERY) request at the Las Vegas crap table in *Diamonds Are Forever*. He starts to play with two stacks of $2,000 each.

10,500 TONS What James Bond (SEAN CONNERY) calculates is the weight of the entire $15 billion gold reserve of the United States, in *Goldfinger*. Under the impression that Goldfinger (GERT FROBE) is planning to steal the bullion, Bond estimates that it would take 60 men 12 days to load the stolen gold onto 200 trucks. Now you know what 007 does when he's stuck in a jail cell for 10 hours.

TERESA BOND 1943–1969 BELOVED WIFE OF JAMES BOND "WE HAVE ALL THE TIME IN THE WORLD" Inscription on the tomb of James Bond's (ROGER MOORE) wife, as seen in the opening teaser of *For Your Eyes Only*. It's one of the few sentimental moments in the series's history.

TERRY, JOHN Boyish actor who portrayed American CIA agent Felix Leiter in *The Living Daylights*. Certainly the youngest of the seven actors to play Leiter, Terry is good in the limited role, which places him aboard a sophisticated surveillance yacht in Tangier monitoring the activities of arms dealer Brad Whitaker (JOE DON BAKER). *See* LEITER, FELIX.

THAI KLONGS A series of narrow canals that crisscross Bangkok, Thailand, and that are featured in a boat chase in *The Man with the Golden Gun*. Instead of racing along in a swift motorboat, as he did in the previous film, *Live and Let Die*, Bond (ROGER MOORE) steals a relatively slow, knife-like Thai motor canoe for his getaway vehicle.

Agent 007 actually gets better results with the canoe's propeller when it's out of the water—scaring the hell out of his pursuers—than when it's in the water. While racing by in the canoe, 007 is spotted by his old bayou buddy Sheriff J. W. Pepper (CLIFTON JAMES),

who's in Thailand on a vacation with his wife, Mabel.

THAMES LAWN A riverfront mansion near Pinewood Studios in Buckinghamshire that became M's (BERNARD LEE) home in *On Her Majesty's Secret Service*. In hiring director Peter Hunt, producers Albert R. Broccoli and Harry Saltzman injected a different style into their sixth film. Whereas on *You Only Live Twice*, Lewis Gilbert and Roald Dahl had been more concerned with the fantasy elements of Bond's world—by creating huge, workable sets and incredible stunts—Hunt pressed for a return to the basics of Fleming's writing.

This new emphasis is quite apparent in several sequences that were transferred to the screen almost word for word from the novel. One of these little bits of nostalgia was a visit to M's house—the only visit of the series, thus far.

Hunt had always wanted to show the admiral's home, complete with a 16th-century cannon guarding the driveway, an oceanfront view, and a servant named Hammond (JOHN GAY). On *OHMSS*, he was given his chance, and Richard Maibaum wrote a sequence in which Bond (GEORGE LAZENBY) comes to tell his chief that Blofeld (TELLY SAVALAS) has been found in Switzerland. The exterior filming of that home, shot at Thames Lawn, was completed on Wednesday, April 9, 1969.

THATCHER, DENIS The husband of British Prime Minister Margaret Thatcher (JANET BROWN). He's portrayed by John Wells, who appears briefly during a humorous sequence at the end of *For Your Eyes Only*. *See* THATCHER, MARGARET.

THATCHER, MARGARET British Prime Minister portrayed by Thatcher look-alike Janet Brown, who appears in a humorous sequence at the end of *For Your Eyes Only*. Telephoning Bond (ROGER MOORE) in Corfu to congratulate him on the success of his latest caper, Thatcher inadvertently starts speaking to Max, the parrot who does not count shyness among his qualities.

"Give us a kiss, give us a kiss," he squawks. Slightly embarrassed by "007's" display of affection, Thatcher blushes, while her equally befuddled husband, Denis (JOHN WELLS), stands by.

"THAT'S A CHARMING TUNE. YOU DO TAKE ENGLISH MONEY?" First phrase of the British Secret Service recognition code, spoken by James Bond (ROGER MOORE) to Vijay (VIJAY AMRITRAJ) when they meet in a New Delhi street market in *Octopussy*. Vijay replies, "Only gold sovereigns."

THIRD FLOOR The location of Tiffany Case's (JILL ST. JOHN) Amsterdam apartment in *Diamonds Are Forever*.

THIRD NIPPLE (aka supercilious papilla) An anatomical abnormality displayed by super-assassin Francisco Scaramanga (CHRISTOPHER LEE) in *The Man with the Golden Gun*. According to legend, in a man it's a sign of invulnerability and great sexual prowess. To gain an audience with ruthless industrialist Hai Fat (RICHARD LOO), Bond (ROGER MOORE) impersonates Scaramanga with the help of a third nipple supplied by Q Branch.

13 G FORCE The amount of pressure that Bond (ROGER MOORE) endures in the sabotaged centrifuge trainer in *Moonraker*. The normal human being is supposed to black out at 7 Gs.

13TH The actual day on which Bond (SEAN CONNERY) and Kerim Bey (PEDRO ARMENDARIZ) launch their surprise raid on the Russian embassy in Istanbul to steal the Lektor decoding machine. To counter any proposed Russian trap, Bond had previously told defecting Russian cipher clerk Tatiana Romanova (DANIELA BIANCHI) that the raid would take place on the 14th. Unfortunately, S.P.E.C.T.R.E. is Bond's true enemy, and they are not fooled.

38 DEGREES 17.1 MINUTES NORTH/22 DEGREES 43.2 MINUTES WEST Mid-Atlantic position of redesignated pirate nuclear submarine Stromberg No. 2 in *The Spy Who Loved Me*. James Bond (ROGER MOORE) uses these coordinates to direct the two Stromberg pirate subs to blow each other up with their nuclear missiles.

3,500 DEGREES FAHRENHEIT Heat level produced by the solar panels in Scaramanga's (CHRISTOPHER LEE) power station in *The Man with the Golden Gun*.

35,000 FEET The altitude of Goldfinger's (GERT FROBE) private Lockheed Jetstar when James Bond (SEAN CONNERY) awakens and is greeted by Pussy Galore (HONOR BLACKMAN). The jet is traveling southwest over Newfoundland, 55 minutes from its destination, en route from Switzerland to Friendship Airport, Baltimore.

30 MINUTES The amount of time that 007 (ROGER MOORE) has to get ashore San Monique and rescue Solitaire (JANE SEYMOUR) before incendiary bombs destroy Kananga's (YAPHET KOTTO) poppy fields in *Live and Let Die*.

39 DEGREES 30.03 MINUTES NORTH/48 DEGREES 00.06 MINUTES WEST Mid-Atlantic position of redesignated pirate nuclear submarine Stromberg No. 1 in *The Spy Who Loved Me*.

31A 9/19/65 Identification number on the back of a photo of François Derval (PAUL STASSINO) and his sister, Domino (CLAUDINE AUGER), that is in 007's (SEAN CONNERY) dossier in *Thunderball*. The number might be either the United Artists publicity department's ID number or that of the British Secret Service's photo research department. I'm inclined to believe it's the former.

31,600 POUNDS Liquid capacity of the Kenworth tanker trailer-trucks that form drug runner Franz Sanchez's (ROBERT DAVI) cocaine convoy in *Licence to Kill*. Each truck's cargo is worth approximately $40 million.

3600 Numbers appearing on the detonator countdown panel when Max Zorin (CHRISTOPHER WALKEN) activates a huge bomb in the Main Strike Mine in *A View to a Kill*. Joining forces, Bond (ROGER MOORE) and May Day (GRACE JONES) are able to remove the bomb from a mountain of explosives and load it onto a railway handcar. Because of a faulty brake, May Day stays with the bomb and sees it safely outside the mine, where she dies in the tremendous explosion.

33 EAST 65TH ST. New York City address of the Oh Cult Voodoo Shop in *Live and Let Die*. It's also the address on Whisper's (EARL JOLLY BROWN) automobile registration certificate, a fact discovered by the CIA—when they check license plate 347 NDG—and passed on to James Bond (ROGER MOORE), who visits the shop.

30-YEAR-OLD VIN As estimated by 007 (SEAN CONNERY), the age of the "disappointing" brandy served at the Bank of England in *Goldfinger*. Bond also tells his dining partners, M (BERNARD LEE) and Colonel Smithers (RICHARD VERNON), that the drink is probably suffering from an indifferent blending process and an overdose of bombois.

"THIS NEVER HAPPENED TO THE OTHER FELLOW" The whimsical bit of dialogue spoken by James Bond (GEORGE LAZENBY) on a Portuguese beach, in *On Her Majesty's Secret Service*, after the girl he rescues (DIANA RIGG) drives off and leaves him holding her shoes. It was screenwriter Richard Maibaum's ultimate "wink" to the audience, which was being introduced to a new James Bond.

Said Maibaum, "It was the first time that we actually spoofed ourselves in the series. We decided this time that we would break the aesthetic distance for once.

"It was a different guy. We knew, and we knew the audience knew. So we decided, what the hell. Let's have a little fun. And the audience laughed and accepted it, and they were pleased that we didn't try some kind of phony B-picture thing to excuse the fact that we had a new James Bond."

THOMAS, VARLEY Silver-haired actress, in *Goldfinger*, who portrayed the friendly Swiss gatekeeper, a tough little woman who later blasts away at Bond's Aston Martin with a submachine gun.

THREE The number of deadly nerve-gas–carrying globes (out of a total of 50) that are successfully launched by Hugo Drax (MICHEL LONSDALE) from his radar-invisible space station, in *Moonraker*. Stealing a shuttle equipped with a nose-mounted laser cannon, Bond (ROGER MOORE) and Dr. Goodhead (LOIS CHILES) must destroy all three globes before they can enter the Earth's atmosphere.

3:00 A.M. According to M's clock (BERNARD LEE), this is the time when 007 (SEAN CONNERY) first enters his office in *Dr. No*.

"THREE BLIND MICE" The first song featured in the James Bond series is this calypso version of the famous nursery rhyme. In this case, the phrase refers to three black assassins hired by Dr. No (JOSEPH WISEMAN) and disguised as blind beggars. A nice touch of local color in Kingston, Jamaica.

THREE DOZEN RED ROSES James Bond's (ROGER MOORE) gift to Russian KGB agent Pola Ivanova (FIONA FULLERTON) when she was a Bolshoi ballerina. It was his way of telling her that he knew she was a communist agent sent to seduce him—as revealed by 007 in a San Francisco hot tub in *A View to a Kill*. See IVANOVA, POLA.

3549-WUU The license plate of James Bond's (TIMOTHY DALTON) new trick Aston Martin in *The Living Daylights*. See ASTON MARTIN DB-5 WITH MODIFICATIONS.

347 NDG The license plate of Whisper's (EARL JOLLY BROWN) white Cadillac "pimpmobile" in *Live and Let Die*. It's equipped with a deadly dart gun built into the right side-view mirror. Calling in the license plate to the local police, Felix Leiter (DAVID HEDISON) refers to the plate letters as "Nelson, David, George."

355 Identification number on James Bond's (ROGER MOORE) phony name tag in the *Octopussy* teaser. Agent 007 is impersonating a South American army officer named Colonel Luis Toro (KEN NORRIS). See TORO, COLONEL LUIS.

359-ETO-75 License plate of the Citroen taxi stolen by Bond (ROGER MOORE) in Paris during the chaotic chase after May Day (GRACE JONES) in *A View to a Kill*.

3:45 P.M. Zero hour for an A-bomb explosion at a U.S. Air Force base in West Germany, in *Octopussy*. Planted by Kamal Khan (LOUIS JOURDAN) inside the base of a circus cannon, the bomb is set to go off in Feldstadt during a performance of the Octopussy Circus. James Bond (ROGER MOORE), disguised as a circus clown, deactivates the bomb, with only seconds to spare.

3 G FORCE On the centrifuge trainer in *Moonraker*, it's equivalent to the takeoff pressure on the space shuttle. Explaining the system to James Bond (ROGER MOORE), astrophysicist Dr. Holly Goodhead (LOIS CHILES) says that a 70-year-old man can take 3 Gs. When the trainer is sabotaged, Bond eventually undergoes 13 Gs.

THREE GIRLS AND THREE BOYS The only present that Tracy (DIANA RIGG) requests from James Bond (GEORGE LAZENBY) at their wedding in *On Her Majesty's Secret Service*.

300 James Bond's (ROGER MOORE) room number at the Miramonte Hotel in Cortina D'Ampezzo in *For Your Eyes Only*. Returning to his room after a day's worth of investigation, he finds teenage ice skater Bibi Dahl (LYNN-HOLLY JOHNSON) waiting for him in bed. Ever the gentleman, 007 offers her an ice-cream cone instead of lovemaking.

$300 MILLION The value in Zurich, Switzerland, of the stolen Kremlin jewels that Kamal Khan (LOUIS JOURDAN) and Octopussy (MAUD ADAMS) smuggle out of East Germany in *Octopussy*. Little does Octopussy know that she's being double-crossed and that Kamal has taken the horde for himself, replacing it with a nuclear device that will explode on a U.S. Air Force base in West Germany.

THREE KNOCKS James Bond's (SEAN CONNERY) recognition signal to Tatiana Romanova (DANIELA BIANCHI) in their compartment on the Orient Express, in *From Russia with Love*.

"THREE MORE TICKS AND MR. GOLD-FINGER WOULD'VE HIT THE JACK-POT" The phrase uttered by James Bond (SEAN CONNERY) when a scientist deactivates the atomic device in *Goldfinger*. It's a confusing phrase, since the counter actually stops at 007.

Editor Peter Hunt offered a simple explanation. The idea of stopping the counter at 007 was an afterthought that was inserted into the film after the actors had already finished their dubbing chores. Since Sean Connery was not available to "loop" his lines, the "three more ticks" quip was left in. Originally, the counter was set to stop at 003.

3:00 P.M. The scheduled performance time for the Octopussy Circus at a U.S. Air Force base in Feldstadt, West Germany. Kamal Khan (LOUIS JOURDAN) intends to explode a nuclear bomb on the base at 3:45 P.M.

304 The number on Bond's (SEAN CONNERY) Nassau hotel room in *Thunderball*. It's a busy room. Quist tries to kill 007 there. Paula Caplan (MARTINE BESWICK) hangs out there until she's kidnapped by a S.P.E.C.T.R.E. goon squad. Fiona Volpe (LUCIANA PALUZZI) takes her celebrated bath there. And after his lovemaking with Fiona, her goons go there to capture 007.

306 The San Francisco City Hall room number of corrupt Division of Oil and Mines official W. G. Howe (DANIEL BENZALI) in *A View to a Kill*.

Determined to frame James Bond (ROGER MOORE) and Stacey Sutton (TANYA ROBERTS) for murder, Max Zorin (CHRISTOPHER WALKEN) shoots Howe, sets his office on fire, and traps Bond and Stacey in a City Hall elevator shaft. He then drops a Molotov cocktail onto their elevator car, setting it ablaze. Bond and Stacey survive and eventually make their escape in a San Francisco Fire Department hook-and-ladder truck.

THREE RAZOR BLADES Concealed weapons carried by Soviet masterspy Le Chiffre

(PETER LORRE) in the TV film "Casino Royale" (1954). Based exactly on author Ian Fleming's description, the blades are carried in his hat band, in the heel of his left shoe, and in his cigarette case.

Bond (BARRY NELSON) uses the blade concealed in the cigarette case to shred his bonds and escape from the bathroom of his hotel room, where's he being held prisoner with Valerie Mathis (LINDA CHRISTIAN) by Le Chiffre and his thugs. Bond then quickly steals a gun and kills the masterspy.

3266 The supposed registration number on the back of James Bond's (ROGER MOORE) watch in *Live and Let Die*. The number is mentioned by Kananga (YAPHET KOTTO) during a tense interrogation sequence in New Orleans.

Suspicious of Solitaire's (JANE SEYMOUR) allegiance, Kananga asks her if the number is correct. If she answers correctly, Tee Hee (JULIUS HARRIS) will not sever 007's right pinkie finger. Solitaire carefully turns over a card and says that Kananga speaks the truth. Kananga doesn't blink, and Tee Hee removes his claw from 007's finger.

Solitaire has answered correctly, so it seems, until Bond is knocked unconscious and is removed from the room. At that point, Ka-nanga tells Solitaire that she was wrong. He slaps her and orders Baron Samedi (GEOFFREY HOLDER) to prepare her execution on San Monique island.

THREE YEARS The amount of time Red Grant (ROBERT SHAW), posing as British agent Captain Nash, claims he's spent in Yugoslavia, in *From Russia with Love*.

THUMPER One of the acrobatic ladies whom Blofeld (CHARLES GRAY) assigns the task of guarding Willard Whyte (JIMMY DEAN) in *Diamonds Are Forever*. Portrayed by American actress Trina Parks, she and her partner Bambi (DONNA GARRATT) give Bond (SEAN CONNERY) plenty of trouble when he comes searching for the missing Whyte.

THUNDERBALL (United Artists, 1965) ★ ★ ★ ½ The fourth James Bond film, produced by Kevin McClory and executive produced by Albert R. Broccoli and Harry Saltz-

Sean Connery, Claudine Auger, and an eavesdropping diver take their final instructions during filming of *Thunderball*'s finale in 1965. (Rex Features Ltd./RDR Productions)

man. U.S. release date: December 29, 1965. Budget: $5.6 million. U.S. film rentals: $28.6 million. Running time: 129 minutes.

Thunderball is an epic film in every sense of the word—a big caper on a big canvas, depicting a sense of worldwide alarm that has never been duplicated in the series. The capers have been equally ambitious in other Bond films, but director Terence Young and screenwriter Richard Maibaum managed to infuse this film with a very realistic menace. In *The Spy Who Loved Me*, Stromberg's nuclear threat is a fantasy. In *Thunderball*, however, you believe that S.P.E.C.T.R.E. can and will detonate an atomic device if their ransom is not paid.

Like the previous films in the series, there are simple touches in *Thunderball* that anchor the film in reality. The hijacking of the NATO bomber is treated realistically, as is the general alarm created by the NATO command. When Bond walks into the Secret Service briefing room and takes his seat with all the other double-0 agents in Europe, you sense that an incredible adventure is about to begin, with the fate of the planet potentially on the line. And although Bond appears to be a bit cavalier at times—spending far too much time bedding one conquest after another—when duty calls, he responds quickly and decisively.

Much has been written over the years

Director Terence Young dons a wet suit during filming on *Thunderball*. (Terence Young Collection)

The Home Secretary (ROLAND CULVER) plays the S.P.E.C.T.R.E. extortion tape in *Thunderball*. Surrounding him, *left to right*, are Lois Maxwell, Bernard Lee, Reginald Beckwith, and Charles Russhon. (Claire Russhon Collection)

The NATO bomber mockup is lowered into the water off Clifton Pier, Nassau during filming on *Thunderball* in 1965. (Ronnie Udell Collection)

Sean Connery in the *Life* magazine cover pose for *Thunderball*. He was 34 when this picture was taken.
(Rex Features Ltd./RDR Productions)

about the ineffectiveness of *Thunderball*'s underwater sequences and how they slow down the pace of the film. Certain fight sequences do appear repetitive, but the underwater arena contributes enormously to the romance of this picture. As a backdrop to the love affair between Bond and Domino, the underwater sequences have a poetic quality. Nowhere is this more evident than in the opening sequence, in which Bond meets Domino in the waters off Nassau.

Directed by Ricou Browning, photographed by Lamar Boren, and scored beautifully by John Barry, this romance sequence is a perfect catalyst for the interplay between the two future lovers. Unlike *Never Say Never Again*, which moved to different locations for no apparent reason, *Thunderball* uses the romantic lure of Nassau as a running character throughout the film. One of the most evocative sequences is a brief moment when Bond arrives for a night of gambling in the Paradise Island casino. As he gets off the boat, he hears the laughter of a group of well-dressed vacationers who are leaving for the night. "See you tomorrow," they shout, and the viewer suddenly gets a tremendous sense of the tropics, of carefree vacations, cool tropical drinks, and moonlight romance.

There's also a super-confident quality that Sean Connery brings to the picture, a kind of comfortable "I know what I'm doing" attitude. Critics might refer to this quality as "sleepwalking through the role," but, in actuality, it's part of the film's self-assurance.

After three films, the 007 character has been established. Now, it's time for Sean to have a little fun—as shown in the scene in the chateau where he kills Jacques Boitier and takes time to throw flowers on the body, or the scene in Shrublands where he discovers the dead Angelo and steals a bit of fruit as he leaves. Touches like these set *Thunderball* apart from other Bond movies.

The film also features one of the most beautiful women ever to grace a 007 adventure. Claudine Auger, a French beauty-contest

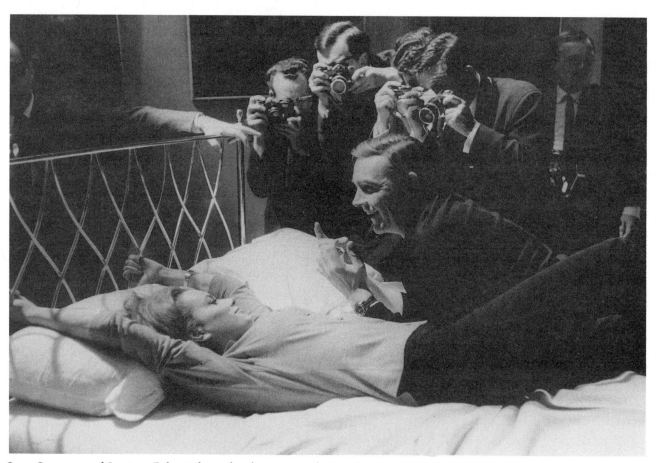

Sean Connery and Luciana Paluzzi clown for the cameras during shooting at Pinewood Studios on *Thunderball*. (Rex Features Ltd./RDR Productions)

winner, is nothing less than stunning. Like Connery, she has an electrifying presence on-screen that gives their romance the requisite fire. Luciana Paluzzi is also a fetching witch, a voluptuous Italian redhead who brings plenty of her own charisma to the part of Fiona, the S.P.E.C.T.R.E. assassin. What are the film's problems? The Shrublands sequence stalls early in the film. Aside from the interplay with the very desirable Patricia Fearing, much of the sequence is just too slow and uninteresting.

THUNDERBALL CAST

James Bond . . . . Sean Connery
Domino . . . . Claudine Auger
Emilio Largo . . . . Adolfo Celi
Fiona Volpe . . . . Luciana Paluzzi
Felix Leiter . . . . Rik Van Nutter
M . . . . Bernard Lee
Paula Caplan . . . . Martine Beswick
Count Lippe . . . . Guy Doleman
Patricia Fearing . . . . Molly Peters
Q . . . . Desmond Llewelyn
Miss Moneypenny . . . . Lois Maxwell
Foreign Secretary . . . . Roland Culver
Pinder . . . . Earl Cameron
Major Derval/Angelo . . . . Paul Stassino
Madame Boitier . . . . Rose Alba
Jacques Boitier . . . . Bob Simmons
Vargas . . . . Philip Locke
Kutze . . . . George Pravda
Janni . . . . Michael Brennan
Group Captain Pritchard . . . . Leonard Sachs
Air Vice Marshall Sir John . . . . Edward Underdown
Kenniston . . . . Reginald Beckwith
Quist . . . . Bill Cummings
Mademoiselle LaPorte . . . . . . Maryse Guy Mitsouko

THUNDERBALL CREDITS

Presented by . . . Albert R. Broccoli, Harry Saltzman
Produced by . . . . Kevin McClory
Director . . . . Terence Young
Screenplay by . . . . Richard Maibaum, John Hopkins
Based on the Original Story by . . . . Kevin McClory, Jack Whittingham, Ian Fleming
Director of Photography . . . . Ted Moore, B.S.C.
Production Manager . . . . David Middlemas
Supervising Film Editor . . . . Peter Hunt
Production Designer . . . . Ken Adam
Assistant Director . . . . Gus Agosti
Art Director . . . . Peter Murton

Special Effects . . . . John Stears
Camera Operator . . . . John Winbolt
Sound Recorders . . . . Bert Ross, Maurice Askew
Location Manager . . . . Frank Ernst
Costume Designer . . . . Anthony Mendleson
Wardrobe Mistress . . . . Eileen Sullivan
Wardrobe Master . . . . John Brady
Stunt Director . . . . Bob Simmons
Makeup . . . . Paul Rabiger, Basil Newall
Continuity . . . . Joan Davis
Hairstylist . . . . Eileen Warwick
Assistant Art Director . . . . Michael White
Set Dresser . . . . Freda Pearson
Underwater Sequences . . . . . . Ivan Tors Underwater Studios, Ltd.
Underwater Director . . . . Ricou Browning
Underwater Cameraman . . . . Lamar Boren
Underwater Engineer . . . . Jordan Klein
Music Composed and Directed by . . . . . John Barry
"Thunderball" Lyrics by . . . . Don Black
Title Song Sung by . . . . Tom Jones
Main Title Designed by . . . . Maurice Binder
Production Company . . . . Eon Productions
Distribution Company . . . . United Artists

THUNDERBALL COMPETITION

Competitive films in release when *Thunderball* opened in Los Angeles on December 21, 1965:
Inside Daisy Clover
The Spy Who Came In from the Cold
Viva Maria
Boeing Boeing
Battle of the Bulge
The Great Race
Pinocchio in Outer Space
Doctor Zhivago
When the Boys Meet the Girls

THUNDERBALL The British Secret Service code name for the double-0 mission to find a missing NATO bomber and its cargo of two atomic bombs, in *Thunderball*.

THUNDERBALL CONTINUITY PROBLEMS One of the major complaints about this 1965 James Bond movie are some glaring continuity errors. As editor Peter Hunt explained, "The whole film doesn't bear watching too closely. And as for continuity slips, there were many.

"One that I love is when Bond (SEAN CONNERY) and Leiter (RIK VAN NUTTER) are looking for the Vulcan bomber from their helicopter. In one shot, Rik is sitting there with a hat on, and in another sequence, he has on a completely different set of clothes. And both sequences are cut together.

"It worked because nobody ever noticed it. My rationale is that if we had nothing else, we had to make it work.

"In another sequence, Bond, having lost his own blue diving mask, swims over to a dead S.P.E.C.T.R.E. frogman and grabs his black mask. However, in the next shot, Bond has his blue mask back on.

"Sometimes when it comes time to juxtapose certain bits of film, you can't. It's not possible, and that's how gaps occur. It's better to maintain the pace of the film than to worry about continuity."

THUNDERBALL TITLE SEQUENCE It was filmed by title specialist Maurice Binder in the Pinewood Studios tank in July 1965. Mickey de Rauch, Billie Bater, and Jean McGrath portrayed the nude swimmers—symbolic of the film's underwater theme.

THUNDERBIRD Felix Leiter's (CEC LINDER) car in *Goldfinger*. It's a white 1964 model, with a black landau top. In *Thunderball*, Emilio Largo (ADOLFO CELI) also drives a Thunderbird in Paris.

TIBBETT, SIR GODFREY British Secret Service agent portrayed by Patrick Macnee in *A View to a Kill*. Working undercover as James Bond's (ROGER MOORE) chauffeur, Tibbett arrives at Max Zorin's (CHRISTOPHER WALKEN) sumptuous French estate to help 007 investigate Zorin's use of steroids to increase the racing abilities of his thoroughbreds.

Fooling the estate security team with a tape-recorded conversation that plays in 007's bedroom, Bond and Tibbett sneak into Zorin's secret underground laboratory beneath his stables and discover a surgical suite where special microchips are being surgically inserted into the horses' legs to trigger the correct dose of steroids. They also discover a huge cache of microchips that are being hoarded by Zorin.

Returning to their quarters, Bond and Tibbett make plans to get the information to M (ROBERT BROWN). Unfortunately, before Tibbett can make an important phone call, he's strangled by May Day (GRACE JONES) in a nearby car wash. Bond is knocked unconscious and thrown into the backseat with his deceased fellow agent, while May Day pushes their Rolls-Royce into a nearby lake. Regaining his senses, Bond escapes from the sinking car and survives by sucking air from one of the Rolls's Michelin tires. *See* MACNEE, PATRICK.

TITLE SONGS AND THE BILLBOARD TOP 100 SINGLES CHART When Duran Duran's title song for *A View to a Kill* hit No. 1 on the Billboard Top 100 in July 1985, it was the first time a James Bond song hit the number-one spot. Here's the record thus far of the Bond songs that have made the Top 100 singles chart:

BOND SONGS HITTING BILLBOARD'S TOP 100

ARTIST	SONG	HIGHEST NO. ON TOP 100
Duran Duran	"A View to a Kill" (1985)	No. 1
Paul McCartney and Wings	"Live and Let Die" (1973)	No. 2 (for three weeks)
Carly Simon	"Nobody Does It Better" from *The Spy Who Loved Me* (1977)	No. 2 (for three weeks)
Sergio Mendez and Brazil '66	"The Look of Love" from *Casino Royale* (1967)	No. 4
Sheena Easton	"For Your Eyes Only" (1981)	No. 4
Shirley Bassey	"Goldfinger" (1964)	No. 8
Tom Jones	"Thunderball" (1965)	No. 25
Herb Alpert and the Tijuana Brass	"Casino Royale" (1967)	No. 27
Rita Coolidge	"All Time High" (1983) from *Octopussy*	No. 36
Nancy Sinatra	"You Only Live Twice" (1967)	No. 44
Shirley Bassey	"Diamonds Are Forever"	No. 57

T.M. The initials inscribed on the case in which Tilly Masterson (TANIA MALLET) carries her hunting rifle, in *Goldfinger*. She lies to Bond (SEAN CONNERY) and says that it contains her ice skates. She also uses the alias Tilly Soames.

"TOFANA 10:00 A.M." Message that appears on the mirror of Bond's (ROGER MOORE) steam-filled bathroom in Cortina, in *For Your Eyes Only*. It refers to a ski-resort meeting place (3,243 meters above sea level) with local Secret Service contact Luigi Ferrara (JOHN MORENO). Their recognition code is "The snow this year is better at Innsbruck," followed by "But not at St. Moritz."

TOKYO Japanese capital city that figures in the plot of many James Bond movies. In *From Russia with Love*, it's where agents of S.P.E.C.T.R.E. capture and torture a British agent to get the Secret Service recognition code.

In the same film, when he's asked to compare Tatiana Romanova's (DANIELA BIANCHI) sexual prowess to that of the women he's known in the West, Bond (SEAN CONNERY) remembers a time when he was in Tokyo with M (BERNARD LEE); his story ends abruptly when M turns off Bond's tape-recorded conversation.

In *You Only Live Twice*, Tokyo is the film's principal location, and it's where Bond meets Tanaka (TETSURO TAMBA), the head of the Japanese Secret Service. During his stay, 007 visits a sumo wrestling match, where he meets Tanaka's agent, Aki (AKIKO WAKABAYA-SHI). And during a chase with agents of S.P.E.C.T.R.E., one of Tanaka's helicopters uses its powerful electromagnet to lift the chasing vehicle into the air, after which it's dropped into Tokyo Bay.

In *Casino Royale*, Tokyo is the site of a British agent's assassination—he was garroted in a geisha house.

TOM Willard Whyte's (JIMMY DEAN) right-hand man, portrayed by Bond favorite Shane Rimmer, in *Diamonds Are Forever*.

TOPOL (Tel Aviv, Israel, September 9, 1935–) (real name, Chaim Topol) Charismatic Israeli leading actor who portrayed Greek smuggler Milos Columbo in *For Your Eyes Only*. In a film that was a throwback to the early, more serious entries in the Bond series, Topol's Columbo was a fascinating character—very much

in the vein of Kerim Bey (PEDRO ARMEND-ARIZ) in *From Russia with Love*.

A big man who's full of life and determined to destroy his enemy, Kristatos (JULIAN GLOVER), at all costs, Columbo is the type of fully realized supporting character that is a fairly consistent element in the Bond series. Topol painted him with layers of likeability, down to his love for pistachio nuts. A real plus for the series. *See* COLUMBO, MILOS.

TOPPING, DON Contortionist who portrayed the strange double-jointed "crab man" during the nightclub sequence in *Live and Let Die*.

TOPPLING What Dr. No (JOSEPH WISE-MAN) is doing to American missiles launched from the Cape Canaveral base in Florida. According to 007's (SEAN CONNERY) definition, toppling means throwing the gyroscopic controls of a guided missile off track with a radio signal. Dr. No's toppling operation is based on an island called Crab Key, where he has an atomic-powered radio beam sequestered in his fortress.

TORO, COLONEL LUIS Mustachioed South American army officer who's portrayed by Ken Norris in the *Octopussy* teaser and impersonated by James Bond (ROGER MOORE). Costumed and made up to look like Toro (with a mustache glued to his upper lip), Bond's mission is to sneak into a heavily guarded air force base hangar and place a demolition charge on a top secret radar system. The ruse works for a moment, but 007 is soon captured when the real Toro shows up.

Placed in an army truck and guarded by two paratroopers, Bond is being driven down the highway when his assistant, sultry Bianca (TINA HUDSON), distracts the paratroopers long enough for Bond to pull the rip cords on their uniforms, catapulting them out of the truck. Agent 007 then jumps into Tina's car, runs back to what appears to be a horse trailer, disconnects it from the car, and bids his lady friend good-bye.

As a swiftly moving convoy bears down on him, Bond enters the horse trailer and starts up the motor on an amazing mini-jet plane. Air-

Agent 007 impersonates Colonel Toro, a South American air force officer, in the *Octopussy* teaser. (Royal Air Force, Northolt)

borne, he is an immediate target for a heat-seeking anti-aircraft missile. Somehow, Bond avoids the missile, flies into the hangar where the radar system is located, and manages to keep the missile on his trail long enough for it to completely obliterate the hangar and everything in it. Running out of gas, he stops at a rural filling station, smiles at the old-timer running the place, and suavely says, as only James Bond can say, "Fill 'er up, please!"

TOWERS, CARLTON British foreign-office agent, portrayed by Bernard Cribbins, who masquerades in West Berlin as Mata Bond's (JOANNA PETTET) cabdriver in *Casino Royale*. He eventually helps her escape from the Mata Hari Dance and Spy School. *See* CRIBBINS, BERNARD.

TOYOTA 2000 Aki's (AKIKO WAKABAYASHI) futuristic white sports car in *You Only Live Twice*. For the film, the Toyota Automobile Corporation offered to create a special version of their new 1966 GT 2000 sports car, complete with a convertible top—the first of its kind ever seen in Japan. Into this dream car, Special Effects Chief John Stears added a functional closed-circuit television that allows Bond (SEAN CONNERY) and Aki to communicate with Tiger Tanaka's (TETSURO TAMBA) Tokyo headquarters.

TRACY The nickname of the spoiled daughter of Marc Ange Draco (GABRIELE FERZETTI), the head of the Union Corse crime syndicate. She's portrayed by Diana Rigg in *On Her Majesty's Secret Service*. Her formal name is Contessa Teresa de Vicenzo (her husband killed himself in a race car).

Introduced as a suicidal burnout case who's ready to end it all in the ocean off Portugal, Tracy is rescued by Bond (GEORGE LAZENBY). She gradually recovers during a whirlwind courtship with 007, until he leaves for Blofeld's (TELLY SAVALAS) Swiss mountain hideaway.

Later, like a female version of the U.S. Cavalry, she comes to Bond's aid, joining him in a mad escape from Switzerland, both in a car and on skis. More than any other woman in the series, she displays the mental and physical skills needed to keep up with Bond.

Hiding out in a barn during a snowstorm, Bond expresses his love for Tracy. And in one of the most dramatic pronouncements of the series, he proposes. However, their wedding plans are cut short when Tracy is captured by Blofeld's men in a mad ski chase. His love for Tracy, combined with his hate for Blofeld, leads Bond on a freelance mission—with the help of Draco—against Blofeld's Piz Gloria fortress (M and the Secret Service refuse to help).

Aki shows off some of the Toyota 2000's more interesting features including a videotape recorder, in *You Only Live Twice*. (Loomis Dean/Camera Press, Globe Photos)

Masquerading as Red Cross workers headed for the Italian flood disaster, Draco's copter-borne attack force arrives at Piz Gloria, rescues Tracy, and obliterates the S.P.E.C.T.R.E. nest. In a thrilling bobsled chase, Bond disables Blofeld, but not enough to prevent him from coming back at the film's conclusion.

Following their wedding, Bond and Tracy, now just another happy wedded couple, pull off a highway in Portugal to remove the conspicuous Just Married signs that have been plastered on 007's Aston Martin. As Bond throws them away, a Mercedes driven by Irma Bunt (ILSE STEPPAT) drives by, and Blofeld opens fire with a machine gun. Bond returns to the car, but Tracy is already dead—shot right between the eyes. *OHMSS* ends on this sad note.

In *For Your Eyes Only*, the 12th Albert R. Broccoli–produced James Bond film, Bond (ROGER MOORE) pays an atmospheric visit to Tracy's grave, prior to one last confrontation with Blofeld in that film's raucous teaser.

TRANQUILIZER GUN The weapon of choice on Octopussy's (MAUD ADAMS) island. Unlike the kill-crazy fanatics hired by evil Kamal Khan (LOUIS JOURDAN), Octopussy's troops are simple smugglers, not killers. Their successful attack on the Monsoon Palace is engineered without a single firearm or death.

TRANSPORT CONSULTANT The occupation on the forged passport used by James Bond (SEAN CONNERY) while impersonating Peter Franks (JOE ROBINSON) in Amsterdam in *Diamonds Are Forever*. Tiffany Case (JILL ST. JOHN) thinks it's "a little cute."

TRANS SIBERIAN PIPELINE Natural-gas pipeline that is defecting Russian General Georgi Koskov's (JEROEN KRABBE) escape route out of Czechoslovakia, in *The Living Daylights*. Helped by Bond (TIMOTHY DALTON) and Rosika Miklos (JULIE T. WALLACE), a friendly gasworks employee, Koskov is placed inside the "pig"—a scouring plug designed to clean the interior of the pipes. This "pig" has been specially modified to carry a human being through the pipeline to Austria.

TREADWAY ESTATE A former Indian reservation in the Louisiana bayou country, that was the site of the madcap motorboat chase through the wedding party in *Live and Let Die*. Three American stuntmen tried to ram their CV-19 powerboats through the wedding cake. After Murray Cleveland and Jerry Comeaux failed, it was Eddie Smith who tasted the icing— at a reduced speed of 60 mph.

TREE, SHADY Wisecracking Las Vegas lounge entertainer and smuggler, portrayed by Leonard Barr, in *Diamonds Are Forever*. He's the leader of a lounge act called Shady Tree and His Acorns, the latter being two showgirls.

The withered, old Tree saves Bond (SEAN CONNERY) from a roasting at Slumber Inc. when he demands to know what happened to the "real" diamonds. Later, while sequestered

in his dressing room backstage at the Whyte House, Tree is assassinated by Blofeld's thugs— Mr. Wint (BRUCE GLOVER) and Mr. Kidd (PUTTER SMITH).

TREMBLE, EVELYN Mild-mannered author and baccarat authority, portrayed by Peter Sellers, who is recruited into the British Secret Service and given the name of James Bond, in *Casino Royale*. A 38-year-old employee at London's Buckingham Club, Tremble is seduced by Vesper Lynd (URSULA ANDRESS), a mysteriously wealthy temptress who owes the British government millions in back taxes and is herself working for Sir James Bond (DAVID NIVEN) to pay it back.

A self-confessed baccarat fiend, Tremble agrees to accept 100,000 pounds in backing from Lynd, to play against Soviet masterspy Le Chiffre (ORSON WELLES) in Monte Carlo. British Intelligence has determined that if Tremble can bankrupt Le Chiffre, who has been losing illegally appropriated Soviet funds, his own KGB will terminate him. Tremble accepts the

Comedy genius Peter Sellers appears in the *Casino Royale* spoof as Evelyn Tremble, a mild-mannered baccarat specialist who is recruited by the British Secret Service and seduced by Vesper Lynd (URSULA ANDRESS).

assignment and goes through a training program at British Secret Service headquarters.

As part of Sir James Bond's plan to confuse enemy agents, Tremble also becomes one of many British agents to be given the name James Bond, Secret Agent 007. Tremble's distinguishing marks include a little scar on his right shoulder and a strawberry-shaped birthmark on his left thigh. He was born in Highgate, England.

Tremble beats Le Chiffre at the tables, but he's later captured and tortured by the huge cardplayer. Eventually Tremble is shot by Vesper Lynd, who turns out to be a double agent (we think). *See* SELLERS, PETER.

TRENCH, SYLVIA The very first Bond girl, portrayed by Eunice Gayson, in the Albert R. Broccoli–produced 007 series. Sylvia is a wealthy, extremely sexy brunette who seduces Bond (SEAN CONNERY) in *Dr. No* and returns to frolic in a canoe on the Thames in *From Russia with Love*.

She meets Bond at the chemin de fer table at Les Ambassadeurs in London, prompting the famous line, "I admire your courage, Miss?" Her hobbies include golf, among other things. Unfortunately, 007 is usually in too much of a hurry to have more than a quick tryst with Sylvia, who looks quite fetching in a man's shirt and high heels.

Gayson was an old friend of director Terence Young, who had planned for her to keep appearing in ensuing 007 movies. When Young left the series during the pre-production on *Goldfinger*, Eunice's part was eliminated. *See* GAYSON, EUNICE.

"TRESPASSERS WILL BE EATEN" Sign on the main gate of Kananga's (YAPHET KOTTO) alligator farm in *Live and Let Die*. A real sign, it belonged to farmer Ross Kananga, the actual owner of the farm.

TRIANA A yacht owned by marine archaeologist and British agent Timothy Havelock (JACK HEDLEY) in *For Your Eyes Only*. Aboard the *Triana*, anchored in Corfu Harbor, Melina Havelock (CAROLE BOUQUET) witnesses the machine-gunning of her parents at the hands of seaplane pilot and Cuban hit man Hector Gonzales (STEFAN KALIPHA).

Later, using the *Triana* as a base of opera- tions, Melina and James Bond (ROGER MOORE) pilot the Havelocks' *Neptune* submarine to the hulk of the *St. Georges* surveillance ship, where they recover the A.T.A.C. computer. Returning to the yacht after their successful assault on Kristatos's (JULIAN GLOVER) St. Cyril's aerie, Bond and Melina dive into the warm waters of the Aegean for a romantic, nude midnight swim.

TRICK GONDOLA Bond's (ROGER MOORE) method of transportation through the Venice canals in *Moonraker*. It helps him fight off a motorboat full of Hugo Drax's (MICHAEL LONSDALE) thugs.

A cousin of the Aston Martin, the Little Nellie autogyro, and the Lotus Esprit, the trick gondola is actually the most ridiculous of all of James Bond's gadgets. Although its conversion from pure oar-driven power to motor launch is plausible, the sequence in which the gondola inflates to Hovercraft size and floats through St. Mark's Square on a cushion of air rates as probably the most idiotic event in the series.

Moore handles the looks of thousands of bystanders with typical upper-class élan, but a double-taking pigeon is just a bit too much for a sequence that is already outrageous. How much of a secret agent is James Bond, anyway?

TRICK KEY-RING FINDER A valuable weapon given to 007 (TIMOTHY DALTON) by Q (DESMOND LLEWELYN) in *The Living Daylights*. Invented for people who are continually misplacing their keys, the normal key-ring finder emits a high-pitched tone when a person triggers its signal—sometimes by a clap of the hands, sometimes by a whistle.

In Bond's case, the key-ring finder has three functions. First, if 007 whistles the first three bars of "Rule Britannia," the ring will emit a stun gas with an effective range of five feet, which will disorient a normal person for about 30 seconds. Second, if 007 offers a wolf whistle (highly appropriate for James Bond), a small quantity of plastic explosive will be detonated. Third, the keys on the ring finder can open 90 percent of the world's locks.

The key-ring finder plays an important part in two key action sequences. In Afghanistan, Bond and Kara Milovy (MARYAM D'ABO) are about to be incarcerated in a jail cell, when Bond whistles "Rule Britannia" and disorients his guards with the stun gas. Later, in Tangier, Bond is about to be blown away by arms dealer Brad Whitaker (JOE DON BAKER), when 007's patented wolf whistle detonates the plastic explosive behind a heavy bust of Wellington. The bust thereupon slams into and kills Whitaker, smashing him against a display case of Waterloo miniatures.

TRICK THREE-WHEELER Modified, high-speed, three-wheel motor cart driven by Vijay (VIJAY AMRITRAJ) during a chaotic chase through the streets of Udaipur, India, in *Octopussy*. Chased by jeep-borne fanatics, Vijay and his passenger, James Bond (ROGER MOORE), maneuver the fast-moving vehicle through the bazaars and literally over the heads of bystanders, until they escape into the nerve center of Q Branch.

TRIESTE The Northern Italian city that is the third stop on the Orient Express in *From Russia with Love* after earlier stops in Belgrade and Zagreb. Bond (SEAN CONNERY) and Tanya (DANIELA BIANCHI) actually leave the train long before Trieste, after 007 kills Grant (ROBERT SHAW).

TRIPLE X Russian KGB agent Anya Amasova's (BARBARA BACH) code name in *The Spy Who Loved Me*. See AMASOVA, MAJOR ANYA.

TROPICANA HOTEL James Bond's (SEAN CONNERY) Las Vegas residence in *Diamonds Are Forever*. It's where he meets Plenty O'Toole (LANA WOOD), who is later thrown out of a hotel window by the diamond-syndicate goons.

TROPIC ROVER Actual name of the catamaran, anchored in Nassau Harbor, that provides James Bond (SEAN CONNERY) with cover in *Thunderball*.

TRUMAN-LODGE, WILLIAM Yuppie financial wizard, portrayed by Anthony Starke, who works for South American drug lord Franz Sanchez (ROBERT DAVI) in *Licence to Kill*. The ever-greedy Truman-Lodge maintains the books for a rapidly expanding cocaine empire based in fictional Isthmus City.

He also monitors the Olimpatec Meditation Institute, a phony religious organization that produces a television show that's used to communicate current drug prices to Sanchez's clientele.

When Bond (TIMOTHY DALTON) begins to destroy Sanchez's operation piece by piece, Truman-Lodge begins to come unglued. His whining irritates an already exasperated Sanchez, who simply turns his submachine gun on him.

TUESDAY, 10:12 A.M. AND 18 SECONDS The time on James Bond's (ROGER MOORE) watch when Magda (KRISTINA WAYBORN) leaves his hotel suite with the Fabergé egg in *Octopussy*.

TULIP What James Bond (SEAN CONNERY) promises to bring back to Miss Moneypenny (LOIS MAXWELL) from Amsterdam in *Diamonds Are Forever*. She had asked for a "diamond in a ring."

TURNBULL & NASSER Famous London men's shop located on Jermyn Street. It's where director Terence Young took Sean Connery for his initial 007 wardrobe in *Dr. No*. The tailor was Anthony Sinclair.

TURO SPOTTITAX Species of exotic tropical fish, with dangerous dorsal spines, identified by James Bond (ROGER MOORE) while posing as marine biologist Robert Sterling in *The Spy Who Loved Me*. The information does not impress 007's host, Karl Stromberg (CURT JURGENS), who already knows that Sterling is Bond.

12 The room number of Honey Ryder's (URSULA ANDRESS) torture chamber on Crab Key in *Dr. No*. Transferred there by Dr. No's (JOSEPH WISEMAN) sadistic guards, who remove her pants—offscreen, of course, for this is 1962—she is chained to the concrete floor as water flows in. Bond (SEAN CONNERY) rescues her, and they both escape as Crab Key is obliterated.

12 NOON The time at which the redesignated nuclear submarines Stromberg No. 1 and Stromberg No. 2 will reach their mid-Atlantic firing positions, in *The Spy Who Loved Me*.

12 SECONDS The amount of time it takes the venom on Morzeny's (WALTER GOTELL) retractable shoe knife to eliminate S.P.E.C.T.R.E. master planner Kronsteen (VLADEK SHEYBAL) in Blofeld's office, in *From Russia with Love*.

20 DAYS The amount of time between the capture of the first U.S. *Jupiter* spacecraft and the launch of the second in *You Only Live Twice*.

28 FLAVORS OF ICE CREAM The dessert selection at CIA equipment section headquarters in Washington, D.C., according to Algernon (ALEC MCCOWEN), the dry-witted British Secret Service equipment officer in *Never Say Never Again*. It's one of the reasons he's thinking about a transfer to the States.

20 G FORCE The maximum speed of the centrifuge trainer in *Moonraker*. Such a force is fatal to humans. Before his wrist dart-gun shoots out the controls of the trainer that is sabotaged by Chang (TOSHIRO SUGA), Bond (ROGER MOORE) undergoes a 13 G force.

$20 MILLION The amount of money promised to Dr. Bechmann (CYRIL SHAPS) and Professor Markovitz (MILO SPERBER) by billionaire shipping magnate Karl Stromberg (CURT JURGENS) for developing the nuclear-submarine tracking system in *The Spy Who Loved Me*. Unfortunately, after they've delivered the system, their helicopter is blown out of the sky by Stromberg, who also cancels the transfer of the $20 million.

20 MINUTES The amount of time on the plastic-explosives detonator that Bond (SEAN CONNERY) places on the nitroglycerin barrels located inside Mr. Ramirez's secret heroin installation, in the *Goldfinger* teaser.

20 PACES The required distance before duelists James Bond (ROGER MOORE) and Francisco Scaramanga (CHRISTOPHER LEE) are allowed to turn and fire in *The Man with the Golden Gun*. Bond takes his paces, but when he turns, Scaramanga has disappeared. The duel then continues in Scaramanga's fabulous "fun house" maze.

In the original script, Bond and Scaramanga actually took shots at each other during a battle on the rocky escarpment of the island, which then segued to the "fun house." This battle was never featured in the finished film, but some of it can be seen in the trailer. *See* MISSING DUEL, THE.

20 SECONDS The amount of time set on the fuse of the bomb 007 (ROGER MOORE) places against the armored control room of the *Liparus* supertanker in *The Spy Who Loved Me*.

20 MILES According to a Russian army officer, it's the minimum safe distance for Kamal Khan (LOUIS JOURDAN) and Gobinda (KABIR BEDI) to survive a nuclear "accident" they've created at a U.S. Air Force base in West Germany, in *Octopussy*. The preset detonator on the 100-kiloton-yield device gives them four hours to cover this ground.

28 YEARS The amount of time that Dikko Henderson (CHARLES GRAY) has spent in Japan, in *You Only Live Twice*.

25 PERCENT The percentage of the annual oil purchases of each NATO country and Japan that S.P.E.C.T.R.E. intends to secure as a ransom for its hijacked nuclear cruise missiles in *Never Say Never Again*.

21 CLUB Proposed rendezvous between Bond (ROGER MOORE) and Felix Leiter (DAVID HEDISON) upon 007's return to New York from New Orleans in *Live and Let Die*.

20.003 GRAMS The individual weight of Francisco Scaramanga's (CHRISTOPHER LEE) golden bullets in *The Man with the Golden Gun*. This fact, plus the fact that the bullets are fired from an unusual 4.2-millimeter automatic pistol, leads Bond (ROGER MOORE) to a gunsmith in Macao (MARNE MAITLAND) who's been supplying Scaramanga with his conspicuous weaponry.

27 James Bond's (ROGER MOORE) hotel room number, in *Octopussy*, in Udaipur's Shianivas Hotel.

26 MILLION FRANCS Amount of gaming funds given to James Bond (BARRY NELSON) by British Secret Service agent Clarence Leiter (MICHAEL PATE) in the TV film "Casino Royale." It's to be used in a Monte Carlo baccarat game against Russian masterspy Le Chiffre (PETER LORRE).

The total equals the sum of Le Chiffre's own remaining funds, which he's illegally taken from Soviet coffers. If Bond can break him at the tables, Le Chiffre will become a target for his own KGB assassins. (*Note*: In 1954 dollars, 26 million francs is equivalent to $78,000.)

20,000 BAHTS The amount of Thai currency that James Bond (ROGER MOORE) offers a beggar boy, in *The Man with the Golden Gun*, if he can make his motor pan go faster. The boy turns on the right switch, but Bond reneges, tossing the boy overboard. When he's being chased by an army of killers, Bond just doesn't have time for gallantry or etiquette.

20,000 FRANCS The bank, or pot, in a game of chemin de fer that Tracy (DIANA RIGG) loses in *On Her Majesty's Secret Service*. Unfortunately, she whispers to the croupier, she has no money. Unbeknownst to the self-destructive Tracy, Bond (GEORGE LAZENBY) is also playing in the game, and he covers her losses.

$22,000 The current price, per kilo, of the cocaine that drug runner Franz Sanchez (ROBERT DAVI) is shipping out of Isthmus City in *Licence to Kill*. The price is communicated to Sanchez through Joe Butcher's (WAYNE NEWTON) televangelist show, where drug distributors call in their figures and the prices are mentioned in code.

22,000 POUNDS Both Sean Connery's salary on *Dr. No* and George Lazenby's salary on the film *On Her Majesty's Secret Service*.

20 YEARS TO LIFE The possible sentence awaiting Tiffany Case (JILL ST. JOHN) for

smuggling, in *Diamonds Are Forever*. For cooperating, however, she gets an all-expenses-paid ocean cruise to England with James Bond (SEAN CONNERY).

TWISS, PETER A former air force pilot who is credited as the first Englishman to break the sound barrier, he was in charge of the motorboat flotilla in *From Russia with Love*.

TWO AIR TICKETS TO LONDON What Bond (SEAN CONNERY) asks for when Sisters Lily (YVONNE SHIMA) and Rose (MICHELE MOK) offer him anything he wants inside Dr. No's (JOSEPH WISEMAN) fortress.

TWO AND A HALF TONS MAXIMUM LOAD Sign on the overhead pulley, above Milton Krest's (ANTHONY ZERBE) shark pen in *Licence to Kill*. Felix Leiter (DAVID HEDISON) is tied to the pulley rope by Sanchez (ROBERT DAVI) and his men. He's then lowered into the pen, where he's mangled by a shark. Traitorous DEA agent Killifer (EVERETT MCGILL) isn't as lucky.

TWO DEAD, TWO IN HOSPITAL The British Secret Service casualty total after Necros (ANDREAS WISNIEWSKI) rescues defecting Russian General Georgi Koskov (JEROEN KRABBE) from the Bladen safe house in *The Living Daylights*.

2827 License plate on the British military police jeep that pulls up in front of James Bond's (SEAN CONNERY) Hong Kong hotel room in *You Only Live Twice*.

2579 SLO6 License plate on Fatima Blush's (BARBARA CARRERA) Renault turbo sports car in *Never Say Never Again*.

2:44 P.M. The time on James Bond's (ROGER MOORE) watch when he's traveling in the company of a slow-moving, fat West German family in *Octopussy*. Stuck in their white Volkswagen, Bond keeps thinking of the A-bomb that will explode on a U.S. Air Force base in Feldstadt at 3:45 P.M.

TWO HOURS The amount of time Bond (SEAN CONNERY) has left when he enters the rocket crater, in *You Only Live Twice*, before the S.P.E.C.T.R.E. *Intruder* rocket intercepts the second U.S. spacecraft—a hostile act that could precipitate World War III.

$280 MILLION The amount of ransom that S.P.E.C.T.R.E. demands from NATO after hijacking two atomic bombs, in *Thunderball*. In English currency in 1965, this amount translated to 100 million pounds sterling. The ransom, to be paid in flawless blue-white diamonds weighing between three and eight carats, was then to be dropped in the Mergui Archipelago off the coast of Burma.

$250,000 The amount of money that S.P.E.C.T.R.E. mercenary Angelo Palazzi (PAUL STASSINO) demands from his organization for impersonating an aerial observer and hijacking a NATO bomber with nuclear bombs on board. His original agreed-upon fee was $100,000.

Agents Fiona Volpe (LUCIANA PALUZZI) and Count Lippe (GUY DOLEMAN) agree to the raise, but Palazzi never collects it. He's murdered by Largo (ADOLFO CELI) in Nassau.

It's also the sum that James Bond (TIMOTHY DALTON) initially loses at the blackjack table in Isthmus City, in *Licence to Kill*. Having raised the limit to $5,000 a hand, Bond starts out slowly, but he eventually reverses his luck and wins $250,000.

250–300,000 POUNDS British Secret Service art expert Jim Fanning's (DOUGLAS WILMER) prediction of what the jeweled Fabergé egg will fetch in a Sotheby's auction in *Octopussy*. When Bond (ROGER MOORE) sees that Kamal Khan (LOUIS JOURDAN) is determined to buy the egg, 007 enters the bidding himself, raising the ante to 500,000 pounds before dropping out. *See* FABERGE EGGS.

200 MILES WEST OF BANGKOK Where the British Secret Service discovers Scaramanga's (CHRISTOPHER LEE) abandoned AMC Matador car/plane in *The Man with the Golden Gun*.

200,000 RUPEES The final bet in the rigged backgammon game between Bond (ROGER MOORE) and Kamal Khan (LOUIS JOUR-

DAN) in *Octopussy*. 007 calls "player's privilege," takes Kamal's rigged dice, and throws a winning double six. "It's all in the wrist," he says. *See* BACKGAMMON GAME.

220 MILES PER HOUR The speed of Champagne Section's Piper Cherokee monoplanes as they prepare to spray what they think is Delta Nine nerve gas above Fort Knox, in *Goldfinger*.

224TH STRATEGIC MISSILE WING/ NORTH DAKOTA An American missile base attached to the Strategic Air Command's 168th Squadron that becomes an early target of Blofeld's (CHARLES GRAY) laser satellite in *Diamonds Are Forever*.

TWO INCHES The thickness of the Armorlite III bulletproof glass that protects the outer windows of South American drug runner Franz Sanchez's (ROBERT DAVI) office in *Licence to Kill*.

TWO MILES The location of the nearest intact bridge crossing once Bond (ROGER MOORE) discovers that Scaramanga's (CHRISTOPHER LEE) car is on the other side of a Thai river in *The Man with the Golden Gun*. This fact prompts 007 to perform the unheard-of 360-degree spiral jump across a ruined bridge.

$2 MILLION A standing cash offer to anyone who will secure the release of South American drug lord Franz Sanchez (ROBERT DAVI) in *Licence to Kill*. DEA agent Killifer (EVERETT MCGILL) succumbs to the bribe and helps Sanchez escape from Key West, Florida. However, Bond (TIMOTHY DALTON) finds Killifer and throws him to the sharks, along with his money. Two million dollars is also Bond's credit limit at Sanchez's casino in Isthmus City.

TWO MOLES ON THE LEFT THIGH The method by which 007 (SEAN CONNERY) recognizes Domino (CLAUDINE AUGER) in *Thunderball*. He spots the identifying marks when she climbs into her motorboat.

2:00 P.M.–3:00 P.M. daily Tanya's (DANIELA BIANCHI) scheduled daily work hours with the Lektor decoding machine in *From Russia with Love*.

2.5 ON THE RICHTER SCALE Magnitude of the tremor felt by James Bond (ROGER MOORE) at Stacey Sutton's (TANYA ROBERTS) northern California mansion in *A View to a Kill*. According to her computer, the epicenter is located near Max Zorin's (CHRISTOPHER WALKEN) oil fields on the Hayward earthquake fault. *See* PROJECT MAIN STRIKE.

$2.492 BILLION Maximillian Largo's (KLAUS MARIA BRANDAUER) net worth in *Never Say Never Again*.

TWO TONS The amount of free heroin Dr. Kananga (YAPHET KOTTO) plans to distribute through his chain of American Fillet of Soul nightclubs in *Live and Let Die*. The shipment has a U.S. street value of $1 billion. The impact should put his competitors out of business and double the number of addicts in the United States.

2:21 P.M. The time on 007's (ROGER MOORE) watch when he hits the highway after killing Grischka (ANTHONY MEYER), one of the twin assassins in *Octopussy*. Bond's headed for the U.S. Air Force base at Feldstadt, where an A-bomb is going to be detonated at 3:45 P.M.

TWO WEEKS The amount of time 007 (SEAN CONNERY) has devoted to the unusual war games conducted by M (EDWARD FOX) in *Never Say Never Again*. M claims that Bond's record is suspect. After all, he was killed once. On another occasion, on a beach in the Black Sea, he lost both legs to a land mine. And on a third outing, he suffered a severe arm injury. That's enough for M to send Bond to the Shrublands health clinic.

TWO WHITE DOTS The familiar animated logo designed by title specialist Maurice Binder for the first James Bond film, *Dr. No* in 1962. The logo introduces each film in the series.

Accompanied by John Barry's staccato signature 007 theme (which was continuously reorchestrated by succeeding composers), two dots—simulating the view down the scope of a sniper's rifle—roll across the screen, merging into one dot through which James Bond takes his patented walk. The dot itself then takes on the characteristics of the inside of a gun barrel.

At a given point, 007 turns and fires at the screen, triggering a red shroud that slowly covers the dot. As it wavers and begins to sink, indicating the death of the sniper, the single dot reappears, through which we see the first scene of the movie's teaser. (Regarding the various orchestrations for the signature 007 theme, I have always felt that the opening of *From Russia with Love* was John Barry at his most dramatic.)

In the first three James Bond movies, which were projected on the screen in the 1:85 ratio—referred to in film jargon as "flat"—stuntman Bob Simmons portrayed James Bond. When *Thunderball* was planned as the first "wide screen," anamorphically projected Bond film—referred to in film jargon as "scope," for "Cinemascope"—title designer Maurice Binder was forced to create a new version of the 007 logo. He asked Sean Connery to take the patented "walk and fire." Since then, George Lazenby, Roger Moore, and Timothy Dalton have all taken the walk in the dot.

20-00 The license plate on Aki's (AKIKO WAKABAYASHI) white Toyota 2000 convertible in *You Only Live Twice*.

TYLER, KELL Shapely actress who portrayed Linda, the bored jet-setter whose "drop-in" yacht guest turns out to be the new 007 (TIMOTHY DALTON), in *The Living Daylights* teaser.

TYNAN, DR. Plastic surgeon who designs the Blofeld clones in the *Diamonds Are Forever* teaser, portrayed by DAVID DE KEYSER, who dubbed the voices of actors GERT FROBE and GABRIELE FERZETTI for previous Bond films.

U

UDAIPUR, INDIA Beautiful city on the subcontinent that became a principal location in *Octopussy*. Founded in 1599 by Maharaja Udai Singh, it is known as the "City of Sunrise." Shooting began there on September 21, 1982, and continued for three weeks.

UDELL, RONALD (South Mimms, Hertfordshire, England, August 20, 1911–) Pinewood Studios construction manager, and production designer Ken Adam's right-hand man on many of the early James Bond films. Udell's motto, which Adam took literally, was "If you can draw it, we can build it."

Udell and his team of craftsmen at Pinewood encouraged Adam during the early days of the Bond series to try out new materials and techniques that were within the series's initially low budgets. When the film series took off, Udell was intimately involved in the huge set constructions that became a trademark of the Bond films, including the interior and exterior of Fort Knox in *Goldfinger* and the huge volcano missile base in *You Only Live Twice*.

Udell's first film at Pinewood was the classic suspense thriller *Green for Danger*. By the middle 1950s, he was one of the studio's six construction managers who supervised all construction at Pinewood. He worked closely with Harold Combden, Bill Surridge, Jock Lyle, Bert Mansell, and Ted Hughes. It was common for Udell to be involved in as many as six to eight films at once. Each team moved from construction to construction, and there was a camaraderie among the various teams that is unknown today.

Udell was appointed chief construction manager for the studio in 1969. Udell's relationship with Ken Adam began on *The Hidden Room* in 1949, an Edward Dmytryk–directed

Pinewood construction manager Ronnie Udell with Michael Redding on *You Only Live Twice*'s volcano set. (Ronnie Udell Collection)

suspense thriller. For *Dr. No* in 1962, Udell was delighted to work on the unusual sets designed by Adam for the film.

"We had a budget of 17,000 pounds for all of the interiors," he recalled. "We had just enough money to finish everything except the most important set—Dr. No's reactor room. Since the producers were extremely happy with the rushes, they went back to United Artists and fought for another 7,000 pounds to finish the reactor room.

"We used a lot of fiberglass on *Dr. No*, which was a new material. We gave it a metallic finish with an Italian jewelry spray. For the reactor room, which was built on Stage E, Ken originally wanted one slick catwalk—where Bond has the fight with Chang, the fuel elements technician—with no visible means of suspension. For safety reasons, we convinced him to design two supports into the set."

While Bill Surridge supervised the constructions for *From Russia with Love*, Udell was heavily involved on *Goldfinger*. One of his initial assignments was to build a ramp for the out-of-control Mercedes Benz that goes over a cliff and slams into a side of the Auric Enterprises building.

"We went to the Harefield Quarry for the stunt," Udell remembered, "and we discovered that the only place we could build the ramp was over a pig sty. So that's exactly where we built it. While John Stears and his crew filled the car with petrol jelly, all of these pigs were constantly bleating."

Six months before *Goldfinger* began principal photography, Udell was planting an avenue of trees that would eventually lead up to the Fort Knox replica that was built full-scale in the Black Park woodland next to the studio. The trees were identical to ones photographed during a helicopter tour of the actual Fort Knox in Kentucky. Udell also remembered the difficulty of maneuvering the one-ton vault door from the interior stage to the outdoor set, where U.S. troops battled Goldfinger's Grand Slam Task Force.

For *Thunderball*, Udell and his team journeyed to a Royal Air Force base in Alton, where a plaster mold was made of a full-scale Vulcan bomber. The mold was then taken to the Bahamas, where the bomber was constructed out of fiberglass and then lowered into the Caribbean off Clifton Pier. A separate bomb bay was constructed and photographed from underneath when Bond explored the wreck of the bomber.

Between February and May 1965, Udell was consumed by the *Thunderball* project—one of the most expensive films ever based at Pinewood. But even *Thunderball* paled beside *You Only Live Twice*, which involved the construction of a full-scale rocket base within the cone of an extinct volcano (See VOLCANO ROCKET BASE). Udell retired from Pinewood Studios in August 1976, a month before principal photography began on *The Spy Who Loved Me*.

UK 40401 The number on James Bond's (SEAN CONNERY) Playboy Club membership card in *Diamonds Are Forever*. Tiffany Case (JILL ST. JOHN) finds the card on the body of Peter Franks (JOE ROBINSON) after Bond switches their billfolds. As a result, Tiffany says, "You've just killed James Bond."

UNCLE Q's (DESMOND LLEWELYN) cover in Isthmus City in *Licence to Kill*. While supplying Bond (TIMOTHY DALTON) with illegal weaponry—007 is a rogue agent—Q also plays 007's chauffeur.

UNDERDOWN, EDWARD (1908–   ) British actor who portrayed Sir John, the Air Vice Marshall in *Thunderball*.

"UNDERNEATH THE MANGO TREE" In capturing the romantic mood of the tropics, "Underneath the Mango Tree" is one of the series's best songs. In the absence of a title song, this is really the theme of *Dr. No*. It's sung at various times by the Byron Lee Band at Puss-Feller's Club and by Honey Ryder (URSULA ANDRESS) and Bond (SEAN CONNERY) on the beach at Crab Key—the only time that Connery ever sings in the series. And a breezy instrumental version plays at the end of the movie.

UNDER THE PRESIDENT'S FEET The site in Washington, D.C., where S.P.E.C.T.R.E. plants one of the hijacked nuclear warheads in *Never Say Never Again*. It's recovered in time, thanks to James Bond (SEAN CONNERY), who also helps recover the second bomb in the Tears of Allah archaeological dig.

UNDERWATER BATTLE The huge action-filled concluding sequence in *Thunderball*. It was filmed in segments over a period of six days in the waters off Nassau, with 60 divers from the Miami-based Ivan Tors unit. One important sequence was filmed around a sunken U.S. Navy landing craft where Bond (SEAN CONNERY) lures two S.P.E.C.T.R.E. frogmen to their deaths. The rest of the battle spread itself across the Nassau seascape.

Filming an underwater war was, at times, almost too realistic. In one scene, Bond flicks a switch on his trick backpack and fires an explosive spear at an enemy diver. In the actual sequence, Courtney Brown, portraying the S.P.E.C.T.R.E. diver, was given a piece of lead explosive head to place on the outside of his wet suit. When the spear was fired—on a line—it was designed to strike the lead and create an underwater explosion of black powder. Unfortunately, Brown placed the lead underneath his wet suit instead so that when the spear hit, it blew a hole right through the diver's wet suit, severely burning his skin and landing him in St. Margaret's Hospital.

Bond's jet-propelled diving backpack—designed by Jordan Klein—which gives him super underwater speed, was actually a prop. A piano wire attached to a speedboat propelled Bond's double, Frank Cousins, through the water. If Cousins had turned his face at any moment, the force of being pulled at such speed would have torn the diver's mask from his face.

Most of the battle took place in 20 feet of water off Clifton Pier. Into the battle, the producers threw every piece of equipment in the *Thunderball* arsenal, including the S.P.E.C.T.R.E. bomb sled, the scooters, and the scores of CO_2 guns that sprayed a lethal underwater rain of spears among the fighting ranks. With the free-swimming, orange-suited Aqua-paras attacking the black-suited enemy underwater flotilla, it was almost a return to the Indians versus the covered wagon fights of the Old West. Seemingly invincible behind their spear-firing sleds, Largo's frogmen are systematically overwhelmed in hand-to-hand combat by Bond and his Aqua-paras.

"The underwater sequences, especially the final battle, were too long," recalled Terence Young, who became disenchanted with *Thunderball* during its final weeks of shooting. "The trouble was that people kept wondering what the hell was going on. Of all the Bond films, *Thunderball* was the only one where the audience had at least a half hour of meditation during those long underwater sequences. People began to ask questions that we didn't want them to ask until they were on their way home.

"I thought that the first underwater scenes were delightful, especially the opening sequence in which the *Disco Volante* sends out her divers to recover the hijacked atomic bombs. But in the later fight sequences, we kept repeating ourselves. There was nothing you could do except fire a spear at somebody, pull his mask off, or cut his lifeline. So when you've done that stuff 45 times, the audience is naturally going to clamor for something new."

UNDERWATER HATCH An important feature of the *Disco Volante* yacht in *Thunderball*. Employing an army of frogmen in Nassau, Largo (ADOLFO CELI) uses the hatch to move the hijacked A-bombs from the wrecked NATO bomber to their underwater storage cave. Later, the *Disco Volante* transports one of the weapons to a wreck off Miami's Buoy Point.

UNDERWATER INFRARED CAMERA One of the gadgets supplied to 007 (SEAN CONNERY) by Q (DESMOND LLEWELYN) in *Thunderball*. Bond uses it to take pictures of the *Disco Volante*'s underwater hatch. It takes eight pictures in rapid succession.

UNITED ARTISTS Motion-picture production and distribution company founded in 1919 by Mary Pickford, Douglas Fairbanks, Charlie Chaplin, and D. W. Griffith. Since 1962, it has released every James Bond film except *Casino Royale* (Columbia Pictures) and *Never Say Never Again* (Warner Brothers).

UNITED NATIONS Site of a British agent's assassination in *Live and Let Die*. It's the first of three killings performed by the agents of island diplomat and drug smuggler Dr. Kananga (YAPHET KOTTO). At the UN, Dawes, the agent, is killed when someone sabotages his translation headset, sending a lethal high-pitched tone to his brain.

UNITED STATES Fourth target selected in the Domination video-game battle between Largo (KLAUS MARIA BRANDAUER) and James Bond (SEAN CONNERY) in *Never Say Never Again*. It's worth $42,000, and Largo wins, sending a powerful shock to Bond, which topples him to the floor. Getting to his feet, Bond challenges his nemesis to one more game for the rest of the world. *See* DOMINATION.

UNIT 25 Code name of the San Monique motorcycle and automobile units in Kananga's (YAPHET KOTTO) employ in *Live and Let Die*. They eventually chase Bond (ROGER MOORE) and Solitaire (JANE SEYMOUR), who have commandeered an old British double-decker bus.

UNIVERSAL STUDIOS BACK LOT Actual site of the madcap parking-lot car chase in *Diamonds Are Forever*. It simulated the parking lot of downtown Las Vegas's Mint Hotel.

UNIVEX The abbreviation for Universal Exports, used by Bond (SEAN CONNERY) when he calls Miss Moneypenny (LOIS MAXWELL) from the car phone in his Bentley, in *From Russia with Love*.

U.S. NAVY AQUA-PARAS Largo's (ADOLFO CELI) nemesis in the final underwater battle in *Thunderball*. Outmanned and outgunned by the superior S.P.E.C.T.R.E. force of black-suited frogmen, the orange-suited Aqua-paras hold their own until Bond (SEAN CONNERY) arrives to even the odds.

V

VA-402 Identification number of the *St. Georges*, a British surveillance and communications ship disguised as a Greek fishing trawler in *For Your Eyes Only*. Carrying the registry of Valletta, a Greek city, the *St. Georges* is sunk when her fishing nets snare a World War II mine.

VANDENBERG U.S. Air Force base in California that is the launch site for Ernst Stavro Blofeld's (CHARLES GRAY) laser satellite in *Diamonds Are Forever*. The same base is also the launch site for a shuttle carrying U.S. space forces in *Moonraker*. Led by Colonel Scott (MICHAEL MARSHALL), the U.S. team is headed for a pitched battle on Hugo Drax's (MICHEL LONSDALE) space station.

VANNER, SUE British actress who portrayed the Austrian log-cabin girl who betrays 007 (ROGER MOORE) to the KGB in the teaser for *The Spy Who Loved Me*.

VAN NUTTER, RIK Handsome, silver-haired American actor who portrayed Felix Leiter in *Thunderball*. Van Nutter (pronounced VAN NOOTER) was married to actress Anita

Felix Leiter (RIK VAN NUTTER), Paula Caplan (MARTINE BESWICK), and James Bond (SEAN CONNERY) prepare to meet Q in *Thunderball*. (Rex Features Ltd./RDR Productions)

Ekberg in the early 1960s, and it was through the couple's friendship with Albert and Dana Broccoli that Van Nutter was first considered for the role of Leiter.

"We were having one of those immense Italian dinners in London with Cubby and Dana," recalled Van Nutter, "when Cubby suddenly came out and said that I looked just like Felix Leiter. Now, I had read all of the Bond books, and I knew that Felix had straw-colored hair, blue eyes, and long legs. So I fit the bill physically. I later met Terence Young, who tested me with some of the Bond girls. The tests worked out fine, and I made plans to travel to Nassau that spring" (1965).

VARGAS Lean, sullen S.P.E.C.T.R.E. henchman, portrayed by Philip Locke, in *Thunderball*. According to his boss, Emilio Largo (ADOLFO CELI), Vargas is a passionless man who doesn't drink, doesn't smoke, and doesn't make love. What does Vargas do? He's a killer, pure and simple. Agent 007 (SEAN CONNERY) disposes of him on Love Beach with a well-aimed shot from his CO_2 speargun.

VARIG FLIGHT 128 Jaws's (RICHARD KIEL) airline flight to Rio de Janeiro in *Moonraker*. In a humorous moment, his cobalt-steel teeth trigger the flight's security device. Jaws smiles at the attendant and moves on.

VASSAR In *Moonraker*, it's where Dr. Holly Goodhead (LOIS CHILES) tells James Bond (ROGER MOORE) she went to college. It's also where she learned to fight.

VAVRA The gypsy leader portrayed by Francis de Wolff, in *From Russia with Love*. Bond (SEAN CONNERY) saves his life when Bulgar assassins attack the Gypsy camp. For that effort, Vavra bestows the honor of "son" on 007. *See* DE WOLFF, FRANCIS.

VENICE Site of the International Grandmasters Chess Championship between Kronsteen (VLADEK SHEYBAL) and McAdams (PETER MADDEN) in *From Russia with Love*. It's also the ultimate destination for Bond (SEAN CONNERY) and Tanya (DANIELA BIANCHI) when they leave Illystria in a stolen motorboat.

VENINI GLASS An Italian subsidiary of Drax Enterprises Corporation in *Moonraker*, its Venice laboratory is testing a nerve gas that can destroy all human life on the planet Earth.

Tipped off by documents he finds at Drax's (MICHEL LONSDALE) California estate, Bond (ROGER MOORE) breaks into the facility by using the five-note *Close Encounters of the Third Kind* entry code, discovers the experiments, and actually uses the nerve gas on the scientists. Later, hoping to expose the facility to M (BERNARD LEE) and Freddie Gray (GEOFFREY KEEN), Bond discovers that Drax has entirely changed the composition of the laboratory, turning it into a huge drawing room.

Venini Glass's public museum is also a setting in the film for a raucous fight between Bond and Chang (TOSHIRO SUGA). After disposing of Chang, who is thrown through an upper-story glass window, Bond finds additional clues that lead him to another Drax facility in Rio de Janeiro.

VENZ One of General Gogol's (WALTER GOTELL) KGB agents, portrayed by Dolph Lundgren, in *A View to a Kill*. Venz can be seen briefly at Max Zorin's (CHRISTOPHER WALKEN) private racecourse in France, where Gogol goes to chastise the industrialist for killing James Bond (ROGER MOORE) without KGB permission.

VERNON, GABOR Actor who portrayed Borchoi, the curator of Leningrad's Hermitage museum who exposes Lenkin's (PETER PORTEOUS) jewel forgeries in *Octopussy*. *See* BORCHOI.

VERNON, RICHARD (1907–) British character actor who portrayed the very intelligent and distinguished Colonel Smithers of the Bank of England in *Goldfinger*. Smithers briefs 007 (SEAN CONNERY) and M (BERNARD LEE) on Goldfinger's (GERT FROBE) legal and very illegal activities. Vernon was also the Hungarian speaker at the UN in *Live and Let Die*. *See* SMITHERS, COLONEL.

VICTORIA CROSS Britain's highest military honor, a bronze Maltese cross. According to *Casino Royale*, this cross was won by Sir

James Bond (DAVID NIVEN) at the Battle of Mafeking in the Boer War.

VIDA Gypsy woman, portrayed by Aliza Gur, who is involved in the celebrated girl fight with Zora (MARTINE BESWICK) in *From Russia with Love.*

VIEW TO A KILL, A (United Artists, 1985) ★ The 14th James Bond film produced by Albert R. Broccoli. U.S. release date: May 24, 1985. U.S. film rentals: $25.3 million. Running time: 131 minutes.

For some reason, after Broccoli had succeeded with *For Your Eyes Only* and *Octopussy,* which effectively followed the *From Russia with Love* formula, it was decided once again to return to the *Goldfinger* approach and create an outrageous fantasy. In many ways, *A View to a Kill* is a veritable remake of *Goldfinger.* And it self-destructs on so many levels that it makes a critical analysis difficult.

Let's start with the villain and his scheme. Max Zorin is a Goldfinger clone. He wants to corner the world market on microchips, instead of gold bullion. Microchips? The idea of creating an earthquake to destroy Silicon Valley, California, home of the microchip, was ridiculous. The earthquake was logical, considering its proximity to the very dangerous San Andreas Fault, but no one cares about microchips, no one cares about Silicon Valley, and thus no one cared about the plot.

In *Goldfinger,* Fort Knox was a much more understandable target. With a simple explanation uttered by Bond, the audience understood the danger to the free world if our gold supply were to be irradiated for 58 years. Max Zorin should have explained why his monopoly on microchips was so dangerous to the free world, but he never really does.

Interestingly, early in the film it's mentioned that Zorin has developed a chip that is impervious to an atomic explosion in outer space, which could neutralize the typical microchip and shut down every computer in England, including an early-warning system. That idea was never elaborated upon in the film and yet it

Zorin's goons try to stop a Bay Area protest in a scene cut from *A View to a Kill.* (San Francisco Chronicle).

was a far more interesting and plausible plot device.

Zorin himself, as portrayed by Christopher Walken, is bland and stupid. The sequence in which he and Scarpine machine-gun the Main Strike Mine crew was a case of literal overkill. As for Grace Jones, who played his superstrong henchwoman, May Day, she was just too androgynous for mainstream audiences. Like *Never Say Never Again*, *A View to a Kill* is another Bond movie with very little action. It's refreshing to see Patrick Macnee, but the entire sequence filmed in France at Zorin's estate was pointless and had nothing to do with the film's main plot, and it seems to go on forever. The teaser was well made, but once again a goofy musical score ruins an action sequence. The Beach Boys and James Bond just don't mix.

Tanya Roberts—a beautiful, sexy, and very photogenic actress— spends most of the film in conservatively cut formal dresses and coveralls—another miscalculation. The fire-truck chase through San Francisco is awful and belongs in a *Ghostbusters* movie, not a Bond film. The raging-fire sequence in San Francisco City Hall is suspenseful, but we've seen it many times before in other films, including *The Towering Inferno*.

The best part of *A View to a Kill* takes place in the Main Strike Mine and includes some excellent production-design work from Peter Lamont. The action sequences are fantastic. But didn't Steven Spielberg cover this same terrain in *Indiana Jones and the Temple of Doom*?

High point: John Barry's score, reminiscent of *Goldfinger*, which repeats instrumental elements of the catchy Duran Duran title song at key moments.

A VIEW TO A KILL CAST

James Bond ....Roger Moore
Max Zorin ....Christopher Walken
Stacey Sutton ....Tanya Roberts
May Day ....Grace Jones
Sir Godfrey Tibbett ....Patrick Macnee
Scarpine ....Patrick Bauchau
Chuck Lee.......................David Yip
Pola Ivanova....................Fiona Fullerton
Bob Conley ....Manning Redwood
Jenny Flex ....Alison Doody
Dr. Carl Mortner ....Willoughby Gray

Q.........................Desmond Llewelyn
M.........................Robert Brown
Miss Moneypenny ....Lois Maxwell
General Gogol ....Walter Gotell
Minister of Defense ....Geoffrey Keen
Achille Aubergine ....Jean Rougerie
W. G. Howe ....Daniel Benzali
Klotkoff....................Bogdan Kominowski
Pan Ho ....Papillon Soo Soo
Kimberley Jones ....Mary Stavin
Butterfly Act Compere ......Dominique Risbourg
Whistling Girl ....Carole Ashby
Taiwanese Tycoon ....Anthony Chin
Paris Taxi Driver.................Lucien Jerome
U.S. Police Captain ....Joe Flood
The Auctioneer ....Gerard Buhr
Venz ....Dolph Lundgren
Mine Foreman....................Tony Sibbald
O'Rourke......................Bill Ackridge
Guard No. 1 ....Ron Tarr
Guard No. 2 ....Taylor McAuley
Tycoon ....Peter Ensor
Helicopter Pilot ....Seva Novgorodtsev
The Girls ...Sian Adey-Jones, Samina Afzal, Celine Cawley, Nike Clark, Helen Clitherow, Maggie Defreitas, Gloria Douse, Caroline Hallett, Deborah Hanna, Josanne Haydon-Pearce, Ann Jackson, Terri Johns, Karen Loughlin, Angela Lyn, Patricia Martinez, Kim Ashfield Norton, Elke Ritschel, Lou-Anne Ronchi, Helen Smith, Jane Spencer, Paula Thomas, Mayako Torigai, Toni White

A VIEW TO A KILL CREW
Producers ..Albert R. Broccoli, Michael G. Wilson
Director ....John Glen
Screenplay by ....Richard Maibaum, Michael G. Wilson
Associate Producer ....Thomas Pevsner
Music by...........................John Barry
Title Song Performed by ....Duran Duran
Production Designer ....Peter Lamont
Main Title Designer ....Maurice Binder
Director of Photography ....Alan Hume
Second-Unit Director and Photographer....Arthur Wooster
Ski Sequence Director and Photographer ....Willy Bogner, Jr.
Costume Designer ....Emma Porteous
Casting ....Debbie McWilliams
Editor.........................Peter Davies
Sound Editor ....Colin Miller
Special Effects Supervisor........John Richardson

Roger Moore and the women of *A View to a Kill*, including, *left to right*, Jenny Flex, (ALISON DOODY), Pola Ivanova (FIONA FULLERTON) and Stacey Sutton (TANYA ROBERTS). (Express Newspapers, London)

Production Supervisor ....Anthony Waye
Production Managers Philip Kohler, Serge Touboul, Ned Kopp & Company, Leonhard Gmur, Jon Thor Hannesson
Unit Manager ....Iris Rose
Production Accountant..........Douglas Noakes
Assistant Director ....Gerry Gavigan
Camera Operator ....Michael Frift
Sound Recorder ....Derek Ball
Continuity ....June Randall
Electrical Supervisor ....John Tythe
Action-Sequences Arranger ....Martin Grace
Driving Stunts Arranger ....Remy Julienne
Art Director ....John Fenner
Set Decorator ....Crispian Sallis
Construction Manager..........Michael Redding
Makeup Supervisor ....George Frost
Hairdressing Supervisor ....Ramon Gow
Production Controller ......Reginald A. Barkshire
Director of Marketing.............Charles Juroe
Location Managers..Nick Daubeny, Agust Baldursson, Stefan Zucher, Jean-Marc Deschamps, Steph Bensman, Rory Enke
Second-Assistant Director ....Peter Bennett
Second-Unit Continuity ...Penny Daniels, Daphne Carr

Additional Assistant Directors ....Edi Hubschmid, Laurent Bregeat, Serge Menard, Terry Madden, Andrew Warren, Simon Haveland, Nick Heckstall-Smith, Barbara Broccoli
Location Accountants ..Hazel Crombie, Mauricette Boisard, Jane Meagher, Christl Kirchner
Production Coordinators ...May Capskis, Nathalie Farjon, Norma Garment, Sally Hayman, Maureen Murphy
Production Secretaries..Joanna Brown, Janine King, Doris Spriggs
U.S. Casting ....Jane Jenkins, Janet Hirshenson
Costume Supervisor ....Tiny Nicholls
Additional Wardrobe for Grace Jones ....Azzedine Alaia
Costumes Made by ......C. & G. Costumers Ltd.
Additional Art Directors ....Michael Lamont, Ken Court, Alan Tomkins, Serge Douy, Armin Ganz, Katharina Brunner
Assistant Art Directors ..James Morahan, Ted Ambrose, Michael Boone
Assistant Set Decorator ....Jillie Brown
Sketch Artists .....Roger Deer, Maciek Piotrowski
Production Buyer ....Ron Quelch
Scenic Artists .....Ernest Smith, Jacqueline Stears
Computer Effects............Ira Curtis Coleman

Boom Operator ....Ken Nightingall
Makeup . . ..Eric Allwright, Bunty Phillips
Hairdressers ....Vera Mitchell, Joan Carpenter
Special Effects ....John Morris, Joss Williams, Ken Morris, Andre Trielli, Larry Cavanaugh, Willy Neuner
Unit Publicist...................Geoff Freeman
Assistant Publicist.........Jennifer Collen-Smith
Stills ....Keith Hampshire, George Whitear
Property Master.................John Chisholm
Model Photography ....Leslie Dear
Second-Unit Camera Operator ...Malcolm Vinson, Robert Hillmann
Focus..............Simon Hume, Michael Evans
Front Projection .....Charles Staffell, Roy Moores
Camera Grips......Colin Manning, Ken Atherfold
Eiffel Tower ........................S.N.T.E.
Zorin's Stable ..Musee Vivant du Cheval, Chantilly
Whitewood House.....Dunsmuir House, Oakland
Chateau Flowers ....Rene Veyrat
Seine Speedboats ....Chantiers Glastron Rocca
Cranes.....................Lee Lifting Services
Ultraviolet Lighting.................Thorn EMI
Cameras and Binoculars ....Nikon UK Limited
Special Properties............The Sharper Image
Iceland Advisers.........................
Iceland Breakthrough, Tony Escritt
Travel and Transport ....Renown Freight Ltd., The Travel Company, D & D International Locations Ltd., Location Facilities
Sound Effects ....Jean-Pierre Lelong
Additional Editors ....John S. Smith, Henry Richardson
Assistant Editor ....John Nuth
Dubbing Editors ..Jack Knight, Nigel Galtt, Stanley Fiferman
Music Mixer ....Dick Lewzey
Music Editor ....Alan Killick
Rerecording Mixers ....Graham Hartstone, John Hayward
Stunt Team Supervisors ....Jim Arnett, Bob Simmons, Claude Carliez
Stunt Team ...Jason White, Bill Weston, Pat Banta, Mike Runyard, Elaine Ford, Tracey Eddon, Doug Robinson
Driving Team ....Michel Julienne, Christian Bonnichon, Jean-Claude Bonnichon, Robert Blasco, Dominique Julienne, Claude Lagniez, Jean-Claude Houbart
Eiffel Tower Jump ....B. J. Worth
Skyship 500 ....Nicholas T. Bennett
Helicopters....Helicopter Hire, Aerospatiale, Helisweiss, Helifrance, Castle Air

Pilots ....Marc Wolff, Rick Holley, Chuck Tamburro, Robert Liechti, Gerry Crayson
Camera ....David Butler, Peter Allwork, Doug Milsome
Horse Team ....Oliver Victor-Thomas, Marcel Riou, Mario Luraschi, Anthony Fairbairn, Christian de Lagarde, Francois Nadal, Brian Bowes
Snow Team ..Peter Rohe, Steven Link, John Eaves, Joe Brown, Thomas Simms, Andrea Florineth
Production Company ....Eon Productions
Distribution Company ....United Artists

A VIEW TO A KILL COMPETITION
Competitive films in release when A View to a Kill opened in Los Angeles on May 24, 1985:
Rambo: First Blood Part II
Mask
Brewster's Millions
Lost in America
Beverly Hills Cop
Ladyhawke
Witness
Amadeus
Gotcha
Hellhole
The Littles

VIJAY Amiable British Secret Service agent based in Udaipur, India, portrayed by professional tennis player Vijay Amritraj in Octopussy. Vijay's posing as a snake charmer when he meets Bond (ROGER MOORE) in a Udaipur street market. His rendition of the James Bond theme (the Bond movies have come a long way, haven't they?) gets Bond's attention.

Vijay hates snakes and prefers his other, more natural cover as a tennis pro at Kamal Khan's (LOUIS JOURDAN) resort club. His mean backhand comes in handy when Gobinda (KABIR BEDI) and his men attack Bond's scooter in the streets of Udaipur. When 007 infiltrates Octopussy's (MAUD ADAMS) island in the middle of Lake Pichola, Vijay stays behind on the mainland to keep watch. Unfortunately, he's jumped by local thugs and killed by the man with the horrifying buzz-saw yo-yo.

VILLAINS AND HENCHMEN The deadly hoods' gallery that has been the Bond series's hallmark. They include the following:

BOND BAD GUYS

FILM	NAME/ACTOR	MANNER OF DEATH
"Casino Royale" (TV)	Le Chiffre/Peter Lorre	Shot
Dr. No	Dr. No/Joseph Wiseman	Drowned
	Professor Dent/ Anthony Dawson	Shot
	Mr. Jones/ Reggie Carter	Poisoned
From Russia with Love	Rosa Klebb/Lotte Lenya	Shot
	Kronsteen/Vladek Sheybal	Stabbed and Poisoned
	Red Grant/Robert Shaw	Strangled
	Morzeny/ Walter Gotell	Blown Up
Goldfinger	Goldfinger/Gert Frobe	Blown Out of a Jet Aircraft Window

FILM	NAME/ACTOR	MANNER OF DEATH
Goldfinger	Oddjob/Harold Sakata	Electrocuted
	Mr. Solo/Martin Benson	Shot and Crushed
Thunderball	Largo/Adolfo Celi	Speared
	Fiona/Luciana Paluzzi	Shot
	Vargas/Philip Locke	Speared
You Only Live Twice	Blofeld/Donald Pleasence	?
	Mr. Osato/Teru Shimada	Shot
	Helga Brandt/ Karin Dor	Eaten by Piranhas
Casino Royale (Film)	Dr. Noah/Woody Allen	Blown Up
	Agent Mimi/ Deborah Kerr	Joined a Convent
	Le Chiffre/Orson Welles	Blown Up
	Vesper Lynd/ Ursula Andress	Blown Up
On Her Majesty's Secret Service	Blofeld/Telly Savalas	Survives
	Irma Bunt/Ilse Steppat	Survives
Diamonds Are Forever	Blofeld/Charles Gray	?
	Mr. Wint/Bruce Glover	Blown Up
	Mr. Kidd/Putter Smith	Set Afire
	Saxby/Bruce Cabot	Shot
Live and Let Die	Kananga/Yaphet Kotto	Blown Up
	Tee Hee/Julius Harris	Thrown Out of a Train Window
	Whisper/Earl Jolly Brown	?
	Baron Samedi/ Geoffrey Holder	Survives
The Man with the Golden Gun	Scaramanga/ Christopher Lee	Shot
	Nick Nack/Herve Villechaize	Captured
	Hai Fat/Richard Loo	Shot
The Spy Who Loved Me	Stromberg/Curt Jurgens	Shot
	Jaws/Richard Kiel	Survives
	Sandor/Milton Reid	Pushed Off Building

The villains of *Licence to Kill, left to right,* Dario (BENICIO DEL TORO), Perez (ALEXJANDRO BRACHO), and Braun (GUY DE SAINT CYR). (Erik Hollander)

FILM	NAME/ACTOR	MANNER OF DEATH
Moonraker	Drax/Michel Lonsdale	Tossed into Outer Space
	Jaws/Richard Kiel	Survives
	Chang/Toshiro Suga	Tossed Off Building
For Your Eyes Only	Kristatos/Julian Glover	Knifed
	Locque/Michael Gothard	Pushed Off Cliff in His Car
	Kriegler/John Wyman	Tossed Out of a Window
	Gonzales/ Stefan Kalipha	Shot with a Crossbow
Octopussy	Kamal Khan/Louis Jourdan	Died in a Plane Crash
	Orlov/Steven Berkoff	Shot
	Gobinda/Kabir Bedi	Fell to His Death
	First Twin/David Meyer	Crushed
	Second Twin/ Tony Meyer	Knifed
Never Say Never Again	Largo/Klaus Maria Brandauer	Speared
	Fatima Blush/ Barbara Carrera	Blown Up
	Lippe/Pat Roach	Impaled
A View to a Kill	Max Zorin/ Christopher Walken	Fell to His Death
	May Day/Grace Jones	Blown Up
	Scarpine/Pat Bauchau	Blown Up
	Karl Mortner/ Willoughby Gray	Blown Up
The Living Daylights	Brad Whitaker/ Joe Don Baker	Crushed
	General Koskov/ Jeroen Krabbe	Captured
	Necros/Andreas Wisniewski	Fell to His Death
Licence to Kill	Sanchez/Robert Davi	Burnt to Death
	Milton Krest/ Anthony Zerbe	Blown Up
	Heller/Don Stroud	Impaled on a Forklift
	Joe Butcher/ Wayne Newton	Survives
	Dario/Benicio Del Toro	Shredded

VILLECHAIZE, HERVE (Paris, France, April 23, 1943–September 4, 1993) Three-

Herve Villechaize poses with a Playboy Bunny during luncheon activities at the James Bond Weekend held in Los Angeles in July 1981.

foot, nine-inch-tall French character actor who portrayed Scaramanga's (CHRISTOPHER LEE) servant, Nick Nack, in *The Man with the Golden Gun*. Villechaize is better known as Ricardo Montalban's partner on the popular U.S. television series "Fantasy Island."

VILLEFRANCHE-SUR-MER City on the French Riviera whose narrow streets played host to the motorcycle stunts in *Never Say Never Again*.

VILLIERS, JAMES (1930–) British character actor who portrayed Secret Service Chief of Staff Tanner in *For Your Eyes Only*. According to Freddie Gray (GEOFFREY KEEN), M was on leave in that film. In reality, actor Bernard Lee had died before the start of production, and Villiers was his temporary replacement until Robert Brown became the new M, on *Octopussy* in 1983.

VIRUS OMEGA A deadly germ-warfare virus that Ernst Stavro Blofeld (TELLY SAVALAS) plans to spread in *On Her Majesty's Secret Service*. Omega creates total infertility in plants and animals and can destroy whole strains forever throughout an entire continent. Blofeld calls it "epidemic sterility."

The virus will be spread by Blofeld's Angels of Death—a group of lovely international allergy patients who are given atomizers as Christmas presents, filled with the virus. Equipped with long-range radio transmitters, and brainwashed to receive a prearranged signal from Blofeld, the girls are programmed to destroy the agricultural and animal productivity of the entire world unless Blofeld gets his price—full pardon for past crimes and official acceptance of his claim to the Count de Bleuchamp title.

Before Blofeld's Alpine base is destroyed in a dawn assault by Marc Ange Draco's (GABRIELE FERZETTI) commandos, Bond (GEORGE LAZENBY) is able to photograph a map that pinpoints the location of Blofeld's angels, once again neutralizing a terrifying S.P.E.C.T.R.E. plot.

VN 75WB Identification number on Kamal Khan's (LOUIS JOURDAN) twin-engined Beechcraft getaway plane in *Octopussy*. Disabled in midflight by Bond (ROGER MOORE), the plane eventually crashes into a mountainside, killing the exiled Afghan prince. Bond and Octopussy (MAUD ADAMS) jump out in the nick of time.

V99060 Serial number on the enemy motorboat that chases James Bond (ROGER MOORE) through the Venice canals in *Moonraker*.

VODKA MARTINI What James Bond (SEAN CONNERY) orders on Maximillian Largo's (KLAUS MARIA BRANDAUER) yacht, the *Flying Saucer*, in *Never Say Never Again*.

VODKA ON THE ROCKS James Bond's (SEAN CONNERY) drink choice when he meets Domino (KIM BASINGER) at Maximillian Largo's (KLAUS MARIA BRANDAUER) charity ball in Nice, in *Never Say Never Again*.

VOLCANO ROCKET BASE Ernst Stavro Blofeld's (DONALD PLEASENCE) fortress in *You Only Live Twice*. It was designed and built full-size by production designer Ken Adam for $1 million. Hidden inside the cone of a dormant Japanese volcano, the base harbors the formidable *Intruder* rocket that is systematically robbing the U.S. and Soviet space programs of their manned space capsules.

Inside the hidden base, in addition to the rocket-firing platform, is a functional heliport, a closing steel curtain that covers the entire cone of the volcano and is camouflaged as a crater lake from the outside, a monorail that transports personnel and equipment throughout the complex, numerous working elevators and cranes, and a labyrinth of stairways and catwalks that ring the fortress.

Remembered Adam, "It was the first time that I had to build something that big. One of the problems on the Bond films is that if these big sets were written completely into the original screenplays, we could probably get away with building part of the sets full-size and faking the rest with models and matte paintings. But since we know only at the time of construction that the big finale or the big shootout takes place in the set, and nothing else, I've got to go for full size. We then work out the action as we go along.

"On *You Only Live Twice*, I designed the volcano rocket base, and then Lewis Gilbert and Roald Dahl came along and helped plan the actual movements within the set. Since, by the time we made *You Only Live Twice*, we had a liberal budget for the set, our main problem was logistics.

"You can't afford to make any mistakes on a set of this size, especially when you're using an enormous amount of structural steel. You have to consult with structural engineers, who calculate your stress factors. And you can't keep changing your mind like you often do on an interior set. We had to create accurate models, and these had to be followed to a T. And when you work with steel, it has to be ordered three months ahead of time."

In January 1967, the *Los Angeles Times* published a few of Adam's more interesting statistics. In constructing the volcano rocket base, his team used 200 miles of tubular steel, more than 700 tons of structural steel, 200 tons of plasterwork, 8,000 railway ties for the set's working monorail, and more than 250,000 square yards of canvas to protect the set from

Observing the finished S.P.E.C.T.R.E. rocket base are, *left to right*, Lois Maxwell, Akiko Wakabayashi, Sean Connery, Karin Dor, and Mie Hama. (Express Newspapers, London)

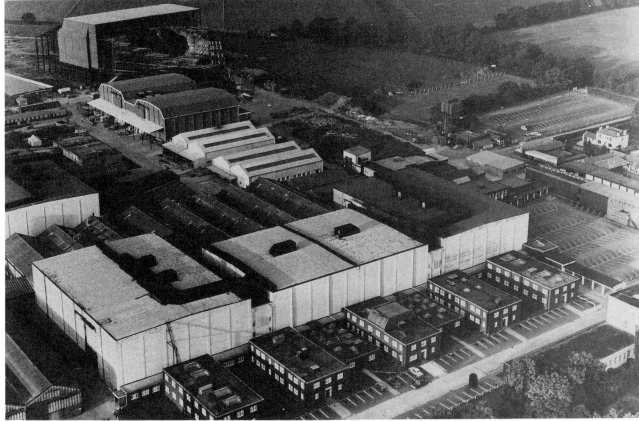

Aerial view of the volcano rocket base's construction phase at Pinewood. (Ronnie Udell Collection)

The finished product, a true miracle of movie engineering and design skill. (Ronnie Udell Collection)

the elements. Two hundred and fifty men worked on the project, and on May 11, 1966, the first of the steel foundations was completed. The finished set, built on the Pinewood Studios lot, was visible from the main London–Oxford Highway some three miles away.

"Such a set," said Adam, "represents both a dream and a nightmare in movie-making. The nightmare comes from suddenly realizing that you have designed something that has never been done before in films, and that it is bigger than any set ever used before. Many times I woke up in the middle of the night wondering whether the whole thing would work. Sometimes the best possible construction engineers can't solve your problems. They may be qualified to build an Empire State Building or an Eiffel Tower—buildings that follow normal construction techniques—but we had to construct a set for which there were no precedents.

"But this type of set is also a designer's dream. To be given the mandate to plan such a complicated structure is a challenge no artist could resist. And seeing your drawings and ideas taking shape and becoming reality in steel, concrete, and plaster is like watching your own child grow into Superman."

Adam, a veteran of many films in the Bond series, would go on to design the equally enormous supertanker interior—the so-called Jonah Set for The Spy Who Loved Me.

VOLPE, FIONA S.P.E.C.T.R.E.'s voluptuous, redheaded assassin who is a key element of the organization's NATO Project. She's portrayed in Thunderball by Italian actress Luciana Paluzzi.

Using her feminine charms, Volpe seduces handsome NATO aerial observer François Derval (PAUL STASSINO), whom she arranges to

Director Terence Young prepares the sequence in which Fiona Volpe gets rid of her motorcycle. First Assistant Director Gus Agosti stands by with the bullhorn. (John Stears Collection)

have murdered by his exact duplicate, a mercenary named Angelo Palazzi. After Palazzi hijacks a NATO bomber with nuclear bombs on board, Volpe's associate, Count Lippe (GUY DOLEMAN), who is keeping Derval's body at the Shrublands health clinic, initiates a personal vendetta against James Bond (SEAN CONNERY), who also happens to be at the clinic.

For Lippe's trouble, he's assassinated by a rocket from Fiona's motorcycle. She then joins Emilio Largo (ADOLFO CELI) in Nassau, where she meets Bond on the highway one night after 007's underwater ordeal in the harbor. Giving him a ride to his hotel in her Mustang, Fiona tries to intimidate him at high speed, but it doesn't work.

After kidnapping Bond's assistant, Paula Caplan (MARTINE BESWICK), who later

takes poison, Fiona steals into 007's hotel room during the Junkanoo celebration. Bond finds her relaxing in his bathtub. When she asks for something to "put on," he hands her some shoes. After their lovemaking, Fiona's S.P.E.C.T.R.E. goons arrive to take Bond away, but he later escapes into the crowd during the height of the Junkanoo Parade.

When Bond is wounded by one of her assistants, Fiona follows 007's trail of blood to the Kiss Kiss Club, where she asks him for a dance. While in her arms, 007 sees an assassin lurking in the shadows and whirls Fiona around at the last moment. She gets a bullet in the back.

In the *Thunderball* remake, *Never Say Never Again*, Fiona's lethal charm is inherited by the luscious Fatima Blush (BARBARA CARRERA) character.

Actress Luciana Paluzzi listens to director Terence Young while Sean Connery sits back and relaxes during shooting in Bond's bathroom in *Thunderball*. (Rex Features Ltd./RDR Productions)

VON SCHELL, CATHERINE Beautiful German actress who portrayed Nancy, the German allergy patient, in *On Her Majesty's Secret Service*.

Actress Catherine Von Schell portrayed Nancy, the allergy victim, in *On Her Majesty's Secret Service*. (C.C.A.)

VON SCHLAF, CONTESSA LISL Milos Columbo's (TOPOL) exotically beautiful mistress, portrayed by Cassandra Harris, in *For Your Eyes Only*. While dining with Aris Kristatos (JULIAN GLOVER) at Columbo's casino in Corfu, Bond (ROGER MOORE) sees Lisl for the first time. Kristatos identifies her as Columbo's mistress who often shills for the casino.

After arguing openly with Columbo and spilling wine in his face, Lisl leaves the casino, encouraging 007 to follow. Sensing a trap, Bond escorts Lisl to her beach house, where he discovers that her Austrian countess pedigree is a sham—she's from Liverpool. They make love, but in the morning while strolling on the beach, they're jumped by Locque (MICHAEL GOTHARD) and his dune-buggy-driving henchmen, who run over and kill Lisl.

VON SYDOW, MAX (Lund, Sweden, July 10, 1929–) Swedish character actor, and a former member of Ingmar Bergman's acting company, who portrayed Ernst Stavro Blofeld in *Never Say Never Again*. More a cameo part than an essential role in the film, von Sydow's Blofeld is an exquisitely mannered, bearded, aristocrat-type who presents S.P.E.C.T.R.E.'s typical blackmail demands in return for the stolen NATO cruise missiles. *See* BLOFELD, ERNST STAVRO.

VOSS, PHILIP British actor who portrayed the Sotheby's auctioneer, in *Octopussy*, who sells a jeweled Fabergé Easter egg to Kamal Khan (LOUIS JOURDAN) for a half-million pounds.

VULCAN The type of English jet bomber hijacked by S.P.E.C.T.R.E. mercenary Angelo Palazzi (PAUL STASSINO) during a NATO training flight in *Thunderball*. Cruising at 45,000 feet, the plane has on board two atomic bombs, MOS-type.

W

WAKABAYASHI, AKIKO Lovely Japanese actress who portrayed Aki, a Japanese Secret Service agent in *You Only Live Twice* who is poisoned by S.P.E.C.T.R.E. *See* AKI.

WALKEN, CHRISTOPHER (Astoria, New York, March 31, 1943–) American actor who portrayed psychotic industrialist Max Zorin in *A View to a Kill*. Walken, who has made a career out of playing quirky, often insane characters (he won a Supporting Actor Oscar for his Russian roulette–playing Vietnam veteran in *The Deer Hunter*), was perfectly cast as Zorin, the product of an abortive Nazi steroid experiment to enhance intelligence in newborns.

The blond (Walken had his hair bleached) East German KGB-operative-turned-French-industrialist was created very much in the image of Auric Goldfinger (GERT FROBE). Both characters were interested in monopolizing a commodity: Goldfinger, gold; Zorin, microchips.

The problem with Zorin is that he's lassoed to a boring scheme. Viewers could identify with Goldfinger's obsession. At one point, talking about his passion for gold, he refers to its enticing color and "divine" heaviness. It is familiar terrain. Microchip manufacturing, on the other hand, is very unfamiliar terrain. And yet microchips are the focus of Zorin's plan to destroy Silicon Valley, which, sadly, is no Fort Knox.

Still, Walken was comfortable playing the various sides of Zorin's personality: the well-heeled horse breeder, the macho lover and playmate of May Day (GRACE JONES), and the psychotic who enjoys mowing down his miners with a submachine gun. *See* ZORIN, MAX.

WALLACE, JULIE T. Comical British character actress who portrayed resourceful Rosika Miklos, a Czechoslovakian gasworks employee who helps James Bond (TIMOTHY DALTON) spirit defecting Russian General Georgi Koskov (JEROEN KRABBE) into Austria in *The Living Daylights*. Wallace also appeared with Timothy Dalton in the bittersweet *Hawks* (1989). *See* MIKLOS, ROSIKA.

WALLIS, WING COMMANDER KENNETH H. (Ely, Cambridge, England, 1916–) Retired RAF officer who designed and built Little Nellie, the auto-gyro that James Bond (SEAN CONNERY) flies in *You Only Live*

Aki (AKIKO WAKABAYASHI) and her Toyota 2000. (Loomis Dean/Camera Press, Globe Photos)

Twice. The tiny aircraft, designated Beagle-Wallis Auto-gyro Type WA-116, military serial number XR 943, Civil Registration G-ARZB, was originally designed for the British Army as a reconnaissance aircraft. *See* LITTLE NELLIE.

WALTHER PPK James Bond's patented handgun, which replaced his Beretta in *Dr. No.*

WARDER, FREDERICK British actor who portrayed doomed Agent 004 in the teaser for *The Living Daylights. See* 004.

WAR GAMES British Secret Service training exercises, one of which is conducted at the beginning of *Never Say Never Again* as Bond (SEAN CONNERY) attempts to rescue a kidnapped millionairess (WENDY LEECH) from fanatical revolutionaries. In a severe test of his agility and perseverance, Bond is sent into the South American jungle to overwhelm a garrison of well-armed killers. Everything appears genuine, down to the painful screams of the men Bond eliminates in his assault.

In actuality, the fighting is fixed and 007

Bond (SEAN CONNERY) prepares to take out a nest of terrorists in the war-game teaser for *Never Say Never Again.* (Taliafilm)

doesn't really kill anyone. Unaware that the millionairess has been brainwashed (à la Patty Hearst), 007 lowers his guard, and she stabs him in the arm with a retractable knife.

Evaluating the exercise on video, M (EDWARD FOX) is thoroughly unimpressed with Bond's ability to break into the enemy nest and downright disgusted that he forgot to check his rescue victim for brainwashing. The upshot is that Bond is sent to the Shrublands health clinic to once again purge his system of body toxins that are obviously slowing down his reflexes.

War games also play a part in *The Living Daylights* teaser. Assigned to penetrate a radar station on Gibraltar that's defended by S.A.S. troops, three double-0 agents—002 (GLYN BAKER), 004 (FREDERICK WARDER), and 007 (TIMOTHY DALTON)—skydive and parachute onto the island, where they each meet a different fate. Agent 002 is immediately captured by the S.A.S. 004 is assassinated by an imposter (CARL RIGG) working for arms dealer Brad Whitaker (JOE DON BAKER) and renegade Russian General Georgi Koskov (JEROEN KRABBE). And 007 exacts his own revenge by jumping on the assassin's land rover, riding it down the mountainside, and forcing it off a cliff—with Bond escaping out the back when he pulls the rip cord on his reserve parachute.

WATER Where James Bond movies invariably end, as shown in the following chart:

Bond Film Endings

Film	Location of Ending
Dr. No	the Caribbean, with Bond and Honey in a motorboat
From Russia with Love	a canal in Venice, with Bond and Tanya in a gondola
Thunderball	the Caribbean, with Bond and Domino in a life raft that is lifted out of the water by a Coast Guard B-17
You Only Live Twice	the Sea of Japan, with Bond and Kissy in a life raft that ends up on the deck of a British nuclear submarine
Diamonds Are Forever	on an ocean liner, where Bond and Tiffany dispose of assassins Mr. Wint and Mr. Kidd
The Man with the Golden Gun	on a Chinese junk with Bond and Mary Goodnight
The Spy Who Loved Me	in the Atlantic, with Bond and Major Amasova floating toward a British warship in the Atlantis escape pod
For Your Eyes Only	in the Aegean, with Bond and Melina diving off the Havelock yacht
Octopussy	on India's Lake Pichola, down which Octopussy's barge floats, while Bond and she make love
Never Say Never Again	in a Nassau Jacuzzi with Bond and Domino
A View to a Kill	above San Francisco Bay, where Bond and Stacey prepare to descend from the top of the Golden Gate Bridge
Licence to Kill	in Sanchez's indoor pool with Bond and Pam Bouvier

WATERLOO Historic land battle of the Napoleonic wars, a miniature version of which is the final resting place for a very dead Brad Whitaker (JOE DON BAKER) in *The Living Daylights*. See WHITAKER, BRAD.

WATTIS, RICHARD (1912–1975) Bespectacled British character actor who portrayed a British army officer involved in the auction of compromising photographs at Mata Hari's dance and spy school in *Casino Royale*.

WAVEKREST Marine research vessel, 155 feet long, owned by drug runner Milton Krest (ANTHONY ZERBE) in *Licence to Kill*. Like the *Disco Volante* in *Thunderball*, the *Wavekrest* is the base of operations for a number of Krest's illegal underwater drug-smuggling activities. Both the *Shark Hunter II* minisub and the *Reef Hunter* remote-control underwater transport are housed inside the *Wavekrest*.

The *Wavekrest* also becomes the pawn in James Bond's (TIMOTHY DALTON) plot to destroy Franz Sanchez (ROBERT DAVI) and his organization from within. Having destroyed a huge cocaine shipment headed for the *Wavekrest*, and stealing $4.9 million of drug loot that was supposed to be headed back to Sanchez, Bond and Pam Bouvier (CAREY LOWELL) plot to destroy Krest's relationship with his drug lord.

Impersonating the Isthmus City harbor pilot, Pam takes command of the *Wavekrest* and expertly rams it into the dock. The distraction gives Bond time to plant the $4.9 million in the *Wavekrest*'s own decompression chamber. To Krest's astonishment, Sanchez finds the pile of cash. Having already heard from 007 that there's a traitor in his midst, Sanchez orders Krest thrown into the decompression chamber, where, à la Dr. Kananga (YAPHET KOTTO) in *Live and Let Die*, he super-inflates and explodes.

"What do we do with the cash?" asks one of Sanchez's men. Straight-faced, Sanchez replies, "Launder it." *Note*: In real life, the *Wavekrest* is the *J. W. Powell*, an oil company supply boat that was turned into a research vessel now owned by Perry Oceanographics of Florida.

WAVEKREST MARINE RESEARCH

Key West–based marine biological research entity run by Milton Krest (ANTHONY ZERBE) in *Licence to Kill*. Although their genetic research into ocean life forms is supposed to help alleviate the Third World's hunger problem, Krest is really just another drug runner, working for Franz Sanchez (ROBERT DAVI).

Operating with a fleet of smuggling vessels and aircraft, Wavekrest is Sanchez's primary drug distribution outlet in North America. Escaping from Drug Enforcement Administration units, Sanchez holes up in the Wavekrest warehouse in Key West, where he orders captured CIA agent Felix Leiter (DAVID HEDISON) thrown into a shark pen. Thanks to revenge-seeking James Bond (TIMOTHY DALTON), the same pen later claims the life of traitorous DEA agent Killifer (EVERETT MCGILL).

WAYBORN, KRISTINA

Swedish beauty who portrayed Magda, the circus performer, pickpocket, and Girl Friday in *Octopussy*. Ac-

Circus hijinks with Roger Moore and Kristina Wayborn. (Express Newspapers, London)

cording to Graham Rye in his book *The James Bond Girls*, Wayborn was born on a small island in the Baltic Sea where she was a Swedish track champion. Prior to her movie career, she led an adventurous life as a race-car driver, jockey, horse and animal trainer, and clothes designer. Her break into acting came when producer David Wolper chose her to play the young Greta Garbo in "The Silent Lovers" segment of his 1980 *Moviola* miniseries. *See* MAGDA.

WAYNE, DR. Physical therapist Patricia Fearing's (MOLLY PETERS) boss at the Shrublands health clinic in *Thunderball*. We never meet Wayne, but he's the man that could fire Fearing if Bond (SEAN CONNERY) reports a malfunction in the clinic's motorized traction table (actually, it was sabotaged by S.P.E.C.T.R.E.).

WAYNE, USS American nuclear submarine that is the third and last sub captured by megalomaniac Karl Stromberg's (CURT JURGENS) supertanker in *The Spy Who Loved Me*.

Captained by Commander Carter (SHANE RIMMER), the sub is left behind when the redesignated Stromberg No. 1 and Stromberg No. 2 nuclear subs leave on their apocalyptic mission. When Bond (ROGER MOORE) leads an eventually successful attack on the *Liparus*'s crew and command center, the surviving submariners board the *Wayne*, which escapes from the doomed supertanker.

W.E.B.S. Miami Beach, Florida, radio station broadcasting during Bond's (SEAN CONNERY) bed play with Jill Masterson (SHIRLEY EATON) in *Goldfinger*. According to their news report, "the president was entirely satisfied."

"WE HAVE ALL THE TIME IN THE WORLD" Wonderful ballad sung by Louis Armstrong in *On Her Majesty's Secret Service*. Although it should have been the title tune, producers Albert R. Broccoli and Harry Saltzman opted for a faster-paced instrumental theme from John Barry instead. Instrumental title themes are uncommon in the series, having been featured in only three films: *Dr. No* (the end of which features the Byron Lee vocal tune "Three Blind Mice"), *From Russia with Love*

(Matt Munro's vocal was featured at the end of the film), and *On Her Majesty's Secret Service*.

W-80 Thermonuclear warheads inserted in the cruise missiles that S.P.E.C.T.R.E. hijacks in *Never Say Never Again*. The switch is accomplished when U.S. Air Force Captain Jack Petachi (GAVAN O'HERLIHY) tricks a government security device with an implanted cornea that has been designed to duplicate the eye print of the president of the United States. With "presidential" authorization, the nuclear devices replace the dummy warheads normally used in NATO training exercises.

S.P.E.C.T.R.E. places one of the hijacked warheads beneath the White House in Washington, D.C. The other is buried in the Tears of Allah archaeological dig in the Middle East, close to a huge oil field. Thanks to James Bond (SEAN CONNERY), both warheads are recovered before they detonate.

WEISLING FOUNDRY A gold-smelting facility in Essen, Germany, where 600 ingots were created by the Nazis in 1940. One of these gold bars, recovered from the bottom of Lake Topliz in Austria's Salz-Kammergut region, becomes the prize in a high-stakes golf match between 007 (SEAN CONNERY) and Auric Goldfinger (GERT FROBE).

WELCH, RAQUEL (September 5, 1940–) (real name, Raquel Tejada) Curvaceous American sex symbol of the late 1960s who was about to be signed to play Domino in *Thunderball* when Twentieth Century Fox film executive Richard Zanuck, with the consent of Cubby Broccoli, won her over to his *Fantastic Voyage* (1966) project instead. Ironically, in the latter film, her debut in a tight wet suit was considered comparable to bikini-clad Ursula Andress's introduction in *Dr. No*. Broccoli had discovered Welch on the cover of the October 1964 edition of *Life* magazine.

"WELCOME TO FORT KNOX, GENERAL RUSSHON" Sign on a hangar wall at Fort Knox during Operation Rockabye Baby in *Goldfinger*. It was actually an inside reference to the film company's military liaison, Charles Russhon, who had helped secure cooperation with local U.S. Army authorities. *See* RUS-SHON, CHARLES JOSEPH ANTHONY "RUSH."

"WELCOME TO MIAMI BEACH" Promotional banner trailing a single-engine plane above the Fontainebleau Hotel in *Goldfinger*. This sequence, which features a smart, brassy uptempo score by John Barry, immediately follows the Shirley Bassey title song.

WELLES, ORSON (Kenosha, Wisconsin, May 6, 1915–October 10, 1985) Avant-garde American writer/director/producer/actor who portrayed Soviet masterspy Le Chiffre in the *Casino Royale* spoof. Well known for his 1938 Halloween "War of the Worlds" radio broadcast, which caused panic along the eastern seaboard of the United States, Welles's own film career started off with a bang in 1941 with his Academy Award–winning film *Citizen Kane*, but he never quite lived up to that promising start. *See* CHIFFRE, LE.

"WE'LL HEAD HIM OFF AT THE PRECIPICE!" Cornball dialogue line uttered straight-faced by Ernst Stavro Blofeld (TELLY SAVALAS) while chasing James Bond (GEORGE LAZENBY) and Tracy (DIANA RIGG) through Switzerland in *On Her Majesty's Secret Service*. Moments like this one reinforced the fact that Savalas was probably too American to play Blofeld.

WELLS, JOHN British comic actor who portrayed Fordise, Q's (GEOFFREY BAYLDON) assistant, in the *Casino Royale* spoof. Wells also portrayed Margaret Thatcher's (JANET BROWN) husband, Denis, in a humorous sequence at the end of *For Your Eyes Only*.

"WE'LL TAKE MORE CARE OF YOU" Slogan on a British Airways billboard in the mountains above Rio, in *Moonraker*. During a fight inside an enemy ambulance, Bond (ROGER MOORE) kicks one of his captors out of the car and through the mouth of the billboard's stewardess, a spokesperson for the airlines.

WERICH, JAN Czechoslovakian actor who was signed to play Ernst Stavro Blofeld in *You Only Live Twice*. Forced to withdraw from the film due to illness, he was replaced by Donald Pleasence.

WESTERLY The direction in which the wind is blowing when Champagne Section's Piper Cherokee monoplanes prepare to spray what they think is Delta Nine nerve gas over Fort Knox, in *Goldfinger*.

WESTON, PAUL British stunt supervisor who started as a stuntman on *The Man with the Golden Gun*, *The Spy Who Loved Me*, and *Moonraker*, and graduated to become a stunt supervisor on *Octopussy*, *The Living Daylights*, and *Licence to Kill*. On *Spy*, Weston worked on the Jonah Set, taking a high fall off a gantry and into the docking bay. On *Moonraker*, he doubled actor Richard Kiel during the incredible 15-foot jump from one cable car to another.

WETBIKE Water motorcycle introduced to international film audiences in *The Spy Who Loved Me*. Bond (ROGER MOORE) uses one to go from the USS *Wayne* to Stromberg's (CURT

British comedian John Wells portrayed Margaret Thatcher's husband in *For Your Eyes Only*. (Michael Whitehall, Ltd.)

JURGENS) Atlantis base. This recreational vehicle, invented by Nelson Tyler, was supplied to the production by Arctic Enterprises of Minnesota.

WET NELLIE Nickname given to the Lotus Esprit submarine car in *The Spy Who Loved Me*. It was a reference to Little Nellie, the auto-gyro from *You Only Live Twice*. *See* LOTUS ESPRIT SUBMARINE CAR.

"WHAT A VIEW!" Comment uttered by May Day (GRACE JONES) when Max Zorin's (CHRISTOPHER WALKEN) blimp arrives above San Francisco in *A View to a Kill*. Zorin's appropriate reply is, "To a kill."

"WHAT HAPPENED?" Original line spoken by the construction worker who observes the destruction of the enemy hearse in *Dr. No*. Director Terence Young changed the dialogue in post-production to "How did it happen?"

"WHAT'S NEW, PUSSYCAT?" Theme music played when Mata Bond (JOANNA PETTET) opens an East Berlin manhole cover in *Casino Royale*.

WHEATLEY, THOMAS British actor who portrayed Saunders, the British Secret Service section chief in Austria who helps James Bond (TIMOTHY DALTON), in *The Living Daylights*. *See* SAUNDERS.

WHISPER Extremely soft-spoken, portly assassin employed by Kananga (YAPHET KOTTO) in *Live and Let Die* and portrayed by Earl Jolly Brown. Whisper is the driver of the white Cadillac "pimpmobile" that kills Bond's (ROGER MOORE) CIA chauffeur (JOIE CHITWOOD) in New York City.

Later, on San Monique, Whisper impersonates a waiter who delivers champagne and threats to Bond's hotel room. In the film's conclusion, Whisper gets into a fight with Bond and is pushed into a drug-ferrying metal canister.

WHISTLER, MRS. Kindly teacher-turned-diamonds-smuggler, portrayed by Margaret Lacey, in *Diamonds Are Forever*. She's bumped off by Mr. Wint (BRUCE GLOVER) and Mr. Kidd

(PUTTER SMITH), the homosexual assassins working for Ernst Stavro Blofeld (CHARLES GRAY). They dump her body into an Amsterdam canal. Before she dies, she delivers a huge diamond cache to the apartment of Tiffany Case (JILL ST. JOHN).

WHITAKER, BRAD Smug international arms dealer and military history buff, portrayed by Joe Don Baker, who joins forces with a renegade Russian general (JEROEN KRABBE) to perpetrate a huge opium-for-diamonds deal in *The Living Daylights*.

Based in Tangier, Whitaker's mansion houses a virtual museum of waxed military figures (Hitler, Napoleon, Attila, Caesar), toy-soldier dioramas, and ancient weaponry. It also houses a devil's cache of the newest weapons, all displayed in drawers operated electronically by a series of remote controls.

Whitaker has made a huge arms deal with the Russians, who have given him a $50 million advance. However, instead of delivering the weapons in quantity to the Soviet Union, Whitaker and his partner, General Georgi Koskov, have taken the advance and converted it into diamonds, which they use to purchase a huge heroin shipment from the Snow Leopard Brotherhood of Afghanistan.

To help their cause, the two partners convince British Intelligence that KGB Chief General Leonid Pushkin (JOHN RHYS-DAVIES), who has replaced General Gogol (WALTER GOTELL), is behind a rash of killings that have targeted British agents. A repeated clue—the words "Smiert Spionam," Russian for "Death to Spies"—is found on or near the bodies of the dead agents.

James Bond (TIMOTHY DALTON) doesn't trust the defecting Koskov, who is briefly housed in an English safe house before he's recaptured by the KGB—actually Koskov's own team. So, when M (ROBERT BROWN) orders him to kill Pushkin, Bond hesitates, eventually giving the KGB chief a chance to prove himself. Together, Pushkin and Bond lay their own trap for Koskov and Whitaker, faking Bond's sniper-shooting of Pushkin the following day.

Thinking that the KGB is now out of the way, Koskov captures Bond and lovely Czechoslovakian cellist Kara Milovy (MARYAM

D'ABO) and takes them with him to a Russian air force base in Afghanistan. Bond foils the drug deal, destroying a cargo plane filled with raw opium, and returns to Tangier to deal with Whitaker.

Helped by Felix Leiter (JOHN TERRY), who has kept a close surveillance on the house, Bond breaks in and engages in a fierce gun battle with Whitaker, who has an inexhaustible supply of high-tech weapons. Bond's trick key-chain wins the day by exploding next to Whitaker. He's killed by a falling bust of Wellington that smashes the arms dealer against a display case depicting the Battle of Waterloo. *See* BAKER, JOE DON.

WHITE CAT, THE The mascot of S.P.E.C.T.R.E. Chief Ernst Stavro Blofeld throughout the James Bond series. Introduced in *From Russia with Love*, it sits on the lap of Blofeld, whose face we never see. (Anthony Dawson was the actor; Eric Pohlmann provided the voice.) After explaining to Colonel Rosa Klebb (LOTTE LENYA) the analogy of the Siamese fighting fish, Blofeld hands one of the dead fish to the cat, who chews it gratefully.

The cat returns in *Thunderball*, once again sitting on the lap of the man whose face we never see. (Eric Pohlmann provided the voice again.) When Donald Pleasence became the first on-screen Blofeld in *You Only Live Twice*, he had his cat, as did Telly Savalas in *On Her Majesty's Secret Service* and Charles Gray in *Diamonds Are Forever*.

In the latter film, since there are two Blofelds, it's not surprising that there are also two white cats. When Bond (SEAN CONNERY) kills the wrong Blofeld in Willard Whyte's penthouse, the real Blofeld says, "Right idea," to which Bond responds, "But wrong pussy."

When Blofeld disappeared from the Albert R. Broccoli–produced Bond films, it became the responsibility of producer Jack Schwartzman to bring the white cat back, which he did in *Never Say Never Again*. In that film, the cat sits on the lap of Max von Sydow, the last actor, to date, to portray the head of S.P.E.C.T.R.E.

WHITE ELEPHANT A London restaurant where, over lunch in 1973, Director Guy Hamilton offered actor Christopher Lee the part of

Francisco Scaramanga in *The Man with the Golden Gun*.

WHITE RIVER A river in Jamaica that served as the location for the Crab Key swamps in *Dr. No*.

WHITTINGHAM, JACK (1910–) British screenwriter, who in 1959 collaborated with Kevin McClory and Ian Fleming on what would eventually become *Thunderball*. When the project fell apart and Fleming published his novel without their permission, Whittingham joined McClory in a major lawsuit against Fleming, which they won in 1963.

Following Ernst Cuneo's original story memorandum, dated May 28, 1959, in which Cuneo had outlined an A-bomb hijacking caper, Fleming wrote a treatment in which the Mafia were the principal villains who break into a U.S. atomic base in England and steal a bomb that they transfer from a helicopter to a tramp steamer to a flying boat and finally to Largo's *Virginia* yacht in the Bahamas. Meanwhile, Fleming had Bond working with a fellow agent named Domino Smith, who infiltrates the Mafia in England.

In discussions, Whittingham had a number of problems with Fleming's treatment. He felt that the method in which the Mafia grabbed the American atomic bomb was unbelievable. The idea of three disguised Mafia henchmen sneaking onto an American base and making off with a bomb was straining reality, he thought, and too much time was spent transferring the bomb from chopper to ship to plane to yacht. Whittingham suggested that in place of all this, the Mafia hijack a NATO bomber with atom bombs on board. They could then crash-land the plane in the Bahamas, where the bombs could still be transferred aboard the Mafia yacht via frogmen.

Whittingham also pointed out that Fleming's story was told too much through dialogue and that there were not enough visuals to carry the story along. Furthermore, he didn't like Domino Smith's easy penetration of the Mafia gang, or the counterespionage plot in which the Secret Service sends only two men and a girl to Nassau.

Whittingham also felt that the Mafia should steal two bombs. The first could be detonated if the NATO powers failed to deliver the

Screenwriter Jack Whittingham cowrote the first *Thunderball* script with Kevin McClory and Ian Fleming.
(National Film Archive, London)

ransom. In addition, he eliminated all passages where Fleming had stopped the script with a Bond narration. He took out an interlude at a public house in England and erased Bond's description of the Mafia. Plans were made instead to introduce the villains visually.

Whittingham decided to begin the script with a Mafia agent named Martelli who journeys to Nassau to tell Largo that a NATO observer named Joe Petachi is now under their control. Largo is pleased, offers him a fee of $10,000, and then promptly has one of his bodyguards shoot Martelli in the back, after which his body is thrown to the sharks.

In the Whittingham script, Largo's home is called Xanadu, and Domino is replaced by a lazy American playgirl named Gaby. The name of the head of the Sicilian-based Mafia was changed from Cuneo to Bastico. He also introduced one of Largo's henchmen as Janni.

Petachi hijacks the plane, but not before Allied Intelligence is able to get a faint trace of it in the mid-Atlantic. Bond is informed by M that this faint trace appears in longitude 78 west, so that is where Bond is sent. The longitude 78

west location became the working title of the script, until Fleming and McClory changed it to *Thunderball*—the code name for the Anglo-American Intelligence operation.

Whittingham's script followed the basic Fleming outline once Bond and Felix Leiter arrive in Nassau. They lead the investigation on the island, where they come across Largo and other Mafia types at a convention.

Whittingham added a scene, however, where Bond fights it out with an underwater sentry while searching the hull of Largo's yacht' (whose name changed from the *Virginia* to the *Sorrento*). A British gunboat—replacing Fleming's submarine—shadows the *Sorrento* until the final underwater battle, which this time takes place off the Grand Bahama Missile Base.

Whittingham's ending has Largo flying off in a seaplane with the other atomic bomb, unaware that Gaby has reset the detonator. As Bond and a wounded Leiter observe, the plane is obliterated.

When the *Thunderball* lawsuit was concluded in 1963 and film rights were sold by McClory to producers Albert R. Broccoli and

Harry Saltzman, Whittingham's script was rewritten by American screenwriters Richard Maibaum and John Hopkins. However, the final film credit reads "Screenplay by Richard Maibaum and John Hopkins, based on an original screenplay by Jack Whittingham, Kevin McClory, and Ian Fleming."

"WHOEVER SHE WAS, I MUST HAVE SCARED THE LIVING DAYLIGHTS OUT OF HER." James Bond's (TIMOTHY DALTON) appropriate comment to Austrian Section Chief Saunders (THOMAS WHEATLEY) after foiling Kara Milovy's (MARYAM D'ABO) assassination attempt on defecting General Georgi Koskov (JEROEN KRABBE) in *The Living Daylights*.

"WHY DON'T YOU PLAY THE WATER BALLOONS?" Message written on the back of a blackjack playing-card dealt to Tiffany Case (JILL ST. JOHN) in *Diamonds Are Forever*. It's all part of a CIA plan, engineered by Felix Leiter (NORMAN BURTON), to give Case a cache of diamonds at the Circus Circus Casino and then tail her to the next stop on a diamond-smuggling pipeline.

WHYTE HOUSE A Las Vegas hotel owned by billionaire recluse Willard Whyte (JIMMY DEAN) in *Diamonds Are Forever*. Whyte is kidnapped and imprisoned by Ernst Stavro Blofeld (CHARLES GRAY), who has literally taken over his global empire.

When *Diamonds Are Forever* was filmed in Las Vegas in 1971, the Whyte House was actually the Las Vegas International Hotel. That hotel was later sold to the Hilton chain, and today it's called the Las Vegas Hilton.

WHYTE, WILLARD Billionaire recluse portrayed effectively by Jimmy Dean in *Diamonds Are Forever*. Based loosely on the character of Howard Hughes, who was producer Albert R. Broccoli's boss in the 1940s, Whyte is the perfect kidnap victim for Ernst Stavro Blofeld (CHARLES GRAY), who is once again at work on an international blackmail scheme. Since no one has seen Whyte for five years, Blofeld finds it easy to take over his global empire, especially when he's supplied with a computerized voice-sampler that perfectly duplicates Whyte's vocal patterns. Whyte is involved in many fields, but it is his aerospace business and ties to the U.S. Air Force that help Blofeld easily launch a laser satellite powered by the diamonds he has been stealing from a crime syndicate. That satellite becomes the instrument of Blofeld's latest blackmail scheme.

Whyte is finally rescued by James Bond (SEAN CONNERY), who has to wade through his two acrobatic bodyguards, Bambi (DONNA GARRATT) and Thumper (TRINA PARKS). Returning to his penthouse in Las Vegas, Whyte takes one look at a huge map of his holdings and discovers one element that doesn't belong—an oil-drilling platform in the Gulf of Baja, a clue that leads Bond to Blofeld's final command post.

Broccoli's familiarity with Howard Hughes was certainly a plus when it came time to make *Diamonds Are Forever*. But a dream Broccoli had one night truly inspired the whole project. In the dream, Broccoli was paying a visit to Hughes at his permanent hotel suite at the Las Vegas Desert Inn. As Broccoli walked past a window, he saw the back of Hughes's head. However, when the man turned around, it wasn't Hughes.

The vision jolted Broccoli and compelled him to contact Richard Maibaum, who was then preparing the story for the new Bond film. Maibaum had, at one point, considered introducing the evil twin brother of Auric Goldfinger (GERT FROBE) as a possible choice for the villain in *Diamonds*. Broccoli's dream became a more suitable inspiration, and thus Willard Whyte was born.

WICHITA FALLS Phony hometown whose name is given to security guards at the Olimpatec Meditation Institute by undercover CIA agent Pam Bouvier (CAREY LOWELL) when she visits Joe Butcher (WAYNE NEWTON) in *Licence to Kill*.

WILLIAMS, JAN English actress who portrayed Red Grant's bosomy masseuse in *From Russia with Love*.

WILLIS, AUSTIN Actor who portrayed Mr. Simmons, the cardplayer in *Goldfinger*. Well-tanned and dapper, Willis was perfect as the vacationing American who is being systematically cheated at gin by Goldfinger (GERT FROBE).

"WILL YOU MARRY ME?" Dramatic proposal uttered by James Bond (GEORGE LAZENBY) to Teresa "Tracy" de Vicenzo (DIANA RIGG) in the sixth 007 adventure, *On Her Majesty's Secret Service.* It is the only time that James Bond has proposed in the series.

Tracy accepted and the couple were married at the conclusion of the film. Unfortunately, it was to be a short-lived marriage, for during a climactic honeymoon drive along the Portuguese coast, Tracy is machine-gunned to death by Irma Blunt (ILSE STEPPAT).

WILMER, DOUGLAS (1920–) British character actor who portrayed Secret Service art expert Jim Fanning in *Octopussy. See* FANNING, JIM.

WILSON, MICHAEL G. (New York, 1943–) An American writer/producer, and the stepson of Albert R. "Cubby" Broccoli, who has been exclusively involved in the production of the James Bond films since *The Spy Who Loved Me* in 1976.

It became apparent after the departure of producer Harry Saltzman in 1975 that Broccoli was in need of an associate to begin sharing the producer chores on the enormously complicated 007 productions. Wilson fit the bill. He was an experienced lawyer and a former partner in a prestigious Washington, D.C., and New York City law firm. He was also a college-trained electrical engineer with an interest in photography and scuba diving.

The son of actor Lew Wilson, who was the cinema's first Batman in 1923, Michael G. Wilson became part of the Broccoli clan when his mother, Dana, married Cubby in 1960. His first experience with the Bond series actually came in February 1964, when he became a production assistant on *Goldfinger* during location shooting in the United States. Wilson was vacationing in London and about to start law school, when Broccoli invited him to join him in the United States for sequences shot at Fort Knox.

Wilson bought cases of beer for the American GI's participating in the sequence in which the entire base is put to sleep by Miss Pussy Galore's Flying Circus. A decade later, Wilson left his law practice to become assistant to the producer on *The Spy Who Loved Me.* He received his stripes as executive producer on *Moonraker,* and he continued in that position on *For Your Eyes Only* and *Octopussy.* He became coproducer on *A View to a Kill, The Living Daylights,* and *Licence to Kill.*

Meanwhile, starting with *For Your Eyes Only,* Wilson began to collaborate with veteran writer Richard Maibaum on the Bond scripts. He has continued in that capacity on *Octopussy, A View to a Kill, The Living Daylights,* and *Licence to Kill.*

WINDUST, BRETAIGNE (1906–1960) American producer/director who produced the 1954 live television adaptation of Ian Fleming's *Casino Royale* for CBS.

WINT, MR. Soft-spoken homosexual assassin employed by Ernst Stavro Blofeld (CHARLES GRAY) in *Diamonds Are Forever* and portrayed by veteran character actor Bruce Glover. Wint's partner and fellow assassin is Mr. Kidd (PUTTER SMITH). Together they give 007 (SEAN CONNERY) plenty of trouble.

Wint and Kidd's first priority is to infiltrate a diamond-smuggling operation that stretches from South Africa to the United States. The diamonds will be used by Blofeld to create a huge laser satellite capable of blackmailing the entire planet.

Disposing of one agent after another, Wint and Kidd first meet Bond—posing as smuggler Peter Franks (JOE ROBINSON)—at Milton Slumber's (DAVID BAUER) mortuary in Las Vegas, where they knock him out and place him in a terrifying crematorium. Bond is about to be burned to death in the series's most desperate situation, when 007 is saved by diamond smugglers Slumber and Shady Tree (LEONARD BARR), who are upset over Bond's phony diamond cache.

After killing another Blofeld duplicate in Willard Whyte's (JIMMY DEAN) penthouse, 007 is later overcome by sleeping gas and thrown into the back of Wint's car. Wint also manages to drop his after-shave lotion in the process, which is smashed under 007's body.

Thus, when the assassins place the unconscious Bond in a concrete pipe that is being placed in an underground flood-control line, 007 smells like, in his own words, "a tart's handkerchief."

The smell of Mr. Wint's after-shave lotion is an important clue in the film's final scene, when Wint and Kidd try to assassinate Bond on the luxury liner. Posing as waiters, the pair have planted a bomb inside the "surprise" dessert. A suspicious 007 first smells Wint's very familiar after-shave, then trips up the "waiter" with a comment about the wine selection, which Wint fails to comprehend. A fight ensues, and both Kidd and Wint are disposed of—the latter with the bomb attached to his torso.

The idea of homosexual assassins was a tad spicy in 1971, when *Diamonds Are Forever* was released. In actuality, the reference to this aspect of Wint and Kidd's relationship was slight and treated in true tongue-in-cheek fashion. The scene in which they walk off into the South African desert holding hands was one of the film's biggest laughs. Wint and Kidd's relationship was perfectly matched to Charles Gray's portrait of Blofeld, which was extremely effeminate, including a scene of him in drag during his escape from the Whyte House.

WISEMAN, JOSEPH (1919–) American actor who portrayed Dr. No in the first James Bond film produced by Albert R. Broccoli and Harry Saltzman. Made up to appear half Asian—in respect to his German/Chinese pedigree—and outfitted with a stylish wardrobe and black metal hands, Wiseman set the tone for every future Bond villain.

Producer Harry Saltzman had remembered Wiseman from his performance as the crazed drug addict in William Wyler's *Detective Story* and he didn't disappoint in *Dr. No*. The measured way in which Wiseman delivered his dialogue—using an unemotional, monotoned "voice of doom"— was a marvelous and memorable touch. *See* NO, DR.

WISNIEWSKI, ANDREAS (Berlin, West Germany, July 3, 1959–) Blond West German actor who portrayed Necros, the formidable assassin who battles Bond (TIMOTHY DALTON) on the cargo nets in *The Living Daylights*. *See* NECROS.

WOMEN OF THE JAMES BOND FILMS They include the following:

BOND CHARACTERS AND THEIR ACTRESSES

Film	Character	Actress
Dr. No	Honey Ryder	Ursula Andress
	Sylvia Trench	Eunice Gayson
	Miss Taro	Zena Marshall
	Miss Moneypenny	Lois Maxwell
From Russia with Love	Tatiana Romanova	Daniela Bianchi
	Sylvia Trench	Eunice Gayson
	Miss Moneypenny	Lois Maxwell
	Ravishing Girl	Nadja Regin
	Zora	Martine Beswick
	Vida	Aliza Gur
Goldfinger	Pussy Galore	Honor Blackman
	Jill Masterson	Shirley Eaton
	Tilly Masterson	Tania Mallet
	Bonita	Nadja Regin
	Dink	Margaret Nolan
	Miss Moneypenny	Lois Maxwell
Thunderball	Domino	Claudine Auger

German actor Andreas Wisniewski brought charisma to the part of Necros, the assassin, in *The Living Daylights*. (Andreas Wisniewski, Richard Schenkman)

Film	Character	Actress
Thunderball	Fiona	Luciana Paluzzi
	Paula	Martine Beswick
	Patricia	Molly Peters
	French Agent	Mitsouko
	Miss Moneypenny	Lois Maxwell
You Only Live Twice	Kissy	Mie Hama
	Aki	Akiko Wakabayashi
	Helga Brandt	Karin Dor
	Miss Moneypenny	Lois Maxwell
	Ling	Tsai Chin
"Casino Royale" (TV)	Valerie Mathis	Linda Christian
Casino Royale (Film)	Vesper Lynd	Ursula Andress
	Mimi	Deborah Kerr
	Miss Moneypenny	Barbara Bouchet
	Mata Bond	Joanna Pettet
	The Detainer	Daliah Lavi
	Buttercup	Angela Scoular
	Miss Goodthighs	Jacqueline Bisset
On Her Majesty's Secret Service	Tracy	Diana Rigg
	Ruby	Angela Scoular
	Nancy	Catherine VonSchell
	Miss Moneypenny	Lois Maxwell
Diamonds Are Forever	Tiffany Case	Jill St. John
	Plenty O'Toole	Lana Wood
	Woman on Beach	Denise Perrier
	Miss Moneypenny	Lois Maxwell
	Bambi	Donna Garratt
	Thumper	Trina Parks
Live and Let Die	Solitaire	Jane Seymour
	Miss Caruso	Madeline Smith
	Rosie Carver	Gloria Hendry
	Miss Moneypenny	Lois Maxwell
The Man with the Golden Gun	Mary Goodnight	Britt Ekland
	Andrea Anders	Maud Adams
	Miss Moneypenny	Lois Maxwell
The Spy Who Loved Me	Major Anya Amasova	Barbara Bach
	Naomi	Caroline Munro
	Hotel Clerk	Valerie Leon
	Log Cabin Girl	Sue Vanner
	Miss Moneypenny	Lois Maxwell
Moonraker	Holly Goodhead	Lois Chiles
	Corinne Dufour	Corinne Clery
	Manuela	Emily Bolton
	Private Jet Hostess	Leila Shenna
	Miss Moneypenny	Lois Maxwell
For Your Eyes Only	Melina Havelock	Carole Bouquet
	Lisl	Cassandra Harris

Film	Character	Actress
For Your Eyes Only	Bibi	Lynn-Holly Johnson
	Miss Moneypenny	Lois Maxwell
Octopussy	Octopussy	Maud Adams
	Magda	Kristina Wayborn
	Midge	Cherry Gillespie
	Gwendoline	Suzanne Jerome
	Miss Moneypenny	Lois Maxwell
Never Say Never Again	Domino	Kim Basinger
	Fatima Blush	Barbara Carrera
	Miss Moneypenny	Pamela Salem
	Girl on Fishing Boat	Valerie Leon
	Agent 326	Saskia Cohen Tanugi
A View to a Kill	Stacey Sutton	Tanya Roberts
	May Day	Grace Jones
	Pola Ivanova	Fiona Fullerton
	Kimberley Jones	Mary Stavin
	Miss Moneypenny	Lois Maxwell
The Living Daylights	Kara Milovy	Maryam d'Abo
	Miss Moneypenny	Caroline Bliss
	Linda	Kell Tyler
Licence to Kill	Pam Bouvier	Carey Lowell
	Lupe Lamora	Talisa Soto
	Miss Moneypenny	Caroline Bliss
	Della Churchill	Priscilla Barnes

WOOD, CHRISTOPHER British screenwriter, and a favorite of director Lewis Gilbert, who wrote *The Spy Who Loved Me* (with Richard Maibaum) and *Moonraker*.

Actress Lana Wood put the Plenty in O'Toole. (Lew Sherrell Agency, Ltd.)

WOOD, LANA (Santa Monica, California, March 1, 1946–) American actress who portrayed Plenty O'Toole in *Diamonds Are Forever*. She is the sister of Natalie Wood. *See* O'TOOLE, PLENTY.

"WORLD IS NOT ENOUGH, THE" The motto on James Bond's coat of arms, as related by Sir Hilary Bray (GEORGE BAKER) to 007 (GEORGE LAZENBY) in *On Her Majesty's Secret Service*. According to the records of the London College of Arms, Bond's lineage can be traced back to 1387. The coat of arms was that of Sir Thomas Bond, who died in 1734. It consisted of an "argent on a chevron sable, with three bezants," or gold balls.

WORLD'S GREATEST MARCHES Phony label on the master satellite control-tape in *Diamonds Are Forever*. It contains the code that guides Blofeld's (CHARLES GRAY) laser satellite. Bond (SEAN CONNERY) first spots it at Professor-Dr. Metz's (JOSEPH FURST) laboratory at Techtronics. Later, on Blofeld's oil-drilling platform, 007 tries unsuccessfully to substitute a phony tape for the real one.

WORTH, B. J. (Whitefish, Montana, 1952–) American stuntman and skydiving expert who jumped off the Eiffel Tower in *A View to a Kill* and parachuted to safety. Worth was doubling Grace Jones's character, May Day. For the sequence in which he parachutes onto a Seine River wedding barge, Worth actually jumped twice from a stationary helicopter.

W6N The call sign for Commander John Strangways's (TIM MOXON) transmitter in Kingston, Jamaica.

WYMAN, JOHN Muscular actor who portrayed East German biathlon champion and Soviet agent Eric Kriegler in *For Your Eyes Only*. *See* KRIEGLER, ERIC.

X

XA-MUA Identification number on South American drug runner Franz Sanchez's (ROBERT DAVI) helicopter in *Licence to Kill*. It transports him from the Olimpatec Meditation Institute to the rendezvous with his tanker trucks at Paso el Diablo.

XB-LOX Identification number on the crop-dusting plane stolen by CIA agent Pam Bouvier (CAREY LOWELL) in *Licence to Kill*. It's the aircraft that ferries Bond to one of the escaping tanker trucks.

XT-7B Designation of the jet-propelled flying platforms utilized by James Bond (SEAN CONNERY) and Felix Leiter (BERNIE CASEY) in *Never Say Never Again*. Fired from inside a U.S. nuclear submarine's Polaris missile tubes, the hovering platforms are designed to transport Bond and Leiter to the Arabian mainland. There the two agents can then dive into a well that connects to the underground Tears of Allah archaeological dig of Maximillian Largo (KLAUS MARIA BRANDAUER).

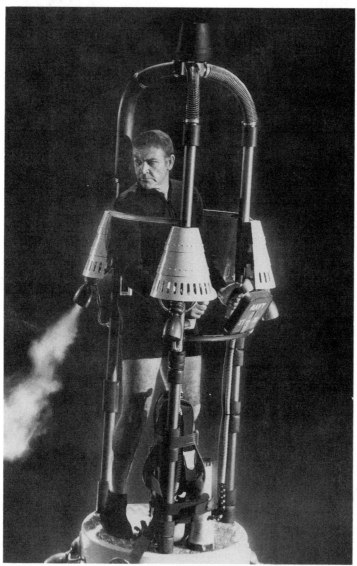

Sean Connery's work with the XT-7B flying platform in *Never Say Never Again* was filmed against a blue screen. (Taliafilm)

Y

YIP, DAVID British actor who portrayed American CIA agent Chuck Lee, Bond's (ROGER MOORE) San Francisco liaison, in *A View to a Kill.* Yip, born in Liverpool to an English mother and a Chinese father, is popular in England as the star of the television series "The Chinese Detective."

"YOUNG COLUMBIANS" Sign on a banner being carried in a circus parade outside the U.S. Air Force base at Feldstadt, West Germany, in *Octopussy.*

YOUNG, FREDDIE (1902–   ) Three-time Academy Award–winning British cinematographer whose exquisite work can be viewed in *You Only Live Twice.* He was part of the new team brought in by producers Albert R. Broccoli and Harry Saltzman to freshen up the series

Cinematographer Freddie Young worked on *You Only Live Twice.* (National Film Archive, London)

in 1966. Other fresh faces on *You Only Live Twice* were director Lewis Gilbert, writer Roald Dahl, and editor Thelma Connell.

YOUNG, RAYMOND British actor who portrayed Sierra, James Bond's (SEAN CONNERY) South American contact, in the *Goldfinger* teaser. *See* SIERRA.

YOUNG, ROBBIN *Playboy* magazine playmate who portrayed the Cortina flower girl in *For Your Eyes Only. See* FLOWER GIRL IN CORTINA.

Model Robbin Young of *For Your Eyes Only* and escort Jerry Buss attended the James Bond Weekend in 1981.

YOUNGSTEIN, MAX (New York City, March 21, 1913–   ) American production executive who was a vice president with United Artists in 1961 when the James Bond film series was initiated with producers Albert R. Broccoli and Harry Saltzman. Youngstein's interest in 007, though, predates the Broccoli/Saltzman deal and involved an English producer/director named Victor Saville.

Saville, the son of an extremely wealthy English banker, had been a successful producer/director with MGM when he left the studio to join United Artists in the early 1950s. Youngstein and UA were interested in Saville because he held the rights to a series of pseudo-erotic, slam-bang Mickey Spillane thrillers. The studio at that time was looking for low-budget productions that had a guaranteed audience.

Saville eventually produced several Spillane films for UA, including *I, the Jury* (1953) and *Kiss Me Deadly* (1955). "But," said Youngstein, "we could never find the right Mike Hammer. We had Ralph Meeker and Biff Eliot. Some of the productions were better than others—Robert Aldrich directed one—but they were B-movies without a name lead."

A personality conflict with UA president Arthur Krim eventually proved the end of Saville's relationship with UA. It was at this point that Saville mentioned the James Bond novels to Youngstein. "He walked into my office," remembered Youngstein, "and said, 'Did you ever hear of James Bond?' He then pulled out a paperback of *From Russia with Love* and we started to talk about the cinematic potential of the books.

"I knew about James Bond because I had close contacts with every book editor in New York. I had read the Fleming books and found them to be terrific, but I didn't have the money

for an option. I told him to take the books in to Arthur and see what kind of result he would get."

Unfortunately, the personality conflict persisted, and Krim wasn't interested. It took political columnist Hugh Sidey's magazine article on President Kennedy's favorite books, which included *From Russia with Love*, to get Krim excited. Youngstein picked up an advance copy of the magazine, shoved it in his briefcase, and called Krim at home.

"He asked me if the rights were available," said Youngstein, "and I told him I'd dropped interest in them through Saville. We ended up calling the publisher and finding out that Cubby Broccoli and Harry Saltzman had the option. We then made the historic deal that led to *Dr. No* and all the rest."

YOUNG, TERENCE (Shanghai, China, June 20, 1915–September 7, 1994) Urbane Irish film director and screenwriter, and a contemporary of Ian Fleming. He directed three of

A youthful Terence Young directs *Paratrooper*, his first picture for Cubby Broccoli. In the trenches, *left to right*, Leo Genn, Alan Ladd, and Harry Andrews. Ted Moore is the cinematographer standing behind Young. (National Film Archive, London)

the best films in the 007 series: *Dr. No, From Russia with Love,* and *Thunderball.*

Since he was the first director on the United Artists series, he was very much responsible for setting the style of the films and guiding Sean Connery in the role that made him an international star. In many ways, Young *was* James Bond.

While Fleming was serving his country as an intelligence officer, Young was a dashing young tanker with the Irish Guards Armored Division. Like Fleming, he was a connoisseur of the finer things in life—gourmet meals, expensive wines, beautifully appointed homes, travel, and adventure. He has always surrounded himself with an eclectic group of artists, authors, filmmakers, and VIPs who have long appreciated his keen wit, sense of humor, and boyish enthusiasm for the filmmaking profession.

Young had been reading Fleming's novels for years and thus was very familiar with the world of 007. Combining Young's sophisticated talents with the contributions of American screenwriter Richard Maibaum and editor Peter Hunt, producers Albert R. Broccoli and Harry Saltzman created a true hybrid in the early 1960s—a stylish international film series with well-crafted production values and action sequences that American audiences could appreciate.

Young noted with pride that he "directed the first James Bond film (*Dr. No*), the best James Bond film (*From Russia with Love*), and the most successful James Bond film of all (*Thunderball*)." His involvement with Broccoli and Maibaum dates back to 1954 and the Alan Ladd World War II adventure *The Red Beret.* One of Young's earliest films was about the Irish Guards and was titled *They Were Not Divided.* It featured several actors who would become regular players in the Bond series, including Peter Burton, Anthony Dawson, Desmond Llewelyn, and Michael Brennan.

YOU ONLY LIVE TWICE (United Artists, 1967) ★ ★ ½ The fifth James Bond film produced by Albert R. Broccoli and Harry Saltzman. U.S. release date: June 13, 1967. U.S.

During Ninja training on *You Only Live Twice,* Bond tangles with an infiltrator. (Rex Features Ltd./RDR Productions)

film rentals: $19.4 million. Running time: 116 minutes.

Every film series has its highs and lows. It's extremely difficult to maintain quality in the film business—given the creative aspirations of filmmakers, who are always looking for new paths and challenges. To be involved in the making of the same type of film every two years is not an attractive thought for any serious artist.

For Sean Connery, the urge to move on was already apparent when he began work on *You Only Live Twice* in 1966. But Connery wasn't the only one ready for a change. For the fifth James Bond film, producers Broccoli and Saltzman changed their lineup considerably. Gone were director Terence Young, writer Richard Maibaum, cinematographer Ted Moore, and editor Peter Hunt (although he was brought back to shoot second-unit footage and to supervise the post-production editing). The new team included director Lewis Gilbert, cinematographer Freddie Young, and short-story writer Roald Dahl.

It was a difficult shoot, and the result is a disappointing Bond entry. While *Thunderball*'s S.P.E.C.T.R.E. nuclear blackmail scheme is believable, Blofeld's scheme to capture U.S. and Soviet spaceships with an *Intruder* rocket is pure science fiction. If anything has been proven in the Bond series, it's that James Bond's arena should be on earth, not in outer space.

Following *Thunderball*'s enormous success (over $50 million gross in the U.S. alone), the emphasis on *You Only Live Twice* was once again size—production designer Ken Adam was given carte blanche to create his enormous volcano rocket-base set: the unit skipped across the Japanese mainland, filming at many picturesque locations (surrounded at all times by the Japanese press corps); and the world was once again threatened with nuclear destruction.

Although the film does develop a flavor for the Far East—with its beautiful women, emerging technology, and ancient customs—the film's story is a less than compelling one. Elaborate set pieces take over center stage at the expense of a sustained dramatic structure. The best Bond films establish the caper and the villain early in the story, and everything moves toward a final confrontation between Bond and his enemy. But *You Only Live Twice* bounces from villain to villain, escapade to escapade, until the final assault on the volcano rocket base puts 007 up against Blofeld for the first time.

The action sequences are also more like those found in comic books, and Connery—so glib and light-footed in *Thunderball*—is given very little to do in the story. The helicopter battle above volcano country, pitting the Little Nellie auto-gyro against a flight of S.P.E.C.T.R.E. killer helicopters, is one of the least dramatic action sequences in the entire series. Pushing the buttons on his defense-mechanism controls, Bond becomes a passive automaton and a very boring hero.

The women in *You Only Live Twice* are actually much more interesting than Bond. Aki, Helga Brandt, and Kissy are the advance guard of the new Bond girl—less breathless females who have more equality on the firing line. In other words, they hold their own with Bond and help him out of more than a few scrapes with death.

High points: John Barry's lush score and Freddie Young's cinematography. Thanks to a long and complicated production schedule, *You Only Live Twice* was scheduled for a summer 1967 release, instead of Christmas 1966. Under those circumstances, it was beaten to the box office by Charles K. Feldman's huge, lumbering 007 spoof *Casino Royale*, which opened on April 28, 1967. *Casino Royale*'s relative failure to duplicate the success of the serious Bond films had a definite negative effect on the release of *You Only Live Twice*.

Although Broccoli and Saltzman's Bond was no failure, it did not repeat the success of *Thunderball*. For the Bond series, a box-office down-spiral began that would last a decade. With the exception of *Diamonds Are Forever* (1971), Bond would not return to big money box-office success until 1977 with the lavish *The Spy Who Loved Me*.

YOU ONLY LIVE TWICE CAST

James Bond . . . . Sean Connery
Aki . . . . Akiko Wakabayashi
Tiger Tanaka . . . . Tetsuro Tamba
Kissy . . . . Mie Hama
Osato . . . . Teru Shimada
Ernst Stavro Blofeld . . . . Donald Pleasence

Helga Brandt........................Karin Dor
Miss Moneypenny ....Lois Maxwell
M..................................Bernard Lee
Q...........................Desmond Llewelyn
Dikko Henderson ....Charles Gray
Ling................................Tsai Chin
American President.............Alexander Knox
President's Aide ....Robert Hutton
S.P.E.C.T.R.E. No. 3..............Burt Kwouk
S.P.E.C.T.R.E. No. 4...........Michael Chow
Hans...............................Ronald Rich

YOU ONLY LIVE TWICE CREW

Producers .....Harry Saltzman, Albert R. Broccoli
Director........................Lewis Gilbert
Screenplay.......................Roald Dahl
Director of Photography ....Freddie Young, B.S.C.
Second-Unit Director ....Peter Hunt
Editor ....Thelma Connell
Production Designer.................Ken Adam
Art Director ....Harry Pottle
Production Supervisor ....David Middlemas
Special Effects ....John Stears
Action Sequences ....Bob Simmons
Main Title Designed by ....,..Maurice Binder
Music Composed, Conducted, and Arranged
  by ....John Barry
Title Song Lyrics by ....Leslie Bricusse
Title Song Sung by ....Nancy Sinatra
Technical Adviser ....Kikumaru Okuda
Second Unit Cameraman ....Bob Huke
Aerial Unit Cameraman.............John Jordan
Underwater Cameraman ....Lamar Boren
Assistant Director ....William P. Cartlidge

Location Manager ....Robert Watts
Camera Operator ....Ernie Day
Continuity ....Angela Martelli
Makeup ....Basil Newall, Paul Rabiger
Dubbing Editors...Norman Wanstall, Harry Miller
Sound Recorder ....John Mitchell
Wardrobe Mistress ....Eileen Sullivan
Hairstylist ....Eileen Warwick
Set Dresser ....David Ffolkes
Production Company ....Eon Productions
Distribution Company ....United Artists

YOU ONLY LIVE TWICE COMPETITION

Competitive films in release when *You Only Live Twice* opened in Los Angeles on June 14, 1967:
Casino Royale (in its last eight days of exclusive engagement)
How to Succeed in Business without Really Trying
The Sand Pebbles
A Man for All Seasons
Deadlier Than the Male
You're a Big Boy Now
A Guide for the Married Man
The Professionals/Georgy Girl
Devil's Angels
Cinderfella
The Caper of the Golden Bulls

YUKON North American crash site of the Royal Air Force Boeing 747 that is destroyed when its space-shuttle cargo is hijacked in the *Moonraker* teaser.

Z

ZAGREB, YUGOSLAVIA The second stop made by the Orient Express in *From Russia with Love*. In this station, S.P.E.C.T.R.E. assassin Red Grant (ROBERT SHAW), in possession of the British Secret Service recognition code, leaves the train first, contacts Captain Nash (BILL HILL)—a Yugoslavia-based British agent who has been assigned to help Bond (SEAN CONNERY)—and kills him in the train station rest room. Stealing the agent's wallet, briefcase, and hat, Grant switches identities, becoming Nash when he meets Bond in the station.

ZAMBORA A sideshow attraction at Las Vegas's Circus Circus Casino that figures in the plot of *Diamonds Are Forever*. Zambora is actually a black woman who changes herself magically into a rampaging gorilla. Having given Tiffany Case (JILL ST. JOHN) a cache of diamonds, Felix Leiter (NORMAN BURTON) and his fellow CIA agents hope to trace her to the next stop on a diamond-smuggling pipeline. Unfortunately, while the agents are distracted by the Zambora transformation, Tiffany slips out the back exit, and they lose her.

ZARA Actress who portrayed the Indian allergy victim in *On Her Majesty's Secret Service*.

ZERBE, ANTHONY American character actor who portrayed boozy drug runner Milton Krest in *Licence to Kill*. See KREST, MILTON.

ZERO ZERO Nickname bestowed upon James Bond (SEAN CONNERY) by Japanese Secret Service chief Tiger Tanaka (TETSURO TAMBA) in *You Only Live Twice*.

ZLY 621 Florida license plate on the white limousine that will carry newlyweds Felix Leiter (DAVID HEDISON) and Della Churchill (PRISCILLA BARNES) to the reception in *Licence to Kill*.

ZOLTAN Balding, gray-haired henchman of Russian masterspy Le Chiffre (PETER LORRE) in the TV film "Casino Royale." British agent Clarence Leiter (MICHAEL PATE) thinks he looks like a basset hound. He carries a gun hidden in a cane that he sticks against the lower spine of James Bond (BARRY NELSON) in the Monte Carlo casino. Bond manages to disarm Zoltan, and he later gives Leiter the cane as a present for Scotland Yard's Black Museum.

ZORA Gypsy woman, portrayed by Martine Beswick in *From Russia with Love*, who is involved in the celebrated girl fight with fellow Gypsy Vida (ALIZA GUR).

ZORIN INDUSTRIES Anglo-French combine run by Max Zorin (CHRISTOPHER WALKEN) in *A View to a Kill*. Its holdings include a large oil field off the northern California coast and a huge microchip manufacturing plant that is supplying a new generation of chips to the Soviets. It also owns and operates the Main Strike—an abandoned silver mine in California that is part of Zorin's scheme to destroy Silicon Valley, the high-technology capital of the world.

ZORIN, MAX Billionaire industrialist and horse breeder, portrayed by Christopher Walken, who intends to monopolize the world's supply of microchips by destroying Silicon Valley in *A View to a Kill*. Born in Dresden, Zorin was the victim of a cruel Nazi experiment conducted by Dr. Karl Mortner (WILLOUGHBY GRAY) on pregnant concentration camp inmates. Attempting to prove his theory that steroid injections could enhance the intelligence of children, Mortner succeeded in killing most of the newborns. Those that survived were, indeed, born with phenomenal IQs, but they each suffered a glaring side effect—they were all psychotics.

Zorin fled East Germany in the 1960s on a French passport. By then he was a top KGB agent, working for General Gogol (WALTER GOTELL). Zorin Industries, his brainchild, was financed by the Russians, who hoped to benefit from its new technologies. Zorin's wealth increased as he made his first fortunes in oil and gas trading, continuing on to electronics and high technology.

Perceived in France as a top industrialist

and anticommunist, Zorin continued his work for Mother Russia, but those ties began to weaken. Surrounded by wealth and power, Zorin mentally snapped when he conceived of Project Main Strike—a plan to destroy Silicon Valley and gain a monopoly on world microchip manufacturing.

That plan is short-circuited by James Bond (ROGER MOORE), who tracks Zorin and his henchwoman, May Day (GRACE JONES), from France to San Francisco and on to the Main Strike silver mine. There 007 manages to stop a bomb from detonating along the San Andreas fault line. That explosion, combined with the pumping of seawater from Zorin's oil wells into the nearby Hayward earthquake fault, could have turned Silicon Valley into a lake.

Bond battles his way aboard Zorin's blimp, and during a climactic fight above the Golden Gate Bridge, he forces the psychotic industrialist to lose his footing and fall to his death. *Note:* Actor/singer David Bowie was considered at one point for the role of Zorin, eventually losing out to Christopher Walken. *See* WALKEN, CHRISTOPHER.

Zorin's blimp soars toward the San Francisco skyline with Bond hanging from one of the mooring cables. (Amberle Chalk Pit Museum)

The mock-up of Zorin's blimp, which was used for closeups of the cockpit. (Amberle Chalk Pit Museum)

ZORIN'S BLIMP   Slow-moving, silver-sided airship that is Max Zorin's (CHRISTOPHER WALKEN) principal means of crossing the globe, in *A View to a Kill*. It's also his getaway vehicle once Bond (ROGER MOORE) neutralizes Project Main Strike. When Bond manages to wrap a mooring rope around the topmost girder of the Golden Gate Bridge, the blimp is immobilized, precipitating the final battle between Bond and Zorin.

To save money, the actual full-size Zorin blimp was painted only on one side. Five percent of the final Golden Gate Bridge battle was filmed on location, and the rest was completed at Pinewood Studios on a set that doubled the uppermost girderwork of the bridge. *See* PROJECT MAIN STRIKE; GOLDEN GATE BRIDGE.

ZURICH, AMSTERDAM, CARACAS, AND HONG KONG   Cities in which Auric Goldfinger (GERT FROBE) has stashed the 20 million in pounds sterling worth of gold he has been smuggling out of Great Britain. As to why he's doing this, Colonel Smithers (RICHARD VERNON) of the Bank of England explains to Bond (SEAN CONNERY) that the price of gold varies from country to country and that by smuggling, Goldfinger can significantly increase the value of his loot. In 1964 Smithers mentioned that the gold price in England was $30 per ounce, while the price in Pakistan was $110.

ADDENDUM

Note: This section includes unusual details about the James Bond film series that have come to light since the first edition of this book was published in 1990. Much of this information was supplied by enthusiastic fans of the series from around the world, whose names are mentioned at the end of this addendum.

"AIR ON THE G STRING" Classic Johann Sebastian Bach background piece played when Stromberg's (CURT JURGENS) lovely assistant is dropped down an elevator shaft into the shark tank in *The Spy Who Loved Me*. Actress/model Marilyn Galsworthy portrayed the unlucky lady.

ALPERT, HERB (Los Angeles, California, March 31, 1935–) Famous composer, band leader, trumpeter, and songwriter who played the trumpet during Burt Bacharach's score for *Casino Royale* in 1967 and who produced the title song for *Never Say Never Again* (performed by his wife, Lani Hall), for which he also performed another patented trumpet solo.

ASHBY, CAROLE Beautiful British actress who portrayed the Whistling Girl in *A View to a Kill*.

BARTLE, JOYCE Top Wilhelmina model whose famous legs were featured in the sexy poster art for *For Your Eyes Only* in 1981.

BASS, ALFIE (1920–1987) British character comedian, best remembered in *The Lavender Hill Mob* (1951), who went on to do three Bond cameos. As the astonished drunk with wine bottle in hand, he does classic double takes at Bond's miraculous feats: in *The Spy Who Loved Me*, as the Lotus Esprit emerges onto the Sardinian beach; in St. Mark's Square in *Moonraker*, as the gondola hovercraft passes by; and at a Cortina ski resort in *For Your Eyes Only*, as Bond is pursued by enemy skiers. Bass is credited only for *Moonraker* in the cast as the Consumptive Italian.

BLACKWELL, CHRIS Multimillionaire record producer who is the current owner of Goldeneye, the former Jamaican home of author Ian Fleming. Ironically, in his youth Blackwell was a location scout for Cubby Broccoli on *Dr. No*.

BMT 216A License plate of the Aston Martin DB-5 in *Goldfinger* and *Thunderball*.

CONNERY, NEIL Younger brother of actor Sean Connery who starred in the appropriately titled Italian spy spoof *Operation Kid Brother* in 1967. The film costarred such Bond veterans as Daniela Bianchi of *From Russian with Love*, Adolfo Celi of *Thunderball*, Bernard Lee, who played M; Anthony Dawson, who played Professor Dent in *Dr. No*; and Lois Maxwell, who played Miss Moneypenny. Alberto De Martino directed this bomb.

CONNERY, JASON Son of actor Sean Connery who, in dashing, tongue-in-cheek fashion, portrayed Ian Fleming in the Turner Network Television film *The Private Life of Ian Fleming*.

DUBIN, GARY Kid actor in *Diamonds Are Forever* who competes against Tiffany Case (JILL ST. JOHN) in the water gun concession to win a stuffed dog at Circus Circus. "I saw the whole thing. The machine's fixed! Who's she? Your mother?!" the boy protests to the barker. Dubin went on to play one of the hapless teenagers victimized by Bruce the Shark in *Jaws 2*.

DUCK INN A 17th-century pub near Canterbury, England, that was a favorite watering hole of Bond author Ian Fleming, who lived nearby. It was featured in the book *Moonraker* and inspired Fleming to give James Bond his famous numerical designation. According to the *London Daily Telegraph* in an item published on September 18, 1991, Fleming always took the 007 bus to the pub. Hence Bond became agent 007.

ELROD HOUSE Real name of the futuristic house featured as Willard Whyte's desert residence in *Diamonds Are Forever*. Designed by the late architect John Lautner and listed for sale in 1995 at just under $2 million, the concrete-and-glass house has nearly 8,000 square feet and is situated on about 23 acres in Palm Springs, California. Built for interior designer Arthur Elrod in 1968, the house, likened to a spaceship, has a circular living room 60 feet across with skylights radiating from the center like the petals of a desert flower. The home also has an indoor/outdoor pool and a two-bedroom guest house.

Lautner, one of the greatest American contemporary architects, was still actively working on projects at the time of his death at age 83, in October 1994.

GIRAUT, LEILA Lebanese-born beauty who played Leila, the gypsy belly dancer, in *From Russia with Love*. Raised in California, Leila performed in Europe where her appearance on BBC-TV attracted the attention of producers Albert R. Broccoli and Harry Saltzman, who signed her to perform in the gypsy camp sequence. She also modeled for Chelsea artist Alex Pottner as the belly dancer in the British and European *From Russia with Love* poster artwork. After the Bond stint, Leila hopped over to England's Shepperton Studios for a similar undulating chore in Hammer's *Curse of the Mummy's Tomb*.

GOLDENEYE Television film, which starred actor Charles Dance (previously a villain in *For Your Eyes Only*) as Ian Fleming.

IAN FLEMING FOUNDATION A non-profit organization devoted to archiving and preserving the legacy of Ian Fleming and the popular culture phenomenon of James Bond. Founded in 1992, the IFF has archived and restored many original film props, including the badly damaged Lotus effects car from *The Spy Who Loved Me* and the *Neptune* submarine from *For Your Eyes Only*. More important, the IFF continues to work on archiving Fleming's professional papers housed at Glidrose Publications. The Ian Fleming Foundation publishes *Goldeneye* magazine and the *Shaken, Not Stirred* newsletter, fan publications that contain current Bond news as well as detailed research articles on James Bond and Ian Fleming's work.

The current (as of 1995) board of directors of the Ian Fleming Foundation consists of Michael VanBlaricum, president; Doug Redenius, vice president; John Cork, editor *Goldeneye* magazine; David Reinhardt, Canadian representative; Dave Worrall, U.K. representative; Peter Janson-Smith, chairman, Glidrose Publications; and Nicholas Fleming, Fleming family representative. The Ian Fleming Foundation can be contacted at the following address: The Ian Fleming Foundation, P.O. Box 6897, Santa Barbara, California 93160, USA.

LOVE, BESSIE (1898–1986) Petite American leading lady of the silent screen (*Intolerance*, *The Lost World*, *Broadway Melody*) who resided in London since the mid-1930s. Love played occasional cameo parts in Bond movies such as the American casino guest in *On Her Majesty's Secret Service*.

MASON, JAMES (1909–1984) Leading British actor (*The Desert Fox*, *Lolita*, *The Prisoner of Zenda*) who in 1976 was under prime consideration for the role of Karl Stromberg in *The Spy Who Loved Me*, probably because of the parallels with his Captain Nemo in *20,000 Leagues Under the Sea*.

MENCONI, LORRIE "Miss February" centerfold in the February 1969 issue of *Playboy* that Bond (GEORGE LAZENBY) steals from Gumbold's (JAMES BREE) office in *On Her Majesty's Secret Service*.

NORMAN, MONTY (London, April 4, 1928–   ) Top British composer who, for *Dr. No*, arranged all of the wonderful Jamaican calypso music ("Three Blind Mice," "Jump Up, Jamaica," and "Underneath the Mango Tree") that served the film so well. And, of course, he is credited with composing the James Bond theme, although history shows us that John Barry (then of the John Barry Seven pop group) revised Norman's theme, replacing it with the plucked guitar signature that has become world-famous).

Norman began his career as a singer with the leading British dance bands of the late '50s and early '60s and graduated to being a solo performer on stage, records, and television. He wrote pop songs for himself and other artists, and when his first show, "Expresso Bongo," scored a West End hit, he abandoned his singing career to become a composer. A string of musicals followed, including the long-running *Make Me an Offer*; *The Art of Living*; *Belle*; *Quick Quick Slow*; *Songbook*, which won the Evening Standard, the SWET (Laurence Olivier), and the Ivor Novello Awards for Best Musical, plus the Broadway Tony nomination; *Poppy*, which brought him yet another SWET Award for Best Musical; and *Pinocchio*, his first children's musical. His many film scores include *Call Me Bwana* (also for Cubby Broccoli and Harry Saltzman), *Irma La Douce*, *Expresso Bongo*, *The Day the Earth Caught Fire*, and *The Two Faces of Dr. Jeckyll*. The James Bond theme has been recorded over 500 times and has sold over 20,000,000 records over the years. Norman was given a special Ivor Novello Award for that theme. Norman's songs have been recorded by scores of top British, American, and European artists, including Cliff Richard, Tommy Steel, Shirley MacLaine, Bob Hope, Mantovani, and Count Basie. His many television credits include "Against the Crowd" and "Dickens of London." In 1988, he received from the British Academy of Songwriters, Composers, and Authors the highly coveted Gold Badge of Merit, for services to British music.

PHIDIAN Artist employed by the College of Arms in *On Her Majesty's Secret Service*, played by British actor Brian Grellis. When Bond (GEORGE LAZENBY) arrives at the college, Sir Hilary Bray (GEORGE BAKER) is complimenting Phidian on a coat of arms he has just completed on Bond's family tree. In the scenes that follow, which were filmed in part but never made the final cut of the film, Bond discovers a tiny radio transmitting "homer" disguised inside a paperweight on Sir Hilary's desk. Realizing Phidian is a Blofeld hireling and that he probably overheard Bond's plan to substitute as the genealogist, 007 takes pursuit. He chases Phidian out of the college, past St. Paul's Cathedral, and into London's Main Post Office. Phidian is eventually struck and killed in an underground tunnel by one of the high-speed automated electric trolleys used to deliver mail. To make Phidian's death appear accidental to Blofeld, an elaborate ruse is devised. Phidian's body is recovered and, along with a dozen other corpses "borrowed" from morgues, planted on a St. Albans commuter train. A terrible train accident is staged, making it appear as if the train has jumped the tracks. It is reported that there are no survivors. Blofeld reads about Phidian's death and finds nothing suspicious. Obviously, these scenes would have added to the movie's already long running time, and therefore they were either never shot or deleted in the final editing.

VAUX-LA-VICOURTE Real castle located outside Paris, which served as Hugo Drax's French estate transplanted to California in *Moonraker*.

Contributors: Terry Baxter (Clacton on Sea, England), John Ewaniuk (Los Angeles, California), Philippe Lombard (Paris, France), Stephen P. Oxenrider (Arlington, Virginia).

GOLDENEYE

BEAN, SEAN (Sheffield, Yorkshire, 1960–) British actor who plays the mysterious Trevelyan (aka 006), a colleague of James Bond's (PIERCE BROSNAN), in *Goldeneye*. Bean received international attention when he portrayed an Irish terrorist who confronts Harrison Ford in *Patriot Games*.

Born in Sheffield (Robin Hood country), Bean was first attracted to acting at his local arts community center. He applied successfully for a grant to study at the Royal Academy of Dramatic Arts, where he won a Silver Medal and two fencing medals. Ultimately, he returned to theater, making his professional acting debut as Tybalt in *Romeo and Juliet*. At the Citizens Theater in Glasgow, he played for a season in *The Last Days of Mankind* and *Der Rosenkavalier*, a play based on the opera. During the Young Writers Festival, Bean was invited to join the

Royal Court Theater Upstairs where he starred in *Who Knew MacKenzie?* and *Gone*. Next came his first major film role as the doomed lover in Derek Jarman's *Caravaggio*. The turning point of Bean's theatrical career came in 1986 when he played Romeo opposite Niamh Cusack's Juliet in the highly acclaimed Royal Shakespeare Company production at Stratford. Bean's film credits include *Stormy Monday*, *The Field*, *Troubles*, *Black Beauty*, and for television, *Titus Andronicus*, *Joey and Spansky*, *Samson and Delilah*, *Winter Flight*, *Lady Chatterley* (for director Ken Russell), and the series "Sharpe's Rifles" and "Betty." *See* TREVELYAN (Addendum).

BMW ROADSTER A two-seat, convertible BMW driven by Bond (PIERCE BROSNAN) on a Caribbean island in *Goldeneye*. It is first introduced during a sequence at Q Branch, where it is undergoing suitable modifications.

Announced in London on January 22, 1995, the Bond-BMW relationship was a new one for the series, which had previously relied on Aston Martin and Lotus to supply automobiles to 007. As the press report said, "A roadster, a two-seat open sports car, of the caliber of the new BMW symbolizes freedom and active mobility, reflecting the essence of James Bond—smart, a little audacious, and always in control of the situation. The roadster will be built in BMW's new plant in South Carolina."

BOND, SAMANTHA Shakespearean stage actress who won the coveted part of Miss Moneypenny in *Goldeneye*. She's not the first Bond to be involved in the series. Trevor Bond handled pre-title sequence work on *From Russia with Love* and *Goldfinger*.

BOURBON Drink of preference of the new M (DAME JUDI DENCH) in *Goldeneye*. It replaced the brandy of her predecessor.

BROCCOLI, BARBARA American film producer and daughter of legendary Bond producer Albert R. Broccoli, who makes her Bond producing debut on *Goldeneye*. Along with Broccoli's stepson, Michael Wilson, she guides the

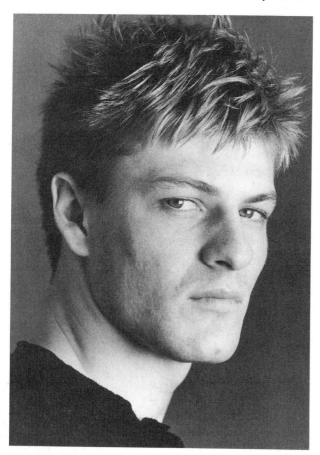

Sean Bean is Alec Trevelyan in *Goldeneye*, an ex-double-0 agent with connections to the Russian underworld. (ICM, London)

future of the James Bond films, fanning the flames that began in 1960 when Albert R. Broccoli teamed up with producer Harry Saltzman to initiate the world's most successful film series. Gaining experience on previous Bond films in virtually every department, including production, casting, and music supervision, Broccoli received credit as an executive assistant on *Octopussy*, graduating to assistant director on *A View to a Kill*. She received associate producer credit on both Timothy Dalton Bond entries, *The Living Daylights* and *Licence to Kill*.

BROSNAN, PIERCE (Ireland, May 16, 1952–   ) The latest actor to play the part of James Bond. At a June 8, 1994, press conference, announcing his casting in the famous 007 role for the movie *Goldeneye*, Brosnan promised "a Bond for the '90s." Brosnan, bearded from his role in a TV version of *Robinson Crusoe*, said he had been "cautiously optimistic" about getting the role. Asked how he could play Bond, he said, "He has to go back to being a more flinty character. But we are now in 1994. I think that has to be addressed." The new Bond would be no "new man," however. "In a piece like this," he continued, "which is fantasy, I think the

A 1984 shot of Pierce Brosnan and his late wife, Cassandra Harris, who costarred in *For Your Eyes Only* as Countess Lisl Von Schlaf. (Janet Gough)

Using the same persona that won him international stardom in the "Remington Steele" television series, future Bond Pierce Brosnan, seen here with Robert Prosky, excelled as the con man antihero in film capers like *The Heist*. (Bob Greene/HBO)

Before he took the 007 part, Pierce Brosnan fine-tuned his action skills in thrillers like *Alistair MacLean's Death Train*, which costarred Bond veteran Christopher Lee. (Branko Hrkac)

political correctness has to be eased up a little." Brosnan also remembered that the earliest film he could remember seeing as a boy was *Goldfinger*. "I remember sitting in that cinema on a Saturday afternoon with my parents, seeing this magnificent thing unfold before me—and I remember Sean!" (*See* BROSNAN, PIERCE.)

BUNGEE JUMPING Special skill that James Bond (PIERCE BROSNAN) utilized in the *Goldeneye* teaser.

CAINE, JEFFREY British screenwriter who cowrote *Goldeneye*.

CAMPBELL, MARTIN New Zealand–born film director who helmed *Goldeneye* in 1995. Campbell enters a small select group of international directors who have directed a United Artists Bond adventure: Terence Young (three times), Guy Hamilton (four times), Lewis Gilbert (three times), Peter Hunt (one time), and John Glen (five times).

Campbell emigrated to England in the late 1960s to pursue his dream of working in the film and television industry. After starting his career as a video cameraman at ATV in London in 1967, where he worked on everything from "The Power Game" to Liberace and Tom Jones specials, Campbell directed his first film in 1975—the ill-fated *Three for All*, presented by the Dick James Music Organization. Turning to producing, he put together director Anthony Simmons's "Black Joy," and served as line producer on Alan Clarke's infamous "Scum" (which was banned by the BBC, which originally commissioned it), as well as "The Great Rock and Roll Swindle." He then did second-unit work before directing again in high-profile British TV series such as "The Professionals," "Shoestring," "Bergerac," and "Minder." It was in long-form television in Britain that Campbell made his mark—first in "Muck in Brass," a six-part British TV production about city corruption, and the acclaimed "Edge of Darkness," an existential thriller that won six British Academy Awards. "Edge of Darkness" brought him to the attention of Hollywood producers, and he made his U.S. film directing debut in 1989 with *Criminal Law*, starring Kevin Bacon and Gary Oldman. The film was not a hit, but Campbell did get a chance to work with actor Joe Don

Baker, who joins him on *Goldeneye* as Jack Wade. Campbell followed with another thriller, *Defenseless*, starring Barbara Hershey, Mary Beth Hurt, and Sam Shepard. He won critical acclaim for an odd period supernatural thriller titled *Cast a Deadly Spell*, which was produced by Gale Anne Hurd for Home Box Office. He also directed an episode of Barry Levinson's acclaimed TV series "Homicide," and prior to *Goldeneye*, Campbell directed *No Escape*, starring Ray Liotta.

CHURCH'S OF NORTHAMPTON British shoe manufacturer that supplied Pierce Brosnan with his footwear for *Goldeneye*.

COLTRANE, ROBBIE (Glasgow, Scotland, 1950–) (real name, Robbie McMillan) Award-winning Scottish actor who portrayed burly arms trader and Russian black market criminal Valentin Zukovsky in *Goldeneye*. Well known to British television fans of the

Long before he took the part of mysterious Russian mafioso Valentin in *Goldeneye*, top British character actor Robbie Coltrane was none other than the pontiff in *The Pope Must Die*. (Sonet)

"Cracker" series, in which he portrayed clinical-psychologist-turned-detective Eddie Fitzgerald, Coltrane is also a respected comedian (he starred in *Nuns on the Run*).

The son of a physician, Coltrane was born in Glasgow and studied art before beginning his acting career. Changing his surname from the family McMillan to that of jazzman John Coltrane, his rise was steady. Passing creditably through a host of small-scale theater productions, his 1973 documentary *Young Mental Health* won him a Film of the Year Award from the Scottish Education Council. Gradually, he began appearing on television in everything from the "The Tube" to "The Young Ones." His success as a member of the Comic Strip comedy troupe enhanced the impression that he was a comedian who could act rather than an actor who could make you laugh, but his aim stayed true. On British television, he was nominated for a British Academy of Film and Television Arts Award as Best Actor for his role in the BBC miniseries "Tutti Frutti."

His film credits include *Britannia Hospital, Scrubbers, Revolution, Krull, Eat the Rich, Absolute Beginners, The Supergrass* (Comic Strip feature film), *Subway Riders, Defense of the Realm, Caravaggio* (opposite Sean Bean), *Bert Rigby, You're a Fool, The Fruit Machine, Slipstream, Let It Ride, Mona Lisa, The Pope Must Die, Henry V* (as Falstaff), *Perfectly Normal, The Adventures of Huckleberry Finn,* etc. *See* ZUKOVSKY, VALENTIN (Addendum).

DENCH, DAME JUDI Veteran British actress who was the first woman to portray double-0 section chief M, in *Goldeneye*. Prior to the Bond film, Dench was well known from a number of British films, including the award-winning *Room with a View*, in which she portrayed Miss Lavish.

DRIVER, MINNIE British TV actress who rose to fame with the gentle romantic drama *Circle of Friends* in 1995 and who took the small part of Valentin's (ROBBIE COLTRANE) singing girlfriend, Irina, in *Goldeneye*. Prior to her U.S. feature debut, Driver was well known in England for her work in "Mr. Wroe's Virgins," "Royal Celebration," and "The Day Today," all

for the BBC. Her film credits include *God on the Rocks, Zebra Man,* and *That Sunday.* For *Circle of Friends,* she gained 25 pounds, which she lost for her brief appearance in *Goldeneye.*

ELECTROMAGNETIC PULSE Space-based satellite weapon first mentioned but never exploited in *A View to a Kill*, it was an important plot element in *Goldeneye*. According to British Intelligence, this type of technology was first developed by the Americans and Soviets during the height of the cold war (i.e., the so-called Star Wars breed of space-based weaponry). If you detonated a nuclear weapon in Earth's ionosphere, it would generate an electromagnetic surge or pulse that could short-circuit and disable all Earth-based electrical appliances. As intimated in *A View to a Kill*, it would destroy every computer in England and blind the entire country to possible attack or invasion. In *Goldeneye*, a well-organized and terror-oriented branch of the Russian Mafia is determined to get control of the *Goldeneye* technology for their own horrific purposes.

Dame Judi Dench takes over the role of James Bond's superior, M, in *Goldeneye*. (Julian Belfrage Associates)

FARREL, ADMIRAL CHUCK U.S. Naval representative in *Goldeneye*, portrayed by actor Billy J. Mitchell, whom Bond (PIERCE BROSNAN) sees escorting Xenia Onatopp (FAMKE JANSSEN) at a Monte Carlo casino. Mitchell

Once a submarine commander in *Never Say Never Again*, actor Billy J. Mitchell is promoted to admiral in *Goldeneye*. (McIntosh Rae Management)

previously portrayed Commander Pederson, commander of the U.S. nuclear sub that is trailing the *Flying Saucer* yacht in *Never Say Never Again*.

FEIRSTEIN, BRUCE Top American humorist, author, columnist, screenwriter, and director, who was intimately involved in the writing of *Goldeneye*. His credit on the final film was still unclear at press time.

Feirstein, who writes a column for the *New York Observer*, started his career in advertising and worked on the "Ultimate Driving Machine" campaign for BMW. His writing career took off in 1983 when he wrote the worldwide bestseller *Real Men Don't Eat Quiche*. Since then he has written for American television shows such as "Mr. President" (with George C. Scott) and "Monsters" (which he also directed), and he wrote and produced "The Best Legs in the Eighth Grade" for Home Box Office. Feirstein came to the Bond series through his longtime friendship with top Broadway and film producer Fred Zollo (Barbara Broccoli's husband).

During the long incubation period of *Goldeneye*, Broccoli and Zollo had discussed the possibility of having Feirstein contribute to the script. They were impressed with his screenwriting talent, and even though a number of his scripts had not been filmed, he had the type of sensibility they were looking for. Feirstein understood the dynamic of Bond to a T.

"Barbara Broccoli and I had talked about Bond many times," he remembers. "I once pointed out something to her that I thought was wrong with *Octopussy*. In that film's teaser, you recall, Bond's baby jet is low on fuel, and he ends up taxiing into a rural gas station in Cuba and tells the attendant to fill it up. That wasn't very Bondian. What he should have done was flown the baby jet into the rear of an inflight C-5 transport plane, where he would be greeted by Miss Moneypenny who would take him to his briefing with M. That was the way the original movies worked. The humor had to be smart."

In September 1994, Feirstein received a phone call from Barbara Broccoli informing him that he had a meeting the next day with Bond director Martin Campbell. All of a sudden the fate of the finished *Goldeneye* script was placed in his hands.

Feirstein is canny about his contribution to the script, but he will admit that he came in primarily to work on the characters, including Bond; the third act of the film; and making the humor smarter.

"My favorite scenes in the movie are the ones with M and Q," he laughs. "Martin Campbell came up with the idea of making M a woman. My assignment was to see if I could make it work. M is not a Maggie Thatcher. She smokes, drinks; she's tough. She's not politically correct and she's certainly not from the same old boy's club as the previous M."

As for Bond himself, Feirstein has a clear

vision of how he should be in 1995. "In order for you to understand Bond, you have to realize that a lot of him is not on screen. There was a great deal of darkness in the original novels and in the first films. Sean Connery brought that to life. You really believed that this was a guy you'd love to go drinking with up to a point. You knew he was dangerous—he's a man who lives every day of his life as if it was his last.

"We have a key scene in *Goldeneye* between M and Bond where Bond says, 'I've never forgotten that a license to kill is also a certificate to die.' That's the character. He's someone who understands that and lives his life accordingly. During one of the love sequences, I heard someone on the set say, 'This is a guy who isn't sure he's going to live for six months, what does he care about safe sex? His job is death.' "

FRANCE, MICHAEL (St. Petersburg, Florida, January 4, 1962–   ) American screenwriter who cowrote the "Goldeneye" screenplay. France always wanted to do a Bond movie, but it wasn't until his spec script for the Sylvester Stallone hit *Cliffhanger* sold in 1991 that he was given the chance. Says France, "I learned how to write action movies from watching Bond films. I always wanted to write one, and I had my agent pester Michael Wilson and Barbara Broccoli. Once they got past the legal problems they had faced for a couple of years, I was invited to lunch with Barbara and Michael at an Italian restaurant on Pico Boulevard in west Los Angeles called Osteria Romano Orsini. This was in January 1993. Before the meeting I crammed on everyone's bios, and as soon as I showed up they started quizzing me, basically on what my attitude toward the character was, what I knew about 007, what I could bring to a new film to make it fresh and different from the blizzard of action movies that had come out in recent years.

"They liked the fact that I knew the movies. Many people didn't know the characters. They were pitching old stories. I decided I wanted to be a writer when I was watching *Goldfinger*. When I was a kid, I wanted to be Richard Maibaum, not Bond." France's meeting with the producers lasted over 90 minutes. But for two months, France heard nothing. Finally in March 1993, they called back, and France was given the opportunity to come up with a new story line.

He explains, "We were all in agreement that we needed to treat Bond seriously and not to do one of the more comedic, sillier Bonds like *Moonraker*. By the same token, they didn't want to be as serious as *Licence to Kill*. *Goldfinger* was considered the model Bond. They didn't lay down the law—no formulas were mentioned. But it was very collaborative. We had meetings twice a week for several months with Michael, Barbara, Cubby, and Dana—either at Cubby's house in Beverly Hills or MGM. I also talked to some technical people like stuntman B. J. Worth and aviation coordinator Corky Fornoff.

"People will react well to the new Bond that Pierce Brosnan portrays. The movies that we kept coming back to as inspiration were the earlier Connery Bonds like *From Russia with Love*. That's where we wanted the character and situations to be. We also wanted a villain on the level of *Goldfinger*—with an elaborate, unsinkable plot. At the same time, we also want him to be credible as a threat—that all of the story elements were based in reality, that these things could happen."

France placed much of the story in Russia—post–Soviet Union—with the island location in Cuba saved for the ending. He finished his final draft in February/March 1994, a full year after his first meeting with Wilson and Broccoli. British writer Jeffrey Caine was brought in to write the next draft of the screenplay. And he, in turn, was followed by Kevin Wade and Bruce Feirstein. Final screenwriting credits for *Goldeneye* were unclear as this book went to press.

GOLDENEYE Coded, credit-card-shaped device that controls access to a secret space-based weapons system introduced in *Goldeneye*, the 17th James Bond movie presented by Albert R. Broccoli.

GOLDENEYE (MGM/United Artists, 1995) The 17th James Bond movie released by United Artists, which marked the debut of

Pierce Brosnan as James Bond. A throwback to the intrigue-laden Bond films of the '60s, such as *From Russia with Love*, *Goldeneye* pits 007 against a fanatical splinter group of the Russian Mafia and the ex-KGB and their heinous scheme to unleash an electromagnetic pulse attack on England's computer grid. Their weapon is secret Soviet space satellites. With a nod to previous female assassins like Fiona Volpe in *Thunderball* and wicked Fatima Blush in *Never Say Never Again*, the producers introduced amazingly athletic Xenia Onatopp (FAMKE JANSSEN), a gorgeous assassin who knocks off her victims with her "killer thighs." Other villains include the mysterious Trevelyan (SEAN BEAN), who carries the double-0 number himself, and renegade Russian General Ourumov (GOTTFRIED JOHN). Helping Bond along the way are another beauty, computer expert and love interest Natalya Simonova (IZABELLA SCORUPCO); CIA agent Jack Wade (*The Living Daylights* veteran JOE DON BAKER); and the usual gadget bag of tricks—even a female M (DAME JUDI DENCH) and a new Moneypenny (SAMANTHA BOND), no less.

(Note: The following cast and crew credits were available at press time and are not necessarily based on contractual obligations. Final screen credits may differ.)

GOLDENEYE CAST

James Bond	Pierce Brosnan
Alec Trevelyan	Sean Bean
Natalya Simonova	Izabella Scorupco
Xenia Onatopp	Famke Janssen
General Ourumov	Gottfried John
Boris Grishenko	Alan Cumming
Mishkin	Tcheky Karyo
Valentin	Robbie Coltrane
M	Dame Judi Dench
Q	Desmond Llewelyn
Miss Moneypenny	Samantha Bond
Jack Wade	Joe Don Baker
Admiral Farrell	Billy J. Mitchell
Irina	Minnie Driver

GOLDENEYE CREW

Executive Producer	Tom Pevsner
Producers	Barbara Broccoli, Michael G. Wilson
Associate Producer	Anthony Waye
Director	Martin Campbell
Screenplay	Michael France, Jeffrey Caine
Cameraman	Phil Meheux
Editor	Terry Rawlings
Production Manager	Phil Kohler
Assistant Director	Gerry Gavigan
Production Designer	Peter Lamont
Art Director	Andrew Ackland-Snow
Set Decorator	Michael Ford
Costume Designer	Lindy Hemming
Production Coordinator	Elena Zokas
Special Effects	Chris Corbould
Casting	Debbie McWilliams
Publicist	Geoff Freeman
Distributor	MGM/United Artists

(Special thanks to Gregory-James Gelet for the *Goldeneye* graphic.)

GRISHENKO, BORIS IVANOVICH

Egocentric computer hacker who works with Natalya Simonova (IZABELLA SCORUPCO) in *Goldeneye*, portrayed by Alan Cumming.

So despicable in *Circle of Friends* as the odious suitor of Minnie Driver, actor Alan Cumming joins the cast of *Goldeneye* as computer genius Boris Grishenko. (ICM, London)

JANSSEN, FAMKE Dutch actress who portrayed a luscious yet lethal post-Soviet assassin in *Goldeneye*. Born in the Netherlands, Janssen has made her home in the United States for over a decade. Her film credits include the thriller *Lord of Illusions*, also released by United Artists. *See* ONATOPP, XENIA (Addendum).

JANUS SYNDICATE Russian organized crime syndicate that plays a nefarious part in the *Goldeneye* caper. It is based in St. Petersburg and named after the two-faced Roman god.

JOHN, GOTTFRIED British actor who portrays ruthless General Arkady Grigorovich Ourumov, head of satellite operations in northern Russia in *Goldeneye*. *See* OURUMOV, ARKADY GRIGOROVICH (Addendum).

In *Goldeneye*, Gottfried John portrays General Ourumov, an ambiguous renegade Russian general. (Pressebüro Peter W. Engelmeier)

KARYO, TCHEKY Celebrated French actor who slipped easily into the role of powerful politburo figure Dimitri Mishkin in *Goldeneye*

and who earlier had won many plaudits for his portrayal of Nostradamus. Karyo's most recent credit includes *Bad Boys* (1995).

MAY 23, 1995 At press time, the projected wrap (end) date of principal photography on *Goldeneye*.

MISCHA Russian orbiting satellite that has the same electromagnetic pulse weapons system as the Petya Satellite in *Goldeneye*.

MISHKIN, DIMITRI Dry-witted Russian politburo figure, portrayed by French actor Tcheky Karyo in *Goldeneye*. I guess they finally retired General Gogol from the series.

"MISOGYNIST DINOSAUR" What the new M (DAME JUDI DENCH) calls James Bond (PIERCE BROSNAN) at one point in *Goldeneye*. What would Bernard Lee say?

MONTE CARLO Mediterranean resort and classic James Bond location that once again hosted Bond in *Goldeneye*. It's where 007 (PIERCE BROSNAN) meets his arch-nemesis, Xenia Onatopp (FAMKE JANSSEN).

MOSKVICH Battered Russian motor car driven by St. Petersburg–based CIA agent Jack Wade (JOE DON BAKER) in *Goldeneye*.

OMEGA Brand of James Bond's (PIERCE BROSNAN) Swiss watch that contains a built-in laser in *Goldeneye*.

ONATOPP, XENIA Sexy, incredibly athletic, and extremely lethal Russian assassin and ex–fighter pilot reputed to have connections to organized crime in Russia, portrayed by Famke Janssen in *Goldeneye*. Beware of her thighs! She's a native of the Republic of Georgia. According to London's *Sun* newspaper, in one scene Xenia leaves Bond shaken and stirred when she tries to finish him off during a steamy sex session in a spa. Brosnan commented, "Thankfully I get away, but only by the skin of my teeth. This woman uses her thighs to kill her victims—at least they die smiling." *See* JANSSEN, FAMKE (Addendum).

OURUMOV, GENERAL ARKADY GRI-GOROVICH Ruthless head of the Russian Space Division which controls orbiting satellite operations in *Goldeneye*, portrayed by actor Gottfried John.

PARKER Brand of James Bond's (PIERCE BROSNAN) ballpoint pen that doubles as a hand grenade in *Goldeneye*.

PETYA Name given to a Russian orbiting satellite that explodes early in *Goldeneye*.

ROLLS-ROYCE FACTORY Located at Leavesden Airfield in Hertfordshire, England, 40 minutes north of London, this enormous complex, in which airplane engines were once built, replaced Pinewood Studios as 007 headquarters for *Goldeneye*. With Pinewood Studios overbooked with the production of the films *Mary Reilly* (with Julia Roberts) and *First Knight* (in which Sean Connery plays King Arthur), the producers chose the Rolls-Royce facility, which is considered the largest covered factory area in the world, featuring 1.2 million square feet of space and boasting five soundstages. Combined with a deserted Royal Air Force military airfield and exterior sets, that makes for 290 acres—about three times as big as Pinewood. Six hundred crew members were reported to be working on the production during its construction phase. During World War II, British Mosquito fighter/bombers and Halifax bombers were built and test-flown at Leavesden. Sources indicated that the property may become a golf course in the near future.

ST. PETERSBURG (Previously, Leningrad) City in northwest Russia on the east end of the Gulf of Finland, which is a primary location in *Goldeneye*. A full second-unit crew shot there in the spring of 1995, capturing background materials that will blend with exterior sets built on the Rolls-Royce Factory property complex in Leavesden, England.

SCORUPCO, IZABELLA (1970–) Stunning Polish-born actress and ex-model who portrayed Natalya Fyodorovna Simonova, a computer expert who works for Northern Russia's Space Weapons Research Centre, in *Goldeneye*. Popular in Swedish films and advertisements, Scorupco was originally discovered on the Baltic island of Gotland. Her character becomes Bond's ally and paramour in the latest 007 adventure. *See* SIMONOVA, NATALYA (Addendum).

SIMONOVA, NATALYA FYODO-ROVNA Beautiful and superintelligent computer expert (referred to as a Level Two Programmer) specializing in satellite guidance systems, portrayed by Polish actress Izabella Scorupco, who teams up with James Bond (PIERCE BROSNAN) in *Goldeneye*. She's the sole survivor of an attack on a Russian Space Complex that controls orbiting satellites—one of which may have the ability to launch an electromagnetic pulse attack on Earth. *See* SCORUPCO, IZABELLA, ELECTROMAGNETIC PULSE (Addendum).

"STAND BY YOUR MAN" Country-western standard (written by and popularized by Tammy Wynette) sung in Russian in *Goldeneye* by Irina (MINNIE DRIVER), the girlfriend of black market arms dealer Valentin (ROBBIE COLTRANE).

T-55 Heavy Russian battle tank commandeered by James Bond (PIERCE BROSNAN) for a hair-raising chase in *Goldeneye*.

TIGRE High-tech French helicopter with stealth capability, featured in *Goldeneye*.

TREVELYAN, AKA 006 Top British double-0 operative, portrayed by actor Sean Bean, in *Goldeneye*. He accompanies Bond (PIERCE BROSNAN) on a mission inside the Soviet Union in the exciting teaser sequence. *See* BEAN, SEAN (Addendum).

WADE, JACK Burly CIA contact based in St. Petersburg and portrayed by American character actor Joe Don Baker in *Goldeneye*. Baker had previously portrayed illegal arms trader Brad Whitaker in *The Living Daylights*.

Already a veteran of *The Living Daylights* as dastardly arms trader Brad Whitaker, Joe Don Baker returns in *Goldeneye*, this time as American CIA agent Jack Wade, Bond's contact in St. Petersburg. (The Artists Agency)

WADE, KEVIN (Bronxville, New York, March 9, 1954–) American playwright and screenwriter who contributed heavily to *Goldeneye*. His credit on the film was still unclear at press time.

Wade first came to prominence in 1980 with the play *Key Exchange*, which was later adapted as a movie for 20th Century–Fox. Wade is better known for the screenplays for *Working Girl* (1988), *True Colors* (1991), *Mr. Baseball* (1992), and *Junior* (1994).

He first met Bond producer Barbara Broccoli in 1990 and attended her wedding to pro-ducer Fred Zollo. In August 1994, Wade was hired to do a rewrite on *Goldeneye*. He was sent to London, and for five weeks (seven days a week), he worked on the script while holed up in the Eon Productions office in Picadilly Circus (next to the Hard Rock Cafe). Wade was asked to work on the character of James Bond, who, in the previous drafts of the script, was more reac-tive than active. "I went to the bookshelf at Eon," says Wade, "and picked up three of the original Fleming novels. I would work from 8 to 6 every day, and then I'd go home and read the books. It helped a lot. James Bond is a fatalistic action hero, and we wanted to give him the edge that Connery once presented when he did Bond. I had to make sure that Pierce Brosnan's Bond was a direct descendent of Connery's.

"When you read the Fleming novels, you see that Bond is always getting the crap beat out of him. He's a real character, not a comic-book hero, but unless you center the action around him, he becomes a mechanic."

Wade also streamlined the plot of the film. A long interlude in a St. Petersburg weapons bazaar was reduced to a single scene. Wade, appropriately, also gave his surname to Bond's CIA contact in Russia, Jack Wade. Since he had pressing screenwriting duties with producer Ivan Reitman on the comedy *Junior*, Wade was unable to finish his work. Bruce Feirstein took over the rewrite.

ZUKOVSKSY, VALENTIN DIMITRE-VEYCH Russian black market criminal based in St. Petersburg in *Goldeneye*, portrayed by British actor Robbie Coltrane. Bond (PIERCE BROSNAN) wounded him on a previous, un-named mission, so he walks with a limp. Al-though there's obviously no love lost between Valentin and Bond, there is a grudging respect between the two men. Valentin reminds one of the colorful character Milos Colombo, the smuggler, played by Topol in *For Your Eyes Only*. *See* COLTRANE, ROBBIE (Addendum).